Cottle

CCDP Self-Study: Designing Cisco Network Architectures (ARCH)

Keith Hutton

Amir Ranjbar, CCIE No. 8669

Cisco Press

800 East 96th Street
Indianapolis, Indiana 46240 USA

CCDP Self-Study: Designing Cisco Network Architectures (ARCH)

Keith Hutton

Amir Ranjbar, CCIE No. 8669

Copyright © 2005 Cisco Systems, Inc.

Published by:

Cisco Press

800 East 96th Street

Indianapolis, Indiana 46240 USA

Printed in the United States of America 1 2 3 4 5 6 7 8 9 0

First Printing December 2004

Library of Congress Cataloging-in-Publication Number: 2003116483

ISBN: 1-58705-185-0

Warning and Disclaimer

This book is designed to provide information about selected topics for the CCDP ARCH exam. Every effort has been made to make this book as complete and as accurate as possible, but no warranty or fitness is implied.

The information is provided on an "as is" basis. The authors, Cisco Press, and Cisco Systems, Inc. shall have neither liability nor responsibility to any person or entity with respect to any loss or damages arising from the information contained in this book or from the use of the disks or programs that may accompany it.

The opinions expressed in this book belong to the author and are not necessarily those of Cisco Systems, Inc.

The Cisco Press self-study book series is as described, intended for self-study. It has not been designed for use in a classroom environment. Only Cisco Learning Partners displaying the following logos are authorized providers of Cisco curriculum. If you are using this book within the classroom of a training company that does not carry one of these logos, then you are not preparing with a Cisco trained and authorized provider. For information on Cisco Learning Partners please visit:www.cisco.com/go/authorizedtraining. To provide Cisco with any information about what you may believe is unauthorized use of Cisco trademarks or copyrighted training material, please visit: http://www.cisco.com/logo/infringement.html.

Trademark Acknowledgments

All terms mentioned in this book that are known to be trademarks or service marks have been appropriately capitalized. Cisco Press or Cisco Systems, Inc. cannot attest to the accuracy of this information. Use of a term in this book should not be regarded as affecting the validity of any trademark or service mark.

Corporate and Government Sales

Cisco Press offers excellent discounts on this book when ordered in quantity for bulk purchases or special sales. For more information please contact: **U.S. Corporate and Government Sales**   1-800-382-3419 corpsales@pearsontechgroup.com

For sales outside the U.S. please contact: **International Sales**   international@pearsoned.com

Feedback Information

At Cisco Press, our goal is to create in-depth technical books of the highest quality and value. Each book is crafted with care and precision, undergoing rigorous development that involves the unique expertise of members from the professional technical community.

Readers' feedback is a natural continuation of this process. If you have any comments regarding how we could improve the quality of this book, or otherwise alter it to better suit your needs, you can contact us through e-mail at feedback@ciscopress.com. Please make sure to include the book's title and ISBN in your message.

We greatly appreciate your assistance.

Publisher	John Wait
Editor-in-Chief	John Kane
Cisco Representative	Anthony Wolfenden
Cisco Press Program Manager	Nannette M. Noble
Executive Editor	Brett Bartow
Acquisitions Editor	Michelle Grandin
Production Manager	Patrick Kanouse
Development Editor	Sheri Cain
Project Editor	Sheila Schroeder
Copy Editor	Katherin Bidwell
Technical Editors	Shawn Boyd, Jesse Herrera, and Diane Teare
Team Coordinator	Tammi Barnett
Cover Designer	Louisa Adair
Composition	Interactive Composition Corporation
Indexer	Eric T. Schroeder

CISCO SYSTEMS

Corporate Headquarters
Cisco Systems, Inc.
170 West Tasman Drive
San Jose, CA 95134-1706
USA
www.cisco.com
Tel: 408 526-4000
800 553-NETS (6387)
Fax: 408 526-4100

European Headquarters
Cisco Systems International BV
Haarlerbergpark
Haarlerbergweg 13-19
1101 CH Amsterdam
The Netherlands
www-europe.cisco.com
Tel: 31 0 20 357 1000
Fax: 31 0 20 357 1100

Americas Headquarters
Cisco Systems, Inc.
170 West Tasman Drive
San Jose, CA 95134-1706
USA
www.cisco.com
Tel: 408 526-7660
Fax: 408 527-0883

Asia Pacific Headquarters
Cisco Systems, Inc.
Capital Tower
168 Robinson Road
#22-01 to #29-01
Singapore 068912
www.cisco.com
Tel: +65 6317 7777
Fax: +65 6317 7799

Cisco Systems has more than 200 offices in the following countries and regions. Addresses, phone numbers, and fax numbers are listed on the **Cisco.com Web site at www.cisco.com/go/offices.**

Argentina • Australia • Austria • Belgium • Brazil • Bulgaria • Canada • Chile • China PRC • Colombia • Costa Rica • Croatia • Czech Republic Denmark • Dubai, UAE • Finland • France • Germany • Greece • Hong Kong SAR • Hungary • India • Indonesia • Ireland • Israel • Italy Japan • Korea • Luxembourg • Malaysia • Mexico • The Netherlands • New Zealand • Norway • Peru • Philippines • Poland • Portugal Puerto Rico • Romania • Russia • Saudi Arabia • Scotland • Singapore • Slovakia • Slovenia • South Africa • Spain • Sweden Switzerland • Taiwan • Thailand • Turkey • Ukraine • United Kingdom • United States • Venezuela • Vietnam • Zimbabwe

About the Authors

Keith Hutton is a senior Cisco network administrator with Magma Communications, Ltd., Canada's leading, full-service Internet company. Prior to joining Magma, Keith worked as a certified Cisco Systems instructor with Global Knowledge Canada. He currently holds CCNP and CCDP certifications.

Amir S. Ranjbar, CCIE No. 8669, is a senior network architect and certified Cisco Systems instructor (CCSI) at Global Knowledge Network (Canada), Inc. Born in Tehran, Iran, Amir moved to Canada in September 1983 and completed his master's degree in computing and information science in January 1991 at the University of Guelph (Guelph, Ontario). Amir worked for Statistics Canada until May 1995 in various computing roles. Then, he joined Digital Equipment Corporation's Learning Services to work as a Microsoft Certified Trainer (MCT). Amir was one of the first Microsoft Certified Systems Engineers in Canada. In May 1998, Amir joined Geotrain corporation (later acquired by Global Knowledge Network) to pursue his career in the internetworking field; he has worked as an instructor ever since. Amir passed the Certified Cisco Internetwork Expert (CCIE, Routing and Switching) lab exam in January 2002. Amir teaches the Cisco Interconnecting Cisco Networking Devices, Building Cisco Remote Access Networks, Building Scalable Cisco Internetworks, Building Cisco Multilayer Switched Networks, Cisco Internetwork Troubleshooting, Cisco Voice over IP, Border Gateway Protocol, and Multiprotocol Label Switching courses on a regular basis and strives to expand his expertise into the IP telephony and security fields. Amir can be contacted by e-mail at amir.ranjbar@globalknowledge.com or aranjbar@rogers.com.

About the Technical Reviewers

Shawn Boyd is a senior network consultant for ARP Technologies, Inc. Shawn is active in course development and is a certified Cisco Systems instructor with ARP Technologies and IBM, and is responsible for teaching most of the CCNP, CCDP, and Security courses. His background is in network security and design at a service-provider level. He has worked for Canada's largest telco providers performing network designs and implementations and was lead contact on many large government contracts.

Jesse J. Herrera is a senior systems analyst for a Fortune 100 company located in Houston, Texas. Mr. Herrera holds a bachelor of science in computer science from the University of Arizona and a master of science in telecommunications management from Southern Methodist University. Current Cisco certifications include CCNP and CCDP. Responsibilities include design and implementation of enterprise network architectures including capacity planning, performance monitoring, and network integration services. Recent activities include wireless and Virtual Private Network initiatives and support of electronic business services.

Diane Teare is a consultant in the networking, training, and e-learning fields. She has more than 20 years of experience in designing, implementing, and troubleshooting network hardware and software and has also been involved in teaching, course design, and project management. She was a Cisco instructor and course director at one of the largest authorized Cisco Learning Partners. She was recently the director of e-learning for the same company, where she was responsible for planning and supporting all of the company's e-learning offerings in Canada, including Cisco courses. Diane has a bachelor's degree in applied science in electrical engineering (BASc) and a master's degree in applied science in management science (MASc). She currently holds her CCNP and CCDP certifications. She edited *Designing Cisco Networks*, authored *CCDA Self-Study: Designing for Cisco Internetwork Solutions (DESGN)*, and coauthored *Building Scalable Cisco Networks* and *CCNP Self-Study: Building Scalable Cisco Internetworks (BSCI)* (first and second editions), all published by Cisco Press.

Dedications

I would like to dedicate this book to my parents, Mr. Kavos Ranjbar and Mrs. Batoul Ghafouri-miadi, whose genuine love, purity, and wisdom made me who I am. My honesty, confidence, and ambition are due to my upbringing. My parents taught me to enjoy the harmony of nature and life and that this short journey can only be pleasant through peace, love, and fairness; I'll love and respect them forever. I hope and will try to be as good of a parent to Thalia, Ariana, and Armando. Finally, I would like to thank Elke Haugen-Ranjbar, for being such a good friend, hardworking partner, and loving wife to me.

—Amir

This book is dedicated to my wife, Ingrid.

—Keith

Acknowledgments

I would like to express my sincere gratitude to Keith Hutton for inviting me to join him in this project. Many thanks to Michelle Grandin, Sheri Cain, Christopher Cleveland, and the rest of the members of the Cisco Press team for their hard work, professionalism, and beautiful attitude. I appreciate the suggestions and the feedback from our technical editors, Shawn Boyd, Jesse Herrera, and Diane Teare. Thank you all!

—Amir

First, I would like to thank Amir Ranjbar for joining me in undertaking this project. Second, I would like to express my thanks and appreciation to Michelle Grandin, Sheri Cain, Christopher Cleveland, and the staff at Cisco Press and Cisco Systems, who helped make this project a reality. Finally, special thanks to the technical editors, Shawn Boyd, Jesse Herrera, and Diane Teare for keeping this book grounded with their valuable input and suggestions.

—Keith

Contents at a Glance

Table of Contents

Icons Used in This Book

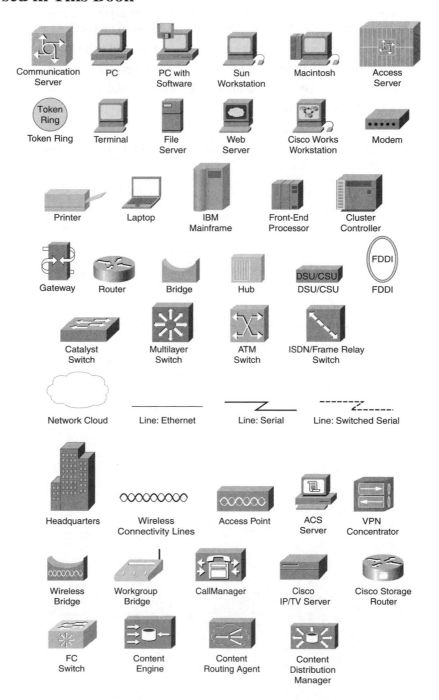

Command Syntax Conventions

The conventions used to present command syntax in this book are the same conventions used in the IOS Command Reference. The Command Reference describes these conventions as follows:

- **Boldface** indicates commands and keywords that are entered literally as shown.
- *Italics* indicate arguments for which you supply actual values.
- Vertical bars (|) separate alternative, mutually exclusive elements.
- Square brackets [ ] indicate optional elements.
- Braces { } indicate a required choice.
- Braces within brackets [{ }] indicate a required choice within an optional element.

Foreword

CCDP Self-Study: Designing Cisco Network Architectures (ARCH) is a Cisco authorized, self-paced learning tool that helps you understand foundation concepts covered on the CCDP ARCH exam. This book was developed in cooperation with the Cisco Internet Learning Solutions group, the team within Cisco responsible for the development of the ARCH exam. As an early-stage exam preparation product, this book teaches the knowledge and skills needed to perform the conceptual and intermediate design of a network infrastructure that supports network solutions over intelligent network services, to achieve effective performance, scalability, and availability. Whether you are studying to become CCDP certified, or are simply seeking to gain a better understanding of design with Quality of Service (QoS), security, network management, fine-tuning routing protocols, switching structures and IP Multicast, you will benefit from the information presented in this book.

Cisco Systems and Cisco Press present this material in text-based format to provide another learning vehicle for our customers and the broader user community in general. Although a publication does not duplicate the instructor-led or e-learning environment, we acknowledge that not everyone responds in the same way to the same delivery mechanism. It is our intent that presenting this material via a Cisco Press publication will enhance the transfer of knowledge to a broad audience of networking professionals.

Cisco Press will present other books in the Certification Self-Study Series on existing and future exams to help achieve the Cisco Internet Learning Solutions Group's principal objectives: to educate the Cisco community of networking professionals and to enable that community to build and maintain reliable, scalable networks. The Cisco Career Certifications and classes that support these certifications are directed at meeting these objectives through a disciplined approach to progressive learning.

In order to succeed with Cisco Career Certifications and in your daily job as a Cisco certified professional, we recommend a blended learning solution that combines instructor-led training with hands-on experience, e-learning, and self-study training. Cisco Systems has authorized Cisco Learning Partners worldwide, which can provide you with the most highly qualified instruction and invaluable hands-on experience in lab and simulation environments. To learn more about Cisco Learning Partner programs available in your area, please go to www.cisco.com/go/authorizedtraining.

The books Cisco Press creates in partnership with Cisco Systems will meet the same standards for content quality demanded of our courses and certifications. It is our intent that you will find this and subsequent Cisco Press certification self-study publications of value as you build your networking knowledge base.

Thomas M. Kelly
Vice President, Internet Learning Solutions Group
Cisco Systems, Inc.

November 2004

Introduction

Designing reliable internetworks poses a difficult challenge for today's IT professional. The very scope and scale of present-day network technologies precipitates the requirement for a structured and formalized approach. To meet this requirement, Cisco has developed a comprehensive structured design architecture called Architecture for Voice, Video, and Integrated Data (AVVID). Cisco AVVID provides network designers with a solid foundation for the engineering of enterprise networks.

Goals of This Book

CCDP Self-Study Guide: Designing Cisco Network Architectures (ARCH) assists administrators in the design process by providing a solid foundation for the study of the AVVID framework. This book serves as a companion reference volume and study guide for those preparing to write the CCDP ARCH certification exam.

This book is organized into 13 chapters, an appendix, and a glossary that cover the key areas of Cisco AVVID architecture. Each chapter is designed to examine a single element of the AVVID framework. At the conclusion of every chapter, the reader is presented with references, review questions, and a case study that reinforce the concepts covered.

This book can be read from cover to cover, or used as a technical reference and consulted in the order required.

Who Should Read This Book

CCDP Self-Study Guide: Designing Cisco Network Architectures (ARCH) is intended for network administrators, designers, consultants, and resellers who are involved in the process of designing and supporting complex networks. This book provides students of the Designing Cisco Network Architectures (ARCH) course a supplementary guide to the official courseware material. If you are preparing for the ARCH certification exam, this book is a perfect self-study reference. Finally, it may serve as a means for students of the previous Cisco Internetwork Design course, as well as owners of the related Cisco Press publication, *Cisco Internetwork Design*, to update their knowledge and skill sets.

How This Book Is Organized

This book can be read cover-to-cover, or on a per-chapter basis as a reference guide. Chapters 1 to 13 cover the following AVVID topics:

- **Chapter 1, "Introducing Cisco Network Service Architectures"**—Chapter 1 introduces the Cisco AVVID framework; it lists and explains the benefits and key components of the Cisco AVVID framework. This chapter also introduces the Enterprise Composite Network model and describes its comprising functional areas. How each functional area of the Enterprise Composite Network model meets the need for performance, scalability, and availability is explained in this module as well.

- **Chapter 2, "Designing Enterprise Campus Networks"**—Chapter 2's topic is designing Enterprise Campus Networks. A review of enterprise network design methodology is followed by a detailed discussion on designing campus infrastructure; topics discussed there include logical and physical campus network, Layer 2 and Layer 3 switching solutions, selecting Cisco hardware and software, IP addressing strategy, and selecting routing protocols. Chapter 2 concludes by a discussion on designing the Server Farm.

- **Chapter 3, "Designing Enterprise Edge Connectivity"**—Chapter 3's focus is on Enterprise Edge: it begins by reviewing the Enterprise Edge Network Design Methodology. Designing the classic Wide Area Network module, the remote access, and the Internet connectivity modules of the enterprise composite model assemble the latter parts of Chapter 3.

- **Chapter 4, "Designing Network Management Services"**—Chapter 4 covers the design of enterprise network management strategies and architectures. It examines network management policies and procedures and reviews the deployment of the CiscoWorks family of products. Chapter 4 concludes with an overview of guidelines and best practices for the design of enterprise network management systems.

- **Chapter 5, "Designing High-Availability Services"**—Chapter 5 discusses high availability; it includes network requirements for high availability, Cisco IOS high availability architecture, hardware redundancy, and options for Layer 3 redundancy and Spanning Tree Protocol. Design guidelines for enterprise campus and enterprise edge, along with best practices for high availability is provided to complete the discussion on high availability.

- **Chapter 6, "Designing Security Services"**—Chapter 6 examines the process of designing and defining network security policies. It presents Cisco security solutions within the context of the Security Architecture for Enterprise security architecture. Chapter 6 concludes with an overview of guidelines and best practices for the design of enterprise network security solutions.

- **Chapter 7, "Designing QoS"**—Chapter 7 is dedicated to designing QoS. QoS mechanisms are identified in the initial section; the topics presented are enterprise requirements for QoS, IntServ and DiffServ QoS architectures, classification and marking, congestion avoidance, congestion management, traffic conditioning, and link efficiency mechanisms. The second section of Chapter 7 is about designing QoS for enterprise networks; the QoS design guidelines for enterprise networks are presented here.

- **Chapter 8, "Designing IP Multicast Services"**—Chapter 8 explains designing of multicast services. Multicast services are first examined by introducing IP multicast and its data delivery principles, multicast forwarding, IP multicast group membership, multicast distribution trees, and protocol independent multicast. Designing IP multicast solutions for enterprise networks is the topic of discussion in the second half of chapter 8. This latter section presents IP multicast design considerations for an enterprise campus. Designing IP multicast for a small and for a large enterprise campus and designing IP multicast over a WAN conclude this section.

- **Chapter 9, "Designing Virtual Private Networks"**—Chapter 9 describes VPN technologies, analyzes VPN management concepts and describes the CiscoWorks VPN management solution. This chapter concludes with an examination of the guidelines and best practices for the design of site-to-site and remote VPN solutions.

- **Chapter 10, "Designing Enterprise Wireless Networks"**—Chapter 10 examines Cisco wireless LAN solutions and the design of enterprise wireless networks. Chapter 10 concludes with an overview of guidelines and best practices for the design of enterprise network wireless solutions.

- **Chapter 11, "Designing IP Telephony Solutions"**—Chapter 11 provides a review of Cisco's IP Telephony solution and examines Cisco's CallManager solution and related technologies. Chapter 11 concludes with an overview of guidelines and best practices for the design of enterprise network IP telephony solutions.
- **Chapter 12, "Designing Content Networking Solutions"**—Chapter 12 provides a review of Cisco's Content Networking Solution. This chapter describes Content Networking Technolgies and Cisco's Content Networking Architecture. Chapter 12 concludes with an overview of guidelines and best practices for the design of enterprise network Content Networking solutions.
- **Chapter 13, "Designing Storage Networking Solutions"**—Chapter 13 provides a review of Cisco Storage Networking Solution. This chapter describes Storage Networking Technolgies and Cisco Storage Networking Architecture. Chapter 13 concludes with an overview of guidelines and best practices for the design of enterprise network Storage Networking solutions.

This book also contains an appendix and a glossary:

- **Appendix A, "Answers to Review Questions"**—This appendix lists the answers to all the chapter-ending review questions.
- **Glossary**—The glossary lists important terms and their definitions for the CCDP ARCH certification exam.

After completing this chapter, you will be able to

- List the three primary concerns while deploying an enterprise network.
- List and explain the benefits and key components of the Cisco Architecture for Voice, Video, and Integrated Data (AVVID) framework.
- Describe the performance, scalability, and availability concerns when deploying an enterprise network.
- List and describe the functional areas that comprise the Enterprise Composite Network Model.
- Explain how each functional area of the Enterprise Composite Network Model meets the need for performance, scalability, and availability.

CHAPTER 1

Introducing Cisco Network Service Architectures

Large enterprises increasingly seek an enterprise-wide infrastructure to serve as a solid foundation for emerging applications such as IP Telephony, content networking, and storage networking. The Cisco Architecture for Voice, Video, and Integrated Data (AVVID) framework, with its open communications interface, is the basis of the Cisco enterprise network architecture. The framework is designed to support the operation of concurrent solutions operating over a single infrastructure. An infrastructure as such is designed, tested, and fully documented with performance, scalability, and availability at a level that fulfills end-to-end enterprise requirements. These are the primary concerns of network development, which will be discussed next, prior to the discussion of AVVID framework.

Primary Concerns of Network Deployment

There are three primary concerns while deploying an enterprise network:

- Performance
- Scalability
- Availability

Performance

Performance might be the least understood term in networking. Typically, *performance* is defined as throughput, or it is referenced in packets per second (pps). These are easy numbers to gauge and report, but these values relate to a single switch or router and make no sense when measuring an entire network's performance. For example, suppose you have a network that you expect to perform at 10,000 pps, but testing data transfer over the network shows a yield of only 5000 pps. One explanation for this might be that the network consists of 1.536-Mbps (T1) WAN links with traffic shaping enabled, which in turn limits the packet rate through the entire network. In addition, forwarding traffic at that rate might impact the processor loads, limiting the overall throughput performance and placing the router at risk of not having enough resources either to converge following a failure in the network or to enable additional features.

We can conclude that no single metric exists for determining or measuring performance. Finally, note that even though specific devices or applications might promise performance, effective performance is achieved only by considering and optimizing each and every component. Only a cohesive, integrated, and optimized network can ensure the best network performance.

Three metrics or parameters allow you to reasonably gauge network performance:

- **Responsiveness**—Important to the user because it indicates how the user or consumer perceives the performance of network applications. Responsiveness is affected by link speeds, congestion, and implemented features, and it includes device and protocol responses. This is the most important metric in the network: If an application does not respond in an acceptable time, the network's claimed speed is rendered irrelevant.

  Network responsiveness might be altered based on how applications respond to changes in the network; for example, many applications use Transmission Control Protocol, which slows the transmission rate if too much congestion or loss is present in the network. The top section of Figure 1-1 shows how responsiveness switches from fast to slow, and ultimately to never, as network utilization increases and approaches 100%.

- **Throughput**—Important to operational management. Throughput specifies the rate of information arriving at, and possibly passing through, a particular point in a network system.

  Throughput is closely related to utilization. As utilization increases, throughput approaches the theoretical maximum until driven to congestive collapse. Typically, throughput is measured in packets per second (pps), kilobits per second (Kbps), megabits per second (Mbps), or gigabits per second (Gbps). The bottom section of Figure 1-1 depicts how throughout increases as network utilization increases, how it suffers as utilization gets into higher levels, and ultimately, how throughput is driven to congestive collapse as network utilization gets at or near 100%.

- **Utilization**—Important to executive management. Utilization measures the use of a particular resource over time, usually expressed as a percentage, where the usage of the resource is compared with its maximum operational capacity. Measuring utilization allows you to identify congestion (or potential congestion) throughout the network. You can also identify underutilized resources.

  Utilization is the principle measure to determine how full the network pipes (links) are. Analyzing CPU, interface, queuing, and other system-related capacity and utilization levels help us determine the extent to which network system resources are being consumed. High utilization is not necessarily bad. Low utilization might indicate traffic flows through unexpected paths. As lines become overutilized, the effects can become significant. Overutilization on a link occurs when there is consistently more traffic than the capacity of the link or interface. Ultimately, overutilization might result in excessive queuing delays and even packet loss. Sudden jumps in resource utilization can indicate a fault condition. Utilization is also an indicator of return on investment. For example, if utilization of a link is less than 30%, it might be economically beneficial to reduce the link's bandwidth. On the other hand, a utilization of 70% or more might be an indicator for the need to increase link capacity (bandwidth).

Figure 1-1   *Effects of Utilization Growth on Responsiveness and Throughput*

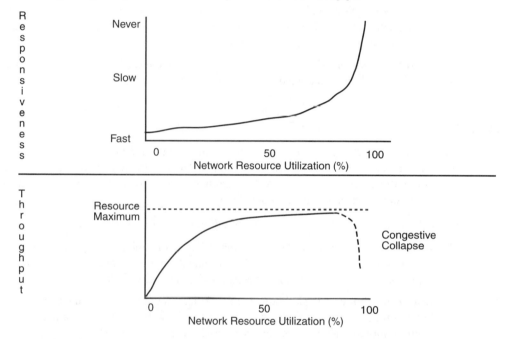

Scalability

Taking scalability into account is an important aspect of designing enterprise networks. A network's size or capacity might have to grow substantially over a period of time. For instance, a network administrator might need to design a WAN that supports only 50 existing branch offices, but it also needs to be able to support an additional 50 branches that require connectivity over a year's time. The design, IP address management, features, and WAN link speeds must all be able to accommodate this need for added connectivity without massive network redesign.

When designing an enterprise network, exercising some basic principles throughout the network will improve scalability. Utilizing specialized devices and card modules for specific functions facilitates the job of upgrading devices as the network grows. Implementing a hierarchy escalates the level of control over a network and its overall manageability.

The following areas of concern and the decisions made about them have major influence on a network's scalability:

- **Topology**—Network topology must be such that additions or deletions to and from the network do not result in major reconfigurations, cause instability, modify deterministic performance, or adversely affect availability levels.

- **Addressing**—Distribution of IP addresses should facilitate route summarization. Additionally, it should be possible to create new subnets with a minimum impact on the addressing scheme and router load.

- **Routing protocols**—The routing protocol of choice must be able to accommodate additions, deletions, and changes without massive redesign.

Availability

Network *availability* is a parameter that, for the most part, must be measured or viewed from the perspective of its users. An application failure, a router malfunction, or a cut strand of fiber are all perceived as the network being unavailable. Network managers want to maximize network availability and convergence.

Network availability can be increased with the following four good practices:

- **Device fault tolerance and redundancy**—Fault-tolerant devices provide a high level of reliability. Cisco offers options for redundant supervisor engines and dual-power supplies, which provide the first backstop against a network failure.

- **Link redundancy**—Link redundancy is critical in the network and provides a high level of reliability in the event of a link failure. However, although some redundancy is good, more redundancy is not necessarily better.

- **Protocol resiliency**—Good design practices guide you in implementing protocol redundancy, load sharing, fast convergence, and so on.

- **Network capacity design**—Good design practices take capacity matters into consideration. For instance, the load volume that different links can handle in the worst-case scenario are accounted for. Another example would be that a designer must ascertain whether a link can handle twice its regular traffic load, in case a redundant link fails.

The key components of the Cisco AVVID framework are as follows:

- Common Network Infrastructure
- Intelligent Network Services
- Network Solutions

These important components are described in the following section.

Cisco AVVID Framework

The Cisco AVVID framework provides an enterprise with a foundation that combines IP connectivity with performance and availability. Layering application solutions, such as voice, video, or content delivery networks, require changes to an existing infrastructure. The Cisco AVVID framework provides effective design principles and practices to plan those changes.

Each enterprise network is different, because it is built to accommodate different topologies, media, and features that the specific enterprise has deployed. Network managers who design and build networks to support converged solutions combining data, voice, and video must consider the components that allow networks to operate properly. The Cisco AVVID framework provides an infrastructure on which to offer intelligent services to support network solutions and business applications.

Figure 1-2 provides a visual representation of how the Cisco AVVID framework defines the infrastructure, services, and solutions to support various markets. As you can see on the left side of this figure, three elements are listed. The bottom element is Common Network Infrastructure and Intelligent Network Services. The Enterprise Composite Network Model (discussed later in this chapter) divides this element into three functional areas: Enterprise Campus, Enterprise Edge, and Service Provider Edge.

Figure 1-2 *Elements of Cisco AVVID Framework*

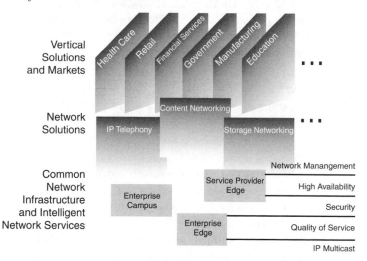

Network management and features such as high availability, security, quality of service (QoS), and support for IP multicast applications, which are listed on the lower right-hand side of Figure 1-2, might be implemented within the Common Network Infrastructure and Intelligent Network Services.

The middle element shown in Figure 1-2 is Network Solutions. Examples of Network Solutions are IP Telephony, content networking, and storage networking. Naturally, these applications will only function if appropriate Common Network Infrastructure and Intelligent Network Services are put in place.

The top element shown in Figure 1-2 is Vertical Solutions and Markets. As its title implies, different segments of the market and economy can benefit from network solutions, but the markets are not part of the AVVID framework. Some of the candidate segments listed in Figure 1-2 are Government, Education, Manufacturing, Financial, Retail, and Health Care services.

Cisco AVVID provides the framework for today's Internet business solutions. Cisco AVVID is an enterprise-wide, standards-based network architecture that provides a roadmap for combining business and technology strategies into a cohesive model. An architecture is important for enterprise networks, because it is a roadmap and guide for ongoing network planning, design, and implementation. A *network architecture* provides a coherent framework that unifies disparate solutions onto a single foundation.

The major components of the Cisco AVVID framework are

- **Common Network Infrastructure**—Several elements comprise the Common Network Infrastructure. The hardware and software used to send, receive, and manage datagrams transmitted between end-user devices throughout the enterprise, and the transmission media and devices that control transmission paths, including private and public transport media, are all components of the Common Network Infrastructure. Routers, LAN switches, WAN switches, and Private Branch Exchanges (PBXs) are examples of the mentioned devices.

- **Intelligent Network Services**—These services essentially add intelligence, extra qualities, and features to the Common Network Infrastructure beyond merely moving datagrams. Subsequently, end users are allowed to operate in a controlled and secure environment that might offer differentiated services as well. Intelligent Network Services include network management, high availability, security, QoS, and IP multicast.

- **Network Solutions**—Network-based applications (including the hardware and software) that use the Common Network Infrastructure and Intelligent Network Services to their advantage and enable an enterprise organization to interact more effectively with customers, suppliers, partners, and employees are also key components of the Cisco AVVID framework. Network solutions allow enterprises to make business decisions about the business itself as well as about networks and the technologies and applications that run on them. Customer service, commerce, and internal applications run over the Common Network Infrastructure enabled by Intelligent Network Services. Some examples of Network Solutions are IP Telephony, content networking, and storage networking.

Some benefits of the Cisco AVVID framework include the following:

- **Integration**—By leveraging the Cisco AVVID framework and applying the network intelligence inherent in IP, organizations can use comprehensive tools to improve productivity. Combining the Common Network Infrastructure and services with new applications, Cisco AVVID accelerates the integration of technology strategy with business activities.

- **Intelligence**—Traffic prioritization and intelligent networking services maximize network efficiency for optimized application performance.

- **Innovation**—Customers have the ability to adapt quickly in a competitive and changing business environment.

- **Interoperability**—Standards-based hardware and software interfaces allow open integration, providing organizations with choice and flexibility.

Cisco AVVID Common Network Infrastructure

The Cisco AVVID Common Network Infrastructure solution provides an enterprise foundation that combines IP connectivity with high performance and availability.

Common Network Infrastructure is the collective set of devices, transmission media, and any other hardware and software that facilitates transportation of data and operation of Intelligent Network Services and Network Solutions. It is clear that AVVID is a layered model with the Common Network Infrastructure residing at the bottom, supporting Intelligent Network Services. Intelligent Network Services, residing in the middle, supports Network Solutions, which forms the top part. Although laycring application solutions such as voice, video, or content delivery networks require changes to the Common Network Infrastructure, this infrastructure provides a basis for good design principles and practices.

The Cisco AVVID Common Network Infrastructure consists of these hardware components:

- **Application servers and clients**—Application servers provide services to clients, and might be located in a data center or another easily accessible, logical network location. Network clients include workstations, portable computers, IP phones, and wireless devices.

- **Network platforms**—Routers, switches, gateways, firewalls, and other devices comprise network platforms. These components of the infrastructure provide the basis for a complete networking solution.

Network managers who design and build networks to support solutions, such as voice and video, must first consider the components that allow networks to operate properly. Thus, the network device often becomes the focus of design decisions. However, you should not focus only on a single element, whether it is a switch, a router, or any other networking device. How the devices connect, what features and protocols are enabled, and the particular configuration of all these elements form the foundation for the services that run on top of the Common Network Infrastructure. If the foundation is unstable, layering solutions over the network can create problems.

This layered model, which facilitates basic connectivity and protocol deployment, is the key to the Cisco AVVID Common Network Infrastructure solution for providing performance, scalability, and availability.

Cisco AVVID Intelligent Network Services

Intelligent Network Services add intelligence to the Common Network Infrastructure and allow user data and applications to exist, transport, and operate in a controlled and secure environment that might also provide differentiated services. Intelligent Network Services operate over and rely on Cisco AVVID Common Network Infrastructure, producing a blueprint that blends equipment, features, and management tools, and satisfies business requirements.

Cisco Systems devices allow you to deploy the following intelligent network services, each of which might play a role in meeting enterprise needs for performance, scalability, and availability:

- **Network management**—A number of related network management tools built upon a Common Management Foundation (CMF) are provided. These tools include the following:
  - The LAN Management Solution for advanced management of Catalyst multilayer switches
  - The Routed WAN Management Solution for monitoring traffic management and providing access control to administer the routed infrastructure of multiservice networks
  - The Service Management Solution for managing and monitoring service-level agreements
  - The VPN/Security Management Solution for optimizing Virtual Private Network (VPN) performance and security administration

- **High availability**—Numerous refined design methodologies and tools are offered to ensure end-to-end availability for services, clients, and sessions. These tools include the following:
  - Reliable, fault-tolerant network devices to automatically identify and overcome failures
  - Resilient network technologies, such as Hot Standby Router Protocol (HSRP), which bring resilience to the critical junction between hosts and backbone links

- **Security**—Network security is provided through authentication, encryption, and failover protection. Security features include application-based filtering (context-based access control), intrusion detection in the network and at the hosts, defense against network attacks, per-user authentication and authorization, and real-time alerts.

- **QoS**—QoS manages the delay, delay variation (jitter), bandwidth, and packet loss parameters on a network to meet the diverse needs of voice, video, and data applications. QoS features provide functionality, such as network-based application recognition (NBAR), for classifying traffic on an applications basis, a Service Assurance Agent (SAA) for end-to-end QoS measurements, and Resource Reservation Protocol (RSVP) signaling for admission control and reservation of resources.

- **IP multicast**—IP multicast provides bandwidth-conserving technology that reduces traffic by simultaneously delivering a single stream of information to thousands of end-system clients. Multicasting enables distribution of videoconferencing, corporate communications, distance learning, distribution of software, and other applications. Multicast packets are forwarded in the network by Cisco routers enabled with Protocol Independent Multicast (PIM) and other supporting multicast protocols, resulting in efficient delivery of data to multiple receivers.

Cisco AVVID Network Solutions

Strategic investment in mission-critical solutions and network applications can provide a competitive edge to enterprises. Cisco Systems, along with third-party companies (through the Cisco AVVID partner program), provide solutions for enterprise business processes and challenges. The Cisco AVVID framework provides a foundation for Network Solutions. Cisco Systems offers the following network solutions to address enterprise application needs:

- **VPN**—VPNs use advanced encryption and tunneling to permit organizations to establish secure, end-to-end, private network connections over third-party or public networks, such as the Internet or extranets.

- **Wireless**—Wireless and IP technology creates anytime, anywhere connections to the Internet and enterprise networks. In a campus environment or distant mobile location, wireless technology allows users to be constantly connected as they move between wireless cells, unconstrained by direct physical connections.

- **IP Telephony**—The convergence of voice, video, and data on a single IP network is changing the way enterprises communicate. You can transport voice, video, and data on a single common network infrastructure, lowering total network costs and optimizing enterprise communications.

- **Content networking**—Content networking provides an architecture that optimizes website performance and content delivery by positioning content near consumers in anticipation of use.

- **Storage networking**—Driven by workforce collaboration, e-commerce, and e-learning, storage networking has emerged as an important networking application. Cisco storage networking solutions provide high-capacity, low-latency networking for disaster recovery, data replication, and storage consolidation.

Enterprise Composite Network Model

The Enterprise Composite Network Model provides a modular framework for designing enterprise networks. The modularity within the model allows flexibility in network design and facilitates implementation and troubleshooting. This model relies on the principles of the Cisco AVVID framework.

Nearly a decade ago, Cisco introduced a hierarchical design model as a tool for network designers to approach network design from the physical, logical, and functional viewpoints (see Figure 1-3). The hierarchical model divided networks into these layers:

- **Access layer**—Grants user access to network devices. At a network campus, the access layer makes shared or switched media/ports available to workstations and servers. In the WAN environment, the access layer can provide sites with access to the corporate network using a WAN technology.

- **Distribution layer**—The distribution layer aggregates the wiring closets and uses Layer 2 and Layer 3 switching to segment workgroups and isolate network problems, preventing them from impacting the core layer. Routing and packet manipulation occur in the distribution layer.

- **Core layer**—The core layer is a high-speed backbone and is designed to switch packets as fast as possible. Because the core is critical for connectivity, it must provide a high level of availability and must adapt to changes quickly.

This hierarchical module was useful, but had weaknesses when implementing large, complex enterprise networks.

Figure 1-3   *The Cisco Classical Hierarchical Design Model*

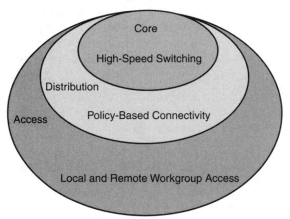

The Enterprise Composite Network Model introduces additional modularity into the network structure. The entire network is divided into functional areas, each of which might contain the hierarchical model's access, distribution, and core layers (see Figure 1-4). The Enterprise Composite Network Model contains three major functional areas:

- **Enterprise Campus**—Contains the modules required to build a hierarchical, highly robust campus network that offers performance, scalability, and availability. This functional area contains the network elements required for independent operation within a single campus. This functional area does not offer remote connections or Internet access. A campus is defined as one or more buildings, with multiple virtual and physical networks, connected across a high-performance, multilayer-switched backbone.

- **Enterprise Edge**—Aggregates connectivity from the various elements at the edge of the enterprise network. The Enterprise Edge functional area filters traffic from the edge modules and routes it into the Enterprise Campus functional area. The Enterprise Edge functional area contains all the network elements for efficient and secure communication between the Enterprise Campus and remote locations, remote users, and the Internet.

- **Service Provider Edge**—Provides functionality implemented by service providers. The Service Provider Edge functional area enables communications with other networks using different WAN technologies and Internet service providers (ISPs).

Figure 1-4   *Enterprise Composite Network Model*

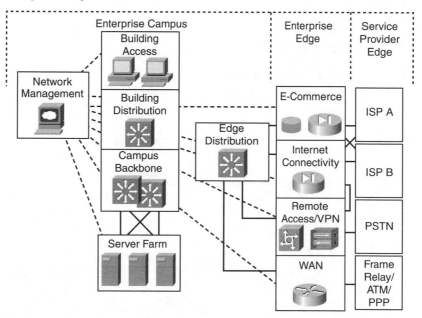

Cisco introduced the Enterprise Composite Network Model to scale the hierarchical model and to make the physical, logical, and functional boundaries of the enterprise network more clear-cut. The Enterprise Composite Network Model meets modern enterprise network criteria and offers the following benefits:

- Defines a deterministic network with clearly defined boundaries between modules. The model has clear demarcation points to aid the designer in identifying the module or submodule that any spot in the network is part of, or belongs to.

- Increases network scalability and eases the design task by making each module discrete.

- Provides scalability by allowing enterprises to add modules easily; as network complexity grows, designers can add new functional modules.

- Offers more integrity in network design, allowing the designer to add services and solutions without changing the underlying network design.

Enterprise Campus Functional Area

This section is dedicated to the Enterprise Campus functional area of the Enterprise Composite Network Model, and the following sections focus on the Enterprise Edge and the Service Provider Edge functional areas, correspondingly. The Enterprise Campus functional area is comprised of four modules, each of which has a specific function within the campus network (see Figure 1-5).

The four modules of the Enterprise Campus functional area are

- Campus Infrastructure module
- Network Management module
- Server Farm module
- Edge Distribution module

Figure 1-5 *Components of the Enterprise Campus Functional Area*

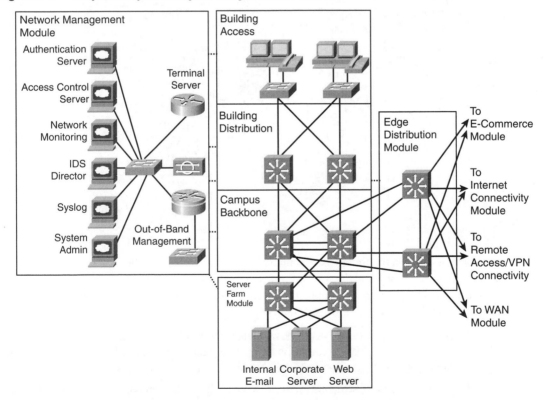

Campus Infrastructure Module

The Campus Infrastructure module connects users within a campus to each other and to the Server Farm and Edge Distribution modules. This module is composed of one or more floors or buildings connected to the Campus Backbone submodule. Each building contains a Building Access layer and Building Distribution layer, in line with the hierarchical model presented earlier.

The Campus Infrastructure module includes these submodules:

- **Building Access layer**—Contains end-user workstations, IP phones, and Layer 2 access switches that connect devices to the Building Distribution submodule. The Building Access layer performs important services such as broadcast suppression, protocol filtering, network access, and QoS marking (if possible).

- **Building Distribution layer**—Provides aggregation of wiring closets, often using Layer 3 switching. The Building Distribution layer performs routing, QoS, and access control. Requests for data flow into the building distribution switches and to the campus core. This module might provide fast failure recovery, if each building distribution switch maintains two equal-cost paths in the routing table to every destination network. When one connection to the campus core fails, all routes immediately switch over to the remaining path, because of a swift routing protocol convergence. This happens shortly (it can be about one second) after the link failure is detected.

- **Campus Backbone**—Provides redundant and fast-converging connectivity between buildings, as well as with the Server Farm and Edge Distribution modules. It routes and switches traffic as fast as possible from one module to another. This module uses Layer 2 or Layer 3 switches for high throughput functions with added routing, QoS, and security features.

Network Management Module

The Network Management module performs intrusion detection, system logging, and authentication, as well as network monitoring and general configuration management functions. For management purposes, an out-of-band connection (that is, a network on which no production traffic resides) to all network components is recommended. The Network Management module provides configuration management for nearly all devices in the network, primarily through using dedicated network-management stations.

Server Farm Module

The Server Farm module contains internal e-mail and corporate servers providing application, file, print, e-mail, and Domain Name System (DNS) services to internal users. Because access to these servers is vital, they are usually connected to two different switches, enabling full redundancy and load-sharing. The Server Farm module switches are cross-connected with core-layer switches, enabling high reliability and availability of all servers.

Edge Distribution Module

The Edge Distribution module aggregates the connectivity from the various elements at the Enterprise Edge functional area and routes the traffic into the Campus Backbone submodule.

Its structure is similar to the Building Distribution submodule. Both modules use access control to filter traffic, although the Edge Distribution module can rely on the edge distribution devices to perform additional security.

Effects of the Enterprise Campus Functional Area on the Enterprise Network

Table 1-1 shows how each module of the Enterprise Campus functional area affects the enterprise network's need for performance, scalability, and availability.

Table 1-1   *How Campus Network Modules Meet Enterprise Needs*

Module	Performance	Scalability	Availability
Building Access	Critical to desktop performance	Should provide port density	Important to provide redundancy
Building Distribution	Critical to campus performance	Should provide switch modularity	Critical to provide redundancy
Campus Backbone	Critical to overall network performance	Should provide switch modularity	Critical to provide redundancy and fault tolerance
Network Management	Monitors performance	Should monitor utilization (capacity)	Monitors device and network availability
Server Farm	Critical to server performance	Should provide switch modularity	Critical to provide redundancy and fault tolerance
Edge Distribution	Critical to WAN and Internet performance	Should provide switch modularity	Critical to provide redundancy

Enterprise Edge Functional Area

This section explains the Enterprise Edge functional area of the Enterprise Composite Network Model. This functional area is also comprised of four modules, each of which connects to the Edge Distribution module of the Enterprise Campus functional area, thus connecting the Enterprise Edge and the Enterprise Campus functional areas (see Figure 1-6).

The four modules of the Enterprise Edge functional area are

- E-commerce
- Internet Connectivity
- Remote Access/VPN
- WAN

Figure 1-6   *Modules of the Enterprise Edge and the Service Provider Edge Functional Areas*

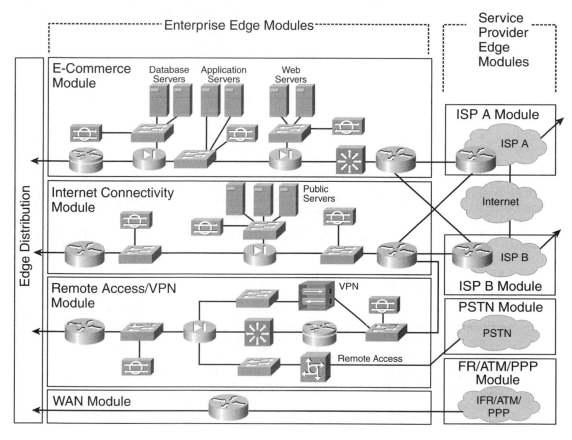

E-Commerce Module

The E-Commerce module enables enterprises to successfully deploy e-commerce applications and take advantage of the powerful competitive opportunities provided by the Internet. All e-commerce transactions pass through a series of intelligent services to provide performance, scalability, security, and availability within the overall e-commerce network design. To build a successful e-commerce solution, enterprises might deploy the following network devices:

- **Web servers**—Act as the primary user interface for the navigation of e-commerce
- **Application servers**—Support enterprise applications including online transaction processing systems and decision support applications
- **Database servers**—Contain the critical information that is the heart of e-commerce business implementation
- **Security devices**—Govern communication between the various levels of security in the system, often using firewalls and intrusion detection systems

Internet Connectivity Module

The Internet Connectivity module provides internal users with secure connectivity to Internet services. Internet users can access the information on publicly available servers. Additionally, this module accepts VPN traffic from remote users and remote sites and forwards the traffic to the Remote Access and VPN module. The major components of the Internet Connectivity module are

- **E-mail servers**—Act as a relay between the Internet and the intranet mail servers
- **DNS servers**—Serve as authoritative external DNS servers for the enterprise and relay internal requests to the Internet
- **Public web servers**—Provide public information about the organization
- **Security devices**—Govern communication between the various levels of security in the system, often using firewalls and intrusion detection systems
- **Edge routers**—Provide basic filtering and Layer 3 connectivity to the Internet

Remote Access and VPN Module

The Remote Access and VPN module terminates VPN traffic, forwarded by the Internet Connectivity module, from remote users and remote sites. It also initiates VPN connections to remote sites through the Internet Connectivity module. Furthermore, the module terminates dial-in connections received through the public switched telephone network (PSTN) and, after successful authentication, grants dial-in users access to the network. The major components of the Remote Access and VPN module are

- **Dial-in access concentrators**—Terminate dial-in connections and authenticate individual users
- **VPN concentrators**—Terminate Internet Protocol Security (IPSec) tunnels and authenticate individual remote users
- **Firewalls and intrusion detection systems**—Provide network-level protection of resources and stateful filtering of traffic; provide differentiated security for remote access users
- **Layer 2 switches**—Provide switched Layer 2 connectivity

WAN Module

The WAN module routes traffic between remote sites and the central site. It supports WAN physical technologies including leased lines, optical, cable, digital subscriber lines (DSLs), and wireless, as well as data-link, protocols such as Frame Relay, Asynchronous Transfer Mode (ATM), and Point-to-Point Protocol (PPP).

Effects of the Enterprise Edge Functional Area on the Enterprise Network

Table 1-2 shows how the four modules of the Enterprise Edge functional area participate in, or affect the total performance, scalability, and availability of an enterprise network.

Table 1-2 *How Enterprise Edge Modules Meet Enterprise Needs*

Module	Performance	Scalability	Availability
E-Commerce	Important to provide performance to partners and customers	Should provide router modularity	Important to provide redundancy
Internet Connectivity	Important to provide performance to Internet	Should provide router modularity	Important to provide redundancy
Remote Access and VPN	Critical to provide performance to remote users	Should provide router modularity	Important to provide redundancy
WAN	Critical to provide good WAN performance	Should Provide router modularity	Critical to provide redundancy

Service Provider Edge Functional Area

The Service Provider Edge is the last functional area of the Enterprise Composite Network Model. The modules of the Service Provider Edge functional area and the functions they provide are as follows (refer to Figure 1-6) :

- **Internet service provider (ISP)**—This module enables enterprise connectivity to the Internet. This service is essential to enable Enterprise Edge services, such as E-commerce, Remote Access and VPN, and Internet Connectivity modules. To provide redundant connections to the Internet, enterprises connect to two or more ISPs. Physical connection between the ISP and the enterprise can be any of the available WAN technologies.

- **Public Switched Telephone Network (PSTN)**—The PSTN module represents the dial-up infrastructure used to access the enterprise network using Integrated Services Digital Network, analog, and wireless (cellular) technologies. Enterprises can also use the PSTN module to back up existing WAN links. Connections are established on demand and terminated shortly after transmission of interesting (intended) traffic completes.

- **Frame Relay/Asynchronous Transfer Mode/Point-to-Point Protocol (FR/ATM/ PPP)**—This module includes all WAN technologies for permanent connectivity with remote locations. Frame Relay, ATM, and PPP are the most frequently used today. However, many technologies can fit into this module's category.

Each module has its own access, distribution, and core layers (in correspondence to the classical hierarchical model).

Figure 1-7 depicts an example of how the Service Provider Edge functional area can be implemented to meet the modern enterprise network needs.

Figure 1-7 *Example Implementation of the Service Provider Edge Functional Area*

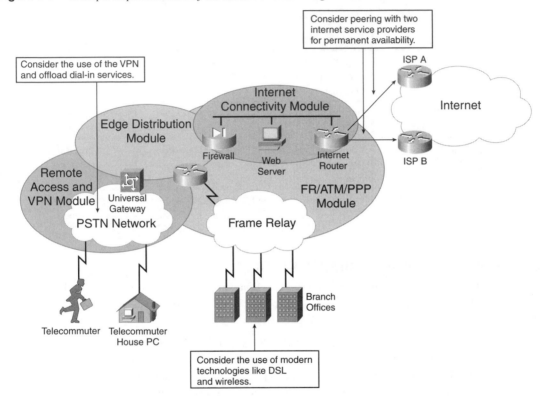

Summary

In this chapter, you learned the following key points:

- Cisco AVVID is an enterprise-wide, standards-based network architecture that provides a roadmap for combining business and technology strategies into a cohesive model.

- The key components of the Cisco AVVID framework are

    — Common Network Infrastructure

    — Intelligent Network Services

    — Network Solutions

- The benefits of Cisco AVVID are
  - Integration
  - Intelligence
  - Innovation
  - Interoperability
- The primary concerns of network deployment are
  - **Performance**—Gauged using these three metrics: responsiveness, throughput, and utilization.
  - **Scalability**—Network scalability is dependent on its topology, addressing, and deployed routing protocols.
  - **Availability**—Network availability can be increased with device fault tolerance and redundancy, link redundancy, protocol resiliency, and network capacity design.
- The Cisco AVVID Common Network Infrastructure consists of these hardware components:
  - Clients and application servers
  - Network platforms
  - Intelligent network services
- Using Cisco Systems tools and solutions, you might deploy the following intelligent network services to keep the network at peak performance:
  - Network management
  - High availability
  - Security
  - QoS
  - IP multicast
- The network solutions provided by Cisco Systems within AVVID framework are
  - VPN (part of the Enterprise Edge)
  - Wireless (part of the Campus Infrastructure)
  - IP Telephony
  - Content networking
  - Storage networking

- The hierarchical design model that Cisco introduced nearly a decade ago divided networks into three layers:
  - Access layer
  - Distribution layer
  - Core layer

  This model was useful but had weaknesses when implementing large, complex enterprise networks.

- The Enterprise Composite Network Model introduces additional modularity into the Common Network Infrastructure and meets the following criteria:
  - Defines a deterministic network
  - Increases network scalability
  - Offers more integrity in network design

- The major functional areas of the Enterprise Composite Network Model are
  - **Enterprise Campus**—Includes these four major modules: Campus Infrastructure, Network Management, Server Farm, and Edge Distribution. The Campus Infrastructure module in turn is comprised of the Building Access submodule, Building Distribution submodule, and Campus Backbone submodule.
  - **Enterprise Edge**—The elements of Enterprise Edge module are E-Commerce, Internet Connectivity, Remote Access and VPN, plus the WAN module.
  - **Service Provider Edge**—The Service Provider Edge modules are ISP, PSTN, and FR/ATM/PPP.

References

Cisco AVVID. http://www.cisco.com/en/US/netsol/ns340/ns19/networking_solutions_market_segment_solutions_home.html.

Product Summary

Table 1-3 provides a brief overview of some of the products available from Cisco Systems that relate to the topics discussed in this chapter. For a more detailed breakdown of the Cisco product line, visit http://www.cisco.com/en/US/products/index.html.

Table 1-3   *Products for Various Modules Within the Enterprise Composite Model*

Product Name	Description
Cisco Routers	
Cisco 1701-K9	ADSLoPOTS Router w/ISDN-BRI-S/T, K9 Image, 32MB Fl, 96MB DR
Cisco 1721	10/100BaseT Modular Router w/2 WAN slots, 16M Flash/32M DRAM. Also Available: Cisco 1721-VPN/K9 (with VPN Bundle)
Cisco 1760	10/100 Modular Router w/ 2WIC/VIC, 2VIC slots, 19-inch Chassis. Also Available: Cisco 1760-V (with Voice) Cisco 1760-VPN/K9 (with VPN Module)
Cisco 2651XM	High Performance Dual 10/100 Modular Router with Cisco IOS IP. Also Available: Cisco 2651XM-DC (DC NEB) Cisco 2651XM-RPS (RPS ADPT) Cisco 2651XM-V (AIM-VOICE-30)
Cisco 2691	High Performance 10/100 Dual Eth Router w/3 WIC Slots, 1 NM. Also Available: Cisco 2691-RPS
Cisco 3631-CO-AC	Cisco 3631-CO with AC Power Supply. Also Available: Cisco 3631-CO-DC
Cisco 3662-AC-CO	Dual 10/100E Cisco 3660 6-slot CO Mod Router-AC w/ Telco SW. Also Available: Cisco 3662-DC-CO
Cisco 3725	Cisco 3700 Series 2-slot Application Service Router. Also Available: Cisco 3725-DC-U
Cisco 3745	Cisco 3700 Series 4-slot Application Service Router
Cisco 7204VXR-CH	Cisco 7204VXR, 4-slot chassis, 1 AC Supply w/IP Software. Also Available: Cisco 7206VXR-CH (6-slot chassis)
Cisco 7304	4-slot chassis, NSE100, 1 Power Supply, IP Software
Cisco 7401ASR-CP	7401ASR, 128M SDRAM, IP Software
Cisco 800 series	Varius ISDN, Ethernet, and DSL routers
Cisco SOHO series	Cisco SOHO 78, 91, 96, 97 (different options)

continues

Table 1-3   *Products for Various Modules Within the Enterprise Composite Model (Continued)*

Product Name	Description
Cisco Switches	
Catalyst 2950-12	12 port, 10/100 autosensing, autonegotiating Catalyst Switch. There are several varieties within the 2950 series Catalyst Switches.
Catalyst 2955C-12	2955 12 TX w/MM Uplinks. Also Available: Catalyst 2955S-12 (with Single-Mode Uplinks) Catalyst 2955T-12 (with copper uplinks)
Catalyst 2970G-24T-E	Catalyst 2970 24 10/100/1000T Enhanced Image
Catalyst 3508G XL	Catalyst 3508G XL Enterprise Edition
Catalyst 3550-12G	10 GBIC ports and 2-10/100/1000BaseT ports. There are several varieties within the 3550 series Catalyst Switches.
Catalyst 3560-24PS-E	Catalyst 3560 24 10/100 PoE + 2 SFP Enhanced Image. There are several varieties within the 3560 series Catalyst Switches.
Catalyst 3750-24PS-E	Catalyst 3750 24 10/100 PoE + 2 SFP Enhanced Image. There are several varieties within the 3750 series Catalyst Switches.
Catalyst 4503	Catalyst 4500 Chassis (3-Slot), fan, no p/s
Catalyst 4506	Catalyst 4500 Chassis (6-Slot), fan, no p/s
Catalyst 4507R	Catalyst 4500 Chassis (7-Slot), fan, no p/s, Red Sup Capable
Catalyst 4510R	Catalyst 4500 Chassis (10-Slot), fan, no p/s, Redundant Sup Capable
Catalyst 6509-NEB	Catalyst 6509 Chassis for NEBS Environments

Review Questions

Answer the following questions to test your comprehension of the topics discussed in this chapter. Refer to Appendix A, "Answers to Review Questions," to check your answers.

1. List the key components of the Cisco AVVID framework.

2. List the benefits that the Cisco AVVID framework offers.

3. What are the primary concerns of network deployment?

4. What are the three metrics for gauging network performance?

5. What are the major areas of concern with respect to network scalability?

6. What are the key availability issues that must be addressed during network deployment?

7. What are the hardware components of the Cisco AVVID Common Network Infrastructure?

8. Name the intelligent network services you might deploy using Cisco Systems products and solutions to keep the network at peak performance.

9. Which network solutions does Cisco provide?

10. The hierarchical model that Cisco introduced nearly a decade ago divided a network into what layers?

11. What are the functional areas that comprise the Enterprise Composite Network Model?

12. What are the modules that the Enterprise Campus functional area is made of?

13. What are the modules that the Enterprise Edge functional area is made of?

14. Name the network devices that might be deployed to build a successful E-Commerce solution.

15. What are the major components of the Internet Connectivity module?

16. What are the major components of the Remote Access and VPN module?

17. What are the functions provided by the Service Provider Edge modules?

After completing this chapter, you will be able to

- Use the Enterprise Network Design Methodology to design campus networks and server farms

- Plan an effective Campus Infrastructure module design, given specific enterprise network requirements

- Plan an effective Server Farm module design, given specific enterprise network requirements

CHAPTER 2

Designing Enterprise Campus Networks

Enterprise sites, whether small or large, need a solid network infrastructure to support emerging solutions, such as IP Telephony, storage networking, broadband solutions, content networking, and the applications that surround them. The network foundation hosting these technologies for an emerging enterprise should be efficient, highly available, scalable, and manageable. The Cisco Architecture for Voice, Video, and Integrated Data (AVVID) network infrastructure is designed to run a converged voice, video, and data network over IP with due consideration for quality of service (QoS), bandwidth, latency, and high performance demanded by network solutions.

This chapter first discusses the Enterprise Network Design Methodology; it then describes how to design the Campus Infrastructure module and the Server Farm module, given specific enterprise requirements.

Enterprise Network Design Methodology

This section introduces a process that Cisco Systems has developed to facilitate effective network design. This process enables the network designer to assess enterprise requirements, design each module of the network, and determine the effectiveness of the design.

The Enterprise Composite Network Model (discussed in Chapter 1, "Introducing Cisco Network Service Architectures") enables network designers to create a campus network made out of modular building blocks, which are scalable to meet evolving business needs. The Enterprise Network Design Methodology is a step-by-step methodology that yields effective campus design and meets enterprise requirements for performance, scalability, and availability. A short coverage of analyzing network traffic patterns, an essential task for designing the logical and physical network, concludes this section.

Campus Design Within the Enterprise Composite Network Model

As explained in the previous chapter, the Enterprise Campus functional area includes Campus Infrastructure, Network Management, Server Farm, and Edge Distribution modules (see Figure 2-1). Hence, to design an enterprise campus network, each of these modules needs to be individually considered and designed.

Figure 2-1   *Enterprise Campus Network*

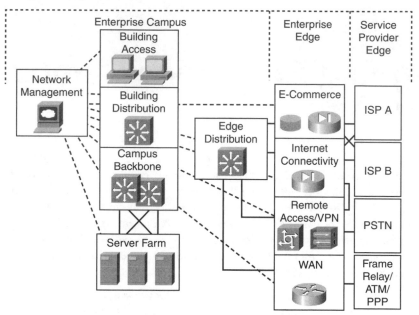

The Campus Infrastructure module connects users within a campus with the Server Farm and Edge Distribution modules. The Campus Infrastructure module is composed of one or more buildings connected to the Campus Backbone submodule. The Campus Infrastructure module includes the following submodules:

- **Building Access**—This submodule contains end-user workstations, IP phones, and data-link layer access switches that connect devices to the Building Distribution submodule. Building Access performs important services such as broadcast suppression, protocol filtering, network access, and QoS marking. Access switches are recommended to be connected to redundant distribution switches via two uplink connections.

- **Building Distribution**—This submodule provides aggregation of wiring closets, often using multilayer switching. Building Distribution performs routing, QoS, and access control. Fast failure recovery is provided through provision of two connections from each Building Distribution switch to the core, thus creating two equal-cost paths in the routing table to every destination network. When one connection to the campus core fails, data flows switch over to the remaining path after the link failure is detected.

- **Campus Backbone**—This submodule provides redundant and fast-converging connectivity between buildings, as well as with the Server Farm and Edge Distribution modules. It routes and switches traffic as fast as possible from one module to another. This submodule uses data-link layer switches and multilayer switches for high throughput functions with added routing, QoS, and security features if required.

NOTE	Readers must beware that the terms multilayer switch/switching and data-link layer switch/switching are recently used more often than their older counterparts, Layer 3 switch/switching and Layer 2 switch/switching.
	The terms Layer 2 and data-link layer are usually used as synonyms. However, because the terms Layer 3 and multilayer have differences, they should not be freely used as synonyms. For instance, a multilayer switch can process information beyond a datagram's Layer 3 header; hence, it is more appropriate to be called a multilayer switch rather than a Layer 3 switch.

Typical Requirements for an Enterprise Campus Network

A designer must ascertain that the following important requirements of an enterprise campus network are satisfied:

- **Functionality**—The enterprise network must support the required applications and data flows. Typical enterprise-wide applications include online transaction processing (OLTP) systems, decision support systems, e-mail, and information sharing. Applications and data might require special peak-time processing, or they might require steady processing throughout a day.

- **Performance**—Includes three primary metrics: responsiveness, throughput (volume), and utilization. Each campus network will be measured in terms of how well it meets these performance metrics.

- **Scalability**—Campus networks must provide scalability for future growth in the number of users and in the amount of data and applications that the network must support.

- **Availability**—One hundred % (or extremely close to 100%) availability is required for most enterprise networks. Networks providing converged services and solutions, and those providing support for critical applications, might be required to meet a standard of availability approaching 99.999%. This is often referred to as the "five-nines" availability rule.

- **Manageability**—An enterprise campus network must be manageable across the entire infrastructure.

- **Cost-effectiveness**—A key concern for most enterprises. The network designer's goal is to design the network for maximum effectiveness based on the given budgetary limitations. It is important to recognize that a perfect design is often not possible; therefore, part of the design process is to evaluate alternatives, consider compromises, and make the most cost-effective decisions.

The preceding needs and requirements have varying levels of significance within the modules and submodules that collectively comprise the enterprise campus network.

Enterprise Campus Design Methodology

Cisco network designers have developed a simple, seven-step process to design an enterprise campus network. This step-by-step campus design methodology will be used, referenced, and followed throughout this book. The following are the seven steps of the Cisco campus design methodology:

Step 1   Determine application and data requirements for each campus location on the enterprise network before beginning any network design.

Step 2   Design the logical network. This step entails identifying the logical networks as virtual LANs (VLANs) or as separate networks.

Step 3   Design the physical network. Transmission media, data-link layer technology, Layer 2 or Layer 3 switching strategy, spanning-tree implementation, and utilization of trunks for interswitch connections are identified in the third step of this methodology.

Step 4   Based on the specific requirements at each location, select appropriate Cisco network devices (hardware and software) and create a network topology diagram.

Step 5   Select an IP addressing strategy and numbering scheme. Determine if logical networks are single networks, subnetworks, or part of the larger network. Usually, a VLAN (logical network) maps to a single IP subnet. Subsequently, determine the numbering scheme for each logical or physical network and when to use route summarization.

Step 6   Select a routing protocol (or as many as justifiably required) that meets the need for performance, scalability, and availability.

Step 7   Design the Edge Distribution module. The Edge Distribution module provides connectivity between the core layer and the WAN modules. It generally consists of one or more multilayer switches.

Analyzing Network Traffic Patterns

Before designing the actual network, you should analyze the network traffic patterns for each application and for each site or campus location on the network. This information helps you determine the performance, scalability, and other requirements for each location and segment, which, are in turn, useful for designing the logical and physical networks. It is an effective technique to tabulate the characteristics of each campus building block. Some useful information to be tabulated about each location is

- Active application
- Type of application

- Number of users

- Number of servers

- QoS requirements such as bandwidth, loss, and delay tolerance

Table 2-1 displays an example of such a table, showing information about the applications within three buildings of a campus network.

Table 2-1   *A Sample Table Characterizing Applications*

Location	Name of Application	Type of Application	Number of Users	Number of Servers	Bandwidth, Delay Tolerance, Loss Characteristics
Building 1	Marketing Digital Signature Standard	Database (OLAP)	137	3	High bandwidth, high delay tolerance, low loss
Building 2	Corporate e-mail	E-mail	65	2	Low bandwidth, low delay tolerance, low loss
Building 3	File server	File sharing (File Transfer Protocol)	48	1	Low bandwidth, medium delay tolerance, low loss

Network designers need a way to properly size network capacity, especially as networks grow. Traffic theory enables network designers to make assumptions about their networks based on past experience. *Traffic* is defined as either the amount of data or the number of messages over a circuit during a given period of time. Traffic engineering addresses service issues by enabling network designers to define a grade of service or blocking factor. A properly engineered network has low blocking and high circuit utilization. Among the many factors that must be taken into account when analyzing traffic, the most important factors are

- **Traffic load measurement**—To measure the traffic load, gather statistics based on past experience in the enterprise and compute the average data rate (number of kbps) per user, and the average data rate (number of kbps) per network segment. Peak loads will also be an important input to network capacity planning and design.

- **Traffic types**—Traffic types that might be present in a network include data, voice, and video. Each traffic type might include elements that are different from one another. For example, the traffic type might include spreadsheets, pictures, graphics, or rich text documents.

- **Sampling methods**—Probability theory suggests that to accurately assess network traffic, you need to consider at least 30 of the busiest hours of a network in the sampling period. Although this is a good starting point, other variables can skew the accuracy of this sample. For example, you cannot take the top 30 out of 32 samples. To obtain the most accurate results, you need to take as many samples of the offered load as possible. Beware, however, that as you take samples throughout the year, your results can be skewed as the year-to-year traffic load increases or decreases. Some of the factors affecting the accuracy of your collected data are the number of samples taken, sample period, and stability of the sample period. For example, samples taken solely during the holiday season or weekends might have little value to year-round network capacity planning.

Now that designing enterprise campus network has been reviewed, the next section discusses designing the campus infrastructure.

Designing the Campus Infrastructure

The availability of hardware-accelerated multilayer switches that also provide intelligent network services allows network designers to achieve data rates previously possible on Layer 2 switches only (at the network and upper layers). Multilayer switching in the Campus Backbone and Building Distribution submodules offers speed and manageability advantages; traditional data-link layer workgroup switching at the Building Access submodule reduces complexity in the wiring closet. Design criteria for selecting data-link layer switches and multilayer switches include functionality, performance, and cost requirements. Cisco Systems recommends the use of data-link layer switches at the network edge to avoid the complexity of extending multilayer switching in the wiring closet. It is also recommended that Building Access devices terminate on a unique subnet at the Building Distribution submodule.

This section focuses on planning an effective Campus Infrastructure module design, given specific enterprise network requirements. This planning entails completion of the following tasks, based on specific internetwork requirements:

- Selecting logical network segments and the segmentation method for the Campus Infrastructure module

- Selecting transmission media, data-link protocols, and spanning-tree strategy for the Building Access, Building Distribution, and Campus Backbone submodules of the Campus Infrastructure module

- Selecting data-link layer switching and multilayer switching solutions for the Building Access, Building Distribution, and Campus Backbone submodules of the Campus Infrastructure module

- Selecting hardware and software for a campus network infrastructure

- Identifying an IP addressing strategy for the campus network

- Selecting routing protocols for the campus network that meet performance, scalability, and availability requirements

Designing the Logical Campus Network

After the step that identifies the application and data needs for an enterprise is complete, the logical network design (based on the specific internetwork requirements) begins. A key design decision to be made is whether to colocate the clients with respect to the resources they often need to access (such as departmental servers and printers). Some network designers consider placing each group of client computers and resources on the same logical network as the ideal situation. The benefit of doing this is the significant reduction in the network-layer processing load on the Building Distribution and Campus Backbone submodules, which forward (route) traffic between segments.

Logical network segments might be created using one of the following two general methods:

- **VLAN**—An extended data-link layer switched domain. If several VLANs coexist across a set of data-link layer switches, each individual VLAN is an independent failure domain, broadcast domain, and spanning-tree domain. This method essentially allows VLANs to span across two or more Layer 2 switches. Hence, even though a number of computers are not necessarily connected to the same cable or even the same switch, they are still within the same logical network (also referred to as a VLAN or broadcast domain).

- **Separate networks**—You can implement one or more bridged physical segments as a separate network. This method, on the other hand, does not use LAN switches to extend VLANs across multiple switches. This model has been considered suitable for very small networks only and is not discussed further in this book.

NOTE   The most recent trend in campus network design places each device in a separate logical network. Each device will need to be connected to a Layer 3 (or multilayer) switch and will be in a unique collision and broadcast domain. Notice that this model marries the concepts of a logical network and a physical network to make them one and the same, which is the opposite to the concept of VLAN. The forwarding speed of Cisco modern Layer 3 and multilayer switches makes this model logically acceptable. However, using multilayer switches in the access layer may render the cost of implementing this model prohibitive for smaller companies that have budgetary limitations. This model also terminates inherent support for most broadcast-based applications and protocols.

Modern campus network designers frown upon models that extend VLANs beyond the boundary of a block (building block). Deploying pervasive VLANs throughout the campus introduces complexity and reduces the deterministic behavior of the network. On the other hand, avoiding loops and restricting a set of unique VLANs to a single data-link layer switch in one wiring closet minimizes the complexity and increases network manageability. Smaller spanning-tree domains can also converge faster in the event of failure. A designer must weigh simplicity in the network design against the potential organizational advantages of logical networks that span site or campus (multiple buildings).

The most common access layer models, which do not span beyond (across) building distribution switches are

- One VLAN per switch
- Unique VLANs per switch
- VLANs spanning multiple access switches

One VLAN Per Switch

The Building Access submodule is the first point of entry into the network and essentially links end users to the remainder of the network. Figure 2-2 shows a one-VLAN-per-switch Building Access submodule model. Each uplink is part of only one VLAN, and, therefore, no trunks are created between the wiring-closet switches and the Building Distribution submodule switches. Therefore, transporting traffic from one switch to another requires going through a multilayer device.

Figure 2-2 *One-VLAN-Per-Switch Access Layer Model*

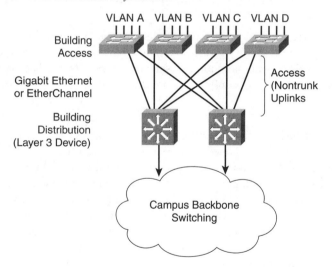

Unique VLANs Per Switch

In the unique-VLANs-per-switch model, more than one VLAN exists per wiring-closet switch; hence, trunks are necessary on uplink connections to transport multiple VLANs. For optimization purposes, unnecessary VLANs are pruned from the trunks. This design still requires a multilayer device to transport traffic between VLANs. Figure 2-3 shows a model with a set of unique VLANs per switch.

Figure 2-3   *Unique VLANs-Per-Switch Access Layer Model*

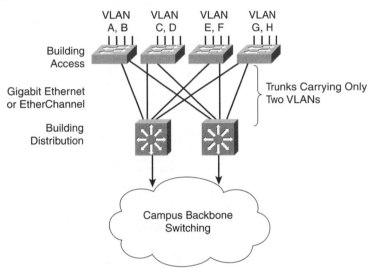

Trunking is a way to carry traffic from several VLANs over a point-to-point link between two devices. You can implement Ethernet trunks in two ways:

- Interswitch Link (ISL) (Cisco proprietary protocol)

- 802.1Q (IEEE standard)

VLANs Spanning Multiple Access Switches

In the VLANs-spanning-multiple-access-switches model, one or more VLANs span several Building Access submodule switches. The uplink connections between the access switch and the redundant distribution switches must be configured as trunks; failing to do so would create segregated networks that might result in suboptimal traffic paths or introduce routing black holes. A routing black hole occurs when a router advertises a network to its peers, even though it cannot properly route traffic to that network. Figure 2-4 shows VLANs A and B spanning across multiple access switches that are connected to two (redundant) distribution switches using uplink trunks.

NOTE   In Figure 2-4, the Spanning Tree Protocol (perhaps with some configuration) causes traffic from VLAN A to cross one uplink trunk, and the traffic from VLAN B to cross the other uplink trunk. Figure 2-4 also describes a more general concept, which is the ability to support distributed workgroup servers attached to the Building Distribution submodule switches. These servers would reside on VLAN A or B.

Figure 2-4   *Access Layer Model Allowing VLANs to Span Multiple Access Switches*

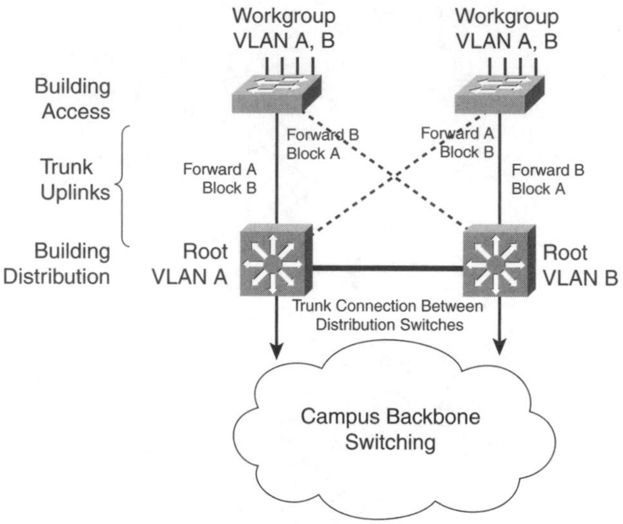

Designing the Physical Campus Network

The physical network design identifies the Layer 1 (physical) and Layer 2 (data link and spanning tree) implementations for the enterprise network. Given specific internetwork requirements, selecting transmission media, data-link protocols, and spanning-tree strategy for the Building Access, Building Distribution, and Campus Backbone submodules of the Campus Infrastructure module are parts of this process.

Selecting Transmission Media and Data-Link Protocols

The primary types of transmission media used in enterprise networks include

- **Twisted pair**—The two types of twisted-pair cabling are unshielded twisted-pair (UTP) and shielded twisted-pair (STP). UTP is widely used to interconnect workstations, servers, and other devices from their network interface card (NIC) to a network device (usually, a Layer 2 access switch). STP is similar to UTP, but cables are wrapped in foil to protect them from external electromagnetic influences.

- **Multimode fiber**—Multimode fiber uses a light emitting diode (LED) as the light source. The low power output and modal dispersion limits the distance at which the signal can be distinguished reliably.

- **Single-mode fiber**—Single-mode optical fiber uses lasers as the light source and is designed for the transmission of a single wave or mode of light as a carrier. The single ray of light can be distinguished more reliably at longer distances compared to multimode fiber.

Table 2-2 provides comparative information about maximum distance, speed, price, and typical place of usage for twisted pair, multimode fiber, and single-mode fiber transmission media.

Table 2-2   *Twisted Pair, Multimode Fiber, and Single-Mode Fiber's Maximum Distance, Speed, Relative Cost, and Typical Uses*

	Twisted Pair	**Multimode Fiber**	**Single-Mode Fiber**
Distance	Up to 100 m	Up to 2 km for Fast Ethernet and up to 550 m for Gigabit Ethernet	Up to 40 km for Fast Ethernet and up to 90 km for Gigabit Ethernet
Speed	Up to 1 Gbps (for the 1 Gbps speed, 100 m is the maximum cable length)	Up to 1 Gbps	1 Gbps, 10 Gbps, or higher
Relative Cost	Low	Moderate	High
Typical Uses	Building Access	Building Distribution, Campus Backbone	Building Distribution, Campus Backbone

Ethernet is the most common data-link technology/protocol deployed in today's campus networks. The Ethernet technology has been constantly evolving since its invention, yielding a number of Ethernet speeds. The following are the most popular variations of Ethernet, plus Long-Range Ethernet, which is the most recent variation of Ethernet:

- **10-Mbps Ethernet**—The slowest of the three technologies. 10-Mbps Ethernet is considered a legacy media, because the prices of the other media are low enough that it is just as economical to build a 100-Mbps Fast Ethernet network as it is to build a 10-Mbps Ethernet network.

- **100-Mbps Ethernet (Fast Ethernet)**—The current media of choice because of its low cost and ability to service most user requirements and many server requirements. Fast Ethernet is relatively inexpensive to implement.

- **1000-Mbps Ethernet (Gigabit Ethernet)**—A little more expensive to implement, but 1000-Mbps Ethernet yields a 10-fold increase in bandwidth, so it is generally used as the uplink between access and distribution and between distribution and core switches.

- **Long-Range (or Long-Reach) Ethernet (LRE)**—For buildings with existing Category 1/2/3 wiring, LRE technology provides connectivity at speeds from 5 to 15 Mbps (full duplex) and distances up to 5000 feet. LRE technology delivers broadband service on the same lines as plain old telephone service (POTS), digital telephone, and Integrated Services Digital Network traffic. LRE also supports modes compatible with asymmetric digital subscriber lines (ADSLs), allowing enterprises to implement LRE to buildings where broadband services currently exist.

Table 2-3 provides comparative information about speed, price, and typical uses of Ethernet, Fast Ethernet, Gigabit Ethernet, and LRE.

Table 2-3 *Speed, Relative Price, and Typical Uses of Ethernet, Fast Ethernet, Gigabit Ethernet, and Long-Range Ethernet*

	Ethernet	Fast Ethernet	Gigabit Ethernet	LRE
Speed	10 Mbps	100 Mbps	1000 Mbps	5 to 15 Mbps
Price	Very Low	Low	Moderate	Very Low
Typical Uses	Building Access	Building Access, Building Distribution	Building Distribution, Campus Backbone	Building Access (for special cases)

EtherChannel technology provides incremental speeds between Fast Ethernet and Gigabit Ethernet. EtherChannel combines multiple Fast Ethernet links up to 800 Mbps or Gigabit Ethernet links up to 8 Gbps. EtherChannel provides fault-tolerant, high-speed links between switches, routers, and servers. Without EtherChannel, connectivity options are limited to the specific line rates of the interface.

Figure 2-5 shows the transmission media for a typical campus network structure. Building Access submodule devices that are no more than 100 meters away from the LAN switch use UTP. The UTP wiring can easily handle the required distance and speed, and its installation is a straightforward task. Multimode and single-mode optical cables handle higher-speed requirements at the Campus Backbone and Building Distribution submodules. Multimode optical cable is usually satisfactory inside a building. For communications between buildings, multimode or single-mode cable is used, depending on distance limitations.

Figure 2-5 *Transmission Media and Data-Link Protocol Selection Example*

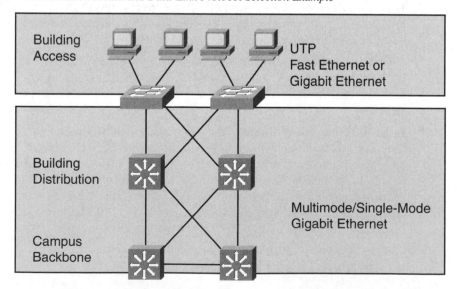

NOTE   When selecting transmission media, scalability for the future is a key concern. Therefore, attention to the properties of the media being installed, such as shifted and nonshifted dispersion fiber, the wavelength, and the diameter of the fiber, is essential.

Selecting a Physical Network Segmentation Strategy

Designing a physical campus network entails selecting a network segmentation strategy based on broadcast domains, failure domains, and policy domains. One must also determine how to implement STP to complement the segmentation strategy.

The effect of broadcast, failure, and policy domains on the campus network includes the following:

- **Broadcast domain**—Media Access Control (MAC)-layer broadcasts flood throughout the data-link layer switched domain. Use multilayer switching in a structured design to reduce the scope of broadcast domains. In addition, intelligent, protocol-aware features of multilayer switches will further contain broadcasts, such as Dynamic Host Configuration Protocol (DHCP), by converting them into directed unicasts. These protocol-aware features are a function of the Cisco IOS Software, which is common among multilayer switches and routers.

- **Failure domain**—A group of data-link layer switches connected together to extend a single network is called a Layer 2 switched domain. The data-link layer switched domain is considered to be a failure domain, because a misconfigured or malfunctioning workstation can introduce errors that have an impact on, or disable the entire domain. A jabbering network interface card (NIC), for instance, might flood the entire domain with broadcasts, and a workstation with an invalid/duplicate IP address can become a black hole for packets. Problems of this nature are difficult to localize. Restricting failure domains to one data-link layer switch in one wiring closet, if possible, reduces the scope of the failure domain. The scope of VLANs must also be restricted; ideally, each VLAN (Internet Protocol subnet) is restricted to one wiring-closet switch. The gigabit uplinks from each wiring-closet switch connect directly to routed interfaces on multilayer switches in the Building Distribution submodule. To achieve load balancing, two such VLANs can connect the wiring-closet switch to the multilayer switch in the Building Distribution submodule.

- **Policy domain**—Policy is usually defined on the routers or multilayer switches in the campus network. A convenient way to define policy is with access control lists (ACLs) that reference specific IP subnet(s). Thus, a group of users or servers with similar QoS or security policies can be conveniently grouped together in the same IP subnet (the same VLAN). Services, such as DHCP, can be defined on an IP subnet basis.

Selecting and Implementing Spanning Tree Protocol

Data-link layer switches run Spanning Tree Protocol (STP) to block loops in the Layer 2 topology. One drawback of allowing loops in the data-link layer design is that redundant links are put in blocking mode and do not forward traffic. It is better to avoid Layer 2 loops by design and have the Layer 3 protocols handle load balancing and redundancy. As a result, all links are utilized and user traffic makes most efficient use of the network bandwidth. The second drawback of having loops in the Layer 2 topology is STP's convergence, which takes 30 to 50 seconds. Therefore, avoiding loops is especially important in the mission-critical parts of the network.

Cisco switches support the 802.1D STP. Unless a device is still running an older operating system, the new 802.1w Rapid STP is supported. To take advantage of the benefits of Rapid STP, one must make sure that the interswitch segments are full-duplex (point-to-point) and that the switches have operating systems supporting the Rapid STP. As its name implies, Rapid STP (802.1w) converges faster than the traditional 802.1D protocol. Rapid STP incorporates features similar to those Cisco has previously recommended into the protocol; examples of those features are port fast, uplink fast, and backbone fast. A one-to-one negotiation on point-to-point (full-duplex) links also plays a role in rapid convergence of 802.1w.

By default, Cisco products operate in per-VLAN spanning-tree (PVST+) mode. This mode builds a spanning-tree instance for each VLAN, and it can interoperate with switches that are in Common Spanning Tree (CST) mode. CST has been the method that non-Cisco vendors following the IEEE recommendations have undertaken. CST builds one single spanning-tree instance and uses it for all VLANs, despite the fact that these VLANs might have quite different topologies. The benefit of PVST is that each spanning tree can be optimized for the topology of its corresponding VLAN, and its drawback is the extra overhead of having many spanning-tree instances that are built and maintained. The CST has minimal overhead, because it builds only one spanning-tree instance; on the other hand, its weakness is that the topology of the single spanning tree it builds might not be optimized for the topology of all VLANs.

The recently developed IEEE 802.1s standard, Multiple Spanning Trees (MST) protocol, is a compromise between PVST and CST. MST allows multiple spanning-tree instances to be built and maintained. Each spanning-tree instance is used for VLANs with similar topologies and can, therefore, be optimized accordingly. Because MST does not build one spanning-tree instance per VLAN, its overhead is substantially less than that of PVST. Building multiple spanning trees renders MST's overhead more than its CST counterpart, although MST wins the optimization battle against CST. In conclusion, using MST and the features of Rapid STP, if possible, is the most preferred choice of STP implementation. Availability of these options is product dependent.

To prevent STP convergence events in the Campus Backbone submodule, ensure that all links connecting backbone switches are routed access links, not trunks carrying switched VLANs. This will also constrain the broadcast and failure domains. Use multilayer switching in a structured design to reduce the scope of spanning-tree domains. Let a Layer 3 routing protocol, such as Enhanced Interior Gateway Routing Protocol (EIGRP) or Open Shortest Path First (OSPF), handle load balancing, redundancy, and recovery in the backbone.

Selecting Data Link or Multilayer Switching Solutions

The development of data-link layer switching in hardware led to network designs that emphasize data-link layer switching. These designs are often characterized as "flat," because they are most often based on the campuswide VLAN model, in which a number of VLANs span the entire network. This type of architecture favored the departmental segmentation approach in which, for example, all marketing or engineering users needed to use their own broadcast domain to avoid crossing slow routers. Because these departments could exist anywhere within the network, VLANs had to span the entire network.

Multilayer switching provides the identical advantages as routing, with the added performance boost from packet forwarding handled by specialized hardware. Adding multilayer switching in the Building Distribution and Campus Backbone submodules of the Campus Infrastructure module segments the campus into smaller, more manageable pieces. This approach also eliminates the need for campuswide VLANs, which allows for the design and implementation of a far more scalable architecture. Today's multilayer switches offer advances in semiconductor technology, enabling Cisco to offer more features; hence, you can implement multilayer functionality and multilayer control in the campus backbone at a cost-effective price point.

Table 2-4 summarizes the selection criteria for data-link layer switching and multilayer switching for a campus network. As Table 2-4 specifies, data-link layer switching supports simple, flat networks. Multilayer switching is useful in hierarchical networks that require complex routing, and it offers advantages of equal-cost path routing, fast convergence, load balancing, and scalability.

Table 2-4   *Data Link and Multilayer Switching Characteristics*

	Cost	Complexity	Versatility	Typical Uses
Data-link layer Switching	Moderate	Simpler	Less versatile	Building Access, Campus Backbone
Multilayer switching	Expensive	More complex	More versatile	Building Distribution, Campus Backbone

How data-link layer switching and multilayer switching are used in the design of different-sized campus networks and complexities are presented through a set of examples:

- Small campus network
- Medium campus network
- Multilayer switched campus backbone
- Large-scale multilayer-switched campus backbone

Small Campus Network

The small campus network design is appropriate for a building-sized network with up to several thousand networked devices. You can collapse the Campus Backbone and Building Distribution submodules into one layer for a small campus network, in which case the Campus Backbone provides aggregation for the Building Access switches. Cost-effectiveness in this model comes with a tradeoff between scalability and investment protection. The lack of distinct Campus Backbone and Building Distribution submodules and limited port density in the Campus Backbone restricts scaling in this model.

The building design shown in Figure 2-6 comprises a single redundant building block. The two multilayer switches form a collapsed Campus Backbone. Data-link layer switches are deployed in the wiring closets for desktop connectivity. Each data-link layer switch has redundant gigabit uplinks to the backbone switches. In a small campus network, servers would either be attached to data-link layer switches, or they would be directly connected to the multilayer backbone switches, depending on performance and density requirements.

Figure 2-6   *Small Campus Network Design*

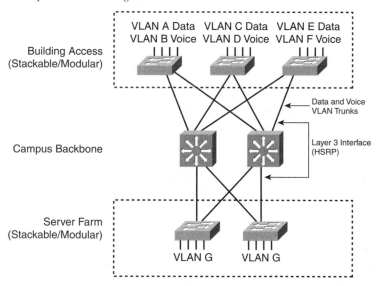

Medium Campus Network

Figure 2-7 shows a medium campus design with higher availability and higher capacity. The most flexible and scalable Campus Backbone consists of multilayer switches.

Figure 2-7   *Medium Campus Network Design*

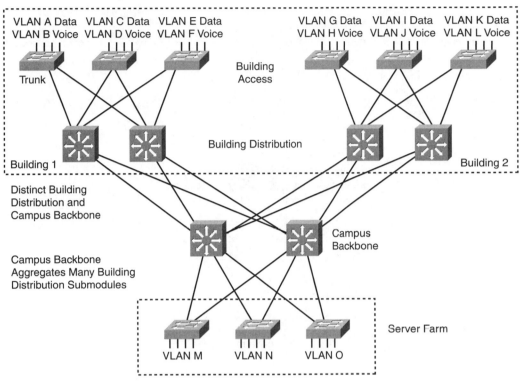

In Figure 2-7, the building distribution switches are connected to the backbone switches by routed Gigabit Ethernet or Gigabit EtherChannel links. Multilayer-switched backbones offer these advantages:

- Reduced router peering
- Flexible topology with no spanning-tree loops
- Multicast and broadcast control in the backbone
- Scalability to an arbitrarily large size

Multilayer Switched Campus Backbone

The most flexible and scalable Campus Backbone consists of multilayer switches, as shown in Figure 2-8. The backbone switches are connected by routed Gigabit Ethernet or Gigabit EtherChannel links.

Figure 2-8 *Multilayer Switched Campus Backbone Design*

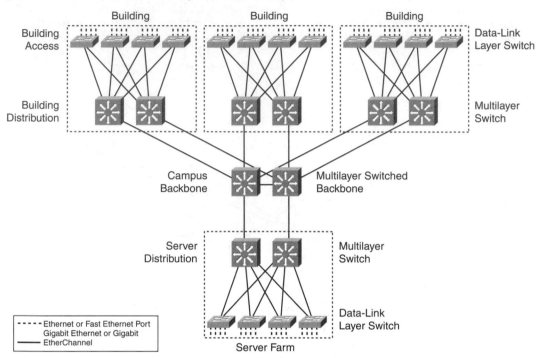

Multilayer-switched backbones have several advantages:

- Reduced router peering
- Flexible topology with no spanning-tree loops
- Multicast and broadcast control in the backbone
- Scalability to an arbitrarily large size

Figure 2-9 shows a large-scale multilayer-switched Campus Backbone. This multilayer-switched backbone has the advantage that arbitrary topologies are supported, because a sophisticated routing protocol, such as EIGRP or OSPF, is used pervasively.

In Figure 2-9, the backbone consists of four multilayer switches with Gigabit Ethernet or Gigabit EtherChannel links. All links in the backbone are routed links, so there are no spanning-tree loops. This figure suggests the actual scale by showing several gigabit links connected to the backbone switches. Note that a full mesh of connectivity between backbone switches is possible, but not required. When allocating link bandwidths, traffic patterns within the backbone must be carefully examined.

Figure 2-9   *Large-Scale Multilayer-Switched Campus Backbone*

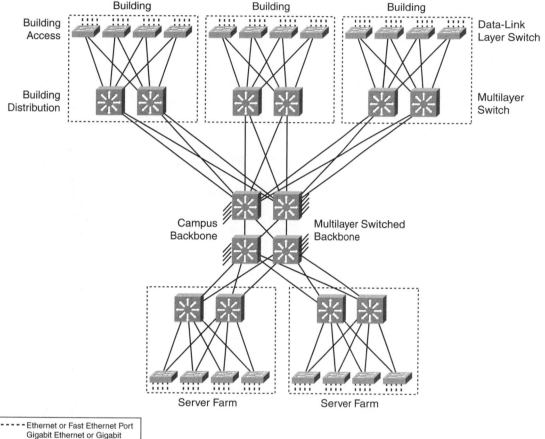

Selecting Cisco Hardware and Software

After designing the logical and physical campus network and selecting data-link layer or multilayer switching solutions, the next step in the campus network design methodology requires that you select the Cisco hardware and software for each location on the network.

Cisco offers the Cisco Product Advisor to help you select the right switch solution for the enterprise campus network. The tool operates in two modes: novice and expert. To access the Product Advisor, go to http://www.cisco.com/en/US/products/prod_tools_index.html, and click the Cisco Product Advisor link. Then, click a device category.

The Product Advisor asks you questions to help you select routers appropriate for your particular needs (see Figure 2-10). Product advisor does not include all products and features, but it does provide helpful information for selecting the adequate Cisco products for your network.

Figure 2-10 *Cisco Online Product Advisor*

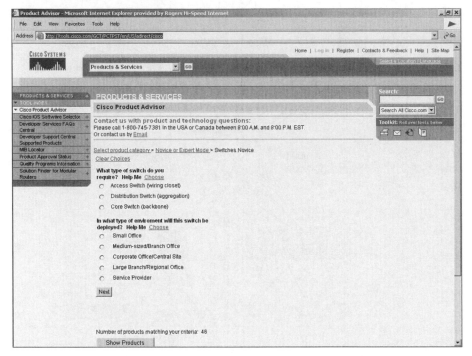

To help in selecting the most appropriate Cisco switch for each campus location, the following questions must be answered:

1 What is the size of the campus location or building? Select one of the following:

- Small campus location/building
- Medium campus location/building
- Large campus location/building

2 What speed is required for most ports (excluding the uplink ports)? Select one of the following:

- 10 Mbps
- 10/100 Mbps
- 10/100/1000 Mbps (copper ports)
- 1000 Mbps (Gigabit Interface Converter [GBIC] ports)

3 How many ports are required on the switch?

4 What media type is needed for uplinks (copper/fiber)?

5 What is the desired speed for uplinks (100 Mbps, 1000 Mbps, or 10 Gbps)?

6 How many uplinks are required (1, 2, or more)?

7 Is redundant power supply required?

8 Does the switch need redundant switching engines?

9 Does the switch need IP routing/multilayer switching?

10 Is the switch required to have Intrusion Detection System (IDS), Server Load Balancing (SLB), or Network Analysis Module (NAM)?

11 Must the switch have inline power for IP phones or wireless access points?

12 Does the switch need to run CatOS or Native IOS, or does it need to operate in Hybrid mode?

13 What CatOS and/or IOS version does the switch need?

14 Which Intelligent Network Services are required to be enabled, configured, and provisioned on the switch?

NOTE   The industry-standard Cisco GBIC is a hot-swappable input/output (I/O) device that plugs into a Gigabit Ethernet port or slot, linking the port with the network. Cisco GBICs can be interchanged on a wide variety of Cisco products and can be intermixed in combinations of 1000BASE-T, 1000BASE-SX, 1000BASE-LX/LH, 1000BASE-ZX, or 1000BASE-CWDM interfaces on a port-by-port basis. As additional capabilities are developed, these modules make it easy to upgrade to the latest interface technology, maximizing investment protection. Cisco GBICs are supported across a variety of Cisco switches, routers, and optical transport devices.

Identifying an IP Addressing Strategy

An effective IP addressing scheme is critical to the success and scalability of the network. Identifying an IP addressing strategy for the campus network, given specific internetwork requirements, is essential.

Step 1   The first step in an IP addressing plan design is to determine the size of the network to establish how many IP addresses are needed. To gather the required information, answer these questions:

- **How big is the network?**—Determine the number of workstations, servers, IP phones, router interfaces, switch management interfaces, firewall interfaces, and so on. The summary defines the minimum overall number of IP addresses required for the network. Because all networks tend to grow, allow a reserve of about 20% to 40% for potential network and application expansion.

- **How many locations are in the network, and what are their sizes?**—The information about the size and number of the individual locations is closely related to the overall network size. These values should correlate to the segmentation strategy chosen for the campus networks. These values impact the subnetwork addressing scheme deployed to accommodate all locations and the number of IP addresses required in each location.

Step 2   Determine if you need private or public addresses based on the following questions:

- Are private, public, or both address types required? The decision about when to use private, public, or both address types depends on the Internet connection presence and the number of publicly visible servers. Possible situations are

  - **There is no Internet connectivity**—The network is isolated, and there is no need to acquire public addresses.

  - **There is Internet connectivity, but there are no public-accessible servers**—The network is connected to the Internet and, thus, at least one public IP address is required. Use one public IP address and a translation mechanism, such as port address translation (PAT), to allow access to the Internet from a single IP address. Private addresses are used to address the internal network.

  - **There is Internet connectivity and public-accessible servers**—The public addresses are required to connect all public-accessible servers to the Internet. The number of public addresses corresponds to the number of Internet connections and public-accessible servers.

  - **All end systems should be publicly accessible**—Only public IP addresses are required and used to address the whole network.

- What class of addresses and how many networks can be obtained from the authority (usually the Internet Service Provider) assigning public numbers? The required IP address classes for the planned network are based on information about the network size, the number of locations, and the size of the individual locations.

- How many end systems need access to the public network only (not publicly visible)? This is the number of end systems that need a limited set of external services (for example, e-mail, FTP, web browsing) and do not need unrestricted external access. The public network does not need to initiate any communication with these devices.

- How many end systems also need to be visible to the public network? This is the number of Internet connections and various servers that needs to be visible to the public (public servers and servers used for e-commerce, such as web servers, database servers, and application servers) and defines the number of required public IPv4 addresses.

- How and where will you cross the boundaries between the private and public IP addresses? When private addresses are used for addressing in a network, and this network needs to be connected to the Internet, a translation mechanism such as Network Address Translation (NAT) must be used to translate from private to public addresses and vice versa.

NOTE   Some applications do not support translation to a single IP address using PAT. Therefore, sufficient IP addresses will be required to support one-to-one NAT for each user concurrently accessing these applications through the Internet.

Step 3   The decision on how to implement the IP addressing hierarchy is an administrative decision that is based on these questions:

- Is hierarchy needed within the IP addressing plan? You will decide how to implement the IP addressing hierarchy based on the network size and the geography and topology of the network. In large networks, a hierarchical IP addressing plan is required to promote a stable network. Also, routing protocols such as OSPF rely on a hierarchical addressing plan.

- What are the criteria to divide the network into route summarization groups? The network is usually divided into route summarization groups based on the network size and topology. To reduce the routing overhead in a large network, a multilevel hierarchy might be required. The depth of hierarchy levels depends on the network size, topology, number of network layers, and the size of the upper-level summarization group.

Selecting Routing Protocols

After the detailed IP addressing strategy is identified, the next step is to select routing protocols for the campus network that meet performance, scalability, and availability requirements. The decision about which routing protocols to implement is based on the design goals, the physical topology of the network, and the configuration of links for remote sites.

Prior to the discussion of comparing and contrasting different routing protocols, it is important to review the circumstances upon which usage of static routing is either necessary or at least justifiable. Subsequently, drawbacks of static routing and the benefits of dynamic routing will be listed in tandem. Finally, it is important to dissect and analyze the exact situations or places where implementing a particular routing protocol would be acceptable or preferable.

Static Versus Dynamic Routing

Static routing is primarily used for

- Routing to and from stub networks. A stub network only carries traffic for local hosts and typically has only one entry/exit point. Even if it has paths to more than one other network, it does not carry traffic for other networks.
- Smaller networks that are not expected to grow significantly.
- Supporting special features such as dial-on-demand routing (DDR) and On-Demand Routing (ODR).
- Specifying routes toward dialing peers in dial-in environments.

Configuration and maintenance of static routes is time consuming. It requires that you have complete knowledge of the entire network to implement it properly. Dynamic routing protocols have two major advantages over static routing protocols:

- Easy configuration, which involves much less work for an administrator (even in small networks)
- Dynamic adaptation to changes in the network

The use of dynamic routing protocols is favored in almost all network scenarios, except for DDR, ODR, a stub network, or a dial-in scenario.

Choosing Routing Information Protocol, IGRP, EIGRP, OSPF, or Integrated Intermediate System-to-Intermediate System must be an informed decision based on organizational policies, design goals, and network topology and architecture. The following sections provide a condensed overview of each protocol and situations/places where these protocols might or might not be beneficial.

RIP and RIPv2

Routing Information Protocol (RIP) is the oldest routing protocol and is simple in its operation. It is a classful distance vector protocol. Its metric is based only on hop count, and it does not support variable-length subnet mask (VLSM), manual route summarization, and classless interdomain routing (CIDR).

Routing Information Protocol version 2 is an enhanced version of the original RIP (now referred to as RIPv1) that supports VLSM. RIPv2 is implemented mainly in small networks, especially small hub-and-spoke networks using point-to-point links. RIPv2 with snapshot routing support is used in dialup networks, because it is able to freeze its routing table and wait for the dialup link to connect to start the exchange of routing information. It is seldom used in LAN environments, because it is chatty and has a low hop count limit. In nonbroadcast multiaccess (NBMA) environments, the main issue of RIPv2 is associated with the split-horizon rule, which prevents the propagation of routing updates to all connected routers reachable through the same physical interface (but over different virtual circuits). The use of RIPv1 and RIPv2 in NBMA networks is not appropriate because of large bandwidth requirements.

IGRP

Interior Gateway Routing Protocol (IGRP) is the original Cisco routing protocol. It is a classful distance vector protocol with a more complex metric calculation than RIP; it takes into account minimum bandwidth and accumulated delay. IGRP might be suitable for small-to-medium networks. Like RIP, it has problems with the split-horizon feature in NBMA networks. Other problems of IGRP include its slow convergence because of its pure distance vector operation and the potential for high bandwidth utilization when propagating entire routing tables to neighbors. IGRP is not typically recommended for new deployments.

EIGRP

Enhanced IGRP (EIGRP), developed based on IGRP, is a very powerful routing protocol. EIGRP is also a Cisco proprietary protocol licensed to limited vendors. It is an advanced distance vector protocol with some link state features (topology table, no periodic route propagation, and triggered updates). This protocol is well suited to almost all environments, including LAN, point-to-point, and NBMA. EIGRP is not suitable for dialup environments, because it must maintain the neighbor relationship and it uses periodic hello packets, effectively keeping the dialup circuits active all the time.

EIGRP offers the following features:

* VLSM support
* Advanced composite metric
* Fast convergence
* Scalability
* Authentication
* Flexible summarization
* Configurable bandwidth usage
* Low bandwidth during normal conditions
* Load balancing across unequal cost paths
* Support for stub networks

OSPF

Open Shortest Path First (OSPF) is a standards-based link-state routing protocol, based on Dijkstra's shortest path first (SPF) algorithm for best path calculation. Initially, OSPF was designed for networks that consisted of point-to-point links, but later, it was successfully adapted for operation in LAN and NBMA environments. OSPF can be tuned for dialup operation by suppressing the hello protocol over dialup lines (sometimes called Demand Circuit operation). Because of the hierarchical design requirement, there are design considerations when using OSPF in larger networks. One backbone area is required and all nonbackbone areas must be attached directly to that backbone area. Expansion of the backbone area can cause design issues, as the backbone area must remain contiguous.

OSPF offers these features:

- There is no limitation on the hop count. The intelligent use of VLSM is very useful in IP address allocation.

- OSPF uses IP multicast to send link-state updates. This ensures less processing on routers that are not listening to OSPF packets. Updates are only sent when routing changes occur rather than periodically. This ensures a better use of bandwidth. Nonetheless, all OSPF routers must send link state advertisements every 30 minutes to ensure that all other OSPF routers have the most recent routing information, and they are all consistent.

- OSPF offers fast convergence, because routing changes are propagated instantaneously and not periodically (a characteristic of distance vector routing protocols).

- OSPF provides for effective load balancing.

- OSPF allows for a logical definition of networks where routers can be divided into areas. This will limit the explosion of link-state updates over the whole network. This also provides a mechanism for aggregating routes and cutting down on the unnecessary propagation of subnet information.

- OSPF allows for routing authentication by using different methods of password authentication.

- OSPF allows for the transfer and tagging of external routes injected into an autonomous system. This keeps track of external routes injected by exterior protocols, such as Border Gateway Protocol (BGP).

IS-IS

Integrated Intermediate System-to-Intermediate System (IS-IS) is a standards-based link-state protocol whose operation is similar to OSPF. IS-IS uses the SPF algorithm for best path calculation as well. An IS-IS network consists of two areas: a backbone and connected nonbackbone areas. In contrast to OSPF, the IS-IS backbone can easily be expanded to accommodate new nonbackbone areas. Integrated IS-IS has the following features:

- Integrated IS-IS is a proven protocol for very large networks.

- Integrated IS-IS has no adaptation for NBMA point-to-multipoint networks, which is one design point to be considered prior to implementation.

- Integrated IS-IS is not suited for dialup networks because, unlike OSPF, it does not include hello protocol suppression capability.

The deployment of Integrated IS-IS in networks requires more knowledge than for other Interior Gateway Protocols (IGPs). Integrated IS-IS is based on the Open System Interconnection (OSI) IS-IS protocol, and the numbering of IS-IS areas is done in an OSI-based environment, not in IP.

Table 2-5 provides a condensed comparison of RIP, IGRP, EIGRP, OSPF, and IS-IS.

Table 2-5   *Routing Protocol Characteristics*

	Support for Classless Summarization	Flat Model (as opposed to Hierarchical)	Supports Multiaccess (LAN)	Supports Point-to-Point	Supports Point-to-Multipoint (Frame Relay)
RIPv1		X	X	X	
IGRP		X	X	X	
EIGRP	X	X	X	X	X
OSPF	X		X	X	X
IS-IS	X		X	X	

Selecting Areas for Networks

After selecting routing protocols, you will identify areas or networks for that routing protocol. The key considerations for routing areas or networks are based on

- Number of multilayer devices and the type of CPU power and media available
- Type of topology (either full mesh or partial mesh)
- Multilayer device memory

Enterprise Campus Design Examples

In this section, three examples or scenarios are presented. Each example begins with a short description of a company and its internetwork requirements. For each case, based on the size of the company and its network applications and other specifications, the design concerns and questions, as discussed in the previous sections, are answered.

Small Enterprise Design Example

A small company has about 200 users in one building with two separate floors. Its primary network user applications include e-mail, FTP, Hypertext Transfer Protocol (HTTP) access to an intranet server, and dedicated Internet access for all employees. Table 2-6 summarizes the design decisions made—and the rationale behind them—to satisfy this company's requirements.

Table 2-6 *Design Questions, Decisions, and Rationale for a Small Company Campus Network*

Design Question	Decision	Notes
What is the logical network design?	Single corporate-wide VLAN.	There is no requirement for voice, so the entire network of 200 users will be in a single VLAN.
What physical network media will be used?	Twisted pair throughout the entire network.	Twisted pair was selected because of its low cost.
What data-link layer protocol will be used?	Fast Ethernet in the Campus Backbone, Fast Ethernet in the Building Access to the desktop.	Fast Ethernet is sufficient today; if more growth is realized in the future, the company could easily upgrade to Gigabit Ethernet.
How will STP be deployed?	Spanning tree will be used and a Campus Backbone switch will be the root.	For simplicity, the Catalyst 3550 was selected as the STP root, because the Catalyst 3550 has the highest processing capability.
What is the data-link layer/ multilayer switching strategy for the network?	Network layer routing is only needed on the Internet edge, and data-link layer switching in the network.	Network layer routing is only needed for Internet access; data-link layer switching is used throughout the rest of the network.
Which Cisco products will be used?	Catalyst 3550 in the Campus Backbone submodule, and Catalyst 2950 in the Building Access submodule.	The redundant Catalyst 3550 in the Campus Backbone is optional and is provided for redundancy.
What IP addressing scheme will be used?	Approximately 254 IP addresses from ISP or regional number authority.	—
Which routing protocols will be used?	No routing protocol will be used; a default route to the Internet will suffice.	A very small network (or a stub network) reaps no benefit from running a routing protocol.

Medium Enterprise Design Example

A medium-sized company's campus network must support about 1000 users. The primary network applications are database applications. The company spreads over two buildings that connect to each other through a 100-foot walkway. This company intends to add voice (support for Voice over IP [VoIP] and IP Telephony) in the future and would like to plan for it in the infrastructure now. Table 2-7 summarizes the design decisions made—and the rationale behind them—to satisfy this company's requirements.

Table 2-7   *Design Questions, Decisions, and Rationale for a Medium-Sized Enterprise Network*

Design Question	Decision	Notes and Comments
What is the logical network design?	Segmentation by type of traffic (voice and data): one VLAN for voice and one for data on each Building Access submodule switch. To get both VLANs back to the Building Distribution submodule, the company chose ISL trunking from the access switch to the distribution switch. The data center will have three server farms in unique VLANs that connect directly to the Campus Backbone submodule.	The Information Technology staff wants voice on one VLAN and data on a separate VLAN, which requires two VLANs in each access switch.
What physical network media will be used?	UTP is implemented from the workstations to the Layer 2 switches in the Building Access submodule. Multimode fiber from the Building Access submodule to the Building Distribution submodule. Multimode fiber from the Building Distribution submodule to the Campus Backbone submodule.	The multimode fiber between the Building Access and Building Distribution submodules, and in the Campus Backbone submodule, provides an upgrade path to Gigabit Ethernet or faster technologies.
What data-link layer protocol will be used?	Gigabit Ethernet in the Campus Backbone and Building Distribution submodules. Fast Ethernet in the Building Access submodule to the desktop.	—

continues

Table 2-7 *Design Questions, Decisions, and Rationale for a Medium-Sized Enterprise Network (Continued)*

Design Question	Decision	Notes and Comments
How will STP be deployed?	Spanning-tree root is the distribution device.	—
What is the data-link layer/ multilayer switching strategy for the network?	Multilayer switching in the Campus Backbone submodule. Data-link layer switching in the Building Distribution and Building Access submodules.	—
Which Cisco products will be used?	Catalyst 6500 and 400x in the Campus Backbone submodule. Catalyst 4006 in the Building Distribution submodule. Catalyst 400x and 3500XL PWR in the Building Access submodule. Catalyst 400x and 3500XL in the server farm.	Need inline power modules for voice equipment.
What IP addressing scheme will be used?	Private addressing. Each VLAN is its own subnet.	Because of the number of IP addresses needed and no Internet access requirement, private addressing will be used in the network. The base network number for the voice VLANs will be different from the base network number for the data VLANs.
Which routing protocols will be used?	EIGRP	OSPF or even RIPv2 would also work, because the network contains only two multilayer-switched devices.

Large Enterprise Design Example

A large enterprise network supports 4000 users in four buildings. It plans to implement voice in the future as part of an incremental deployment. Hence, the company wants to ensure that the infrastructure it plans today will support future requirements.

The information systems department has decided that each of the Building Distribution submodule devices will perform multilayer switching to limit broadcast and failure domains within each Building Distribution and Building Access switch.

The company has the budget to put in the required multiple strands of fiber between the buildings for redundancy purposes. Single-mode fiber is already installed in the risers of the buildings, enough to support the bandwidth needs. Table 2-8 summarizes the design decisions made—and the rationale behind them—to satisfy this company's requirements.

Table 2-8   *Design Questions, Decisions, and Rationale for a Large Enterprise Network*

Design Question	Decision	Notes and Comments
What is the logical network design?	Segmentation by type of traffic (voice and data). One VLAN for voice and one for data on each access layer switch.	Each department will have its own VLAN. There will be separate subnetworks and VLANs designed for voice.
What physical network media will be used?	UTP is implemented from the desktop all the way to the Layer 2 switches in the Building Access submodule. Fiber to the Building Distribution and Campus Backbone submodules.	Fiber runs between the buildings to create the meshed core and will provide redundant connections between the Building Distribution and Campus Backbone submodules.
What data-link layer protocol will be used?	Gigabit EtherChannel in the Building Distribution and Campus Backbone submodules. Fast Ethernet in the Building Access submodule to the desktop.	—
How will spanning-tree protocol be deployed?	Spanning-tree root will be the distribution switch in each building.	Eight separate spanning-tree domains, two per building.
What is the data-link layer/ multilayer switching strategy for the network?	Multilayer switching in the Building Distribution and Campus Backbone submodules. Data-link layer switching in the Building Access submodule.	—
Which Cisco products will be used?	Catalyst 6500 in the Campus Backbone submodule. Catalyst 6500 or 4006 in the Building Distribution submodule. Catalyst 400x in the Building Access submodule.	—

continues

Table 2-8 *Design Questions, Decisions, and Rationale for a Large Enterprise Network (Continued)*

Design Question	Decision	Notes and Comments
What IP addressing scheme will be used?	Class B addresses. Private addressing two networks: one for data and one for voice.	There will be multiple subnets used within each address range. The purpose of having two networks is to segregate the voice from the data completely. The company needs one Class C address from the service provider to support public access to the Internet.
Which routing protocols will be used?	OSPF Core will be area 0, and each building will be a different area.	Given the size of the network, either EIGRP or OSPF is acceptable. If the company wants standards-based routing protocols, they should use OSPF, with each building being its own area and the core being area 0.

Designing the Server Farm

A server farm is a controlled environment that houses enterprise servers. The server farm's servers support the business applications accessed by users over the corporate intranet. These servers can be centralized or distributed strategically, thus offering high levels of performance, scalability, and availability. The remainder of this chapter is dedicated to design objectives for the server farm and its infrastructure architecture. How the server farm can be designed for scalability and the considerations for server farm security and manageability is also discussed.

Design Objectives for the Server Farm

The primary objectives in the design of a large-scale, shared-enterprise server farm are

- **Performance**—Up to 10 Gbps outbound bandwidth capacity is required from the server farm for most enterprises.

- **Scalability**—A critical requirement in every server farm. Server load balancing is most often deployed. As the number of servers requiring higher-bandwidth connections increases, port densities can exceed the capacity of a single switch or server farm block. Applying a modular block design to server farm deployments permits flexible growth.

- **Availability**—Availability is generally ensured through the overall network design. Networks are designed to minimize the occurrence of service problems and the time to recover from problems, for example, with backup recovery policies and procedures. Redundancy and failover provisions at the physical, data link, and network layers ensure high availability at all layers. The most effective solutions are those with consistent engineering considerations tightly integrated throughout the server farm.

- **Security**—Security is an integral part of the network design. A single vulnerability could compromise the enterprise. Specialized security expertise is often required. There are challenges in offering encryption, certification, directory services, network access, and other security capabilities that make a network fully secure.

- **Manageability**—Manageability means much more than knowing if a server or other network element is up or down. The ability to assess service levels on a "per-user" basis is important to offering and maintaining required service levels. An operations center support system might track network configuration and application performance, and maintain and resolve errors and alarms. Good manageability tools and qualified personnel lower operations costs and reduce wasted time, and they yield higher overall satisfaction.

NOTE   Other considerations for the Server Farm module design are locality of access (single or multiple site), number of applications, data volume (small, medium, or large), transaction frequencies (seldom to often), and control of access points to the Server Farm module.

Server Farm Infrastructure Architecture

Similar to the campus infrastructure, the enterprise server farm infrastructure might contain an access layer and a distribution layer, and it is connected to the Campus Backbone submodule (see Figure 2-11).

Figure 2-11 *Server Farm Infrastructure Architecture*

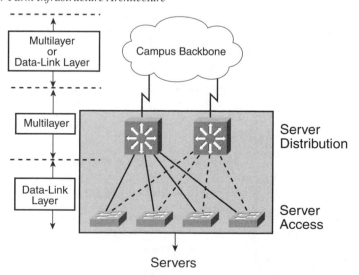

The server access layer provides data-link layer-based transport to directly connected servers. The data-link layer provides flexibility and speed in provisioning. It also allows deployment of applications and systems, which might inherently expect data-link layer-level connectivity.

The server distribution layer consists of multilayer switches, which provide servers with Layer 2 (intra VLAN) and Layer 3 (inter VLAN) connectivity to the rest of the campus and enterprise network. The Server Distribution layer leverages multilayer switching scalability characteristics while benefiting from the flexibility of data-link layer services.

The Campus Backbone is shared between the Campus Infrastructure distribution devices, Enterprise Edge distribution devices, and the Server Farm distribution devices. It is composed of high-end switches providing network layer transport between the distribution and edge layers. Optionally, you can combine the Server Distribution and Campus Backbone layers physically and logically into a collapsed backbone.

Best practices for supporting the Server Farm module at the server access layer, the server distribution layer, and the Campus Backbone are summarized in Table 2-9.

Table 2-9   *Summary of Best Practices at Different Layers of the Server Farm Infrastructure Architecture*

	Best Practices
Server Farm Campus Backbone (or simply Campus Backbone)	• Deploy high-end switches (such as the Catalyst 8500 or Catalyst 6500 series). • Implement highly redundant switching and links with no single points or paths of failure. • Implement web cache redirection (using Cisco Content Networking solutions). • Implement Hot Standby Router Protocol (HSRP) for failover protection. • Implement intrusion detection with automatic notification of intrusion attempts in place.
Server Farm Distribution Layer	• Deploy mid-range to high-range switches (such as Catalyst 6500 series). • Implement redundant switching and links with no single points or paths of failure. • Deploy caching systems where appropriate (using Cisco Content Networking solutions). • Implement server load balancing (using Cisco Content Networking solutions). • Implement server content routing (using Cisco Content Networking solutions).
Server Farm Access Layer	• Deploy mid-range switches (Catalyst 6500 or 4000 series). • Dual-home all servers.

Designing the Server Farm for Scalability

The Server Farm architecture addresses scalability by providing flexible growth paths to deliver high bandwidth rates to the connected IP core. Some methods that can be used to augment the server farm's performance and scalability include

- **Increase port density**—You can increase raw port density for both end-user devices and infrastructure interconnecting links using a modular approach to add connectivity to the existing installation. You can consider the distribution layer and access layer switches as a module, which provides a predetermined number of data-link layer ports. Expanding data-link layer ports is only a matter of adding another module and updating the configuration to include new modules.

- **Add higher-speed interfaces**—Migrating to a higher-speed interface or EtherChannel technology is a way to deliver greater bandwidth capacity between devices.

- **Consider the spanning-tree implementation**—One of the main limiting factors in designing large Layer 2 implementations is the capacity of the system to handle and scale STP. You can implement Multiple (or Multiinstance) STP (802.1s) to reduce the total number of spanning-tree instances needed to support the infrastructure. This reduces the total overhead associated to STP.

- **Implement a modular design**—Choose devices that are easily upgradeable. Allow for addition of new Server Farm module(s), either at the same location or at another location. Both the complications and available solutions increase greatly if the Server Farm module is part of a geographically dispersed set. A geographically dispersed Server Farm module allows content to be served closer to the requesting client. However, the multilocation Server Farm design has to face challenges in management of content, distribution of updates, synchronization of different sources, proper routing of requests, handling of downed servers, security, and so on.

Considerations for Server Farm Security and Manageability

Physical and network security policies, physical security devices, security software implementation, and security architecture are some of the important items to be considered to meet the Server Farm module's requirements for security.

Good manageability tools and qualified personnel supporting the infrastructure reduce operations costs. Moreover, time and efforts are not wasted on addressing or trying to resolve conflicting indications from management systems. Well-managed server farms yield higher user satisfaction as well. To meet Server Farm module manageability requirements, consider the following items:

- Identify critical devices and applications.
- Create an operations and support plan.
- Implement 24/7 monitoring of servers and network equipment.

- Implement problem/resolution procedures.
- Create a business continuity plan in case of natural disaster.

Security design and designing to ensure manageability are both fully explained in Chapter 4, "Designing Network Management Services," and Chapter 6, "Designing Security Services," respectively.

Summary

In this chapter, you learned the following key points:

- Because the Enterprise Campus functional area is comprised of Campus Infrastructure, Network Management, Server Farm, and Edge Distribution modules, design of an enterprise campus network entails design of each of these modules. The design of an enterprise campus network must meet these requirements:
  - Functionality
  - Performance
  - Scalability
  - Availability
  - Manageability
  - Cost effectiveness
- To design an enterprise campus network, Cisco recommends the following series of steps to be completed:

  Step 1 Determine application and data requirements for each campus location.

  Step 2 Design the logical network.

  Step 3 Design the physical network.

  Step 4 Select appropriate Cisco network devices (hardware and software).

  Step 5 Select an IP addressing strategy and numbering scheme.

  Step 6 Select a routing protocol.

  Step 7 Design the Edge Distribution module.

- Network traffic patterns must be analyzed before designing the actual network. The most important factors one must take into account when analyzing traffic are
  - Traffic load measurement
  - Traffic types
  - Sampling methods

- After the application and data needs for an enterprise are identified, the logical network design may begin by selecting logical network segments and a segmentation method. Logical network segments might be created by
  - Using VLANs
  - Using separate networks (only applicable to very small networks)
- It is recommended that campuswide VLANs should be avoided; within the access layer, you can choose to have one VLAN per switch, unique VLANs per switch, or allow VLANs to span multiple access switches. The choices for trunk protocols are ISL (Cisco proprietary) and 802.1Q (IEEE Standard).
- Transmission media, usually selected from among twisted pair, multimode fiber, and single-mode fiber, have different distance limitations, speed, and costs. Twisted pair is typically used for building access, while multimode and single-mode fiber are used for Building Distribution and Campus Backbone.
- Ethernet (10 Mbps), Fast Ethernet (100 Mbps), and Gigabit Ethernet (1000 Mbps) are today's popular data-link layer protocols; they are progressively faster and more expensive to implement. Ethernet might be used for Building Access, Fast Ethernet is usually used for Building Access and/or Building Distribution, and Gigabit Ethernet can be used for Building Distribution and Campus Backbone.
- With regard to STP, you have the choice between PVST, CST, and MST. It is best to avoid Layer 2 loops, and let Layer 3 protocols handle load fault tolerance, redundancy, and load sharing; otherwise, the scope of the spanning-tree domain must be reduced using multilayer switches. Multilayer switches, used in building distribution and campus backbone, are more complex, more versatile, and more expensive than data-link layer switches, which are used in Building Access and perhaps in Campus Backbone (in some cases).
- Cisco offers the Product Advisor to help you select the correct Cisco network device. The Product Advisor is available at this website: http://www.cisco.com/en/US/products/prod_tools_index.html.
- Identifying an IP addressing strategy can be organized into the following steps:

  Step 1   Determine the size of the network.

  Step 2   Determine if you need private or public addresses.

  Step 3   Determine a method to implement the IP addressing hierarchy.

- The decision about which routing protocols to implement is based on the design goals and the physical topology of the network and the configuration of links for remote sites.
  - Static routing is primarily used for stub networks and/or small networks or to support special features, such as on-demand and dial-on-demand routing.

- — Except in special circumstances, dynamic routing protocols are preferred over static routes. Choosing from among the variety of dynamic routing protocols available is usually based on

    1 The enterprise policy on usage of standard as opposed to proprietary protocols, plus the knowledge and comfort of the network engineers with particular protocols

    2 Size of the enterprise and whether it has multiple locations (requiring hierarchical routing and summarization)

    3 Existence of and, hence, the need to support Multiaccess, Nonbroadcast-Multiaccess, Point-to-Point, and Stub networks

    4 The need for special features, such as manual/classless/per-link summarization, authentication, fast convergence, unequal metric load sharing, and so on

- A server farm is the controlled environment that houses enterprise servers. The data center servers support the business applications accessed by users over the corporate intranet and can be centralized or distributed, thus offering high levels of performance, scalability, and availability. The primary objectives in the design of an enterprise server farm (or data center) are

    - — Performance

    - — Scalability

    - — Availability

    - — Security

    - — Manageability

- The enterprise server farm infrastructure might contain an access layer and a distribution layer, similar to the Campus Infrastructure, and is connected to the Campus Backbone submodule.

- Some methods that can be used to augment the server farm's performance and scalability include

    - — Increase port density

    - — Add higher-speed interfaces

    - — Consider the spanning-tree implementation

    - — Implement a modular design

- Physical and network security policies, physical security devices, security software implementation, and security architecture are some of the important items to be considered to meet the Server Farm module's requirements for security.

- To meet Server Farm module manageability requirements, consider the following items:

    - — Identify critical devices and applications

— Create an operations and support plan

— Implement 24/7 monitoring of servers and network equipment

— Implement problem/resolution procedures

— Create a business continuity plan in case of a natural disaster

References

White Paper. "Gigabit Campus Network Design—Principles and Architecture" at http://www.cisco.com/warp/public/cc/so/neso/lnso/cpso/gcnd_wp.htm.

White Paper. "Data Centers: Best Practices for Security and Performance" at http://www.cisco.com/warp/public/cc/so/neso/wnso/power/gdmdd_wp.pdf.

Product Summary

Tables 2-10 and 2-11 provide a brief overview of some of the products available from Cisco Systems that relate to the topics discussed in this chapter. For a more detailed breakdown of the Cisco product line, visit http://www.cisco.com/en/US/products/index.html.

Table 2-10 lists a few examples of Cisco switches with the following features:

- **Topology**—Access
- **Architecture**—Layer 2 Switching (Intelligent Services)

Table 2-10   *Sample/Example of Access Switches Suitable for Corporate Office/Central Site*

Product Name	Description
Catalyst 3550-24-PWR-EMI	24-10/100 inline power + 2 GBIC ports: EMI
Catalyst 3550-24-PWR-SMI	24-10/100 inline power + 2 GBIC ports: SMI
Catalyst 3560-48PS-E	Catalyst 3560 48 10/100 PoE + 4 SFP Enhanced Image
Catalyst 3560-48PS-S	Catalyst 3560 48 10/100 PoE + 4 SFP Standard Image
Catalyst 4503	Catalyst 4500 Chassis (3-Slot), fan, no p/s
Catalyst 4506	Catalyst 4500 Chassis (6-Slot), fan, no p/s
Catalyst 4507R	Catalyst 4500 Chassis (7-Slot), fan, no p/s, Red Sup Capable
Catalyst 4510R	Catalyst 4500 Chassis (10-Slot), fan, no p/s, Red Sup Capable
Catalyst 6509-NEB	Catalyst 6509 Chassis for Network Equipment Building Systems Environments

- **Environment**—Corporate Office/Central Site
- **Connectivity**—Ethernet (10/100 w/inline power)
- **Port density**—25–48
- **System features**—Integrated Inline Power

Table 2-11 *Cisco Switches to Be Used Within the Server Farm Module*

Product Name	Description
Catalyst 4503	Catalyst 4500 Chassis (3-Slot), fan, no p/s
	Catalyst 4500 Chassis (6-Slot), fan, no p/s
Catalyst 4506	Catalyst 4500 Chassis (7-Slot), fan, no p/s, Red Sup Capable
Catalyst 4507R	Catalyst 4500 Chassis (10-Slot), fan, no p/s, Red Sup Capable
Catalyst 4510R	Catalyst 6509 Chassis for NEBS Environments
Catalyst 6509-NEB	Catalyst 4500 Chassis (3-Slot), fan, no p/s

The Cisco Catalyst 6509-NEB (WS-C6509-NEB) is an excellent distribution or core layer product that satisfies the following specifications:

- **Topology**—Distribution or Core
- **Architecture**—Multiprotocol Routing, Layer 3 Switching (multilayer switching), Layer 4 to Layer 7 Switching
- **Environment**—Corporate Office/Central Site
- **Connectivity**—Ethernet (Gigabit) (GBIC)
- **Port density**—0–24
- **System features**—Redundant Power Supply, Redundant Supervisor Engine, Specialized Service Modules (IDS, NAM, Call switching module)
- **Form Factor**—Modular

Table 2-11 lists a few examples of Cisco switches that are good candidates to be used within the Server Farm module with the following features:

- **Topology**—Server Farm
- **Environment**—Corporate Office/Central Site
- **Connectivity**—Ethernet (Gigabit) (GBIC)
- **Port density**—0–24
- **Form factor**—Modular

Standards and Specifications Summary

Request For Comments (RFCs) can be downloaded from the following website: http://www.rfc-editor.org/rfc.html.

- RFC 1918, "Address Allocation for Private Internets."

Review Questions

Answer the following questions to test your comprehension of the topics discussed in this chapter. Refer to Appendix A, "Answers to Review Questions," to check your answers.

1. The design of an enterprise campus network entails design of each of which modules?

2. What requirements must the design of an enterprise campus network meet?

3. List the seven steps of the campus design methodology.

4. Name at least two important factors that need to be considered when analyzing network traffic?

5. What are the two methods used to create logical network segments?

6. What are the drawbacks of campus-wide VLANs?

7. List at least two methods of deploying VLANs at the access layer.

8. What are the common transmission media for campus networks? Identify which one is suitable for which layer of the campus infrastructure.

9. What are the common data-link layer protocols used in campus networks? Identify the typical uses of each one.

10. Specify the wiring/cable category used for Long-Range Ethernet (LRE) plus its speed range and distance limitation.

11. Network segmentation strategies are based on consideration of which three domain types?

12. How many spanning-tree instances exist when PVST is used? How many if CST is used? What is the modern compromise between PVST and CST called?

13. Briefly compare data-link layer switching and multilayer switching.

14. What tool does Cisco offer to help in selecting a Cisco network device?

15. List at least two factors that affect IP addressing strategy.

16. Name at least two situations that justify usage of static routing.

17. List at least two considerations that influence the choice of dynamic IP routing protocol deployed.

18. Name three of the server farm design objectives.

19. Specify at lease two methods that can augment the server farm's performance and scalability.

20. Name at least three server farm manageability considerations.

Case Study: OCSIC Bottling Company

The purpose of this case study is to practice the key design skills discussed in this chapter. The project is to design a campus network that meets the needs of OCSIC Bottling Company. Specifically, you have been asked to design the headquarters' campus network, design the headquarters' server farm, and, finally, design a typical North American plant network for OCSIC. As each component of the design will have multiple options, consider each option carefully, based on the given constraints. For each identified component of the design, you are required to provide justification for your decision. The justification will provide an explanation for the options considered and the reason behind choosing the selected option.

Background

OCSIC Bottling Company is a United States–based soft drink and beverage distributor. OCSIC's products include colas, flavored soft drinks, and bottled juices. Most of its products, particularly its soft drinks, are recognized throughout the world. Other products, such as juices, are currently available only in selected regions, although the company would like to distribute them worldwide. OCSIC owns and operates 12 bottling, distribution, and sales facilities in North America. In South America, Europe, and the Asia Pacific regions, its products are sold, manufactured, and distributed by independently owned and operated distribution companies. These international distribution companies can sell any products they choose and often do not carry the entire line of OCSIC products.

Business Goals of OCSIC

The company is completing a 10-year plan to move its business into the next century. The company is concerned about losing its competitiveness if it does not innovate and become more responsive to its customers and distributors. Through a series of planning sessions, the company has defined these goals:

- Develop and bring new products to market more quickly
- Provide faster order fulfillment to customers
- Increase product distribution outside the United States
- Improve communications between employees, customers, and partners

- Implement a supply chain management system that provides better integration and responsiveness to the plants and distributors
- Reduce operating costs and increase profitability

Headquarters Location, Network, and Applications

The facilities in North America consist of one main headquarters campus located in Memphis, Tennessee, and 12 wholly owned bottling, distribution, and sales facilities in the United States and Canada. Table 2-12 describes each building in the headquarters' campus. The campus has developed over a long period of time, and users continually move around the campus.

Table 2-12 *OCSIC Headquarters*

Building	Function	Estimated Number of Users	Building Characteristics
Building A	Executive Finance	1400	Six-story building 210,000 square feet
Building B	Accounting Order Processing	600	Two-story building 90,000 square feet
Building C	Marketing Distributor Relations	1200	Four-story building 180,000 square feet
Building D	Research and Development	800	Three-story building 120,000 square feet
Building E	Research and Development	900	Four-story building 120,000 square feet
Building F	Information Systems Data Center Help Desk	400	Two-story building 80,000 square feet

The headquarters' location has an aging Token Ring network, which supports traditional applications such as database, file and print sharing, and e-mail. Over the past 10 years, the company has added IP capabilities to its existing network but is finding the network increasingly difficult and expensive to maintain. The company now wants to "move into the 21st century," replacing its campus network with a complete IP-based solution. Figure 2-12 depicts the current headquarters' campus network. The cabling plant on the headquarters' Token Ring network backbone and risers consists of copper using shielded twisted-pair wiring. Copper unshielded twisted-pair wiring goes to the desktops. Fiber is not currently used anywhere in the network.

Figure 2-12 *OCSIC Headquarters Network*

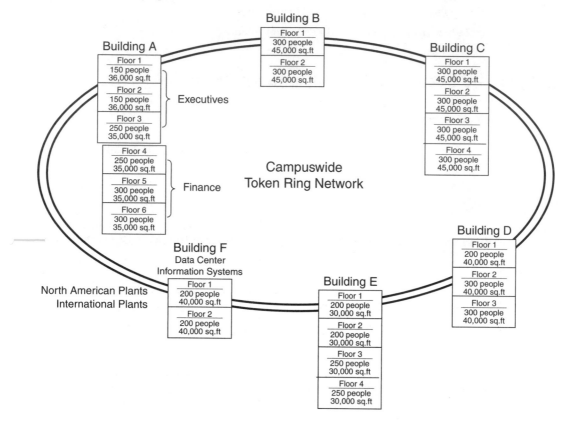

The IT department at OCSIC develops and maintains a variety of enterprise-wide applications. Some are available only at headquarters, and others are available to the North American plants and international manufacturing, distribution, and sales centers. Table 2-13 summarizes the primary applications that the company uses.

Table 2-13 *Primary Applications at OCSIC*

Application	Data Characteristics*	Primary Users	Notes and Description
SAP	Heavy	Accounting Finance Marketing Manufacturing Distribution Order Processing	SAP is used throughout the company to manage manufacturing, inventory, distribution, and order processing.

Table 2-13   *Primary Applications at OCSIC (Continued)*

Application	Data Characteristics*	Primary Users	Notes and Description
PeopleSoft	Moderate	Everyone	PeopleSoft applications are used for financial management and reporting throughout the company.
Custom Oracle database applications	Moderate	Everyone	The company has developed a number of custom Oracle database applications that are used throughout the company, primarily for reporting and decision support.
E-mail	Moderate	Everyone	E-mail is used as the primary means of electronic communication throughout the company. E-mail messages consist primarily of text, but some users send e-mail with graphics and video.
Intranet website	Moderate	Everyone	The company maintains an intranet website that provides up-to-date, corporate-wide information to the employees.
Extranet website (planned)	Moderate	International distributors	The company wants to add an extranet website that provides up-to-date information for the international distributors. Information to be contained on the extranet website includes: Marketing information, such as product data Order status information Sales data Inventory data

* See following Note.

NOTE   Applications are classified into the following four categories based on their data characteristics:

- **Light application**—Generates hundreds of bytes of data per minute
- **Moderate application**—Generates thousands of bytes of data per minute
- **Heavy application**—Generates tens of thousands of bytes of data per minute
- **Extremely heavy application**—Generates hundreds of thousands of bytes per minute

The traffic volume on the network from each building to the data center in Building F is documented as follows:

- From Building A to Building F—1900 Kbps
- From Building B to Building F—1200 Kbps
- From Building C to Building F—2300 Kbps
- From Building D to Building F—500 Kbps
- From Building E to Building F—500 Kbps
- From Building F to Building F—300 Kbps

North American Plants and Their Applications

Each district and local (regional) building facility is similar. They each include a manufacturing floor, warehouse facilities, distribution and logistics offices, and sales offices. The district office facilities have slightly more staff to handle the administrative and logistical functions of their district. Table 2-14 describes each district and local facility in North America.

Table 2-14 *Description of Each OCSIC District and Regional Facility*

Function	Location	Estimated Number of Users	Building Characteristics
Eastern District Office/Plant	Boston, MA	175	60,000-square-foot manufacturing, distribution, and sales office building
Midwestern District Office/Plant	Kansas City, MO	175	60,000-square-foot manufacturing, distribution, and sales office building
Southern District Office/Plant	Dallas, TX	175	60,000-square-foot manufacturing, distribution, and sales office building
Western District Office/Plant	Los Angeles, CA	175	60,000-square-foot manufacturing, distribution, and sales office building
New York Regional Office/Plant	New York, NY	150	50,000-square-foot manufacturing, distribution, and sales office building
Toronto Regional Office/Plant	Toronto, Canada	150	50,000-square-foot manufacturing, distribution, and sales office building
Chicago Regional Office/Plant	Chicago, IL	150	50,000-square-foot manufacturing, distribution, and sales office building
Omaha Regional Office/Plant	Omaha, NB	150	50,000-square-foot manufacturing, distribution, and sales office building

Table 2-14   *Description of Each OCSIC District and Regional Facility (Continued)*

Function	Location	Estimated Number of Users	Building Characteristics
Orlando Regional Office/Plant	Orlando, FL	150	50,000-square-foot manufacturing, distribution, and sales office building
Denver Regional Office/Plant	Denver, CO	150	50,000-square-foot manufacturing, distribution, and sales office building
San Francisco Regional Office/ Plant	San Francisco, CA	150	50,000-square-foot manufacturing, distribution, and sales office building
Seattle Regional Office/Plant	Seattle, WA	150	50,000-square-foot manufacturing, distribution, and sales office building

The North American plants use the same applications as headquarters, although their usage varies. The data center is located at the Memphis headquarters, so each plant accesses the headquarters' applications over the network on a regular basis. Table 2-15 describes the current and planned applications at the North American plants.

Table 2-15   *Applications at OCSIC North American Plants*

Application	Data Characteristics	Primary Users	Notes and Description
SAP	Moderate	Accounting Finance Marketing Manufacturing Distribution	SAP is used in the plants to manage manufacturing, inventory, and distribution.
PeopleSoft	Light	Everyone	PeopleSoft applications are used to obtain financial reports.
Custom Oracle database applications	Moderate	Everyone	The plants access custom Oracle database applications, primarily for reporting and decision support.
E-mail	Heavy	Everyone	E-mail is used as the primary means of electronic communication throughout the company. Most e-mail messages are sent within a plant, with lighter traffic to the headquarters.

continues

Table 2-15 *Applications at OCSIC North American Plants (Continued)*

Application	Data Characteristics	Primary Users	Notes and Description
Intranet website	Heavy	Everyone	The company maintains an intranet website that provides up-to-date, corporate-wide information to the employees in the plants, who would not be able to obtain information otherwise. Information contained on the intranet website includes: Forms used for human resources functions • Accounting functions, such as purchase requests and supply ordering • Marketing information, such as product data • IT application and help desk information

Networking Strategies and Goals

To better support the overall business goals and reduce costs, OCSIC is developing an integrated information systems project plan that includes six building blocks or components:

- Replacement of older, slower PCs with new, faster personal computer workstations while maintaining the current workload

- Implementation of advanced network solutions, such as IP Telephony

- Implementation of a corporate intranet and extranet that better serves employees, customers, and partners

- Replacement of the existing campus and plant networks

- Upgrade to the WAN

- Streamline operations and lower total costs through business process reengineering

Proposed Headquarters Campus Network Solution

Figure 2-13 shows a campus network diagram proposed for OCSIC headquarters' site. Note that the network diagram includes each building and the Campus Backbone submodule; each item is appropriately labeled.

Figure 2-13 *Proposed Network Diagram for OCSIC Headquarters*

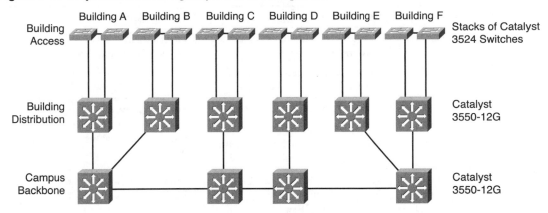

Table 2-16 summarizes one possible set of design decisions that meets OCSIC's requirements for its headquarters' campus network.

Table 2-16 *Design Decisions for OCSIC Headquarters*

Design Question	Decision	Justification
What is the logical network design?	Use logical Layer 2 segmentation by VLAN for each floor by department	The network is logically segmented based on departments.
What type of VLAN trunking will be used?	802.1Q	802.1Q is an industry standard that provides interoperability with other vendors' equipment.
What physical network media will be used in the Campus Backbone submodule?	Multimode fiber in the Campus Backbone and building risers	The current cabling plant is outdated and will not support the Gigabit Ethernet requirements of the company. Multimode fiber provides the bandwidth required in the Campus Backbone submodule.
What physical network media will be used in the Building Distribution submodule?	Multimode fiber in the Building Distribution submodule	Multimode fiber provides the bandwidth required in the Building Distribution submodule.
What physical network media will be used in the Building Access submodule?	Category 5 cabling to the desktop	Category 5 cabling provides the bandwidth required in the Building Access submodule.

continues

Table 2-16   *Design Decisions for OCSIC Headquarters (Continued)*

Design Question	Decision	Justification
Which data-link layer protocol will be used at each location?	Fast Ethernet from the switch to the desktops Gigabit Ethernet through the risers and between the floor switches	Fast Ethernet and Gigabit Ethernet provide the performance required.
What spanning-tree deployment and version will be used?	Spanning tree (Rapid STP/MST) will be used. The associated Building Distribution switch will be the root.	For simplicity, the Catalyst 3550 was selected as the STP root, because it provides a logical break between the data link and network layers.
What is the data-link layer/ multilayer strategy for the Campus Backbone submodule?	Multilayer switched in the Campus Backbone submodule with 12 fiber pairs to each building	Multilayer switching in the Campus Backbone provides flexibility.
What is the data-link layer/ multilayer strategy for the Building Distribution submodule?	Multilayer switched in the Building Distribution submodule with 4 fiber pairs	Multilayer switching in the Building Distribution submodule provides flexibility.
What is the data-link layer/ multilayer strategy for the Building Access submodule?	Data-link layer switched in the Building Access submodule with inline power.	Data-link layer switching provides performance and simplicity at the wiring closet.
Which Cisco products and options will be used in the Campus Backbone submodule?	Catalyst 3550-12G switches in the Campus Backbone submodule	The selected switches provide a cost-effective solution, supporting effective performance, scalability, and availability.
Which Cisco products and options will be used in the Building Distribution submodule?	Catalyst 3550-12G switches in the Building Distribution module	The selected switches provide a cost-effective solution, supporting effective performance, scalability, and availability.
Which Cisco products and options will be used in the Building Access submodule?	Stacks of Catalyst 3524 switches in the Building Access submodule (24-port 10/100 with integrated inline power + two-port 1000BASE-X, Enterprise Edition)	The selected switches provide a cost-effective solution, supporting effective performance, scalability, and availability.
What IP addressing scheme will be used? Is NAT/PAT required?	Class B addresses (RFC 1918) Private Class B address with NAT to the Internet	The company wants a private address space for ease of implementation. The Class B addresses allow for simple segmentation on an 8-bit boundary.

Table 2-16   *Design Decisions for OCSIC Headquarters (Continued)*

Design Question	Decision	Justification
Which routing protocols will be used in each area of the network?	OSPF throughout the network	Each building is a separate area, and area 0 is comprised of the Campus Backbone Catalyst 3550 switches. The interface from the Campus Backbone switch into each building is the OSPF boundary. Each building is a separate OSPF area to simplify management issues.
What type of switching will be deployed at the Edge Distribution module?	Multilayer switching	Multilayer switching in the Edge Distribution module provides flexibility.

Proposed Headquarters Server Farm Solution

Figure 2-14 shows a proposed network diagram for OCSIC's server farm. This network diagram shows the physical layout and how the server farm relates to the Campus Backbone module.

Figure 2-14   *Proposed Network Diagram for OCSIC Server Farm*

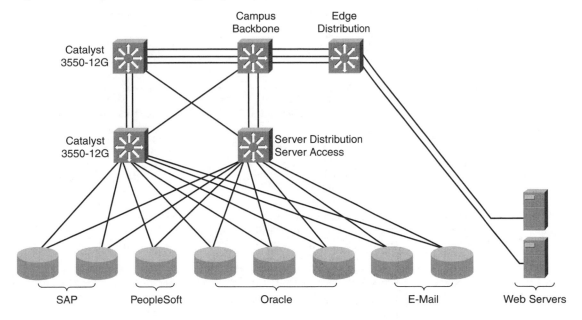

Table 2-17 summarizes one possible set of design decisions that meets OCSIC's server farm requirements.

Table 2-17 *Design Decisions for OCSIC Server Farm*

Design Question	Decision	Justification
What is the logical network design?	Use logical Layer 2 segmentation by VLAN for each type of server as follows: Web server network: VLANFD31 Server farm network: VLANFD32 Edge distribution: VLANFD33	The network is logically segmented based on the application.
What type of VLAN trunking will be used?	802.1Q	802.1Q is an industry standard that provides interoperability with other vendors' equipment.
What physical network media will be used?	Multimode fiber for all links in the Server Farm module	The physical network media provides the bandwidth required at each location.
What data-link layer protocol will be used?	Gigabit Ethernet	Gigabit Ethernet provides the performance required.
What spanning-tree deployment will be used?	Spanning tree will be used, with a Server Distribution switch as the root.	For simplicity with the rest of the network, the Catalyst 3550 is selected as the STP root.
What is the data-link layer/ multilayer strategy for the Server Distribution layer?	Multilayer switched in the Server Distribution layer	Multilayer switching in the Server Distribution layer provides flexibility.
What is the data-link layer/ multilayer strategy for the Server Access layer?	Data-link layer switched in the Server Access layer with inline power	Data-link layer switching provides performance and simplicity at the wiring closet.
Which Cisco products and options will be used in the Server Distribution layer?	Server Distribution and Server Access combined in one switch: Catalyst 3550-12G	The company wants to deploy a cost-effective solution that provides the optimal performance, scalability, and availability.
Which Cisco products and options will be used in the Server Access layer?	Server Distribution and Server Access combined in one switch: Catalyst 3550-12G	The company wants to deploy a cost-effective solution that provides the optimal performance, scalability, and availability.
What IP addressing scheme will be used? Is NAT/PAT required?	Class B addresses (RFC 1918) Private Class B address with NAT to the Internet	The Server Farm module has its own set of subnets within the Class B address range.
Which routing protocols will be used?	OSPF	The Server Farm module will be its own OSPF area.

Proposed North American Plan Model

Figure 2-15 shows a proposed campus network diagram for a typical OCSIC plant in North America.

Figure 2-15 *Proposed Network Diagram for a Typical OCSIC Plant in North America*

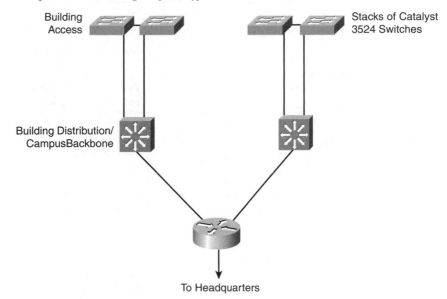

Table 2-18 summarizes one possible set of design decisions that meet OCSIC's North American plant requirements.

Table 2-18 *Design Decisions for a Typical OCSIC Plant in North America*

Design Question	Decision	Justification
What is the logical network design?	Use logical Layer 2 segmentation by VLAN for each plant.	The network is logically segmented based on a plant.
What type of VLAN trunking will be used?	802.1Q	802.1Q is an industry standard that provides interoperability with other vendors' equipment.
What physical network media will be used in the Campus Backbone submodule?	Given the collapsed Campus Backbone/Building Distribution submodule, multimode fiber will be used.	Multimode fiber provides the bandwidth required in the Building Distribution submodule.

continues

Table 2-18 *Design Decisions for a Typical OCSIC Plant in North America (Continued)*

Design Question	Decision	Justification
What physical network media will be used in the Building Distribution submodule?	Given the collapsed Campus Backbone/Building Distribution submodule, multimode fiber will be used.	Multimode fiber provides the bandwidth required in the Building Distribution submodule.
What physical network media will be used in the Building Access submodule?	Category 5 cabling to the desktop	Category 5 cabling provides the bandwidth required in the Building Access submodule.
What data-link layer protocol will be used?	Fast Ethernet	Fast Ethernet provides the performance required.
What spanning-tree deployment will be used?	Spanning tree will be used. The Campus Backbone/Building Distribution switches will be the root of the spanning tree.	For simplicity, the Campus Backbone/Building Distribution switches are selected.
What is the data-link layer/multilayer strategy for the Campus Backbone submodule?	Multilayer switched out of each plant through a router to headquarters	Multilayer switching in the Campus Backbone submodule provides flexibility.
What is the data-link layer/multilayer strategy for the Building Distribution submodule?	Included in the Campus Backbone submodule	Multilayer switching in the Building Distribution submodule provides flexibility.
What is the data-link layer/multilayer strategy for the Building Access submodule?	Data-link layer switched in the Building Access submodule with inline power	Data-link layer switching provides performance and simplicity at the wiring closet.
Which Cisco products and options will be used in the Campus Backbone submodule?	Catalyst 3550-12G in the Campus Backbone submodule	The company deploys a cost-effective solution that provides the optimal performance, scalability, and availability.
Which Cisco products and options will be used in the Building Distribution submodule?	Included in the Campus Backbone submodule	The company deploys a cost-effective solution that provides the optimal performance, scalability, and availability.
Which Cisco products and options will be used in the Building Access submodule?	Stacks of Catalyst 3524 switches in the Building Access submodule (24-port 10/100 with integrated inline power + two-port 1000BASE-X, Enterprise Edition)	The company deploys a cost-effective solution that provides the optimal performance, scalability, and availability.

Table 2-18 *Design Decisions for a Typical OCSIC Plant in North America (Continued)*

Design Question	Decision	Justification
What IP addressing scheme will be used? Is NAT/PAT required?	Class B addresses (RFC 1918) Private Class B address with NAT to the Internet	Each regional and branch office has their own /24 (254 hosts) address from the corporate Class B addresses for ease of address manipulation.
Which routing protocols will be used?	OSPF	Each plant is a separate OSPF area to simplify management issues.

After completing this chapter, you will be able to

- Use the Enterprise Edge Design Methodology to design Wide Area Network, Remote Access, and the Internet Connectivity modules

- Design small, medium, and large enterprise site-to-site WANs, given enterprise WAN needs

- Design an enterprise remote access solution, given enterprise remote access needs

- Design the Internet Connectivity module, given enterprise needs to access the Internet

CHAPTER **3**

Designing Enterprise Edge Connectivity

Enterprises commonly use WANs, on-demand connections, and the Internet to build an intranet (site-to-site private connection) between corporate offices, connect with customers and business suppliers over the Internet, conduct electronic commerce, and provide remote access capabilities to their partners and employees. This chapter discusses how you can design enterprise edge network infrastructures for effective functionality, performance, scalability, and availability, given specific network requirements.

Reviewing the Enterprise Edge Network Design Methodology

To facilitate effective network design, Cisco Systems has developed a process that enables the network designer to assess requirements, design each module of the network, and determine the effectiveness of the design. The Enterprise Composite Network Model, discussed in Chapter 1, "Introducing Cisco Network Service Architectures," enables network designers to design the Enterprise Edge functional area from modular building blocks, which are scalable enough to meet evolving business needs. By deploying a step-by-step methodology, network designers can create an effective enterprise edge design that meets enterprise needs for performance, scalability, and availability.

This section identifies the modules of the Enterprise Edge functional area and lists what criteria it must meet and what needs it must fulfill. The step-by-step design methodology for the Enterprise Edge is presented next, followed by a discussion on traffic analysis within this particular functional area of the Enterprise Composite Network Model.

Enterprise Edge Design

The Enterprise Edge functional area is comprised of E-Commerce, Internet Connectivity, Remote Access/Virtual Private Network, and WAN modules, each with its own unique design requirements. As shown in Figure 3-1, each module of the Enterprise Edge functional area connects to the Edge Distribution module of the Enterprise Campus functional area on one side, and it connects to a module of the Service Provider Edge on the other side.

Figure 3-1   *Enterprise Edge Functional Area of the Enterprise Composite Network Model*

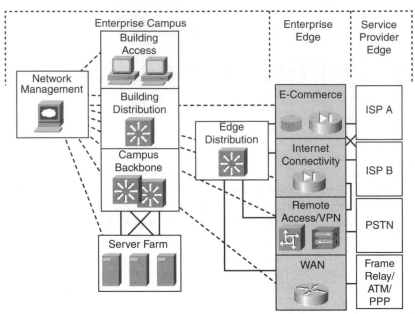

The Enterprise Edge modules perform these functions:

- **E-Commerce**—Enables enterprises to deploy e-commerce applications and take advantage of the Internet. All e-commerce transactions pass through a series of intelligent services to provide performance, scalability, and availability within the overall e-commerce network design.

- **Internet Connectivity**—Provides internal users with connectivity to Internet services. Internet users can access the information on publicly available servers. Additionally, this module accepts VPN traffic from remote users and remote sites and forwards it to the Remote Access and VPN module.

- **Remote Access and VPN**—This module terminates dial-in connections received through the Public Switched Telephone Network (PSTN) and upon successful authentication, it grants dial-in users access to the network. Furthermore, the Remote Access and VPN module terminates VPN traffic forwarded by the Internet Connectivity module from remote users and remote sites, and initiates VPN connections to remote sites through the Internet Connectivity module.

- **WAN**—Routes traffic between remote sites and the central site using dedicated media or circuits. The WAN module supports any WAN technology, including leased lines, Frame Relay, Asynchronous Transfer Mode (ATM), optical, and cable. The WAN module might also use Integrated Services Digital Network (ISDN) or PSTN dial-on-demand for occasional access and availability.

Typical Requirements for the Enterprise Edge

The features and functionalities of the Enterprise Edge functional area must be identified before its design can commence. The typical, and at the same time, important requirements that the Enterprise Edge functional area must fulfill are

- **Functionality**—An enterprise network must support the applications and data flows required within the required timeframes. Typical enterprise-wide applications include online transaction processing (OLTP) systems, decision support systems (DSS), e-mail, information sharing, and many other functions. Applications and data might require special peak-time processing, or they might require steady processing throughout a day.

- **Performance**—Includes three primary metrics: responsiveness, throughput, and utilization. Each Enterprise Edge link and device will be measured in terms of how well it meets all three of the performance metrics.

- **Scalability**—The Enterprise Edge functional area must provide scalability for future growth in the number of users and in the amount of data and applications that the network might support.

- **Availability**—Users perceive that the network is down, regardless of where a failure might occur. A typical standard for most enterprise data networks is 99.9% availability.

- **Manageability**—The Enterprise Edge module must be manageable across the entire infrastructure.

- **Cost effectiveness**—Cost effectiveness is a key concern for most enterprises, given limited budgets. The network designer's goal is to design the network for maximum efficiency given affordability limitations. Affordability for the Enterprise Edge functional area includes one-time costs for equipment, as well as ongoing tariffs or service charges.

Table 3-1 describes how Enterprise Edge modules meet enterprise needs for functionality, performance, scalability, availability, manageability, and cost effectiveness; and the importance of each component in meeting that need. Each need is ranked in terms of its relative importance, where Critical is highest in relative importance, followed by Important and Normal (no elements in Table 3-1 are marked as Normal). For example, functionality is critical (that is, absolutely required) to the E-Commerce module, while scalability is important (desirable) to the E-Commerce module.

Table 3-1   *How the Enterprise Edge Functional Area Modules Fulfill Enterprise Needs*

	Functionality	Performance	Scalability	Availability	Manageability	Cost Effectiveness
E-Commerce	Critical	Important	Important	Critical	Important	Important
Corporate Internet	Critical	Important	Important	Important	Important	Important
Remote Access/VPN	Critical	Important	Important	Important	Important	Important
WAN	Critical	Important	Important	Critical	Important	Critical

Enterprise Edge Design Methodology

Cisco has developed a step-by-step methodology that you can use to design the Enterprise Edge functional area. The design is based on application Characteristics and involves selecting topology, an Internet service provider (ISP), data-link layer and physical layer technologies, specific Cisco devices, routing protocols, and perhaps special features. This methodology is comprised of eight steps, each of which must be completed in turn:

Step 1   Characterize applications for the Enterprise Edge functional area. The important application characteristics are minimum bandwidth needed, plus delay, jitter, and loss tolerance.

Step 2   Select and diagram the WAN topology. The WAN topology is designed based on the geography and data-sharing requirements.

Step 3   Select an ISP and negotiate price and features. Each ISP will offer different services, rates, and quality guarantees. After you select a service provider, you can complete the remaining steps based on the features available to you.

Step 4   Select a data-link layer WAN, remote access, or Internet technology for each link on the enterprise network. The data-link layer technology selection is based on application requirements and the features a service provider has to offer.

Step 5   Select a physical layer WAN, remote access, or Internet technology for each link on the enterprise network. Based on the data-link layer technology selection and the services offered by the service provider, you can select the physical layer technology.

Step 6   Select specific WAN, remote access, and Internet features for each link on the enterprise network. WAN features are based on application requirements and the features a service provider has to offer.

Step 7   Select specific Cisco network devices and hardware and software options at each location, and create a network topology diagram. Based on the specific requirements at each location, select specific Cisco network devices that meet specified criteria.

Step 8   Select routing protocols and Internet Protocol (IP) addressing for the Enterprise Edge functional area. Similar to the Enterprise Campus functional area, you will select routing protocols and an IP addressing strategy for the Enterprise Edge functional area.

Analyzing Network Traffic Patterns

Assessing and analyzing network traffic patterns typically found in the Enterprise Edge functional area is an important part of network design. The applications that are shared between any two or more sites on the network must be characterized. The gathered information will then be useful to determine the performance, scalability, and requirements for each WAN, remote access, or Internet link. A table that looks similar to Table 3-2 can aid in characterizing the applications at each network campus location. Give special attention to the information that must be recorded in each column.

Table 3-2   *An Example of Characterizing Applications*

To/From Location	Name of Application	Type of Application	Number of Users	Number of Servers	Bandwidth/Delay Tolerance/Loss Characteristics
Building 1 to Building 2	Web Content	Hypertext Markup Language/ Hypertext Transfer Protocol/Java	137	2	High Bandwidth High Delay Medium Loss
Headquarters to NY Office	Order Processing	Database	512	5	High Bandwidth High Delay Low Loss
San Francisco Office to Asia Pacific	Web Content	HTML/HTTP	427	2	Medium Bandwidth High Delay Medium Loss

The types of data that applications process, access, and transfer vary in volume and, hence, in bandwidth demands. Table 3-3 shows a sample of typical volumes of various kinds of data that applications process.

Table 3-3   *An Example of Typical Volumes of Different Data Types*

Data Type	Volume (in MB)
Text e-mail message	0.01
Spreadsheet	0.1
Computer screen	0.5
Rich e-mail message	1
Still image	10
Multimedia object	100
Database replication	1000

The first of the main modules comprising the Enterprise Edge functional area is the WAN module. The effective design methodology and techniques related to this module are discussed next.

Designing the Classic WAN Module

Wide-area networking provides communications to users across a broad geographic area. WANs typically include routers and switches that link sites and remote offices around the world. Network designers can select WAN links of different capacities and those that use different technologies, depending on the particular requirements. Cisco WAN solutions help network designers build scalable networks and deliver business-critical services using the communications infrastructure. A designer must be able to design small, medium, and large enterprise site-to-site WANs, given enterprise WAN needs and objectives. This design task entails several decisions and tasks, including, but not limited to, the following:

- Identifying enterprise needs for site-to-site WANs
- Recommending WAN topology and features
- Identifying the services and service level agreements
- Recommending data-link layer technologies and physical layer protocols
- Selecting edge routing solutions and IP addressing strategies

Enterprise Needs for the WAN

Applications drive the design of the site-to-site WAN. Understanding the number of users at each location and the applications used will dictate the service and bandwidth requirements for each regional and branch site. Traditionally, WAN communication has been characterized by relatively low throughput and high error rates. Because the WAN infrastructure is generally rented (leased) from a service provider, WAN network designs optimize the cost of bandwidth and pursue bandwidth efficiency.

Based on application needs, enterprises typically have these requirements for a site-to-site WAN solution:

- **Bandwidth**—Sufficient bandwidth is required to support applications.
- **Link quality**—High link quality is required to ensure end-to-end delivery of packets.
- **Reliability**—Reliability and availability are critical to ensure end-to-end delivery of packets.
- **Data-link protocol characteristics**—Each data-link protocol offers services that make the protocol ideal for certain applications.
- **Always-on or on-demand characteristics**—Some applications require that a WAN be available all the time (always on); other applications can function even if the WAN link is established as needed (on demand).
- **Cost**—Cost effectiveness is a concern for any network solution. The WAN solution needs to consider fixed and recurring costs.

Selecting the WAN Topology

The WAN topology includes the physical and logical WAN topology. The topology is closely related to the geographical structure of the enterprise. Figure 3-2 shows an enterprise with a mix of full-mesh and partial-mesh WAN topologies. In Figure 3-2, sites 1 to 4 are connected through a full-mesh topology, although the Regional Edge and Branch Edge are connected to sites 1 to 4 via partial-mesh topologies.

Figure 3-2   *A Typical Enterprise WAN Topology*

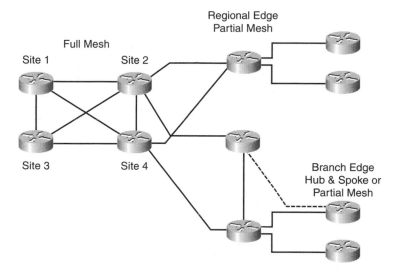

The site-to-site WAN might include a branch, regional, and central hierarchy. The designer must identify the reliability, availability, and service levels for each level of the hierarchy in the WAN during the design phase. The actual design will often mirror the enterprise's organizational structure. The WAN requirements at each point in the network will be unique. Although you can group sites that have similar requirements, the actual bandwidth and service requirements usually end up different for each site on the network.

To determine bandwidth requirements, it is preferable to work from the branch and remote-access devices into the central site(s). This allows you to determine the aggregation needs and to identify bandwidth limitations early in the process. Starting with the branch office and working back to the Campus Backbone submodule make it easier to see bottlenecks or potential aggregation issues. For example, given that the required bandwidth from a branch office to its regional office is 256 kbps, what amount of bandwidth is needed from the regional office that supports four branch offices to the central site? In the calculation, you cannot forget to include the bandwidth requirements for the regional office itself, and then add it to the total bandwidth (4 * 256 kbps) required to support all four branch offices. In other words, if the regional office requires x kbps of bandwidth and each of the four branch offices it supports needs 256 kbps, the total bandwidth needed between the regional office and the central office would be $x + (4 * 256$ kbps$)$.

Branch Office WAN

The branch office is typically the end of the network. The regional office typically sits between the Campus Backbone submodule and the branch offices. The regional office might house the application servers that the branch sites use, or it might simply provide access to the Campus Backbone submodule. The regional office will have its own set of requirements for WAN connectivity. Figure 3-3 depicts a regional edge device with dual connections to a branch office.

Figure 3-3 *Branch Office WAN*

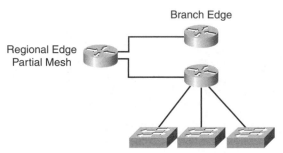

If the branch office requires redundant links, the design will use either dual WAN links to two different regions or connect to another branch, which connects to a regional site. In the latter case, the link between two branch offices is generally set up to be the minimum amount of bandwidth to support each branch. Another method for connecting a branch office to a regional site is to implement a dial-on-demand circuit through either ISDN or PSTN.

When designing the WAN to reach the branch office, you must answer the following questions:

- How many users are in the branch?
- What are the per-application bandwidth requirements?
- What is the total bandwidth needed for applications?
- What type of routing protocol is going to be used?
- What are the redundancy needs of the site?
- What is the effect on the business if the site is unreachable or if the site cannot reach the central servers?
- Is the site supporting on-demand connectivity to other sites or users?

Regional Office WAN

It is common for the regional office to be an aggregation point for multiple branch offices. When aggregation is done, it is imperative to ensure there is enough bandwidth from the regional office to the core to provide the expected level of service to all branch offices that connect to that regional site. The regional office typically has multiple load-sharing links between the regional office and the central site Enterprise Edge functional area. Figure 3-4 shows a regional office in the middle with dual (load-sharing) connections to the central site. The regional office aggregates traffic from the branch and sends it to the central site.

Figure 3-4 *Regional Office WAN*

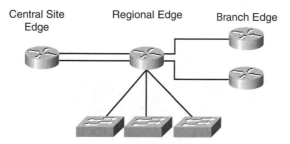

The central site Enterprise Edge functional area is typically a fully meshed environment with multiple load-sharing links, which are able to distribute all of their aggregated traffic from the regional office. When load balancing, attempt to avoid asymmetrical routing. Before developing the WAN module to support a regional office WAN, you must answer the following questions:

- How many users are in the regional office?
- What are the per-application bandwidth requirements?
- What is the total bandwidth needed for applications?
- What type of routing protocol is going to be used?
- What are the redundancy needs of the site?
- What is the effect on the business if the site is not reachable, or the site cannot reach the central servers?
- Is the site supporting on-demand connectivity to other sites or users?
- Is the site a rally (aggregation) point for traffic from other sites to pass through?
- Does the regional site have servers or services that are shared with other offices, either branch or central (core) locations? Does this change the amount of bandwidth that the branch offices need to the core?

Enterprise WAN Backbone

The enterprise WAN backbone is normally the focal point of the enterprise. The server farms are usually placed in the central campus/site. The requirement for high-speed connectivity between routers is critical to ensure that all the outlying regions and branches/remote sites maintain their service levels. If the core site is accessed through a single router or the Enterprise Edge routers of a large-scale enterprise, it must support the total aggregation of all the traffic from the rest of the network.

A full-mesh solution, such as the one shown in Figure 3-5, might have an impact on convergence time, depending on the routing protocol implemented. The fiber reliability that is available today eliminates the need for a full-mesh design. Before provisioning (or ordering it), the impact of every additional link on the overall network convergence must be carefully considered.

Figure 3-5   *Enterprise WAN Backbone*

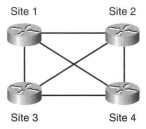

When designing the enterprise WAN backbone, you must answer the following questions:

- What are the per-application bandwidth requirements?
- What is the total bandwidth needed for applications?
- What type of routing protocol is going to be used?
- What are the redundancy needs of the site?
- What is the effect on the business if the site is not reachable?
- Is the site supporting on-demand connectivity to other sites or users?
- Is the site a rally point for traffic from other sites to pass through?

Selecting a Service Provider

After the bandwidth, redundancy, and service level requirements are defined, different providers must be contacted to determine what transport is available to implement the design. After a service provider is selected, the site-to-site WAN might need to be redesigned based on the services available to you; in other words, based on the features, services, and costs that the provider offers, some redesign might be necessary. Each service provider offers a range of prices, speeds, features, and geographical coverage, which affects the ultimate selection. Hence, the selection of a service provider depends on these criteria:

- **Price**—Price, including one-time and recurring (fixed and variable) costs, is one of the most important criteria when selecting a service provider.

- **Speeds supported**—Different service providers offer a different range of speeds for different technologies. Speed is often closely related to price. Distance might also affect price. Make sure the service provider you select offers the speeds you require.

- **Features supported**—Different service providers offer different WAN features and technologies. Features offered might affect price. From the technologically possible group of features, make sure the service provider you select offers an appropriate subset of those features.

- **Geographies covered**—The service provider must service the geographies you need to include in the WAN. Several different service providers might be needed to provide the full geographical coverage the network requires.

- **Service level agreements**—A service level agreement (SLA) is a key component of a service level contract (SLC). The SLC specifies connectivity and performance agreements for an end-user service from a provider of service. A service provider might provide wide-area or hosted application services. Bandwidth, round-trip response, loss characteristics, and network services are part of the SLA specifications. Table 3-4 describes an example SLA and how it is measured.

Table 3-4   *A Sample Service Level Agreement*

Network Area	Availability Target	Measurement Method	Average Network Response Time Target	Maximum Response Time Accepted	Response Time Measurement Method
WAN	99.90%	Impacted user minutes	Under 100 ms (Round-trip ping)	150 ms	Round-trip ping response
Critical WAN and extranet	99.95%	Impacted user minutes	Under 100 ms (Round-trip ping)	150 ms	Round-trip ping response

Selecting the Data-Link Layer

For the data-link layer, commonly selected WAN technologies are Point-to-Point Protocol (PPP), Frame Relay, ATM, Multiprotocol Label Switching (MPLS), and X.25. Table 3-5 provides a comparative presentation of the characteristics of these WAN data-link layer technologies. Selecting a data link technology depends on the services offered by the service provider(s) and the features required.

Table 3-5   *Data-Link Layer Protocols Characteristics*

	Bandwidth	Link Quality	Network Delay	Reliability	Cost
PPP	Moderate	Low	Low	Moderate	Low
Frame Relay	Moderate	High	Low	Low	Moderate
ATM	High	High	Low	Low	Moderate

continues

Table 3-5   *Data-Link Layer Protocols Characteristics (Continued)*

	Bandwidth	Link Quality	Network Delay	Reliability	Cost
MPLS	High	High	Low	Low	Moderate
X.25	Low	Low	High	High	Moderate

The following are common data-link layer technologies for site-to-site WANs:

- **PPP**—PPP provides router-to-router and host-to-network connections over synchronous and asynchronous circuits. PPP is typically used for the transmission of IP packets over serial lines and ISDN.

- **Frame Relay**—Frame Relay is a switched data-link layer protocol that handles multiple virtual circuits using High-Level Data Link Control (HDLC)-derived encapsulation between connected devices. Frame Relay is more bandwidth efficient than X.25, and the protocol is generally considered as Frame Relay's predecessor. Frame Relay provides cost-effective, high-speed, low-latency virtual circuits between sites. Frame Relay runs over DS0, T1/E1, and serial links.

- **ATM**—ATM is the international standard for cell relay in which multiple service types (such as voice, video, or data) are conveyed in fixed-length (53-byte) cells. Fixed-length cells allow cell processing to occur in hardware, reducing transit delays. ATM is designed to take advantage of high-speed transmission media, such as T1/E1, T3/E3, and optical.

- **MPLS**—MPLS is a switching mechanism that allows packet forwarding to be based on a label enclosed in the MPLS header, which resides between Layer 2 and Layer 3 headers. The MPLS forwarding table is processed without process switching and can be downloaded to line card/interface memory, similar to distributed Cisco Express Forwarding (CEF) processing. A label either maps to the IP address of an MPLS Traffic Engineering (TE) tunnel's tail, to the IP address of an egress edge router in an autonomous system, or to a VPN client's site identification on the edge router. The MPLS header might enclose quality of service (QoS) information in its experimental (EXP) field as well.

- **X.25**—X.25 is an International Telecommunication Union Telecommunication Standardization Sector (ITU-T) standard for use in packet data networks. X.25 is an older protocol that has been or is being replaced by Frame Relay. X.25 runs over DS0, T1/E1, and serial links.

Selecting the Physical Layer

The common physical layer technologies to choose from include leased line, digital subscriber line (DSL), dialup, ISDN, or optical carrier. Table 3-6 displays and compares bandwidth range, link quality, on-demand properties, and cost of those physical layer technologies.

Table 3-6   *Physical Layer Technologies/Protocols Characteristics*

	Bandwidth Range	Link Quality	On-Demand/ Always On	Cost
Leased line	Any	Moderate	Always on	Low to Moderate
DSL	Moderate	Moderate	Always on	Moderate
Dialup	Low	Low	On Demand	Low to Moderate
ISDN	Moderate	Moderate	Control: Always on Link: On Demand	Moderate
Optical	High	High	Always on	Moderate

The following physical layer technologies can be used for site-to-site WANs:

- **Leased line**—Leased lines can be used for PPP networks, for hub-and-spoke topologies, or as backup for another type of link. Leased lines can be provisioned over synchronous serial, asynchronous serial, or time-division multiplexing (TDM) (T1 interface, for instance).

- **DSL**—DSL is becoming widely available as an always-on Internet connectivity option.

- **Dialup**—Dialup is a low-speed but cost-effective technology for intermittent, on-demand WAN requirements including access to corporate data networks.

- **ISDN**—ISDN can be used for cost-effective remote access to corporate networks. It provides support for voice and video, as well as a backup for other links.

- **Synchronous Optical Network (SONET)/Synchronous Digital Hierarchy (SDH)**—Establishes Optical Carrier (OC) levels from 51.8 Mbps (capable of transporting a T3 circuit) to 40 Gbps.

Selecting WAN Features

After selecting the data-link layer and physical layer technologies, you must choose the desired WAN features. Each data-link layer technology has its own WAN features. The WAN features available depend on the selected service provider. The features offered by each of the common data-link layer technologies are

- **PPP**—The rates available for PPP depend on the type of connection: synchronous or asynchronous. Multilink PPP (MP) allows devices to send data over multiple point-to-point data links to the same destination by implementing a virtual link. The MP connection has a maximum bandwidth equal to the sum of the bandwidths of the component links. MP can be configured for either multiplexed links, such as ISDN and Frame Relay, or for multiple asynchronous lines. Link quality and round-trip time (RTT), however, should be equivalent; otherwise, some packets might arrive out of sequence or might not arrive at all.

- **Frame Relay**—You can select a number of ports, committed information rate (CIR), and maximum burst size for Frame Relay. The number of ports depends on the number of connections required at any point in time as well as bandwidth requirements. The CIR is fixed.

- **ATM**—You can select the number of ports and one of these service classes:
  - **Constant Bit Rate (CBR)**—This traffic category has a bandwidth guarantee. Use it for traffic least tolerant of delay or loss.
  - **Available Bit Rate (ABR)**—This traffic type is scheduled at the same priority as non-real time (NRT) variable bit rate (VBR). Use it for medium priority traffic.
  - **Unspecified Bit Rate (UBR)**—This traffic category is best effort. Use it only for least important traffic.
  - **Real-Time Variable Bit Rate (RT-VBR)**—This traffic category has a higher priority than NRT-VBR and a lower priority than CBR. Use it for medium priority traffic.
  - **Non Real-Time Variable Bit Rate (NRT-VBR)**—This traffic type has a higher priority than UBR, but lower than RT-VBR. Use it for medium priority traffic.
- **X.25**—You can select the number of ports and speed for X.25, although rates will be lower than those available for Frame Relay.

Selecting Cisco Edge Routing Solutions

For selecting edge routing solutions, the Cisco Product Advisor is a useful tool; it is interactive, and it presents you with a list of options to choose from, in a step-by-step fashion. Cisco offers the Product Advisor to help designers select the right internetworking solution for the enterprise edge network. The tool operates in two modes: novice and expert. Cisco Product Advisor can be accessed by clicking the Cisco Product Advisor link on http://www.cisco.com/en/US/products/prod_tools_index.html page. The Product Advisor page displays a list of product categories and expects the user to choose one. After a product category is selected (clicked) and the expert/novice choice is made, the Product Advisor asks questions to help you select devices for particular needs. Even though Product Advisor might not include all products and features, it does provide helpful information to aid selection of appropriate Cisco products.

For example, assume that you are interested in selecting a Cisco edge router using Product Advisor. After the Product Advisor page is loaded, you must select **Routers** from the list of product categories. Next, you click **Novice** as opposed to **Expert** to go through a dialog for product specification and selection. Product Advisor presents you with a set of questions, along with notes and choices:

1. Determine the type of environment in which the router will be deployed. Your choices are

   - Small office/branch office
   - Corporate office/central site
   - Large branch/regional office

2. Determine how the router will be used. One or more of the following must be selected:

   - To connect to the Internet

   - To connect offices together

   - To connect employees to the network remotely

   - To deploy IP Telephony on the network

   - To provide security for the network

3. Determine the type of configuration required. Your choices are

   - Fixed configuration (less expensive, not highly scalable)

   - Modular configuration (more expensive, highly scalable)

   - No preference

4. Determine the type of LAN connectivity required. Select one or more:

   - Ethernet (10BASE-T)

   - Fast Ethernet (10/100)

   - Gigabit Ethernet

5. Determine the number of LAN ports required. Choose one:

   - 1

   - 2

   - More than 2

6. Select the types of WAN connectivity required. One or more of the following can be chosen:

   - T1/E1

   - Fractional T1/E1

   - ISDN Primary Rate Interface (PRI)/Channelized T1/E1

   - ISDN Basic Rate Interface (BRI)

   - Synchronous Serial

   - Asynchronous Serial

   - T3/E3/OC3

   - DSL

   - ATM

   - Frame Relay

7. Determine the number of WAN ports required. Select one:

   - 1

   - 2 to 10

   - 11 to 30

   - More than 30

8. Determine if voice will be deployed on the WAN, now or in the future. Answer Yes or No.

9. Determine if a redundant power supply is required. Answer Yes or No.

10. Determine if a rack-mountable router is required. Answer Yes or No.

11. Determine which software features are required now and in the future. Select one or more:

    - VPN

    - Firewall

    - Internet/WAN access

12. Select the Cisco IOS version for each router you selected.

Routing Protocol and IP Addressing Considerations

The decision about which routing protocols to implement is based on the design goals, the physical topology of the network, and the configuration of links for remote sites. Routing protocol selection is closely related to IP addressing strategies as well. Edge routing protocols include static routes, Enhanced Interior Gateway Routing Protocol (EIGRP), Open Shortest Path First (OSPF), and Routing Information Protocol version 2 (RIPv2). Table 3-7 provides a brief comparison between these choices. Static routing is useful in smaller environments where there are few WAN connections. EIGRP is suitable for nonbroadcast multiaccess (NBMA) environments where there are split-horizon issues, such as with Frame Relay or ATM multipoint interfaces. When equipment from multiple vendors is part of the overall design, the use of EIGRP is restricted. OSPF is useful in NBMA and dialup environments. OSPF requires more knowledge for proper configuration. RIPv2 is useful for small- to medium-sized networks that do not exceed the 15-hop limit.

Table 3-7 *IP Routing Protocols for a Site-to-Site WAN*

	Hierarchical	Flat	Point-to-Point Support	Multipoint (Frame Relay) Support
Static		X	X	
EIGRP	X	X	X	X
OSPF	X		X	X
RIPv2		X	X	

The routing protocol and IP addressing design considerations are closely related:

- With EIGRP, the query range can be reduced using summarization, distribution lists, and stubs; route summarization is highly recommended to be used whenever possible.

- OSPF allows for the division of a network into smaller areas. Each area is a logical collection of OSPF routers and links. An OSPF router within an area must maintain a topological database for the area to which it belongs. The router does not have any detailed information about networks outside of its area, thereby reducing the size of its database. An address hierarchy can be created to match the created OSPF topology while maintaining address contiguity. Route summarization can be performed on Area Border Routers (ABRs) for interarea routes, and it can be done on Autonomous System Boundary Routers (ASBRs) for external routes.

- RIPv2 is a good choice for hub-and-spoke environments. To design RIPv2, send the default route from the hub to the spokes. The spokes then advertise their connected interface via RIPv2. RIPv2 can be used when secondary addresses on the spokes need to be advertised or if several vendors' routers are used. RIPv2 supports summarization (classless), but because of its metric limitation, it is only suitable for networks whose diameters (the number of hops) do not exceed 15.

The questions you need to ask to help identify the IP addressing strategy for the WAN are the same as those you would ask for the enterprise campus network. The first step in IP addressing plan design is to determine the size of the network to establish how many IP addresses are needed. To gather the required information, answer these questions:

- How big is the network?

  Determine the number of workstations, servers, IP Phones, router interfaces, switch management interfaces, firewall interfaces, and so on. The summary defines the minimum overall number of IP addresses required for the network. Because all networks tend to grow, allow a reserve of about 20% to 40% for potential network expansion.

- How many locations are in the network, and what are their sizes?

  The information about the sizes of the individual locations is closely related to the overall network size.

- What class of addresses and how many networks can be obtained from the public number authority?

  The required IP address classes for the planned network are based on information about the network size, the number of locations, and the size of the individual locations.

- How many addresses will be needed throughout the network?

  Determine the number of addresses needed for workstations, servers, IP phones, network devices, and so on.

Next, you must determine whether public IP addresses are needed (as opposed to private IP addresses), and how many addresses are required, based on how the following questions are answered:

- Are private, public, or both address types required?

  The decision when to use private, public, or both address types depends on the Internet presence and the number of publicly visible servers. Four situations are possible:

  — **No Internet connectivity is required**—The network is isolated, and there is no need to acquire public addresses.

  — **Internet connectivity is required, but there is no public accessible servers**—The network is connected to the Internet and, thus, public addresses are required. Use one public address and translation mechanism to allow access to the Internet. Private addresses are used to address the internal network.

  — **Internet connectivity is required, and there are public accessible servers**—The public addresses are required to connect all public accessible servers to the Internet. The required number of public addresses varies, but in most instances, a public address is required for the routers that connect to the Internet and any publicly accessible servers, plus a range of addresses needs to be available for the corporate users that are accessing the Internet.

  — **All end systems should be publicly accessible**—Only public addresses are required and used to address the whole network.

- How many end systems need access to the public network only?

  This is the number of end systems that need a limited set of external services (for example, e-mail, File Transfer Protocol (FTP), web browsing) and do not need unrestricted external access.

- How many end systems need to be visible to the public network?

  This is the number of Internet connections and servers that need to be visible to the public (public servers and servers used for e-commerce, such as web servers, database servers, and application servers), which defines the number of required public addresses. These end systems require addresses that are globally unambiguous.

- How and where will you cross the boundaries between the private and public addresses?

  When private addresses are used for addressing in a network, and this network needs to be connected to the Internet, a translation mechanism, such as Network Address Translation (NAT), must be used to translate from private to public addresses and vice versa.

The decision on how to implement the IP addressing hierarchy is an administrative decision that is based on these questions:

- Is hierarchy needed within an IP addressing plan?

  Implementation of the IP addressing hierarchy is based on the network size and the geography and topology of the network. In large networks, the hierarchy within the IP addressing plan is required to have a stable network.

- What are the criteria to divide the network into route summarization groups?

  The network is usually divided into route summarization groups based on the network size and topology.

An Enterprise WAN Design Example

A national insurance brokerage has four main data centers; each data center has four regional offices, and each regional office has four branch offices. There are a total of 64 branch offices, 16 regional offices, and 4 core offices. The company's primary WAN applications are e-mail and database applications with low bandwidth requirements. The information technology (IT) department has done a study and determined that each branch office needs 128 kbps worth of bandwidth, and each regional office needs 256 kbps of bandwidth.

The first part of the design project was to determine how the branch offices will be connected to the regional offices. The company identified these network needs:

- Total bandwidth required for applications—128 kbps per branch.
- Redundancy needs of the site—The IT staff determined that 32 of the 64 offices did not require a redundant link, because the downtime at those offices would not drastically impact the company. The other 32 sites needed redundancy. The decision was to have those branch offices dual-homed to two different regional offices.

From the information gathered, the company decided to implement two different design scenarios. The requested bandwidth for a site with a single connection will be 128 kbps. For the dual-homed branch offices, each link will be 128 kbps. Figure 3-6 shows two different types of branch offices, with and without dual connections.

The next goal was to design the regional office WAN layout. The IT department wanted the regions to be connected through a closed delta design, each region connected to two different core sites. To determine the amount of bandwidth needed between the regions and the enterprise central site (Campus Backbone submodule), the company calculated the aggregate bandwidth from the branches ($4 * 128 = 512$) and then added it to the bandwidth requirements for the regional site ($512 + 256 = 768$). Because there were two load-sharing paths, they were sized using the current requirements of 768 kbps per link, as shown in Figure 3-7.

Figure 3-6 *Single and Dual-Connected Branch Offices*

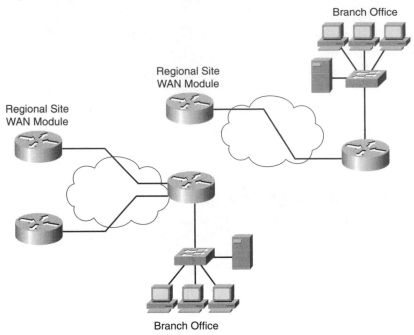

Figure 3-7 *Site-to-Site Regional Office to Campus Backbone*

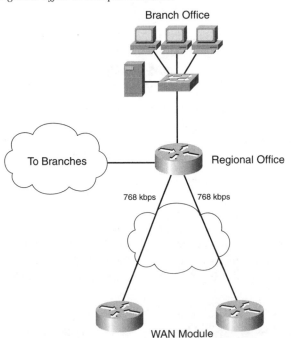

The next step was to design the Campus Backbone connectivity. As noted earlier, between each core and its regional offices, 768-kbps links were implemented. The IT team determined that each core could be self-sufficient, but the company wanted sufficient bandwidth to support database and server replication between the cores; according to their experts, two T1s of bandwidth were required for this. Therefore, from each core site, they required 768 * 4 = 3072 kbps of bandwidth (to the regional offices) plus two T1s for connecting to the other core sites, for a total of four T1s worth of bandwidth. The service provider was willing to provide a T3 for the price of four T1s, so each core site had three T3s going to the other core sites. Figure 3-8 shows a complete core office network.

Figure 3-8   *Site-to-Site Completed Network*

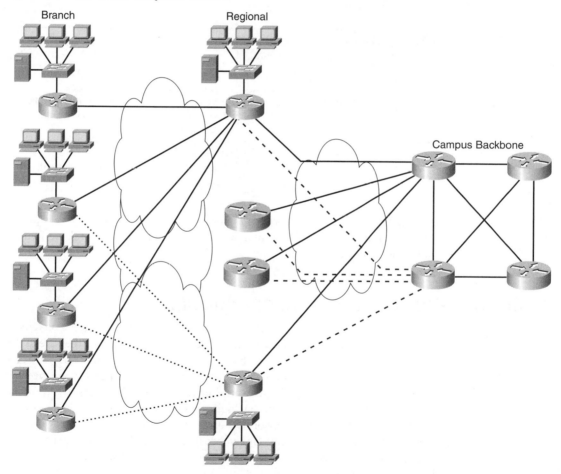

Table 3-8 summarizes the design decisions that the company made to meet these requirements.

Table 3-8   *Design Questions, Decisions, and Comments*

Design Question	Decision	Notes
What topology will be used for the WAN?	Mixture of partial mesh and full mesh in the core	Given the size and requirements of the network, several topologies are used.
What service provider will be selected?	National carrier	A national carrier is required to provide geographical coverage.
What data-link layer protocol will be used?	Frame Relay where available and PPP leased lines where Frame Relay is not available	
What physical network media will be used?	Copper or fiber	
Which Cisco products will be used?	Branch offices: Cisco 1720 Regional offices: Cisco 2620 Core: Cisco 3640	
Which routing protocols will be used?	OSPF hierarchical design	Given the number of sites and the way the design leads to an easy division of areas, OSPF was chosen.
What IP addressing scheme will be used?	Access to the Internet and NAT are required.	A single Class C address provides Internet connectivity. A Class B is used internally and NAT is used.

The second of the main modules comprising the Enterprise Edge functional area is the Remote Access module. The effective design methodology and techniques related to this module are discussed next.

Designing the Remote Access Module

Easy connectivity solutions and consistency are important for enterprises relying on remote access. Customers, employees, and partners should be able to connect as if they are at the company site. They also must count on the ability to log in and to remain connected at an expected level of performance. The number of telecommuters and mobile users are growing every day. Their communications needs are expanding from simple data transmission to the need for voice, fax, and data transmission, including conferencing. The remote access server is an integral part of the total network solution and must scale to meet growing demand. A comprehensive remote access module design entails identifying enterprise needs for remote access, selecting the appropriate type of remote access, selecting appropriate physical and data-link layer protocols for the remote access solution, and, finally, selecting proper Cisco access routing solutions for users and aggregation points, all based on specific enterprise requirements.

Enterprise Needs for Remote Access

Telecommuters, remote users, and branch offices all require remote access to a central site. The key concerns for an IT department are functionality, performance, scalability, availability, manageability, and security. Remote connections link single users (mobile users and/or telecommuters) and branch offices to a local campus or the Internet.

Typically, a remote site is a small site that has few users and, therefore, needs a smaller WAN connection. The remote requirements of an internetwork, however, usually involve a large number of remote single users or sites, and, therefore, an internetwork usually needs a larger WAN connection. With so many remote single users or sites, the aggregate WAN bandwidth cost is proportionally greater in remote connections than in WAN connections. The WAN media rental charge from a service provider is the largest cost component of a remote network. Unlike WAN connections, smaller sites or single users seldom need to connect 24 hours a day. Easy connections and consistency are crucial to companies relying on remote access. Customers, employees, and partners should be able to connect seamlessly, as if they were in one office. They must also count on the ability to log in and remain connected at an expected level of performance. Security is a high priority for remote access.

When designing the remote access connectivity, four important questions need to be addressed. After these questions are answered, the remote access Layer 1, Layer 2, and Layer 3 networking decisions are based on functionality, reliability, and cost effectiveness. The basic questions to ask are

- What type of remote access is needed?—Determine if a group of users in a remote location need intermittent data exchanges with an enterprise site or if individuals located in different places need their own connectivity solution.

- What types of access connectivity is needed in the environment?—The solution might consist of a single-access methodology or a combination of different methodologies. The most common method today is to run PPP through either an analog dialup circuit, a digital trunk, or through a VPN tunnel that goes across a service provider's network or a public network. A company might decide to build a remote access VPN if it has analog and digital circuits that terminate with a service provider, and the expense of moving those circuits is prohibitive.

- Where is the remote access termination point going to be?—Most often, the remote access termination point is located at a central site, but it could be at a remote site or even within a service provider network. If the enterprise decides to host its own remote access termination point, it must decide if it is less expensive to bring all the termination back to the central office or to distribute it between regional or remote branches to save on toll charges.

- Who is going to provide the actual endpoint for termination of the remote access device? —The options include having the equipment in-house with internal IT management, or outsourcing with a link to the outsourced party.

The Remote Access and VPN module of the Enterprise Composite Network Model provides remote access to end users. The primary components within this model are the circuits, the access server (which provides authentication and authorization), firewalls, and, optionally, Intrusion Detection Systems (IDSs) (see Figure 3-9). From the PSTN to the Remote Access and VPN module, you can deploy many effective Layer 2 technologies.

Figure 3-9 *Components of the Remote Access and VPN Module*

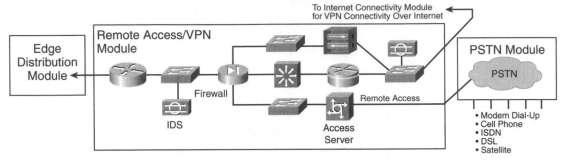

Selecting the Remote Access Type and Termination

The two primary types of remote access are site-to-site and user-to-site.

The *site-to-site* remote access model is appropriate when a group of users in the same vicinity can share an on-demand connection to either their local branch office or central site. The criteria for selecting a site-to-site remote access solution includes the following:

- Sporadic need for enterprise network connectivity, not requiring an "always-up" connection
- Multiple users at a facility sharing the on-demand access
- Prohibitive cost of putting in a dedicated always-on connection

The most common remote access model is called *user-to-site*, which involves a single user who needs connectivity to the corporate network. This single user is located where no immediate network resources are available to connect to. The user might dial in through a dialup mechanism or connect through an always-on connection, and access the network through a VPN.

The choice on where to terminate the physical remote access connectivity—at the corporate site, remote site, or service provider—depends on who is doing the termination. If a service provider provides termination, remote users will dial into a local point of presence (POP) to limit toll charges. If a company is going to provide the remote access physical termination at one of its sites, a number of questions need to be answered. Based on those answers, the physical and data-link protocols must be selected. The questions are

- What are the requirements on the termination ports? Do they have to support voice, data, and fax?
- What is the cost of bringing all the users into a central site, versus the cost of maintaining modem pools in several sites? Where will the connectivity be most reliable?
- How many users are going to simultaneously use the remote access system?
- Are the users mobile or fixed?

- How many fixed users have access to always-on technology?
- Are sites or individual users being terminated?

Selecting the Remote Access Physical Connectivity

The physical connectivity technologies include remote dialup access and broadband technologies. The following physical layer technologies are available for remote dialup access to an enterprise site:

- **Modem dialup**—Analog modems using basic telephone service are asynchronous transmission-based. Basic telephone service is available everywhere, is easy to setup, dials anywhere on demand, and is very inexpensive.

- **ISDN**—ISDN offers digital dialup connections and a short connection setup time. ISDN is a good solution for telecommuters. Instead of leasing a dedicated line for high-speed digital transmission, ISDN offers the option of dialup connectivity, incurring charges only when the line is active.

- **Cell phone**—Cell phones use the public cell phone network to access the central site. The primary benefit of using cell phones is mobility, although the expense can be high with limited functionality.

The following physical layer technologies offer broadband remote access:

- **DSL**—Enterprises are increasingly turning to DSL to expand the use of telecommuting, reduce costs, and provide Internet-based services. DSL offers always-on access, allowing users to work at remote offices as if they were on site.

- **Cable**—Cable is increasingly available. Cable offers always-on access, allowing users to work at remote offices, such as their homes, as if they were on site.

- **Satellite**—Wireless communications devices usually connect to a satellite. A transponder receives and transmits radio signals at a prescribed frequency range. After receiving the signal, a transponder will broadcast the signal at a different frequency. Satellites provide high quality, at a high cost, primarily to support mobility.

Table 3-9 compares these physical layer technologies using criteria such as offered bandwidth range, link quality, and cost.

Table 3-9   *A Comparison of Remote Access Physical Connectivity Choices*

	Dialup or Broadband	Offered Bandwidth (Range)	Link Quality	On Demand/ Always On	Cost
Modem Dialup	Dialup	Low	Low	On Demand	Low to Moderate
ISDN	Dialup	Moderate	Moderate	Control: Always On Link: On Demand	Moderate

continues

Table 3-9 *A Comparison of Remote Access Physical Connectivity Choices (Continued)*

	Dialup or Broadband	Offered Bandwidth (Range)	Link Quality	On Demand/ Always On	Cost
Cell Phone	Dialup	Low	Low	On Demand	High
DSL	Broadband	Moderate	Moderate	Always On	Moderate
Cable	Broadband	Moderate	Moderate	Always On	Moderate
Satellite	Broadband	Moderate to High	Moderate	Always On/ On Demand	High

Selecting the Remote Access Protocol

The most common method used to transport packets from user equipment to a termination point is a form of PPP. Each version of PPP has its targeted purpose, but each basically encapsulates the IP packet and delivers it at the other end. The following data-link protocols are typically deployed for remote-access networks:

- **PPP**—PPP in a remote-access environment defines methods of sending IP packets over circuit lines and is an inexpensive way of connecting PCs to a network. Refer to Requests for Comments (RFCs) 1661 and 2153 for more information about PPP.

- **PPP over Ethernet (PPPoE)**—Allows a PPP session to be initiated on a simple Ethernet-connected client. PPPoE can be used on existing customer premise equipment. PPPoE preserves the point-to-point session used by ISPs in the current dialup model. It is the only protocol capable of running point-to-point over Ethernet without requiring an intermediate IP stack. PPPoE is most often used to connect a host to a cable (or DSL) modem.

- **PPP over ATM (PPPoA)**—PPPoA adaptation Layer 5 (AAL5) (specified in Request for Comments (RFC) 2364) uses AAL5 as the framed protocol, which supports both permanent virtual circuits (PVCs) and switched virtual circuits (SVCs). PPPoA is primarily implemented as part of an asymmetric digital subscriber line (ADSL). PPPoA relies on RFC 2684, operating in either Logical Link Control-Subnetwork Access Protocol (LLC-SNAP) or virtual circuit multiplexer mode. A customer premises equipment (CPE) device encapsulates the PPP session for transport across the ADSL loop and the DSL Access Multiplexer (DSLAM).

Table 3-10 compares these data-link layer technologies using criteria such as bandwidth, link quality, and reliability.

Table 3-10 *Comparison of Remote Access Data-Link Layer Characteristics*

	Bandwidth	Typical Physical Media	Link Quality	Reliability
PPP	Moderate	PSTN	Low	Low
PPPoE	Moderate	Cable	Moderate	Moderate
PPPoA	Moderate	DSL	Moderate	Moderate

Selecting Cisco Access Routing Solutions

For a company that is providing its own remote access termination, access routing solutions are required at both the remote location and at a central site. The requirements at each site will be different. Product Advisor is an excellent tool that can be used to select Cisco access routing solutions for both the remote site and central site, based on specific enterprise requirements. Cisco Systems offers the Product Advisor to help customers select the correct routing solution for their Enterprise Edge network. The tool operates in two modes: novice and expert. You can access the Product Advisor by clicking the Cisco Product Advisor link on the following page:

> http://www.cisco.com/en/US/products/prod_tools_index.html

After the device category is selected, and if the user specified that he or she is a novice user, the Product Advisor will ask questions to help select routers based on the specific needs of the customer. Even though Product Advisor does not include all products and features, it does provide helpful information that facilitates selecting appropriate Cisco products.

Sizing the Central Site Remote Access Connection

To size the central site remote access solution, one must determine the total number of remote users, percentage of remote users that log in at once, and bandwidth required per user. Planning for peak usage is crucial. The mix and time of connections help determine the peak requirements. For example, 200 modem users calling between 1:00 P.M. and 3:30 P.M. would require 200 DS-0s (digital signal level 0) or 9 PRI circuits. To determine the peak bandwidth, use the following formula:

Total bandwidth required =

> Total number of remote users *
> Percentage of users logged in at one time (expressed as 0.nn) *
> Bandwidth required per user (expressed as kbps)

Based on the number of simultaneous users, you can make the assumption that the number of circuits equals the number of simultaneous users. Most telephony circuits are 64 kbps each and, unless there is a methodology for multiplexing multiple steams over the same circuit, the end point will expect a 64-kbps circuit.

An Enterprise Remote Access Design Example

Assume that the executive management of a tool and dye company has identified a number of factors that point to the need for some form of dial-in access for cost reduction and to improve employee morale and productivity. The company's pool of 25 engineers spends more than 90% of its time sitting at a workstation working on computer-aided design and manufacturing program-based projects. Some engineers are on part-time contracts, yet the company pays for office space to put them in front of a PC all day. Some of the full-timers put in long hours and aren't happy about the time spent away from home. Others would work more if they could do it from home. Additionally, the company employs five telesales representatives and two customer-service representatives who, using their phones and PCs, almost never leave their cubes. They are questioning why they must deal with their ugly commutes when they could do it all from home. In addition, company management is wondering why it pays for their office space.

One possible set of design decisions that the company can make to meet its requirements is summarized in Table 3-11.

Table 3-11   *A Possible Remote Access Solution for the Tool and Dye Company*

Design Questions	Decision	Notes
What topology will be used for the WAN?	Hub and spoke	ISDN is a hub-and-spoke technology, in which each user authenticates with the hub to use the services in the network.
What service provider will be selected?	Local phone company	The local phone company is capable of providing the services and geographic coverage required.
What data-link layer protocol will be used?	PPP	PPP is easy to configure and maintain.
What physical network media will be used?	ISDN (always on)	ISDN provides the bandwidth requirements and the always-on feature needed for continuous remote access.
Which Cisco products will be used?	Engineers: Cisco 802* Telesales representatives: Cisco 804* Central site: Cisco 3640 with T1 controller module for PRI*	The 800 series routers provide ISDN remote access. The Cisco 802 and 804 include integrated network termination 1 (NT-1), and the Cisco 804 provides phone ports for the telesales representatives. The 3600 series provides sufficient features and modularity to support current needs and future expansion.
Which routing protocols will be used?	OSPF (used on backbone network)	OSPF routing supports the remote routing needs of this application.
What IP addressing scheme will be used?	Dynamic Host Configuration Protocol (DHCP) is used to dynamically assign addresses	Automatic IP addressing simplifies administration of the remote sites.

* The example platforms are accurate as of the date this book was published.

The third of the main modules comprising the Enterprise Edge functional area is the Internet Connectivity module. The effective design methodology and techniques related to this module are discussed next.

Designing the Internet Connectivity Module

Not long ago, companies owned and operated numerous networks to deliver multiple services to their customers and employees. Voice communications required the telephone network, video broadcasting used a broadband cable network to broadcast video onto the network and to transport computer application data, and companies built data networks. Companies can now share information throughout the network that previously existed in isolation and was accessed through one medium. Customers, partners, and remote employees can now access that information when they are connected across the Internet. A network designer must be able to identify a company's needs for Internet connectivity and understand if/when NAT must be used for Internet connectivity. Familiarity with Cisco ISP connectivity solutions and design guidelines to support availability and load balancing is considered a great asset for network designers.

Enterprise Requirements for the Internet

Companies frequently require access from the internal network to the Internet and might provide access to public servers for outside users over the Internet. Connectivity initiated from the company-owned sites to the Internet and from the Internet to the company-owned sites must both be supported. Functionality, performance, scalability, availability, manageability, and cost-effectiveness are required in both directions. The Internet-to-company site case requires an increased level of security to ensure that unauthorized users do not gain access to the corporate network.

The first step in developing a network design for the Internet Connectivity module is to determine connectivity requirements. The following questions with regard to Internet connectivity must be answered:

- Does the company need a single Internet connection or multiple Internet connections? Will multiple Internet connections be furnished by a single ISP or by different ISPs?

- If multiple ISPs are used, how will load balancing be done?

- Which routing protocol will advertise the Internet internally, and advertise publicly available subnets externally?

- Is NAT or Port Address Translation (PAT) required at a router or transition device between the public and corporate network?

- What security measures are required to protect the corporate network?

The Internet Connectivity module of the Enterprise Composite Network Model provides services to enterprise (employees) who want to access the Internet and to outside users who want access to company public services, typically web servers or application servers. The primary components at the central site are the Internet access device (a router, access server, or VPN equipment), a publicly available network with publicly accessible servers, and, optionally, firewalls and Intrusion Detection Systems (IDS) nodes (see Figure 3-10).

Figure 3-10 *Internet Connectivity Module*

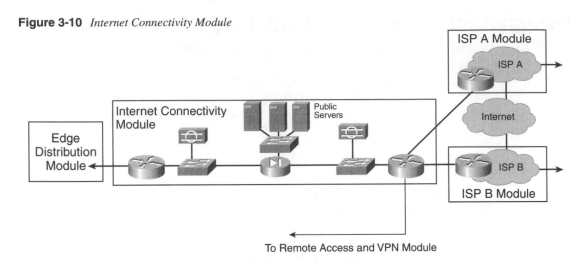

To Remote Access and VPN Module

Using NAT at the Enterprise Edge

NAT is designed to conserve IP addresses, because it enables large IP internetworks that use private IP addresses to connect to the Internet with a small set of registered/public IP addresses. Understanding the functionality of NAT and when and how NAT is used properly is a crucial topic of Internet connectivity. NAT operates on a router, usually connecting two networks together, and translates private addresses in the internal network into legal public addresses before forwarding packets onto another/external network. As part of NAT's functionality, one can configure NAT to advertise only one address for the entire network to the outside world. Figure 3-11 depicts the main terminology of NAT.

Figure 3-11 *Network Address Translation*

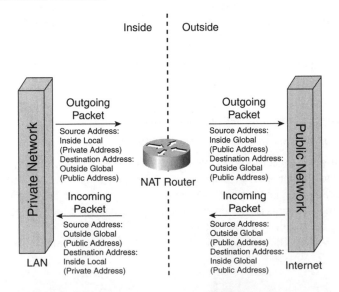

A company that uses public/registered addresses on its IP devices does not need to perform address translation, but it needs one IP address per device, and it is at a higher security risk (than its NAT counterpart). On the other hand, a company that uses private IP addressing needs to perform address translation, does not need one IP address per device, and it is at a lower security risk. NAT provides additional security, effectively hiding the entire internal network from the world behind that address. NAT takes these forms:

- **Static NAT**—Maps an unregistered IP address to a registered IP address on a one-to-one basis. Static NAT is particularly useful when a device needs to be accessible from outside the network.

- **Dynamic NAT**—Maps an unregistered IP address to a registered IP address from a group/pool of registered IP addresses.

- **Overloading**—A form of dynamic NAT that maps multiple unregistered IP addresses to a single registered IP address by using different ports, known also as PAT, single-address NAT, or port-level multiplexed NAT.

- **Overlapping**—When the IP addresses used on the internal network are registered IP addresses in use on another network, the NAT router must maintain a lookup table so that it can intercept and replace these registered addresses with unique IP addresses. The NAT router must translate the internal addresses into registered unique addresses. It must also translate the external registered addresses to addresses that are unique to the private network through static NAT or with dynamic NAT with Domain Name System (DNS).

Designing ISP Connectivity Solutions

An enterprise (company) might connect to the Internet as a single-homed or as a dual-homed (multihomed in general) autonomous system. An *autonomous system* is a network or group of networks under common administration with a registered autonomous system number. An autonomous system without a registered autonomous system number might use a private autonomous system number from the range 64512 to 65535. The simpler method is to provision a single connection to an ISP. If redundancy and load sharing are requirements, the multihomed model must be adopted.

The ISP connectivity that has no redundancy and is the easiest to configure is the single-run, or single-homed system, which connects the corporate site to a single ISP (see Figure 3-12). When implementing a single-homed system, the routing decision is to use a default route (gateway of last resort) pointing to the network that connects the site to the ISP. The gateway of last resort (referred to as default route by some) is then advertised into the corporate site pointing to the edge router, so that any packets with an unknown destination are forwarded to the ISP. The IP addressing is accomplished with real addressing, if it is available, or through NAT. If NAT is used, the publicly available servers must have addresses that are statically mapped either to a public address or to a PAT table. The ISP will use static routes that point to the enterprise site and then advertise those routes within their network and to those with whom they have peering arrangements.

Figure 3-12 *Single-Homed Site (Single ISP Connectivity)*

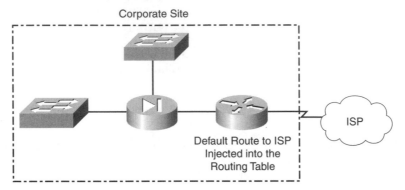

The questions and concerns with regard to implementing a single-homed connection are

- What are the consequences if the Internet connection is lost?
- Can the enterprise afford the consequences of an outage?
- Will public addressing or private addressing be used in the network?
- If private addressing is used inside, how many public addresses are needed to support the hosts that need static addressing? How many addresses are needed in the address pool for the users?
- When selecting the ISP, what services and support does it provide?

ISP multihoming solutions improve availability and load balancing for WANs that use the Internet. Multiple connections, known as multihoming, reduce the chance of a potentially catastrophic shutdown if one of the connections should fail (see Figure 3-13). In addition to maintaining a reliable connection, multihoming allows a company to perform load balancing (or at least load sharing) by lowering the number of computers connecting to the Internet through any single connection. Distributing the load through multiple connections optimizes performance and can significantly decrease wait times.

Multihomed networks are often connected to several different ISPs. Each ISP assigns an IP address (or range of IP addresses) to the company. Routers use Border Gateway Protocol (BGP) to route between networks of different administrative domains (autonomous systems). In a multihomed network, the corporate edge routers have Internal BGP (IBGP) relations among themselves and have External BGP (EBGP) relations with the ISP routers. Multihoming makes a significant difference when the connection to one of the ISPs fails. As soon as the router assigned to connect to that ISP determines that the connection is down, it will reroute all data through one of the other routers or paths.

Figure 3-13 *Multihomed Enterprise*

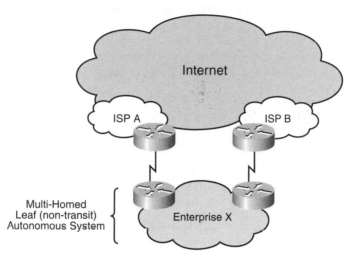

Two common methods are used when implementing a multihomed enterprise (ISP customer) solution. The first method is to inject (advertise) a default route into the customer network by each of the edge devices or by each of the ISP routers. This will yield multiple paths to the Internet, and it facilitates some load sharing across the multiple paths as well. The second method is to connect the enterprise edge routers and to set up an IBGP session between them. This method will provide a much more superior ground for load sharing and implementing enterprise routing policies. For a single-homed customer pointing the gateway of last resort (default route) toward the ISP, injecting a default route into the internal network will suffice. However, for a multihomed customer that desires to enforce symmetry, load balancing, and other policies, the second method (IBGP between enterprise edge routers) is a better solution.

Internet Connectivity Design Example

Jessie and Partners, Inc. has outgrown its current single ISP connection and wants to move to a multihomed network connection using two different ISPs to provide them with reliable, redundant service. It currently has 3400 employees and, at any given time, 400 people need simultaneous access to the Internet. The company recently developed a new process for ordering its products online and expects a large demand for its online ordering and online technical support services.

The IT staff has decided to use ISP A and ISP B as its service providers, and each provider is willing to create BGP connections into Jessie and Partners' network (as shown in Figure 3-14). The selected ISPs provide solutions and services, POPs, and high reliability and support. Both ISPs are willing to support BGP peer advertising of both public addresses that have been assigned to Jessie and Partners. Jessie and Partners have received two individual Class C addresses from the InterNIC (an accredited registrar of the InterNIC, to be exact) that they want both ISPs to advertise.

Figure 3-14 *Internet Connectivity Solution for Jessie and Partners Inc.*

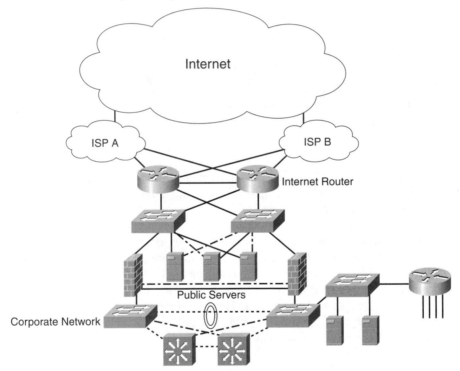

The company expects a large response from the outside to the publicly accessible or corporate network, but it will be difficult to judge without baselining the time it takes to use the products.

The following decisions were made with regard to the services that shall be provided and how addressing and routing will be handled:

- Basic security is currently provided by firewalls that keep outsiders out of the corporate network.

- The services provided will be FTP for drivers, and support documentation and HTTP access for papers and documentation. The internal users are expected to have the same kinds of traffic; that is, FTP and HTTP.

- NAT will be used in two ways: overloading for most employees, and static addresses for several key systems. The public addresses will be used in the isolated LAN and on the routers that connect to the ISPs. There will be no public addressing behind the firewalls.

- The company will accept full BGP routes from both services providers and will run IBGP between its edge routers. This approach will facilitate load sharing and implementing the company's routing policies.

Summary

In this chapter, you learned the following key points:

- The Enterprise Edge functional area is comprised of E-commerce, Internet Connectivity, Remote Access/VPN, and WAN modules, each of which is connected to the Edge Distribution module of the Enterprise Campus functional area on one side, and connected to a module of the Service Provider Edge on the other. Typical requirements of the Enterprise Edge are

  — Specific functionalities

  — Performance

  — Scalability

  — Availability

  — Manageability

  — Cost effectiveness

- The important characteristics of network applications at the Enterprise Edge functional area are

  — Bandwidth

  — Delay

  — Loss

  Assessing and analyzing network traffic patterns typically found in the Enterprise Edge functional area is an important part of network design.

- Based on application needs, enterprises typically have the following requirements for a site-to-site WAN solution:

  — Cost effectiveness

  — Sufficient bandwidth

  — High link quality

  — Reliability

  — Specific/appropriate data-link protocol characteristics

  — Either always-on or on-demand characteristics

- The branch office is typically the end of the network. The regional office typically sits between the Campus Backbone submodule and the branch offices, and it might house the application servers that the branch sites use, or it might simply provide access to the Campus Backbone submodule. The total amount of bandwidth for a branch site can be determined after the number of users, bandwidth requirements per user, and the branch applications and protocol characteristics are identified.

- It is common for the regional office to be an aggregation point for multiple branch offices. When aggregation is done, it is imperative to ensure there is enough bandwidth from the regional office to the core to provide the expected level of service to all branch offices that connect to that regional site. The regional office typically has multiple load-sharing links between the regional office and the central site Enterprise Edge functional area.

- The Campus Backbone WAN is normally the center of the enterprise. The server farms are usually placed in the central campus/site. The requirement for high-speed connectivity between routers is critical to ensure that all the outlying regions and branches/remote sites maintain their service levels. If the core is a single router or the Enterprise Edge routers of a large-scale enterprise, it must support the total aggregation of all of the traffic from the rest of the network.

- Each service provider offers a range of prices, speeds, features, and geographical coverage; hence, the selection of a service provider will depend on these factors considered together. The common data-link layer technologies for site-to-site WANs are

    — PPP

    — Frame Relay

    — ATM

    — MPLS

    — X.25

  The common physical layer technologies to choose from include

    — Leased line

    — DSL

    — Dialup

    — ISDN

    — Optical carrier

- The decision about which routing protocols to implement is based on the design goals, the physical topology of the network, and the configuration of links for remote sites. Routing protocol selection is also closely related to IP addressing strategies. Edge routing protocols include

    — Static routes

    — EIGRP

    — OSPF

    — RIPv2

References

"Wide Area Network Design." http://www.cisco.com/warp/public/779/largeent/design/wan_index.html.

"Remote Access Networking." http://www.cisco.com/warp/public/779/largeent/learn/topologies/remote_access.html.

Product Summary

Tables 3-12 and 3-13 provide a brief overview of some of the products available from Cisco Systems that relate to the topics discussed in this chapter. For a more detailed breakdown of the Cisco product line, visit http://www.cisco.com/en/US/products/index.html.

Table 3-12 lists a few Cisco routers that are good candidates as WAN aggregation devices for a corporate central office. They all provide the following features:

- **Product features**—Modular Configuration
- **Environment**—Corporate Office/Central Site
- **Application space**—WAN Aggregation
- **WAN connectivity**—Frame Relay

Table 3-12   *Examples of Cisco WAN Aggregation Routers for Central Sites*

Product Name	Description
Cisco 3725	Cisco 3700 Series 2-slot Application Service Router
Cisco 3725-DC-U	3725 router w/Universal Power Supply 24/48 volts
Cisco 3745	Cisco 3700 Series 4-slot Application Service Router
Cisco 7204VXR-CH	Cisco 7204VXR, 4-slot chassis, 1 AC Supply w/IP Software
Cisco 7206VXR-CH	Cisco 7206VXR, 6-slot chassis, 1 AC Supply w/IP Software
Cisco 7304	4-slot chassis, NSE100, 1 Power Supply, IP Software
Cisco 7401ASR-CP	7401ASR, 128M SDRAM, IP Software

Table 3-13 lists a few Cisco routers that can be used in the Remote Access/VPN module of an Enterprise Central Site, providing the following features:

- **Product Features**—Modular Configuration/VPN

- **Environment**—Corporate Office/Central Site
- **Application Space**—Remote Access

Table 3-13 *Examples of Cisco Remote Access/VPN Routers for Central Sites*

Product Name	Description
Cisco 3725	Cisco 3700 Series 2-slot Application Service Router
Cisco 3725-DC-U	3725 router w/Universal Power Supply 24/48 volts
Cisco 3745	Cisco 3700 Series 4-slot Application Service Router
Cisco 7204VXR-CH	Cisco 7204VXR, 4-slot chassis, 1 AC Supply w/IP Software
Cisco 7206VXR-CH	Cisco 7206VXR, 6-slot chassis, 1 AC Supply w/IP Software
Cisco 7304	4-slot chassis, NSE100, 1 Power Supply, IP Software
Cisco 7401ASR-CP	7401ASR,128M SDRAM, IP Software

Standards and Specifications Summary

Request For Comments (RFCs) can be downloaded from the following website: http://www.rfc-editor.org/rfc.html.

- RFC 1661, "The Point-to-Point Protocol (PPP)."
- RFC 2153, "PPP Vendor Extensions."
- RFC 2364, "PPP Over AAL5."
- RFC 2684, "Multiprotocol Encapsulation over ATM Adaptation Layer 5."

Review Questions

Answer the following questions from the material provided in this chapter. To check your answers, refer to Appendix A, "Answers to Review Questions."

1. Name the four modules that the Enterprise Edge functional area is comprised of.

2. Name at least four of the typical requirements for the Enterprise Edge functional area.

3. List the eight steps of the Cisco Enterprise Edge Design methodology.

4. Name at least two important characteristics of network applications that need to be noted while analyzing network traffic patterns.

5. List at least three enterprise requirements for a site-to-site WAN solution.

6. What are some of the valid questions for designing a branch office WAN connection? (List at least three.)

7. When developing the WAN module to support a regional office WAN, what questions need to be answered? (List at least three.)

8. What questions/concerns need to be answered/addressed when designing the enterprise WAN backbone? (List at least three.)

9. Name at least three criteria for selection of a service provider.

10. What are the commonly selected data-link layer WAN technologies? (Name at least two.)

11. What are the commonly selected physical layer WAN technologies? (Name at least two.)

12. Explain the MP feature of PPP.

13. Name at least three service classes of ATM.

14. What is the name of the online tool Cisco provides for choosing the best Cisco product for your particular needs?

15. Name three routing protocols that are suitable for site-to-site WAN. Which is the most scalable and nonproprietary protocol?

16. When designing the remote access connectivity, what important questions need to be answered?

17. In what situation would an on-demand remote access solution be viable for a group of employees at a remote site?

18. What are some questions to be asked about remote access physical termination?

19. What are five common physical layer technologies (dialup and broadband) for enterprise remote access?

20. To size the central site remote access solution, what parameters need to be determined? How would the peak bandwidth be determined?

21. To determine Internet connectivity requirements, what are some of the basic questions that must be answered?

22. Name the major forms of NAT.

23. What are some the common questions that must be asked when implementing a single-homed connection?

24. What are the advantages of multihoming?

25. What are the two routing options for a multihomed solution?

Case Study: OCSIC Bottling Company

The purpose of this case study is to practice the key design skills discussed in this chapter. The project is to design the enterprise edge network that meets the needs of the OCSIC Bottling Company. Specifically, you have been asked to do the following for OCSIC:

- Design the site-to-site WAN
- Design a remote access edge solution
- Design the Internet Connectivity module

As each component of the design will have multiple options, you need to consider each option carefully, based on the given constraints. For each identified component of the design, you are required to provide justification for your decision. The justification will provide an explanation for the options considered and the reason behind choosing the selected option.

The background information and network diagram for OCSIC were provided in the case-study section of Chapter 2, "Designing Enterprise Campus Networks."

North American Plant Headquarters WAN

The networks at each of OCSIC's plants were developed at different times and, therefore, are quite different from each other. The support and maintenance expenses have grown out of control and are placing an increasing burden on IT today. The company wants to replace the existing networks with a complete IP-based solution. Figure 3-15 shows the current network between the North American district and regional plants, and the headquarters office.

The plants currently use a Frame Relay over Fractional T1 WAN to the headquarters office. Although relatively inexpensive, the company finds these links too slow. Table 3-14 describes the traffic volume on the network from each North American plant office to the data center at headquarters.

Figure 3-15 *OCSIC's Current North American Plant Headquarters WAN Diagram*

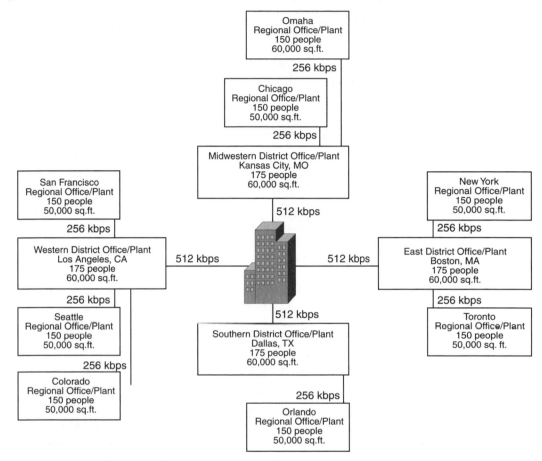

Table 3-14 *Traffic Volumes Between Server Farm and District Office(s) and Regional Office(s)*

Building From	Building To	Volume (in kbps) (To Nearest 50 kbps)
District Office/Plant	Building F (server farm)	600
Regional Office/Plant	District Office/Plant	450

Remote Access and Internet Connectivity Requirements

The salespeople work out of their local plant offices but are often on the road visiting with existing and potential customers. From the road, the salespeople need access from their PCs to the service access point (SAP) and custom Oracle applications. Each office has approximately 20 to 30 users that require remote access to the network. Security is key for those users, because much of the data is financial in nature. It is assumed that 300 people are on the road at one time. If 40% are active at one time, 120 ports will be required. All remote access is through the headquarters office.

The company wants all employees at headquarters to have access to the Internet. The projected traffic is 512 kbps.

International Manufacturing, Distribution, and Sales Plants

The international manufacturing, distribution, and sales plants are similar to their North American equivalents. That is, each location supports 150 to 175 users in a 50,000- to 60,000-square-foot facility. However, each plant is independently owned and operated.

The South American manufacturing, distribution, and sales plants are located in these cities: Sao Paolo (Brazil), Santiago (Chile), Caracas (Venezuela), San Jose (Costa Rica), and Mexico City (Mexico). The European manufacturing, distribution, and sales plants are located in these cities: Hanover (Germany), London (England), Paris (France), Rome (Italy), Dublin (Ireland), Madrid (Spain), and Prague (Czech Republic). The Asia-Pacific manufacturing, distribution, and sales plants are located in these cities: Singapore, Tokyo (Japan), Hong Kong, Taiwan (China), and Sydney (Australia).

International Plant Networks and Applications

Because the international plants are independently owned and operated, they have their own networks, applications, and IT staff. The offices do not communicate among themselves. To meet its own corporate goals, OCSIC wants to enhance communications and information sharing with its distributors, which require a higher-speed, inexpensive connection between the headquarters and each plant. Today, distributors use high-speed dialup connections to headquarters, as their needs are intermittent. However, many have very high toll calls to support this connectivity. OCSIC believes that the Internet will provide an ideal mechanism to share applications on an as-needed basis with these companies. Security will be a key consideration as the company implements a networking solution between its headquarters and its international partners. The international plants need access to these applications at headquarters: SAP, e-mail, and extranet website (planned). Table 3-15 describes the anticipated traffic volume on the network from international location to the data center at headquarters.

Table 3-15 *Traffic Volumes from International Location to the Data Center (HQ)*

Building From	Building To	Estimate Volume (kbps)
Each Office/Plant (today)	Building F (server farm)	90
Each Office/Plant (with extranet)	Building F (server farm)	170

WAN Module Design

Table 3-16 summarizes one possible set of design decisions that meets OCSIC's requirements for its WAN module. The top section of Figure 3-16 depicts an example design for the Edge Distribution module and the WAN module, with connections to the district offices; the bottom part of Figure 3-16 shows an example design for the WAN connections to the regional offices.

Table 3-16   *WAN Module Design Decisions for OCSIC*

Design Question	Decision	Justification
What topology will be used for the WAN?	Implement a simple hub-and-spoke configuration. Planning some redundancy is recommended.	The simple hub-and-spoke topology works with the headquarters hub connecting to the district plants, and the district plant hubs connecting to the regional plants.
What service provider will be selected?	A national carrier	A national carrier is required to provide geographical coverage.
What data-link layer protocol will be used?	Frame Relay	Frame Relay provides the bandwidth required at an affordable price.
What physical network media will be used?	Headquarters: T1 Each district plant: T1 Each regional plant: T1 (See the Note following this table.)	See the Note following this table.
What additional services would you select for each WAN link? If you selected Frame Relay, choose the number of ports, committed information rate (CIR), committed burst (Bc), excess burst (Be), transmission convergence (TC), and maximum burst size. If you selected ATM, choose the service class, either CBR, ABR, UBR, RT-VBR, or NRT-VBR. If you selected PPP, the services depend on the Layer 1 technology you selected.	The company is implementing the following features: • Permanent virtual circuits with • backward explicit congestion notification (BECN)/forward explicit congestion notification (FECN) acknowledgement and • Quality of service (QoS)	The features provide the QoS that the company requires.
Which Cisco products will be used?	Headquarters: Cisco 3640 District plants: Cisco 1760 Regional plants: Cisco 1750	Each product provides the capacity and features required.

continues

Table 3-16 *WAN Module Design Decisions for OCSIC (Continued)*

Design Question	Decision	Justification
Which routing protocols will be used?	OSPF hierarchical design	Given the number of sites and the way the design leads to an easy division of areas, OSPF is chosen.
What IP addressing scheme will be used?	Access to the Internet is required, and NAT must be deployed.	A single Class C address provides Internet connectivity. A Class B will be used internally, and NAT shall be used for external communication.

NOTE   **Headquarters** requires **two T1 access lines** to the Frame Relay provider. Each T1 has two Frame Relay permanent virtual circuit (PVC), each to a district office in a different time zone, at 640 kbps CIR with a committed burst up to 768 kbps and an excess burst up to 1024 kbps.

Eastern district requires **two T1 access lines** to the Frame Relay provider. Three PVCs are provisioned: one to headquarters with a 640 kbps CIR with a committed burst up to 768 kbps and an excess burst up to 1024 kbps on a dedicated T1, and two to the associated regional offices at a CIR of 512 kbps with a committed burst up to 640 kbps and an excess burst up to 768 kbps on the other T1.

Midwestern district requires **two T1 access lines** to the Frame Relay provider. Three PVCs are provisioned: one to headquarters with a 640 kbps CIR with a committed burst up to 768 kbps and an excess burst up to 1024 kbps on a dedicated T1, and two to the associated regional offices at a CIR of 512 kbps with a committed burst up to 640 kbps and an excess burst up to 768 kbps on the other T1.

Southern district requires **one T1 access line** to the Frame Relay provider. Two PVC are provisioned: one to headquarters with a 640 kbps CIR with a committed burst up to 768 kbps and an excess burst up to 1024 kbps, and one to the associated regional office at a CIR of 512 kbps with a committed burst up to 640 kbps and an excess burst up to 768 kbps.

Western district requires **two T1 access lines** to the Frame Relay provider. Four PVCs are provisioned: one to headquarters with a 640 kbps CIR with a committed burst up to 768 kbps and an excess burst up to 1024 kbps, and three to the associated regional offices at a CIR of 512 kbps with a committed burst up to 640 kbps and an excess burst up to 768 kbps. The PVC to headquarters and one West Coast regional office share a T1, and the two PVC to the other regional offices share the other T1.

Each **regional office** has a single **768 kbps fractional T1 access line** to the Frame Relay provider. There is a single PVC at a CIR of 512 kbps with a committed burst up to 640 kbps and an excess burst up to 768 kbps.

Figure 3-16 *WAN Connections Between Headquarters WAN Module, District Offices, and Regional Offices*

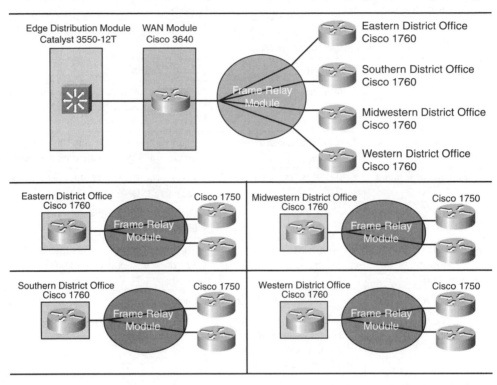

Remote Access Design

Figure 3-17 shows an example design for the connectivity between the Edge Distribution module and the Remote Access module.

Figure 3-17 *Remote Access Design*

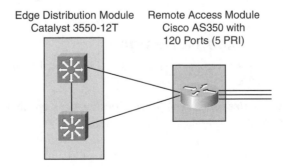

Table 3-17 summarizes one possible set of design decisions that meet OCSIC's requirements for Remote Access.

Table 3-17 *Remote Access Design Decisions for OCSIC*

Design Questions	Decision	Justification
What topology will be used for remote access?	Centralized	ISDN is deployed. Each user authenticates with the access servers at the hub to use the services in the network.
What service provider will be selected?	Local phone company	The local phone company provides the services and geographic coverage required.
What data-link layer protocol will be used?	PPP over ISDN or Dialup	ISDN provides bandwidth for users with access to ISDN. Dialup provides access for other remote users.
What physical network media will be used? How many trunks are required?	T1 with 5 PRIs	The physical media meets the need for 120 ports to support remote users.
Which Cisco products will be used?	Cisco AS5350 with 120 ports at headquarters Client devices require appropriate client software for dialup and applications	Each product provides the capacity and features required.
Which routing protocols will be used?	Not applicable	
What IP addressing scheme will be used?	Dynamic Host Configuration Protocol (DHCP) is used to dynamically assign addresses	Automatic IP addressing simplifies administration of the remote locations. An appropriate subnet address (/24) derived from the Class B address is dedicated to remote access.

Internet Connectivity Module Design

Figure 3-18 shows an example design for the Edge Distribution module and the Internet Connectivity module.

Table 3-18 summarizes one possible set of design decisions that meets OCSIC's requirements for Internet connectivity.

Figure 3-18 *Internet Connectivity Design*

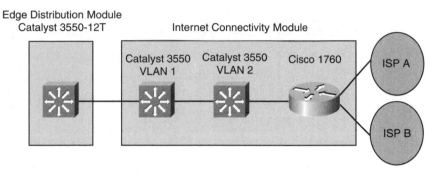

Table 3-18 *Internet Connectivity Design Decisions for OCSIC*

Design Questions	Decision	Justification
What topology will be used for Internet connectivity?	Point-to-point	Point-to-point provides the link required.
What service provider will be selected?	Local ISP	The local phone company provides the services and geographic coverage required.
What data-link layer protocol will be used?	PPP	Along with the data-link layer protocol, the following features are implemented: • Cisco IOS Firewall • Access lists
What physical network media will be used?	DSL	DSL provides a point-to-point link to the service provider at a cost-effective price point.
Which Cisco products will be used?	Catalyst 3550 in the Edge Distribution module Cisco 1760 to the Internet	Each product provides the capacity and features required.
Which routing protocols will be used?	Default routes throughout the OSPF network that point to the Cisco 1760 as the Internet gateway	
What IP addressing scheme will be used?	Two Class C networks NAT addressing	Two Class C networks are acquired from the provider to use with NAT. NAT provides public and private addressing.

After completing this chapter, you will be able to

- Develop an enterprise network management strategy
- Design the network management architecture
- Review CiscoWorks
- Create network management design scenarios

CHAPTER 4

Designing Network Management Services

The complexities associated with today's network-based services have increased significantly in the past decade. For example, the addition of voice and video to the network infrastructure has increased the demands for quality of service versus quantity. As the capacity and complexity of network services increase so, too, does the network's vulnerability to malicious attacks and unauthorized usage. For example, high-speed and broadband residential access, along with wireless LAN services have increased the footprint of the network, presenting multiple challenges from a security and capacity planning perspective. One task for network management is to reduce the potential negative influences on the enterprise infrastructure that these services might have. Another task is to plan for the implementation and preparation of the network for the deployment of these and other services to leverage their benefits. Network management, therefore, is a fundamental service within the enterprise network infrastructure.

To ensure that the enterprise network management design enhances availability, performance, and security, special consideration must be given to network management design principles. This chapter defines these principles with respect to the functional areas of network management. To reinforce these concepts, three network management models are presented and explained.

NOTE   Network management is defined as the process by which network administrators ensure the availability, performance, and security of network resources and services on behalf of the end user(s).

Developing an Enterprise Network Management Strategy

Network management includes a broad range of policies and procedures, combined with purpose-built hardware and software solutions. It is within the context of these various policies, procedures, and solutions that the appropriate network management strategy is developed. This strategy is not defined in isolation, but built upon sound technical and business requirements. Once defined, the goals for your network management system need to be developed. To assist you in this process, this section provides a definition of network management goals and explains the concept of network policy and procedure definition. The Cisco network management strategy is reviewed, and CiscoWorks is introduced as an example of a purpose-built software solution for enterprise network management.

Functional Areas of Network Management

Network management is an expanding field that evolves constantly. Initially, network management was based upon a simple fault notification system. Problems associated with resource availability and performance were communicated to network administrators after they had occurred—typically by the end user. In the past, network management was reactive; it provided little capacity to plan for future resource availability, performance, and security requirements. The capabilities and expectations of network management were, for the most part, low. However, as our dependency upon, and usage of network-based services increased, so did the expectations and requirements for better service by the end user. Reactive network management was no longer a palpable approach, so the requirement of a proactive network management system became the norm. Fortunately, as network capabilities and services evolve, so do the procedures and products that are used to manage them. Today, network management has grown to incorporate multiple stages including fault, configuration, accounting, performance, and security management (FCAPS).

Evolution of Network Management

Here is a brief summary of the evolution of network management services:

- **Network availability**—Initial network management systems (NMS) were based on the simple principle of network availability. There was no systematic way to determine if a fault occurred. When something went wrong in the network, the people in charge of the network were told via word of mouth that there was a problem.

- **Device reachability**—Basic device reachability was established. This allowed the people in charge of the network to see when a device failed or became unreachable but it did not give any reason for the outage.

- **Statistics collection**—The people managing the network began gathering statistics on the behavior of devices. When a device went down, historical data was available that may have helped solve the problem. This statistics gathering was extremely helpful for resolving recurring problems that were difficult to reproduce. Statistics collection also helped administrators become more proactive in their network management efforts.

- **Performance monitoring**—The statistics gathering became the input for measuring the performance of the devices being monitored. By monitoring the performance of the devices, the management staff could then tell when a device was about to have problems based on the device performance.

- **Baseline and configuration**—The performance data was used to create a baseline of normal network performance. Thresholds could then be set to determine when the network was performing outside the expected thresholds. The baseline and configuration data was used to monitor the network and be proactive in network management efforts.

- **Network modeling**—Took a snapshot of the network and then modeled the network so "what if" scenarios could be run to determine when and where a failure of the network might occur. Having this information beforehand allowed the management staff to predict when a problem would happen and proactively fix the potential trouble area before it ever occurred. Modeling also provided capacity planning to help determine which upgrades might be necessary to support a proposed architecture, new applications, and growth.

FCAPS

As network management became an integral part of the enterprise, the International Organization for Standardization (ISO) developed a standardized framework that defined the goals for modern NMS. Popular NMS solutions are designed around the ISO model, with tools and services oriented toward one or more of the functional areas. (These tools and services are covered in the section, "CiscoWorks.")

The five functional areas of network management as defined by the ISO are

- **Fault management**—The ability to detect, isolate, notify, and correct a fault that occurs within the network.

- **Configuration management**—The ability to track and maintain device configurations within the network. This includes configuration file management, device inventory, and software management.

- **Accounting management**—The ability to track the usage of the devices and the network resources. Accounting management tracks the hardware and software inventory, and should provide change control (versioning).

- **Performance management**—The ability to gather performance information from the devices and then interpret that information to determine the performance levels of the links and devices within the network. The collection of this information allows proactive identification and correction of performance problems.

- **Security management**—The ability to restrict and log access to the network resources to provide a system of defense against malicious attacks and track unauthorized access to resources.

NOTE   This chapter primarily focuses on the ISO areas of fault, configuration, and performance management. These three components are interpreted as the nucleus of the network management model and are reflected in the design of various network management systems.

Security is covered in Chapter 6, "Designing Security Services."

Network Management Policies and Procedures

As network management systems are implemented, it is vital to put policies and procedures in place to regulate the systems' deployment and usage. Policies and procedures are living documents that must evolve with the enterprise network. The significance of having clearly defined and implemented policies and procedures becomes evident when a network fault or security breach occurs. Lack of planning and preparation will lead to confusion and inactivity, both of which compound the situation rather than alleviate it. Therefore, having poorly defined policies and procedures is better than having none at all because at least you have somewhere to start.

Policies are implemented to define the plan for the network management system, and procedures define how to respond to an event or how to interpret collected performance data.

Policies

Individual policies provide the details about who and what is to be managed. In the context of network management, this means outlining which devices are monitored for reachability, which devices are monitored for performance measurements, the plan for escalation, and when users are to be notified of network issues. The following list outlines some key considerations when defining a network policy:

- **Monitoring**—The process of defining which devices are to be monitored (servers, routers, switches), the frequency at which polling should be conducted, and what software applications and protocols (SNMP, RMON, protocol analyzer) are to be employed. It specifies who is responsible or authorized to conduct the monitoring of select network resources (network services group), and where monitoring occurs (which segments, on which interfaces, and so on).

- **Security**—The process of protecting the network from malicious and unauthorized usage. The security policy defines what is acceptable usage of network resources. It dictates what services are to be deployed and who will manage them to protect the network and ensure its availability. Security also defines the kind of action taken to respond to a security threat (for example, temporarily shunning a connection on a firewall or taking a network resource offline).

- **Escalation**—The process of defining who is authorized to contact various personnel or outside agencies in response to a network event.

- **Client notification**—The process of defining who is authorized to notify clients and at what point in time clients can be notified.

- **Change control**—The process of defining who is authorized to change network configurations. It also defines what process to follow when implementing network and configuration changes.

Procedures

Procedures describe the steps taken when an event occurs. Procedures instruct the administrator on how to correct a problem and, if required, escalate it for resolution and document the entire incident.

The following list outlines important procedures and processes that require development:

- "What if" scenarios are developed for events as minor as an interface state change on a desktop switch, or cover an incident as significant as implementing disaster recovery procedures in the event of the destruction of a Network Operations Centre.

- "How to" instructions include step-by-step actions that an administrator or technician can take when a device fails or a network resource is compromised by a hacker.

- The staff notification process provides instructions that define names and contact numbers of the appropriate staff, how they should be notified, and what information should be provided to them regarding the incident.

- Trouble ticket procedures provide templates for how to complete and record the appropriate documentation associated with network incidents.

- The documentation process defines how different types of records are to be completed for various network administration or management events.

Network Management Methods

The approach that someone adopts to network management is dictated by the availability, performance, and security goals defined during the design process of the network strategy. Despite this process, the ability to implement an effective network management service is also shaped by the availability of resources to perform the task. The relationship between desirability and availability strongly influences how the two management styles of reactive and proactive are balanced.

Reactive—Event Driven

The reactive management method is common in the enterprise that has either not thought out its network management strategy, or lacks the required resources to effectively execute it. Many enterprise IT departments are understaffed, or their network is so poorly planned that the staff is constantly on the defensive, reacting to network issues. Another form of reactive management occurs when management makes a decision to only monitor events sent from the device(s) adjacent to the device that is having a problem. The problem with such an event-driven solution is that it keeps the staff in reactive mode. The staff only learns of a problem after the problem has manifested itself as a network issue, when a device sends an event out to the network management station.

NOTE   For example, if monitoring and retrieval of statistical information from a device is conducted, such as memory usage on a router, thresholds can be established. When the threshold is exceeded, alerts can be generated to advise network administrators that the resource is being excessively taxed. This allows a proactive approach to identifying potential performance-related failures or problems. Event driven is having the switch connected to the router report that an interface changed from up to down. The administrators have no indication of what caused the event to occur and are only aware of an issue with the router because of the event notification from the switch. Nor are they provided with an opportunity to avert the situation by upgrading the router's memory prior to its failure.

Proactive—Polling and Event Driven

The proactive management style is the preferred style by management staff. It uses event-driven information and polling to determine the health of the network. The polling and collection of data from devices allow the management team to identify problems before they happen so they can take steps to reduce or remove issues before users see any problems. Though in the proactive style, it is still necessary to put out fires, there should be fewer issues and better plans developed to resolve issues as they occur.

Network Management Strategy Process

Network management requires the development of a solid strategy and sound methodology to succeed. The following list outlines the recommended steps required to develop a network management strategy for the enterprise:

Step 1   Plan which devices are to be managed and which are not. Create an inventory of your network resources and services and classify their importance in relationship to their overall impact on network availability, performance, and security. Classify network devices relative to the services they provide and the impact their absence will have on the enterprise mission or objective.

Step 2   Determine what information to gather or receive from network devices. If the management system is going to be event-driven, determine what kind of information to collect from the traps. Traps are events sent to the management station via Simple Network Management Protocol (SNMP) from a device. If the management style is poll-driven, determine what information to collect from the devices to meet the management goals.

Step 3 Set realistic, measurable goals for network management. If the management style is event-driven, set goals that you can measure based on the events received. If the management style is based on polling or a combination of polling and events, set measurable goals to determine if the network management system is performing as expected.

Step 4 Identify the tools available to collect the required data. Are you going to rely on a commercial solution, such as CiscoWorks, or native features, such as Cisco Cluster Manager, to achieve your goal. Perhaps an open source solution, such as Multi-Router Traffic Grapher (MRTG), can meet certain requirements. Various services might be deployed in isolation or combined to achieve the task(s) at hand. Do you require an enterprise solution, such as HP OpenView, or independent element solutions, such as MRTG, for performance management?

Step 5 Identify the monitoring goals and thresholds. Then set the appropriate traps and alerts on the specific devices best positioned to report the activity. To be effective in setting thresholds and alerts, it is important to not only have intimate knowledge of the platform that is being monitored, but also to have conducted network modeling derived from baseline statistics that have been collected over time.

Step 6 Create plans and procedures to handle "what if" scenarios, so that when a network problem is identified, some basic procedures are in place to resolve the problem. Plans and procedures are only effective if they are based on realistic data collected from network modeling and baselining. Furthermore, procedures must be tested regularly to provide training and ensure their effectiveness.

NOTE   MRTG is a management tool that provides real-time reporting of activity on network links. MRTG uses SNMP to poll network interfaces and converts the data into graphics that are viewable via HTML pages. Detailed information about MRTG can be obtained from www.mrtg.org.

HP OpenView is a comprehensive network management solution from Hewlett-Packard. Detailed information can be obtained from www.openview.hp.com.

The Cisco Cluster Manager is a native management product included with select Catalyst switch operating systems. It provides an HTML-based interface for configuring and managing up to 16 geographically dispersed Catalyst products.

Network Management Module Functions

To implement network management goals, enterprises will implement individual infrastructure components that meet specific needs. This section identifies the infrastructure components that the Network Management module provides.

The Enterprise Composite Network Model includes the Network Management module, which contains one or more of the following:

- **Authentication server**—Provides authentication services for remote and local users on the network

- **Access control server**—Provides centralized command and control for all user authentication, authorization, and accounting (AAA)

- **Network monitoring server**—Responsible for monitoring the devices in the network

- **Intrusion Detection System (IDS) Director**—Provides a comprehensive, pervasive security solution for combating unauthorized intrusions, malicious Internet worms, and bandwidth and application attacks

- **Syslog**—Provides a collection point for network events and traps

- **System administration server**—Management station used to configure network management and other network devices

The following tools provide a network administrator with access to the devices in the Network Management module:

- **Out-of-band management**—Provides the ability to access devices through a path external to that taken by production network traffic. For example:

  - **Terminal server**—Provides a way to perform out-of-band management to multiple devices connected serially to the terminal server, which, in turn, might be connected to a modem

  - **Auxillary port**—Provides a way to perform out-of-band management to a single device connected serially to a modem

  - **Console port**—Provides a way to perform out-of-band management to a single device connected serially to a terminal communications port

  - **Separate physical network**—Each managed device is connected to an independent switched network. This allows usage of IP-based services, but restricts traffic to a completely separate physical path from end-user data.

- **In-band management**—Provides the ability to access devices through a path shared by production network traffic. For example:

  - **NMS**—Provides a way to perform in-band management to multiple devices using the SNMP protocol over an existing Transmission Control Protocol/ Internet Protocol (TCP/IP) network infrastructure

  - **Telnet**—Provides a way to perform in-band management to a single device using the Telnet protocol over an existing TCP/IP network infrastructure

— **SSH**—Provides a secure way to interact with remote IP-enabled devices at the command-line interface similar to Telnet.

— **Management VLAN**—All NMS devices are placed in a separate broadcast domain that does not permit, nor contain end-user devices or resources. Access to the Management VLAN is controlled via trunking and routing. All management traffic—SNMP, Telnet, SSH, TFTP, VTP, and so on—coexist on the same physical paths as regular enterprise users, but are isolated logically at Layer 2 by being tagged as belonging to a unique VLAN.

— **VPN**—Provides the most secure in-band management alternative by moving all traffic over an encrypted tunnel between the NMS and the Management Agent. The Management Agent is the network management process running on the managed device. It is this agent process that enables the network management station to remotely monitor and manage the platform. Communication between the Management Agent and NMS occurs via the TCP/IP protocol SNMP.

Table 4-1 describes the most common protocols used for network management.

Table 4-1 *Common Network Management Protocols*

Protocol	Identifier	Description
Telnet	TCP 23	Telnet is an application protocol that provides terminal-based access to remote network devices. One of the oldest TCP/IP protocols in use today, it is inherently insecure because of its transmission of payload contents in plain text. This fact limits its safe deployment to isolated or encrypted (VPN) management networks.
SSH	TCP 22	Secure Shell (SSH) is an application protocol that provides terminal-based access to remote network devices. It was designed to overcome the weakness of Telnet by encrypting its payload contents allowing secure management over insecure networks. Its use has not become ubiquitous in the world of network management because it is not supported by all vendor products or versions.
HTTP	TCP 80	Hypertext Transfer Protocol (HTTP) is an application protocol that provides an integrated common interface to network resources for the purpose of management. Its appeal is based upon the broad familiarity of its interface and simplicity of its deployment. It is, however, insecure and, therefore, limits its safe deployment to isolated or encrypted (VPN) management networks.
SSL	TCP 443	Secure Socket Layer (SSL) is an application protocol that provides an integrated common interface to network resources for the purpose of management. Its appeal is based upon the broad familiarity of its interface and simplicity of its deployment. It overcomes the security limitations of HTTP by encrypting the application payload. This allows it to be used over insecure networks with a relative degree of security assurance.

continues

Table 4-1 *Common Network Management Protocols (Continued)*

Protocol	Identifier	Description
Syslog	UDP 513	Syslog is an application protocol that provides logging messages based upon a predefined standard. It is not a secure service because its payload data is unencrypted. As a result, location of syslog resources should be on isolated management networks or across encrypted tunnels to protect them from exploitation.
TFTP	UDP 69	Trivial File Transfer Protocol (TFTP) is an application that is used to remotely store device configurations and operating systems (IOS). This allows for a managed remote storage and retrieval system. It is not a secure service because its payload data is unencrypted. As a result, location of TFTP resources should be on isolated management networks or across encrypted tunnels to protect them from exploitation.
SNMP	UDP 161/162	Simple Network Management Protocol (SNMP) is the most ubiquitous application protocol that is used to manage devices remotely. It defines the format for the collection and exchange of data between managed devices and the network management station.
RMON		Remote Monitoring (RMON) is an extension of the SNMP database specification known as the Management Information Base (MIB), which defines information sets and formats.
CDP	Layer 2 SNAP	Cisco Discovery Protocol (CDP) is a proprietary Layer 2–based application that allows the discovery of directly connected Cisco devices. CDP is not routed and cannot be used for remote management purposes. It provides predefined information about the platform it is enabled on. Security issues arise when this information is generated on insecure networks because the payload contents are clear text and could be used to exploit a device by unintentionally revealing critical information, such as addressing and OS version.

NOTE   For more information regarding these protocols, refer to the section, "References," at the end of this chapter.

Cisco Network Management Strategy

Enterprise network managers are faced with the task of developing a strategy for managing very large networks. As enterprise networks continue to grow in size, and the number of different management tools and products multiply, developing an appropriate strategy is becoming more difficult. Cisco Systems approached this problem by developing a common architecture for its management products. This framework is made accessible through a standard interface for the user to simplify implementation of the network management strategy.

A key component of the Cisco network management strategy is built around a web-based model that possesses the following characteristics:

- Simplification of tools, tasks, and processes
- Flexible but secure user access via a common web browser
- Web-level integration with NMS platforms and general management products
- Capability to provide end-to-end solutions for managing routers, switches, and access servers
- Creation of a management intranet by integrating discovered device knowledge with Cisco Connection Online (CCO) and third-party application knowledge

The Cisco network management strategy is reflected in their suite of software management products known as CiscoWorks. In the following section, an overview of two solutions from the CiscoWorks family known respectively as the LAN and Remote WAN management solutions will be examined.

CiscoWorks

CiscoWorks is a family of products based on Internet standards for managing enterprise networks and devices. This section describes the CiscoWorks network management solution, given specific network management requirements.

The CiscoWorks product line, shown in Figure 4-1, offers a set of solutions designed to manage the enterprise network. These solution sets are built upon the ISO framework of FCAPS. The core components of FCAPS—fault, configuration, and performance management—are implemented by Cisco in its LAN Management Solution (LMS) and Routed WAN Management Solution (RWAN). These two solutions focus on key areas in the network such as optimization of the WAN, administering switch-based LANs, and measuring service level agreements (SLAs) within all types of networks. The expanding CiscoWorks product line offers the flexibility to deploy end-to-end network management solutions.

Cisco Architecture for Voice, Video, and Integrated Data (AVVID) solutions rely on a stable foundation of optimally functioning Catalyst multiprotocol, multilayer LAN switches. Proper network management is essential to maintain such an environment. However, administrators often find that it is difficult to adequately manage a converged network using manual processes.

CiscoWorks network management can provide the network administrator with a scalable tool that is easily learned, and is capable of automating the most common network management tasks. When properly deployed, the CiscoWorks network management solution can provide considerable savings by reducing labor cost and increasing network availability.

Figure 4-1 *CiscoWorks Product Line*

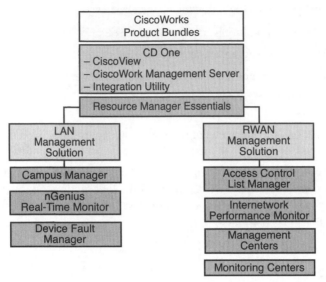

<table>
<tr><td colspan="2">CiscoWorks
Product Bundles</td></tr>
</table>

CD One
– CiscoView
– CiscoWork Management Server
– Integration Utility

Resource Manager Essentials

LAN Management Solution	RWAN Management Solution
Campus Manager	Access Control List Manager
nGenius Real-Time Monitor	Internetwork Performance Monitor
Device Fault Manager	Management Centers
	Monitoring Centers

NOTE

Cisco offers a comprehensive set of network management products that provide IP Telephony, Security, and Wireless network support. This chapter focuses on LMS and RWAN. Here is a brief description of three other key solution sets that are available from Cisco Systems:

- **CiscoWorks IP Telephony Environment Monitor (ITEM)**—A powerful suite of applications and tools that continuously evaluate and report the operational health of your Cisco IP Telephony implementation. ITEM is used to manage Cisco AVVID and Cisco IOS software-based IP Telephony environments and provides specialized operations and security tools beneficial to large and small IP Telephony implementations. CiscoWorks ITEM consists of a product bundle as well as several optional components that can be downloaded from the Cisco Systems website.

- **CiscoWorks Small Network Management Solution (SNMS)**—A bundle of network management applications designed to manage the Cisco devices in a small- to medium-sized network. SNMS includes CiscoView, 40-device Resource Manager Essentials, and Ipswitch What's up Gold.

- **CiscoWorks VPN/Security Management Solution (VMS)**—A bundle of applications providing centralized management of the security components of Cisco SAFE-based networks. VMS includes CiscoView, Security Management Centers (PIX, IOS), Resource Manager Essentials, IDS Host Console, CSPM, VPN Monitor, and the CiscoWorks Server.

This material was derived from the Cisco website located at http:// http://www.cisco.com/ en/US/products/sw/netmgtsw/index.html#products.

CiscoWorks Common Management Foundation

The CiscoWorks architecture consists of a Common Management Foundation (CMF) with a web-based desktop as a single point of management. An additional component provides data collection services using SNMP, CDP, and Interim Local Management Interface (ILMI) tables, Syslog, Telnet, Cisco Interactive Monitor/extensible markup language (CIM/XML), and Hypertext Markup Language (HTML).

NOTE   ILMI specification provides the exchange of management information between ATM user-to-network (UNI) management interfaces.

Discovery of the network occurs via a seed device, typically a Catalyst switch, through which the CMF starts discovery of the network by reading its CDP or ILMI table and SNMP variables. This information permits the discovery of the seed's neighboring devices, which, in turn, are queried for CDP/ILMI and SNMP information. This process continues outward from each discovered device to build a network topology map. The CMF also provides granular security, process control, and device information retrieval via SNMP.

NOTE   CiscoWorks CMF is the core basis for Cisco Common Services. Common Services provides a foundation of application infrastructure for all CiscoWorks applications to share a common model for data storage, login, user role definitions, access privileges, and security protocols, as well as for navigation and launch management. It creates a standard user experience for all common management functions and integrates CiscoWorks applications at multiple levels.

CiscoWorks Common Services provides the common framework for all basic system-level operations such as installation; data management, including backup-restore and import-export; event and message handling; job and process management; and so on. It also packages industry standard services, such as web, SNMP, XML parsing, XSLT processing, logging, email, and so on, used by CiscoWorks applications. In addition, CiscoWorks Common Services allows third-party management applications to be integrated and data to be shared.

The following information was derived from the Cisco website located at http://www.cisco.com/en/US/products/sw/cscowork/ps3996/index.html.

CiscoWorks LAN Management Solution

The CiscoWorks LMS provides a solid foundation of the basic and advanced management applications that enable network operators to efficiently manage the LAN. This section helps you select CiscoWorks LAN management tools, given specific network management requirements.

Figure 4-2 illustrates the modules associated with the Cisco LMS.

Figure 4-2 *CiscoWorks LAN Management Solution*

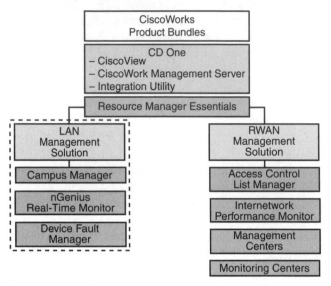

All CiscoWorks product bundles include these two common modules:

- **CD One**—The first component to install on the management server. This collection of base packages includes these applications:

  — **CiscoView**—A web-based device management application providing dynamic status, monitoring, and configuration for a managed Cisco device.

  — **CiscoWorks Management Server**—Includes the database engine, online help, security, login, application launching (from the CiscoWorks desktop), job and process management, and a web server for client access. CiscoWorks Server also includes Common Management Foundation services and Cisco Management Connection (CMC) to integrate other web-based management applications and tools into the CiscoWorks desktop.

  — **Integration Utility**—Offers integration with third-party network management platforms by adding CiscoView device-specific information to the platform and provides launch points to other Cisco applications.

- **Resource Manager Essentials (RME)**—Contains the configuration management tools necessary for Cisco devices. RME contains these six applications to aid the administrator's efforts:

  — **Inventory Manager**—Provides current inventory of all Cisco devices (routers, switches, firewalls) in the network, including support for Cisco CallManager, VPN concentrators, and WAN switches. Hardware and software summary information includes detailed reports for groups of devices, memory, flash, software version, interface, and stack modules.

— **Device Configuration Manager**—Maintains an active archive of configuration changes, and can modify stored configuration changes across multiple Cisco routers and switches. When Configuration Manager detects a configuration change (applied via CLI, Telnet, or CiscoWorks), it automatically updates the archive data, and logs the change information to the Change Audit Service. Configuration Manager also provides powerful editing capabilities of the archived configuration data, including find, search, replace, copy, cut, paste, as well as compare and change detail. Modified files can be saved locally or downloaded to the target device.

Cisco-provided templates simplify the configuration change process for SNMP community, Terminal Access Controller Access Control System plus (TACACS+), enable, Syslog, SNMP trap destinations, CDP, and Domain Name System (DNS).

— **Software Image Manager**—Simplifies the version management and routine deployment of software updates to Cisco routers and switches through wizard-assisted planning, scheduling, downloading, and monitoring of software updates. Links to Cisco.com compare the latest Cisco online software update information with the Cisco IOS and Catalyst software images deployed in the network. Software Image Manager also allows the administrator to validate the target switch or router's inventory data with the hardware requirements of a new image to help ensure a successful upgrade. When multiple devices are being updated, Software Image Manager synchronizes download tasks and allows the user to monitor job progress. Scheduled jobs are controlled through a signoff process, enabling managers to authorize a technician's activities before initiating each upgrade task.

— **Change Audit**—Displays changes made to managed devices. Summary information includes types of changes made, the person responsible for the change, time of change, and whether the changes were made from a Telnet or console CLI or from a CiscoWorks application. Reports detailing the nature of the changes, such as cards added or removed, memory changes, and configuration changes, are available as well.

— **Availability Manager**—Displays the operational status of critical routers and switches. Drilling down on a particular device allows the administrator to view historical information with regard to a given device, including response time, availability, reloads, protocols, and interface status.

— **Syslog Analyzer**—Filters syslog messages logged by Cisco switches, routers, access servers, and Cisco IOS firewalls, and generates reports in an easily digested format. Its reports are based on user-defined filters that highlight specific errors or severity conditions, and help identify when specific events occurred (such as a link-down condition or a device reboot). Syslog Analyzer also allows syslog messages to be linked to customized information, such as web-based administrative tips or to launch a Common Gateway Interface (CGI) script to take corrective actions.

CiscoWorks LMS is composed of these three modules:

- **Campus Manager**—Provides the administrator with tools to configure, manage, and understand the physical and logical aspects of a Catalyst-based LAN. Campus Manager offers these applications and services:

  - **Topology Services**—The principle interface to a variety of large-scale topology maps, tabular summaries, reports, and configuration services of the Layer 2 network. A directory-like tree interface lists physical Layer 2 and logical, VLAN Trunking Protocol (VTP), and ATM domain views, along with table summaries of the devices and the interface associated with these views. This tree structure acts as the launching point for topology maps, discrepancy reporting functions, and configuration services.

  - **User Tracking**—Designed to assist in locating end-station connections at the access switch, this application is used in troubleshooting or connectivity analysis. Through automated acquisition, a table of end-user stations and Layer 2 connection information is constructed. This table can be sorted and queried, allowing administrators to easily find users. Users can be identified by name, IP handset, or MAC and IP address, as well as the switch port and switch on which they are connected; the VLAN and VTP assignment of the port can also be identified. Predefined reports, such as duplicate MAC address per switch port, or duplicate IP addresses, enable managers to locate mobile users or violations in port policies.

  - **Path Analysis**—An application for switched network management, this is an extremely powerful tool for connectivity troubleshooting. Path Analysis uses user tracking, topology services, and real-time spanning-tree information to determine Layer 2 and Layer 3 connectivity between two endpoints in the network. The resulting trace is presented in graphical views that illustrate the Layer 2 and Layer 3 devices, path direction, and link types. A tabular format provides specific interface, IP address, VLAN, and link-type information.

  - **VLAN Port Assignment**—Campus Manager provides graphical means for creating, modifying, or deleting VLANs and LAN emulation (LANE) elements, plus assigning switch ports to VLANs. As VLANs are created or modified, port and user changes are updated and transmitted to the switches, eliminating the need to update and configure each participating switch individually. As VLANs are selected, the table view shows the participating ports, port status, and switch information, and the topology map can be launched to graphically highlight participating devices and links for the VLAN connections. Additional map tools allow managers to show spanning-tree states, VTP trunks, switch port links, and existing LANE service elements.

— **Discrepancy Reports**— Used to view the physical and logical discrepancies discovered on the network.

- **nGenius Real-Time Monitor**—A web-based tool that delivers multiuser access to real-time RMON and RMON2 information, and is used for monitoring, troubleshooting, and maintaining network availability. Real-Time Monitor (RTM) can graphically analyze and report device-, link-, and port-level RMON-collected traffic data obtained from RMON-enabled Catalyst switches, internal Network Analysis Modules, and external LAN and WAN probes.

- **Device Fault Manager**—Provides real-time fault analysis for managed Cisco devices. Device Fault Manager actively monitors a wide range of problems that Cisco has identified can occur within Cisco devices. Depending on the type of device, Device Fault Manager will actively monitor different conditions via Internet Control Message Protocol (ICMP) polling, SNMP MIB interrogation, and SNMP trap reception, and track only those conditions known to help cause higher-level problems in that particular device.

NOTE   MIB is an essential component of the SNMP management architecture. The MIB is a hierarchical database that identifies what type of information can be retrieved from a managed device using SNMP-enabled applications. The RMON specification is an extension to the SNMP MIB defining new information sets and actions that can be performed on RMON-enabled devices.

NOTE   This section contained information regarding the CiscoWorks product line. To retain faithfulness to the course material for those who are using this book to prepare for certification, the material was not changed in its content or presentation. However, it is important to note that various changes have occurred to the product line that affect the accuracy of the previous information. Here is a brief list of some of the changes that affect the text. For accurate information regarding the CiscoWorks product line, visit http://www.cisco.com/go/ciscoworks/:

- CiscoWorks CD One has reached "end of life"; see http://www.cisco.com/en/US/products/sw/cscowork/ps4737/index.html.

- CMC is now part of RME; see http://www.cisco.com/en/US/products/sw/cscowork/ps2073/index.html.

Best Practices for Managing the LAN Using LMS

Network management tasks will differ depending on the needs and capabilities of the network and available support resources. However, you should plan to conduct these tasks with Resource Manager Essentials regardless of the network's individual characteristics:

- **Maintain a configuration archive**—Automatically conducted by RME on all devices in the RME inventory

- **Maintain a software image archive**—RME can import the software images on all devices, and then automatically poll devices to determine if their image is backed up in the archive for disaster recovery purposes

- **Create a change management inventory**—Automatically conducted on all inventoried devices

- **Run custom reports**—RME Syslog Analyzer can run custom reports based on a device level, syslog message priority, or timeframe

Use Campus Manager to perform these tasks:

- **Detect configuration discrepancies**—Use Campus Manager Path Analysis to automatically validate connectivity for proper duplex, speed, and trunking configuration

- **Locate switch ports with multiple IP addresses**—Campus Manager's user tracking function will locate switch ports with multiple IP addresses

Use nGenius Real-Time Monitor to perform this task:

- **Monitor RMON statistics**—Monitor RMON statistics using RTM to detect application errors and link usage

CiscoWorks Routed WAN Management Solution

The CiscoWorks Routed WAN (RWAN) Management Solution extends the CiscoWorks product family by providing a collection of powerful management applications to configure, administer, and maintain a Cisco RWAN. This section helps you select CiscoWorks WAN management tools, given specific network management requirements.

The RWAN solution addresses the management needs of WANs by improving the accuracy, efficiency, and effectiveness of your network administrators and operations staff, as well as increasing the overall availability of your network through proactive planning, deployment, and troubleshooting tools.

NOTE   Many management tasks that are essential in the LAN environment are also equally important in the WAN environment. Therefore, some overlap exists in the functionality between LMS and RWAN.

The Common Management Foundation (CMF) is common in all CiscoWorks solutions. RWAN also shares the RME with LMS.

Figure 4-3 shows each of the modules associated with CiscoWorks RWAN Management Solution.

Figure 4-3   *CiscoWorks RWAN Management Solution*

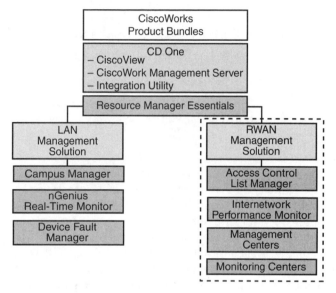

Specific RWAN modules include

- **Access Control List Manager (ACLM)** — Manages the access lists of Cisco devices. ACLM provides tools to set up and manage IP and IPX filtering and device access control. These tools include
  - Access list editors
  - Policy template managers
  - Network and service class managers for scalability
  - Access list navigation tools for troubleshooting
  - Optimization of access lists
  - Automated distribution of access list updates

- **Internetwork Performance Monitor (IPM)** — Measures network performance based on synthetic traffic generation technology generated by the Service Assurance Agent (SAA) contained in Cisco IOS. IPM gives the network manager the ability to obtain baseline performance data, useful in troubleshooting situations and to validate the network infrastructure for new multiservice applications. IPM can generate a network response time baseline for any of these network traffic types:
  - Internet Control Message Protocol (ICMP) echo
  - IP path echo

- Systems Network Architecture (SNA) echo

- User Datagram Protocol (UDP)

- UDP jitter

- Voice over IP (VoIP)

- Transmission Control Protocol (TCP) connect

- Domain Name System (DNS)

- Dynamic Host Configuration Protocol (DHCP)

- HTTP

- Data-link switching (DLSw)

NOTE   The Cisco Service Assurance Agent (SAA) is embedded software within Cisco IOS that performs active monitoring. Active monitoring is the generation and analysis of traffic to measure performance between Cisco IOS devices or between Cisco IOS devices and network application servers. Active monitoring provides a unique set of performance measurements: network delay or latency, packet loss, network delay variation (jitter), availability, one-way latency, website download time, as well as other network statistics. SAA can be used to measure network health, verify SLAs, assist with network troubleshooting, and plan network infrastructure. SAA is supported on almost all Cisco IOS devices. Enterprises and service providers routinely deploy SAA for network performance statistics and within IP networks that utilize quality of service (QoS), VoIP, security, Virtual Private Network (VPNs), and Multiprotocol Label Switching (MPLS). SAA provides a scalable and cost-effective solution for IP service-level monitoring and eliminates the deployment of dedicated active monitoring devices by including the "probe" capabilities within Cisco IOS.

This material was derived from the Cisco website located at http://www.cisco.com/en/US/tech/tk447/tk823/tech_protocol_family_home.html.

Best Practices for Managing the WAN Using RWAN

As was already explained in the section, "Best Practices for Managing the LAN Using LMS," regardless of the network's individual characteristics, to best manage the WAN using RWAN

- **Maintain a configuration archive**—RME automatically conducts configuration archives on all devices in the RME inventory.

- **Maintain a software image archive**—RME can import the software images on all devices, and then automatically poll devices to determine if the images are backed up in the archive for disaster recovery purposes.

- **Change management**—Automatically conducted on all inventoried devices.

- **Syslog reporting and monitoring**—RME Syslog Analyzer can run custom reports based on a device level, syslog message priority, or timeframe.

In addition, best practices include performing these WAN-specific management tasks:

- **Use IPM to monitor critical network services**—Monitor critical network services such as DNS and DHCP, as well as response times to critical servers with IPM.

- **Use ACL Manager to standardize and optimize access control lists**—ACL Manager presents a user-friendly graphical user interface that allows you to concentrate on the security of your network without having to learn complex IOS syntax.

Designing the Network Management Architecture

Enterprise network managers are often faced with the problem of managing very large networks. To alleviate the inherent difficulties associated with this task, you must ensure proper attention is paid to the design of the network management architecture.

While designing the network management architecture, multiple elements must be considered, such as data collection, management strategy, and server sizing. Deployment of the correct solution requires calculating the correct number of management servers to deploy, selecting a scalable solution, and determining whether or not partitioning your network is required. This section assists you with these processes by reviewing network management design considerations and making deployment recommendations.

Remember, the network management architecture affects the network management system itself as well as the network as a whole. Selecting the right components and defining strategies are critical to the success and availability of the enterprise network.

Network Management Design Considerations

Network management is an integral part of the overall network design because network management can adversely affect network performance. This section identifies design considerations for a network management system.

Network Management Infrastructure Considerations

To develop a network management strategy for the network management infrastructure, you need to answer the following questions:

- **Is a single network management station required or are multiple network management stations required?** The number of network management stations required depends on the number of end-user devices to be managed.

- **Is it best to have a centralized or distributed deployment of network management stations?** The decision often depends on the organization's ability to support the solution.

- **Is a hierarchical design required to mirror the network infrastructure?** Many enterprises implement a hierarchical network management system design that mirrors the network infrastructure from the campus, to the enterprise edge, to the branch offices. The decision depends on the size of the organization, and the organization's ability to support the solution.

- **Does network management require a dedicated network, or can it be part of the campus network?** You need to decide if you want to establish an independent broadcast domain (VLAN) that possesses a unique physical and logical connection to each device for management purposes.

- **Which management tools are required: element management tools or end-to-end policy-based tools?** The size of the enterprise usually dictates the types of tools required.

NOTE   Two types of network management systems exist. One type is called an element manager, which is responsible for managing a particular aspect of the network. It usually covers only one of the areas defined by FCAPS. An example of an element management application is Cisco Access Router Manager, which provides configuration management for Cisco 2600, 3600, and 3700 access routers. Element managers are part of the second type of management system: enterprise management system. Enterprise management systems such as CiscoWorks RWAN are responsible for the overall network, not just a singular component or platform.

- **How do Network Address Translation (NAT) and firewalls affect the network management strategy?** Enterprises often use NAT and firewalls that can have the unwanted side effect of blocking or breaking access via common management protocols. Solutions are to disable SNMP on security devices, or use more advanced authentication options such as certificates, and limit SNMP access to trusted interfaces and from specific devices only. Management can be conducted remotely using SSH and be further locked down by limiting SSH access to trusted interfaces and from specified addresses only. If external accesses to devices are required, configure a VPN and force all external administrators to VPN into the network and then from a trusted internal server interact with the network devices over internal trusted networks.

Network Management Data Collection and Management Considerations

To develop a network management strategy for data collection and management, you need to answer these questions:

- **Is polling required or will the solution be event driven?** To maintain a proactive management strategy, you will generally choose to implement polling. However, polling can place a large burden on the network infrastructure. Some enterprises implement a separate infrastructure to support network management and polling.

NOTE   SNMP polling can increase CPU usage on devices by 50 percent or more based on the rate and extent a device is polled. To help reduce the impact of SNMP, ensure that the SNMP process is set to low on all managed platforms. Limit the types of traps that are sent, or turn off traps where not needed. If you are using Syslog messages to track certain events, it is unnecessary to also deploy SNMP traps for those same events. This can help reduce the bandwidth and resource utilization caused by network management.

- **What data should be collected? How long should the data be stored?** Consider which data is critical to the management effort and whether the data will actually be used before storing it. Stored data should be purged at regular intervals.

NOTE   Management data storage is an important aspect of the network policy. Information that has been collected by network management processes is vital to the operation of any organization. Management data provides a window into the history of network performance and security-related events. It is important that a policy be developed that specifies how long critical data, such as logs, reports, and traffic graphs, be kept. The policy should also specify storage procedures and backup policies for this data.

- **How much bandwidth is required for polling, particularly across low-bandwidth WAN links?** To reduce bandwidth requirements, you can reduce polling intervals, implement RMON, and distribute network management systems so they are close to the devices they manage.

- **What issues regarding management protocols, such as SNMP and RMON, should you address?** SNMP and RMON pose inherent security risks. Managing devices that connect to less secure areas of the network require security to be considered. For example, when deciding which protocol to use for remote management, many administrators will select SNMP. However, the decision process does not stop here. What version of SNMP? Currently, SNMPv1, SNMPv2, SNMPv2c, and SNMPv3 exist. SNMPv3 might appear to be a good choice because of its enhanced security features, but it is not supported by all NMS solutions.

> **NOTE**   You need to review all the applications that you are going to deploy for management purposes and create an inventory of the protocols they require to function. For example, if you plan to deploy the RME Availability Manager, it requires the use of SNMP, Telnet, and ICMP. This information is important when designing your management network and establishing an appropriate policy.

- **What issues regarding access protocols, such as HTTP and Telnet, should you address?** Web-based management tools that use HTTP or Telnet access are not usually options because of security concerns. If you want to deploy SSL and SSH as secure alternatives, be sure to deploy services that support them.

> **NOTE**   **Telnet versus SSH**
>
> Telnet is clear text over IP and, therefore, subject to interception and playback. SSH provides a secure alternative by encrypting the Telnet payload and establishing a secure tunnel between both endpoints. The complexities of the decision-making process become evident when you consider that SSH is the preferred protocol for remote access, but is not supported by all platforms (in other words, set and clear-based Catalyst products). Availability and desirability are two features that have to be considered during the planning process.
>
> For more information regarding these two protocols, refer to the section, "References," at the end of this chapter.

- **Is out-of-band or in-band management required?** Depending on the network management solution deployed and the location of support personnel, out-of-band and/or in-band management will be required.

Ensuring the availability of the devices being managed can be one challenge of developing a network management strategy. The network management station will poll the essential data to determine the status of the device and to meet the goals for managing each type of device.

To provide availability, you need to build a reliable, redundant network and network management system. Then, if one link goes down, the entire network management system does not go down. You should have a plan for disaster recovery if the situation dictates that the system be manageable from another location (in case the primary location goes down).

Another challenge is to implement a proactive system versus a totally reactive system. To build the proactive system, you need to have the staff, procedures, and policies in place and train users to use the network management tools.

Network Management Station Sizing Considerations

Correctly sizing network management stations is important because a server can easily become overloaded, which can adversely affect performance. Each network management vendor publishes guidelines to help you select the right-size platform for your needs. To size a network management station, consider these items:

- Determine the number of managed devices.

- Determine which operating systems are used in the enterprise (Windows or Solaris).

- Select the appropriate CPU type, number, and speed.

- Consider the amount of RAM and swap space required for polling.

- Consider the amount of hard disk space required for polling data and reporting data.

System Management Resource Considerations

Resources not considered might adversely impact the overall effectiveness of the network management system.

To manage the network, you need to consider management system servers and agents as part of the network management plan. In today's management environment, no single platform can do everything. Most platforms are based on the UNIX or Microsoft Windows operating systems. The devices being managed might utilize their own internal agents.

Depending on the data collection requirements, the network management system may use a substantial amount of the bandwidth over WAN links. Monitoring remote devices across a WAN requires that you plan for the bandwidth and connectivity requirements to the remote sites. The bandwidth requirements for management and user traffic might exceed the total amount of bandwidth available.

If a full-scale enterprise management system is implemented, an appropriate staff is required to monitor and maintain the systems. A staff needs training on the procedures, goals, and the use of the tools to properly manage the network.

Network Management Deployment Recommendations

For networks that require more than a single workstation or server, you may need to use multiple workstations for a single management domain (a single managed network) by distributing applications across multiple workstations. The result will be better performance and maximum scaling. This section provides strategies to help you design network management deployments, given specific enterprise management needs.

Single Server Deployment

A LMS is recommended for networks with up to 2000 managed network devices or 40,000 user end stations. The addition of other applications depends on specific application scaling factors and the size of your network. A single server or workstation deployed as a network management platform is capable of supporting this solution. Performance, however, can be an issue, so it is important to monitor system resources, and use a multiprocessor platform if appropriate, and/or provide additional memory and disk space as needed. Using a single server may not be practical if all bundled applications are on one server. For performance reasons, it may still be necessary to use more than one machine and distribute individual applications across several machines.

Multiserver, Split Applications—Single Management Domain

If a workstation cannot handle the load because of lack of capacity, when multiple applications are required, one solution is to distribute the applications across several servers. Applications should be distributed based on the biggest resource users.

In Figure 4-4, three management workstations manage a network of 2000 network devices, with the heaviest applications from the LMS distributed across the three workstations.

Figure 4-4 *Multiserver, Split Applications—Single Management Domain*

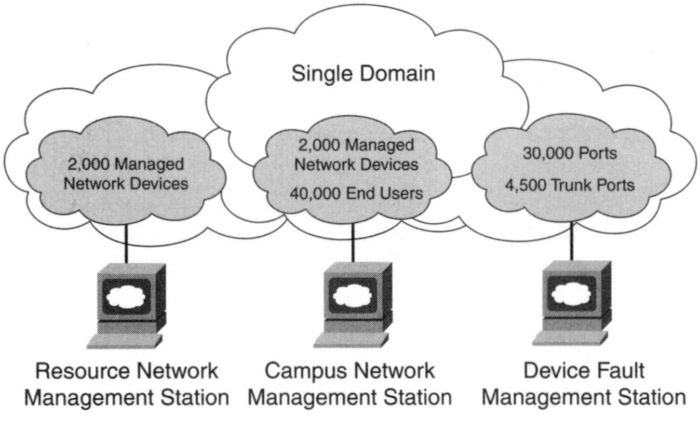

Other bundled applications can be installed where it makes sense.

Larger networks will have to be split into multiple management domains, or multiple groups managed by individual management servers or groups of servers. When a network is split into multiple domains, you can make the division by administrative groups, geographically, or whatever fits your needs.

Multiple Management Domains

When the size of the network is larger than 2000 network devices, you should divide the network into multiple management domains, and multiple management servers (or groups of servers) to ensure that you do not exceed the resource requirements for each server. In some cases, it may be preferable to implement multiple management domains for administrative reasons, even if the numbers do not require the division.

Look for logical ways to segment the network based on the following:

- VTP domains
- IP address blocks
- LAN/WAN boundaries

Look for administrative logic with separate management teams, regions, or administrative groupings. You need to determine which management workstation is managing which device (and vice versa), and remember to leave room for future growth.

Consider the scenario shown in Figure 4-5. A network of 6000 devices is broken into three groups with up to 2000 devices each (with no more than 40,000 end stations), with a separate LAN server for each segment of the network.

Figure 4-5 *Multiple Management Domains Example*

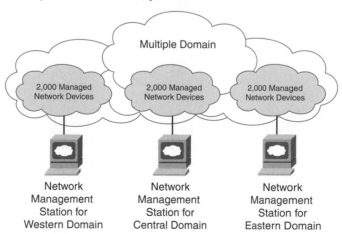

Centralized WAN Management with LAN Management

Figure 4-6 shows one option for networks of up to 5000 managed devices. This option indicates that it desirable to install a single central resource management (RME) server, and combine that with multiple campus management servers.

Figure 4-6   *Centralized WAN Management with LAN Management Example*

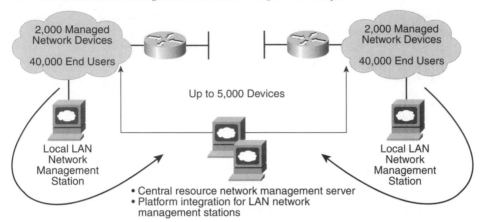

A centralized RME design can provide a single reporting server for inventory, configurations, changes, software distribution, and bulk changes for up to 5000 network devices. For larger networks, one centralized resource server per network partition might be another option. The local LAN management server would have campus and other management applications, but resource management would not be installed on these machines. The resource management server would receive inventory data from each local LAN management machine, and push changes in device credentials back to each local LAN management machine.

For large deployments, it might be necessary to distribute network management applications across multiple servers, either for performance reasons or simply to accommodate larger numbers of network devices.

Key Questions to Consider

The most common question to deploying a network management solution is, "What size workstation do I need for a network management station to manage *x* number of devices?" This question is difficult to answer. Consider the following questions as you define network management services to manage an enterprise network:

- How many network management servers are needed?

- What specific bundles and products will be deployed?

- What components and functions of the products are most important to the network managers?

- What other management tools will be present? Will any other applications be installed on a CiscoWorks network management server, for example?

- How many users will the network management tools have? How many of them will use the tools simultaneously?

- In the case of very large networks, what are the administrative groupings of the network devices and network management users?
- Is a separate network required for network management?

Availability Manager Issues

If a CiscoWorks RME Availability Manager application is to be used, Cisco recommends that there be no more than 500 devices monitored from a single RME server on an adequately equipped system. If a high-end system is used with multiple processors, each RME server can support up to 1000 network devices, depending on the full usage of the system running the RME software.

NOTE   The functions provided by RME's Availability Manager are often provided by third-party SNMP management platforms. Therefore, the 500-device limitation might not be an issue with common deployment scenarios, which include these other management servers.

Network Management Design Scenarios

When designing a small or large network management solution, you will consider the number of management stations, functionality requirements, resource utilization, and many other factors. This section teaches you how to design Cisco network management solutions for small, medium, and large enterprise networks, given specific network management requirements.

Small Site Network Management Design Scenario

For a small site with fewer than 200 network devices, a single CiscoWorks system with LMS and RWAN Management Solutions is likely sufficient. A single instance of RME can manage the entire network.

Table 4-2 summarizes the design decisions that a small enterprise would make to meet its requirements.

Table 4-2   *Small Site Design Decisions*

Design Question	Decision	Notes and Comments
How many management domains does the enterprise require?	One domain for the company	The domain will be managed centrally.
How many devices need to be managed?	Fewer than 200	

continues

Table 4-2 *Small Site Design Decisions (Continued)*

Design Question	Decision	Notes and Comments
What key components and functions are required?	LAN Management Solution RWAN Management Solution	For a small network, one network management server suffices.
How many servers are required?	One server with LAN Management Solution and RWAN Management Solution	
What administrative grouping of network devices will work for this enterprise?	All network devices within a single administrative grouping	Given the small size of the network, only one administrative grouping of network devices is required.
What administrative grouping of network management users will work for this enterprise?	All management users within a single administrative grouping	Given the small size of the network, only one administrative grouping of management users is required.

Medium Site Network Management Design Scenario

In the scenario shown in Figure 4-7, two main sites exist: the west site in Los Angeles, California and the east site in Pensacola, Florida. The west site supports 4500 users with 350 managed network devices. It is the hub for the West Coast branch offices and connects to ten branch offices with six managed devices at each office. The east site supports 7000 users with 300 managed network devices. The east site is the hub for 15 East Coast branch offices with six managed devices per branch. There is a T3 between the east and west facilities. The company wants to use the Availability Manager to determine the status of its key devices. Each site has up to 450 key devices to be managed. The network operations center is located in Los Angeles. All management will be done from the Los Angeles site.

Figure 4-7 *Medium Site Network Management Design Scenario*

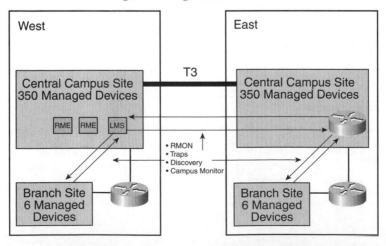

The company factors these considerations into how it will design its network:

- The company plans to use Cisco RME for configuration and software management.
- The IT staff expects to use a single domain while splitting management functions over multiple servers.
- Availability Manager will be used to determine device operational status.

Table 4-3 summarizes the design decisions that the company made to meet its requirements.

Table 4-3   *Medium Site Design Decisions*

Design Question	Decision	Notes and Comments
How many management domains does the enterprise require?	One domain for the company	The domain will be managed from a central site.
How many devices need to be managed?	West: 410 managed devices East: 390 managed devices	
What key components and functions are required?	LMS, including the following: RME Availability Manager Campus Manager Fault Manager RWAN Management Solution including: Performance Monitor ACL Manager	
How many servers are required?	Three total: two RME with Availability Manager and one for LMS/RWAN Management	The recommended number of devices associated with the Availability Manager is 500, so two servers are required.
What administrative grouping of network devices will work for this enterprise?	One administrative grouping	Given the requirements, there is one domain and one administrative group.
What administrative grouping of network management users will work for this enterprise?	One administrative group for all locations	

Large Site Network Management Design Scenario

When designing large and very large network management solutions, dividing the network into regions or domains, each with its own set of servers that manage individual domains, becomes a viable solution.

Table 4-4 shows the scaling issues for a large site network management design.

Table 4-4 *Scaling Issues for a Large Site Network Management Design*

Cisco Product	Scaling Issue
Cisco RME	Total number of objects in inventory
	Inventory updates of largest devices
	Availability monitoring
	Web GUI performance
	Software update jobs for large numbers of devices at one time
	Configuration-change jobs for large numbers of devices at one time
	Syslog traffic level
Cisco Campus Manager	Total number of devices or objects discovered and kept in database
	Campus topology maps, which get very crowded and difficult to use for a large number of devices
	User tracking limit on total number of end stations (number of rows in table)
	User tracking discovery time
	User tracking **ping** sweep (can disrupt network traffic)
Cisco Device Fault Manager	Intelligent fault interpretation and device modeling resident in memory
	Number of managed objects (chassis, modules, ports, and so on)
	CPU and I/O utilization, which depend on polling intervals
ACL Manager	The major scaling issue is the size of the Access Control Lists (ACLs).
CiscoView	Server performance can be affected if too many simultaneous users are active. Five to 10 is the recommended limit on the number of simultaneous users.
Bundles	Bundles combine various products; they can be mixed together in a single deployment.
	It is usually possible to run all products in the bundle on a single server for small to moderate size networks if sufficient system resources are available; for larger networks, it will be necessary to deploy multiple servers.
	Plan around largest resource users.

In the scenario presented in Figure 4-8, the IT staff for AngelFish (a global fish reseller) wants to implement a centralized RME approach with each domain having its own LMS functionality. In this design, the planners have decided to split the global network into four manageable domains: the U.S. headquarters in Chicago, the Americas in Sao Paolo, Europe in Munich, and Asia-Pacific in Seoul. Each domain will monitor and discover the devices within its own domain.

Figure 4-8 *Large Site Network Management Design Scenario*

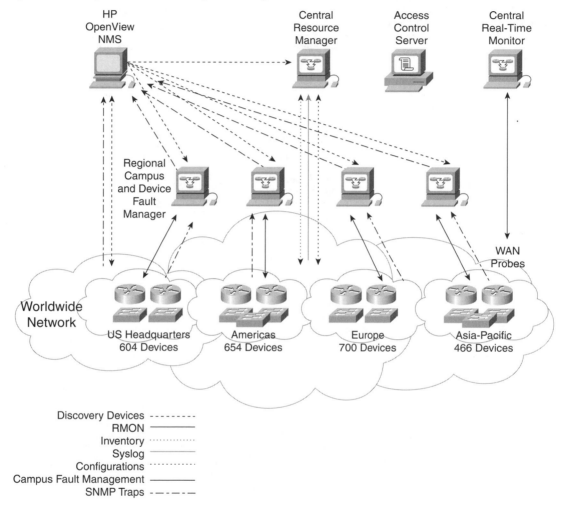

Each site manages approximately 600+ routers. Chicago is designated as the primary site where the RME system will be located. All four of the LMS systems will discover their regional asset information based on IP addresses. They will synchronize the device credential information with the central RME system. The Chicago site will need an RME and LMS server; all other domains would only need an LMS server. Any necessary polling is done by each of the four workstations, with polling intervals set appropriately.

Regional and local management of switched networks is performed with Cisco Campus Manager (under 1000 network devices) as well as RME. IP address ranges segment the regional networks. Different management groups do not share community strings, making configuration of CiscoWorks more difficult, but this policy is the preferred one for this customer.

Table 4-5 summarizes the design decisions that the company made to meet its requirements.

Table 4-5   *Large Site Design Decisions*

Criteria	Decision	Notes and Comments
How many managed domains are there?	Four domains	The headquarters domain is assumed to be where the RME server will be located.
How many managed devices are there?	Headquarters: 604 Americas: 654 Europe: 700 Asia-Pacific: 466	
What key components and functions are required?	LAN Management System with: RME Campus Manager Fault Manager RWAN Management Solution with: Performance Monitor ACL Manager	
How many servers are required?	One server for RME in headquarters One HP OpenView server One LMS/RWAN server at headquarters One LMS/RWAN server for Americas One LMS/RWAN server for Europe One LMS/RWAN server for Asia-Pacific	All domains will have at least one LMS/RWAN server Corporate headquarters will utilize three servers: One for HP OpenView One for RME One for LMS/RWAN
What administrative grouping of network devices will work for this enterprise?	Headquarters Americas Europe Asia-Pacific	
What administrative grouping of network management users will work for this enterprise?	Headquarters Americas Europe Asia-Pacific	

Summary

In this chapter, you learned the following key points:

- Network management is a growing field that is under constant change. Initially, network management included only fault notification. Today, it has grown to incorporate multiple functions including fault, configuration, accounting, performance, and security management.

- As network management systems are implemented, it is vital to put policies and procedures in place.

- To implement network management goals, enterprises will implement individual infrastructure components that meet specific needs.

- Networks continue to grow in size, and the number of different management tools and products is often large as well, making the management task difficult.

- CiscoWorks is a family of products based on Internet standards for managing Cisco enterprise networks and devices.

- The CiscoWorks LAN Management Solution provides a foundation of basic and advanced management applications that enable network operators to efficiently manage the LAN.

- The CiscoWorks RWAN Management Solution provides a collection of powerful management applications to configure, administer, and maintain a Cisco RWAN.

- Network management must be an integral part of the overall network design, because network management can adversely affect network performance.

- For networks that require more than a single workstation or server, you may need to use multiple workstations for a single management domain (a single managed network) by distributing applications across multiple workstations. The result will be better performance and maximum scaling.

- When designing a small or large network management solution, you should consider number of management stations, functionality requirements, resource utilization, and many other factors.

References

White paper—Network Management System: Best Practices. http://www.cisco.com/warp/public/126/NMS_bestpractice.html.

White paper—CiscoWorks in Large-Scale Network Environments. http://www.cisco.com/warp/public/cc/pd/wr2k/prodlit/ckspp_wp.htm.

Cisco Network Management CiscoWorks web site. http://www.cisco.com/en/US/products/sw/netmgtsw/index.html.

CiscoWorks Common Management Solution web site. http://www.cisco.com/en/US/
products/sw/cscowork/ps3996/index.html.

Cisco Service Assurance Agent web site. http://www.cisco.com/en/US/tech/tk447/tk823/
tech_protocol_family_home.html.

Solutions Reference Network Design (SRND) Networking Solutions Design Guides.

To locate these documents, do the following:

Step 1 Go to http://www.cisco.com/.

Step 2 In the Search box, enter **SRND** and click **Go**. A list of SRND Networking
Solutions Design Guides appears.

Step 3 Select the Networking Solutions Design Guide that meets your needs.

Product Summary

Table 4-6 provides a brief overview of some of the products available from Cisco Systems
that relate to the technologies discussed in this chapter. For a more detailed breakdown
of the Cisco product line, visit http://www.cisco.com/en/US/products/index.html.

Table 4-6   *Cisco Network Management Products*

Network Management Software Contents	
Product	
CiscoWorks Enterprise Network Management Solutions	Cisco Ethernet Subscriber Solution Engine 1.1 (ESSE)
	CiscoWorks LAN Management Solution 2.2 (LMS)
	CiscoWorks QoS Policy Manager 3.1 (QPM)
	CiscoWorks Routed WAN Management Solution 1.3 (RWAN)
	CiscoWorks Network Connectivity Monitor 1.0 (NCM)
	CiscoWorks Security Information Management Solution 3.1
	CiscoWorks Service Management Solution 2.0 (SMS)
	CiscoWorks Small Network Management Solution 1.5 (SNMS)
	CiscoWorks Voice Manager for Voice Gateways 2.1 (CWVM)
	CiscoWorks IP Telephony Environment Monitor 2.0 (ITEM)
	CiscoWorks VPN/Security Management Solution 2.2
	CiscoWorks for Windows 6.1 (CWW)
	CiscoWorks Wireless LAN Solution Engine 2.0 (WLSE)
	Cisco Secure User Registration Tool Software Version 2.5 (URT)

Table 4-6   *Cisco Network Management Products (Continued)*

Network Management Software Contents	
Product	
CiscoWorks Blue for IBM Environments	CiscoWorks Blue Maps
	CiscoWorks Blue SNA View
	CiscoWorks Blue Internetwork Status Monitor for the S/390 Series
Cisco Element Managers	Cisco 10000 Manager
	Cisco 12000/10720 Router Manager
	Cisco 6400 Service Connection Manager
	Cisco 7000 Series Manager
	Cisco Access Router Manager
	Cisco Cable Manager 2.0
	Cisco Catalyst 8500 Manager
	Cisco DSL Manager
	Cisco MGC Node Manager
	Cisco Universal Gateway Manager (UGM)
	Element Manager Software (EMS) for the Catalyst 6500 Series and the Cisco 7600 Series
Cisco Internet Operations Support Software	Cisco Broadband Access Center for Broadband Aggregation
	Cisco Broadband Access Center for Cable Version 2.5
	Cisco Broadband Access Center Convergent Network Subscriber Provisioning
	Cisco CNS Address and Name Registrar 2.0
	Cisco CNS Configuration Engine v.1.3
	Cisco CNS NetFlow Collection Engine Version 4.0
	Cisco CNS Network Registrar 5.0
	Cisco CNS Notification Engine
	Cisco CNS Performance Engine
	Cisco CNS Subscriber Edge Services Manager 3.1(7)
	Cisco Info Center
	Cisco IP Solution Center
	Cisco Mobile Wireless Center
	Cisco Packet Telephony Center Monitoring and Troubleshooting
	Cisco Packet Telephony Center Virtual Switch
	Cisco Provisioning Center
	Cisco VPN Solution Center 2.2

continues

Table 4-6 *Cisco Network Management Products (Continued)*

Network Management Software Contents	
Product	
Windows and Windows NT Platform	Total Control Manager/SNMP
Building Broadband Service Manager Version 5.0	
Cisco ConfigMaker Configuration Software	
Cisco DNS/DHCP Manager	
Cisco Networking Services Access Registrar 3.0	
Cisco Resource Policy Management System (RPMS)	
Cisco Server Suite 1000 and DNS/DHCP Manager	
Cisco Transport Manager R3.0	
Cisco Universal Gateway Call Analyzer (UGCA)	
Cisco Universal Gateway Manager (UGM)	
Cisco ViewRunner for HP OpenView	
Cisco VPN Device Manager (VDM)	
Cisco WAN Manager	

Standards and Specification Summary

SSH Transport Layer Protocol draft-ietf-secsh-transport-17.txt. http://www.ietf.org/ids.by.wg/secsh.html

SSH Protocol Architecture draft-ietf-secsh-architecture-15.txt. http://www.ietf.org/ids.by.wg/secsh.html

The SSL Protocol Version 3.0 draft-freier-ssl-version3-02.txt. http://wp.netscape.com/eng/ssl3/

The BSD Syslog Protocol. http://www.rfc-editor.org/rfc.html

CDP. http://www.cisco.com/en/US/tech/tk648/tk362/tk100/tech_protocol_home.html

Request For Comments (RFCs) can be downloaded from the following website: http://www.rfc-editor.org/rfc.html.

- **RFC 854**—Telnet Protocol Specification
- **RFC 1350**—The TFTP Protocol (Revision 2)
- **RFC 2819**—Remote Network Monitoring Management Information Base
- **RFC 3411**—An Architecture for Describing Simple Network Management Protocol (SNMP) Management Frameworks
- **RFC 2616**—Hypertext Transfer Protocol—HTTP/1.1

Review Questions

1 What role(s) does network modeling play in the development of a Network Management System?

2 What are the five functional areas defined by the ISO for Network Management?

3 Network management policies differ from network management procedures in what way?

4 What are two management styles typically found in Network Management?

5 Define the six steps required to develop an enterprise network management strategy.

6 Identify the services the Network Management Module might contain.

7 Give an example of out-of-band management.

8 What protocols are used by the Common Management Foundation component of CiscoWorks to discover the network?

9 What are the two core components of the CiscoWorks product line used to manage LANs and WANs?

10 Define the common elements that are found in both the LMS and RWAN CiscoWorks product lines.

11 In the Resource Manager Essentials application, describe the function of the Change Audit Service.

12 What are the three modules that CiscoWorks LMS is composed of?

13 Define the four RME tasks that Cisco recommends as best practices?

14 The Internetwork Performance Monitor (IPM) uses what service within IOS to generate synthetic traffic for performance measurement?

15 What are the RWAN modules in addition to CD One and RME?

16 List three traffic types the IPM can generate a network response time baseline for.

17 What should you consider when sizing your network management station?

18 What are some of the issues that should be considered when considering data collection strategy?

19 A single server deployment LAN Management Solution is recommended for networks with up to how many devices or end-user stations?

20 If multiple management domains are required because of sizing limitations, what are some of the logical ways to base segmentation on?

21 How many devices does Cisco recommend monitoring from a single RME server?

22 What are some of the scaling issues associated with Cisco RME in a large site network?

23 What are the key questions to consider when conducting your network management design process?

Case Study: OCSIC Bottling Company

The purpose of this case study is to design network management services that meet the needs of the OCSIC Bottling Company. Each component of the design will have multiple options. As each component of the design is identified, justification for the decision is provided. The justification explains the options considered and why that option was selected.

Table 4-7 shows the details about the network management solution for the OCSIC Bottling Company.

Table 4-7 *Design Details for the Network Management Solution*

Design Question	Decision	Justification
How many management domains does the enterprise require?	One domain for the company	The domain is managed centrally.
How many devices need to be managed?	Fewer than 500 network devices and fewer than 50 servers	—
What are the key components and functions required?	LAN Management Solution RWAN Management Solution	—
How many servers are required?	Two servers at headquarters with: LAN Management Solution RWAN Management Solution One LMS server at each district office	Two servers are required at headquarters to manage the network. One server for the RWAN software and one for the LAN Management software. The LMS servers at the district offices manage the regional offices.
What administrative grouping of network devices will work for this enterprise?	All network devices within a single administrative grouping	Given the size of the network, only one administrative grouping of network devices is required.
What administrative grouping of network management users will work for this enterprise?	All management users within a single administrative grouping	Given the size of the network, only one administrative grouping of management users is required.

The company implements a proactive network management strategy that incorporates the FCAPS model for network management. Periodic polling of only key managed network devices is implemented in an effort to minimize the effect on the network. Polling information is stored for seven days and then purged to minimize storage requirements. Finally, the campus network diagram is updated to indicate the components of the Network Management module.

Figure 4-9 shows an example network management design for the OCSIC Bottling Company.

Figure 4-9   *OCSIC Bottling Company Solution*

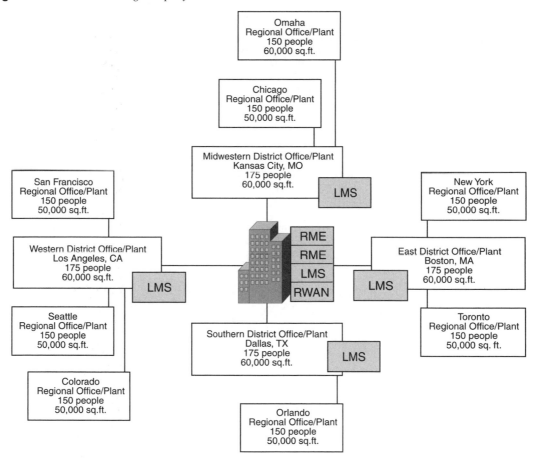

After completing this chapter, you will be able to

- List and discuss high-availability features and options
- Design high-availability enterprise networks

CHAPTER 5

Designing High-Availability Services

Today's enterprises progressively rely more heavily on their IP network for core business practices. High degree of network availability has become a critical requirement, as system downtime usually translates into significant productivity and revenue losses for many enterprises. Maximizing network uptime requires the use of operational best practices and redundant network designs in conjunction with high-availability technologies within network elements. Several high-availability technologies are embedded in Cisco IOS Software. Designers need to identify the necessary components of a high-availability solution and design high-availability solutions for the Enterprise Campus and the Enterprise Edge functional areas based on specific enterprise availability requirements. This chapter briefly reviews high-availability services; it then presents best practices and guidelines for designing highly available Enterprise Campus and the Enterprise Edge functional areas.

High-Availability Features and Options

Cisco IOS high-availability technologies provide network redundancy and fault tolerance. Reliable network devices, redundant hardware components with automatic failover, and protocols like Hot Standby Router Protocol (HSRP) are used to maximize network uptime. This section examines these topics.

Network Requirements for High Availability

An enterprise requires its network to be highly available to ensure that its mission-critical applications are available. Increased availability translates into higher productivity, and perhaps higher revenues and cost savings. Reliability implies that the system performs its specified task correctly; availability, on the other hand, means that the system is ready for immediate use. Today's networks need to be available 24 hours a day, 365 days a year. To meet that objective, 99.999 or 99.9999 percent availability is expected. Table 5-1 shows what each availability rate translates to, in terms of days, hours, and minutes; the bottom two rows (which are shaded), namely 99.999 percent and 99.9999 percent availability, represent highly available networks.

Table 5-1   *Network Availability Percentage versus Actual Network Downtime*

Availability	Defects per Million	Downtime per Year (24 * 365)
99.000	10,000	3 days, 15 hours, 36 minutes
99.500	5000	1 day, 19 hours, 48 minutes
99.900	1000	8 hours and 46 minutes
99.950	500	4 hours and 23 minutes
99.990	100	53 minutes
99.999	10	5 minutes
99.9999	1	30 seconds

NOTE   Number of defects in a million is used to calculate availability. For example, 5000 defects in a million yields 99.5-percent *availability*:

$(1,000,000 - 5,000) / 1,000,000 = 0.995 = 99.5\%$

And *downtime* over 1 year would be:

$5000 / 1,000,000 = 0.005$ year $= 0.005 * 365 * 24 * 60$ minutes

$= 2628$ minutes

$= 43$ hours, 48 minutes

$= 1$ day, 19 hours, 48 minutes

Enterprises implement high availability to meet the following requirements:

- **Ensure that mission-critical applications are available**—The purpose of an enterprise network is to facilitate operation of network applications. When those applications are not available, the enterprise ceases to function properly. Making the network highly available helps ensure that the enterprise's mission-critical applications are functional and available.

- **Improve employee and customer satisfaction and loyalty**—Network downtime can cause frustration among both employees and customers attempting to access applications. Ensuring a highly available network helps to improve and maintain satisfaction and loyalty.

- **Reduce reactive information technology (IT) support costs, resulting in increased IT productivity**—Designing a network to incorporate high-availability technologies allows IT to minimize the time spent fire-fighting and makes time available for proactive services.

- **Reduce financial loss**—An unavailable network, and therefore an unavailable application, can translate directly into lost revenue for an enterprise. Downtime can mean unbillable customer access time, lost sales, and contract penalties.

- **Minimize lost productivity**—When the network is down, employees cannot perform their functions efficiently. Lost productivity means increased cost to the enterprise.

Availability is a measurable quantity. The factors affecting availability are mean time to repair (MTTR), which is the time it takes to recover from a failure, and mean time between failure (MTBF), which is the time that passes between network outages or device failures. Decreasing MTTR and increasing MTBF increase availability. Dividing MTBF by the sum of MTBF and MTTR results in a percentage indicating availability:

Availability = MTBF / (MTBF + MTTR)

A common goal for availability is to achieve 99.999 percent (called "five nines"). For example:

Power supply MTBF = 40,000 hours
Power supply MTTR = 8 hours
Availability = 40,000 / (40,000 + 8) = 0.99980 or 99.98% availability

As system complexity increases, availability decreases. If a failure of any one part causes a failure in the system as a whole, it is called serial availability. To calculate the availability of a complex system or device, multiply the availability of all its parts. For example:

Switch fabric availability = 0.99997
Route processor availability = 0.99996
System availability = 0.99997 * 0.99996 = 0.99992

Cisco IOS High-Availability Architecture

The following are the requirements for a Cisco high-availability solution:

- **Reliable, fault-tolerant network devices**—Hardware and software reliability to automatically identify and overcome failures.

- **Device and link redundancy**—Entire devices, modules within devices, and links can be redundant.

- **Load balancing**—Allows a device to take advantage of multiple best paths to a given destination.

- **Resilient network technologies**—Intelligence that ensures fast recovery around any device or link failure.

- **Network design**—Well-defined network topologies and configurations designed to ensure there is no single point of failure.

- **Best practices**—Documented procedures for deploying and maintaining a robust network infrastructure.

High availability implies that a device or network is ready for use as close to 100 percent of the time as possible. Fault tolerance indicates the ability of a device or network to recover from the failure of a component or device. Achieving high availability relies on eliminating any single point of failure and on distributing intelligence throughout the architecture. You can increase availability by adding redundant components, including redundant network devices and connections to redundant Internet services. With the proper design, no single point of failure will impact the availability of the overall system.

Fault Tolerance and Hardware Redundancy

One approach to building highly available networks is to use extremely fault-tolerant network devices throughout the network. Fault-tolerant network devices must have redundant key components, such as a supervisor engine, routing module, power supply, and fan. Redundancy in network topology and provisioning multiple devices and links is another approach to achieving high availability. Even though these approaches are different, they are not mutually exclusive. Each approach has its own benefits and drawbacks.

Using Fault-Tolerant Devices

Utilizing fault-tolerant devices minimizes time periods during which the system is unresponsive. Failed components can be detected and replaced while the system continues to operate. Disaster protection can be optimized if redundant components were not interdependent. For example, it is best if redundant power supplies are on different electrical circuits. Figure 5-1 depicts a part of a campus network that uses fault-tolerant devices but has a single forwarding path.

Figure 5-1 *Campus Network Utilizing Fault-Tolerant Devices, but Lacking Topological Redundancy*

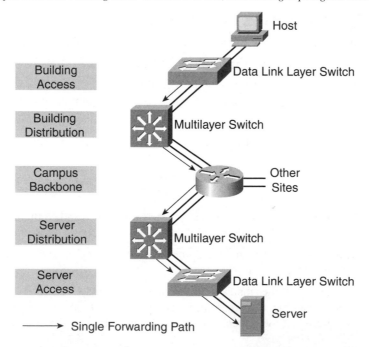

Achieving high network availability solely through device-level fault tolerance has the following drawbacks:

- Massive redundancy within each device adds significantly to its cost, while at the same time reducing physical capacity by consuming slots that could otherwise house network interfaces or provide useful network services.

- Redundant subsystems within devices are often maintained in a hot standby mode, in which they cannot contribute additional performance because they are only fully activated when the primary component fails.

- Focusing on device-level hardware reliability might result in overlooking a number of other failure mechanisms. Network elements are not standalone devices, but they are components of a network system in which internal operations and system-level interactions are governed by configuration parameters and software.

Providing Redundancy in the Network Topology

A complementary way to build highly available networks is to provide reliability through redundancy in the network topology rather than primarily within the network devices themselves. In the campus network design shown in Figure 5-2, a backup exists for every link and every network device in the path between the client and server.

Figure 5-2 *Campus Network with Redundant Paths, Links, and Devices*

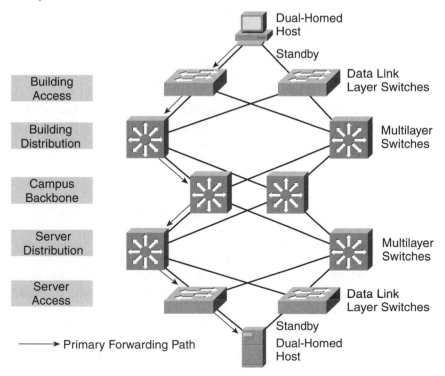

Provisioning redundant devices, links, and paths might have increased media costs and be more difficult to manage and troubleshoot, but this approach offers the following advantages:

- The network elements providing redundancy need not be co-located with the primary network elements. This reduces the probability that problems with the physical environment will interrupt service.

- Problems with software bugs and upgrades or configuration errors and changes can be dealt with separately in the primary and secondary forwarding paths without completely interrupting service. Therefore, network-level redundancy can also reduce the impact of nonhardware failure scenarios.

- With the redundancy provided by the network, each network device no longer needs to be configured for optimal standalone fault tolerance. Device-level fault tolerance can be concentrated in the Campus Backbone and Building Distribution submodules of the network, where a hardware failure would affect a larger number of users. By partially relaxing the requirement for device-level fault tolerance, the cost per network device is reduced, to some degree offsetting the requirement for more devices.

- With carefully designed and implemented resiliency features, you can share the traffic load between the respective layers of the network topology (that is, Building Access and Building Distribution submodules) between the primary and secondary forwarding paths. Therefore, network-level redundancy can also provide increased aggregate performance and capacity.

- You can configure redundant networks to automatically failover from primary to secondary facilities without operator intervention. The duration of service interruption is equal to the time it takes for failover to occur. Failover times as low as a few seconds are possible. Fast and Gigabit Ethernet channeling technologies allow grouping a number of Fast or Gigabit Ethernets to provide fault-tolerant high-speed link bundles between network devices with a few milliseconds or better recovery times. Finally, as a data link layer feature, deterministic load distribution (DLD) adds reliability and predictable packet delivery with load balancing between multiple links.

Route Processor Redundancy

Route Processor Redundancy (RPR) provides a high system availability feature for some Cisco switches and routers. A system can reset and use a standby Route Switch Processor (RSP) in the event of a failure of the active RSP. RPR reduces unplanned downtime and enables a quicker switchover between an active and standby RSP in the event of a fatal error on the active RSP. When you configure RPR, the standby RSP loads a Cisco IOS image upon bootup and initializes itself in standby mode (but MSFC and PFC are not operational). In the event of a fatal error on the active RSP, the system switches to the standby RSP, which reinitializes itself as the active RSP, reloads all the line cards, and restarts the system; switchover takes 2 to 4 minutes. (Note that the 2- to 4-minute recovery is only possible without core dump. If core dump is performed, recovery might take up to *XX* minutes.)

NOTE   MSFC (Multilayer Switch Feature Card) is an optional supervisor daughter card for 6xxx Catalyst switches, and it provides routing and multilayer switching functionalities. PFC (Policy Feature Card) is also an optional supervisor daughter card for 6xxx Catalyst switches, and it adds support for access lists, quality of service (QoS), and accounting to the capabilities furnished by MSFC.

RPR+ allows a failover to occur without reloading the line cards. The standby route processor takes over the router without affecting any other processes and subsystems. The switchover takes 30 to 60 seconds (if core dump upon failure is disabled). In addition, the RPR+ feature ensures that

- The redundant processor is fully booted and the configuration is parsed (MSFC and PFC are operational).
- The IOS running configuration is synchronized between active and standby route processors.
- No link flaps occur during failover to the secondary router processor.

The Cisco Catalyst 6500 offers software redundancy features that include Dual Router Mode (DRM) and Single Router Mode (SRM). These features provide redundancy between MSFCs within the device.

Network Interface Card Redundancy

Nowadays, dual-homing end systems is an available option for consideration. Most network interface cards (NICs) operate in an active-standby mode with a mechanism for MAC address portability between them. During a failure, the standby NIC becomes active on the new access switch. Other end-system redundancy options include NICs operating in active-active mode, in which each host is available through multiple IP addresses. Table 5-2 contrasts various aspects of active-standby NIC redundancy to its active-active counterpart.

Table 5-2   *Comparison Between NIC Redundancy Methods*

	Active-Active	Active-Standby
Predictable Traffic Path	Many	One
Predictable Failover Behavior	More complex	Simple
Supportability	Complex	Simple
Ease of Troubleshooting	Complex	Simple
Performance	Marginally higher	Same as single switch
Scalability	Switch architecture dependent	Same as single switch

Either end-system redundancy mode requires more ports at the Building Access submodule. Active-active redundancy implies that two redundant switches in a high-availability pair are concurrently load balancing traffic to server farms. Because both switches are active, you can support the same virtual IP address on each switch at the same time. This is known as shared Versatile Interface Processor (VIP) address. However, the use of active-active schemes supporting shared VIP configurations is not recommended.

Active-standby redundancy implies an active switch and a standby switch. The standby switch does not forward or load balance any traffic. The standby switch is only active in participating in the peering process that determines which switch is active and which is on standby. The peering process is controlled by the redundancy protocol used by the content switches.

Options for Layer 3 Redundancy

HSRP and Virtual Router Redundancy Protocol (VRRP) enable a set of routers to work together to present the appearance of a single virtual router or default gateway to the hosts on a LAN. HSRP is a Cisco proprietary protocol and it was introduced before its standards-based counterpart VRRP. Protocols for router redundancy allow one router to automatically and transparently assume the function of another router should that router fail.

HSRP is particularly useful in environments where critical applications are running and fault-tolerant networks have been designed. From among a group of routers (their interfaces, to be exact) configured to belong to a common HSRP group, one is elected as the active router and will assume the responsibility for a virtual IP and MAC address. If this router (or its interface) fails, another router in the group (in fact, its interface) will take over the active routers role, being responsible for the virtual IP and MAC address. This enables hosts on a LAN to continue to forward IP packets to a consistent IP and MAC address, enabling the changeover of devices doing the routing to be transparent to them and their sessions.

Each router (its interface) participating in an HSRP group can be given a priority for the purpose of competing for the active router or the standby router role. Of the routers in each group, one will be selected as the active forwarder, and one will be selected as the standby router; other routers in this group will monitor the active and standby routers' status to provide further fault tolerance. All HSRP routers participating in a standby group will watch for hello packets from the active and the standby routers. From the active router in the group, they will all learn the hello and dead timer as well as the standby IP address to be shared. If the active router becomes unavailable because of an interface or link failure, scheduled maintenance, power failure, or other reasons, the standby router will promptly take over the virtual addresses and responsibility; an active router's failure is noticed when its periodic hello packets do not show up for a period of time equal to the dead interval (timer).

Multigroup HSRP (MHSRP) is an extension of HSRP that allows a single router interface to belong to more than one hot standby group. MHSRP requires the use of Cisco IOS

Software Release 10.3 or later and is supported only on routers that have special hardware that allows them to associate an Ethernet interface with multiple unicast MAC addresses, such as the Cisco 7000 series.

VRRP defines a standard mechanism that enables a pair of redundant (1 + 1) devices on the network to negotiate ownership of a virtual IP address (and MAC address). The virtual address could, in fact, belong to one of the routers in the pair. In that case, the router whose IP address is used for the virtual address must and will become the active virtual router. If a third IP address is chosen, based on a configurable priority value, one device is elected to be active and the other serves as the standby. If the active device fails, the backup takes over. One advantage of VRRP is that it is standards based; another advantage is its simplicity. However, this scheme only works for n = 1 capacity and k = 1 redundancy; it will not scale above 1 + 1. RFC 2338 describes VRRP.

In addition to HSRP and VRRP, Cisco IOS Software provides additional network redundancy features:

- **Fast routing protocol convergence with IS-IS, OSPF, or EIGRP**—EIGRP provides superior convergence properties and operating efficiency for Layer 3 load balancing and backup across redundant links and Cisco IOS devices to minimize congestion.

  OSPF and IS-IS, unlike EIGRP, are nonproprietary and are classified as link-state routing protocols, based on Dijkstra's Shortest Path First algorithm. OSPF and IS-IS protocols support large-scale networks, hierarchical addressing and architectures, classless interdomain routing, and they provide fast IP routing convergence.

- **EtherChannel technology**—Uses multiple Fast or Gigabit Ethernet links to scale bandwidth between switches, routers, and servers. Channeling a group of Ethernet ports also eliminates loops, simplifying spanning-tree's topology; hence, it reduces the number of STP blocking (discarding) ports.

- **Load sharing**—Provided across equal-cost Layer 3 paths and spanning trees (for Layer 2–based networks through PVST+ or MST).

- **Cisco Express Forwarding (CEF)**—A topology driven route-caching technology that, unlike its traffic-driven route-caching predecessors, does not need to perform multiple lookups, and its maintenance overhead is less. CEF is the main prerequisite feature for the Multiprotocol Label Switching (MPLS) technology.

NOTE   Gateway Load Balancing Protocol (GLBP) is a new Cisco solution and alternative to HSRP. The main advantage of GLBP over its predecessors (HSRP and VRRP) is its ease of configuration and built-in capability for load sharing among the participating routers.

Redundancy and Spanning Tree Protocol

The Spanning Tree Protocol (STP) was designed to prevent loops. Cisco spanning-tree implementation provides a separate spanning-tree domain for each VLAN; hence, it is called per-VLAN spanning tree (PVST). PVST allows the bridge control traffic to be localized within each VLAN and supports configurations where the traffic between the access and distribution layers of the network can be load balanced over redundant connections. Cisco supports PVST over both Inter-Switch Link (ISL) and 802.1Q trunks. Figure 5-3 depicts a campus model with Layer 2 access switches and multilayer distribution layer switches running Cisco PVST. One distribution switch is the root for odd VLAN spanning trees, and the other is the root for even VLAN spanning trees. The distribution switches are multilayer switches, and belong to a common HSRP group in each VLAN. On odd VLANs, one distribution multilayer switch is made the active HSRP router and the other is configured as the standby HSRP router. The standby router on odd VLANs is configured as the active HSRP router on even VLANs, and the other is naturally configured as the standby HSRP router on the even VLANs.

Figure 5-3   *PVST and HSRP in Campus Networks*

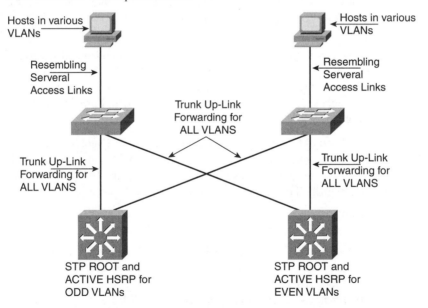

ISL and 802.1Q VLAN tagging also play an important role in load sharing across redundant links. All the uplink connections between Building Access and Building Distribution switches are configured as trunks for all the access VLANs. Each uplink interface/port of an access switch is in forwarding state for half of the VLANs and in blocking (discarding) mode for the other half of the VLANs; or the link might be forwarding for all VLANs (see Figure 5-3). In the event that one of the uplinks or distribution switches has a failure, the other uplink starts forwarding the traffic of all VLANs. Workgroup servers might be connected with dual, high-speed, trunk connections to both of the distribution switches. (The servers, however, should not bridge traffic across their redundant links).

Rapid Spanning Tree Protocol (RSTP), as specified in IEEE 802.1w, supersedes STP specified in 802.1D, but remains compatible with STP. RSTP shows significant convergence improvement over the traditional STP. RSTP's advantage is most experienced when the inter-switch links (connections) are full-duplex (dedicated/point-to-point), and the access port connecting to the workstations is in port fast mode. In segments that older spanning-tree bridge protocol data units (BPDUs) are seen, Cisco devices switch to the traditional STP.

Multiple Spanning Tree (MST), as specified in IEEE 802.1s, allows you to map several VLANs to a reduced number of spanning-tree instances, because most networks do not need more than a few logical topologies. Figure 5-4 shows a topology with only two different final logical topologies, so only two spanning-tree instances are really necessary. There is no need to run 1000 instances. If you map half the 1000 VLANs to a different spanning-tree instance, as shown in the figure, the following is true:

- The desired load-balancing scheme is realized, because half the VLANs follow one separate instance.
- The CPU is spared by only computing two instances.

Figure 5-4   *Multiple Spanning Tree Example*

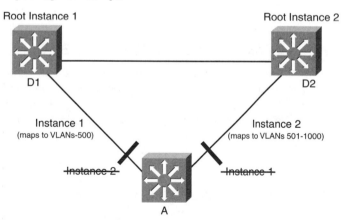

From a technical standpoint, MST is the best solution. From the network engineer's perspective, the only drawbacks associated with migrating to MST are mainly caused by the fact that MST is a new protocol; the following issues arise:

- The protocol is more complex than the traditional CST (or the Cisco PVST+) and requires additional training of the staff.
- Interaction with legacy bridges is sometimes challenging.

PortFast and UplinkFast

The STP (802.1D) was designed for robust, plug-and-play operation in bridged networks, or arbitrary connectivity (looping), and almost unlimited flatness. To improve spanning-tree convergence, Cisco offers a number of features, including PortFast and UplinkFast.

PortFast is a feature that you can enable on Catalyst switch ports dedicated to connecting single servers or workstations. PortFast allows the switch port to begin forwarding as soon as the end system is connected, bypassing the listening and learning states and eliminating up to 30 seconds of delay before the end system can begin sending and receiving traffic. PortFast is used when an end system is initially connected to the network or when the primary link of a dual-homed end system or server is reactivated after a failover to the secondary link. Because only one station is connected to the segment, there is no risk of PortFast creating network loops. In the event of a failure of a directly connected uplink that connects a Building Access switch to a Building Distribution switch, you can increase the speed of spanning-tree convergence by enabling the UplinkFast feature on the Building Access switch.

With *UplinkFast*, each VLAN is configured with an uplink group of ports, including the root port that is the primary forwarding path to the designated root bridge of the VLAN, and one or more secondary ports that are blocked. When a direct uplink fails, UplinkFast unblocks the highest priority secondary link and begins forwarding traffic without going through the spanning-tree listening and learning states. Bypassing listening and learning reduces the failover time after uplink failure to approximately the BPDU hello interval (1 to 5 seconds). With the default configuration of standard STP, convergence after uplink failure can take up to 30 seconds.

Designing High-Availability Enterprise Networks

The Enterprise Campus and the Enterprise Edge need maximum availability of the network resources; hence, network designers must incorporate high-availability features throughout the network. Designers must be familiar with the design guidelines and best practices for each component of an enterprise network. There are specific guidelines for designing a highly available Campus Infrastructure functional area and an Enterprise Edge functional area. Adopting a high-availability strategy for an enterprise site is a must.

Design Guidelines for High Availability

Designing a network for high availability requires designers to consider the reliability of each network hardware and software component, redundancy choices, protocol attributes, circuits and carrier options, and environmental and power features that contribute to the overall availability of the network.

To design high-availability services for an enterprise network, designers must answer the following types of questions:

- Where should module and chassis redundancy be deployed in the network?
- What software reliability features are required for the network?

- What protocol attributes need to be considered?
- What high-availability features are required for circuits and carriers?
- What environmental and power features are required for the network?
- What operations procedures are in place to prevent outages?

Redundancy Options

The options for device redundancy include both module and chassis redundancy. Both types of redundancy are usually most important at the Building Distribution and Campus Backbone submodules. The decision about which type of redundancy to use is based on the criticalness of the resource and the cost of redundancy.

With module redundancy, only selected modules are selected for failover. In the event that the primary module fails, the device operating system determines the failover. Module redundancy is typically the most cost-effective redundancy option available, and is the only option (over chassis redundancy) for edge devices in point-to-point topologies.

With chassis redundancy, the entire chassis and all modules within it are redundant. In the event of a failure, the protocols running on the network, such as HSRP or VRRP, determine how the failover occurs. Chassis redundancy increases the cost and complexity of the network, which are factors to consider when selecting device redundancy. Chassis redundancy is also limited for point-to-point edge networks. To calculate the theoretical advantage gained with redundant modules or chassis, use the following formula:

Availability $= 1 - [(1 -$ availability of device1) $* (1 -$ availability of device2)]

The preceding availability formula is for parallel redundant devices, as opposed to the earlier formula, which was for serial availability. For example, if you implement a redundant switch fabric with 100-percent failure detection and each device's availability is 99.997 percent, the overall availability is calculated as follows:

Availability $= 1 - [(1 - .99997) * (1 - .99997)]$
Availability $= 1 - [(.00003) * (.00003)] = 1 - [.0000000009]$
Availability $= 0.99999$

Therefore, redundant switch fabrics increase the availability of the component to 99.9999 percent. As mentioned, this is known as *parallel availability*.

Link redundancy, implemented through parallel or serial implementations, can significantly increase availability. The following formula calculates the availability resulting from redundant parallel links and shows the theoretical advantage gained:

Availability $= [1 - (1 -$ availability1$)^2] * [1 - (1 -$ availability2$)^2] * [1 - (1 -$ availability3$)^2]$

In the example shown in Figure 5-5, a serial available network is available 99.86 percent of the time, while the parallel available network is available 99.97 percent of the time (based on the preceding formula).

Figure 5-5   *Parallel versus Serial Implementations*

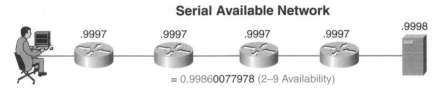

To fully determine the benefit of device, chassis, and link redundancy, designers should discover the answers to the following questions:

- Will the solution allow for load sharing?
- Which components are redundant?
- What active-standby fault detection methods are used?
- What is the MTBF for a module? What is the MTTR for a module? Should it be made redundant?
- How long does it take to upgrade?
- Are hot swapping and online insertion and removal (OIR) available?

Software Features and Protocol Attributes

Cisco Systems recommends implementation of the following software features:

- Protect gateway routers with HSRP or VRRP
- Implement resilient routing protocols, such as EIGRP, OSPF, IS-IS, RIPv2, BGP
- Use floating static routes and access control lists (ACLs) to reduce load in case of failure

Network designers also need to consider protocol attributes, such as complexity to manage and maintain, convergence, hold times, and signal overhead.

Carrier and Circuit Types

Because the carrier network is an important component of the enterprise network and its availability, careful consideration of the following points about the carrier network is essential:

- **Understand the carrier network**—Model and understand carrier availability, including the carrier diversity strategy and how that will affect the availability of your network design. Make sure you have a service level agreement (SLA) that specifies availability and offers alternate routes in case of failure. Ensure that the carrier offers diversity and that dual paths to the ISP do not terminate at the same location (a single point of failure).

- **Consider multihoming to different vendors**—Multihoming to different vendors provides protection against carrier failures.

- **Monitor carrier availability**—Determine if the carrier offers enhanced services, such as a guaranteed committed information rate (CIR) for Frame Relay, or differentiated services. Use carrier SLAs.

- **Review carrier notification and escalation procedures**—Review the carrier's notification and escalation procedures to ensure that they can reduce downtimes.

Power Availability

Power and environmental availability affect overall network availability. According to a prediction by Worldwatch institute, electrical interruptions will cost U.S. companies $80 billion a year. By implementing uninterruptible power supplies (UPS), availability is increased. Table 5-3, from American's Power Conversion's Tech Note #26, describes the effect of UPS and power array generators on overall availability.

Table 5-3   *Power Supply Availability Options*

	RAW AC Power	5 Minute UPS	1 Hour UPS	UPS with Generator	Power Array with Generator
Event Outages	15 events	1 event	.15 events	.01 events	.001 events
Annual Downtime	189 minutes	109 minutes	10 minutes	1 minute	.1 minute
Availability	99.96%	99.979%	99.998%	99.9998%	99.99999%

For power and grounding sensitive electronic equipment, refer to IEEE-recommended practice, Standard 1100-1992.

High-Availability Design Goals and Conclusions

The general network design conclusions with respect to high availability are as follows:

- Reduce complexity, increase modularity and consistency
- Consider solution manageability
- Minimize the size of failure domains
- Consider protocol attributes
- Consider budget, requirements, and areas of the network that contribute the most downtime or are at greatest risk
- Test before deployment

Consider the following cost and budget issues when designing high-availability networks:

- **One-time costs**—Calculate the cost of additional components or hardware, software upgrades, new software costs, and installation.

- **Recurring costs**—Consider the costs of additional WAN links and the recurring cost of equipment maintenance.

- **Complexity costs**—Keep in mind that availability might be more difficult to manage and troubleshoot. More training for the support staff might be required.

Best Practices for High-Availability Network Design

Cisco has developed a set of best practices for network designers to ensure high availability of the network. The five-step Cisco recommendations are

Step 1 **Analyze technical goals and constraints**—Technical goals include availability levels, throughput, jitter, delay, response time, scalability requirements, introductions of new features and applications, security, manageability, and cost. Investigate constraints, given the available resources. Prioritize goals and lower expectations that can still meet business requirements. Prioritize constraints in terms of the greatest risk or impact to the desired goal.

Step 2 **Determine the availability budget for the network**—Determine the expected theoretical availability of the network. Use this information to determine the availability of the system to help ensure the design will meet business requirements.

Step 3 **Create application profiles for business applications**—Application profiles help the task of aligning network service goals with application or business requirements by comparing application requirements, such as performance and availability, with realistic network service goals or current limitations.

Step 4   **Define availability and performance standards**—Availability and performance standards set the service expectations for the organization.

Step 5   **Create an operations support plan**—Define the reactive and proactive processes and procedures used to achieve the service level goal. Determine how the maintenance and service process will be managed and measured. Each organization should know its role and responsibility for any given circumstance. The operations support plan should also include a plan for spare components.

To achieve 99.99-percent availability (often referred to as "four nines"), the following problems must be eliminated:

- Single point of failure
- Inevitable outage for hardware and software upgrades
- Long recovery time for reboot or switchover
- No tested hardware spares available on site
- Long repair times because of a lack of troubleshooting guides and process
- Inappropriate environmental conditions

To achieve 99.999-percent availability (often referred to as "five nines"), you also need to eliminate these problems:

- High probability of failure of redundant modules
- High probability of more than one failure on the network
- Long convergence for rerouting traffic around a failed trunk or router in the core
- Insufficient operational control

Enterprise Campus Design Guidelines for High Availability

Each submodule of the Campus Infrastructure module should incorporate fault tolerance and redundancy features to provide an end-to-end highly available network. In the Building Access submodule, Cisco recommends that you implement STP along with the UplinkFast and PortFast enhancements. Rapid Spanning Tree Protocol (802.1w) and Multiple Spanning Tree Protocol (802.1s), offer benefits such as faster convergence and more efficiency over the traditional STP (802.1D). You can implement HSRP (or VRRP) in the Building Distribution submodule, with HSRP hellos going through the switches in the Building Access submodule. At the Building Distribution submodule, Cisco recommends that you implement STP and HSRP for first-hop redundancy. Finally, the Campus Backbone submodule is a critical resource to the entire network. Cisco recommends that you incorporate device and network topology redundancy at the Campus Backbone, as well as HSRP for failover.

By leveraging the flexibility of data-link layer connectivity in the Building Access switches, the option of dual-homing the connected end systems is available. Most NICs operate in an active-standby mode with a mechanism for MAC address portability between pairs. During a failure, the standby NIC becomes active on the new Building Access switch. Another end-system redundancy option is for a NIC to operate in active-active mode, in which each host is available through multiple IP addresses. Either end-system redundancy mode requires more ports in the Building Access submodule.

The primary design objective for a server farm is to ensure high availability in the infrastructure architecture. The following are the guidelines for server farm high availability:

- Use redundant components in infrastructure systems, where such a configuration is practical, cost effective, and considered optimal

- Use redundant traffic paths provided by redundant links between infrastructure systems

- Use optional end-system (server) dual homing to provide a higher degree of availability

Enterprise Edge Design Guidelines for High Availability

Each module of the Enterprise Edge functional area should incorporate high-availability features from the service provider edge to the enterprise campus network. Within the Enterprise Edge functional area, consider the following for high availability:

- **Service level agreement**—Ask your service provider to write into your SLA that your backup path terminates into separate equipment at the service provider, and that your lines are not trunked into the same paths as they traverse the network.

- **Link redundancy**—Use separate ports, preferably on separate routers, to each remote site. Having backup permanent virtual circuits (PVCs) through the same physical port accomplishes little or nothing, because a port is more likely to fail than any individual PVC.

- **Load balancing**—Load balancing occurs when a router has two (or more) equal cost paths to the same destination. You can implement load sharing on a per-packet or per-destination basis. Load sharing provides redundancy, because it provides an alternate path if a router fails. OSPF will load share on equal-cost paths by default. EIGRP will load share on equal-cost paths by default, and can be configured to load share on unequal-cost paths. Unequal-cost load sharing is discouraged because it can create too many obscure timing problems and retransmissions.

- **Policy-based routing**—If you have unequal cost paths, and you do not want to use unequal-cost load sharing, you can use policy-based routing to send lower priority traffic down the slower path.

- **Routing protocol convergence**—The convergence time of the routing protocol chosen will affect overall availability of the Enterprise Edge. The main area to examine is the impact of the Layer 2 design on Layer 3 efficiency.

Several of the generic high-availability technologies and Cisco IOS features might also be implemented at the Enterprise Edge functional area. Cisco Nonstop Forwarding enables continuous packet forwarding during route processor takeover and route convergence. Stateful failover allows a backup route processor to take immediate control from the active route processor while maintaining WAN connectivity protocols. RPR allows a standby route processor to load an IOS image configuration, parse the configuration, and reset and reload the line cards, thereby reducing reboot time. HSRP enables two or more routers to work together in a group to emulate a single virtual router to the source hosts on the LAN. Alternatively, VRRP enables a group of routers to form a single virtual router by sharing one virtual router IP address and one virtual MAC address.

High-Availability Design Example

Providing high availability in the enterprise site can involve deploying highly fault-tolerant devices, incorporating redundant topologies, implementing STP, and configuring HSRP. Figure 5-6 shows an example enterprise-site design that incorporates high-availability features.

Figure 5-6   *High-Availability Design Example*

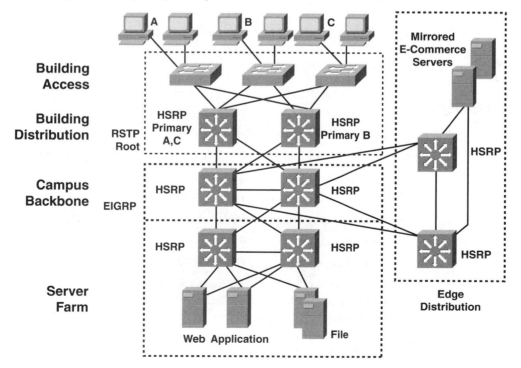

According to the example depicted in Figure 5-6, each module and submodule is utilizing the necessary and feasible high-availability technologies as follows:

- **Building Access submodule**—The Building Access switches all have uplinks terminating in a pair of redundant multilayer switches at the Building Distribution submodule, which act as an aggregation point. Only one pair of Building Distribution switches is needed per building. The number of wiring-closet switches is based on port density requirements. Each Building Access switch includes fault tolerance to reduce MTBF. Because the failure of an individual switch would have a smaller impact than a device failure in the Building Distribution and Campus Backbone submodules, device redundancy is not provided.

- **Building Distribution submodule**—First-hop redundancy and fast failure recovery are achieved with HSRP, which runs on the two multilayer switches in the distribution layer. HSRP provides end stations with a default gateway in the form of a virtual IP address that is shared by a minimum of two routers. HSRP routers discover each other via hello packets, which are sent through the Building Access switches with negligible latency.

- **Campus Backbone submodule**—In the Campus Backbone submodule, two multilayer switches are deployed; each one is configured for high fault tolerance. HSRP is implemented to allow for device redundancy. The EIGRP routing protocol is used to provide load balancing and fast convergence.

- **Server Farm module**—In the Server Farm module, two multilayer switches with HSRP configured provide redundancy. The file servers are mirrored for added protection.

- **Enterprise Edge module**—At the Enterprise Edge, fault-tolerant switches are deployed with link redundancy and HSRP to enable failover. Outward-facing e-commerce servers are mirrored to ensure availability.

Summary

In this chapter, you learned the following key points:

- Enterprises implement high availability to meet the following requirements:
  - Ensure that mission-critical applications are available
  - Improve employee and customer satisfaction and loyalty
  - Reduce reactive IT support costs, resulting in increased IT productivity
  - Reduce financial loss
  - Minimize lost productivity
- Availability is a measurable quantity. The factors that affect availability are MTTR and MTBF. Decreasing MTTR and increasing MTBF increase availability. Using the following equation results in a percentage that indicates availability (99.999 percent is a common goal):

Availability = MTBF / (MTBF + MTTR)

- A Cisco high-availability solution has the following requirements:
  - Reliable, fault-tolerant network devices
  - Device and link redundancy
  - Load balancing
  - Resilient network technologies
  - Network design
  - Best practices
- One approach to building highly available networks is to use extremely fault-tolerant network devices throughout the network. Fault-tolerant network devices must have redundant key components, such as supervisor engine, routing module, power supply, and fan. Redundancy in network topology and provisioning multiple devices and links is another approach to achieving high availability. Each approach has its own benefits and drawbacks.
- Cisco IOS Software provides the following Layer 3 redundancy features:
  - HSRP or VRRP
  - Fast routing protocol convergence
  - EtherChannel technology
  - Load sharing
  - CEF
- The Cisco spanning-tree implementation provides a separate spanning-tree domain for each VLAN called PVST+. RSTP as specified in 802.1w supersedes STP specified in 802.1D, but remains compatible with STP. RSTP shows significant convergence improvement over the traditional STP. RST's advantage is experienced when the inter-switch links (connections) are full-duplex (dedicated/point-to-point), and the access port connecting to the workstations are in PortFast mode. MST allows you to map several VLANs to a reduced number of spanning-tree instances because most networks do not need more than a few logical topologies.
- To design high-availability services for an enterprise network one must answer the following types of questions:
  - Where should module and chassis redundancy be deployed in the network?
  - What software reliability features are required for the network?
  - What protocol attributes need to be considered?
  - What high-availability features are required for circuits and carriers?
  - What environmental and power features are required for the network?
  - What operations procedures are in place to prevent outages?

- To fully determine the benefit of device, chassis, and link redundancy, one should discover the answers to the following questions:

  — Will the solution allow for load sharing?

  — Which components are redundant?

  — What active-standby fault detection methods are used?

  — What is the MTBF for a module? What is the MTTR for a module? Should it be made redundant?

  — How long does it take to do an upgrade?

  — Are hot swapping and online, insertion and removal (OIR) available?

- Cisco Systems recommends implementing the following software features:

  — Protect gateway routers with HSRP or VRRP

  — Implement resilient routing protocols, such as EIGRP, OSPF, IS-IS, RIPv2, BGP

  — Use floating static routes and access control lists to reduce load in case of failure

- Consider protocol attributes such as complexity to manage and maintain, convergence, hold times, and signal overhead

- Because the carrier network is an important component of the enterprise network and its availability, careful consideration of the following points about the carrier network is essential:

  — Understand the carrier network

  — Consider multihoming to different vendors

  — Monitor carrier availability

  — Review carrier notification and escalation procedures to reduce repair times

- The general network design conclusions with respect to high availability are

  — Reduce complexity, increase modularity and consistency

  — Consider solution manageability

  — Minimize the size of failure domains

  — Consider protocol attributes

  — Consider budget, requirements, and areas of the network that contribute the most downtime or are at greatest risk

  — Test before deployment

- Cisco has developed a set of best practices for network designers to ensure high availability of the network. The five-step Cisco recommendations are

  Step 1 Analyze technical goals and constraints.

Step 2   Determine the availability budget for the network.

Step 3   Create application profiles for business applications.

Step 4   Define availability and performance standards.

Step 5   Create an operations support plan.

- Within the Enterprise Edge functional area, the following must be considered for high availability:
  - Service level agreement
  - Link redundancy
  - Load balancing
  - Policy-based routing
  - Routing protocol convergence

Reference

"High Availability Services." http://www.cisco.com/warp/public/779/largeent/learn/technologies/availability.html.

Product Summary

Tables 5-4, 5-5, and 5-6 provide a brief overview of some of the products available from Cisco Systems that relate to the topics discussed in this chapter. For a more detailed breakdown of the Cisco product line, visit http://www.cisco.com/en/US/products/index.html.

Table 5-4   *Examples of Cisco Catalyst Switches with Supervisor and Power Supply Redundancy Options*

Product Name	Description
Catalyst 4507R	Catalyst 4500 Chassis (7-slot), fan, no p/s, redundant supply capable
Catalyst 4510R	Catalyst 4500 Chassis (10-slot), fan, no p/s, redundant supply capable
Catalyst 6509-NEB	Catalyst 6509 Chassis for NEBS environments

Table 5-5   *Examples of Cisco Routers That Are Capable of Having a Redundant Power Supply*

Product Name	Description
Cisco 2651XM-RPS	High Performance Dual 10/100 mod router w/IP-RPS ADPT
Cisco 3662-AC-CO	Dual 10/100E Cisco 3660 6-slot CO mod router-AC w/Telco SW
Cisco 3745	Cisco 3700 Series 4-slot application service router

continues

Table 5-5   *Examples of Cisco Routers That Are Capable of Having a Redundant Power Supply (Continued)*

Product Name	Description
Cisco 7206VXR-CH	Cisco 7206VXR, 6-slot chassis, 1 AC supply w/IP software
Cisco 7304	4-slot chassis, NSE100, 1 power supply, IP software
Cisco 7401ASR-CP	7401ASR, 128M SDRAM, IP software

Table 5-6   *A Cisco Router That Is Capable of Having a Redundant Route Processor and a Redundant Fan Module*

Product Name	Description
Cisco 7304	4-slot chassis, NSE100, 1 power supply, IP software

Standards and Specifications Summary

Request For Comments (RFCs) can be downloaded from the following website: http://www.rfc-editor.org/rfc.html.

- RFC 2338, "Virtual Router Redundancy Protocol."

Review Questions

Answer the following questions to test your comprehension of the topics discussed in this chapter. Refer to Appendix A, "Answers to Review Questions," to check your answers.

1 List at least three requirements for high availability.

2 List at least three requirements or techniques to achieve high network availability.

3 Name at least one benefit of fault tolerance.

4 What is the major drawback of achieving high availability solely through device-level fault tolerance?

5 What is RPR?

6 Name at least two Layer 3 redundancy features offered by Cisco IOS Software.

7 What is MST?

8 Name at least one of the software features recommended by Cisco Systems to achieve high availability.

9 Name at least two essential points that must be considered about the carrier network with regards to high availability.

10 What are the five steps of the process recommended by Cisco as best practices for high availability?

11 Name at least two problems that must be eliminated to achieve 99.99-percent availability.

12 Name at least two problems that must be eliminated to achieve 99.999-percent availability?

13 List at least two of the guidelines for server farm high availability.

Case Study: OCSIC Bottling Company

The purpose of this case study is to practice the key design skills discussed in this chapter. For this project, you must revisit the earlier design for OCSIC Bottling Company and ensure that the Campus Infrastructure, Server Farm, WAN, Remote Access, and Internet Connectivity modules are highly available. Specifically, you have been asked to develop a high-availability design for the Campus Infrastructure module, and to develop a high-availability strategy for the Server Farm, WAN, Remote Access, and finally, the Internet Connectivity modules. For each identified component of the design, you are required to provide justification for our decision. The justification will provide an explanation for the options considered, and the reason behind choosing the selected option.

High-Availability Design for the Campus Infrastructure Module

Table 5-7 summarizes one possible set of design decisions that meet the OCSIC Bottling Company's requirements for high-availability solutions for the headquarters' campus network.

Table 5-7 *Design Decisions Made to Develop a High-Availability Strategy for the Headquarters Campus Network*

Design Question	Decision	Justification
Which devices should be fault tolerant?	None	It is deemed not cost effective to add fault-tolerant devices in the campus network.
Which devices should be redundant?	Cisco Catalyst 3550-12G is a good candidate for the distribution layer. For every Catalyst 3550-12G in the design, a second 3550-12G switch is added to provide device redundancy. Catalyst 4006s with Supervisor IIIs, and two 8-port GB Ethernet (4908G) modules would be good candidates for the backbone layer.	Device redundancy provides high availability as needed in the campus network.

continues

Table 5-7   *Design Decisions Made to Develop a High-Availability Strategy for the Headquarters Campus Network (Continued)*

Design Question	Decision	Justification
Which links should be redundant?	Catalyst 3524 stacks have redundant links to the Building Distribution switches.	Redundant links provide backup in case of a link failure.
What spanning-tree implementation and root devices are required?	Spanning-tree root at the Building Distribution switches using RSTP/MST.	For simplicity, the Building Distribution is used as the STP root because it provides a logical break between the data link and network layers.
What is the router availability strategy?	HSRP	HSRP implemented in the multilayer switches provides high availability.

High-Availability Strategy for the Server Farm Module

Table 5-8 summarizes one possible set of design decisions that meet the OCSIC Bottling Company's requirements for high-availability solutions for the Server Farm module.

Table 5-8   *Design Decisions Made to Develop a High-Availability Strategy for the Server Farm Module*

Design Question	Decision	Justification
Which devices should be fault tolerant?	All devices	Fault tolerance is critical in the Server Farm module.
Which devices should be redundant?	None	Fault tolerance is preferred to device redundancy in the Server Farm module.
Which links should be redundant?	Redundant links throughout the Server Farm module.	Redundant links are required for high availability.
What spanning-tree implementation and root devices are required?	Spanning-tree root at the Server Distribution switches using RSTP/MST.	For simplicity, the Server Distribution is used as the STP root because it provides a logical break between the data link and network layers.
What is the router availability strategy?	HSRP	HSRP implemented in the multilayer switches provides high availability.

High-Availability Strategy for the WAN Module

Table 5-9 summarizes one possible set of design decisions that meet the OCSIC Bottling Company's requirements for high-availability solutions for the WAN module.

Table 5-9   *Design Decisions Made to Develop a High-Availability Strategy for the WAN Module*

Design Question	Decision	Justification
Which devices should be fault tolerant?	None	Fault tolerance is not cost effective in the WAN module.
Which devices should be redundant?	The module should have two Cisco 3640 routers for WAN redundancy.	The second Cisco 3640 WAN router provides the necessary high availability for the WAN module.
Which links should be redundant?	Redundant links to the Edge Distribution module.	Redundant links provide backup in case of a link failure.
What spanning-tree implementation and root devices are required?	None	Not applicable
What is the router availability strategy?	HSRP will run on the Cisco 3640 routers in the WAN module.	HSRP provides high availability.

High-Availability Strategy for the Remote Access Module

Table 5-10 summarizes one possible set of design decisions that meet the OCSIC Bottling Company's requirements for high-availability solutions for the Remote Access module.

Table 5-10   *Design Decisions Made to Develop a High-Availability Strategy for the Remote Access Module*

Design Question	Decision	Justification
Which devices should be fault tolerant?	None	Fault tolerance is not cost effective in the Remote Access module.
Which devices should be redundant?	None	Device redundancy is not cost effective in the Remote Access module.
Which links should be redundant?	Redundant links to the Edge Distribution module.	Redundant links provide backup in case of a link failure.
What spanning-tree implementation and root devices are required?	None	Not applicable
What is the router availability strategy?	HSRP	HSRP provides high availability.

High-Availability Strategy for the Internet Connectivity Module

Table 5-11 summarizes one possible set of design decisions that meet the OCSIC Bottling Company's requirements for high-availability solutions for the Internet Connectivity module.

Table 5-11 *Design Decisions Made to Develop a High-Availability Strategy for the Internet Connectivity Module*

Design Question	Decision	Justification
Which devices should be fault tolerant?	None	Fault tolerance is not cost effective in the Internet Connectivity module.
Which devices should be redundant?	None	Device redundancy is not cost effective in the Internet Connectivity module.
Which links should be redundant?	Redundant links to the Edge Distribution module.	Redundant links provide backup in case of a link failure.
What spanning-tree implementation and root devices are required?	None	Not applicable
What is the router availability strategy?	HSRP	HSRP provides high availability.

Revised Network Diagrams

Figures 5-7 and 5-8 show the updated network diagrams to reflect the high-availability strategies presented.

Figure 5-7 *Revised Network Diagram for the Headquarters' Location with High-Availability Services*

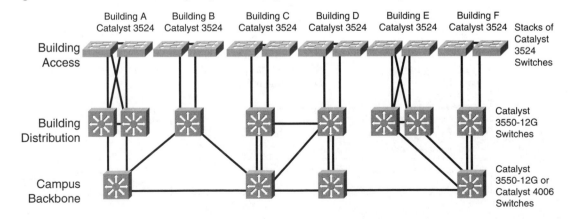

Figure 5-8   *A Network Diagram for the WAN with Redundant Links for Load Sharing and High Availability*

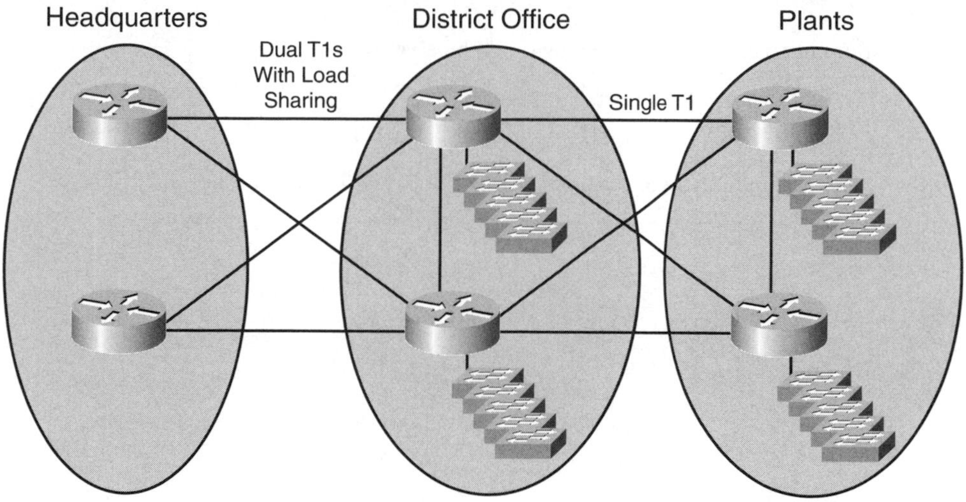

Headquarters   District Office   Plants

Dual T1s
With Load
Sharing

Single T1

After completing this chapter, you will be able to

- Evaluate network security policies
- Review Cisco security solutions
- Implement network security using the Cisco SAFE security blueprints

CHAPTER 6

Designing Security Services

As enterprises continually expand their mission-critical networks with new intranet, extranet, and e-commerce applications, network security is increasingly vital to prevent corruption and intrusion, and eliminate network security vulnerabilities. Without precautions, enterprises could experience major security breaches that result in serious damages or data loss.

A key component of Cisco Architecture for Voice, Video, and Integrated Data (AVVID), network security services improve the network's ability to support mission-critical Internet applications while providing authentication, authorization, and data integrity.

This chapter describes how to evaluate network security policies and develop associated security strategies. It defines the components of a Cisco security solution and the selection of the appropriate features and functions. This chapter concludes with a review of the Cisco Security Architecture for Enterprise (SAFE) network blueprint and how to propose a security strategy.

Evaluating Network Security Policies

Network security policies are critical to the overall security architecture for an enterprise. The three main phases of developing network security policies are

1 Establish a security policy

2 Implement network security technologies

3 Audit the network on a recurring basis

You will use the results of the audits to modify the security policy and the technology implementation as needed.

The enterprise security strategy includes establishing a security policy that defines the security goals of the enterprise, and implementing network security technologies in a comprehensive and layered approach so that the enterprise does not rely upon only one type of technology to solve all security issues.

Maintaining a high level of network security requires a continuous effort. Evaluating network security on an ongoing basis is critical to maintaining the most effective security.

This section describes the primary network vulnerabilities and their countermeasures, the purpose and components of a security policy, the process of maintaining network security and how to assess an existing network's risk from network attacks.

Network Vulnerabilities

As time has passed, the sophistication of tools used to attack a network has increased while the technical knowledge needed to use those tools has decreased. Networks are vulnerable to a variety of threats, as shown in Figure 6-1. This section describes the primary network vulnerabilities and their countermeasures.

Figure 6-1   *Threat Capabilities*

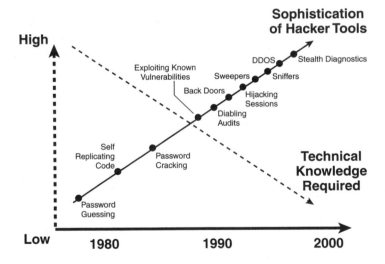

Many people have the impression that Internet hacking incidents are highly complex, technical attacks that take a genius to create. The reality is that a few sophisticated people develop these highly complex, technical attacks, but they use the Internet to share the information and the tools required to execute the attack. The open sharing of hacking information and tools allows individuals with minimal technical knowledge to duplicate an attack. Often, it is as easy as downloading the attack tool from the Internet and launching it against targets. A hacker need not know anything other than how to run the attack tool.

Total data security assurance results from a comprehensive strategy that addresses each type of network vulnerability shown in Figure 6-2.

Figure 6-2   *Network Vulnerability Categories*

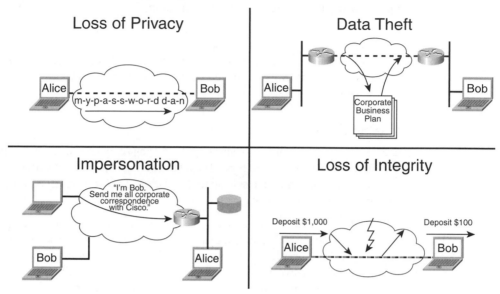

To counteract the problems of loss of privacy and data theft, where data is accessed or even removed, security protocols provide confidentiality for sensitive information as it travels across an untrusted or public network. Protocols that provide confidentiality typically employ encryption techniques that scramble data in a way that is undecipherable to unauthorized access attempts.

To counteract problems associated with impersonation, authentication protocols both validate and guarantee the identity of communicating parties. Authentication protocols are implemented in many ways, but most commonly take the form of digital signatures, digital certificates, or shared keys.

To counteract the problem of loss of integrity, where an external entity might not be able to see the data content but still alter it, security protocols validate the integrity of information traveling across an untrusted or public network. Such protocols are typically hashing algorithms that generate a value unique to the data content. Hashing algorithms do not prevent alteration of data, but rather allow communicating parties to detect when alteration occurs.

NOTE   Message Data 5 (MD5) is an example of a protocol that validates the integrity of data and indicates whether it has been altered or modified. This protocol might provide integrity monitoring of host file systems through the generation of a unique value called a hash for each file stored on that system. The hash result, called a baseline, is then securely stored. At regular intervals, the hashing process is rerun and the baseline is used to compare the results to determine if the integrity of the file(s) has been modified.

Effective data security assurance, from a protocol perspective, requires methods for ensuring data confidentiality, integrity, and authentication.

<table>
<tr><td>NOTE</td><td>An acronym in the security industry that summarizes this security concept is **CIA**. In this context, CIA stands for Confidentiality, Integrity, and Availability of data.</td></tr>
</table>

Defining a Security Policy

Network security efforts are based on a security policy. The policy identifies what is being protected, how users are identified and trusted, how the policy is to be enforced, the consequences of a violation, and the response to a violation. This section describes the purpose and components of a security policy.

As stated in RFC 2196, a security policy "is a formal statement of the rules by which people who are given access to an organization's technology and information assets must abide." Security policies apply to all aspects of running an organization, including building, maintaining, and using the network. Maintaining a high level of network security requires a continuous cycle of efforts based on a security policy. At the minimum, a security policy contains these elements:

- **Definition**—What data and assets will the policy cover?
- **Identity**—How do you identify the users affected by the policy?
- **Trust**—Under what conditions is a user trusted to perform an action?
- **Enforceability**—How will the policy's implementation be verified?
- **Risk assessment**—What is the impact of a policy violation? How are violations detected?
- **Incident response**—What actions are required upon a violation of the security policy?

At the minimum, network security policies typically define these situations:

- **Acceptable use policy**—What constitutes acceptable and appropriate use of the network? What uses are not allowed? How does the policy differ for different types of users, for example, partners and administrators?
- **Identification and authentication policy**—What standards and methodologies are used to identify and authenticate network users?
- **Internet use policy**—What is the policy regarding the purposes for which users are allowed to access the Internet? Are any specific uses identified?
- **Campus access policy**—Under what conditions are users allowed to access the campus network internally?
- **Remote access policy**—What is the policy for users accessing the network from a remote location?

Network Security as a Process

Maintaining network security is based on a security policy. Network security is a continuous process built around a security policy. The ongoing steps shown in Figure 6-3 include securing the network, monitoring network security, testing security, and improving security. This section describes the process of maintaining network security.

Figure 6-3   *Steps to Maintaining Network Security*

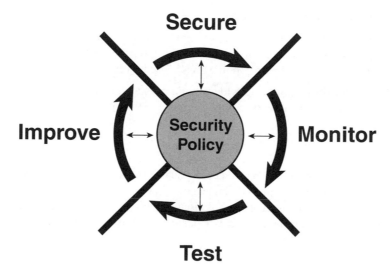

After setting appropriate policies, a company or organization must methodically consider security as part of normal network operations. The policy could be as simple as configuring routers to reject unauthorized addresses or services, or as complex as installing firewalls, intrusion detection systems, centralized authentication servers, and encrypted virtual private networks (VPNs).

After developing a security policy, secure your network by using a variety of products (firewalls, intrusion detection systems, and so on). Implementing a secure network will also involve the deployment of authentication, encryption, firewalls, and vulnerability patching. These solutions are examined in more detail in the next sections.

NOTE   Figure 6-3 also illustrates another important aspect of the security process, that it is an iterative process. For a security process to be effective, the process must constantly be revisited and modified to meet the current requirements of your enterprise network.

Securing the Network

The four solutions that you can implement to secure a network are as follows:

- **Authentication**—The recognition of each individual user, and mapping of his identity, location, and use policy, plus authorization of his network services.

- **Encryption**—A method for ensuring the confidentiality, integrity, and authenticity of data communications across a network. The Cisco solution combines several standards, including the Data Encryption Standard (DES), Triple DES (3DES), and the Advanced Encryption Standard (AES).

- **Firewalls**—A set of related programs located at a network gateway server, which protects the resources of a private network from users from other networks. (The term also implies the security policy that is used with the programs.)

- **Vulnerability patching**—Identifying and patching possible security holes that could compromise a network.

Monitoring Security

To ensure that a network remains secure, you need to monitor the state of security preparation. Intrusion detection systems (IDSs) can monitor and respond to security events as they occur. Using security monitoring solutions, organizations can obtain visibility into both the network data stream and the security posture (profile) of the network.

Testing Security

Testing security is as important as monitoring security. Testing the policy allows you to verify the effectiveness of the policy or identify weaknesses. Network vulnerability scanners can proactively identify areas of weakness.

Improving Security

Monitoring and testing security provide the data necessary to improve network security. With the information gathered during monitoring and testing, you can improve the security implementation to better enforce the security policy and modify the policy to incorporate responses to new risks.

Risk Assessment and Management

A risk assessment identifies risks to your network, network resources, and data. The information gathered during a risk assessment aids in assessing the validity of a network security implementation and, therefore, needs to be performed periodically to be effective. This section describes how to assess an existing network's risk from network attacks.

Risk analysis does not mean you should identify every possible entry point to the network, nor every possible means of attack. The intent of a risk analysis is to identify portions of your network, assign a threat rating to each portion, and apply an appropriate level of security. This helps maintain a workable balance between security and required network access. The risk assessment should be carried out in conjunction with the established security policy.

Assign each network resource one of these three risk levels:

- **Low-risk systems or data**—If compromised (data viewed by unauthorized personnel, data corrupted, or data lost), these systems would not disrupt the business or cause legal or financial ramifications. The targeted system or data can be easily restored and does not permit further access of other systems.

- **Medium-risk systems or data**—If compromised (data viewed by unauthorized personnel, data corrupted, or data lost), these systems would cause a moderate disruption in the business, minor legal or financial ramifications, or provide further access to other systems. The targeted system or data requires a moderate effort to restore, or the restoration process is disruptive to the system.

- **High-risk systems or data**—If compromised (data viewed by unauthorized personnel, data corrupted, or data lost), these systems would cause an extreme disruption in the business, cause major legal or financial ramifications, or threaten the health and safety of a person. The targeted system or data requires significant effort to restore, or the restoration process is disruptive to the business or other systems.

Assign a risk level to each of the following:

- Core network devices
- Distribution network devices
- Access network devices
- Network monitoring devices (Simple Network Management Protocol [SNMP] monitors and remote monitoring [RMON] probes)
- Network security devices
- E-mail systems
- Network file servers
- Network print servers
- Network application servers
- Data application servers
- Desktop computers
- Other network-based devices

Network equipment, such as switches, routers, Domain Name System (DNS) servers, and Dynamic Host Configuration Protocol (DHCP) servers, can allow further access into the network, and are, therefore, either medium- or high-risk devices. It is also possible that corruption of this equipment could cause the network itself to collapse. Such a failure can be extremely disruptive to the business.

After you assign a risk level, you should identify the types of users of that system. The five most common types of users are as follows, although you might consider including nonhuman users, such as applications:

- **Administrators**—Internal users responsible for network resources
- **Privileged**—Internal users with a need for greater access
- **Users**—Internal users with general access
- **Partners**—External users with a need to access some resources
- **Others**—External users or customers

NOTE   Application classification is a useful part of the overall risk-assessment process. Defining risk levels and formulating an appropriate policy toward applications strengthen your overall security posture. An example of this process would be identifying the Berkley Internet Name Daemon (BIND) as a high-risk application. Thus, the network security policy would specify that systems running BIND must be deployed outside of the trusted network. Furthermore, when BIND is installed on a host, the application would have to be run in a confined and isolated virtual environment called Jailed or Change Root (ChRoot). This would help prevent any compromise of the BIND application from allowing the compromise of the entire platform.

The identification of the risk level and the type of access required of each network system forms the basis of the security matrix. The security matrix provides a quick reference for each system and a starting point for further security measures, such as creating an appropriate strategy for restricting access to network resources. Table 6-1 shows an example of a security matrix.

Table 6-1   *Example Risk-Assessment Matrix*

System	Description	Risk Level	Types of Users
Network switches	Core network device	High	Administrators All other for use as a transport
Network routers	Edge network device	High	Administrators All other for use as a transport

Table 6-1   *Example Risk-Assessment Matrix (Continued)*

System	Description	Risk Level	Types of Users
Closet switches	Access network device	Medium	Administrators All other for use as a transport
ISDN or dialup servers	Access network device	Medium	Administrators Partners and privileged users for special access
Firewall	Access network device	High	Administrators All other for use as a transport
DNS and DHCP servers	Network applications	Medium	Administrators General and privileged users for use
Internal e-mail server	Network application	Medium	Administrators All other internal users for use
Oracle database	Network application	Medium or high	Administrators Privileged users for data updates General users for data access All other for partial data access

Use Table 6-2 to create your own security matrix.

Table 6-2   *Security Matrix*

System	Description	Risk Level	Types of Users

NOTE   To assist you in the risk-assessment process, the Centre for Internet Security (http://
www.cisecurity.org) provides free security benchmarking tools for all major operating
systems (OSs), as well as Cisco IOS and Oracle databases.

Another risk-assessment product is the open source vulnerability scanner called Nessus,
which is available from http://www.nessus.org.

Education is a critical component of conducting a successful risk assessment and
classification of your network. Software applications are only as efficient as the user who
deploys them. To assist you in maintaining an up-to-date level of knowledge on current
threats you should subscribe to mail lists and visit the following websites as often as
possible:

- The Computer Emergency Response Team (http://www.cert.org/)

- The Computer Security Resource Centre (http://csrc.ncsl.nist.gov/)

- SANS (SysAdmin, Audit, Network, Security) Institute (http://www.sans.org)

- National Security Agency—Security Recommendation Guides (http://nsa2.www.
  conxion.com/)

- Cisco Product Security Advisories and Notices (http://cisco.com/warp/public/707/
  advisory.html)

Reviewing Cisco Security Solutions

Cisco offers an array of enterprise network security solutions to make the implementation
and maintenance of good network security easier and more cost effective. These solutions
include dedicated appliances, software, and security capabilities embedded into Cisco
network products.

The enterprise security strategy does not include a single product or solution, but
encompasses a range of solutions, strategies, and ongoing audits to provide optimal
security.

This section discusses the following topics:

- Key elements of network security

- Network security attacks and solutions

- Firewall design options

- IDS design options

- Authentication, authorization, and accounting

Key Elements of Network Security

An effective security solution includes the following:

- **Secure connectivity**—When you must protect information from eavesdropping, the ability to provide authenticated, confidential communication on demand is crucial. Sometimes, data separation using tunneling technologies, such as generic routing encapsulation (GRE) or Layer 2 Tunneling Protocol (L2TP), provides effective data privacy. Often, however, additional privacy requirements call for the use of digital encryption technology and protocols such as IP Security (IPSec). This added protection is especially important when implementing VPNs.

NOTE	*VPN* is used to define a data conversation that is occurring between two endpoints over a public network, but whose nature and contents are concealed from view by untrusted entities. GRE and L2TP allow the creation of a tunnel connection, but are subject to confidentiality and integrity violation because of their nonencrypted payload. IPSec might remedy this potential weakness, where required, because it can encrypt the contents.

- **Perimeter security**—This element provides the means to control access to critical network applications, data, and services so that only legitimate users and information can pass through the network. Routers and switches with access control lists (ACLs), stateful firewall implementations, and dedicated firewall appliances provide perimeter security control. Complementary tools, including virus scanners and content filters, also help control network perimeters.

NOTE	*Stateful firewalls* have the ability to monitor, track, and interpret a communication session between two entities. Stateful firewalls monitor sessions initiated by devices and only permit responses associated with that session from passing through the firewall. In essence, the software creates a dynamic rule that is only valid for the duration of the data conversation after which it is removed.

- **Intrusion protection**—To ensure that a network remains secure, it is important to regularly test and monitor the state of security preparation. Network vulnerability scanners can proactively identify areas of weakness, and IDSs can monitor and respond to security events as they occur. Using security-monitoring devices, organizations can obtain unprecedented visibility into both the network data stream and the security posture of the network.

- **Identity**—The accurate and positive identification of network users, hosts, applications, services, and resources. Standard technologies that enable identification include authentication protocols, such as Remote Authentication Dial-In User Service (RADIUS) and Terminal Access Controller Access Control System plus (TACACS+), Kerberos, and one-time password tools. New technologies such as digital certificates, smart cards, and directory services are beginning to play increasingly important roles in identity solutions.

- **Security management**—As networks grow in size and complexity, the requirement for centralized policy management tools grows as well. Sophisticated tools that can analyze, interpret, configure, and monitor the state of the security policy, with browser-based user interfaces, enhance the usability and effectiveness of network security solutions.

Figure 6-4 shows these five key elements that make up an effective security solution.

Figure 6-4   *Components of a Cisco Security Solution*

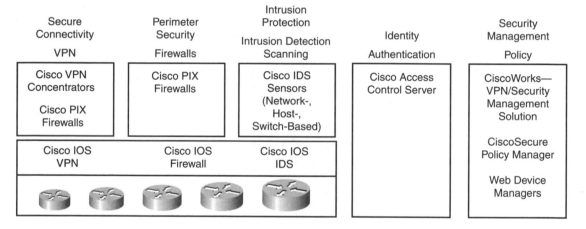

Network Security Attack Types and Their Solutions

Attacks against network security come in many forms. Each type of attack has corresponding actions that you can take to prevent or mitigate the consequences of an attack. This section describes the different types of attacks, and lists the necessary Cisco security-solution elements that defend your network against each attack.

Packet Sniffers

A *packet sniffer* is a software application that uses a network adapter card in promiscuous mode (a mode in which the network adapter card sends all packets received on the physical network wire to an application for processing) to capture all network packets that are sent across a particular collision domain. Sniffers are used legitimately in networks today to aid in troubleshooting and traffic analysis. However, because several network applications send data in clear text, a packet sniffer can access meaningful and often sensitive information, such as usernames and passwords.

NOTE   Ethereal is an excellent open-source protocol analyzer available from http:// www.ethereal.com/. Using an analyzer can assist you in determining the weaknesses that can be exploited on your network.

It is important that you first ensure you have the correct permissions to deploy an analyzer, or other software, on your system and interact with corporate traffic. If you do not, you might be violating your own security policy and find yourself liable to dismissal or criminal charges.

You can mitigate the threat of packet sniffers in several ways:

- **Authentication**—Using strong authentication. (This option is recommended as a first step.)
- **Switched infrastructure**—Deploying a switched campus network infrastructure.

NOTE   Switched networks help mitigate the impact of sniffers because each data conversation is occurring point to point through the switches' architecture, rather then across a shared infrastructure.

However, techniques exist that can circumvent this behavior. One technique is to flood the switch with fake MAC addresses. This fills the MAC table with false entries. After the MAC table is full, the switch will typically flood all subsequent frames. The switch now behaves like a repeater (hub), allowing frames to be captured and sniffed by any device terminated on the platform, regardless of their location. A tool that can provide this type of capability is called DSniff.

As a network administrator, it is imperative that you become familiar with the type of threats that exist so that you can better identify and impede their success.

To reduce the likelihood of such an attack, you must deploy vigilant monitoring of your switched architecture and, where deemed necessary, use techniques for MAC address–level security, such as port security. Port security restricts access to the switched architecture by mapping MAC addresses to ports and preventing unauthorized MAC addresses from generating traffic on the port.

- **Anti-sniffer tools**—Employing software and hardware that are designed to detect the use of sniffers on a network.

NOTE   *Anti-sniffing technologies* rely on the process of detecting if network interface cards (NICs) have been placed in promiscuous mode. This typically is a good indication that the platform has packet-sniffing software installed. The majority of the tools that exist are hand-crafted solutions that largely rely on installing a detection tool on the suspect platform, or analyzing the configuration of the NIC manually.

- **Cryptography**—An effective method to counter packet sniffers; it does not prevent or detect packet sniffers, but renders them irrelevant.

IP Spoofing

An *IP spoofing* attack occurs when a hacker inside or outside a network pretends to be a trusted computer. A hacker can use an IP address that is within the range of trusted IP addresses for a network, or an authorized external IP address that is trusted and to which access is provided to specified resources on a network. IP spoofing attacks are often a launch point for other attacks. A classic example is to launch a denial of service (DoS) attack using spoofed source addresses to hide the hacker's identity. The spoofed address need not be trusted.

You can reduce, but not eliminate, the threat of IP spoofing through these measures:

- **Access control**—The most common method is to properly configure access control. Configure access control to deny any traffic from the external network that has a source address that should reside on the internal network.

- **RFC 2827 filtering**—You can prevent a network's users from spoofing other networks by preventing any outbound traffic on your network that does not have a source address in your organization's own IP range. Your Internet service provider (ISP) can also implement this type of filtering, which is collectively referred to as RFC 2827 filtering (see RFC 2827, "Network Ingress Filtering: Defeating Denial of Service Attacks which Employ IP Source Address Spoofing"). This filtering denies any traffic that does not have the source address that was expected on a particular interface.

- **Authentication**—IP spoofing can function correctly only when devices use IP address–based authentication. Therefore, if you use additional authentication methods, IP spoofing attacks are irrelevant.

DoS Attacks

DoS attacks focus on making a service unavailable for normal use, which is typically accomplished by exhausting some resource limitation on the network or within an operating system or application.

One form of DoS involves attacking applications, such as a web server or a File Transfer Protocol (FTP) server, by opening all the available connections supported by that server, which locks out valid users of that server or service. Hackers can implement DoS attacks using common Internet protocols, such as Transmission Control Protocol (TCP) and Internet Control Message Protocol (ICMP).

Most DoS attacks exploit a weakness in the overall architecture of the system being attacked rather than a software bug or security hole. Some attacks compromise the performance of your network by flooding the network with undesired—and often useless—network packets, and by providing false information about the status of network resources. This type of attack is often the most difficult to prevent because it requires coordination with your upstream network provider. If traffic meant to consume your available bandwidth is not stopped there, denying it at the point of entry into your network does little good because your available bandwidth has already been consumed. When this type of attack is launched from many different systems at the same time, it is referred to as a DDoS attack.

You can reduce the threat of DoS attacks by using these three methods:

- **Anti-spoof features**—Properly configure the anti-spoof features on your routers and firewalls. This includes RFC 2827 filtering at a minimum. If hackers cannot mask their identities, they might not be able to attack.

- **Anti-DoS features**—Properly configure the anti-DoS features on your routers and firewalls. These features often involve limits on the amount of half-open connections that a system allows open at any given time.

NOTE   A TCP half-open connection is one in which the TCP three-way handshake that is used to establish a connection-orientated data session has not been completed or terminated in an orderly fashion. As a result, the server keeps allocated to the connection attempt valuable memory and processing assets. Multiple such attempts might consume all available resources, resulting in an inaccessible service or even a locked or crashed system.

TCP synchronization attacks can be limited in effectiveness by controlling how many half-open connections are allowed to be initiated through a router or firewall. Features such as TCP Intercept in Cisco IOS provide this type of functionality.

- **Traffic-rate limiting**—An organization can implement traffic-rate limiting with its ISP. This type of filtering limits the amount of nonessential traffic that crosses network segments. A common example is to limit the amount of ICMP traffic allowed into a network that is used only for diagnostic purposes.

NOTE
Attempting to prevent or reduce the effects of DDoS attacks can be difficult. In some cases, the countermeasures used to prevent DoS attacks can themselves disrupt services. For example, firewalls and routers running TCP SYN half-open protection services might be brought to a halt if flooded with a high volume of such requests. As the firewall or router attempts to track and terminate the half-open connections, it becomes preoccupied with this task, which prevents it from forwarding legitimate user traffic. In the end, if the condition persists, the gateway might even lock up or crash. If a network's gateway or firewall is removed from service, the network has become inoperative—in essence, the DoS succeeds.

Password Attacks

Hackers can implement *password attacks* using several different methods, including brute-force attacks, Trojan horse programs, IP spoofing, and packet sniffers. Although packet sniffers and IP spoofing can yield user accounts and passwords, password attacks usually amount to repeated attempts to identify a user account and/or password, called brute-force attacks.

A *brute-force attack* is often performed using a program that runs across the network and attempts to log in to a shared resource, such as a server. When hackers successfully gain access to resources, they have the same rights as the compromised account users to gain access to those resources. If the compromised accounts have sufficient privileges, the hackers can create back doors for future access without concern for any status and password changes to the compromised user accounts.

Another problem is created when users have the same password on every system they use, including personal systems, corporate systems, and systems on the Internet. Because a password is only as secure as the host that contains it, if that host is compromised, hackers can try the same password on a range of hosts.

You can most easily eliminate password attacks by not relying on plain-text passwords in the first place. Using a one-time password (OTP) and/or cryptographic authentication can virtually eliminate the threat of password attacks. Unfortunately, not all applications, hosts, and devices support these authentication methods. When standard passwords are used, it is important to choose a password that is difficult to guess. Passwords should be at least eight characters long and contain uppercase letters, lowercase letters, numbers, and special characters (#, %, $, and so on). The best passwords are randomly generated but are very difficult to remember, often leading users to write down their passwords.

NOTE   Password generation and memorization is a serious process for network administrators and for most individuals. In a society where every aspect of our life, from personal banking, video renting, and network access, relies on the use of passwords, a methodology needs to be established and adopted to assist in this process. It is recommended that you develop a process to prioritize your resources that require passwords and use it as a guide to determine the complexity of the passwords you generate. Do not reuse passwords and never write them down. When formulating a password, use the rules previously defined, but try to be practical by generating passwords that can be associated with a common word. For example, "firewall" may be used as a password, but spell it creatively, like F!r3W@ll., which makes it difficult to guess, but easy to remember.

Man-in-the-Middle Attacks

A *man-in-the-middle attack* requires that the hacker have access to network packets that come across a network. An example of such a configuration could be someone who is working for an ISP, who has access to all network packets transferred between his employer's network and any other network. Such attacks are often implemented using network packet sniffers, and routing and transport protocols. The possible uses of such attacks are theft of information, hijacking of an ongoing session to gain access to private network resources, traffic analysis to derive information about a network and its users, denial of service, corruption of transmitted data, and introduction of new information into network sessions.

Man-in-the-middle attacks are effectively mitigated only through the use of cryptography. If someone hijacks data in the middle of a cryptographically private session, all the hacker will see is cipher text—not the original message. If a hacker can learn information about the cryptographic session (such as the session key), man-in-the-middle attacks are still possible.

NOTE   Cryptographically protected sessions that use transport-level security technologies, such as SSL or SSH, can still be hijacked by a man-in-the-middle attack. The attacker places herself in the middle of the conversation by posing as the legitimate site. This can be achieved by poisoning local DNS records and forcing all traffic destined for the legitimate website to the hijacked system where a phony copy of the website exists. After redirection occurs, the hijacker offers the client a new illegitimate certificate. The client application will indicate that the certificate credentials are changed or illegitimate and ask if the user still wishes to accept. An uneducated user might not suspect anything, and not even bother to check the certificate to ensure it is signed by a trusted certification authority (CA). After the new key is installed, the hijacker captures the login credentials and then offers them to the legitimate site posing as the user, but can now capture all transmitted data as it passes between the user and the legitimate website.

Application Layer Attacks

Application layer attacks exploit well-known or newly discovered weaknesses in software that are commonly found on servers, such as sendmail, HTTP, and FTP. By exploiting these weaknesses, hackers can gain access to a computer with the permissions of the account running the application, which is usually a privileged system-level account. These application layer attacks are often widely publicized to encourage administrators to correct the problem with a patch. Unfortunately, many hackers also subscribe to these same mailing lists, which results in their learning about the vulnerabilities in the software.

The primary problem with application layer attacks is that they often use ports that allow traffic through a firewall. For example, a hacker executing a known vulnerability against a web server often uses TCP port 80. Because the web server serves pages to users, a firewall needs to allow access on that port. From the perspective of a firewall, the hacker's input is merely standard port 80 traffic.

You can never completely eliminate application layer attacks. Hackers continually discover and publicize new vulnerabilities. The best way to reduce your risk is to practice good system administration. You can take a few measures to further reduce your risks:

- Read operating system and network log files and analyze them using log analysis applications.

- Subscribe to mailing lists that publicize vulnerabilities, such as Bugtraq (http://www.securityfocus.com) and CERT (http://www.cert.org).

- Keep your operating systems and applications current with the latest patches.

- Use IDSs to minimize application-layer attacks.

Network Reconnaissance

Network reconnaissance refers to the act of learning information about a target network by using publicly available information and applications. When hackers attempt to penetrate a particular network, they often need to learn as much information as possible about the network before launching attacks, often using DNS queries and ping sweeps. DNS queries can reveal information such as who owns a particular domain and what addresses are assigned to that domain. Ping sweeps of the addresses revealed through DNS queries present a picture of the live hosts in a particular environment. The hackers can examine the characteristics of the applications that are running on the hosts. This can lead to specific information that is useful when the hacker attempts to compromise that service.

You cannot prevent network reconnaissance entirely. If ICMP echo and echo-reply is turned off on the edge routers, for example, you can stop ping sweeps, but it comes at the expense of network diagnostic data. However, you can run port scans without full ping sweeps; they simply take longer because they need to scan IP addresses that might not be live. IDSs at the network and host levels can usually notify an administrator when a reconnaissance gathering attack is underway. This allows the administrator to better prepare for the coming attack or to notify the ISP who is hosting the system that is launching the reconnaissance probe.

NOTE	Today, many advanced probing tools are available publicly on the Internet. One of the most popular open-source applications is Nmap. Nmap is an excellent freeware tool that demonstrates how networks can be probed using services other than ICMP. Nmap not only can identify which IPs belong to active platforms by using TCP or UDP sweeps, it can also identify services and operating systems.

Trust Exploitation

Trust exploitation refers to an attack where a hacker takes advantage of a trust relationship within a network. A classic example is a perimeter network connection from a corporation, which often houses enterprise-wide servers. Because they all reside on the same segment, a compromise of one system can lead to the compromise of other systems, because they might trust other systems attached to the same network. Another example is a system on the outside of a firewall that has a trust relationship with a system on the inside of a firewall. When the outside system is compromised, it can leverage that trust relationship to attack the inside network.

You can mitigate trust exploitation-based attacks through tight constraints on trust levels within a network. Systems on the inside of a firewall should never absolutely trust systems on the outside of a firewall. Limit trust to specific protocols and authenticate with more than an IP address where possible.

NOTE	Trust exploitation is a commonly used mechanism for gaining access to a trusted network and its resources. The most infamous example of such exploitation was the attack and abuse of Tsutomu Shimomura's computer system by Kevin Mitnick. Through reconnaissance, Kevin discovered that a trust relationship existed between an external system on the Internet and the target Shimomura's own PC. Armed with this knowledge, Kevin posed as the trusted host through IP spoofing, thus allowing him to bypass the requirement for presenting login authentication credentials. The only credential required in this trust relationship was the correct IP address. To ensure the legitimate spoofed system could not interact with the target during the exploitation, he conducted a DoS against it. After he accessed Shimomura's system, he modified the trust relationship to allow his illegally compromised systems to connect to it without having to log in. Now, he was free to access the system at anytime from anywhere.

Port Redirection Attacks

Port redirection attacks are a type of trust exploitation attack that uses a compromised host to pass traffic through a firewall that would otherwise be dropped. Consider a firewall with three interfaces and a host on each interface. The host on the outside can reach the host on the public services segment (commonly referred to as a perimeter LAN), but not the host on the inside. The host on the public services segment can reach the host on both the outside and the inside. If hackers could compromise the public services segment host, they could install software to redirect traffic from the outside host directly to the inside host. Though neither communication violates the rules implemented in the firewall, the outside host has now achieved connectivity to the inside host through the port redirection process on the public services host.

You can mitigate most port redirection using proper trust models. Assuming a system is under attack, host-based IDSs can help detect and prevent a hacker installing such utilities on a host.

Unauthorized Access Attacks

Although not a specific type of attack, *unauthorized access attacks* refer to the majority of attacks executed in networks today. For someone to use a brute-force attack on a Telnet login, he must first get the Telnet prompt on a system. Upon connection to the Telnet port, a message might indicate "authorization required to use this resource." If the hacker continues to attempt access, the actions become unauthorized. A hacker can initiate these kinds of attacks both from the outside and inside of a network.

Mitigation techniques for unauthorized access attacks are very simple. They involve reducing or eliminating the ability of hackers to gain access to a system using an unauthorized protocol. An example would be preventing hackers from having access to the Telnet port on a server that needs to provide web services to the outside. If a hacker cannot reach that port, it is difficult to attack it. The primary function of a firewall in a network is to prevent simple unauthorized access attacks.

Viruses and Trojan Horses

The primary vulnerabilities for end-user workstations are viruses and Trojan horse attacks. *Viruses* refer to malicious software that is attached to another program to execute a particular unwanted function on a user's workstation. An example of a virus is a program that is attached to command.com (the primary interpreter for Windows systems), which deletes certain files and infects any other versions of command.com that it can find. A *Trojan horse* is different only in that the entire application was written to look like something else, when, in fact, it is an attack tool. An example of a Trojan horse is a software application that runs a simple game on the user's workstation. While the user is occupied with the game, the Trojan horse mails a copy of itself to every user in the user's address book. Then other users get the game and play it, thus spreading the Trojan horse.

You can contain Trojan horse applications through the effective use of antivirus software at the user level and potentially at the network level. Antivirus software can detect most viruses and many Trojan horse applications and prevent them from spreading in the network. Keeping current with the latest mitigation techniques can also lead to a more effective posture against these attacks. As new viruses or Trojan horse applications are released, enterprises need to keep up to date with the latest antivirus software and application versions.

NOTE   A new addition to the family of Trojan horses and viruses is the application type classified as Malware. Malicious software (Malware) behaves much the same way as a Trojan horse application in that it appears as one service, yet performs other functions without the user's knowledge or consent. Malware applications modify system parameters, monitor system and application usages, and report this information back to the originator of the software. Many freeware and file-sharing software applications use Malware to track and monitor their application usage and track statistical information about their clients. There exists various freeware and commercial software applications that focus on this variant of unwanted software and specialize in their detection and removal.

For more information on Malware and related software solutions, visit http://www.lavasoft.de/software/adaware/.

Firewall Design Options

Firewalls provide perimeter security by preventing unauthorized access to the internal network. Identifying the type of traffic that is not allowed to pass the firewall and how such traffic will be prevented are two of the primary decisions to make about a firewall implementation. This section describes features and functionality for firewall solutions.

You need to answer these questions to decide what firewall design is best for your network:

- What is the role of the firewall? Is the firewall in place explicitly to deny all services except those critical to the mission of connecting to the Internet, or is the firewall in place to provide a metered and audited method of queuing access in a nonthreatening manner?

- What level of monitoring, redundancy, and control do you want? You can form a checklist of what should be monitored, permitted, and denied.

- Is the firewall placement exposed on the outside network to run proxy services for Telnet, FTP, news, and so on, or set up as screening filter, permitting communication with one or more internal machines? Both approaches have pluses and minuses, with the proxy machine providing a greater level of audit and security in return for increased cost in configuration and a decrease in the level of service that might be provided, because a proxy needs to be developed for each desired service.

- Will a firewall be deployed as a dedicated hardware appliance or will an integrated software solution be deployed? The integrated functionality is often attractive because you can implement it on existing equipment, or because the features can interoperate with the rest of the device to provide a better functional solution. Appliances are often used when the depth of functionality required is very advanced or when performance needs require using specialized hardware. Make your decisions based on the capacity and functionality of the appliance versus the integration advantage of the device.

Implementing a Perimeter LAN

Perimeter LAN is another term for a Demilitarized Zone (DMZ). Figure 6-5 shows an example of a perimeter LAN.

Figure 6-5 *Implementing a Perimeter LAN*

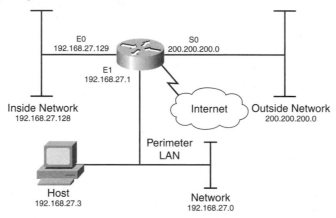

Consider breaking the perimeter LAN into several security zones.

The LAN connected to E1 provides an environment in which services that require public access can be positioned on a segment that offers security, but does not expose the internal network to risk if they become compromised. In the context of firewalls, the perimeter LAN (DMZ) refers to a part of the network that is neither part of the internal network nor directly part of the Internet. Typically, this is the area between the Internet access router and the bastion host, though it can be between any two policy-enforcing components of the network architecture.

NOTE   Bastion host refers to a computer system that has been hardened to reduce its vulnerability to attacks. This is achieved through the removal of unneeded services and applications and might also involve the installation of host-based IDS and/or firewall solutions.

You can create a perimeter LAN by putting ACLs on your access router. This minimizes the exposure of hosts on the perimeter LAN by allowing only recognized and managed services on those hosts to be accessible by hosts on the Internet. For example, a web server running Microsoft Windows NT might be vulnerable to a number of DoS attacks against NetBIOS-based services. These services are not required for the operation of a web server, so blocking connections to NetBIOS services on that host will reduce the exposure to a DoS attack. In fact, if you block everything but HTTP traffic to that host, an attacker will only have one service to attack.

Common approaches for an attacker is to break into a host that is vulnerable to attack, and exploit trust relationships between the vulnerable host and more interesting targets.

If you are running a number of services that have different levels of security, you might want to consider breaking the perimeter LAN into several security zones. For example, the access router could feed two Ethernet segments, both protected by ACLs, and, therefore, in the perimeter LAN.

On one of the Ethernet segments, you might have hosts that provide Internet connectivity. These will likely relay mail, news, and host DNS. On the other Ethernet segment, you could have web servers and other hosts that provide services for the benefit of Internet users.

In many organizations, services for Internet users tend to be less carefully guarded and are more likely to be doing insecure things. (For example, in the case of a web server, unauthenticated and untrusted users might be running CGI or other executable programs. This might be reasonable for the web server, but brings with it a certain set of risks that need to be managed. It is likely that these services are too risky for an organization to run them on a bastion host, where a slip-up can result in the complete failure of the security mechanisms.)

By splitting services not only by host, but by network, and limiting the level of trust between hosts on those networks, you can greatly reduce the likelihood of a break-in on one host being used to break into another host.

You can also increase the scalability of your architecture by placing hosts on different networks. The fewer machines that there are to share the available bandwidth, the more bandwidth that each will get.

Firewall Filtering Rules

Figure 6-6 shows an example where the Cisco firewall is used as the filtering device to enforce a specific network security policy. The company in this example has a Class C network address 195.55.55.0. The company network is connected to the Internet via an ISP. Company policy is to allow access to all Internet-based services; therefore, all outbound connections are permitted. Mail and DNS are the only inbound service requests permitted. To enforce this policy, only inbound packets from the Internet are inspected.

Figure 6-6 *Firewall Filtering Rules*

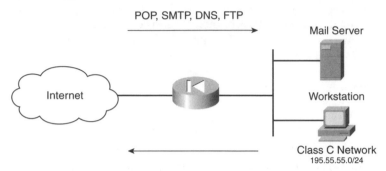

The firewall in Figure 6-6 provides these security services:

- Allows all outgoing TCP connections. This provides support for HTTP, FTP, SMTP, POP, and other popular TCP-based services
- Allows incoming SMTP and DNS to mail server
- Allows incoming FTP data connections to high TCP port (over port 1024)
- Tries to protect services that live on high port numbers

NOTE   A Cisco router can be deployed as a filtering router to control access to network resources. Generally, a packet-filtering router is a device that deploys ACLs to regulate traffic flow, but does not understand connection states and, therefore, cannot build dynamic ACL entries—it is stateless. If a stateless packet filtering router is used with ACLs, rules must be defined to account for all inbound and outbound (return) traffic. For example, if you allow outbound HTTP, you would also have to define a rule on a packet-filtering router to permit the inbound reply from the HTTP server (assuming you were following a policy where you are denying all traffic unless explicitly permitted). If this is not done, your connection request would reach the server, but you would never see the reply.

Perimeter Security: PIX Firewall

The Cisco Private Internet Exchange (PIX) firewall is a dedicated hardware appliance that implements firewall services.

Built upon a proprietary operating system for security services called PIX OS, PIX firewalls provide a range of security services, including

- Network Address Translation (NAT)
- Port Address Translation (PAT)

- Content filtering (Java/ActiveX)
- URL filtering
- Authentication, authorization, and accounting (AAA), RADIUS/TACACS+ integration
- Support for X.509 public key infrastructure (PKI) solutions
- Dynamic Host Configuration Protocol (DHCP) client/server
- PPP over Ethernet (PPPoE) support

PIX firewalls support VPN clients, including Cisco hardware and software VPN clients, and Point-to-Point Tunneling Protocol (PPTP) and L2TP clients found within Microsoft Windows operating systems.

Other features supported by PIX firewalls include

- Site-to-site VPN capabilities
- Limited IDS services
- Enforcement of an organization's security policy
- Restricting access to network resources
- Determining whether traffic crossing in either direction is authorized
- Reduced impact on network performance

Perimeter Security: IOS Firewall

As an alternative to a dedicated hardware device, the Cisco IOS firewall is an add-on software module that allows a router, such as the 2500 series, to provide firewall services without additional hardware. It integrates firewall functionality and intrusion detection by providing stateful, application-based filtering; dynamic per-user authentication and authorization; defense against network attacks; Java blocking; and real-time alerts. In combination with IPSec and other Cisco IOS Software technologies, the Cisco IOS firewall provides a complete VPN solution.

IOS firewalls support VPN clients, including Cisco hardware and software VPN clients, and PPTP and L2TP clients found within Microsoft Windows operating systems.

Other features supported by IOS firewalls include

- Site-to-site VPN capabilities
- Limited IDS services
- Intranet protection
- Context-Based Access Control (CBAC)
- Proxy services

Intrusion Detection System Design Options

An intrusion detection system (IDS) detects and responds to attacks. IDSs act like an alarm system in the physical world. Figure 6-7 shows the two complementary IDS design options:

- **Host-based IDS (HIDS)**—Operates by inserting agents into the host to be protected. It is then concerned only with attacks generated against that one host. They are designed to protect the integrity of individual system file structures, operating system kernels, and services from attacks and unauthorized access.

- **Network-based IDS (NIDS)**—Operates by watching all packets traversing a particular collision domain. When NIDS sees a packet or series of packets that match a known or suspect attack, it can flag an alarm and/or terminate the session. NIDS protect the integrity of resources on the overall network from attacks and unauthorized access.

Figure 6-7   *Intrusion Detection Systems*

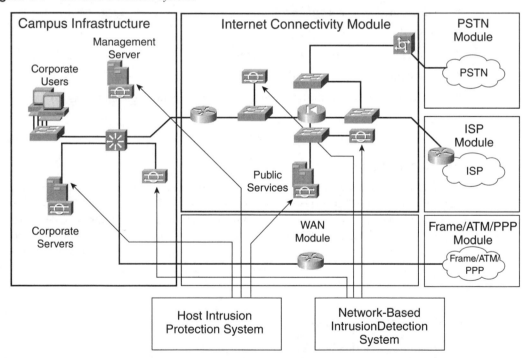

This section describes the features and functionality of both types of IDSs.

IDS Operation

IDSs operate by using attack signatures. *Attack signatures* are the profile for a particular attack or kind of attack. They specify certain conditions that must be met before traffic is deemed to be hostile. In the physical world, IDSs are most closely compared to an alarm system or security camera. When an IDS detects something that it considers an attack, it can either take corrective action itself or notify a management system for intervention by the administrator.

HIDSs work by intercepting operating system and application calls on an individual host. They can also operate by after-the-fact analysis of local log files. The former approach allows better attack prevention, whereas the latter approach dictates a more passive attack-response role. Because of the specificity of their role, HIDSs are often better at preventing specific attacks than NIDS systems, which usually only issue an alert upon discovery of an attack. However, that specificity causes a loss of perspective to the overall network. This is where NIDS excels. Cisco recommends a combination of the two systems, HIDS on critical hosts and NIDS looking over the entire network, for a complete IDS.

IDS Deployment

When you deploy an IDS, you must tune its implementation to increase its effectiveness and remove false positives. False positives are alarms caused by legitimate traffic or activity. False negatives are attacks that the IDS system fails to see. When you tune an IDS, you can configure it more specifically to its threat-mitigation role. You should configure HIDS to stop most valid threats at the host level, because it is well prepared to determine that certain activity is a threat. However, configuring HIDS is often difficult.

Remember that the first step prior to implementing any threat-response option is to adequately tune NIDS to ensure that any perceived threat is legitimate. When deciding on mitigation roles for NIDS, you have two primary options:

- The first option, and potentially the most damaging if improperly deployed, is to shun traffic by using access-control filters on routers and firewalls. When a NIDS detects an attack from a particular host over a particular protocol, it can block that host from coming into the network for a predetermined amount of time (shunning). Use it only in cases where the threat is real and the chance that the attack is a false positive is very low.

- The second option for NIDS mitigation is the use of TCP resets. As the name implies, TCP resets operate only on TCP traffic and terminate an active attack by sending TCP reset messages to the attacking and attacked host. Keep in mind that NIDS operation in a switched environment is more challenging than when a standard hub is used, because all ports do not see all traffic without the use of a Switched Port Analyzer (SPAN) or mirror port. Make sure this mirror port supports bidirectional traffic flows and can have SPAN port MAC learning disabled.

NOTE   SPAN is a feature supported on Cisco Catalyst switches that enables traffic from one port or set of ports to be redirected to another port on the switch. This feature is commonly used for traffic analysis and troubleshooting because it allows traffic to be redirected to a port that has a protocol analyzer or NIDS residing on it.

Both mitigation options require around-the-clock staffing to watch the IDS consoles. Because an IT staff is often overworked, consider outsourcing your IDS management to a third party. Another option for reducing monitoring requirements is to deploy a third-party event correlation engine.

From a performance standpoint, NIDS observes packets on the wire. If packets are sent faster than the NIDS can process them, there is no degradation to the network because the NIDS does not sit directly in the flows of data. However, the NIDS will lose effectiveness and packets could be missed, causing both false negatives and false positives. Be sure to avoid exceeding the capabilities of IDSs, so that you can benefit from their services.

From a routing standpoint, IDS, like many state-aware engines, does not operate properly in an asymmetrically routed environment. Packets sent out from one set of routers and switches and returning through another will cause an IDS system to see only half the traffic, causing false positives and false negatives.

Figure 6-8 illustrates various deployment strategies for IDSs.

Figure 6-8 *Intrusion Detection Deployment Scenarios*

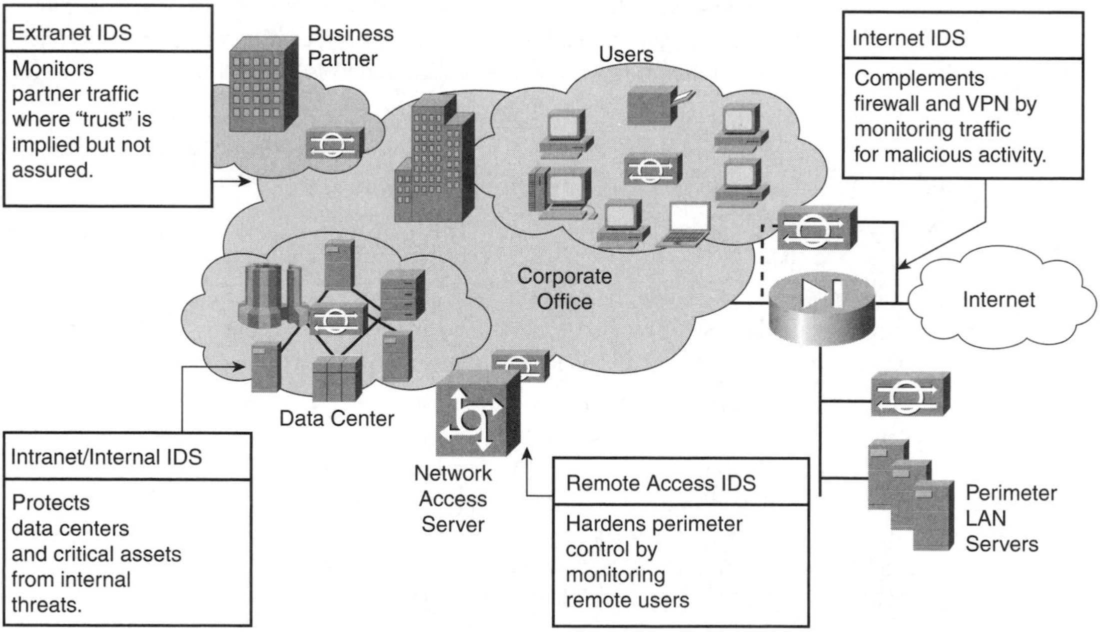

Consider placing an IDS wherever there is a need to protect critical assets from the threat of intrusion. Network ingress points, such as the connections with the Internet and extranets, are prime candidates, as are remote access points. Also consider placing an IDS internally at critical points to protect assets from internal threats.

Authentication, Authorization, and Accounting

Authentication, authorization, and accounting (AAA) is a term used to describe software mechanisms that enhance network security. AAA is designed to primarily provide centralized access control for the network through managed authentication services. AAA might also be configured to provide accounting services. All three features are described in this section.

RADIUS

The RADIUS protocol, shown in Figure 6-9, was developed by Livingston Enterprises, Inc., as an access server authentication and accounting protocol. The RADIUS authentication protocol is documented separately from the accounting protocol, but you can use the two together for a comprehensive solution.

Figure 6-9   *AAA: RADIUS*

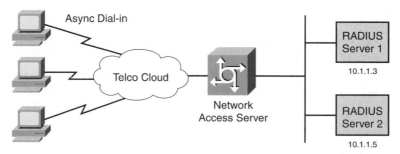

A client/server model forms the basis for the RADIUS protocol. A network access server (NAS) such as a Cisco access server operates as a client of RADIUS. The client is responsible for passing user information to a designated RADIUS server and then acting on the response that is returned.

A RADIUS server (or daemon) can provide authentication and accounting services to one or more client NAS devices. RADIUS servers are responsible for receiving user connection requests, authenticating users, and then returning all configuration information necessary for the client to deliver service to the users. A RADIUS access server is generally a dedicated server connected to the network.

Communication between a NAS and a RADIUS server is transported by the UDP protocol port 1812; accounting services use port 1813. The authors of the RADIUS protocol selected UDP as the transport protocol for technical reasons. Generally, the RADIUS protocol is considered to be a connectionless service. The RADIUS-enabled devices, rather than the transmission protocol, handle issues related to server availability, retransmission, and timeouts.

Typically, a user login consists of a query (Access-Request) from the NAS to the RADIUS server and a corresponding response (Access-Accept or Access-Reject) from the server. The Access-Request packet contains the username, encrypted password, NAS IP address, and port. The format of the request also provides information on the type of session that the user wants to initiate.

Authentication is the most troublesome aspect of remote security because of the difficulty associated with positively identifying a user. To ensure the identity of a remote user, the RADIUS protocol supports several methods of authentication, including Password Authentication Protocol (PAP), Challenge Handshake Authentication Protocol (CHAP), and token cards.

The RADIUS accounting functions allow data to be sent at the start and end of sessions, indicating the amount of resources (such as time, packets, bytes, and so on) used during the session.

TACACS+

TACACS+, shown in Figure 6-10, is a security application that provides centralized validation of users attempting to gain access to a router or network access server. TACACS+ services are maintained in a database on a TACACS+ daemon running, typically, on a UNIX or a Microsoft Windows NT server.

Figure 6-10 *AAA: TACACS+*

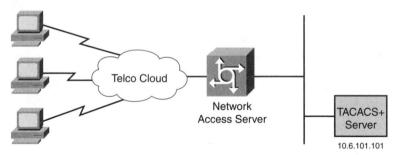

You must have access to and configure a TACACS+ server before the configured TACACS+ features on your network access server are available. TACACS+ provides for separate and modular AAA facilities. TACACS+ allows for a single-access control server (the TACACS+ daemon) to provide each service—AAA—independently. You can tie each service into its own database to take advantage of other services available on that server or on the network, depending on the capabilities of the daemon.

TACACS+ has three major components:

- Protocol support within the access servers and routers

- Protocol specification
- Centralized security database

Similar to an internal security database, TACACS+ supports these features:

- **Authentication**—The TACACS+ protocol forwards many types of username and password information. This information is encrypted over the network with MD5, an encryption algorithm. TACACS+ can forward the password types for AppleTalk Remote Access (ARA), Serial Line Internet Protocol (SLIP), PAP, CHAP, and standard Telnet. This allows clients to use the same username and password for different protocols. TACACS+ is extensible to support new password types.

- **Authorization**—TACACS+ provides a mechanism to tell an access server which access list that a user connected to a port uses. The TACACS+ server and location of the username and password information identify the access list through which the user is filtered. The access list resides on the access server. The TACACS+ server responds to a username with an Accept and an access list number that causes that list to be applied.

- **Accounting**—TACACS+ provides accounting information to a database via TCP to ensure a more secure and complete accounting log. The accounting portion of the TACACS+ protocol contains the network address of the user, username, service attempted, protocol used, time and date, and packet-filter module originating the log. For Telnet connections, it also contains source and destination port, action carried (communication accepted, rejected), log, and alert type. Formats are open and configurable. The billing information includes connect time, user ID, location connected from, start time, and stop time. It identifies the protocol that the user is using and might contain commands being run if the users are connected through EXEC and Telnet.

Kerberos

Kerberos is a secret-key network authentication protocol, developed at MIT, which uses the DES cryptographic algorithm for encryption and authentication. Kerberos was designed to authenticate requests for network resources. Kerberos, like other secret-key systems, is based on the concept of a trusted third party that performs secure verification of users and services. In the Kerberos protocol, this trusted third party is called the key distribution center (KDC).

The primary use of Kerberos is to verify that users and the network services they use are really who and what they claim to be. To accomplish this, a trusted Kerberos server issues tickets to users. These tickets, which have a limited lifespan, are stored in a user's credential cache. You can use the tickets in place of the standard username and password authentication mechanism.

Each of its clients trusts the Kerberos servers' judgment as to the identity of each of its other clients. Timestamps (large numbers representing the current date and time) have been added to the original model to aid in the detection of replay, which occurs when a message is stolen off the network and resent later.

Kerberos uses private key encryption. Each Kerberos database entry is assigned a large number, its private key, known only to that user and Kerberos. In the case of a user, the private key is the result of a one-way function applied to the user's password.

Because the Kerberos server knows these private keys, it can create messages that convince one client that another is really who it claims to be. The Kerberos server also generates temporary private keys, called session keys, which are given to two clients and no one else. A user or application can use a session key to encrypt messages between two parties.

Public Key Infrastructure

A public key infrastructure (PKI) is a management system designed to administer asymmetrical cryptographic keys and public key certificates. It acts as a trusted component that guarantees the authenticity of the binding between a public key and security information, including identity, involved in securing a transaction with public key cryptography.

NOTE   Symmetrical key systems, also known as secret keying, is an encryption methodology that requires both communicating parties to use the same (shared) key to perform the encryption and decryption process.

Asymmetric key systems, also known as private/public keying, use a technique where an entity that wishes to communicate via secure (encrypted) means generates a key pair. The key pair contains a public and private key. The public key is distributed to a key server. The private key is retained by the generating host. Any system that wishes to secure their communications to the owner of the key pair uses the public key to encrypt the data. The recipient uses his private key to decrypt.

Authenticity of the public key might be an issue. To guarantee that the public key is from whom it purports to be, you can use a digital certificate issued from a certification authority (CA).

A certificate is a cryptographically signed structure, called the digital certificate, which guarantees the association between at least one identifier and a public key. It is valid for a limited period of time (called the validity period), for a specific usage, and under certain conditions and limitations described in a certificate policy. The authority that issues this certificate is called the CA.

The initialization process consists of setting the necessary configuration for a PKI entity to communicate with other PKI entities. For example, the initialization of an end entity involves providing it with the public key certificate of a trusted CA. The initialization of a CA involves the generation of its key pair.

During the registration process, an end entity makes itself known to a CA through a registration authority, before that CA issues a certificate. The end entity provides its name and other attributes to be included in its public key certificate, and the CA (or the registration authority [RA], or both) verifies the correctness of the provided information.

The key pair generation for an end entity might either take place in its own environment or is done by the CA (or RA). If the key pair is not generated by the end entity itself, the generated private key must be distributed to the end entity in a secure way (for example, through a secure key distribution protocol, or by using a physical token such as a smart card).

The certification process takes place at the CA. The CA verifies the correctness of the end entity's name and attributes and ensures that the end entity possesses the corresponding private key. If these conditions are met, the CA issues a certificate for the end entity's public key. That certificate is then returned to the end entity and/or posted in a repository where it is publicly available.

IP Security

IP Security (IPSec) provides security for transmission of sensitive information over unprotected networks, such as the Internet. IPSec, as shown in Figure 6-11, acts at the network layer, protecting and authenticating IP packets between participating IPSec devices. This section describes the functionality of IPSec.

Figure 6-11 *IPSec*

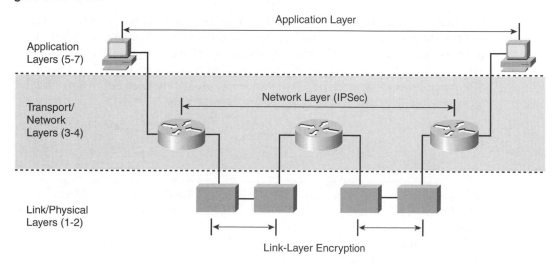

IPSec is a framework of open standards developed by the Internet Engineering Task Force (IETF). IPSec provides security for transmission of sensitive information over unprotected networks such as the Internet. IPSec acts at the network layer, protecting and authenticating IP packets between participating IPSec devices (peers), such as routers.

IPSec provides these optional network security services, dictated by local security policy:

- **Data confidentiality**—The IPSec sender can encrypt packets before transmitting them across a network.

- **Data integrity**—The IPSec receiver can authenticate packets sent by the IPSec sender to ensure that the data has not been altered during transmission.

- **Data origin authentication**—The IPSec receiver can authenticate the source of the IPSec packets sent. This service is dependent upon the data integrity service.

- **Antireplay**—The IPSec receiver can detect and reject replayed packets.

IPSec offers a standard way of establishing authentication and encryption services between endpoints. This means not only standard algorithms and transforms, but also standard key negotiation and management mechanisms. Using the Internet Security Association and Key Management Protocol (ISAKMP) and Oakley to promote interoperability between devices, IPSec allows for the negotiation of services between endpoints.

NOTE   An IPSec transform is used to define which IPSec protocol (either Authentication Header or Encapsulating Security Payload) is to be used along with the associated security algorithms (DES, 3DES, AES, HMAC) and mode (transport or tunnel).

Negotiation refers to the establishment of policies or security associations (SAs) between devices. An SA is a policy rule that maps to a specific peer, with each rule identified by a unique security parameter index (SPI). A device might have many SAs stored in its security association database, created in dynamic random-access memory (DRAM) and indexed by SPI. As an IPSec datagram arrives, the device will use the enclosed SPI to reference the appropriate policy that needs to be applied to the datagram.

SAs are negotiated for both Internet Key Exchange (IKE) and IPSec, and it is IKE itself that facilitates this SA establishment.

NOTE   An SA is a record of the security policy that was negotiated between two devices. It is stored by each peer (one SA per direction) in a database that references the SA entries using a value called the security parameter index (SPI). All IPSec packets carry the SPI value, which is used by the receiving device to look up the correct SA. The SA contains the Security Policy, which defines how to process the packet.

Internet Key Exchange

Internet Key Exchange (IKE) is a form of ISAKMP/Oakley specifically for IPSec:

- ISAKMP describes the phase of negotiation.

- Oakley defines the method to establish an authenticated key exchange. This method might take various modes of operation and is also used to derive keying material via algorithms, such as Diffie-Hellman.

Figure 6-12 shows how IKE derives a symmetric, data encryption session key using the Diffie-Hellman Key Exchange Protocol by using public and private key pairs. The figure also shows an example of how IKE negotiates session-specific IKE and IPSec protocol usage.

Figure 6-12 *Internet Key Exchange*

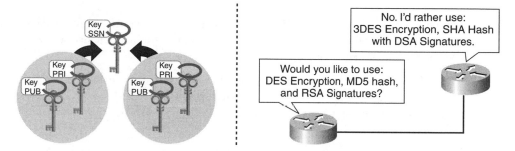

ISAKMP Phase 1, also known as IKE Phase 1, is used when two peers establish a secure, authenticated channel with which to communicate. Oakley main mode is generally used here. The result of main mode is the authenticated bidirectional IKE security association and its keying material.

NOTE   IKE Phase 1 is used to authenticate the IPSec peers, negotiate an IKE SA policy, exchange a shared secret key using Diffie-Hellman, and set up a secure tunnel over which to negotiate IKE Phase 2 using the shared secret key.

IKE Phase 2 is used to set up IPSec SAs, which, in turn, are required to set up the IPSec tunnel. The IPSec tunnel, or VPN, is then used to exchange user data between participating parties.

ISAKMP Phase 2 is required to establish SAs on behalf of other services, such as IPSec, which needs key material or parameter negotiation and uses Oakley quick mode. The result of quick mode is two to four (depending on whether Authentication Header [AH] or Encapsulating Security Payload [ESP] is used) unidirectional IPSec security associations and their keying material.

Authentication Header

The Authentication Header (AH), pictured in Figure 6-13, is a mechanism for providing strong integrity and authentication for IP datagrams. It might also provide nonrepudiation, depending on which cryptographic algorithm is used and how keying is performed. When using AH, the data is not encrypted.

Figure 6-13 *Authentication Header*

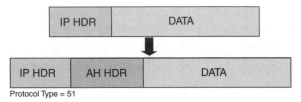

In tunnel-mode AH, the original IP datagram is placed behind the AH within the datagram. In transport-mode AH, the AH is inserted into the IP datagram immediately before the transport-layer protocol header, such as TCP, UDP, or ICMP.

The AH might appear after any other headers that are examined at each hop, and before any other headers that are not examined at an intermediate hop. The IPv4 or IPv6 header immediately preceding the AH will contain the value 51 in its Next Header (or Protocol) field.

Using AH is resource-intensive in terms of bandwidth and the networking device.

Encapsulating Security Payload

The ESP might appear anywhere after the IP header and before the final transport-layer protocol. The Internet Assigned Numbers Authority (IANA) has assigned protocol number 50 to ESP. The IP ESP seeks to provide confidentiality and integrity by encrypting data to be protected and placing the encrypted data in the data portion of the IP ESP.

In tunnel-mode ESP, shown in Figure 6-14, the original IP datagram is placed in the encrypted portion of the ESP and the entire ESP frame is placed within a datagram having unencrypted IP headers.

Figure 6-14 *Encapsulating Security Payload*

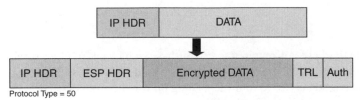

The information in the unencrypted IP headers is used to route the secure datagram from origin to destination. In transport-mode ESP, the ESP header is inserted into the IP datagram immediately before the transport-layer protocol header, such as TCP, UDP, or ICMP. In this mode, bandwidth is conserved because no encrypted IP headers or IP options exist.

Using ESP is resource intensive in terms of bandwidth and the networking device.

Device Security Options

To secure a network, the individual components that make up the network must be secure. You can take actions to ensure security specific to the following:

- Routers
- Switches
- Hosts
- Network as a whole
- Applications

This section describes security options for the specific components of a network.

Routers

Routers, like the one pictured in Figure 6-15, control access from network to network. They advertise networks and filter traffic, and they are a huge potential threat for a hacker. Router security is a critical element in any security deployment. By their nature, routers provide access and, therefore, you should secure them to reduce the likelihood that they will be directly compromised.

Figure 6-15 *Router as a Security Device*

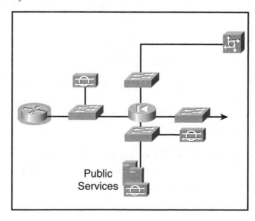

You can complete several tasks to secure a router:

- Restrict Telnet access.
- Lock down SNMP access.
- Control administrative access through the use of TACACS+.
- Turn off unneeded services.
- Log at appropriate levels.
- Authenticate routing updates.
- Deploy secure commands and control.

NOTE   For more information on securing Cisco routers, read the Cisco white paper, "Improving Security on Cisco Routers" (http://cisco.com/warp/public/707/21.html).

Switches

Data link layer and multilayer switches, shown in Figure 6-16, have their own set of security considerations.

Figure 6-16 *Switches as Security Devices*

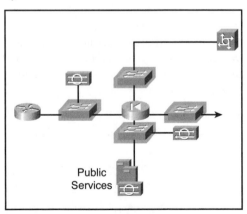

Public
Services

Most of the security techniques that apply to routers also apply to switches. In addition, consider taking these precautions:

- **Use the same options as for routers**—For example, lock down Telnet and SNMP access, use TACACS+, turn off unneeded services, log at appropriate levels, and deploy secure commands and control.

- **Remove user ports from auto-trunking**—For ports without any need to trunk, set any trunk settings to off, as opposed to auto. This setup prevents a host from becoming a trunk port and receiving all traffic that would normally reside on a trunk port.

- **Keep all trunk ports in an unused LAN**—If you are using older versions of software for your Ethernet switch, make sure that trunk ports use a virtual LAN (VLAN) number not used anywhere else in the switch. This setup prevents packets tagged with the same VLAN as the trunk port from reaching another VLAN without crossing a Layer 3 device.

- **Disable all unused ports on a switch**—This setup prevents hackers from plugging in to unused ports and communicating with the rest of the network.

- **Ensure VLAN separation where appropriate**—Avoid using VLANs as the sole method of securing access between two subnets. The capability for human error, combined with the understanding that VLANs and VLAN tagging protocols are not designed with security in mind, makes their use in sensitive environments inadvisable. When VLANs are needed in security deployments, pay close attention to the security configurations and guidelines. Within an existing VLAN, private VLANs provide some added security to specific network applications.

NOTE   Private VLANs allow you to control the flow of traffic between ports that coexist within the same VLAN. Ports can be limited to only receiving and transmitting data to devices outside of their VLAN, and/or restricted to communicating with specified members of their shared VLAN. This can greatly mitigate the threat of trust exploitation within the DMZ. You can set up the private VLAN so that bastion hosts can receive all traffic to them, send traffic from their VLAN, but be denied the capability of sending traffic to other members of the same VLAN. If one bastion host is compromised, the attacker is prevented from using it as a launching point to compromise other DMZ bastion hosts.

For more information on securing Cisco switches, read the Cisco presentation, "Securing the LAN with Cisco Catalyst Switches" (http://cisco.com/go/switching).

Hosts

Because hosts, as shown in Figure 6-17, are the most likely target during an attack, they present some of the most difficult challenges from a security perspective. There are numerous hardware platforms, operating systems, and applications, all of which have updates, patches, and fixes available at different times. Because hosts provide the application services to other hosts that request them, they are extremely visible within the network. Because of the visibility, hosts are the most frequently attacked devices in any network intrusion attempt.

Figure 6-17 *Hosts as Security Devices*

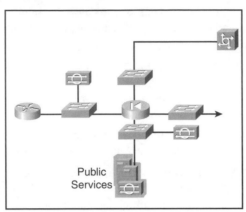

To secure hosts, pay careful attention to each of the components within the systems. Keep any systems up to date with the latest patches and fixes. Pay attention to how these patches affect the operation of other system components. Evaluate all updates on test systems before you implement them in a production environment. Failure to do so might result in the patch itself causing a DoS.

Network-Wide

Network attacks are among the most difficult attacks to deal with because they typically take advantage of an intrinsic characteristic in the way your network operates. These attacks include Address Resolution Protocol (ARP) and Media Access Control (MAC)-based Layer 2 attacks, sniffers, and DDoS attacks. You can mitigate some of the ARP and MAC-based Layer 2 attacks through best practices on switches and routers.

DDoS attacks work by causing tens or hundreds of machines to simultaneously send spurious data to an IP address. Only through cooperation with its ISP can a company hope to thwart such an attack. An ISP can configure rate limiting on the outbound interface to the company's site. This rate limiting can drop most undesired traffic when it exceeds a prespecified amount of the available bandwidth. The key is to correctly flag traffic as undesired.

Common forms of DDoS attacks are ICMP floods, TCP SYN floods, or UDP floods. In an e-commerce environment, this type of traffic is fairly easy to categorize. Only when limiting a TCP SYN attack on port 80 (HTTP) does an administrator run the risk of locking out legitimate users during an attack. Even then, it is better to temporarily lock out new legitimate users and retain routing and management connections than to have the router overrun and lose all connectivity. One approach to limiting this sort of attack is to follow filtering guidelines for networks outlined in RFC 1918 and RFC 2827.

NOTE   DDoS can be a very effective tool when launched from multiple machines spread across the Internet. Often spread through file-sharing applications and e-mail, a worm can infect the host machine and then launches a DDoS against a select target(s) at a preconfigured date and time. Using the Internet to populate and recruit drones allows a DDoS to quickly increase its volume and effectiveness. Attempting to thwart such an attack becomes very difficult.

In a DoS/DDoS based scenario, ISPs can implement rate-limiting features at the gateway routers to reduce the flow of specified traffic. Using NetFlow or IDS-based systems, sources can be identified and shunned at the firewall or blocked using ACLs at perimeter routers. Switches can attempt to mitigate the effect of such traffic using storm control features that shut down the switch port when a specified level of traffic flow is reached.

If the attacker is from a remote network not associated with the ISP, pursuing and stopping the attack can be a long and difficult process. ISPs that have identified infected hosts can contact the owner and inform them of the situation. Customers are typically asked to patch and clean their systems. If this process is not done, acceptable usage policies come into play and the ISP may deny access to the offending customer.

Applications

Applications are coded by human beings and, as such, are subject to numerous errors. These errors can be benign, such as an error that causes your document to print incorrectly, or malignant, such as an error that makes the credit card numbers on your database server available via anonymous FTP.

Care needs to be taken to ensure that commercial and public-domain applications are up to date with the latest security fixes. Public domain applications, as well as custom-developed applications, also require code review to ensure that the applications are not introducing any security risks caused by poor programming. This programming can include scenarios such as how an application makes calls to other applications or the operating system itself, the privilege level at which the application runs, the degree of trust that the application has for the surrounding systems, and finally, the method the application uses to transport data across the network.

Implementing Network Security Using the Cisco SAFE Security Blueprints

The Security Architecture for Enterprise (SAFE) blueprints are frameworks for security and are based on the Cisco AVVID.

SAFE serves as a guide for network designers considering the security requirements of their networks. It takes a defense-in-depth approach to network security design. This type of design focuses on the expected threats and their methods of mitigation based on the best practices that Cisco has developed. The SAFE strategy results in a layered approach to security where the failure of one security system is not likely to lead to the compromise of network resources.

NOTE   The guidelines in this section do not guarantee a secure environment, or that a designer will prevent all intrusions. However, designers will achieve reasonable security by establishing a good security policy, following the best practices outlined here, staying up to date on the latest developments in the hacker and security communities, and maintaining and monitoring all systems using sound system administration practices.

This section covers the following topics:

- Introduction to Cisco SAFE architecture
- SAFE security strategies for small networks
- SAFE security strategies for medium networks
- SAFE security strategies for large networks
- SAFE security strategies for the enterprise edge

Introduction to Cisco SAFE Architecture

The principal goal of the Cisco secure blueprint for enterprise networks (SAFE) is to provide best practice information to interested parties on designing and implementing secure networks. SAFE serves as a guide to network designers considering the security requirements of their network. This section describes the Cisco SAFE architecture and its design objectives.

SAFE emulates as closely as possible the functional requirements of today's networks. Implementation decisions vary, depending on the network functionality required. However, these design objectives, listed in order of priority, guide the decision-making process:

- Security and attack mitigation based on policy
- Security implementation through the infrastructure (not just on specialized security devices)
- Secure management and reporting
- Authentication and authorization of users and administrators to critical network resources
- Intrusion detection for critical resources and subnets

First and foremost, SAFE is a security architecture. It must prevent most attacks from successfully affecting valuable network resources. The attacks that succeed in penetrating the first line of defense, or originate from inside the network, must be accurately detected and quickly contained to minimize their effect on the rest of the network. However, in being secure, the network must continue to provide critical services that users expect. Proper network security and good network functionality can be provided at the same time. The SAFE architecture is not a revolutionary way of designing networks, but merely a blueprint for making networks secure.

SAFE is resilient and scalable. Resilience in networks includes physical redundancy to protect against a device failure, whether through misconfiguration, physical failure, or network attack. The SAFE architecture for small, midsize, and remote networks was designed without resiliency, because of the cost-effectiveness and limited complexity of smaller designs.

At many points in the network design process, you need to choose between using integrated functionality in a network device and using a specialized functional appliance. The integrated functionality is often attractive because you can implement it on existing equipment, and because the features can interoperate with the rest of the device to provide a better functional solution.

Appliances are often used when the depth of functionality required is very advanced or when performance needs require using specialized hardware. Make your decisions based on the capacity and functionality of the appliance rather than on the integration advantage of the device. For example, sometimes you can choose an integrated higher-capacity Cisco IOS router with IOS firewall software as opposed to a smaller IOS router with a separate firewall. When design requirements do not dictate a specific choice, you should choose to go with integrated functionality to reduce the overall cost of the solution.

Although most networks evolve with the growing IT requirements of an organization, the SAFE architecture uses a modular approach. A modular approach has two main advantages:

- It allows the architecture to address the security relationship between the various functional blocks of the network.
- It permits designers to evaluate and implement security on a module-by-module basis, instead of attempting the complete architecture in a single phase. The security design of each module is described separately, but is validated as part of the complete design.

Although it is true that most networks cannot be easily dissected into clear-cut modules, this approach provides a guide for implementing different security functions throughout the network. The authors of the SAFE blueprint do not expect network engineers to design their networks identical to the SAFE implementation, but rather to use a combination of the modules described and integrate them into the existing network.

SAFE Security Strategies for Small Networks

The SAFE design for a small network includes only an Internet Connectivity module that provides access to the external network, and the Campus Infrastructure module containing the internal network. This section describes the Cisco SAFE architecture and security strategies for a small network.

The small network design shown in Figure 6-18 has two modules:

- **Internet Connectivity module**—Has connections to the Internet and terminates VPN and public services (DNS, HTTP, FTP, SMTP) traffic.

- **Campus Infrastructure module**—Contains Layer 2 switching and all the users, as well as the management and intranet servers.

Figure 6-18 *SAFE Design for Small Networks*

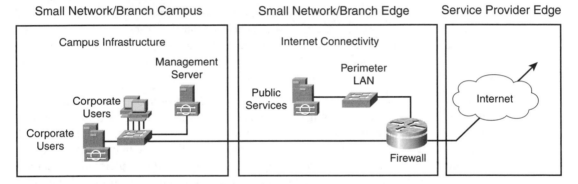

Small Network Internet Connectivity Module

The Internet Connectivity module, shown in Figure 6-19, provides internal users with connectivity to Internet services and Internet users access to information on public servers. This module is not designed to serve e-commerce type applications.

Figure 6-19 *Components of the Small Network Internet Connectivity Module*

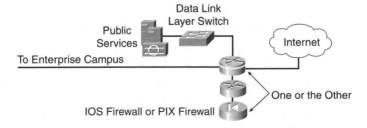

The primary devices included in this module are

- **SMTP server**—Acts as a relay between the Internet and the intranet mail servers
- **DNS server**—Serves as authoritative external DNS server for the enterprise; relays internal DNS requests to the Internet
- **FTP/HTTP server**—Provides public information about the organization
- **Firewall or firewall router**—Provides network-level protection of resources, stateful filtering of traffic, and VPN termination for remote sites and users
- **Layer 2 switch (with private VLAN support)**—Ensures that data from managed devices can only cross directly to the IOS firewall
- **HIDS**—Provides host-level intrusion detection

The Internet Connectivity module includes publicly addressable servers that are the most likely points of attack. The expected threats to this module and the security features used to mitigate their effect are

- **Unauthorized access**—Mitigated through filtering at the firewall.
- **Application-layer attacks**—Mitigated through HIDS on the public servers.
- **Virus and Trojan horse attacks**—Mitigated through virus scanning at the host level.
- **Password attacks**—Limited services available to brute-force attack; operating systems and IDSs can detect the threat.
- **DoS**—Committed access rate (CAR) at ISP edge. CAR allows the ISP to limit the amount of traffic through a router interface using packet rate-limiting controls and access lists. TCP setup controls at the firewall, such as syn cookies and TCP intercept, restrict and reduce the number of half-open TCP connections that can be established through the firewall limiting exposure.
- **IP spoofing**—RFC 2827 and 1918 filtering at ISP edge and local firewall.
- **Packet sniffers**—Switched infrastructure and host IDS to limit exposure.
- **Network reconnaissance**—HIDS detects reconnaissance; protocols filtered to limit effectiveness.
- **Trust exploitation**—Restrictive trust model and private VLANs to limit trust-based attacks.
- **Port redirection**—Restrictive filtering and host IDS to limit attack.

Small Network Campus Infrastructure Module

The Campus Infrastructure module contains end-user workstations, corporate intranet servers, management servers, and the associated Layer 2 infrastructure required to support the devices. Within the small network design, the Layer 2 functionality is combined into a single switch.

Figure 6-20 shows these key devices for the Campus Infrastructure module:

- **Layer 2 switching (with private VLAN support)**—Provides Layer 2 services to user workstations

- **Corporate servers**—Provides e-mail (SMTP and POP3) services to internal users, as well as delivering file, print, and DNS services to workstations

- **User workstations**—Provide data services to authorized users on the network

- **Management host**—Provides HIDS, Syslog, TACACS+/RADIUS, and general configuration management

Figure 6-20 *Small Network Campus Infrastructure Module Components*

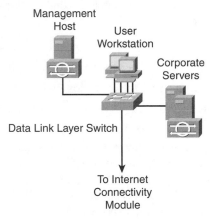

Figure 6-21 shows the expected threats for the Campus Infrastructure module and the associated mitigating factors, which are as follows:

- **Packet sniffers**—A switched infrastructure limits the effectiveness of sniffing.

- **Virus and Trojan horse applications**—Host-based virus scanning prevents most viruses and many Trojan horses.

- **Unauthorized access**—This type of access is mitigated through the use of host-based intrusion detection and application access control.

- **Application-layer attacks**—Operating systems, devices, and applications are kept up to date with the latest security fixes, and are protected by HIDS.

- **Trust exploitation**—Private VLANs prevent hosts on the same subnet from communicating unless necessary.

- **Port redirection**—HIDS prevents port redirection agents from being installed.

Figure 6-21 *Small Network Attack Mitigation Roles for Campus Infrastructure Module*

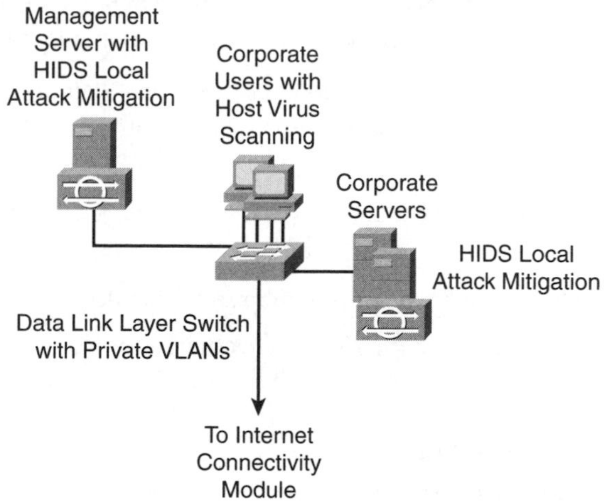

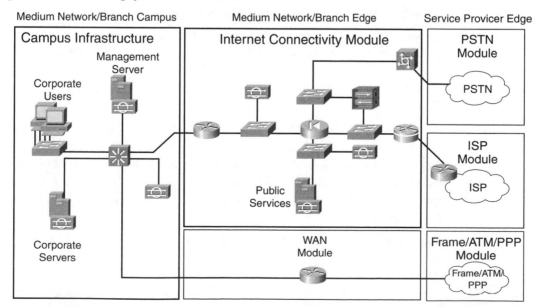

SAFE Security Strategies for Medium Networks

The SAFE medium network design consists of the following modules (see Figure 6-22):

- Internet Connectivity module
- Campus Infrastructure module
- WAN module

This section describes the SAFE architecture and security strategies for a medium network.

Figure 6-22 *SAFE Design for Medium Networks*

As in the small network design, the Internet Connectivity module has the connection to the Internet and terminates VPNs and public services (DNS, HTTP, FTP, and SMTP) traffic. Dial-in traffic also terminates at the Internet Connectivity module.

The Campus Infrastructure module contains the Layer 2 and Layer 3 switching infrastructure along with all the corporate users, management servers, and intranet servers.

From a WAN perspective, two options exist for remote sites connecting into the medium design:

- A private WAN connection using the WAN module
- An IPSec VPN into the Internet Connectivity module

Medium Network Internet Connectivity

The goal of the Internet Connectivity module is to provide internal users with connectivity to Internet services and Internet users access to information on the public servers (HTTP, FTP, SMTP, and DNS). Additionally, this module terminates VPN traffic from remote users and remote sites as well as traffic from traditional dial-in users. (The Internet Connectivity module is not designed to serve e-commerce type applications.)

The Internet Connectivity module shown in Figure 6-23 contains these devices:

- **Dial-in server**—Authenticates individual remote users and terminates analog connections
- **DNS server**—Serves as authoritative external DNS server for the medium network; relays internal DNS requests to the Internet
- **FTP/HTTP server**—Provides public information about the organization
- **Firewall**—Provides network-level protection of resources and stateful filtering of traffic; provides differentiated security for remote access users; authenticates trusted remote sites and provides connectivity using IPSec tunnels
- **Layer 2 switches (with private VLAN support)**—Provides Layer 2 connectivity for devices
- **NIDS appliance**—Provides Layer 4 to Layer 7 monitoring of key network segments in the module
- **SMTP server**—Acts as a relay between the Internet and the intranet mail servers; inspects content
- **VPN concentrator**—Authenticates individual remote users and terminates their IPSec tunnels
- **Edge router**—Provides basic filtering and Layer 3 connectivity to the Internet

Figure 6-23 *Medium Network Internet Connectivity Module*

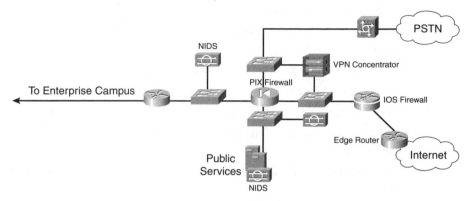

The publicly addressable servers are likely points of attack within the Internet Connectivity module. The expected threats and the security features used to address them are shown in Figure 6-24 and are described in the list that follows.

Figure 6-24 *Medium Network Attack Mitigation Roles for the Internet Connectivity Module*

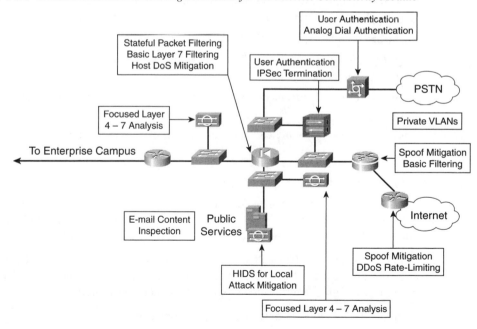

- **Unauthorized access**—Mitigated through filtering at the ISP, edge router, and corporate firewall
- **Application-layer attacks**—Mitigated through IDS at the host and network levels

- **Virus and Trojan horse attacks**—Mitigated through e-mail content filtering, HIDS, and host-based virus scanning
- **Password attacks**—Limited services available to brute-force attack; OS and IDS can detect the threat
- **DoS**—CAR at ISP edge and TCP setup controls at firewall
- **IP spoofing**—RFC 2827 and 1918 filtering at ISP edge and medium network edge router
- **Packet sniffers**—Switched infrastructure and host IDS to limit exposure
- **Network reconnaissance**—IDS detects reconnaissance, protocols filtered to limit effectiveness
- **Trust exploitation**—Restrictive trust model and private VLANs to limit trust-based attacks
- **Port redirection**—Restrictive filtering and host IDS to limit attacks

The remote access and site-to-site VPN services are also points of attack. Expected threats in these areas are

- **Network topology discovery**—ACLs on the ingress router limit access to the VPN concentrator and firewall (when used to terminate IPSec tunnels from remote sites) to IKE and ESP from the Internet.
- **Password attack**—OTPs mitigate brute-force password attacks.
- **Unauthorized access**—Firewall services after packet decryption prevent traffic on unauthorized ports.
- **Man-in-the-middle attacks**—These attacks are mitigated through encrypted remote traffic.
- **Packet sniffers**—A switched infrastructure limits the effectiveness of sniffing.

Medium Network Campus Infrastructure Module

The Campus Infrastructure module shown in Figure 6-25 contains end-user workstations, corporate intranet servers, management servers, and the associated Layer 2 and Layer 3 infrastructure required to support the devices.

This configuration reflects the smaller size of medium networks, and reduces the overall cost of the design. As in the Internet Connectivity module, the redundancy normally found in an enterprise design is not reflected in the medium network design.

The Campus Infrastructure module includes these devices:

- **Layer 3 switch**—Routes and switches production and management traffic within the Campus module, provides distribution-layer services to the building switches, and supports advanced services, such as traffic filtering
- **Layer 2 switches (with private VLAN support)**—Provides Layer 2 services to user workstations

- **Corporate servers**—Provides e-mail (SMTP and POP3) services to internal users, as well as delivering file, print, and DNS services to workstations
- **User workstations**—Provides data services to authorized users on the network
- **SNMP management host**—Provides SNMP management for devices
- **NIDS host**—Provides alarm aggregation for all NIDS devices in the network
- **Syslog host**—Aggregates log information for firewall and NIDS hosts
- **Access control server**—Delivers authentication services to the network devices
- **OTP server**—Authorizes one-time password information relayed from the access control server
- **System admin host**—Provides configuration, software, and content changes on devices
- **NIDS appliance**—Provides Layer 4 to Layer 7 monitoring of key network segments in the module

Figure 6-25 *Components of the Medium Network Campus Infrastructure Module*

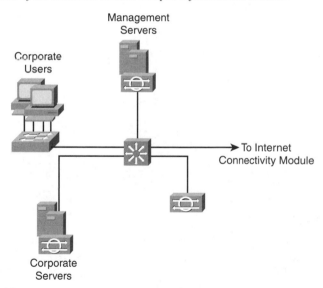

Figure 6-26 and the list that follows illustrate the expected threats for the Campus Infrastructure module and their solutions.

- **Packet sniffers**—A switched infrastructure limits the effectiveness of sniffing.
- **Virus and Trojan horse applications**—Host-based virus scanning prevents most viruses and many Trojan horses.
- **Unauthorized access**—These types of attacks are mitigated through the use of host-based intrusion detection and application access control.
- **Password attacks**—The access control server allows for strong authentication for key applications.

- **Application-layer attacks**—Operating systems, devices, and applications are kept up to date with the latest security fixes, and they are protected by HIDS.

- **IP spoofing**—RFC 2827 filtering prevents source-address spoofing.

- **Trust exploitation**—Trust arrangements are very explicit; private VLANs prevent hosts on the same subnet from communicating unless necessary.

- **Port redirection**—HIDS prevents port redirection agents from being installed.

Figure 6-26 *Medium Network Attack Mitigation Roles for the Campus Infrastructure*

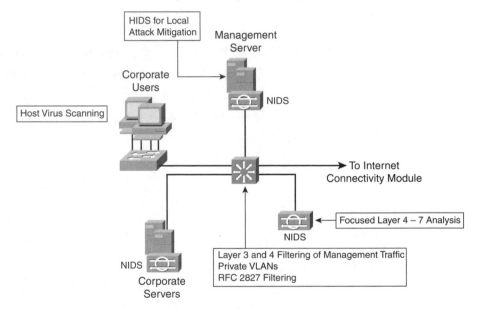

Medium Network WAN Module

The WAN module shown in Figure 6-27 is included in the medium network only when connections to remote locations over a private network are required. This requirement might occur when an IPSec VPN cannot meet stringent quality of service (QoS) requirements, or when legacy WAN connections are in place without a compelling cost justification to migrate to IPSec.

Figure 6-27 *Medium Network WAN Module*

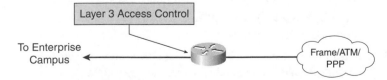

The key device for this module is a Cisco router, which provides routing, access control, and QoS mechanisms to remote locations.

The threats mitigated by the IOS router include

- **IP spoofing**—IP spoofing can be mitigated through Layer 3 filtering.
- **Unauthorized access**—Simple access control on the router can limit the types of protocols, applications, networks, and devices to which branches have access.

SAFE Security Strategies for Large Networks

The SAFE large network design consists of the entire Enterprise Campus functional area. This section describes the SAFE architecture and security strategies for a large network.

Campus Infrastructure Module

Figure 6-28 illustrates the modules of the Enterprise Campus functional area. Security considerations for each module differ based on the function of the module.

Figure 6-28 *SAFE Security Modules for the Enterprise Campus*

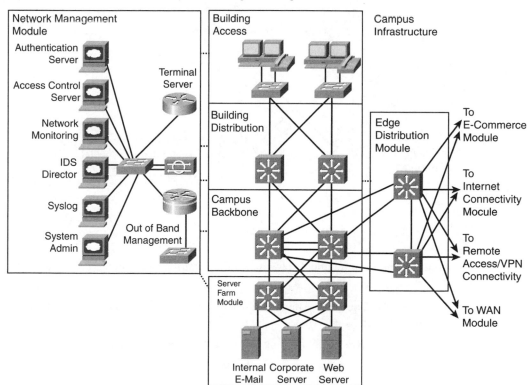

The Campus Infrastructure module is composed of three submodules:

- Campus Backbone
- Building Distribution
- Building Access

As shown in Figure 6-28, Layer 3 switches are used to route and switch production network data from one module to another. By using a switched Campus Backbone, the effectiveness of packet sniffers is limited.

The goal of the Building Distribution submodule shown in Figure 6-29 is to provide distribution-layer services to the building access layer. Services include routing, QoS, and access control. Requests for data flow into these switches and onto the core, and responses follow the identical path in reverse.

Figure 6-29 *Secure Building Distribution and Access Submodules*

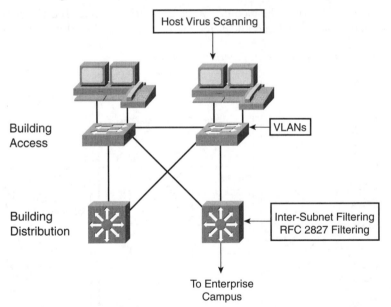

The security features implemented by the building distribution switches help mitigate these attacks:

- **Unauthorized access**—Attacks against resources are limited by Layer 3 filtering of specific subnets.
- **IP spoofing**—RFC 2827 filtering stops most spoofing attempts.
- **Packet sniffers**—A switched infrastructure limits the effectiveness of sniffing.

SAFE defines the Building Access submodule shown in Figure 6-29 as the extensive network portion that contains end-user workstations, phones, and their associated Layer 2 access points. Its primary goal is to provide services to end users.

The security strategy implemented at the Building Access submodule addresses these types of attacks:

- **Packet sniffers**—A switched infrastructure and default VLAN services limit the effectiveness of sniffing.

- **Virus and Trojan horse applications**—Host-based virus scanning prevents most viruses and many Trojan horses.

Secure Network Management Module

The primary goal of the Network Management module (see Figure 6-30) is to facilitate the secure management of all devices and hosts within the enterprise SAFE architecture. Logging and reporting information flows from the devices through to the management hosts, while content, configurations, and new software flow to the devices from the management hosts.

Figure 6-30 *Secure Network Management Module*

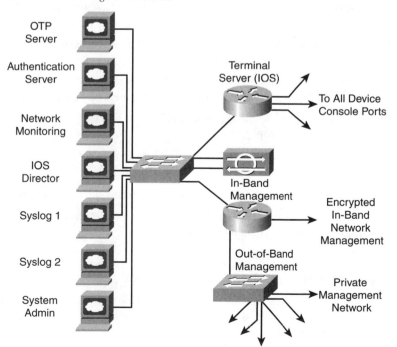

These primary devices are used in the Network Management module:

- **SNMP management host**—Provides SNMP management for devices
- **NIDS host**—Provides alarm aggregation for all NIDS devices in the network
- **Syslog hosts**—Aggregates log information for firewall and NIDS hosts
- **Access control server**—Delivers one-time, two-factor authentication services to the network devices
- **OTP server**—Authorizes one-time password information relayed from the access control server
- **System administration host**—Provides configuration, software, and content changes
- **NIDS appliance**—Provides Layer 4 to Layer 7 monitoring of key network segments
- **Cisco IOS firewall**—Allows granular control for traffic flows between the management hosts and the managed devices
- **Layer 2 switch (with private VLAN support)**—Ensures data from managed devices can only cross directly to the IOS firewall

The security features implemented in the Network Management module help mitigate the attacks in the list that follows:

- **Unauthorized access**—Filtering at the IOS firewall stops most unauthorized traffic in both directions.
- **Man-in-the-middle attacks**—Management data is crossing a private network making man-in-the-middle attacks difficult.
- **Network reconnaissance**—Because all management traffic crosses this network, it does not cross the production network where it could be intercepted.
- **Password attacks**—The access control server allows for strong two-factor authentication at each device.
- **IP spoofing**—Spoofed traffic is stopped in both directions at the IOS firewall through Layer 3 filtering.
- **Packet sniffers**—A switched infrastructure limits the effectiveness of sniffing.
- **Trust exploitation**—Private VLANs prevent a compromised device from masquerading as a management host.

Secure Server Farm Module

The Server Farm module's primary goal is to provide application services to end users and devices. On-board intrusion detection within the Layer 3 switches inspect traffic flows in the Server Farm module.

The security strategy shown in Figure 6-31 addresses the threats in the list that follows.

Figure 6-31 *Secure Server Farm Module Features*

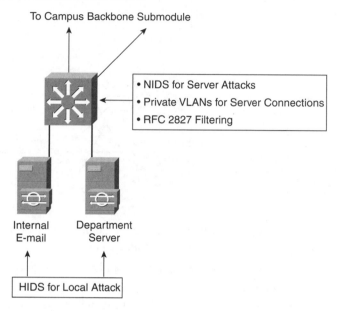

- **Unauthorized access**—Mitigated through the use of host-based intrusion detection and application access control.

- **Application-layer attacks**—Operating systems, devices, and applications are kept up to date with the latest security fixes and protected by host-based IDS.

- **IP spoofing**—RFC 2827 filtering prevents source address spoofing.

- **Packet sniffers**—A switched infrastructure limits the effectiveness of sniffing.

- **Trust exploitation**—Trust arrangements are very explicit; private VLANs prevent hosts on the same subnet from communicating unless necessary.

- **Port redirection**—Host-based IDS prevents port redirection agents from being installed.

Secure Edge Distribution Module

The Edge Distribution module aggregates the connectivity from the various elements at the edge. Traffic is filtered and routed from the edge modules and routed into the core.

The key devices in this module are Layer 3 switches used to aggregate edge connectivity and provide advanced services.

The security strategy illustrated in Figure 6-32 addresses the threats in the list that follows.

Figure 6-32 *Secure Edge Distribution Features*

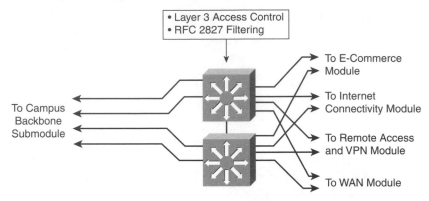

• **Unauthorized access**—Filtering provides granular control over specific edge subnets and their capability to reach areas within the campus.

• **IP spoofing**—RFC 2827 filtering limits locally initiated spoof attacks.

• **Network reconnaissance**—Filtering limits nonessential traffic from entering the campus, limiting a hacker's ability to perform network reconnaissance.

• **Packet sniffers**—A switched infrastructure limits the effectiveness of sniffing.

SAFE Security Strategies for the Enterprise Edge

The SAFE architecture, shown in Figure 6-33, defines the Enterprise Edge functional area as containing the Internet Connectivity module, E-Commerce module, Remote Access and VPN module, and the WAN module. This section describes a security strategy for the enterprise edge.

E-commerce Module

As illustrated in Figure 6-33, these key devices are deployed in the E-commerce module:

• **Web server**—Acts as the primary user interface for the navigation of the e-commerce store

• **Application server**—Platform for the various applications required by the web server

• **Database server**—Critical information that is the heart of the e-commerce business implementation

• **Firewall**—Governs communication between the various levels of security and trust in the system

• **NIDS appliance**—Provides monitoring of key network segments in the module

• **Layer 3 switch with IDS module**—The scalable e-commerce input device with integrated security monitoring

Figure 6-33 *SAFE Security Strategies for the Enterprise Edge*

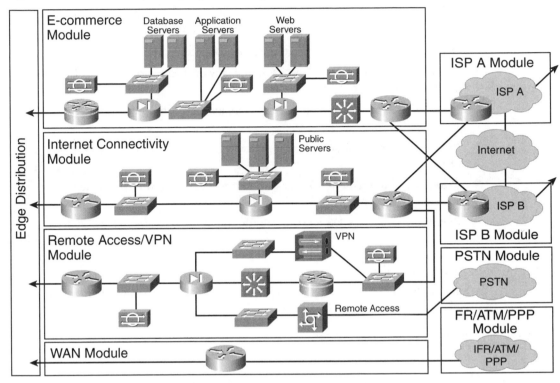

The security features illustrated in Figure 6-34 for the E-Commerce module mitigate the threats in the list that follows.

Figure 6-34 *E-commerce Module Security Features*

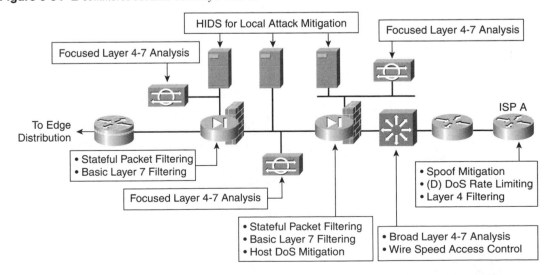

- **Unauthorized access**—Stateful firewalls and ACLs limit exposure to specific protocols.

- **Application-layer attacks**—Attacks are mitigated through the use of IDS.

- **DoS**—ISP filtering and rate limiting reduce DoS potential.

- **IP spoofing**—RFC 2827 and 1918 filtering prevent locally originated spoofed packets and limit remote spoof attempts

- **Packet sniffers**—A switched infrastructure and HIDS limit the effectiveness of sniffing.

- **Network reconnaissance**—Ports are limited to only what is necessary. ICMP is restricted.

- **Trust exploitation**—Firewalls ensure communication flows only in the proper direction on the proper service.

- **Port redirection**—HIDS and firewall filtering limit exposure to these attacks.

Internet Connectivity Module

The security features illustrated in Figure 6-35 for the Internet Connectivity module mitigate the threats in the list that follows.

Figure 6-35 *Internet Connectivity Module Security Features*

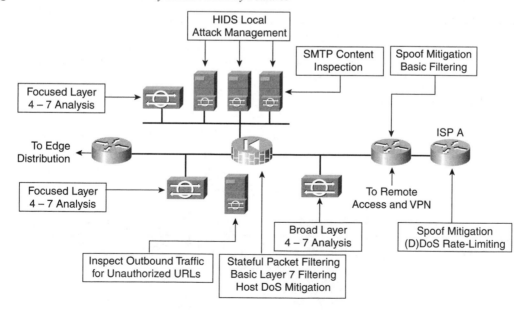

- **Unauthorized access**—Mitigated through filtering at the ISP, edge router, and corporate firewall.
- **Application-layer attacks**—Mitigated through IDS at the host and network levels.
- **Virus and Trojan horse**—Mitigated through e-mail content filtering and host IDS.
- **Password attacks**—Limited services available to brute-force attacks; operating systems and IDSs can detect the threat.
- **DoS**—Rate limiting at ISP edge and TCP setup controls at firewall.
- **IP spoofing**—RFC 2827 and 1918 filtering at ISP edge and enterprise-edge router.
- **Packet sniffers**—Switched infrastructure and host IDS limits exposure.
- **Network reconnaissance**—IDS detects reconnaissance; protocols filtered to limit effectiveness.
- **Trust exploitation**—Restrictive trust model and private VLANs limit trust-based attacks.
- **Port redirection**—Restrictive filtering and host IDS limit attacks.

Remote Access and VPN Module

The security features illustrated in Figure 6-36 for the Remote Access and VPN module mitigate the threats in the list that follows.

Figure 6-36 *Remote Access and VPN Module Security Features*

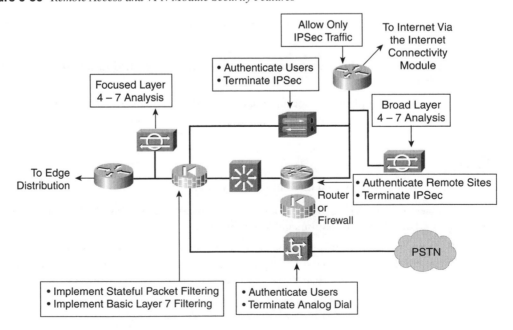

- **Network topology discovery**—Only IKE and ESP are allowed into this segment from the Internet.

- **Password attack**—OTP authentication reduces the likelihood of a successful password attack.

- **Unauthorized access**—Firewall services after packet decryption prevent traffic on unauthorized ports.

- **Man-in-the-middle**—Mitigated through encrypted remote traffic.

- **Packet sniffers**—A switched infrastructure limits the effectiveness of sniffing.

WAN Module Features

The WAN module shown in Figure 6-37 is often not addressed in a security context. You can mitigate man-in-the-middle attacks initiated through an ISP with the features in the list that follows.

Figure 6-37 *WAN Module Security Features*

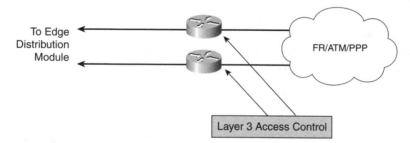

- **Access control**—Access control is required for Layer 3 and Layer 4 network functionality.

- **IPSec encryption**—IPSec encryption is needed if the level of trust for Layer 2 WAN technology is not high.

Summary

In this chapter, you learned the following key points:

- Networks are vulnerable to a variety of threats that can be classified as loss of privacy, data theft, impersonation, and loss of integrity.

- Network security efforts are based on a security policy. The policy should contain information about what is being protected, how users are identified and trusted, how the policy is to be enforced, the consequences of a violation, and the response to a violation.

- The ongoing steps of a security policy include securing the network, monitoring network security, testing security, and improving security.

- A risk assessment identifies risks to your network, network resources, and data. The risk assessment helps determine the validity of a network security implementation and should be performed periodically.

- An effective security solution includes secure connectivity, perimeter security, intrusion protection, identity, and security management.

- Attacks against network security come in many forms. Each has corresponding actions that you can take to prevent or mitigate the consequences of an attack.

- Dedicated firewalls provide perimeter security by preventing unauthorized access to the internal network. Identifying the type of traffic that is not allowed to pass the firewall and how such traffic will be prevented are the primary decisions about a firewall implementation.

- An IDS detects and responds to attacks. Host IDSs protect individual hosts, and network IDSs protect the overall network.

- AAA is a software mechanism that enhances network security by providing authentication services.

- IPSec provides security for transmission of sensitive information over unprotected networks such as the Internet. IPSec acts at the network layer, protecting and authenticating IP packets between participating IPSec devices.

- To secure a network, the individual components that make up the network must be secure. You can take actions to ensure security specific to routers, switches, hosts, applications, and the network as a whole.

- SAFE serves as a guide for network designers considering the security requirements of their network.

- The SAFE design for a small network includes only a Internet Connectivity module that provides access to the external network, and the Campus Infrastructure module containing the internal network.

- The SAFE medium network design consists of the Internet Connectivity module, the Campus Infrastructure module, and the WAN module.

- The SAFE large network design consists of the entire Enterprise Composite Network Model.

- The SAFE architecture defines the Enterprise Edge functional area as containing the Internet Connectivity, E-commerce, Remote Access and VPN, and WAN modules.

NOTE   Wireless technology is not covered in this chapter, but is a critical component of current Enterprise Networks. For information on securing your deployment of this technology, visit the Cisco SAFE website and read the white paper, "SAFE: Wireless LAN Security in Depth—version 2" (http://www.cisco.com/en/US/ netsol/ns340/ns394/ns171/ns128/networking_solutions_white_ paper09186a008009c8b3.shtml).

References

Network Security Policy: Best Practices White Paper at http://www.cisco.com/warp/public/126/secpol.html.

Network Security at http://www.cisco.com/warp/public/779/largeent/issues/security/.

Cisco SAFE Blueprint at http://www.cisco.com/warp/public/779/largeent/issues/security/safe.html.

http://www.securityfocus.com.

Cisco SAFE Homepage—http://www.cisco.com/go/safe/.

SAFE—Wireless LAN Security in Depth—version 2—http://www.cisco.com/en/US/netsol/ns340/ns394/ns171/ns128/networking_solutions_white_paper09186a008009c8b3.shtml.

Cisco Product Security Advisories and Notices at http://cisco.com/warp/public/707/advisory.html.

Nmap—http://www.insecure.org/nmap/.

Adaware—http://www.lavasoft.de/software/adaware/.

The Computer Emergency Response Team at http://www.cert.org/.

The Computer Security Resource Centre at http://csrc.ncsl.nist.gov/.

SANS (SysAdmin, Audit, Network, Security) Institute at http://www.sans.org/.

Centre for Internet Security at http://www.cisecurity.org.

National Security Agency—Security Recommendation Guides at http://nsa2.www.conxion.com/.

SNORT—http://www.snort.org/.

Ethereal—http://www.ethereal.com.

Product Summary

Table 6-3 provides a brief overview of some of the products available from Cisco Systems that relate to the technologies discussed in the preceding chapter. For a more detailed breakdown of Cisco's product line, please visit http://www.cisco.com/en/US/products/index.html.

Table 6-3   *Cisco Security Product*

Firewalls	PIX 535	Cleartext throughput: 1.7 Gbps
		Concurrent connections: 500,000
		168-bit 3DES IPSec VPN throughput: Up to 440 Mbps with VAC+ or 100 Mbps with VAC
		128-bit AES IPsec VPN throughput: Up to 535 Mbps with VAC+
		256-bit AES IPsec VPN throughput: Up to 440 Mbps with VAC+
		Simultaneous VPN tunnels: 2000
	PIX 525	Cleartext throughput: 330 Mbps
		Concurrent connections: 280,000
		168-bit 3DES IPsec VPN throughput: Up to 155 Mbps with VAC+ or 72 Mbps with VAC
		128-bit AES IPsec VPN throughput: Up to 165 Mbps with VAC+
		256-bit AES IPsec VPN throughput: Up to 170 Mbps with VAC+
		Simultaneous VPN tunnels: 2000
	PIX 515E	Cleartext throughput: 188 Mbps
		Concurrent connections: 130,000
		168-bit 3DES IPsec VPN throughput: Up to 140 Mbps with VAC+ or 63 Mbps with VAC
		128-bit AES IPsec VPN throughput: Up to 135 Mbps with VAC+
		256-bit AES IPsec VPN throughput: Up to 140 Mbps with VAC+
		Simultaneous VPN tunnels: 2000
	PIX 506E	Cleartext throughput: 100 Mbps
		Concurrent connections: 25,000
		56-bit DES IPsec VPN throughput: 20 Mbps
		168-bit 3DES IPsec VPN throughput: 17 Mbps
		128-bit AES IPsec VPN throughput: 30 Mbps
		Simultaneous VPN peers: 25

continues

Table 6-3 *Cisco Security Product (Continued)*

Firewalls	PIX 501	Cleartext throughput: 60 Mbps
		Concurrent connections: 7500
		56-bit DES IPsec VPN throughput: 6 Mbps
		168-bit 3DES IPsec VPN throughput: 3 Mbps
		128-bit AES IPsec VPN throughput: 4.5 Mbps
		Simultaneous VPN peers: 10
	FWSM Cisco 7600 Series Router Catalyst 6500 Series Switch	5 Gbps throughput 1 million concurrent connections More than 100,000 connection setup and teardowns/sec Up to 128,000 access lists Supports up to 100 firewall VLANs
Intrusion Detection Systems	4250	500 Mbps 10/100/1000BASE-TX Monitoring Interfaces Up to 5 sniffing interfaces
	4250 XL	1000 Mbps 10/100/1000BASE-TX and Dual 1000BASE-SX Monitoring Interfaces Up to 5 sniffing interfaces
	4235	250 Mbps 10/100/1000BASE-TX Monitoring Interfaces Up to 5 sniffing interfaces
	4215	80 Mbps 10/100BASE-TX Monitoring Interfaces Up to 5 sniffing interfaces
	IDSM-2	This product efficiently integrates full IDS capabilities into the Cisco Catalyst Switch via a dedicated module, providing integrated protection at 600 Mbps.
	Cisco IDS Network Module Cisco 2600, 3600, and 3700 Series Routers	500 new TCP connections per second 500 HTTP transactions per second Average packet size of 445 bytes Running Cisco IDS 4.1 Sensor Software Cisco 2600XM up to 10 Mbps Cisco 3745 up to 45 Mbps

Table 6-3   *Cisco Security Product (Continued)*

Virtual Private Networks	VPN 3080 Concentrator	10,000 Simultaneous IPSec Remote Access Users
		500 Simultaneous WebVPN (Clientless) Users (SSL VPN)
		1000 Maximum LAN-to-LAN Sessions
		100 Mbps Encryption Throughput
		HW Encryption Method
	VPN 3060 Concentrator	5000 Simultaneous IPSec Remote Access Users
		500 Simultaneous WebVPN (Clientless) Users (SSL VPN)
		1000 Maximum LAN-to-LAN Sessions
		100 Mbps Encryption Throughput
		HW Encryption Method
	VPN 3030 Concentrator	1500 Simultaneous IPSec Remote Access Users
		500 Simultaneous WebVPN (Clientless) Users (SSL VPN)
		500 Maximum LAN-to-LAN Sessions
		50 Mbps Encryption Throughput
		HW Encryption Method
	VPN 3020 Concentrator	750 Simultaneous IPSec Remote Access Users
		200 Simultaneous WebVPN (Clientless) Users (SSL VPN)
		250 Maximum LAN-to-LAN Sessions
		50 Mbps Encryption Throughput
		HW Encryption Method
	VPN 3015 Concentrator	100 Simultaneous IPSec Remote Access Users
		75 Simultaneous WebVPN (Clientless) Users (SSL VPN)
		100 Maximum LAN-to-LAN Sessions
		4 Mbps Encryption Throughput
		SW Encryption Method

continues

Table 6-3 *Cisco Security Product (Continued)*

Virtual Private Networks	VPN 3005 Concentrator	100 Simultaneous IPSec Remote Access Users
		50 Simultaneous WebVPN (Clientless) Users (SSL VPN)
		100 Maximum LAN-to-LAN Sessions
		4 Mbps Encryption Throughput
		SW Encryption Method
	VPN 3002 Client	Eliminates the need to add or support VPN applications on a PC or workstation
	IPSec VPN Service Module Cisco 7600 Series Router Catalyst 6500 Series Switch	Provides up to 1.9 Gbps 3DES IPsec throughput

The following Cisco Products support VPN, firewall, and IDS services in software and/or with the addition of hardware modules.

- Small/Home Office:
    - Cisco 800 Series Router
    - Cisco UBR900 Series Router
    - Cisco 1700 Series Router
- Branch/Extranet:
    - Cisco 2600 Series Router
    - Cisco 3600 Series Router
    - Cisco 3700 Series Router
- VPN and WAN aggregation:
    - Cisco 7100 Series Router
    - Cisco 7200 Series Router
    - Cisco 7400 Series Router
    - Cisco 7500 Series Router

NOTE   This information was derived from the Cisco website (http://www.cisco.com/go/safe/).

Standards and Specification Summary

PKCS #3: Diffie-Hellman Key Agreement Standard. http://www.rsasecurity.com/rsalabs/node.asp?id=2126.

Federal Information Processing Standard (FIPS) for the Advanced Encryption Standard (FIPS-197). http://csrc.nist.gov/CryptoToolkit/aes/.

Federal Information Processing Standard (FIPS) for the Data Encryption Standard (FIPS-46-2). http://www.itl.nist.gov/fipspubs/fip46-2.htm.

Federal Information Processing Standard (FIPS) for the Data Encryption Standard (FIPS-46-3). http://www.itl.nist.gov/fipspubs/fip46-2.htm.

X9.52-1998, "Triple Data Encryption Algorithm Modes of Operation."

Request For Comments (RFCs) can be downloaded from the following website: http://www.rfc-editor.org/rfc.html.

- RFC 1321, "The MD5 Message-Digest Algorithm."
- RFC 1492, "An Access Control Protocol, Sometimes Called TACACS."
- RFC 1510, "The Kerberos Network Authentication Service (V5)."
- RFC 1701, "Generic Routing Encapsulation (GRE)."
- RFC 1828, "IP Authentication Using Keyed MD5."
- RFC 2085, "HMAC-MD5 IP Authentication with Replay Prevention."
- RFC 2196, "Site Security Handbook."
- RFC 2402, "IP Authentication Header."
- RFC 2406, "IP Encapsulating Security Payload (ESP)."
- RFC 2408, "Internet Security Association and Key Management Protocol (ISAKMP)."
- RFC 2409, "The Internet Key Exchange (IKE)."
- RFC 2459, "Internet X.509 Public Key Infrastructure Certificate and CRL Profile."
- RFC 2510, "Internet X.509 Public Key Infrastructure Certificate Management Protocols."
- RFC 2516, "Method for Transmitting PPP Over Ethernet (PPPoE)."
- RFC 2631, "Diffie-Hellman Key Agreement Method."
- RFC 2637, "Point-to-Point Tunneling Protocol (PPTP)."
- RFC 2661, "Layer Two Tunneling Protocol "L2TP"."
- RFC 2764, "A Framework for IP Based Virtual Private Networks."
- RFC 2827, "Network Ingress Filtering—Defeating Denial of Service Attacks Which Employ IP Source Address Spoofing."
- RFC 2865, "Remote Authentication Dial in User Service (RADIUS)."

- RFC 2866, "RADIUS Accounting."
- RFC 3193, "Securing L2TP Using IPsec."
- RFC 1938 (2289), "A One-Time Password System."

Review Questions

Answer the following questions to test your comprehension of the topics discussed in this chapter. Refer to Appendix A, "Answers to Review Questions," to check your answers.

1 What are the four types of threats that networks are vulnerable to?

2 Provide a definition of a security policy as stated in RFC 2196.

3 Typically, which situations are defined in a network security policy?

4 What are the four solutions you can implement to secure a network?

5 Define the three risk levels that can be used to categorize network resources during a risk assessment.

6 List the five key elements that make up the Cisco security solution.

7 List the type of network security attacks a network should attempt to defend against.

8 List three measures that can be used to mitigate the effects of denial of service.

9 List standard technologies that can be used to enable identification services.

10 To mitigate the success of password attacks, what steps should be used when selecting a password?

11 List some of the measures that you can take to reduce the risk of application-layer attacks.

12 What is port redirection?

13 List two of the primary vulnerabilities for end-user workstations.

14 Define a Trojan horse.

15 Define a perimeter LAN.

16 List some of the security services provided by the PIX firewall.

17 What are the two complementary IDS technologies?

18 Define the term attack signature.

19 What are some intrusion detection design considerations?

20 Define the term false positives.

21 List at least three authentication, authorization, and accounting protocols.

22 What cryptographic algorithm for encryption authentication does Kerberos use?

23 Define the term certificate within the context of PKI.

24 List the services provided by IPSec.

25 List the two protocols IPSec provides for transporting user data.

26 List some of the tasks that you can perform to secure a router.

27 What are some common forms of DDoS?

28 List the SAFE design objectives.

29 List the primary devices included in the small network Internet Connectivity module.

30 Which three modules comprise the SAFE Design for Medium Networks?

Case Study: OCSIC Bottling Company

The purpose of this case study is to practice the key design skills discussed in this chapter. The project is to revisit the earlier design for OCSIC Bottling Company and ensure that the security solution provides secure access to data and reduces the risk to network intrusions and attacks. For each identified component of the design, we are required to provide justification for our decision. The justification will provide an explanation for the options considered, and the reason behind choosing the selected option.

Your first task is to develop a security policy for the network by proposing a comprehensive security policy for the company network.

Your security policy should contain these elements:

- **Definition**—All corporate data and devices will be covered by this policy.

- **Identity**—Hosts and applications must be authorized to access the network.

- **Trust**—A multilevel trust system, based on levels within the organization, will define the conditions under which a user is trusted to perform an action.

- **Enforceability**—Hardware and software features will be used to enforce the security policy.

- **Risk assessment**—The risk assessment identifies all assets within the corporation and assigns a relative risk.

- **Incident response**—All incidents will be handled based on a hierarchy that defines severity of the infraction.

Your next task is to develop a security design for the headquarters' campus network. Table 6-4 summarizes the design decisions that the enterprise made to meet their requirements.

Table 6-4   *Design Matrix for the Campus Network*

Design Questions	Decision	Justification
What is your firewall strategy? What features would you implement?	None	Firewalls are not required on the campus network.
What is your intrusion detection strategy? What features would you implement?	None	Intrusion detection is not required on the campus network.
What software features would you implement?	Authentication Host-based virus scanning	Authentication is provided for network device access. Host-based virus scanning prevents most viruses and many Trojan horses.

Now, you must develop a security design for the Server Farm module. Table 6-5 summarizes the design decisions that the enterprise made to meet their requirements.

Table 6-5   *Design Matrix for the Server Farm Module*

Design Questions	Decision	Justification
What is your firewall strategy? What features would you implement?	None	Firewalls are not necessary in the server farm.
What is your intrusion detection strategy? What features would you implement?	Use host intrusion protection systems (HIDS)	HIDS mitigates unauthorized access. Operating systems, devices, and applications are kept up to date with the latest security fixes and protected by HIDS. HIDS prevents port redirection agents from being installed.
What software features would you implement?	Implement AAA security with RADIUS authentication RFC 2827 filtering	RFC 2827 filtering prevents source address spoofing.

You now must develop a security design for the WAN module. Table 6-6 summarizes the design decisions that the enterprise made to meet their requirements.

Table 6-6   *Design Matrix for the WAN Module*

Design Questions	Decision	Justification
What is your firewall strategy? What features would you implement?	Implement a firewall Within the firewall, implement NAT and access control features	Firewalls prevent unauthorized access. TCP setup controls at the firewall limit DoS attacks.
What is your intrusion detection strategy? What features would you implement?	An intrusion detection system installed on both sides of the firewall Include IDS monitoring on the inside network and outside network Use the software application built into the firewall to parse log files	Intrusion detection mitigates application-layer attacks, password attacks, attacks by packet sniffers, reconnaissance, and port redirection.
What software features would you implement?	Authentication provided for WAN access	Authentication ensures that only authorized users have access to network resources.

Next, you need to develop a security design for the Remote Access module. Table 6-7 summarizes the design decisions that the enterprise made to meet their requirements.

Table 6-7   *Design Matrix for the Remote Access Module*

Design Questions	Decision	Justification
What is your firewall strategy? What features would you implement?	Implement a firewall Within the firewall, implement NAT and access control features	Firewalls prevent unauthorized access. TCP setup controls at the firewall limit DoS attacks.
What is your intrusion detection strategy? What features would you implement?	An intrusion detection system installed on both sides of the firewall Include IDS monitoring on the inside network and outside network Use the software application built into the firewall to parse log files	Intrusion detection mitigates application-layer attacks, password attacks, attacks by packet sniffers, reconnaissance, and port redirection.

continues

Table 6-7 *Design Matrix for the Remote Access Module (Continued)*

Design Questions	Decision	Justification
What software features would you implement?	Authentication provided for remote access IP spoofing security runs inside the Cisco AS5350	Authentication ensures that only authorized users have access to network resources. IP spoofing detects unwanted guests.

Finally, you must develop a security design for the Internet Connectivity module. Table 6-8 summarizes the design decisions that the enterprise made to meet their requirements.

Table 6-8 *Design Matrix for the Internet Connectivity Module*

Design Questions	Decision	Justification
What is your firewall strategy? What features would you implement?	Implement a firewall Within the firewall, implement NAT and access control features	Firewalls prevent unauthorized access. TCP setup controls at the firewall limit DoS attacks.
What is your intrusion detection strategy? What features would you implement?	An intrusion detection system installed on both sides of the firewall Include IDS monitoring on the inside network and outside network Use the software application built into the firewall to parse log files	Intrusion detection mitigates application-layer attacks, password attacks, attacks by packet sniffers, reconnaissance, and port redirection.
What software features would you implement?	Authentication provided for Internet access Only HTTP access to the Internet is provided Only web-based traffic is allowed to and from the Internet	Authentication ensures that only authorized users have access to network resources.

Update your campus network diagram to reflect your security design.

Figure 6-38 shows a security design for the company network.

Figure 6-38 *Campus Network*

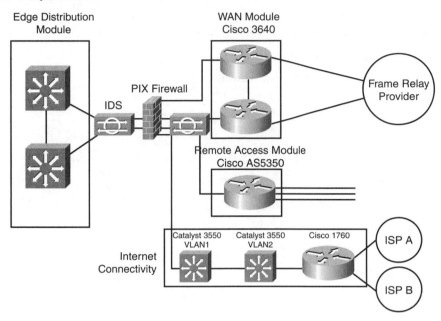

After completing this chapter, you will be able to

- Identify QoS mechanisms
- Design QoS for enterprise networks

CHAPTER 7

Designing QoS

The backbone of a successful enterprise is an efficient, well-designed network that can transport many applications and data, including high-quality voice and video, and critical application data. Bandwidth-intensive applications might stretch network capabilities and resources. Networks must provide secure, predictable, measurable, and sometimes guaranteed levels of service. Achieving the required quality of service (QoS) by managing delay, delay variation (jitter), bandwidth, and packet loss on a network is a critical task.

The first part of this chapter identifies the necessary components of a QoS solution, given specific quality and application requirements. The second part of this chapter provides guidelines for making scalable QoS designs for enterprise networks.

Identifying QoS Mechanisms

Cisco IOS Software provides a range of QoS tools that address the needs of voice, video, and data applications. Cisco IOS QoS technology allows a network designer to implement complex networks that predictably control services to a variety of networked applications and traffic types. Using the QoS toolset in Cisco IOS Software, enterprises can design and implement networks that conform to either the Internet Engineering Task Force (IETF) Integrated Services (IntServ) model, or the Differentiated Services (DiffServ) model. Cisco IOS QoS tools provide additional functionality, such as network-based application recognition (NBAR) for classifying traffic on an application basis, a service assurance agent (SAA) for end-to-end QoS measurements, and Resource Reservation Protocol (RSVP) signaling for admission control and reservation of resources.

Enterprise Network Requirements for QoS

QoS tools are required to manage bandwidth and minimize loss, delay, and delay variation between enterprise sites and within a campus. Between sites, bandwidth availability is the most frequent concern. Within the campus infrastructure, buffer management issues are the primary concern.

QoS is the application of features and functionality needed to satisfy networking requirements for packet loss, delay, and delay variation (jitter). QoS is also needed to guarantee the availability of bandwidth for critical application flows. QoS provides control and predictable service for a variety of networked applications and traffic types in complex networks. Almost any network can take advantage of QoS to optimize efficiency.

The benefits of effective QoS configurations are as follows:

- **Control over resources**—You have control over which resources (bandwidth, equipment, wide-area facilities, and so on) are being used. For example, you can limit the bandwidth consumed over a backbone link by FTP transfers or give priority to an important database access.

- **More effective use of network resources**—Using network analysis management and accounting tools, you will know what your network is being used for and you can configure the system to make the most effective use of resources.

- **Tailored services**—The control and visibility provided by QoS enables carefully tailored grades of service differentiation to applications and customers within large enterprises and service provider networks.

- **Coexistence of mission-critical applications**—QoS technologies make certain that the WAN is used efficiently by mission-critical applications that are most important to the business, and that bandwidth and minimum delays required by time-sensitive multimedia and voice applications are available. Finally, QoS technologies ensure that other applications using the link get fair service without interfering with mission-critical traffic.

An enterprise network may experience some or all of these main types of network-reliability problems:

- Long end-to-end delay
- Delay variation (jitter)
- Packet loss

Delay

Delay (or latency) is the amount of time it takes a packet to reach the receiving endpoint after being transmitted from the sending endpoint. This time period is referred to as the *end-to-end delay* and includes two components:

- **Fixed network delay**—Includes encoding and decoding time (for voice and video), as well as the time required for the electrical and optical pulses to traverse the media en route to their destination

- **Variable network delay**—Generally caused by network conditions, such as congestion, that may affect the overall required transit time

In converged data networks, three types of fixed delay exist:

- **Packetization delay**—The amount of time it takes to packetize the content. With voice and video, this includes the time to sample and encode the analog signals.

- **Serialization delay**—The amount of time it takes to place the bits of the data packets onto the physical media.

- **Propagation delay**—The amount of time it takes to transmit the bits of a packet across the physical media links.

Delay Variation

Delay variation (or jitter) is the difference in the end-to-end delay between packets. For example, if one packet required 100 ms to traverse the network from the source-endpoint to the destination-endpoint, and the following packet required 125 ms to make the same trip, the delay variation is calculated as 25 ms. The major factors affecting variable delays are queuing delay, dejitter buffers, and variable packet sizes.

Each end station in a voice or video conversation has a jitter buffer. Jitter buffers smooth out changes in arrival times of data packets that contain voice. A jitter buffer is often dynamic and can adjust for approximately 30-ms changes in arrival times of packets. If you have instantaneous changes in arrival times of packets that are outside of the capabilities of a jitter buffer's ability to compensate, you will have one of the following situations:

- **Underrun**—A jitter buffer underrun occurs when the arrival time of packets increases to the point where the jitter buffer is exhausted and contains no packets to be processed. The effect is unnatural silence in the case of voice, or a black screen in the case of video.

- **Overrun**—A jitter buffer overrun occurs when packets containing voice or video arrive faster than the jitter buffer can dynamically resize itself to accommodate. When this happens, packets are dropped. When it is time to play voice or video samples, voice quality is degraded.

Packet Loss

Packet loss measures the packets faithfully transmitted and received and compares it to the total number of transmitted packets. Packet loss is expressed as the percentage of packets that were dropped or lost.

QoS-Enabled Network

Managing QoS becomes increasingly difficult in a converged network because many applications deliver individually unpredictable bursts of traffic. For example, usage patterns for web, e-mail, and file transfer applications are virtually impossible to predict, yet network managers need to be able to support mission-critical applications even during peak periods.

QoS technologies allow IT managers and network managers to make the network QoS-enabled. In a QoS-enabled network, managers and engineers can perform the following tasks:

- Predict response times for end-to-end network services
- Manage jitter-sensitive applications, such as audio and video playbacks
- Manage delay-sensitive traffic, such as real-time voice
- Control loss in times of inevitable bursty congestion
- Set traffic priorities across the network
- Support dedicated bandwidth
- Avoid and manage network congestion

QoS Architectures

Two major QoS architectures or models are used in IP networks when designing a QoS solution:

- Integrated Services (IntServ) architecture
- Differentiated Services (DiffServ) architecture

IntServ

IntServ is a multiple service model; in other words, it can accommodate multiple QoS requirements. Each application is expected to request a specific kind of service from the network before it sends data. The request is made using explicit signaling:

1 The application informs the network of its traffic profile and requests a particular kind of service that can encompass its bandwidth and delay requirements.

   The application is expected to send data only after it gets a confirmation from the network.

2 After the network gives a confirmation, the application is expected to send data that only lies within its predescribed traffic profile.

3 The network performs admission control based on the information from the application and available network resources.

4 The network commits to meeting the QoS requirements of the application as long as the traffic remains within the profile specifications.

   The network also fulfills its commitment by maintaining the per-flow state and then performing packet classification, policing, and intelligent queuing based on that state.

The IntServ model is similar to the Public Switched Telephone Network (PSTN); a user dials a number to be connected to, and if the network distinguishes the destination and has the resources to build an end-to-end circuit and the destination device is available, the circuit is built and the user can have a conversation with the party answering the call at the other end. The consumed resources are taken away when the call terminates and are made available to other requestors.

Cisco IOS includes the following features that provide controlled load service (which is a kind of integrated service):

- **RSVP**—Used by applications to signal their QoS requirements to the routers through the network
- **Intelligent queuing mechanisms**—Used with RSVP to provide the following:
  - Guaranteed rate service
  - Controlled load service

Guaranteed rate service allows applications to reserve bandwidth to meet their requirements. For example, a Voice over IP (VoIP) application can reserve 32 kbps end-to-end using this kind of service. IOS QoS uses weighted fair queuing (WFQ) with RSVP to provide this kind of service. Guaranteed rate service is implemented using a queue-service discipline.

Controlled load service allows applications to have low delay and high throughput even during times of congestion. For example, adaptive real-time applications, such as playback of a recorded conference, can use this kind of service. IOS QoS uses RSVP with weighted random early detection (WRED) to provide this kind of service. Controlled load service is a queue-entry discipline that accelerates packet discard as congestion increases.

DiffServ

DiffServ is a multiple service model that can satisfy differing QoS requirements. However, unlike the IntServ model, an application using DiffServ does not explicitly signal (to the router), before it sends data. For DiffServ, the network tries to deliver a particular kind of service based on the QoS per-hop behavior (PHB) associated with the differential services code point (DSCP) within each packet. The DSCP field (6 bits) plus the two explicit congestion notification (ECN) bits, adding up to 8 bits, used to be called the type of service (ToS) byte on the IP header. The DSCP field might be set based on different criteria. The network uses the QoS specification to classify, mark, shape, and police traffic, and to perform intelligent queuing. The DiffServ model performs a relatively coarse level of traffic classification, and no information about individual flows is required in the network. Therefore, DiffServ consumes fewer network resources than IntServ.

Cisco IOS QoS includes these features that support the DiffServ model:

- **Committed access rate (CAR)**—Performs packet classification through IP Precedence and QoS group settings. CAR performs metering and policing of traffic, providing bandwidth management.

NOTE   Class-Based Policing is the newer and more capable tool that is currently used; it is considered the superior substitution to CAR.

- **Intelligent queuing schemes**—Includes distributed WRED (DWRED) and distributed WFQ and their equivalent features on the Versatile Interface Processor (VIP). You can use these features with CAR to deliver differentiated services.

QoS Service Levels

QoS service levels differ in their level of QoS strictness, which describes how tightly the services are bound by specific bandwidth, delay, jitter, and packet loss characteristics. Three basic levels of end-to-end QoS can be provided across a heterogeneous network (see Figure 7-1):

- **Best-effort service (also called lack of QoS)**—Basic connectivity with no guarantees. This service is often characterized by queues that have no differentiation between flows.

- **Differentiated service (also called soft QoS)**—Some traffic classes (aggregates) are treated better than the rest. (For example, the better-treated classes have faster handling, higher average bandwidth, and lower average loss rate.) This is a statistical preference, not a hard-and-fast guarantee to any particular traffic flow. You can provide differentiated services by classifying traffic and using QoS tools such as low-latency queuing (LLQ), class-based weighted fair queuing (CBWFQ), priority queuing (PQ), custom queuing (CQ), WFQ, and so on.

- **Guaranteed service (also called hard QoS)**—An absolute reservation of network resources for specific traffic. Guaranteed services use QoS tools including RSVP and CBWFQ.

Figure 7-1   *QoS Service Levels*

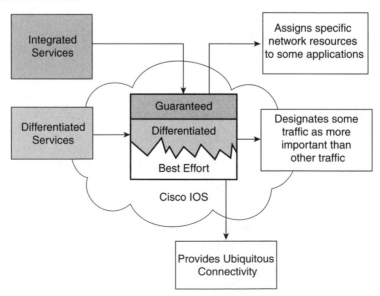

Selecting the type of service to deploy in the network depends on these factors:

- **Application supported or problem being solved**—Each type of service is appropriate for certain applications. This does not imply that an enterprise must migrate to differentiated and then to guaranteed service (although many probably eventually will). A differentiated service, or even a best-effort service, might be appropriate, depending on the application requirements.

- **Speed to upgrade the infrastructure**—A natural upgrade path exists from the technology needed to provide differentiated service to that needed to provide guaranteed service.

- **Cost**—The cost of implementing and deploying guaranteed service is likely to be more than that for differentiated service.

Classification and Marking

Classification tools mark packets with a value used for prioritization, shaping, or policing within the network. This marking establishes a trust boundary that must be enforced. You can apply policy only after traffic is positively identified. For scalability reasons, classification should be implemented as close to the endpoint (sender) as possible. The network edge where markings are accepted (or rejected) is referred to as the trust boundary. Figure 7-2 shows three levels (or places) of the trust boundary—the first and second rows are optimal, and the third row is acceptable.

Figure 7-2   *Classification Tools: Trust Boundaries*

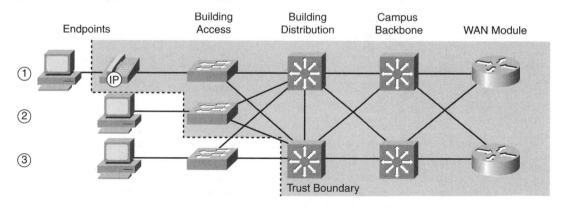

The first element of a QoS policy is to identify the traffic that is to be treated differently. Classification tools mark a packet or flow with a specific identifier. Classification at the trust boundary marks packets by examining any of the following:

- **Layer 2 parameters**—802.1Q/P class of service (CoS) bits, MAC address, Multiprotocol Label Switching (MPLS) label
- **Label switching**—MPLS experimental values

- **Layer 3 parameters**—IP Precedence, DSCP, source or destination address, protocol
- **Layer 4 parameters**—Transmission Control Protocol (TCP) or User Datagram Protocol (UDP) ports
- **Layer 7 parameters**—Application signatures

Packet classification features provide the capability to partition network traffic into multiple priority levels or classes of service. For example, by using the three precedence bits in the ToS field of the IP packet header, you can categorize packets into a limited set of up to six traffic classes. (Two of the eight possible values are reserved for other purposes.) After you classify packets, you can use other QoS features to assign the appropriate traffic-handling policies, including congestion management, bandwidth allocation, and delay bounds for each traffic class (see Figure 7-3).

Figure 7-3 *Classification and Marking*

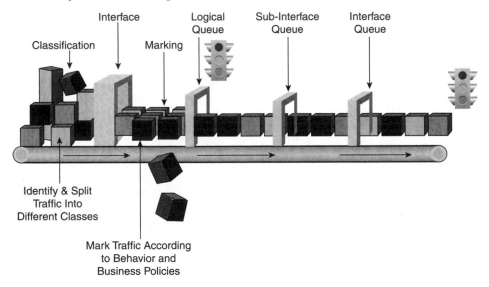

You may classify packets by external sources, that is, by a location or by a downstream service provider. Furthermore, a network can accept the classification of the entering packets or override their classifications, which means entering packets can be reclassified according to local policies. Finally, classification can be based on physical port, source, or destination IP or MAC address, application port, IP protocol type, and other criteria that may be specified using different types of access lists.

Congestion Avoidance

Congestion-avoidance techniques monitor network traffic loads in an effort to anticipate and reduce the impact of congestion at common network and internetwork bottlenecks before it becomes a significant problem. These techniques are designed to provide preferential treatment for premium (priority) traffic under congestion situations while concurrently maximizing network throughput and capacity utilization and minimizing packet loss and delay. The IOS QoS congestion-avoidance features are WRED and DWRED.

Default router behavior allows interface queues to fill during periods of congestion using tail drop to resolve the problem of full queues, unless WRED is configured. When the queue has filled, a potentially large number of packets from numerous connections are discarded because of lack of buffer capacity. This behavior can result in waves of congestion followed by periods during which the transmission link is not fully used. WRED mitigates this situation proactively and preferentially. Congestion avoidance for selected traffic is provided by monitoring buffer depth and performing a probabilistic (random) discard on packets from traffic streams configured for early discard, instead of waiting for buffers to fill and dropping all arriving packets.

WRED is a Cisco implementation of the random early detection (RED) class of congestion-avoidance algorithms. When WRED is used with TCP and the source detects the dropped packet, the source slows its transmission. WRED can also be configured to use the DSCP value when it calculates the drop probability of a packet. Figure 7-4 shows a case of DSCP-based WRED, where drop probability of AF 13 goes from 0 (0%) to 1 (100%), and it begins dropping while the queue is not too long yet. The drop probability of AF 12 goes from 0 to 1, but it begins when the queue is a bit longer and after AF 13 has begun dropping packets (but before AF 11 begins dropping). The drop probability of AF 11 also goes from 0 to 1, but it begins dropping packets when the queue is longer and both AF 13 and AF 12 have begun dropping packets. AF 11, AF 12, and AF 13 are three of several classifications (or DSCP variations) within the DiffServ model.

Figure 7-4   *Congestion Avoidance*

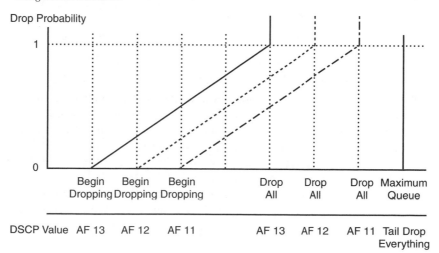

WRED combines the capabilities of the RED algorithm with IP Precedence to provide preferential traffic handling for higher-priority packets. It can selectively discard lower-priority traffic when the interface begins to get congested and can provide differentiated performance characteristics for different classes of service.

The DiffServ-compliant WRED feature extends the functionality of WRED to enable support for DiffServ and Assured Forwarding (AF) PHB. This feature enables customers to implement AF PHB by coloring packets according to DSCP values and then assigning low, preferential drop probabilities to those packets.

DWRED is the high-speed version of WRED. The DWRED algorithm was designed with service providers in mind; it allows an ISP to define minimum and maximum queue depth thresholds and drop capabilities for each class of service. DWRED is implemented on VIP-capable routers.

The flow-based WRED feature forces WRED to afford greater fairness to all flows on an interface with regard to how packets are dropped. To provide fairness to all flows, flow-based WRED has these features:

* It ensures that flows that respond to WRED packet drops by backing off packet transmission are protected from flows that do not respond to WRED packet drops.

* It prohibits a single flow from monopolizing the buffer resources at an interface.

Congestion Management

Congestion management features control congestion when it occurs. One way that network elements handle an overflow of arriving traffic is to use a queuing algorithm to sort the traffic into one or more logical queues, and then determine a method of prioritizing it onto an output link. Each queuing algorithm solves a specific network traffic problem and has a particular effect on network performance.

The software congestion management features include the following:

* **First-in, first-out (FIFO)**—Provides basic storage and forward capability. FIFO is the default queuing algorithm on high-speed interfaces, requiring no configuration.

* **WFQ (flow-based, class-based, and distributed)**—Applies priority (or weights) to identified traffic to classify traffic into conversations and determine how much bandwidth each conversation is allowed relative to other conversations. WFQ classifies traffic into different flows based on such characteristics as source and destination address, protocol, and port and socket of the session. WFQ is the default queuing discipline on links at and below 2.048 Mbps. To provide large-scale support for applications and traffic classes requiring bandwidth allocations and delay bounds over the network infrastructure, IOS QoS includes a version of WFQ that runs only in distributed mode on VIPs. This version is called distributed WFQ (DWFQ). It provides

increased flexibility in terms of traffic classification, weight assessment, and discard policy, and delivers Internet-scale performance on the Cisco 7500 series platforms.

- **LLQ**—Provides strict priority queuing on ATM virtual circuits (VCs) and serial interfaces. This feature allows you to configure the priority status for a class within CBWFQ, and is not limited to UDP port numbers, as is IP RTP priority. IP RTP is a queuing mechanism that was created specifically for Real-Time Transport Protocol (RTP) traffic; IP RTP is explained in a later bullet. LLQ and IP RTP Priority can be configured at the same time, but IP RTP Priority takes precedence. Additionally, the functionality of LLQ has been extended to allow you to specify the committed burst (Bc) size in LLQ and to change (or vary) the number of packets contained in the per-VC hold queue (on ATM adapters that support per-VC queuing). The distributed LLQ feature provides the ability to specify low-latency behavior for a traffic class on a VIP-based Cisco 7500 series router. LLQ allows delay-sensitive data such as voice to be dequeued and sent before packets in other queues are dequeued. The distributed LLQ feature also introduces the ability to limit the depth of a device transmission ring.

- **LLQ for Frame Relay**—Provides strict PQ for voice traffic and WFQ for other classes of traffic. Before the release of this feature, LLQ was available at the interface and ATM VC levels. It is now available at the Frame Relay VC level when Frame Relay traffic shaping is configured. Strict PQ improves QoS by allowing delay-sensitive traffic, such as voice, to be pulled from the queue and sent before other classes of traffic. LLQ for Frame Relay allows you to define classes of traffic according to protocol, interface, or access lists. You can then assign characteristics to those classes, including priority, bandwidth, queue limit, and WRED.

- **PQ**—Designed to give priority to important traffic, PQ ensures that important traffic gets the fastest handling at each point where PQ is used. PQ can flexibly prioritize according to network protocol (such as IP, Internetwork Packet Exchange [IPX], or AppleTalk), incoming interface, packet size, source/destination address, and so on. Priority queuing scheme can starve traffic flows with a lower priority. There is no minimum service guarantee.

- **Frame Relay PVC Interface Priority Queuing (FR PIPQ)**—Provides an interface-level PQ scheme in which prioritization is based on destination PVC rather than packet contents. For example, FR PIPQ allows you to configure PVC transporting voice traffic to have absolute priority over a PVC transporting signaling traffic, and a PVC transporting signaling traffic to have absolute priority over a PVC transporting data. FR PIPQ provides four levels of priority: high, medium, normal, and low. The Frame Relay packet is examined at the interface for the data-link connection identifier (DLCI) value. The packet is then sent to the correct priority queue based on the priority level configured for that DLCI.

- **CQ**—Reserves a percentage of the available bandwidth of an interface for each selected traffic type. If a particular type of traffic is not using the bandwidth reserved for it, other traffic types may use the remaining reserved bandwidth.

- **CBWFQ and distributed CBWFQ (DCBWFQ)**—Extend the standard WFQ functionality to provide support for user-defined traffic classes. They allow you to specify the exact amount of bandwidth to be allocated for a specific class of traffic. Taking into account available bandwidth on the interface, you can configure up to 64 classes and control distribution among them. DCBWFQ is intended for use on the VIP-based Cisco 7000 series routers with the Route Switch Processors (RSPs), and the Cisco 7500 series routers.

- **IP RTP Priority**—Provides a strict priority queuing scheme that allows delay-sensitive data, such as voice, to be dequeued and sent before packets in other queues are dequeued. Use this feature on serial interfaces in conjunction with either WFQ or CBWFQ on the same outgoing interface. Traffic matching the range of UDP ports specified for the priority queue is guaranteed strict priority over other CBWFQ classes or WFQ flows; packets in the priority queue are always serviced first.

- **Frame Relay IP RTP Priority**—Provides a strict priority queuing scheme on a Frame Relay PVC for delay-sensitive data such as voice. Voice traffic can be identified by its Real-Time Transport Protocol (RTP) port numbers and classified into a priority queue. The result of using this feature is that voice is serviced as strict priority in preference to other nonvoice traffic.

- **Modified Deficit Round Robin (MDRR)**—A traffic latency control function that allows the operators to guarantee traffic latency for differentiated flows by controlling the packet dequeuing process. Packet classification is based on IP precedence. Two basic modes of operation govern how packets are dequeued from the low-latency queue in relation to other queues:

    - **Alternate priority**—Queues are serviced by alternating between the low-latency queue and the other queues in round robin.

    - **Strict priority**—The low-latency queue is continually serviced to keep it empty, but its bandwidth is capped.

Consideration of the behavior of congested systems is not simple because traffic rates do not simply rise to a level, stay there a while, and then subside. Periods of traffic congestion can be quite long, with losses that are heavily concentrated. A slight increase in the number of active connections can result in a large increase in the packet-loss rate. This understanding of the behavior of congested networks suggests that, because the level of busy period traffic is not predictable, it is difficult to economically size networks to reduce congestion.

Traffic Conditioning

Cisco IOS QoS offers two kinds of traffic regulation or conditioning mechanisms: policing and shaping. The CAR rate-limiting features and the traffic-policing feature provide the functionality for policing traffic. The features of generic traffic shaping (GTS), class-based shaping, distributed traffic shaping (DTS), and Frame Relay traffic shaping (FRTS) provide the functionality for shaping traffic (see Figure 7-5). You can deploy these features throughout your network to ensure that a data source complies with a service agreement and to determine how your network should treat that data. Figure 7-5 provides an example demonstrating the difference between unshaped and traffic-shaped traffic.

Figure 7-5   *Traffic Conditioning*

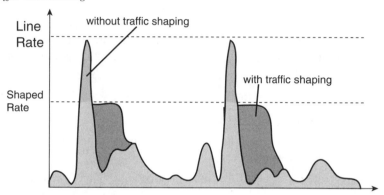

Traffic shaping limits the transmit rate to a value lower than line rate.

CAR: Managing Access Bandwidth Policy and Performing Policing

QoS provides traffic prioritization by either raising the priority of one flow or by limiting the priority of another. CAR is used to limit the bandwidth of a flow in favor of another flow. The IOS implementation of CAR transmits, drops, sets IP Precedence bits, and continues (this refers to cascading CAR statements). This provides a flexible tool that allows you to perform different types of actions upon the traffic. Conforming traffic can be transmitted, and exceeding traffic can be reclassified to a lower IP Precedence setting and then sent to the next CAR statement for additional conditions. The IOS CAR implementation also provides an excess burst capability. Excess burst allows additional tokens above the original (or normal) burst. When these tokens are used, the packet has the possibility of being dropped (even if the action is to transmit). A RED-like algorithm enforces the following policy: The more excess burst tokens a flow uses, the higher probability that its next packet will be dropped. This allows the flow to be scaled back slowly as in WRED, while still maintaining the opportunity to send traffic in excess of the normal burst.

Traffic policing allows you to control the maximum rate of traffic sent or received on an interface, and to partition a network into multiple priority levels. The traffic-policing feature manages the maximum rate of traffic through a token bucket algorithm. The token bucket algorithm can use the user-configured values to determine the maximum rate of traffic allowed on an interface at a given moment in time. The token bucket algorithm is affected by all traffic entering or leaving (depending on where the traffic policy with traffic policing is configured) and is useful in managing network bandwidth in cases where several large packets are sent in the same traffic stream.

The token bucket algorithm provides users with three actions for each packet: conform, exceed, and optional violate. Traffic entering the interface with traffic policing configured is placed into one of these categories. Within these three categories, users can decide packet treatments. For example, packets that conform can be transmitted, packets that exceed can be sent with a decreased priority, and packets that violate can be dropped.

Traffic policing is often configured on interfaces at the edge of a network to limit the rate of traffic entering or leaving the network. In the most common traffic policing configurations, traffic that conforms is transmitted and traffic that exceeds is sent with a decreased priority or is dropped. Users can change these configuration options to suit their network needs.

Traffic Shaping: Controlling Outbound Traffic Flow

Cisco IOS QoS contains the following traffic-shaping features to manage traffic and congestion on the network:

- **Generic traffic shaping (GTS)**—Provides a mechanism to control the flow of outbound traffic on a particular interface. It reduces outbound traffic flow to avoid congestion by constraining specified traffic to a particular bit rate. Traffic adhering to a particular profile can be shaped to meet downstream requirements, eliminating bottlenecks in topologies with data-rate mismatches.

- **Class-based shaping**—Provides the means for configuring GTS on a class, rather than only on an access control list (ACL). You can enable class-based shaping on any interface that supports GTS. Using the class-based shaping feature, you can perform these tasks:

  — Configure GTS on a traffic class.

  — Specify average rate or peak rate traffic shaping.

  — Configure CBWFQ inside GTS.

- **Distributed traffic shaping (DTS)**—Provides the means for managing the bandwidth of an interface to avoid congestion, meet remote site requirements, and conform to a service rate that is provided on that interface. DTS uses queues to buffer traffic surges that can congest a network.

- **Frame Relay traffic shaping (FRTS)**—Applies only to Frame Relay PVCs and switched virtual circuits (SVCs). FRTS provides parameters that are useful for managing network traffic congestion, such as the following:

  — Committed information rate (CIR)

  — Forward and backward explicit congestion notification (FECN/BECN)

  — Discard eligible (DE) bit

Signaling

QoS *signaling* is a form of network communication that allows an end station or network node to communicate with (or signal) its neighbors to request special handling of certain traffic. QoS signaling is useful for coordinating the traffic-handling techniques provided by other QoS features. It plays a key role in configuring successful overall end-to-end QoS service across your network.

True end-to-end QoS requires that every element in the network path, including switches, routers, firewalls, hosts, and clients, deliver its part of QoS, and that all of these entities be coordinated with QoS signaling. Many viable QoS signaling solutions provide QoS at some places in the infrastructure, but they often have limited scope across the network. To achieve end-to-end QoS, signaling must span the entire network. An IP network can achieve end-to-end QoS, for example, by using part of the IP packet header to request special handling of priority or time-sensitive traffic. Given the ubiquity of IP, QoS signaling that takes advantage of IP provides powerful end-to-end signaling. Both RSVP and IP Precedence fit this category.

IOS QoS software takes advantage of IP to meet the challenge of finding a robust QoS signaling solution that can operate over heterogeneous network infrastructures. It overlays data-link layer technology-specific QoS signaling solutions with network layer IP QoS signaling methods of the RSVP and IP Precedence features. To achieve the end-to-end benefits of IP Precedence and RSVP signaling, Cisco IOS/QoS Software offers ATM User-Network Interface (UNI) signaling and the Frame Relay Local Management Interface (LMI) to provide signaling into their respective backbone technologies. To provide support for controlled load service using RSVP over an ATM core network, IOS QoS software offers the RSVP-ATM QoS Internetworking feature.

To achieve centralized monitoring and control of RSVP signaling, IOS Software offers Common Open Policy Service (COPS) with RSVP. To enable admission control over IEEE 802-styled networks, IOS QoS software offers Subnetwork Bandwidth Manager (SBM).

Link-Efficiency Mechanisms

Cisco IOS/QoS software offers three link-efficiency mechanisms that work in conjunction with queuing and traffic shaping to improve the predictability of the application services levels:

- Link Fragmentation and Interleaving (LFI)
- Compressed Real-Time Transfer Protocol (cRTP) and Distributed Compressed Real-Time Transfer Protocol (dcRTP)

LFI

Interactive traffic, such as Telnet and VoIP, is susceptible to increased latency and jitter when the network processes large packets, such as LAN-to-LAN FTP transfers traversing a WAN link. This susceptibility increases as the traffic is queued on slower links. QoS LFI reduces delay and jitter on slower-speed links by breaking up large datagrams and interleaving low-delay traffic packets with the resulting smaller packets. Using LFI with multilink Point-to-Point Protocol (PPP) reduces delay on slower-speed links by breaking up large datagrams and interleaving low-delay traffic packets with the smaller packets resulting from the fragmented datagram. Alternatives to using LFI include the following:

- Reduced maximum transmission unit (MTU)
- Frame Relay fragmentation (FRF.12)
- ATM

cRTP and dcRTP

RTP is a host-to-host protocol used for carrying newer multimedia application traffic (including packetized audio and video) over an IP network. RTP provides end-to-end network transport functions intended for applications sending real-time requirements, such as audio, video, or simulation data multicast or unicast network services.

To avoid the unnecessary consumption of available bandwidth, the RTP header compression feature, referred to as cRTP, is used on a link-by-link basis. The cRTP feature compresses the combined 40-byte IP/UDP/RTP packet headers into 2 to 4 bytes. It must be configured on both ends of each link on which it is desired. This compression reduces the packet size, improves the speed of packet transmission, and reduces packet latency.

The dcRTP feature is the implementation of cRTP on a Cisco 7500 series router with a VIP in distributed fast-switching and distributed Cisco Express Forwarding (dCEF) environments. It offers the same benefits and costs.

Summary of Key Cisco IOS Software QoS Categories and Features

Each QoS feature plays an important role in the network. Figure 7-6 summarizes the key IOS Software QoS categories and features.

The bottom layer (media) contains the transport protocols. The middle section lists the tools that are used in deploying the QoS: classification and marking, congestion avoidance, traffic conditioners, congestion management, and link efficiency. The very top row contains the different applications that benefit from QoS.

Just below the top row are IntServ and DiffServ. In the bars below that are RSVP and DSCP, which are the two marking tools of IntServ and DiffServ, respectively. The IntServ architecture defines fine-grained (flow-based) methods of performing IP traffic admission control that uses RSVP. The DiffServ architecture defines methods of classifying IP traffic into coarse-grained service classes and defines forwarding treatment based on these classifications.

Figure 7-6   *Key Cisco IOS Software QoS Categories and Features*

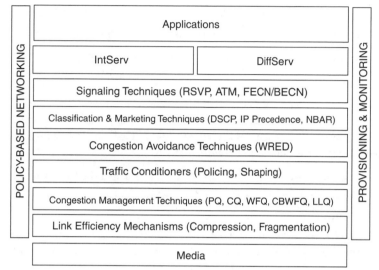

Designing QoS for Enterprise Networks

Enterprise network applications have different requirements for bandwidth, delay, jitter, and packet loss. Voice applications, for example, have stringent delay requirements and can tolerate limited packet loss. On the other hand, a commercial transaction might be less sensitive to delay but very sensitive to packet loss. Cisco QoS features provide the ability to manage traffic intelligently across the network infrastructure.

QoS includes mechanisms that enable network managers to control the mix of bandwidth, delay, variances in delay (jitter), and packet loss in the network, and, hence, deliver a network service, such as VoIP. QoS also allows you to define different service level agreements (SLAs) for different divisions, applications, and/or organizations. You can also prioritize traffic across a WAN link using QoS tools.

This section provides QoS design guidelines for data, voice, and video conferencing. Furthermore, the places for applying QoS tools in a campus network will be discussed. Finally, an example for a QoS implementation will be presented.

QoS Design Guidelines

QoS features are configured throughout a network to make sure that QoS is deliverable end-to-end. The following are some of the important questions or factors to consider:

- What problems will (implementing) a QoS solution attempt to solve?
- Which model will be used for solving the stated problems?

- Are there multiple possible solutions?
- What are the benefits and drawbacks of each of the alternative solutions?
- How do the costs of implementing different solutions compare?

The QoS tools are a set of mechanisms that increase voice quality on data networks by decreasing dropped voice packets during times of network congestion and by minimizing both the fixed and variable delays encountered in a given voice connection. In general, QoS provides resources and services to applications as per those applications' requirements; however, voice is mentioned more often here, as it is the dominant reason for most of today's QoS efforts. When deploying end-to-end QoS, the following important tasks need be performed throughout the network:

- **Classification**—Mark the packets to denote a specific CoS offered on the network.
- **Determining the trust boundary**—Define and enforce a trust boundary at the network edge.
- **Scheduling**—Assign packets to one of multiple queues (based on classification) for expedited treatment throughout the network. Use congestion avoidance for data.
- **Provisioning**—Accurately calculate the required bandwidth for all applications plus element overhead.

Classification tools recognize the type of packet (in a flow), using tools like access lists or NBAR, and subsequently, mark the packet. Only classifications made, or confirmed, at a trust boundary are honored through the network.

Scheduling tools refer to the set of tools that determines how a frame or packet exits a node. When packets enter a device faster than they can exit, a point of congestion will occur at some output interface. Multiple inputs being directed to a single output or a higher-speed input bursting to a lower-speed output might also cause congestion. Devices queue packet buffers to allow for scheduling higher-priority packets to exit sooner than lower-priority ones. Most prioritized queuing mechanisms use multiple logical queues to separate the traffic. The queues are then serviced on a strict priority basis or in some kind of a round-robin scheme that achieves a fairer service for all traffic.

Queues have a finite capacity and act very much like a funnel for water. If water continually enters the funnel faster than it exits, eventually, the funnel will begin overflowing from the top, and water is lost. When queues begin overflowing, packets drop as they arrive (tail-drop). Traffic congestion-management algorithms begin to drop packets arriving from selected low-priority traffic flows before the queue fills. Three mechanisms are involved in queue management:

- Placement of packets into queues on arrival based on prior marking or other values in the packet header
- Servicing of queues as output capacity becomes available
- Determination of which arriving packets are sacrificed as a queue fills to preserve space for other traffic

When calculating the required amount of bandwidth for a converged WAN, remember that, when added together, all the application traffic (voice, video, and data traffic) should equal no more than 75 percent of the provisioned bandwidth. The remaining 25 percent is reserved for short-demand peaks or outages, and administrative overhead, such as routing and signaling protocols.

Table 7-1 lists packet priority classifications and the corresponding IP Precedence and DSCP values.

Table 7-1   *Corresponding Layer 2 CoS, IP Precedence, and IP DSCP Values*

Packet Priority Classification Layer 2 Class of Service	IP Precedence	DSCP
CoS 0	Routine (IP Precedence 0)	0–7
CoS 1	Priority (IP Precedence 1)	8–15
CoS 2	Immediate (IP Precedence 2)	16–23
CoS 3	Flash (IP Precedence 3)	24 31
CoS 4	Flash-Override (IP Precedence 4)	32–39
CoS 5	Critical (IP Precedence 5)	40–47
CoS 6	Internet (IP Precedence 6)	48–55
CoS 7	Network (IP Precedence 7)	56–63

QoS Design Guidelines for Data

Different data applications have different traffic characteristics. Even different versions of the same application can have different traffic characteristics. You can classify data into a relative priority model in one of four classes: gold, silver, bronze, and less-than-best effort.

Traffic analysis and lab testing are required to determine bandwidth requirements for data applications.

Cisco Systems recommends that you implement a relative priority model of these four classes, which has been proven to work well in most enterprise environments. For highly mission-critical data, Cisco recommends that you implement the following:

* DSCP AF21-23
* IP Precedence 2
* CoS 2

For second-tier mission-critical data, Cisco recommends that you implement the following:

- DSCP AF11-AF13
- IP Precedence 1
- CoS 1

Figure 7-7 displays all the DSCP classes, namely Class-Selector, Assured Forwarding (AF), and Expedited Forwarding (EF), along with their corresponding IP Precedence (CoS) values).

Figure 7-7   *Currently Defined DSCP Values and Their Corresponding IP Precedence*

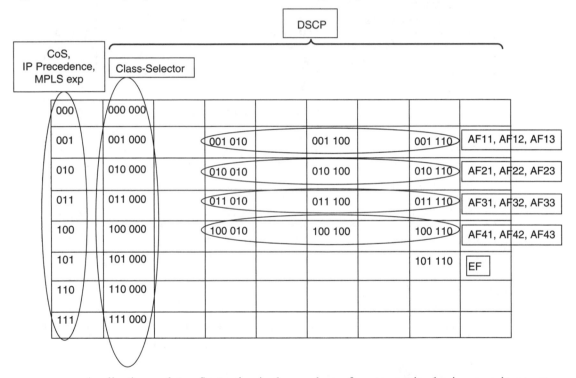

Application updates, fluctuation in the numbers of users, varying business environments, and the time of day, month, and year, all affect the bandwidth requirements of data applications. Therefore, rather than attempting to determine exact kbps of bandwidth requirements for data applications, a simpler and proven approach is to assign relative priorities to data applications.

QoS Design Guidelines for Voice

The bandwidth per call for voice depends on the codec, the duration of the sample or number of predictors, and data-link layer media. To calculate the bandwidth that voice streams consume, add the packet payload and all headers (in bits), and then multiply by the packet rate per second. In centralized call-processing designs, the IP Phones use a TCP control connection to communicate with a call-processing server. If enough bandwidth is not provisioned for these lightweight control connections, the end user might be adversely affected. When addressing voice traffic's QoS needs, the following important facts must be considered:

- One-way latency should be no more than 150 to 200 ms.
- Jitter should be no more than 30 ms.
- Packet loss should be no more than 1 percent.
- 17 to 106 kbps of guaranteed priority bandwidth is required per call (depending on the sampling rate, codec, and Layer 2 overhead).
- 150 bps (and Layer 2 overhead) per phone of guaranteed bandwidth is required for voice control traffic.

In an enterprise Architecture for Voice, Video, and Integrated Data (AVVID) network, you should classify packets that contain voice and video traffic into the appropriate queues, as follows:

- **Voice**—The IETF (draft) recommends a DSCP PHB label of EF for VoIP traffic. To remain backward compatible with IP Precedence, use an IP Precedence value of five and a CoS marking of five. These markings can be used as selection criteria for entry into the priority queue, where it exists, or the queue with the highest service weight and lowest drop probability in a weighted round-robin (WRR)/WRED scheduling scheme.

- **Video**—Use a value that is different from that used for VoIP traffic. In places where policing is needed, you can protect voice from video or vice versa. To accomplish this separation, you should use a DSCP PHB label of AF41, an IP Precedence value of 4, and a CoS marking of 4.

If both voice and video are marked as EF, IP Precedence 5, and CoS 5, it would be more difficult to differentiate between the two types of traffic in case you wanted to rate-limit (police) or otherwise control the amount of voice or video traffic through the network. Typically, a voice gateway or voice application server will mark RTP and control traffic with the appropriate DSCP and CoS markings. However, some end devices might not have the capability to correctly classify their own traffic. To provide control and security, CoS and markings that end devices assign must not be trusted. Assign signaling traffic a DSCP PHB label of AF31, IP precedence value of 3, and a CoS marking of 3.

QoS Design Guidelines for Video Conferencing

The two main types of video applications are streaming video (such as IP/TV, which may be either on-demand or multicast) and interactive video (such as video conferencing). Table 7-2 compares the QoS considerations for video conferencing versus streaming video.

Table 7-2   *QoS Considerations for Video Conferencing and Streaming Video*

Video Conferencing	Streaming Video
One-way latency should be no more than 150 to 200 ms.	Latency should be no more than 4 to 5 seconds, depending on the video application's buffering capabilities.
Jitter should be no more than 30 ms.	There are no significant jitter requirements.
Loss should be no more than 1 percent.	Loss should be no more than 2 percent.
The minimum bandwidth guarantee is the size of the video conferencing session plus 20 percent.	Bandwidth requirements depend on the encoding and rate of video stream.
	Nonentertainment streaming video should be provisioned into the silver (guaranteed bandwidth) data-traffic class.

For video content distribution, the following facts are important to remember:

- Streaming video content distribution is delay and delay-variation insensitive.
- Streaming video requires large file transfers (traffic patterns similar to FTP sessions).
- Distribution must be restricted to less-busy times of day.
- Video must be provisioned as less-than-best-effort data.

In enterprise networks, video conferencing over IP has similar packet loss, delay, and delay-variation requirements to that of VoIP traffic. You must classify IP video conferencing traffic so that network devices can recognize it and provide the appropriate treatment during periods of congestion. In enterprise networks, video conferencing packets should be marked with a DSCP PHB label of AF41. For backward compatibility, an IP Precedence of 4 should be used. Additionally, a Layer 2 802.1p CoS value of 4 should be used for IP Video Conferencing (IPVC) traffic in 802.1Q environments.

Streaming-video applications, such as IPTV video on demand (VoD) programs, are relatively high-bandwidth applications with a high tolerance for packet loss, delay, and delay variation. As such, significant QoS tools are not required to meet the needs of these applications. However, in most enterprise environments, these types of applications are considered more important than regular background applications (such as e-mail and web browsing) and should be given preferential treatment. A Layer 2 classification of CoS 1 in 802.1Q/802.1p environments should be used for these applications. To remain backward compatible, an IP Precedence classification of 1 should be used. Because streaming video is not drop or delay sensitive, you can use the high-drop precedence DSCP PHB: AF13 is recommended.

Designing QoS for the Enterprise Network

The QoS implementation for a campus network differs at the Campus Backbone, Building Access, and Building Distribution submodules. Not all QoS tools are appropriate in all areas of the network. Figure 7-8 shows you the types of QoS tools and techniques to deploy in each module and submodule of the Enterprise Composite Model. As shown in the figure, you would select different QoS solutions based on where QoS is being implemented in the network.

Figure 7-8   *QoS Tools Mapped to Design Requirements*

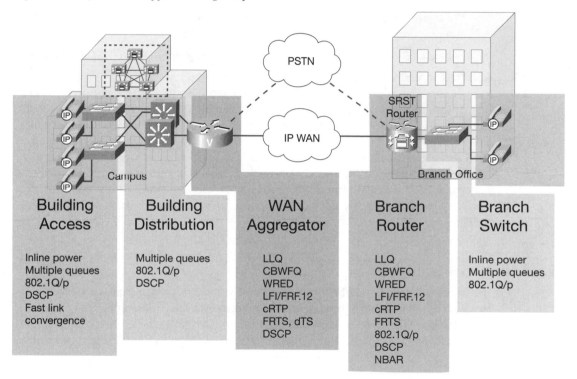

Building Access	Building Distribution	WAN Aggregator	Branch Router	Branch Switch
Inline power	Multiple queues	LLQ	LLQ	Inline power
Multiple queues	802.1Q/p	CBWFQ	CBWFQ	Multiple queues
802.1Q/p	DSCP	WRED	WRED	802.1Q/p
DSCP		LFI/FRF.12	LFI/FRF.12	
Fast link		cRTP	cRTP	
convergence		FRTS, dTS	FRTS	
		DSCP	802.1Q/p	
			DSCP	
			NBAR	

The Building Access submodule is typically where the trust boundary is formed. That is where the precedence is set for the packets and then trusted throughout the rest of the network. A switch at the Building Access submodule must support the following capabilities:

- Multiple VLANs on the access port to which an end user is attached
- Manipulation of the QoS or CoS values provided by an end device
- Extension of the trust boundary for the CoS or DSCP marking toward the end devices

There are times when the devices attached to the campus network do not classify their traffic with the appropriate Layer 2 and Layer 3 markings. When considering your choices for access layer devices, consider the switch's ability to classify and mark traffic at the edge of the network using ACLs and service policies. This allows you to offer QoS as a service throughout the network, and administer it at the edge of the network where CPU resources are plentiful, rather than at the Campus Backbone and Building Distribution submodules, where QoS classification and marking could adversely affect network responsiveness and utilization.

QoS at the Building Distribution layer requires implementation of the following:

- Enable QoS.

- Change the default CoS to the DSCP marking that is desired (use a default CoS to DSCP map table).

- Configure service policies to classify traffic that does not contain a CoS to DSCP marking that you can trust.

- Enable CoS or DSCP trust on the ports where trust is appropriate, DSCP for Layer 3 aware access, and CoS for Layer 2 only access.

To maintain the QoS policy throughout the network, the core device can provide some QoS congestion-management features. The traffic going to the Campus Backbone should already be classified and marked at the Building Access or Building Distribution submodules, so the Campus Backbone should be able to process the traffic quickly using a simple queuing mechanism. There should be no need to run QoS classification and marking tools within the Campus Backbone of the network. If QoS is implemented in the Campus Backbone, keep it to a minimum to facilitate high-speed queuing with some form of intelligent dropping. The typical queue service mechanisms are LLQ and modified deficit round-robin scheduling.

Example: QoS Solution

The Celestal Curtain Manufacturing Company headquarters has recently redesigned its network and has come up with plans to implement a QoS solution for its network, particularly on WAN links. Its new design includes voice and access to critical applications. Voice applications have top priority, and the other critical applications take second priority. All other traffic can be processed on a best-effort service.

The company has a choice of three QoS models:

- **Best-effort model**—Works for the best-effort type of traffic, but not for the other two types of traffic.

- **IntServ model**—Works for all types of traffic but is more difficult to configure and maintain, because RSVP must be enabled throughout the network and traffic flow is actively managed.

- **DiffServ model**—Allows fairly easy configuration to maintain traffic priority by packet type.

The company selected the DiffServ model for its ease of implementation and traffic type-based prioritization. The company decided to build the trust boundary at the access layer (see Figure 7-9).

Figure 7-9   *Celestal QoS Implementation at the Company Headquarters*

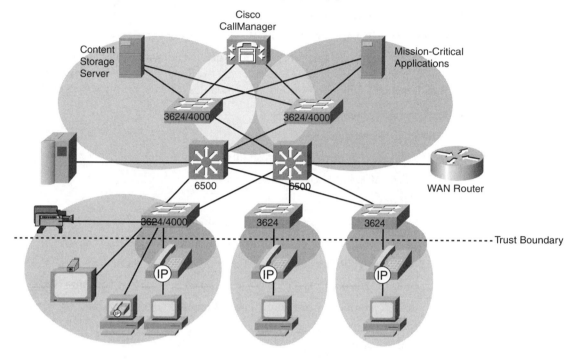

The Catalyst 3524 switch is the base access device, and supports these QoS enablers:

- Two transmit queues
- CoS-based QoS (802.1p)
- Trust CoS
- Port-based CoS marking for unmarked traffic
- GigaStack (only point-to-point stacks are recommended)
- Inline power

On the access devices, the company enabled multiple VLAN identifiers per port. IP Phones classify their traffic. The Catalyst 3524 reclassifies the traffic from behind the end-user device to the low queue. The access layer includes one Catalyst 4000 that supports these QoS enablers:

- Two transmit queues
- CoS (802.1p)-based QoS
- CoS values mapped to output queues in pairs
- Queues are serviced in a round-robin fashion

- Switch-wide CoS marking for unmarked traffic
- All ports are considered trusted
- Inline power via Power Entry Module (PEM) and power shelf

After QoS is enabled, all CoS values are mapped to queue number 1 by default. CoS queue values must be mapped. The company implemented two Catalyst 6500 switches in the Campus Backbone and Building Distribution submodules that support these QoS enablers:

- Redundant supervisors
- Transmit and receive queues
- Priority queues and multiple-drop thresholds
- CoS, DSCP, or ACL-based QoS (policy maps)
- Trust DSCP or CoS
- Settings by port DSCP or CoS (marked or unmarked)
- Mapping from CoS to DSCP or DSCP to CoS
- Port can trust DSCP, IP Precedence, or CoS
- It is recommended to use trust CoS, with access to receive priority queuing (Rx PQ)
- 10/100 network interface cards require an additional step of configuring ACL to trust traffic

Output scheduling consists of

- Assigning traffic to queues based on CoS
- Configuring threshold levels
- Modifying buffer sizes (expert mode)
- Assigning weights for WRR (expert mode)

The Building Distribution submodule is the aggregation point in this network. Because the Catalyst 3524 switches cannot mark and classify multiple data types, classification and marking takes place in the distribution layer. On the Building Distribution devices, the administrator creates ACLs to classify the mission-critical data into a higher priority. The company implemented a gold, silver, bronze, and best-effort model. Voice is classified as gold, signaling is classified as silver, and critical data is classified as bronze. All other traffic goes to the best-effort queue.

Summary

In this chapter, you learned the following key points:

- QoS technologies and tools enable control and predictable service for different network applications and traffic types.

- Network reliability is mainly a function of the following factors and how much control the network administrators have over them:
  - Delay (packetization, serialization, propagation)
  - Delay variation (jitter)
  - Packet loss
- Using QoS technologies, network engineers/administrators can do the following:
  - Predict response times for end-to-end network services
  - Manage jitter-sensitive applications and delay-sensitive traffic
  - Control loss in times of congestion
  - Set traffic priorities across the network
  - Support dedicated bandwidth
  - Avoid and manage network congestion
- The two QoS architectures used in IP networks are
  - Integrated Services (IntServ) model
  - Differentiated Services (DiffServ) model
- The three basic levels of end-to-end QoS that can be provided across a heterogeneous network are
  - Best-effort service
  - Differentiated service
  - Guaranteed service
- The type of service to be deployed in a network depends on the type of application being supported, how fast the migration needs to take place, and cost.
- To deploy QoS in a network, the following tasks need to be performed; each task requires certain tools and technologies, and needs to be implemented at specific spots:
  - Classification and marking
  - Congestion avoidance
  - Congestion management
  - Traffic conditioning
  - Signaling
  - Link efficiency mechanisms
- The Cisco-recommended QoS specifications for voice traffic are
  - One-way latency should be no more than 150 to 200 ms.
  - Jitter should be no more than 30 ms.

- — Packet loss should be no more than 1 percent.
- — 17 to 106 kbps of guaranteed priority bandwidth is required per call (depending on the sampling rate, codec, and Layer 2 overhead).
- — 150 bps (+ Layer 2 overhead) per phone of guaranteed bandwidth is required for voice control traffic.

- The Cisco-recommended QoS specifications for video conferencing are
  - — One-way latency should be no more than 150 to 200 ms.
  - — Jitter should be no more than 30 ms.
  - — Packet loss should be no more than 1 percent.
  - — The minimum bandwidth guarantee is the size of the video conferencing session plus 20 percent.

- The Cisco-recommended QoS specifications for streaming video traffic are
  - — Latency should be no more than four to five seconds, depending on the video application's buffering capabilities.
  - — There are no significant jitter requirements.
  - — Packet loss should be no more than 2 percent.
  - — Bandwidth requirements depend on the encoding and rate of video stream.
  - — Nonentertainment streaming video should be provisioned into the silver (guaranteed bandwidth) data-traffic class.

- The Cisco-recommended QoS implementation for a campus network differs at the Campus Backbone, Building Distribution, and Building Access submodules. A trust boundary is formed at the Building Access submodule; the marking is usually set there, and then trusted throughout the rest of the network. The traffic going to the Campus Backbone should already be classified and marked at the Building Access or Building Distribution submodules, so the Campus Backbone should be able to process the traffic quickly using a simple queuing mechanism.

Reference

Cisco IOS QoS Articles and Reports. http://www.cisco.com/warp/public/732/Tech/qos/.

Product Summary

Table 7-3 provides a brief overview of some of the products available from Cisco Systems that relate to the topics discussed in this chapter. For a more detailed breakdown of the Cisco product line, visit http://www.cisco.com/en/US/products/index.html.

Table 7-3   *Examples of Cisco Catalyst Switches and Their Corresponding QoS Capabilities*

Product Name	Description
Catalyst 3524	Catalyst 3524 can be used as a base access device, and it supports the following QoS enablers: • Two transmit queues • CoS-based QoS (802.1p) • Trust CoS • Port-based CoS marking for unmarked traffic • For stacking (GigaStack), point-to-point stacks are recommended • Inline power (for IP Phones)
Catalyst 4000	Catalyst 4000 can also be used as an access device, and it supports the following QoS enablers: • Two transmit queues • CoS-based QoS (802.1p) • CoS values mapped to output queues in pairs • Queues are serviced in a round-robin fashion • Switch-wide CoS marking for unmarked traffic • All ports are considered trusted • Inline power via Power Entry Modules (PEMs) and power shelf
Catalyst 6500	Catalyst 6500 switches are suitable for Campus Backbone and Building Distribution submodules. They support the following QoS features: • Redundant supervisors • Transmit and receive queues • Priority queues and multiple drop thresholds • CoS, DSCP, or access control list–based QoS (policy maps) • Trust DSCP or CoS • Settings by port DSCP or CoS • Mapping from CoS to DSCP or DSCP to CoS

Standards and Specifications Summary

Request For Comments (RFCs) can be downloaded from the following website: http://www.rfc-editor.org/rfc.html.

• RFC 2474, "Definition of the Differentiated Services Field (DS Field) in the IPv4 and IPv6 Headers."

- RFC 2475, "An Architecture for Differentiated Service."
- RFC 1349, "Type of Service in the Internet Protocol Suite."

Review Questions

Answer the following questions to test your comprehension of the topics discussed in this chapter. Refer to Appendix A, "Answers to Review Questions," to check your answers.

1 Choose three items that require QoS to manage them.

   a   Reliability

   b   Delay

   c   Packet loss

   d   Load

   e   Delay variation

2 Name at least two benefits of effective QoS configurations?

3 Name the three types of fixed delay.

4 Explain delay variation (jitter).

5 What is a jitter buffer?

6 List at least three tasks that IT managers can accomplish using QoS technologies:

7 Name the two QoS architectures (models) used in IP networks.

8 Within the IntServ model, which protocol is used by applications to signal their QoS requirements?

9 Which two of the following items are *not* in line with the IntServ model?

   a   Manages the traffic on a per-flow basis

   b   Manages the traffic on a type-of-traffic basis

   c   Provides customized services per traffic stream

   d   Does not provide individual stream visibility

   e   Results in greater network costs

10 Which two of the following items are *not* in line with the DiffServ model?

   a   Manages the traffic on a per-flow basis

   b   Manages traffic on a type-of-traffic basis

      c Provides customized services per traffic stream

      d Does not provide individual stream visibility

      e Provides a lower implementation cost

11 Name the three basic levels of QoS that can be provided across a heterogeneous network.

12 Classification at the trust boundary can mark packets by examining different fields. Name at least three of those fields.

13 Name and briefly explain the technique (supported by Cisco IOS) for congestion avoidance.

14 Name at least three congestion management features supported by Cisco IOS.

15 Name at least two Cisco IOS–supported traffic conditioning tools and techniques?

16 Name at least two QoS software traffic-shaping features within Cisco IOS?

17 Name the three link-efficiency mechanisms (offered by IOS QoS software) that work in conjunction with queuing and traffic shaping to improve the predictability of application services.

18 Name at least two properties or benefits of LFI?

19 cRTP can reduce the IP/UDP/RTP headers down to how many bytes?

20 Based on the design guidelines for voice and video, what are the one-way requirements for these types of traffic?

Case Study: OCSIC Bottling Company

The purpose of this case study is to practice the key design skills discussed in this chapter. OCSIC Bottling Company wants to prioritize the traffic going over the WAN links to ensure that the SAP/Oracle traffic always gets first priority in the network. The PeopleSoft and e-mail applications get second priority. All traffic within the intranet receives third priority, and all other traffic not specified gets a low priority. OCSIC wants the WAN links to adjust their rate based on Frame Relay BECN and FECN activity. A VoIP solution is also included, which means that voice traffic will require the highest priority.

The objective of this project is to design QoS services that meet the needs of the OCSIC Bottling Company; specifically, a QoS design must be developed for OCSIC's WAN links and for its Campus Infrastructure module. As each component of the design will have multiple options, each option must be considered carefully based on the constraints at hand.

Furthermore, as each component of the design is identified, a justification must be provided for that decision. The justification explains the options considered and why a certain option is selected.

QoS Design for the Site-to-Site WAN

The QoS design for OCSIC's site-to-site WAN requires that the tools and settings for each of the following items be identified:

- Classification and marking
- Congestion avoidance
- Congestion management
- Traffic conditioning
- Signaling
- Link efficiency

Table 7-4 provides one possible solution for the choice of tools and settings for the items listed; it also provides the justification for the decision made.

Table 7-4   *Design Decisions for OCSIC's Site-to-Site WAN QoS*

Design Questions	Decision	Justification
What classification and marking tools and settings are required?	Each type of traffic is classified as close to the source as possible with marking as follows: • Voice packets will be marked with an IP Precedence 5, CoS 5 • Signaling traffic will be marked with an IP Precedence 4, CoS 4 • Mission-critical data will be marked with a precedence 4, CoS 4 • Important data will be marked with an IP Precedence 3, CoS 3 • Corporate data will be marked with an IP Precedence 2, CoS 2 • All other traffic will be marked with an IP Precedence of 0, CoS 0 • Classification for the data is done via CAR utilizing access lists to determine which traffic goes in which queue	Packets are classified and then scheduled on the egress from every device that forwards traffic. The WAN devices are more critical than the LAN devices because of the bandwidth restrictions.

Table 7-4   *Design Decisions for OCSIC's Site-to-Site WAN QoS (Continued)*

Design Questions	Decision	Justification
What congestion avoidance tools and settings are required?	Use WRED	WRED is used to drop packets from lower priority data queues.
What congestion management tools and settings are required?	Use LLQ with alternate priority as the scheduling mechanism. Use three queues to support data traffic.	SAP/Oracle goes in queue 3; PeopleSoft and e-mail go in queue 2; and intranet traffic goes in queue 1. All other traffic goes in default queue 0. The company uses a 25, 50, and 75 packet threshold for dropping packets out of the queues with a CoS 0, 1, and 2.
What traffic conditioning tools and settings are required?	Use Frame Relay traffic shaping	Frame Relay traffic shaping is used to ensure that the far ends can handle the amount of traffic sent to them from the headquarters site.
What signaling tools and settings are required?	Classify the voice signaling as an IP Precedence 4, CoS 4	The precedence values ensure that voice receives priority on the network.
What link efficiency tools and settings are required?	No link efficiency to the district office. Use Frame Relay traffic shaping from the district plants to the regional offices.	Because all the links to the district offices are T1, the solution does not need LFI going to the districts. From the district offices to the regional plants, Frame Relay traffic shaping will be used. The MTU to the remote plants will be set to 512 bytes.

QoS Design for the Campus Infrastructure Module

The QoS design for OCSIC's headquarter campus infrastructure module requires that the tools and settings for each of the following items be identified:

- Classification and marking
- Congestion avoidance
- Congestion management

- Traffic conditioning
- Signaling
- Link efficiency

Table 7-5 provides one possible solution for the choice of tools and settings for the items listed. It also provides the justification for the decision made.

Table 7-5 *Design Decisions for OCSIC Headquarters' Campus Infrastructure Module*

Design Questions	Decision	Justification
What classification and marking tools and settings are required?	Each type of traffic is classified as close to the source as possible with marking as follows: • Voice packets will be marked with an IP Precedence 5, CoS 5 • Signaling traffic will be marked with an IP Precedence 4, CoS 4 • Mission-critical data will be marked with an IP Precedence 4, CoS 4 • Important data will be marked with an IP Precedence 3, CoS 3 • Corporate data will be marked with an IP Precedence 2, CoS 2 • All other traffic will be marked with an IP Precedence 0, CoS 0 • Classification for the data is done via CAR utilizing access lists to determine which traffic goes in which queue	Packets are classified and then scheduled on the egress from every device that forwards traffic. The WAN devices are more critical than the LAN devices because of the bandwidth restrictions.
What congestion-avoidance tools and settings are required?	Use WRED	WRED is used to drop packets from lower priority data queues.

Table 7-5 *Design Decisions for OCSIC Headquarters' Campus Infrastructure Module (Continued)*

What congestion management tools and settings are required?	Use LLQ with alternate priority as the scheduling mechanism. Use three queues to support data traffic.	SAP/Oracle goes in queue 3; PeopleSoft and e-mail go in queue 2; and intranet traffic goes in queue 1. All other traffic goes in default queue 0. The company uses a 25, 50, and 75 packet threshold for dropping packets out of the queues with a CoS 0, 1, and 2.
Design Questions	**Decision**	**Justification**
What traffic conditioning tools and settings are required?	None	Traffic conditioning is not needed on the campus network.
What signaling tools and settings are required?	None	Signaling is not needed on the campus network.
What link efficiency tools and settings are required?	None	Link efficiency is not needed on the campus network.

After completing this chapter, you will be able to

- Examine Internet Protocol (IP) multicast services
- Design IP multicast solutions for enterprise networks

CHAPTER 8

Designing IP Multicast Services

Multicasting facilitates delivery of a single stream of information to multiple recipients without excessive utilization of available network bandwidth. Video conferencing, corporate communications, distance learning, and distribution of software are some of the popular applications of IP multicasting. Multicast packets are replicated in the network by routers enabled with Protocol Independent Multicast (PIM) and other supporting multicast protocols, resulting in efficient delivery of data to multiple receivers at different network locations.

The first part of this chapter focuses on identifying the IP multicast implementation options based on a set of application requirements. The second part of this chapter covers designing an IP multicast solution in an existing unicast infrastructure based on specific network and application needs.

Examining IP Multicast Services

Traditional IP communication allows a host to send packets to a single host (unicast) or to all local hosts (broadcast transmission). IP multicast provides a third possibility: It allows a host to send packets to a group address. Through deployment of multicast technologies, only some subnets and some host(s) within those subnets (interested in the specific multicast group) will receive those packets. As one of the many capabilities of Cisco IOS Software, the IP multicast technologies facilitate scalable, efficient distribution of data, voice, and video streams to hundreds, thousands, or even millions of users. IOS multicast is used by corporate communications, video conferencing, e-learning, Internet broadcast, hoot 'n' holler, and streaming media applications. Internetwork designers ought to be able to identify the IP multicast implementation options and the enterprise requirements for IP multicast intelligent network services.

NOTE   Hoot 'n' holler are multiuser conference networks that do not require users to dial into a conference bridge. Even though it is expensive, hoot 'n' holler broadcast audio network systems are used heavily by brokerages, news agencies, publishers, emergency response agencies, weather bureaus, and so on. The Cisco Hoot 'n' Holler over IP provides an affordable solution while it protects investments in existing hoot 'n' holler equipment, such as turrets, bridges, and four-wire phones.

IP Multicast Basics

IP multicast, as an alternative to unicast and broadcast, sends packets to a group address, which results in a subset of network hosts receiving those packets. By requiring only a single copy of each packet to be sent out of appropriate interface(s), multicast helps reduce network traffic and yields bandwidth to other applications.

With a unicast design, an application sends one copy of each packet to every client; hence, unicast transmission requires a large amount of bandwidth. With unicast, the same information has to be sent multiple times, even on shared links. A large number of clients can impact the scalability of the network. If unicast is used as the means for transmitting the same data to multiple recipients, network managers must take the number of user connections and the amount of replicated unicast transmissions into consideration. If the number of user connections and/or the amount of data to be sent becomes large, the network, or at least parts of it, might get very overloaded.

Figure 8-1 shows the heavy data load a network incurs when a server in a unicast environment sends a separate video stream (1.5 Mbps) to each client requesting access to the application.

Figure 8-1   *Using Unicast to Deliver Data to Many Recipients*

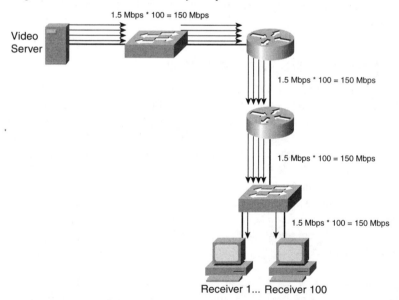

In the example illustrated in Figure 8-1, 100 clients receive the same information, which demonstrates that a large number of clients receiving multiple copies of the same data can quickly consume lots of bandwidth. Additionally, you must also consider the number of router and switch hops that exist in the path between the server and the recipients.

Intermediate devices might become overloaded as a result of having to process, replicate, and forward large volumes of data.

A multicast server sends out a single data stream to multiple clients using a special multicast address. Client devices voluntarily listen or do not listen to the multicast address. Figure 8-2 demonstrates how multicasting saves bandwidth and controls network traffic by forcing the network to replicate and send packets only to the parts of the network where the data is wanted.

Figure 8-2   *Using Multicast to Deliver Data to Many Recipients*

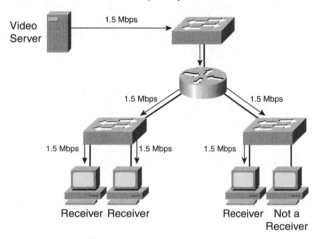

Any application that requires information to be delivered to multiple users concurrently can benefit from IP multicast. Table 8-1 displays two sets of examples for IP multicast applications: The first set is today's common applications, and the second set is comprised of applications that are anticipated to be popular in the future.

Table 8-1   *IP Multicast Applications*

Today	Tomorrow
Video conferencing	Broadband access
IP telephony music-on-hold	Video conferencing
Corporate-wide communications	Digital TV
Distance learning	Digital audio
Software distribution	Entertainment
Any one-to-many data push applications	Personal digital assistants and home appliances

IP Multicast Data-Delivery Principles

IP multicast delivers source traffic to multiple receivers without wasting any network bandwidth. Multicast packets are replicated in the network where paths diverge at routers enabled with PIM and other supporting multicast protocols, resulting in the most efficient delivery of data to multiple receivers.

Many alternatives to IP multicast require the source to send more than one copy of the data. Some, such as application-level multicast, require the source to send an individual copy to each receiver. Even low-bandwidth applications can benefit from using IP multicast when there are thousands of concurrent receivers. High-bandwidth applications, such as Motion Picture Experts Group (MPEG) video, might require a large portion of the available network bandwidth for a single stream. In these applications, IP multicast is the only practical way to simultaneously send data to more than one receiver.

IP multicast is the transmission of an IP data frame to a host group that is defined by a single IP address. IP multicasting is an extension to the standard IP network-level protocol and is described in Request for Comments (RFC) 1112, "Host Extensions for IP Multicasting." IP multicasting has the following characteristics:

- Transmits IP datagrams to a host group that is identified by a single IP destination address. A host group is dynamic and can contain zero or more host devices at any given time.

- Delivers a multicast packet to all members of the destination host group with the same best-effort reliability as regular unicast IP datagrams.

- Supports dynamic membership of a host group.

- Supports all host groups regardless of the location or number of members.

- Supports the membership of a single host in one or more multicast groups.

- Upholds multiple data streams at the application level for a single group address.

- Supports a single group address for multiple applications on a host.

Multicast transmission has many advantages over unicast transmission in a one-to-many or many-to-many environment:

- **Enhanced efficiency**—Available network bandwidth is utilized more efficiently, because multiple streams of data are replaced with a single transmission.

- **Optimized performance**—Fewer copies of data require forwarding and processing.

- **Distributed applications**—In a unicast transmission, multipoint applications will not be possible as demand and usage grow, because unicast transmission will not scale.

Traffic levels and clients increase at a 1:1 rate with unicast transmission. Traffic levels increase at a greatly reduced rate compared to clients when you use multicast transmission. Figure 8-3 displays how the amount of generated traffic increases when the number of data recipients increases in a unicast environment as opposed to a multicast environment.

Figure 8-3   *Unicast Versus Multicast in Traffic Generation*

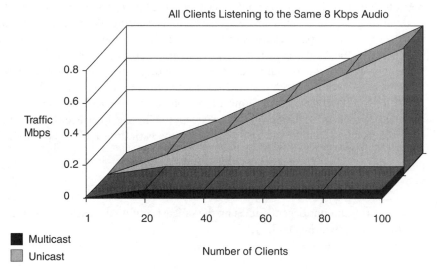

IP multicast intrinsically has several disadvantages. Most IP multicast applications are User Datagram Protocol (UDP)-based. This results in some undesirable side effects when compared to unicast Transfer Control Protocol (TCP) applications. Best-effort delivery results in occasional packet drops. Many multicast applications that operate in real time (such as audio and video) might be impacted by these losses. It is not feasible to request retransmission of the lost data at the application layer for real-time applications. There also can be heavy drops on voice applications. Packet drops can result in jerky, missed speech patterns that make content unintelligible when the drop rate gets high enough. Moderate-to-heavy drops in video are sometimes fairly well-tolerated by the human eye, appearing as unusual artifacts on the picture. However, some compression algorithms can be severely impacted by even low drop rates, causing the picture to become jerky or freeze for several seconds while the decompression algorithm recovers. Lack of congestion control and quality of service (QoS) can result in overall network degradation as the popularity of UDP-based multicast applications grows. The network can occasionally duplicate packets as multicast network topologies change. Multicast applications should tolerate occasional duplicate packets.

Multicast Forwarding

In multicast forwarding, a router makes part of its forwarding decision based on the packet source address. This is opposite to how unicast forwarding works, which is mostly dependent on packet destination. In multicast forwarding, the source IP address of a packet denotes the multicast source (S), and the destination IP address denotes a multicast group (G). The IP hosts interested in receiving IP packets destined to specific multicast groups are not generally co-located and are, for the most part, unknown.

Reverse Path Forwarding (RPF), a common multicast forwarding mechanism, only forwards packets that come in through an interface that is the best egress interface toward the source of the multicast; hence, the name Reverse Path Forwarding. Whether the interface through which the multicast packets are coming into the router is the best egress interface toward the source of the multicast or not can be determined by consulting the multicast routing table or by referring to the familiar IP unicast routing table. The reason for performing the RPF check is to eliminate duplicate forwarding of the multicast traffic. If the interface is determined to be the best egress toward the source (it is the RPF interface), the incoming packets are forwarded out all interfaces except the ingress interface (the interface that the packets came into the router from [with some variations and exceptions]). Figure 8-4 illustrates RPF.

NOTE   Multicast routing has dependencies on the unicast routing data structures and information (routing and forwarding tables).

Figure 8-4   *Reverse Path Forwarding*

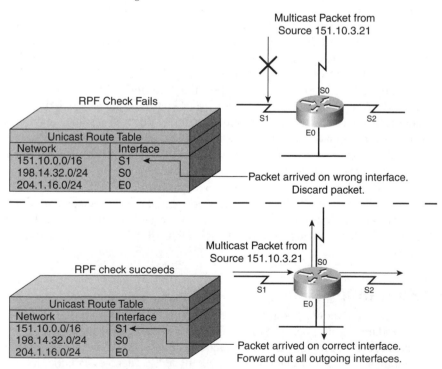

Two cases are shown in Figure 8-4. The top portion of Figure 8-4 shows an RPF check on multicast data received on interface S0. The RPF check fails because, according to the routing table, data was not received on the best egress interface toward the 151.10.3.21 address. Data is silently dropped. The bottom portion of Figure 8-4 shows an RPF check on multicast data received on interface S1. The RPF check succeeds because, according to the routing table, data was received on the best egress interface toward the 151.10.3.21 address. The data is forwarded out of all outgoing interfaces (on the multicast distribution tree) except the interface data from which it came.

IP Multicast Group Membership and Distribution Trees

IP multicast relies on the concept of a virtual group address. In normal Transfer Control Protocol/Internet Protocol (TCP/IP) routing, a packet is routed from a source address to a destination address, traversing the IP network on a hop-by-hop basis. In IP multicast, the packet's destination address is not assigned to a single destination. Instead, receivers join a group and, when they join, packets addressed to that group begin flowing to the members. Senders can be—but do not have to be—members of the group they are sending multicast data to.

Multicast-capable routers create distribution trees that control the path that IP multicast traffic takes through the network to deliver traffic to all receivers. The two basic types of multicast distribution trees are

- Source trees
- Shared trees

Source Trees

The simplest form of a multicast distribution tree is a source tree with its root at the router closest to the multicast source and branches forming a spanning tree through the network to the receivers or to the ultimate routers connected to the multicast group members. Because this tree uses the shortest path through the network, it is also referred to as a shortest path tree (SPT). Figure 8-5 shows an example of a source-based distribution tree delivering multicast traffic from Host A (sender) to Hosts B and C (receivers or group members).

Figure 8-5 shows an example of an SPT for group 224.1.1.1 rooted at router A, which is closest to the source. The branches of the SPT tree for this multicast group extend from router A to router C, and from router C to router E. The special notation of (S,G), pronounced "S comma G," enumerates an SPT, where S is the IP address of the source and G is the multicast group address. Using this notation, the SPT for the example shown in the figure would be (192.168.1.1, 224.1.1.1). The (S,G) notation implies that a separate SPT exists for each individual source sending to each group, which is correct. For example, if Host B is also sending traffic to group 224.1.1.1 and Hosts A and C are receivers, a separate (S,G) SPT would exist with a notation of (192.168.2.2, 224.1.1.1).

Figure 8-5 *IP Multicast Source-Based Distribution Tree Example*

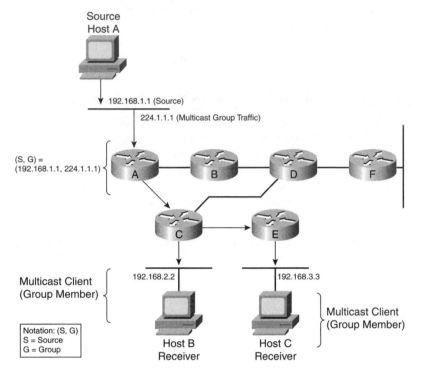

Shared Trees

Unlike source-based multicast distribution trees that have their root at the router closest to the source, shared multicast distribution trees use a single common root (for one or more or all multicast groups) placed at some administratively chosen point in the network. This shared root is called a rendezvous point (RP). Figure 8-6 shows a shared tree for the group 224.1.1.1 with the root located at router D. Source traffic is sent toward the RP on a source tree. The traffic is then forwarded down the shared tree from the RP to reach all the receivers, unless the receiver is located between the source and the RP, in which case, it will be serviced directly.

In the example illustrated in Figure 8-6, multicast traffic from the sources, Hosts A and D, travels to the root (router D) and then down the shared tree to the two receivers, Hosts B and C. Because all sources in the multicast group use a common shared tree, a wildcard notation written as (*,G), pronounced "star comma G," represents the tree.

Figure 8-6   *IP Multicast Shared Distribution Tree Example*

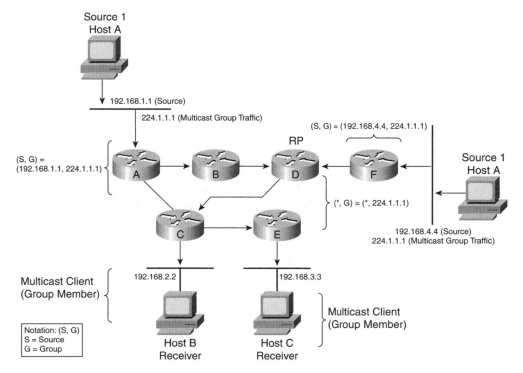

Comparison of Source Trees and Shared Trees

Both source trees and shared trees are loop-free. Messages are replicated only where the tree branches. Members of multicast groups can join or leave at any time; therefore, the distribution trees must be dynamically updated. When all the active receivers on a particular branch stop requesting the traffic for a particular multicast group, the routers prune that branch from the distribution tree and stop forwarding traffic down that branch. If one receiver on that branch becomes active and requests the multicast traffic, the router will dynamically modify the distribution tree and start forwarding traffic again.

Source trees have the advantage of creating the optimal path between the source and the receivers. This advantage guarantees the minimum amount of network latency for forwarding multicast traffic. However, this optimization comes at a cost: the routers must maintain path information for each source. In a network that has thousands of sources and thousands of groups, this overhead can quickly become a resource issue on the routers. Memory consumption from the size of the multicast routing table is a factor that network designers must take into consideration. The multicast routing table is required to maintain current values, called *state*, that determine multicast routing behavior.

Shared trees have the advantage of requiring the minimum amount of state in each router. The disadvantage of shared trees is that under certain circumstances the paths between the source and receivers might not be the optimal paths, which might introduce some latency in packet delivery. For example, in Figure 8-6, the shortest path between Host A (source 1) and Host B (a receiver) would be router A and router C. Because we are using router D as the root for a shared tree, the traffic must traverse routers A, B, D, and then C.

The following characteristics describe the two types of multicast distribution trees:

- **Source (or shortest path) trees**—Because one is built for each source, these trees use more router memory but benefit from optimal paths from the source to all receivers. They also minimize delay.

- **Shared trees**—Because the same tree is used for a multicast group (address) regardless of the source, these trees use less memory, but might result in suboptimal paths from the source to all receivers. Hence, they might encounter extra delays.

Protocol Independent Multicast

The Protocol Independent Multicast version 1 (PIMv1) routing protocol was introduced and used by Cisco Systems and, hence, was considered a proprietary protocol. PIM version 2, however, is standards based and endorsed by industry authorities. PIM leverages the unicast routing information to perform the multicast forwarding function. In other words, PIM uses the unicast routing table to perform the RPF check function, instead of building up a completely independent multicast routing table for that purpose. PIM can operate either in dense mode (DM) or in sparse mode (SM).

PIM Dense Mode

PIM dense mode (PIM-DM) uses a push model to flood multicast traffic to all parts of the network. This push model is a brute-force method for delivering data to the receivers. (It reminds me of the flyers stores send/flood into the vicinity of their businesses!) The PIM-DM method is efficient in deployments where active receivers are on every subnet in the network. PIM-DM initially floods multicast traffic throughout the network. Routers that have no downstream neighbors or have neighbors that are not interested in the multicast traffic prune back (on specific interfaces) and do not flood the unwanted traffic in the unwanted direction. This process repeats every 3 minutes (or 180 seconds) in this fashion:

1 The flood begins (see Part A of Figure 8-7).

2 Prune requests are sent and received. Prune timer starts (see Part B of Figure 8-7).

3 Multicast packets are forwarded to needed subnets only (see Part C of Figure 8-7).

4 Prune times out in 3 minutes and flooding begins again, which brings the process full-circle.

Routers accumulate state information by receiving data streams through the flood and prune mechanism. These data streams contain the source and group information so that downstream routers can build up their multicast forwarding table. PIM-DM supports only source trees, that is, (S,G) entries, and cannot be used to build a shared distribution tree.

Figure 8-7   *PIM-DM Flood and Prune Process*

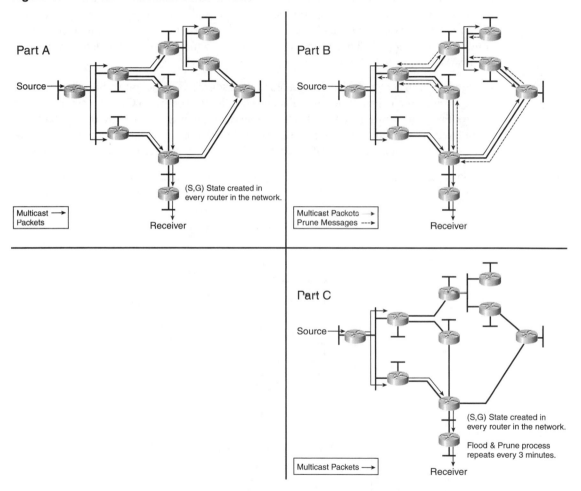

PIM Sparse Mode

PIM sparse mode (PIM-SM) uses a pull model to deliver multicast traffic. Only network segments with interested receivers that have explicitly requested the data will receive the traffic. Because PIM-SM uses shared trees (at least initially), it requires the use of an RP, which must be administratively configured in the network.

Routers closest (connected) to the multicast sources register with the RP; this informs the RP about the currently existing multicasts and their sources. If downstream routers send join messages toward the RP, the RP will request the multicast data to be sent to it so that it can forward the data down the shared tree toward the interested receivers. The edge routers learn about a particular source (address) when they actually receive data packets on the shared tree from that source through the RP. The edge router can send PIM (S,G) join messages toward the source of the multicast (as opposed to sending join messages toward the RP). A router only does that if, based on its unicast routing table, the data from the source has a better path than coming through the RP (which is the normal data flow path in PIM-SM).

In Figure 8-8, an active receiver has joined multicast group G. The router closest/connected to the interested receiver knows the IP address of the RP for group G, and it sends a (*,G) join for this group toward the RP. This (*,G) join travels hop-by-hop toward the RP, building shared tree branches that extend from the RP to the last-hop router directly connected to the receiver. At this point, group G traffic can flow down the shared tree root (RP) to the receiver.

Figure 8-8 *PIM-SM Join Messages Toward RP Cause Branches to Be Grafted and Path(s) Built from RP to the Recipients*

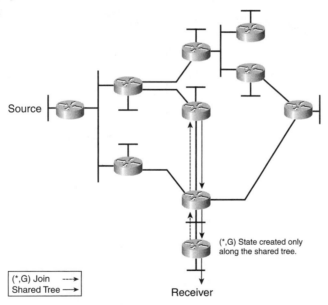

PIM-SM Source Registration

As soon as an active source for group G sends a packet to the router that is attached to this source, the router is responsible for registering the multicast address and its source with the RP. The source router encapsulates the multicast data from the source in a special PIM-SM message called the Register message and unicasts that data to the RP. This is called *source registration* (see Figure 8-9).

Figure 8-9   *PIM-SM Source Registration*

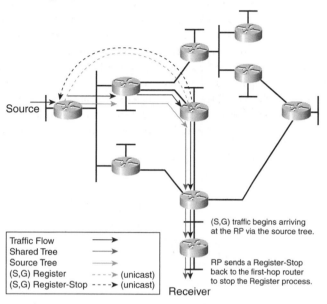

When the RP receives the Register message, it does two things:

1 The RP de-encapsulates the multicast data packet from the Register message and forwards it down the shared tree.

2 The RP sends an (S,G) join back toward the source network **S** to create a branch of an (S,G) SPT.

The SPT extends from the router closest to the sender, called the source router, all the way to the RP. As soon as the SPT is built from the source router to the RP, multicast traffic begins to flow from source **S** to the RP. After the RP begins receiving data through the SPT from source **S**, it sends a *register stop* to the source router. Hence, the data stops going from source **S** to RP using unicast; it will flow toward RP using multicast. The multicast flow from source **S** to RP happens over the source tree with the router closest to the sender as its root. After the multicast packets arrive at the RP, they flow through the branches of the shared tree that has the RP as its source.

Figure 8-9 shows the unicast source registration with dotted lines from the source router to the RP. The RP's acknowledgment of source registration (the stop register message) is shown with a dotted line in the opposite direction. One set of solid arrows shows the flow of data over the source tree to the RP. Another set of solid arrows shows the flow of data from the RP down to recipients on the shared tree. Finally, a third set of arrows shows the flow of data all the way from the source to the destination.

PIM-SM SPT Switchover

PIM-SM includes the capability for last-hop routers (that is, routers with directly connected members/recipients) to switch to the SPT, and bypass the RP if the traffic rate is above a set threshold, called the SPT-threshold. The default value of the SPT-threshold in Cisco routers is 0. This means that the default behavior for PIM-SM leaf routers attached to active receivers is to immediately join the SPT to the source as soon as the first packet arrives via the (*,G) shared tree. In Figure 8-10, the last-hop router sends an (S,G) join message toward the source to join the SPT and bypass the RP. The (S,G) join messages travel hop-by-hop to the first-hop router (the router connected directly to the source), thereby creating another branch of the SPT. This also creates (S,G) state in all the routers along this branch of the SPT. This behavior is called SPT switchover and is followed by prune requests toward the RP, meaning that the traffic flow over the shared tree is no longer necessary.

Figure 8-10   *PIM-SM SPT Switchover*

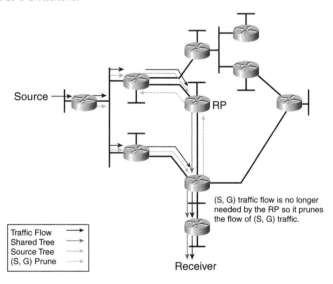

Source

RP

(S, G) traffic flow is no longer
needed by the RP so it prunes
the flow of (S, G) traffic.

Traffic Flow	→
Shared Tree	⇢
Source Tree	⇢
(S, G) Prune	⇢

Receiver

Sparse Mode, Dense Mode, and Sparse-Dense Mode

PIM-DM is appropriate for a large number of densely distributed receivers located in close proximity to the source. PIM-DM offers these advantages:

- Minimal number of commands required for configuration

- Simple mechanism for reaching all possible receivers and eliminating distribution to uninterested receivers

- Simple behavior is easier to understand and, therefore, easier to debug

When configuring a Cisco router interface for PIM, you have three choices available: IP PIM sparse mode, IP PIM dense mode, and IP PIM sparse-dense mode. It is best to use the sparse-dense mode. The router operates in sparse mode if it is configured with the address of the RP; otherwise, it operates in dense mode. A potential issue with PIM-DM is the need to flood frequently, because prunes expire every 3 minutes.

Use PIM-SM for sparse or dense distribution of multicast receivers. The main advantages of PIM-SM are

- Traffic is sent only to registered receivers that have explicitly joined the multicast group.

- RP can be switched to the optimal SPT when high-traffic sources are forwarding to a sparsely distributed receiver group.

Potential issues with PIM-SM include

- PIM-SM requires an RP during the initial setup of the distribution tree.

- RPs can become bottlenecks if not selected with great care.

- PIM-SM's complex behavior is difficult to understand and, therefore, difficult to debug.

IP Multicast Control Mechanisms

By default, a data-link layer switch will forward all multicast traffic to every port that belongs to the destination LAN. IP multicast control mechanisms limit multicast traffic to the ports that need to receive the data. Several IP multicast control mechanisms exist to complement IP multicast routing. Intradomain multicast supports multicast applications within an enterprise campus. IOS multicast technologies leverage network resources for massively scalable content distribution applications. Table 8-2 provides brief descriptions for the IP multicast control mechanisms that Cisco IOS supports.

Table 8-2   *IP Multicast Control Mechanisms Supported by IOS*

Feature	Description
CGMP[1]	A protocol developed by Cisco that allows data-link layer switches to leverage IGMP[2] information on Cisco routers to make data-link layer forwarding decisions.
	Provides management of group membership on switched Ethernet LANs.
	Allows switches to forward multicast traffic to only those ports that are interested in the traffic.
IGMP	Used by Internet Protocol, version 4 (IPv4) hosts to communicate multicast group membership to the connected routers.
	Version 3 of IGMP adds support for source specific multicast.

continues

Table 8-2   *IP Multicast Control Mechanisms Supported by IOS (Continued)*

Feature	Description
IGMP snooping	Requires the LAN switch to examine (snoop) IGMP packets sent from the IP host to the router, so that it can adjust its MAC table and avoid flooding multicast traffic.
PIMv2	PIM was originally developed by Cisco as a multicast routing protocol. PIMv2 is standards based; hence, it is not considered Cisco proprietary.
	PIM can coexist with any intradomain unicast routing protocol (hence, the term protocol independent).
	Supports explicit join (Sparse Mode), flood and prune (Dense Mode), or hybrid Sparse-Dense modes:
	• **Sparse Mode**—Relies upon an explicit joining method before attempting to send multicast data to receivers of a multicast group.
	• **Dense Mode**—Actively attempts to send multicast data to all potential receivers (flooding) and relies upon their self-pruning (removal from group) to achieve desired distribution.

[1] CGMP = Cisco Group Management Protocol

[2] IGMP = Internet Group Management Protocol

IGMP

Internet Group Management Protocol (IGMP) is a protocol that is mainly used between IP hosts and their local router(s). Using IGMP, hosts report to their local multicast router what multicast group(s) they want to join. The multicast router keeps track of all multicast groups that need to be forwarded to the local subnet. Similar to other internetworking protocols, IGMP is a work in progress: each new version of this protocol addresses the limitations of the previous version and introduces new capabilities.

Joining a group and maintaining a group happen as follows: hosts joining a group do not have to wait for a query from the router to join. They send in an unsolicited report indicating their interest. This reduces join latency for the end-system joining if no other members are present. However, to maintain the group membership, the router multicasts periodic IGMPv1 membership queries to the all hosts' group address (224.0.0.1). Only one member per group responds with a report to a query to save bandwidth on the subnet and to impose less processing on the hosts. This process is called response or report suppression. The response suppression mechanism is accomplished using the following rules:

- When a host receives the query, it starts a countdown timer for each multicast group of which it is a member. The countdown timers are each initialized to a random count within a given time range. (In IGMPv1, this was a fixed range of 10 seconds. Therefore, the countdown timers were randomly set to some value between 0 and 10 seconds.)

- When a countdown timer reaches 0, the host sends a membership report for the group associated with the countdown timer to notify the router that the group is still active.

- If a host receives a membership report before its associated countdown timer reaches 0, it cancels the countdown timer associated with the multicast group, thereby suppressing its own report.

In Figure 8-11, H2's time expired first, so it responded with its membership report. H1 and H3 cancelled their timers associated with the group, thereby suppressing their reports.

Figure 8-11 *IGMP General Query, Membership Report, and Report/Response Suppression*

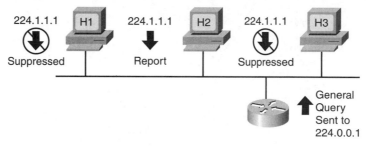

IGMP leave is the opposite of join. In brief, this process happens as follows: assume that a number of IP hosts and a router are interconnected using a LAN switch. When hosts want to leave a multicast group, they can either ignore the periodic general queries sent by the multicast router (IGMPv1 host behavior), or they can send an IGMP leave (IGMPv2 host behavior). When the switch receives a leave message, it sends out a MAC-based general query on the port on which it received the leave message to determine if any devices connected to this port are interested in traffic for the specific multicast group. If no IGMP report is received for any of the IP multicast groups that map to the MAC multicast group address, the port is removed from the multicast forwarding entry. If the port is not the last nonmulticast–router port in the multicast forwarding entry, the switch suppresses the IGMP leave (it is not sent to the router). If the port is the last nonmulticast-router port in the multicast forwarding entry, the IGMP leave is forwarded to the multicast router ports, and the MAC group forwarding entry is removed. When the router receives the IGMP leave, it sends several IGMP group-specific queries. If no join messages are received in response to the queries, and no downstream routers are connected through that interface, the router removes the interface from the IP multicast group entry in the multicast routing table.

IGMPv3 is the third version of the Internet Engineering Task Force (IETF) standards-track protocol in which hosts signal membership to last-hop routers of multicast groups. IGMPv3 introduces the ability for hosts to signal group membership with filtering capabilities with respect to sources. A host can either signal that it wants to receive traffic from all sources sending to a group except for some specific sources (called Exclude mode), or that it wants to receive traffic only from some specific sources sending to the group (called Include mode). In the example illustrated in Figure 8-12, host H1 has joined group 224.1.1.1 but only wants to receive traffic from source 1.1.1.1. Using a IGMPv3 source-specific join, the host can inform the local router, R3, that it is only interested in multicast traffic from source 1.1.1.1 for group 224.1.1.1.

Figure 8-12 *IGMPv3 Source-Specific Multicast*

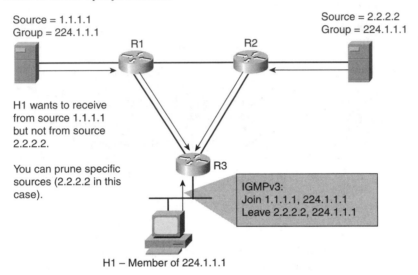

CGMP and IGMP Snooping

The default behavior for a Layer 2 switch is to flood multicast traffic to all the ports that are in the same virtual LAN (VLAN) broadcast domain as the port where the multicast was generated or came in from. This behavior reduces the bandwidth efficiency of the switch, because it does not limit traffic to only the ports that need/want to receive the multicast data. Two methods handle IP multicast more efficiently in a Layer 2 switching environment:

- **CGMP**—A Cisco-developed protocol that allows Catalyst switches to leverage IGMP information on Cisco routers to make data-link layer forwarding decisions. You must configure CGMP on the multicast routers and the data-link layer switches. With CGMP, IP multicast traffic is delivered only to those Catalyst switch ports that are attached to interested receivers. All other ports that have not explicitly requested the traffic will not receive it unless these ports are connected to a multicast router.

- **IGMP snooping**—An IP multicast constraining mechanism that runs on a data-link layer LAN switch. IGMP snooping requires the LAN switch to examine (snoop) some network layer information (IGMP join/leave messages) in the IGMP packets sent between the hosts and a router or multilayer switch. When the switch hears the IGMP host report from a host for a particular multicast group, the switch adds the port number of the host to the associated multicast table entry. When the switch hears the IGMP leave group message from a host, the switch removes the table entry of the host.

Designing IP Multicast Solutions for Enterprise Networks

Multicast deployments require three elements: the application, the network infrastructure, and client devices. Cisco IOS multicast technologies reside in the network infrastructure in Cisco routers and switches. Unlike first-generation video broadcast applications that require a separate stream for each viewer, IOS multicast is highly scalable. Multicast comprises a single content stream that is replicated by the network at branch points closest to viewers. This uses bandwidth more efficiently and greatly decreases the load on content servers, reaching more users at a lower cost per user.

Most enterprises find it essential to deploy customer care, e-learning, e-commerce, and supply-chain management applications over their data networks. Companies are investing in these and other network-enabled applications to attain and keep a competitive edge in an increasingly fast-paced economy. IP multicast technologies enable the efficient deployment of these applications. Network designers must be intimately familiar with the design considerations for IP multicast implementations and be able to design IP multicast services for small and large enterprise campus networks and for multicast services that operate over a wide-area network (WAN).

IP Multicast Design Considerations for an Enterprise Campus

When designing a network for IP multicast, servers and hosts, IP multicast control mechanisms, PIM mode, and router provisioning must all be given thought. The questions to ask when designing a network for IP multicast are as follows:

- Who is the source (server)?

  For each IP multicast application, you must identify the source or server, such as a Cisco IP/TV server.

- How do hosts join a conversation?

  To avoid Layer 2 flooding of multicast traffic, implement either IGMP snooping or CGMP. IGMP snooping is best in devices that provide application-specific integrated circuit (ASIC) hardware support for this purpose. Without hardware support, snooping can seriously degrade device performance, and CGMP should be implemented instead. Verify the IP multicast support for each platform prior to design and implementation.

- Should you use PIM-DM or PIM-SM?

  PIM-DM is easy to configure and provides a simple flood and prune mechanism. However, it causes inefficient flood and prune behavior and does not support shared trees. PIM-SM is very efficient, using an explicit join model and flowing traffic only where it is needed. Cisco recommends that you use PIM-SM whenever possible.

- If you are using PIM-SM, where should rendezvous points be placed?

  Place rendezvous points close to the source of the multicast traffic. Determine the routers that will be used as RPs.

- How should routers be provisioned to support IP multicast?

  Links that support IP multicast need sufficient bandwidth. Similarly, each router that supports IP multicast needs sufficient processing power. The IP multicast routing table stores an entry for each source and host. As the number of sources and hosts grows, the memory requirement for the router grows also.

To implement IP multicast efficiently in enterprise networks, you must first ensure that all data-link layer switches are able to constrain multicast flooding. Second, the network must support a sparse-mode multicast routing protocol. Clients and servers must have an IP protocol stack supporting multicast as specified in the Internet RFC 1112 or 2236 standard, and enterprise applications must support IP multicast. All modern operating systems support IGMP and IP multicast. All IOS software-based platforms support multicast, including the Cisco Catalyst family of switches and routers. The IP multicast design recommendations for addressing and security are

- **IP addressing**—Unless IP multicast traffic will be originating from or sent outside the enterprise, you should use the multicast limited scope addresses. You can aid network management by subdividing the available addresses into separate ranges for different purposes. For example, you can use a different range of addresses for each multicast application.

NOTE   Multicast limited scope, also called administratively scoped multicast, controls the number of hops a particular multicast traffic's packets go through. This is done by releasing the multicast packets with smaller Time to Live (TTL) than normal and/or configuring the routers to only forward multicast packets whose TTL values are larger than a certain value.

- **Security**—Security is an important topic for all areas of network design. Consider protecting your IP multicast traffic from denial-of-service attacks or stream hijacking by rogue sources and/or rogue RPs. You can configure your RPs to accept source registrations only from a defined access control list (ACL) or route map, eliminating rogue multicast sources, and can filter the source of RP announcements, eliminating rogue RPs.

Designing IP Multicast for a Small Campus

In a small campus design with a collapsed core and distribution layer, the backbone switches act as the RPs for multicast forwarding. Figure 8-13 shows a small campus that consists of two small buildings with no more than 200 users and end devices. The network uses a collapsed Campus Backbone and Building Distribution layer referred to as the Campus Backbone. The backbone switches have network layer interfaces to be used for Hot Standby Router Protocol (HSRP). The multicast sources are Cisco CallManager with music on hold and a Cisco IP/TV server attached through the Server Farm module.

Figure 8-13 *IP Multicast Small Campus Design*

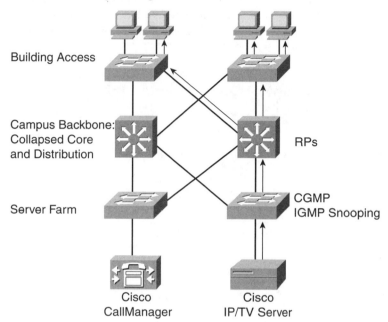

As an IP multicast control mechanism, IGMP snooping is enabled on all switches, except for those switches that do not provide hardware support for IGMP snooping. CGMP will be implemented on those devices. The two backbone switches act as multicast RPs. The Campus Backbone would not normally do anything other than transmit packets. However, it must take over the function of the Building Distribution submodule when you implement a collapsed backbone.

Designing IP Multicast for a Large Enterprise Campus

IP multicast design for a large campus must balance between granular administrative control and simplicity. Multicast design in a large enterprise network can be difficult to administer if the design is too granular. For example, you could place redundant RPs throughout the network, each having responsibility for a specific multicast address range. The optimal design is one that provides fast failover, proper RP placement, and a simplistic approach to traffic control. Although many possible combinations of multicast deployment exist in a large campus, and even more combinations for each type of multicast application, it is generally best to focus on keeping administration simple and the traffic reliable.

Figure 8-14 depicts a model for large campus network design. Each access switch in the Building Access submodule and the Server Farm module is dual-connected to a pair of distribution routers running HSRP. For multicast, one of the two routers is the designated router (DR) and the other is the IGMP querier. The DR for an IP subnet is the router that forwards the necessary multicast traffic to that subnet. The IGMP querier, on the other hand, is the router that keeps track of what multicast groups have an active member in a segment. The IP unicast routing protocol is configured such that the trunk from the access switch to the DR is always preferred, forcing unicast and multicast paths to be the same.

Figure 8-14 *IP Multicast Large Campus Design*

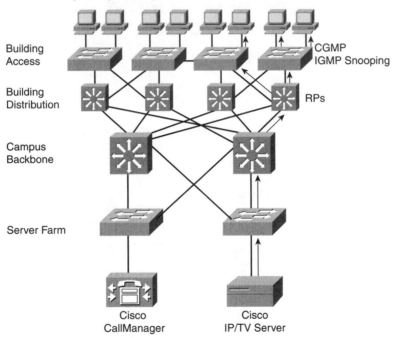

The Building Access submodule uses switches that support IGMP snooping and good port density to serve the end stations. The Building Distribution and Campus Backbone modules both use switches that have good multicast forwarding performance, can support large multicast routing tables, and are able to house multiple-gigabit links. The Server Farm module uses switches that support IGMP snooping. The Campus Backbone switches need to support a dense population of gigabit ports for connectivity to the Building Distribution submodule and other Campus Backbone switches. The multicast applications in this design use an architecture with few sources to many receivers. The sources are located in the Server Farm module. The Campus Backbone switches are designated as the multicast RPs. An alternate choice would be to have the Server Farm access switches serve this role.

Designing IP Multicast Over a WAN

When IP multicast traffic must cross a WAN link, the primary consideration is that the WAN bandwidth not be overwhelmed by unnecessary traffic. In the example illustrated in Figure 8-15, the design decisions for the headquarters' network are the same as in any large campus design: Place the RPs close to the multicast source, and constrain Layer 2 flooding with IGMP snooping or CGMP. The primary focus in this design is the filtering of multicast traffic at the WAN access router. The IP addressing scheme will facilitate the design goals.

Figure 8-15   *IP Multicast Over a WAN Connection*

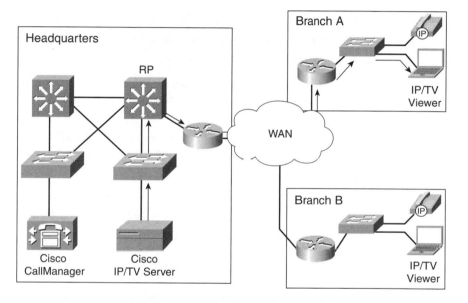

As Table 8-3 shows, you can assign multicast group address ranges based on bandwidth requirements for particular types of multicast traffic. With this scheme in place, you can configure the WAN access router with filters and multicast boundaries to ensure that multicast traffic is only forwarded to sites over links that support the necessary bandwidth.

Table 8-3   *Example for IP Multicast Addressing Scheme*

	Multicast Groups	Address Range	Scope	Restrictions
IP/TV High-Rate Traffic	239.255.x.y/16	239.255.0.0– 239.255.255.255	Site-Local	Restricted to Local Campus
IP/TV Medium-Rate Traffic	239.192.248.x/22	239.192.248.0– 239.192.251.255	Enterprise-Local	Restricted to 768 kbps + Sites
IP/TV Low-Rate Traffic	239.192.244.x/22	239.192.244.0– 239.192.247.157	Enterprise-Local	Restricted to 256 kbps + Sites
Multicast Music-on-Hold	239.192.240.x/22	239.192.240.0– 239.192.243.255	Enterprise-Local	No Restrictions

Summary

In this chapter, you learned the following key points:

- IP multicast allows a host to send packets to a group address. Through deployment of multicast technologies, only some subnets and some host(s) within those subnets (interested in the specific multicast group) will receive those packets.

- As one of the many capabilities of Cisco IOS Software, the IP multicast technologies facilitate scalable, efficient distribution of data, voice, and video streams to hundreds, thousands, even millions of users.

- IOS multicast is used by corporate communications, video conferencing, e-learning, Internet broadcast, hoot 'n' holler, and streaming media applications.

- IP multicasting has the following characteristics:
  - Transmits IP datagrams to a host group identified by a single IP destination address. A host group is dynamic and can contain zero or more host devices at any given time.
  - Delivers a multicast packet to all members of the destination host group with the same best-effort reliability as regular unicast IP datagrams.
  - Supports dynamic membership of a host group.
  - Supports all host groups regardless of the location or number of members.
  - Supports the membership of a single host in one or more multicast groups.
  - Upholds multiple data streams at the application level for a single group address.
  - Supports a single group address for multiple applications on a host.

- Some of the advantages of multicast transmission over unicast transmission are
  - **Enhanced efficiency**—Available network bandwidth is utilized more efficiently, because multiple streams of data are replaced with a single transmission.
  - **Optimized performance**—Fewer copies of data require less forwarding and processing.
  - **Distributed applications**—In a unicast transmission, multipoint applications will not be possible as demand and usage grow, because unicast transmission will not scale.

- Some disadvantages of multicast transmission are
  - **Best-effort delivery**—Drops are expected to happen.
  - **No congestion avoidance**—Lack of TCP windowing and slow-start mechanisms can result in network congestion.

- **Duplicates**—Some protocol mechanisms result in the occasional generation of duplicate packets.

- **Out-of-order delivery**—Some protocol mechanisms result in out-of-order delivery of packets.

- Muticast forwarding has the following characteristics:

  - **Multicast routing is different from unicast routing**—Unicast routing is concerned about where the packet is going, but multicast forwarding is concerned about where the packet came from and where the interested recipients might be.

  - **Multicast routing uses Reverse Path Forwarding**—A router forwards a multicast datagram only if received on the upstream interface toward the source; the routing table used for multicasting is checked against the source IP address in the packet.

- Multicast-capable routers create distribution trees that control the path that IP multicast traffic takes through the network to deliver traffic to all receivers. The two basic types of multicast distribution trees are source trees and shared trees.

- PIMv2 is a standards-based multicast routing protocol. PIM leverages the unicast routing information to perform multicast forwarding function: It uses the unicast routing table to perform the RPF check function. PIM can operate either in DM or in SM. PIM-DM uses a periodic flood and prune model on source-based trees, whereas PIM-SM uses an on-demand model on shared distribution trees.

- In addition to multicast routing protocols, other supporting multicast protocols and control mechanisms are needed for efficient operation of multicast traffic in a network:

  - IGMP is used by IPv4 hosts to communicate multicast group membership to the connected routers.

  - CGMP is a Cisco-developed protocol that allows data-link layer switches to leverage IGMP information on Cisco routers to make data-link layer forwarding decisions. CGMP allows switches to forward multicast traffic to only those ports that are interested in the traffic.

  - IGMP snooping serves the same purpose as CGMP; it requires the LAN switch to examine (snoop) IGMP packets sent from IP hosts to the router so that it can adjust its MAC table and avoid flooding multicast traffic.

- When designing a network for IP multicast, servers and hosts, IP multicast control mechanisms, PIM mode, router provisioning, and addressing and security must all be given thought.

- Although many possible combinations of multicast deployment exist in a large campus, and even more combinations for each type of multicast application, it is generally best to focus on keeping administration simple and the traffic reliable. When IP multicast traffic is to cross a WAN link, the primary consideration is that the WAN bandwidth not be overwhelmed by unnecessary traffic.

References

Multicast Services at http://www.cisco.com/warp/public/732/Tech/multicast/index.shtml.

Solutions Reference Network Design (SRND) Networking Solutions Design Guides. To locate these documents, perform the following:

Go to http://www.cisco.com/.

In the Search box, type **SRND** and click **Go**. A list of SRND Networking Solutions Design Guides appears.

Select the Networking Solutions Design Guide that meets your needs.

Product Summary

Table 8-4 provides a brief overview of some of the products available from Cisco Systems that relate to the topics discussed in this chapter. For a more detailed breakdown of the Cisco product line, visit http://www.cisco.com/en/US/products/index.html.

Table 8-4 *Examples of Cisco Products with Multicast-Related Capabilities*

Product Name	Description
Cisco IP/TV 3426 Broadcast Server (Cisco IP/TV 3400 Series Video Servers)	The Cisco IP/TV 3426 Broadcast Server addresses the need for formats, such as Internet Streaming Media Alliance (ISMA) MPEG-4, through software-based compression. It can encode up to four different streams simultaneously in real time. Alternatively, it can take in one video feed and encode at multiple bit rates for webcasts that need to reach audiences with varying bandwidth requirements.
Cisco IP/TV 3427 Broadcast Server (Cisco IP/TV 3400 Series Video Servers)	The Cisco IP/TV 3427 Broadcast Servers offer the ability to encode from five to eight streams in a single Broadcast Server, saving rack space and simplifying manageability. This high-performance hardware platform includes dual CPUs for multistream software encoding, front-serviceable disks as well as hot-swappable and redundant power supplies and cooling fans for high system availability.

Table 8-4   *Examples of Cisco Products with Multicast-Related Capabilities (Continued)*

Product Name	Description
Cisco IP/TV Software Version 3.5	Cisco IP/TV software version 3.5 contains features such as: New Broadcast Servers with multistream capability, MPEG-4 AAC "Advanced Audio Coding," Internet Streaming Media Alliance (ISMA) compatibility, and QuickTime support.
Cisco CRS-1 Single-Shelf System (Cisco Carrier Routing System)	The Cisco CRS-1 offers continuous system operation, unprecedented service flexibility, and system longevity; it is powered by Cisco IOS XR Software, a unique self-healing and self-defending operating system designed for always-on operation while scaling system capacity up to 92 Terabits per second (Tbps). The innovative system architecture combines the Cisco Silicon Packet Processor, the first programmable 40-Gbps ASIC, with the Cisco Service Separation Architecture for unprecedented service flexibility and speed to service. The Cisco CRS-1 marks a new era in carrier IP communications by powering the foundation for network and service convergence today while protecting investments for decades to come.
	The CRS-1 Single-Shelf System consists of a single, 16-slot line-card shelf with total switching capacity of 1.2 Tbps. The line-card shelf is built from a line-card chassis featuring a midplane design. There are slots for 16 modular services cards and eight fabric cards in the rear of the chassis, and 16 interface modules, two route processors, and two fan controllers in the front of the chassis. All three stages of the switching fabric are done in a single switch fabric card that supports Stage 1, Stage 2, and Stage 3 switching.

continues

Table 8-4   *Examples of Cisco Products with Multicast-Related Capabilities (Continued)*

Product Name	Description
Cisco Catalyst 8500 Series Multiservice Switch Routers	The Cisco Catalyst 8500 is a Layer 3-enhanced ATM switch that seamlessly integrates wire-speed Layer 3 switching and ATM switching, eliminating the need to make a technology choice. The Catalyst 8500 family delivers campus and metropolitan network solutions with scalable performance, lower cost of ownership, and intranet-based application features to deliver increased business productivity. Unlike old first- or second-generation ATM switches that force customers to have a costly, inefficient, multisystem solution, the Catalyst 8500 switch provides an integrated ATM and Gigabit Ethernet solution in a single chassis.

Standards and Specifications Summary

Request For Comments (RFCs) can be downloaded from the following website: http://www.rfc-editor.org/rfc.html.

- RFC 1112, "Host Extensions for IP Multicasting."
- RFC 2236, "Internet Group Management Protocol, Version 2."

Review Questions

Answer the following questions to test your comprehension of the topics discussed in this chapter. Refer to Appendix A, "Answers to Review Questions," to check your answers.

1 If an application on one host wants to send packets to three hosts on the same subnet, usage of which of the following methods will generate more traffic?

   a Unicast

   b Multicast

   c Anycast

   d Broadcast

2 Which of the following applications is a good candidate as a multicast application?

   a   Video conferencing

   b   Software distribution

   c   Digital TV

   d   All of the above

3 Which of the following is not one of the characteristics of IP multicast?

   a   Transmission to a host group

   b   Dynamic membership

   c   Reliable transport

   d   Membership in more than one group

4 Which of the following is not a potential disadvantage of IP multicast?

   a   Inefficient data delivery

   b   Out-of-order or duplicated data delivery

   c   Best-effort data delivery

   d   Lack of congestion avoidance

5 Multicast forwarding is based on which of the following techniques?

   a   Destination-based forwarding

   b   Reverse Path Forwarding

   c   Multiprotocol Label Switching

   d   Anycast

6 Which of the following is not a characteristic of IP multicast source distribution trees?

   a   Use more memory

   b   Support optimal paths from source to all receivers

   c   Require initial configuration of root (RP)

   d   Minimize delay

7 Which of the following is not a characteristic of IP multicast shared distribution trees?

   a Use less memory

   b Might result in suboptimal paths from source to receivers

   c Might introduce extra delay

   d Require easier configuration than source-based trees

8 Which of the following best describes PIM-DM?

   a Flood and prune, shared tree

   b Flood and prune, source tree

   c On-demand join, shared tree

   d On-demand join, source tree

9 Which of the following best describes PIM-SM?

   a Flood and prune, shared tree

   b Flood and prune, source tree

   c On-demand join, shared tree

   d On-demand join, source tree

10 Which of the following is not related to PIM-SM?

   a Periodic Flooding

   b Source registration

   c Rendezvous point

   d SPT switchover

11 Which of the following is not a characteristic of CGMP?

   a Cisco-developed protocol that allows data-link layer switches to leverage IGMP on Cisco routers to make data-link layer forwarding decisions.

   b Used by IPv4 hosts to communicate multicast group membership to the connected routers.

c Provides management of group membership on switched Ethernet LANs.

d Allows switches to forward multicast traffic to only those ports that are interested in the traffic.

12 Which of the following is a characteristic of IGMP?

a Cisco-developed protocol that allows Cisco routers to make data-link layer forwarding decisions.

b Provides management of group membership on switched Ethernet LANs.

c Allows switches to forward multicast traffic to only those ports that are interested in the traffic.

d Used by IPv4 hosts to communicate multicast group membership to the connected routers.

13 Which of the following is an IP multicast control mechanism that Cisco IOS supports?

a CGMP

b IGMP

c IGMP snooping

d All of the above

14 Which of the following is not a major IP multicast design consideration?

a What is the multicast server's OS?

b Should PIM-DM or PIM-SM be used?

c In case of PIM-SM, which routers should be RP?

d What are the multicast addressing and security policies?

15 When designing IP multicast for a collapsed core (small campus) network, which device is considered the best candidate for RP?

a Access switch

b Distribution switch

c Distribution bridge

d Core router

Case Study: OCSIC Bottling Company

The purpose of this case study is to design IP multicast services that meet the needs of the OCSIC Bottling Company. OCSIC headquarters is sending massive updates to the North American plants for new product kickoffs. The kickoff events contain a live video feed. The updates are usually saved so people can view the video at their leisure. Each component of the design must have multiple options; each option must be considered carefully, given the constraints. Each design decision and identified component must be presented with sufficient justification. The justification explains the options considered and why one option was chosen over the other.

IP Multicast Design for OCSIC's New Application

Table 8-5 summarizes one possible set of design decisions that meet OCSIC's new application requirements. The left-most column presents the design considerations; the middle column reveals the decision made, and the right-most column includes the explanations for some of the decisions.

Table 8-5   *IP Multicast Design Decisions for OCSIC's New Product Kickoffs Application*

Design Questions	Decision	Justification
Where should multicast applications be implemented on the network?	Data applications are unicast applications. Voice music on hold and video are multicast applications. The servers (senders) should be in the enterprise server farm.	Sever farms provide reliable and optimal service.
What IP multicast control mechanism should be used?	CGMP is implemented on the switches. PIM-SM and IGMPv3 are implemented on the routers. Non-RPF traffic is routed via the rules of the routing table.	CGMP is more efficient than IGMP snooping. IGMPv3 offers source-specific multicast. PIM-SM is less resource intensive than PIM dense mode.
Will PIM-DM or PIM-SM be used? If PIM-SM is selected, where will the RPs be located?	Use PIM-SM with the RP at the Enterprise Edge router.	RP should be centric, in other words, as equal-distant as possible to the multicast servers and recipients.

Table 8-5   *IP Multicast Design Decisions for OCSIC's New Product Kickoffs Application (Continued)*

Design Questions	Decision	Justification
What security is needed to support IP multicasting on the network?	Connections to the district and plants are a "private" network.	Security depends on how much the service provider is trusted. If need be, encrypted tunnels could be created to send the traffic across the WAN.
Which network devices require an upgrade (memory, IOS version, new hardware) to support the IP multicast applications?	Ensure that the proper IOS is selected to support all the features for multicasting and the other features.	Because video is being added, the load will not diminish on any of the systems. The load actually increases to support the video streams.

After completing this chapter, you will be able to

- Identify Virtual Private Network (VPN) technologies
- Design site-to-site VPNs
- Design remote-access VPNs

CHAPTER 9

Designing Virtual Private Networks

Virtual private networks (VPNs) are networks deployed on a public or private network infrastructure. VPNs are useful for telecommuters, mobile users, and remote offices as well as for customers, suppliers, and partners.

For enterprises, VPNs are an alternative wide-area network (WAN) infrastructure, replacing or augmenting existing private networks that use dedicated WANs based on leased-line, Frame Relay, Asynchronous Transfer Mode (ATM), or other technologies. Increasingly, enterprises are turning to their service providers for VPNs and other complete service solutions tailored to their particular business.

This chapter examines the key technologies associated with the Cisco VPN solution. It explains how to design simple and complex site-to-site VPNs and concludes with examples of each.

VPN Technologies

VPNs use advanced encryption and tunneling to permit organizations to establish secure, end-to-end, private network connections over third-party networks, such as the Internet or extranets. VPNs are included in the Cisco Architecture for Voice, Video, and Integrated Data (AVVID), the enterprise architecture that provides an intelligent network infrastructure for today's Internet business solutions.

VPNs do not inherently change private WAN requirements, such as support for multiple protocols, high reliability, and extensive scalability. They often meet these requirements cost-effectively and with great flexibility.

This section examines how to

- Identify enterprise VPN requirements
- VPN tunneling
- VPN security
- VPN termination
- VPN management

Enterprise VPN Requirements

VPNs enable network connectivity for an organization, its business partners, and customers over a shared infrastructure, delivering the same policies as a private network. This section identifies enterprise requirements for site-to-site and remote-access VPNs.

For VPNs, the Internet protocol (IP)-based infrastructure can be a private enterprise network, an Internet service provider (ISP) network, or the Internet, providing organizations with flexibility in connectivity and cost. To deliver the same policies as a private network, organizations must consider implementing enhanced security, sophisticated traffic engineering, and policy-based management.

Because VPNs are typically new technologies to most enterprise networks, it is important to use a four-phase structured methodology to implement VPNs:

- **Strategy phase**—You should analyze the business requirements for implementing a VPN.
- **Design phase**—Sets the technical and functional requirements for the VPN.
- **Implementation phase**—Focuses on evolving the existing network and rolling out new network components.
- **Administrative phase**—Defines the metrics and tools to ensure that the new technology meets the technical and business goals of the project.

VPN applications in enterprise networks are divided into two main categories (see Table 9-1):

- Site-to-site
- Remote access

Table 9-1   *Comparison of Site-to-Site and Remote-Access VPNs*

Remote-Access VPN	Site-to-Site VPN
Evolution away from dialup	Extension of classic WAN
Per-user manageability	Compatibility with diverse network traffic types
Multioperating system (desktop) support	Integration with routing (route traffic using standard routing protocols across the VPN)
Deployment scalability	Deployment scalability

Site-to-site VPNs focus on connecting geographically dispersed offices without requiring dedicated circuits. Extranet VPNs, a type of site-to-site VPN, add interconnections between multiple organizations. Remote-access VPNs focus on remote users and partners who access the network on an as-needed basis. Table 9-2 describes various alternatives and benefits associated with both remote-access and site-to-site VPN types.

Table 9-2 *VPN Alternatives and Benefits*

	Application	Alternative To	Benefits
Site-to-Site VPN	Site-to-site intranet	Leased line	Extends connectivity
	Internet connectivity	Leased line	Increased bandwidth Offers lower cost than a dedicated circuit
Remote-Access VPN	Site-to-site extranet	Dedicated dial	Provides ubiquitous access
	Remote dial connectivity	Dedicated dial	Offers lower cost than a dedicated circuit

NOTE   Remote VPN solutions are seen as a viable alternative to dedicated dial; however, VPN services can also be enabled across your dialup architecture through the use of a Virtual Private Dialup Networking (VPDN) solution. The role of VPDNs is to replace expensive long-distance dialup charges associated with remote users. Rather than dialing up the corporate Registration, Admission, and Status Protocol (RAS), the user dials up the local ISP point of presence (PoP) and creates a Layer 2 tunnel across the shared Internet to the corporate network.

VPN Tunneling

Virtual point-to-point connectivity is typically provided by a tunneling protocol. This section describes the tunneling technology that enables VPNs.

Tunneling is a technique where packets of one type of protocol are encapsulated by another protocol. Tunneling, as shown in Figure 9-1, is often used to transport or route packets across networks of disparate protocols. In the context of VPN, tunneling is used to encapsulate private messages and apply encryption algorithms to the payload.

Figure 9-1 *VPN Tunneling*

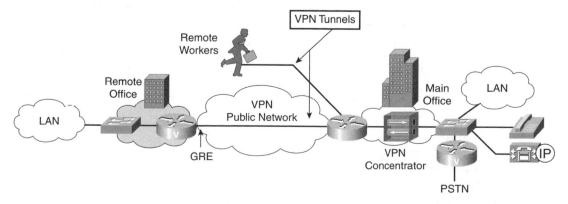

Several different tunneling protocols have evolved, and each is based on encapsulating a Layer 2 protocol (Layer 2 tunneling) or a Layer 3 protocol (Layer 3 tunneling).

You can implement Layer 3 tunneling in native form or nest it within other tunneling protocols, such as Layer 2 Tunneling Protocol (L2TP). For example, Microsoft Windows 2000 includes a native VPN desktop client that uses L2TP over IP Security (IPSec) as the transport protocol. This combination provides the routing advantages of L2TP with the security of IPSec.

In site-to-site VPNs, the principal tunneling is generic routing encapsulation (GRE). If only IP-unicast packets are being tunneled, simple encapsulation provided by IPSec is sufficient. GRE is used when multicast, broadcast, and non-IP packets need to be tunneled.

VPN Security

VPN security is provided by these primary security technologies that enable VPNs:

- IPSec
- User authentication
- Encryption

IPSec

A VPN solution based on an IP network must provide secure services. Without security measures, standard IP packets are susceptible to numerous security breaches. For example, individual packets or streams of packets might be intercepted in transit and modified by a third party without the knowledge of the user or application. Source and destination addresses might be changed. TCP/IP does not provide any methods of securing a data stream.

IPSec is a set of standards that specifies various options for providing VPN data privacy. Packet authentication protects the information flow from being tampered with or even repeated, thereby minimizing disruption to the communication.

An IPSec networking architecture has been specifically designed to address these issues. The framework set forth by the IPSec working group, Internet Engineering Task Force (IETF), provides data integrity checks for tamper detection, source address verification, and data privacy for the packet data and data path.

IPSec provides privacy and integrity and it can be implemented transparently in the network infrastructure. It scales from small to very large networks and offers hardware and software acceleration. The details of this specification are defined in Request For Comments (RFC) 2401, "Security Architecture for the Internet Protocol."

Today, IPSec is widely accepted as a robust and secure method of securing IP traffic. A range of services is performed in IPSec-compliant implementations, including key management, data encryption, and data authentication.

User Authentication

VPN implementations cannot afford to ignore security threats. One of the primary reasons VPNs are popular is the ubiquity and easy access afforded by IP services. This results in security threats, which must be guarded against. In many cases, enterprises that are migrating to VPN from a dialup remote-access infrastructure want to use their existing authentication servers, such as Remote Authentication Dial In User Service Microsoft Windows NT domain authentication, and token-based security servers.

In cases where a selected VPN device does not support the authentication database of choice, you can use RADIUS proxy. Authentication requests are sent from the VPN device through the VPN gateway to the RADIUS server, which communicates with the actual authentication server. In some cases, both the RADIUS server executable and the authentication database might reside on a single server. After the proxy service is defined, the authentication process is seamless to the remote-access user.

Public key infrastructure (PKI) can be used for authenticating remote-access users and generating keys used for Internet Key Exchange (IKE) negotiations. X.509 digital certificates are used to exchange key information for each remote-access user. The PKI provides a suite of security services for distribution, management, and revocation of digital certificates. A certification authority (CA) digitally signs each certificate and validates the integrity of the certificate.

NOTE   Prior to establishing a tunnel between two IPSec peers, mutual authentication must occur. Each peer needs to verify that the other peer is who he says he is. PKI and X.509 digital certificates can be used to provide this service. Issued from an established and trusted CA, the certificates contain each peer's public key and verify the key's authenticity. This process occurs during IKE Phase 1, when a secure channel is established between two IPSec peers prior to the exchange of encrypted data (IKE Phase 2).

Encryption

Encryption is the process of converting data through an algorithm to a form that cannot be easily read. The resultant encrypted data stream cannot be read without decrypting the contents of the packets that transport the data. Figure 9-2 demonstrates the encryption/decryption process.

Data encryption algorithms are generally configurable. Today, Triple Data Encryption Standard (3DES) is widely used. It is considered secure enough for enterprise deployments and sensitive data applications. The National Institute of Standards and Technology has endorsed 3DES since 1975. Advanced Encryption Standard (AES) is also gaining in popularity in addition to Data Encryption Standard (DES) and 3DES. Cisco is now using AES as well in VPN devices. Data authentication protocols are also configurable—the most popular today being the Secure Hash Algorithm 1 (SHA-1) and Message Digest 5 (MD5). Key exchanges identify each party in the remote-access session. A popular, automated method of key exchange is called IKE (formally known as Internet Security Association and Key Management Protocol (ISAKMP)/Oakley).

Figure 9-2 *Security Through Encryption*

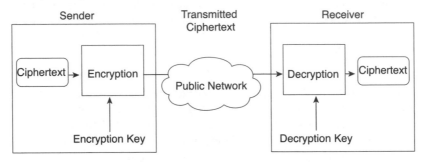

Encryption and Authentication Standards

To create a secure VPN tunnel between two security gateways, IKE Phases 1 and 2 must occur.

IKE Phase 1: Management Tunnel Setup

The purpose of IKE Phase 1 is to create a secure management tunnel between two IPSec peers for the purpose of establishing, maintaining, and tearing down a VPN tunnel.

In IKE Phase 1, the following steps occur:

Step 1 **Security Association negotiation and exchange**—A secure communications channel is created between two IPSec peers through the negotiation and exchange of IKE policy information known as Security Associations (SAs).

IKE Phase 1 SAs carry policy parameters in constructs called transforms. Transforms define the following:

— **Encryption algorithm used**—DES, 3DES, AES

— **Hashing algorithm to be used (integrity check)**—MD5, SHA-1

— **Authentication algorithm to be used**—Preshare, Rivest, Shamir, and Adelman (RSA) certificates, or RSA nounces

— **Mode (method of transferring the policy information)**—Main or aggressive

— **Diffie-Hellman key length**—Group 1 768 or Group 2 1024

Both sides must agree to the same parameters for all values defined in the transform, or no tunnel will be established.

Step 2 **Diffie-Hellman Key Exchange**—Used to allow both parties to create and exchange a shared secret key over an insecure channel. After the key is exchanged, all subsequent tunnel management traffic between the peers will be encrypted using the shared secret.

Step 3   **Authentication**—Peer authentication can be done using either preshared keys configured manual on both peers, RSA certificates using the PKI X.509 specification, or RSA nounces, which use random number generation encryption and exchanges to authenticate.

IKE Phase 2: IPSec Tunnel Setup

The purpose of IKE Phase 2 is to create a VPN tunnel between two IPSec peers for the purpose of exchanging data across a secure channel over an untrusted network. IKE Phase 2 is conducted over the secure channel created in IKE Phase 1.

In IKE Phase 2, the following steps occur:

Step 1   **SA negotiation and exchange**—To establish the IPSec tunnel, both peers must negotiate and agree upon a security policy. Just as in IKE Phase 1, SAs must be established that define how the packets are to be processed when they are received from their IPSec peer. This is done through the definition and exchange of transforms. Transforms for IKE Phase 2 define the following:

- **Encryption algorithm**—DES, 3DES, or AES

- **Authentication algorithm**—MD5 or SHA-1

- **IPSec protocol**—Encapsulating Security Payload (ESP) or Authentication Header (AH)

- **Mode**—Transport or tunnel

- Lifetime of the SA

After the policy is defined and agreed upon by both ends, each participant creates an SA for the session containing all the defined parameters and stores the information in their respective security policy databases. It is important to note that the security policy has to be identical for each participant on either end of the tunnel. The SA is used when a packet arrives to define the processing that is required to decrypt and authenticate the data. To ensure that the correct policy is applied to a received packet, each packet sent across a VPN tunnel carries a Security Parameter Index (SPI). The SPI is used to look up the appropriate security policy in the database for that peer so that the correct policy is applied to the packet.

Step 2   IPSec peers can change security policy parameters associated with a session through the renegotiation of SAs. The Diffie-Hellman key can also be renegotiated but only if Perfect Forward Secrecy (PFS) has been enabled.

VPN Termination

A wide variety of VPN products are available on the market. This section helps you select the necessary termination components of a VPN solution, given specific enterprise VPN requirements.

VPN Concentrators

For high availability and scalability in enterprise applications, it is best to seek out a dedicated VPN platform called a VPN concentrator. The VPN concentrator is a purpose-built device designed to aggregate a large volume of simultaneous remote VPN sessions. Table 9-3 classifies and defines the difference between small, medium, and large VPN sites. The table defines the number of remote VPN users, data throughput, and tunnels that are supported by each category.

Table 9-3   *VPN Concentrators*

	Small	Medium	Large
Simultaneous Users	100	1500	Up to 10,000
Performance	4 Mbps	50 Mbps	100 Mbps
Site-to-Site Tunnels	100	500	1000

When evaluating the capabilities of VPN concentrators, answer these questions:

- **Is it a purpose-built communications platform?** Many vendors have attempted to enter the market with a general-purpose PC to build their VPN devices. This approach suffers from the low mean time between failures (MTBF) of consumer-grade PC technology, introduction of failure-prone mechanical components, such as disk drives, and lack of scalability to deal with performance requirements. Similar to routers and switches, the VPN device is part of the communications infrastructure and should be implemented using a purpose-built communications platform.

- **Is physical redundancy designed in?** A high-availability platform should provide fully redundant power, multiple fans, field-swappable components, and easy swapping of a failed unit. Look for a form factor that readily allows rack mounting and hot swapping in case of failure, with a size and weight that allows overnight shipment of replacement parts.

- **Does the product use a proven software operating system?** Even if the hardware uses a robust, fault-tolerant design, system uptime can still be compromised by a software architecture that uses proprietary, unproven operating system software. Ideally, the software platform will be based on an industry-standard operating system (OS) with significant field experience in embedded system products.

- **Can the device be proactively managed for high availability?** The VPN design should include tools that monitor critical components and warn in advance of potential failure conditions. It should provide status monitoring for power supply, fan speed, and internal temperature. System failure from these elements tends to occur over time, so proactive monitoring and reporting can allow intervention before an actual system failure occurs. In addition, the system software should provide automatic recovery in case of a system crash. To ensure high availability, the unit should recover from software failure without external intervention.

To support fewer than 70 individual tunnels, a router would be acceptable. Between 70 and 100 individual tunnels, you could select a router or a VPN concentrator. The main design question to answer is: Do you want all of your WAN and VPN termination through one device, or do you want to split the functionality?

NOTE

Cisco positions its VPN products as follows:

- **Router**—Primarily for site-to-site VPN
- **Concentrator**—Primarily for remote-access VPN
- **PIX firewall**—Either remote-access or site-to-site VPNs

VPN Client Software

Remote-access client software runs on the remote desktop and provides the user interface and transparent underlying VPN security protocols for establishing the tunnel to the VPN termination device. Table 9-4 defines the common protocols used by VPN client software, their associated tunnel type, and encryption algorithms as well as common deployment.

Table 9-4 *VPN Software*

Protocol	Tunneling Type	Encryption	Implementation
Point-to-Point Tunneling Protocol	Layer 2 (GRE)	Up to 128-bit RC4 (Encapsulation Security Payload Protocol)	Integrated client available for Microsoft Windows clients Requires service pack for best encryption and hot fixes
IP Security	Layer 3 (Encapsulation Security Payload Protocol)	Up to 168-bit 3DES	VPN vendor-specific Limited based on VPN termination equipment Might support enhanced remote-access features
L2TP within IP Security	Layer 2, Layer 3	Up to 168-bit 3DES	Integrated with some Microsoft Windows 2000 clients Requires Microsoft digital certificates for key negotiation Might include other non-IP protocols in tunnel

The enterprise must weigh the pros and cons of vendor-specific VPN client software implementations versus the embedded clients in Windows 95, Windows 98, Windows NT, and Windows 2000. There are also third-party offerings for MacOS, Solaris, and Linux. OS-integrated desktop clients can be easier to deploy, especially if no service packs are required. However, consider carefully any security and compatibility trade-offs with existing remote-access infrastructure (token security, digital certificates, or RADIUS).

The client software should be easy to install and simple to operate. Open software distribution licenses provide the network administrator with fixed costs during the implementation and upgrade phases. With this model, spikes in demand do not trigger uncapped incremental expenses.

When evaluating proprietary client software, the development philosophy behind the implementation needs to be understood. The following questions should be asked:

- Is this a client application that can be modified or tuned by the end user? If so, support calls and misconfigurations might plague a large-scale deployment.
- Is the client well integrated with a dialer?
- Does the client support roaming dial services for traveling users?
- How is the client distributed to end users? Can it be preconfigured for mass deployment?
- Are there methods for revision control and automatic software updates?
- Does the client support a larger policy management strategy?
- How is split tunneling handled?
- Can users be grouped together and assigned common LAN privileges?
- Does the client interoperate with antivirus and personal firewall software?

NOTE Split tunneling is a remote VPN feature that can be enabled if required. With split tunneling any traffic not directed for the network address block(s) associated with the VPN tunnel is routed by the client locally outside of the tunnel.

VPN Management

Robust VPN management is another critical success factor for any large remote-access deployment. Management features can be grouped into broad categories such as configuration, monitoring, and alert functionality. This section helps you select the necessary VPN management components of a Cisco VPN solution, given specific enterprise VPN requirements.

VPN Management Considerations

Consider the flexibility of management tools and the varied audiences that might interface with them. In many cases, having both a browser interface and command-line interface (CLI) is beneficial. Consider the following deployment issues in the management context:

- **Ease of configuration**—VPN is a sophisticated technology with many configuration options. A VPN solution should provide an intuitive interface, and allow the systems administrator to quickly configure and manage new devices. The management functionality should also provide flexibility for extended configurations so that the VPN might be optimized for specific applications.

- **Dynamic reconfiguration**—All configuration changes should take effect without requiring a reboot of the device. Disruption of service with a fully loaded VPN device can potentially impact thousands of individual users.

- **Robust configuration**—Any time the device is reconfigured or new software is loaded, there is a real possibility of disrupted operation because of operator error (incorrect configuration or faulty download of a software image). It is critical for the unit to be able to check the validity of the configuration and downloaded software, and automatically restore operation to the last known configuration or software image in case of error.

- **Proactive monitoring and alerts**—To ensure high availability, the device must support a wide range of system monitoring (both hardware and software) to constantly monitor operational status. At a minimum, the solution should include tools that can allow rapid isolation, diagnosis, and reporting of faults to allow rapid repair and recovery. Ideally, the system will also incorporate intelligence to identify trends that can predict a potential failure, alerting the system manager to take action before a fault condition occurs.

- **Multiple device monitoring**—In a redundant topology, VPNs need a management tool to allow status viewing of multiple devices as a single service entity. This tool should allow top-level monitoring of overall service operation, as well as automatic highlighting and notification of abnormal operating conditions. Facilities that allow an operator to aggregate and analyze a high volume of data are essential. Archival, graphing, and trend analysis of management status are also critical.

CiscoWorks VPN/Security Management Solution

CiscoWorks VPN/Security Management Solution offers web-based applications for configuring, monitoring, and troubleshooting enterprise VPNs, firewall security, and network and host-based intrusion detection systems (IDSs).

The CiscoWorks VPN/Security Management Solution includes these modules:

- **VPN Monitor**—Collects, stores, and reports on IPSec-based site-to-site and remote-access VPNs. VPN Monitor supports the Cisco VPN concentrators and routers.

- **Cisco Intrusion Detection System Host Sensor**—Provides prevention and reporting of security threats to critical servers. Includes both the management console and the evaluation sensor agents. Agents provide protection to operating systems and protection to servers. Agents are purchased separately.

- **Cisco Secure Policy Manager (CSPM)**—Used to define and enforce security policies on Cisco PIX firewalls, and to report and alert about intrusions when Cisco Network Intrusion Detection Systems (NIDSs) are deployed. CSPM is also used to define IDS and IOS security policies.

- **Resource Manager Essentials (RME)**—Provides the operational management features required by enterprises—software distribution, change audit and authorization, device inventory, credentials management, and syslog analysis for problem solving and notification of VPN and security operational problems.

- **CiscoView (CD One)**—Provides administrators with browser access to real-time device status, and operational and configuration functions.

Designing Site-to-Site VPNs

Site-to-site VPNs are an alternative WAN infrastructure used to connect branch offices, home offices, or business partners' sites to all or portions of an enterprise's network. VPNs do not inherently change private WAN requirements, such as support for multiple protocols, high reliability, and extensive scalability, but instead meet these requirements more cost-effectively and with greater flexibility. Site-to-site VPNs utilize the most pervasive transport technologies available today, such as the public Internet or service provider IP networks, by employing tunneling and encryption for data privacy, and quality of service (QoS) for transport reliability.

Using Internet transport, site-to-site VPNs often reduces WAN costs and can be easily and quickly extended to new locations and business partners. VPNs enable secure use of cost-effective, high-speed links. VPNs encrypt and authenticate traffic traversing the WAN to deliver true network security in an insecure, networked world.

This section explains the following:

- Site-to-site VPN requirements
- Key design considerations for site-to-site VPNs
- High availability and resiliency considerations
- Using a routing protocol over the VPN
- Minimizing packet fragmentation
- Implementing IPSec

Site-to-Site VPN Requirements

Site-to-site VPNs extend the classic WAN by providing large-scale encryption (high data rates) between multiple fixed sites, such as remote offices and central offices, over a shared private or public network, such as the Internet. This section identifies typical requirements for site-to-site VPNs.

Site-to-site VPNs are primarily deployed to connect office locations of an enterprise. They provide an alternative to the WAN infrastructure, as well as offer significant cost benefits. They enable new infrastructure applications, such as an extranet, and extend and enhance network connectivity. The key characteristics of site-to-site VPNs are

- Full mesh or hub and spoke
- Uses tunneling
- Uses a routing protocol
- Data plus voice and video

Enterprise WAN requirements for traditional private WAN services, such as multiprotocol support, high availability, scalability, and security, are also requirements for VPNs. VPNs can often meet these requirements more cost-effectively and with greater flexibility than private WAN services using leased lines or virtual circuit technologies, such as Frame Relay and ATM.

The key components of site-to-site VPN design include

- **Cisco head-end VPN routers**—Serve as VPN head-end termination devices at a central campus (head-end devices)
- **Cisco VPN access routers**—Serve as VPN branch-end termination devices at branch office locations (branch-end devices)
- **IPSec and GRE tunnels**—Interconnect the head-end and branch-end devices in the VPN
- **Internet services from ISPs**—Serve as the WAN interconnection medium

The first decision for an enterprise is whether to replace a traditional WAN with a VPN. The enterprise needs to compare the features and benefits of each technology.

Table 9-5 describes the advantages and disadvantages associated with traditional private WAN solutions and VPN solutions.

Table 9-5   *Comparison of Private WANs and VPNs*

	Private WAN	Site-to-Site VPN
Advantages	Reliability	Globally available
	Secure	Redundant
	Controlled	Less expensive
	Self-managed	Greater connectivity
		Simplified WAN
		Alternative to dial-on-demand for backup
Disadvantages	Scaling challenge	Reliance on third parties
	Local skill required	Requires encryption and client management
	Investment in technology	Lack of control

Key Design Considerations for Site-to-Site VPNs

When designing the site-to-site VPN, you need to design the topology, and incorporate resiliency and failover mechanisms. Cisco products support all of these design criteria. This section lists the design considerations for enterprise site-to-site VPNs.

The four major steps to design a site-to-site VPN solution are

Step 1   Determine the application and data needs for the VPN solution.

Step 2   Design the VPN topology between sites. These types of site-to-site VPNs are deployed most often:

— Hub-and-spoke topology and multiple hub-and-spoke topology

— Mesh topology

— Hierarchical network topology

Step 3   Incorporate design resiliency and failover mechanisms.

Step 4   Choose head-end products based on predicted VPN capacity requirements.

Hub-and-Spoke VPN Topologies

The hub-and-spoke designs in Figure 9-3 are used when a single regional or headquarters location has a large number of remote offices, and the majority of all traffic is between the remote sites and the regional or headquarters location.

Figure 9-3   *Hub-and-Spoke VPN Topologies: One-to-Many and Many-to-Many*

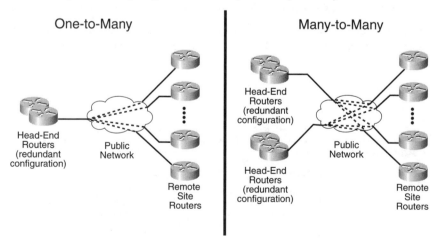

The variations of the hub-and-spoke topology are

• The remote sites communicate exclusively to the head-end location.

• The remote sites require communication with each other as well as to the head-end location.

A hub-and-spoke design typically minimizes the device configuration and complexity of the solution by having a single IPSec connection or a single GRE tunnel from each remote location back to the regional or headquarters location. However, this design does not scale well when there is a requirement for a high degree of traffic flow between remote sites. Traffic flow between remote sites can be accomplished by using GRE tunneling with IPSec, and routing traffic through the regional or headquarters location. Nor does it allow for any redundancy in the VPN network in the event of a failure of the single headquarters or regional office location.

Simple Full-Mesh VPN Topology

Mesh VPN designs, as shown in Figure 9-4, can either be fully meshed, providing any-to-any connectivity, or partially meshed, providing some-to-some connectivity, depending upon the customer requirements. The meshed topology is the appropriate design to use when there are a small number of total locations (regional, headquarters, or remote locations), with a large amount of traffic flowing between some (partial mesh) or all (full mesh) of the sites.

Figure 9-4   *Simple Full-Mesh VPN Topology*

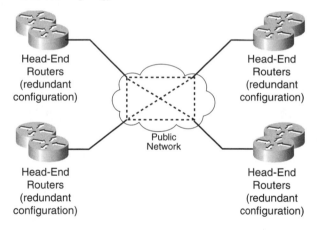

In a full-mesh design, the loss of a single location only affects traffic to or from that location. All other locations remain unaffected. However, this design does not scale well when there are a large number of sites because of the large number of straight IPSec connections and/or GRE tunnels with IPSec that have to be configured on each device.

Hierarchical VPN Topology

A hierarchical VPN topology design consists of a full- or partial-mesh core, with peripheral sites connecting into the core using a hub-and-spoke design.

A hierarchical topology, as shown in Figure 9-5, is the appropriate design to use with larger networks that contain both a large number of remote offices, which have little traffic interaction between them, and a smaller number of headquarters or regional offices, with a large amount of traffic flowing between them. Hierarchical designs are the most scalable design for large networks, which require either partial or full connectivity between sites.

Figure 9-5   *Hierarchical VPN Topology*

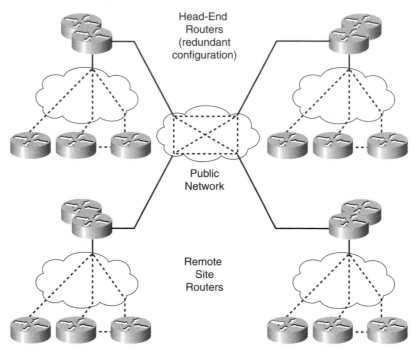

The criteria for the core components are similar to those for a meshed design. Likewise, the criteria for the peripheral components are similar to those for a hub-and-spoke design. The design differences depend upon whether a single set of routers will be used for both the head-end VPN termination device for the core component and the VPN termination device for the peripheral component; or if two sets of routers will be used.

This design is the most complex of the designs in terms of configuration, and might have a combination of GRE tunnels with IPSec running over them, or straight IPSec connections.

High-Availability and Resiliency Considerations

When remote user or branch office connectivity is critical to the successful operation of the enterprise, downtime for the VPN is not an option. Enterprises need a systematic approach to examine all the essential elements in delivering a high-availability site-to-site VPN. This section lists the high-availability and resiliency design considerations for enterprise site-to-site VPNs.

A typical IPSec VPN might involve a number of site-to-site connections. IPSec protects information as it travels from one part of the private network to another part over the public network. For each unique connection across the public network, a unique IPSec connection is established between the two peer points at the boundary of the private and public networks. An IPSec connection consists of one IKE security association and at least two dependent IPSec security associations. Security associations, identified by a unique security parameter index, are stateful relationships between the two peer points. The state information includes common secret keys, security parameters, and peer identity. This state information is established during the main-mode negotiation for the IKE SA and the quick-mode negotiation for IPSec security associations. If there is a prolonged loss of IP connectivity between the two peers, you must set up a new set of relationships through stateless failover.

Two steps must occur for stateless failover before the process is successful:

Step 1   One of the peers must detect the loss of connectivity.

Step 2   After detected, the peer must take action to reconnect with another peer to reach the part of the private network at the same site.

Loss of IP connectivity can be caused by local-link failure, full-loss connectivity by the service provider, or device failure. For a typical remote site, a dedicated or dial-on-demand path to the head-end site can protect against failure. Protection against a local-device failure at a remote site is not usually provided unless the importance of connectivity for the remote site warrants the cost. For a typical head-end site, you can achieve redundancy by implementing multiple provider connections and by deploying multiple head-end routers.

High availability and resiliency can be enhanced by using primary and secondary tunnels as follows:

- Implement primary and secondary tunnels between each branch device and the central site for resiliency
- Allocate primary tunnels to balance load on head-ends
- Allocate secondary tunnels to balance load after failover

Using a Routing Protocol Over the VPN

When using a routing protocol over the VPN, the tunnel now becomes the wire. The VPN tunnel offers the same benefits as a traditional WAN and is subject to the same bandwidth and delay considerations. With a dynamic routing protocol, you can verify connectivity by observing the routing table updates.

A site-to-site VPN solution will support static and dynamic routing protocols that are implemented elsewhere in the network. This section defines the routing protocol design considerations for enterprise site-to-site VPNs.

Routing functionality enables a central-site VPN device to efficiently learn a remote network during initial installation and dynamically update the connections over time. This scenario drastically reduces installation time and the management overhead of maintaining static routing tables.

Routing functionality in VPN devices dramatically improves the flexibility of these devices. In many cases, enterprises will choose to connect one or more remote sites through a remote-access–based VPN deployment. You can implement routing protocols within GRE tunnels to support functionality, such as any-to-any connectivity of remote sites within a hub-and-spoke design, without creating a full mesh of IPSec security associations. This can be particularly useful in large implementations, which require all remote sites to communicate with each other. Redundancy, through the use of routing protocols within GRE tunnels, is an additional functionality that can be supported.

Figure 9-6 shows an example of how a routing protocol can use two paths, both IPSec-protected GRE tunnels, to send network reachability information. A remote site using routing protocols for high availability will establish two IPSec-protected GRE tunnels, one to each head-end. Routing updates traverse both tunnels to the remote site, which will then forward the traffic to the head-end that has reachability to the destination network. From the perspective of the remote site, there are two paths to the head-end. Consider defining one of the tunnels as the primary tunnel to avoid asymmetric routing by adjusting the routing protocol cost for one of the links. In case of tunnel failure, convergence will occur as soon as the routing protocol realizes the path is no longer available. After failure recovery, remote sites using routing protocols will optionally revert back to their primary preferred path.

Figure 9-6 *Routing Protocol*

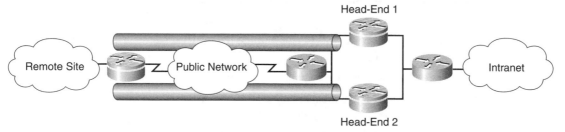

Concentrator and firewall head-ends often support failover capabilities in an active or standby configuration. When the primary fails, the secondary unit assumes the IP and MAC address of the primary, and the tunnel reestablishment commences. Routers function in an active-active configuration. Both head-end devices will allow tunnel establishment. You could consider using IKE keepalives in the head-end for heterogeneous remote-site device support. No IETF standard exists for keepalives today, and thus, this mechanism will work only with products from a single vendor. If a momentary loss of connectivity occurs at a remote site, it might establish a new tunnel with the secondary (but always active) head-end device.

Because tunnel establishment does not affect the routing table unless routing protocols are running over the tunnel, the routing state in the head-end will not change. Flapping occurs when the remote site temporarily loses WAN connectivity. When the tunnel switches between the head-ends because of remote-site flapping, the next-hop router will not be able to determine which active head-end device has a valid path to the remote site. Failover of IPSec between devices today is stateless and requires new tunnel establishment on the secondary device.

In summary, when using VPN concentrators or firewalls at the head-end, use IKE keepalives for high availability. When using VPN routers at the head-end, use routing protocol resilience for high availability.

Minimizing Packet Fragmentation

IPSec and GRE headers increase the size of packets being transported over a VPN. In Figure 9-7, the size of the packet before encryption is near the maximum transmission unit (MTU) of the transmission media; the encrypted packet with the additional IPSec and GRE headers, therefore, exceeds the MTU of the transmitting interface. This section describes the packet fragmentation design considerations for enterprise site-to-site VPNs.

Figure 9-7   *Anticipating Packet Fragmentation*

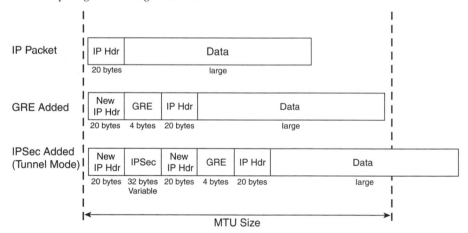

IP MTU discovery can eliminate the possibility of fragmentation when the end stations support it. This is a procedure that is run between two end stations with the participation of the network devices between them. For this process to work over an IPSec network with GRE, the GRE tunnel MTU should be set to a value low enough to ensure that the packet will make it through the encryption process without exceeding the MTU on the outbound interface, usually 1400 bytes.

Layer 3 packet fragmentation requires these packets to be reassembled prior to the decryption process. In some enterprise networks, fragmentation results in less-than-optimal throughput performance.

To avoid the fragmentation problem, you can do the following:

- Employ the MTU discovery.
- Set the MTU to allow for packet expansion, such as 1400 bytes.

For some networks, it might not be possible to easily manage MTU size. For these situations, Cisco has implemented prefragmentation for IPSec VPNs.

Implementing IPSec

IPSec tunnels are not virtual interfaces. They can only carry unicast IP packets, and have no end-to-end interface management protocol. To add resiliency to IPSec tunnels, you can implement it in transport mode on top of a robust tunnel technology, such as GRE. This section describes the IPSec design considerations for enterprise site-to-site VPNs.

A GRE tunnel is a virtual interface in a router and provides many of the features associated with physical interfaces. This is generally preferable except when the head-end router connects to thousands of remote sites.

GRE tunnels provide the ability to encapsulate multicast and broadcast packets and packets from non-IP protocols. Enabling this feature might enhance performance and scalability for site-to-site VPN services. Because GRE tunnels are unique interfaces, they can each be assigned their own cryptographic maps. When the source router needs to send a packet on the VPN destined for the other end of the GRE tunnel, it first makes a routing decision to send it out an interface and then does a search of the SPI table to find the corresponding SA. With GRE tunnels, the router must make a routing decision across a multitude of GRE tunnels. After the GRE tunnel is chosen, a limited number of SAs are available from which to choose.

Because GRE provides the tunneling mechanism, IPSec can be configured in transport mode, eliminating a portion of the IPSec overhead that is present in IPSec tunnel mode. By using transport mode, the IPSec packets do not need to be tunneled in IPSec as well as GRE for traffic when the endpoints are both the source and destination of the traffic.

For VPN resilience, configure the remote site with two GRE tunnels: one to the primary head-end VPN router and the other to the backup VPN router. Both GRE tunnels are secured via IPSec. Because GRE can carry multicast and broadcast traffic, it is possible and often desirable to configure a routing protocol for these virtual links.

After a routing protocol is configured, it provides failover capabilities. The hello/keepalive packets sent by the routing protocol over the GRE tunnels provide a mechanism to detect loss of connectivity. In other words, if the primary GRE tunnel is lost, the remote site will detect this event by the loss of the routing protocol hello packets. After virtual-link loss is detected, the routing protocol will choose the next best route: the backup GRE tunnel. VPN resilience is obtained by the automatic behavior of the routing protocol. Because the backup GRE tunnel is already up and secure, the failover time is determined by the hello packet mechanism and the convergence time of the routing protocol.

Using GRE tunnels with IPSec in transport mode provides a robust resilience mechanism for hub-and-spoke topologies. The three main issues when using this feature are

- Manageability of the Cisco IOS configuration for the head-end router
- Overhead on the network and the router processor
- Scalability

Site-to-Site VPN Examples

You can implement site-to-site VPNs in both small and large enterprise environments. This section provides examples of simple and complex site-to-site VPN solutions that meet specific enterprise VPN requirements.

Example: Small Site-to-Site VPN

The small publishing company shown in Figure 9-8 has done a comparative analysis between a leased-line WAN solution and a VPN. The company is using a centralized data store that resides in the corporate network. It accesses the data store through a web-based interface. The company uses e-mail as a primary means of communication and the Microsoft Office package for office productivity. Employees use extensive file sharing with files that include large graphics.

Figure 9-8   *Simple Site-to-Site VPN Example*

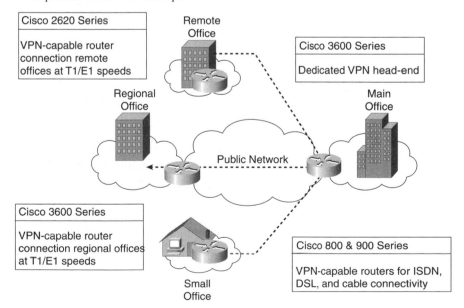

The company's main office has 150 people who access the corporate network. In addition, these offices need access to the corporate network:

- **Regional office**—75 users
- **Remote office**—26 users
- **Six small offices**—15 users each

The regional office and remote office have T1 access to the headquarters office. The small offices are using asymmetric digital subscriber line (ADSL) at 512 kbps to connect to the Internet. Each office has two physical connections to the Internet.

Small Site-to-Site VPN Solution

Table 9-6 summarizes the design decisions that the small publishing company made to meet its requirements.

Table 9-6   *Site-to-Site VPN Solution*

Design Questions	Decision	Notes
What topology will be used for the site-to-site VPN?	Hub-and-spoke topology	All corporate traffic will pass through the corporate network, because all the shared file storage, database, and e-mail engines are at the main office.
What type of tunneling will be deployed?	GRE between each site and the main office Single tunnel to each location without VPN client software on each client computer	This solution maintains simplicity. Because the company has two interfaces to the Internet, one is designated for the tunnel and one for Internet access.
What type of security will be deployed?	Basic security on each tunnel using IPSec Eight tunnels connect from the hub to individual sites Firewall at each site	Basic security keeps any confidential traffic from going over the Internet in plain text. Each site has a firewall either in the same device as the VPN tunnels or separate from the VPN tunnels.
Is Network Address Translation (NAT) required?	Yes	NAT is not needed over the VPN tunnels but will be used on the link going to the Internet.
What VPN hardware will be used?	Main office: Cisco 3600 series Regional office: Cisco 3600 series	Given the requirement for dedicated VPN hardware with hardware encryption, the company selected the Cisco 3600 series at the main office.

Table 9-6   *Site-to-Site VPN Solution (Continued)*

Design Questions	Decision	Notes
What VPN hardware will be used? (*Cont.*)	Remote office: Cisco 2620 Small office: Cisco 800/900	Given 75 users at the regional office, the company selected the Cisco 3600 series. The remote office has 26 users. Because there is no need for dedicated VPN hardware, a Cisco 2621 was selected to support two Ethernet segments, and a one- to two-port serial WAN interface card (WIC). The Cisco 2621 leaves growth for voice and the capability to insert a hardware encryption card. The small office requires VPN access over DSL. The two most common hardware solutions are standard routers and DSL specialty devices. The company selected a DSL specialty device: the Cisco 800.
What type of high availability will be deployed?	No additional redundancy or failover, but a separate interface will be used for Internet access at each site	A separate interface for Internet traffic means that Internet traffic will not affect the performance of the entire network. The IT department agreed that a temporary outage would not stop the business from running.

Example: Large Site-to-Site VPN

A large publishing company, as shown in Figure 9-9, needs a VPN solution between its headquarters office and a number of large branch offices. VPN access is required from the remote sites to the regional sites.

The headquarters office has 1600 people, and contains master file servers and data servers. It has a file distribution system that pushes a copy of the production files to a server in each region. It relies heavily on e-mail with attachments for corporate correspondence. The primary e-mail server is located at the headquarters corporate network.

Each regional office has approximately 286 people, and has a support server farm where they get a copy of the latest data store and published files on a nightly basis. Each regional facility has multiple T1s for access to its service provider.

Figure 9-9   *Large Site-to-Site VPN Example*

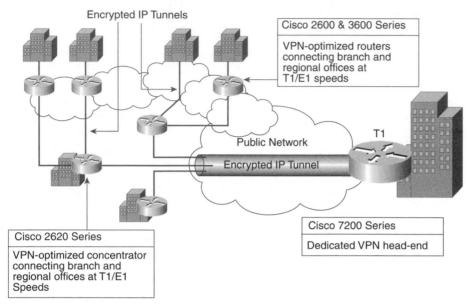

The remote site offices have approximately 45 people at each facility. They are logically part of their regional office and retrieve all their data store information from their regional office. The remote site offices also submit their updated data to their regional office at the end of each business day.

Large Site-to-Site VPN Solution

Table 9-7 summarizes the design decisions that the enterprise made to meet its requirements.

Table 9-7   *Large Site-to-Site VPN Solution*

Design Questions	Decision	Notes
What topology will be used for the site-to-site VPN?	Meshed VPN solution	The company implemented a meshed VPN solution between headquarters and the regional offices, and between the regional offices and the remote sites. The final design is a hierarchical design.
		All Internet traffic goes through the headquarters office. Headquarters needs the ability to forward out to the Internet.

Table 9-7   *Large Site-to-Site VPN Solution (Continued)*

Design Questions	Decision	Notes
What type of tunneling will be deployed?	14 site-to-site tunnels using IPSec and GRE	A total of six tunnels is required between the headquarters and the regional sites. From the regional office to the remote offices, eight tunnels are required. Hardware encryption was required in all devices and dedicated VPN hardware at the headquarters and regional sites.
What type of security will be deployed?	Any data sent over the Internet will have the original IP header and data encrypted Basic security required through tunneling and firewalls	No outside access exists to the Internet except through the headquarters facility. Each site requires a firewall, either in the same device as the VPN tunnels or separate from the VPN tunnels.
Is NAT required?	Yes	Because the headquarters site handles Internet access, a need exists for NAT going out to the Internet, offered on a separate system from the VPN solution.
What VPN hardware will be used?	Headquarters: Cisco 7200 Regional offices: Cisco 2600 and 3600 series Remote offices: Cisco 2620	Because a requirement for dedicated VPN hardware with hardware encryption exists at the headquarters site, the Cisco 7200 series was selected to provide hardware encryption and cryptography. At the regional offices, based on the number of users, the Cisco 2600 or 3600 series was selected. Because there was no need for dedicated VPN hardware at the remote offices, the Cisco 2621 was selected, leaving room for growth.
What type of high availability will be deployed?	Redundant paths between headquarters and regional site, and paths between regional sites Failover from regional sites to the remote sites	—

Designing Remote-Access VPNs

Remote-access VPNs permit secure, encrypted connections between mobile or remote users and their corporate networks via a third-party network, such as a service provider. Deploying a remote-access VPN enables enterprises to reduce communications expenses by leveraging the local dial-up infrastructures of ISPs.

To fully realize the benefits of high-performance remote-access VPNs, an organization needs to deploy a robust, highly available VPN solution to their mobile and remote authorized users.

This section explains the following:

- Remote-access VPN requirements
- Remote-access VPN design considerations
- Capacity planning for remote-access VPNs
- NAT translation issues for remote-access VPNs

Remote-Access VPN Requirements

Remote-access VPNs typically begin as a replacement technology for traditional remote-access servers. As high-speed Internet access and broadband connectivity continue to emerge as cost-effective choices for consumers and businesses, the VPN paradigm takes on greater strategic significance. This section identifies typical requirements for a remote-access VPN.

Remote-access VPNs encompass analog, dialup, ISDN, digital subscriber line (DSL), mobile IP, and cable technologies to securely connect mobile users, telecommuters, or branch offices (see Figure 9-10).

Figure 9-10 *Remote-Access VPN*

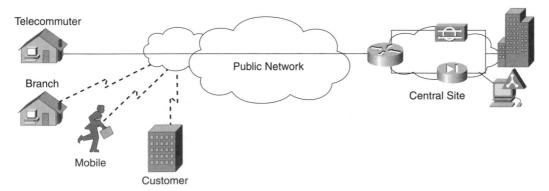

Remote-access VPNs require high-density, relatively low-bandwidth connections between remote users and a central site.

Typical remote-access VPN requirements include

- VPN clients
- Network devices with centralized authentication services, such as authentication, authorization, and accounting (AAA)

Figure 9-11 demonstrates a typical remote-access VPN network design that connects small or home offices to a central site.

Figure 9-11 *Typical Remote-Access VPN Network Design*

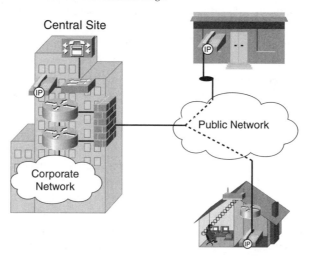

Remote VPN technology is used to connect small- or home-based offices to a central site. Connectivity is provisioned using DSL, cable, or dialup services depending upon their availability and the end-users' requirements. After the tunnel has been established, it is capable of providing secure transport services for data, voice, and video. Remote VPN tunnels are typically provisioned using IPSec, GRE, and L2TP protocols.

The principal advantages of a remote-access VPN solution include

- **Reduced access charges**—VPNs use the Internet or a service provider's shared IP network as the transport medium for private LAN access. Typically, enterprises deploy remote-access infrastructures in centralized topologies or in multiple locations for redundancy purposes. Toll-free access is the norm, but this becomes expensive as companies engage large numbers of remote workers. However, ubiquitous low-cost Internet access through ever-increasing Post Office Protocol (POP) coverage means that corporate users can connect to the enterprise using local numbers, thereby dramatically reducing or eliminating long-distance access charges.

- **Reduced overhead cost**—VPNs reduce the management overhead and capital investments required for remote access. In traditional remote-access infrastructures, modems are a core technology. In many cases, however, the modem is the weak link, frequently compromising the service availability and performance of the access infrastructure, because of the need for revision control, upgrades, and patches. This costly overhead consumes valuable IT resources. When this infrastructure is not maintained, remote-access users experience degraded service and service-call spikes.

- **Reduced service and support costs**—VPNs allow IT managers to take advantage of their service provider's modem pool and remote-access server infrastructure for remote access from local POPs. Because top-tier service providers constantly monitor, maintain, and upgrade their dialup infrastructure, you do not have to perform these functions. This drastically reduces primary service calls, because the service provider can offer technical support at all times for any and all modem connectivity issues. This benefit is subtle but extremely important, because a large percentage of remote-access usage typically occurs after normal business hours.

- **More successful connections**—By dialing a local POP, end users typically achieve higher connection rates than by dialing directly into the enterprise over long-distance lines.

- **Improved scalability**—The cost and complexity of scaling and delivering remote-access services is drastically reduced with VPNs. With remote-access servers, scalability is limited to the number of integrated modems, typically 24 to 48 modems. To increase capacity, the IT manager must install additional systems and the T1/Primary Rate Interface (PRI) feeder lines (or individually measured business lines). Telco installation times vary greatly, and adding new remote-access systems is a considerable cost. With VPN devices, maximum capacities approach thousands of simultaneous sessions in a single chassis. The IT manager can simply add new logins and distribute client software as demand for the remote-access service increases, incrementally increasing the bandwidth of the connection to the ISP as actual use requires.

- **Improved availability**—A relatively unknown feature of modem-based, remote-access servers is that IT managers must estimate a suitable port ratio for the usage pattern of their particular enterprise, because, under normal circumstances, remote-access users dial in at different times during the day and stay online for different duration periods. Port ratios enable the enterprise to significantly reduce the cost of their remote-access infrastructure (cost savings are proportional to the port ratio) and conserve equipment charges.

Remote-Access VPN Design Considerations

To design a remote-access VPN, you will determine the primary applications and requirements for the system. This section lists the design considerations for remote-access VPNs.

The VPN concentrator supports a remote-access VPN solution that resides within the Remote Access and VPN module. Generally, enterprises place a AAA server between the public network and the first router within the Remote Access and VPN module. As shown in Figure 9-12, the VPN concentrator then resides between routers so that all traffic goes through the VPN concentrator before being routed to the campus network.

Figure 9-12 *Placement of the VPN Concentrator*

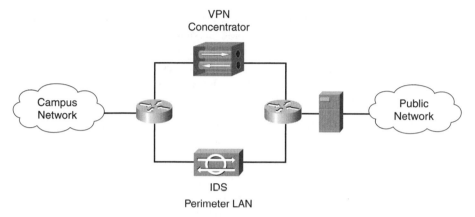

To design a remote-access VPN, ask the following questions:

- Is remote-access connectivity the main focus of the solution?
- What operating systems will remote users use? Determine if the VPN hardware and software client supports these operating systems.
- Which VPN tunneling protocol will be used in this solution?
- What type of routing protocols will be used on the VPN concentrator?
- How will user authentication be achieved in this solution?

To design a firewall solution for the VPN, ask the following questions:

- Is there an existing firewall in the current Internet access network topology? If not, is there any plan to introduce a firewall into the new VPN design?
- Is there an internal corporate security policy in place that mandates that all traffic going to the Internet must pass from the private interface of the firewall to the public interface of the firewall, and vice versa, rather than traversing a perimeter LAN interface off the firewall?
- Is it feasible to use one or more available firewall interfaces to create VPN perimeter LAN segments?

At this point in the design formulation, we have determined that there exists at least one available firewall interface that can be used to protect one of the interfaces (public, private, or both) of the VPN concentrator.

- Are there two available firewall interfaces to protect both the public and private interfaces of the VPN concentrator?

- If only one firewall interface is available, which VPN interface (public or private) should be protected by this firewall perimeter LAN interface?

Broadband Access Design Considerations

Broadband can play an important role in an enterprise VPN strategy. Today, cable and DSL service providers can offer corporate accounts, centralized billing, and turnkey VPN solutions. Always-on broadband connections are typically more cost-effective than toll-free dialup for high-usage users. In addition, user satisfaction is directly proportional to the speed of their remote-access connection. However, broadband VPN does have security implications. Key areas to consider are

- **Persistent connections**—The remote computer can be on all the time, either to the Internet, the corporate LAN via a tunnel, or both simultaneously.

- **Shared medium**—The enterprise LAN is being accessed over a shared medium. In some cases, the service provider might bridge traffic from one or more residential areas.

- **Security**—Abuse of the high-bandwidth connection can occur. For example, a disgruntled employee can easily download megabytes of confidential information in a very short period of time, which would be impractical at dialup speeds. In some cases, the corporate PC will be attached to a private home LAN. Policies must ensure that sensitive corporate data is protected from family members, cohabitants, and visitors. You can use several protective measures, including

  - A password-protected screen saver

  - Strong authentication methods, including token-based security and digital certificates

  - Workstation encryption packages

  - Inactivity timeouts for tunnels to protect the remote desktop from intrusion over the Internet or home LAN

  - Split-tunneling restrictions and personal firewall hardware or software

Capacity Planning for Remote-Access VPNs

You must select a VPN concentrator for a remote-access VPN based on current and future capacity projections. This section will help you plan the capacity for remote-access VPNs, given the number of users.

Answer the following questions to help document the capacity planning design aspects of the remote-access VPN solution:

- What is an estimate for the total number of users who plan to take advantage of the remote-access VPN solution in the initial phase of deployment?

- What is an estimate for the number of concurrent users who plan to connect to the remote-access VPN solution in the initial phase of deployment?
- What is the current bandwidth of the links to the ISP or Internet?
- List the estimated number of users connecting to the remote-access VPN solution using each of the following methods:
  - Analog dial
  - Dedicated line
  - ISDN
  - Wireless
  - DSL
  - Frame Relay
  - Cable modem
  - Other (list)
- List any forecasted growth estimates for the remote-access VPN solution.
- Is the peak number of simultaneous users accessing the VPN concentrator expected to reach 100, or is the estimated amount of user traffic expected to exceed 4 Mbps in the near future? If the answer is yes, a VPN concentrator is required.

Based on the capacity information, choose the appropriate VPN concentrator model.

NAT Issues

NAT is the function used to disguise source addresses from network eavesdroppers and is a method used by companies to conserve IP addresses. NAT, which can be used statically or dynamically, along with IPSec, presents potential problems for the remote-access VPN. This section describes various issues with NAT for remote-access VPNs.

NAT refers to the process of converting an IP address to a virtual IP address either to protect—or hide—the original IP address, or to convert a private (RFC 1918, "Address Allocation for Private Internets") IP address to an address that can be legally used and routed over the public Internet.

IPSec runs directly on top of IP and encrypts all information regarding the connection. Although this provides a very high degree of security, it poses a problem for devices performing NAT. To operate correctly, NAT needs access to some basic information in the transmitted packets (in particular, a unique identifier per session) that does not exist with IPSec packets. In short, because IPSec runs directly over IP, there is no port information and no unique unencrypted identifier for NAT to examine and map. Most devices that can perform NAT support two types of translations:

- One-to-one translation
- Many-to-one translation

One-to-One Translation

One-to-one translation does not require the use of ports and, therefore, does allow IPSec traffic to pass. Using this mechanism, an internal IP address block (for example, 10.2.4.0/24) is mapped to an external address block (for example, 125.100.2.0/24). A machine on the internal network (for example, 10.2.4.44) that would like to reach an external site, such as Yahoo!, can have all packets translated so that they are sent out with a source address of 125.100.2.44. This type of NAT, while not common in most enterprise deployments, will allow IPSec traffic to pass, because one-to-one NAT mapping does not involve changing anything associated with ports, only modifying the source IP address on outbound packets and the destination address of inbound packets.

Many-to-One Translation

The most common NAT scenario is many-to-one translation. With this setup, a block of internal addresses (for example, 10.2.4.0/24) are all mapped to appear as a single external IP address (for example, 125.100.2.254), allowing an administrator to hide internal IP addresses from the outside world while conserving IP address space. Routers and firewalls supporting NAT keep a translation table that contains a map of the internal source address and port to the external address and port (the globally visible address) for outgoing packets. This setup will allow return packets to come back to the source destination, mapped to the correct internal address based on the unique identifier, and then be routed to the appropriate device. Many-to-one NAT is also known as Port Address Translation (PAT).

For the many-to-one type of NAT, most routers support mapping of only two main protocols, TCP and User Datagram Protocol (UDP). When TCP/UDP is used, source and destination ports are available for NAT so that the substitution can take place. This scenario is not possible with IPSec, which does not have any ports and encrypts all critical information, making parameters, such as internal addresses, invisible to the NAT process. This is why NAT typically fails when used with IPSec.

NAT Traversal

NAT Traversal (NAT-T) lets IPSec peers establish a connection through a NAT device. It does this by encapsulating IPSec traffic in UDP datagrams, using port 4500, thereby providing NAT devices with port information. NAT-T auto detects any NAT devices, and only encapsulates IPSec traffic when necessary.

Remote-access clients that support both NAT-T and IPSec encapsulated in UDP methods first attempt NAT-T and then IPSec/UDP (if enabled) if a NAT device is not auto detected. This allows IPSec traffic to pass through firewalls that disallow IPSec. The VPN concentrator implementation of NAT-T supports IPSec peers behind a single NAT or PAT device, such as

- One Microsoft L2TP IPSec client
- One LAN-to-LAN IPSec connection

Either a LAN-to-LAN connection or multiple remote-access clients, but not a mixture of both, are allowed.

VPN Split-Tunnel Communication

Split tunneling is a configuration that involves tunnel interfaces or protocols that encapsulate packets so data can flow either inside or outside of a particular tunnel.

This tunnel could be an IPSec tunnel, a GRE tunnel, a combination of these, or almost any other tunneling protocol. When split tunneling is not enabled, all the data flowing out a router's (or a client's PC) egress interface will be encapsulated by the tunneling protocol and be sent directly to the peer router or concentrator of that particular tunnel. When split tunneling is enabled, that traffic might or might not be encapsulated in the tunneling protocol. This decision is normally made on a destination-by-destination basis by routing table entries, or via an access list entry.

In Figure 9-13, the split-tunneling feature is enabled, and all the traffic leaving the site through the router is forwarded directly to the next hop closest to the destination of that traffic. Only traffic destined to the remote site served by the tunnel is encapsulated. This decreases the load on a head-end or central site device when access is made to hosts not at that central site, such as the Internet. In the case of a home office network, this keeps traffic not specifically business-related out of the core of the network, and casual Internet surfing by family members does not appear as if it originated from the corporate network.

Figure 9-13 *VPN Split-Tunnel Communication*

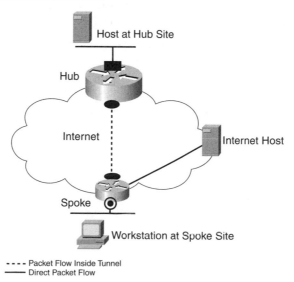

Because traffic is no longer guaranteed to be tunneled, access to the remote site might be made directly from outside networks without passing through any access controls placed at the central site. In the case of the Internet, this access will constitute a security problem, because access to the remote site might not be authenticated. For this reason, the use of a stateful inspection firewall feature is recommended at each remote site with split tunneling enabled when the Internet is used for the VPN. Then two instances of firewalls must be managed at the remote and the central sites.

Management of the firewalls includes ensuring that the policies implemented on each router and firewall are synchronized. Failure to keep these policies synchronized causes a possible vulnerability. Managing the firewalls also might include intrusion detection. If an IDS is deployed at the corporate location, you should replicate this function at each remote location that uses split tunneling.

When split tunneling is involved with a network that uses the Internet to create a VPN, it is highly recommended that a stateful inspection firewall function be configured at the spoke sites. Split tunneling allows an end station to directly access those hosts on the Internet. These end stations will not be protected by any firewall configured at the hub location. NAT is not a complete firewall solution. When running a routing protocol, a tunnel method other than IPSec tunnel mode must be used, because IPSec currently supports IP unicast traffic only.

When tunnels are present, the routing device should see two paths to a particular end point: one path through the tunnel and another path (that would appear longer from a routing standpoint) through the network unencapsulated. When data is encapsulated inside the tunnel, the destination might appear many hops closer than it actually is. This can cause problems if the state of the tunnel is not properly fed back into the routing table. This is often the case with static routes and GRE tunnels.

When running a routing protocol, do not mix routes from the inside networks with the outside routes, because a routing loop or recursive routing could occur. A routing loop occurs if the route from the tunnel interface is many hops shorter than the route learned via the outside routing protocol. A packet could be sent into a router to be encapsulated and then sent out the same interface it entered the router on.

Remote-Access VPN Examples

You can implement remote-access VPNs in any network, from a small company to large enterprise environments. This section provides examples of a small and a large remote-access VPN solution that meets specified VPN requirements.

Example: Small Remote-Access VPN

A small training company has 19 office-based employees, 8 salespeople who work either in the office or from home, and 160 instructors and 55 course developers. Remote users need secure remote access to information on the corporate network, including e-mails and documents such as course materials, learner lists, and administration forms.

Internally, a single-switch network connects to all the office equipment. The company has a DSL router that connects to the Internet, and it has a public Class C address assigned to it.

The company thought about allowing Internet access to its corporate File Transfer Protocol (FTP) server, but a new client needing courseware development is providing the company with highly sensitive material on a new product to be released in a year. The arrangement to win the bid specified that the technical materials be safeguarded and, if transmitted over the Internet, the confidential material would need to be secured through VPN tunnels.

Small Remote-Access VPN Solution

Table 9-8 summarizes the design decisions that the enterprise made to meet its client's requirements. Figure 9-14 shows the primary components associated with the VPN solution.

Table 9-8   *Small Remote-Access VPN Solution*

Design Questions	Decision	Notes
What topology will be used for the remote-access VPN?	Hub-and-spoke topology	The corporate LAN is the hub and each individual user becomes a spoke.
What type of tunneling will be deployed?	Encrypted tunnels using IPSec	—
What type of security will be deployed?	RADIUS server Firewall	The RADIUS server authenticates remote users. The firewall augments a DSL router. It allows access to the Internet for the IP addresses specified in a filter list. Users who dial in will be given an IP address from a pool of addresses that are blocked from Internet access.
Is NAT required?	No	All addresses are public, and the remote users are not allowed access to the Internet through the corporate network.
What VPN hardware will be used?	Dial-in access provided by an ISP	By allowing remote users to dial in to an ISP, the company avoids maintaining its own modem pool. As a restriction, none of the remote users can access the Internet while they are connected to the corporate LAN.

continues

Table 9-8 *Small Remote-Access VPN Solution (Continued)*

Design Questions	Decision	Notes
What VPN hardware will be used? (*Cont.*)	Headquarters: Cisco 3005 VPN Concentrator VPN client for remote users	At headquarters, there is no requirement for specialized hardware except that it has to connect to DSL and provide VPN termination with the ability to authenticate against a RADIUS server. Therefore, a Cisco 3005 VPN Concentrator is used at the corporate site. Each remote system has a VPN client installed to allow for authentication against the RADIUS server over an encrypted IPSec connection.
What type of high availability will be deployed?	None, except services offered by the ISP	The only resiliency incorporated into the design is that the ISP offers the VPN service and has many numbers that users can call to access their global system. If the corporate network fails, there is no corporate access.

Figure 9-14 *Small Remote-Access VPN Solution*

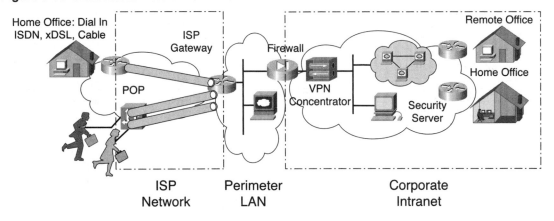

Example: Large Remote-Access VPN

An old-fashioned cosmetics and cleaning material manufacturer is looking for a way to keep its sales force updated on the latest inventories, while using the Internet as the basis of connectivity for its remote salespeople. The company is enlisting the help of a nationwide service provider to provide access points for dial-in connectivity. Each remote user will be able to use the VPN to access the corporate network and then access the Internet from within the corporate backbone. The primary applications are e-mail and file sharing between users and corporate data devices.

The company has 1400 users in the local corporate campus and 1100 salespeople in the field. Forty small and home office combinations have fewer than 30 people at each site. The IT department wants to have only one VPN device at each of the fixed small and home office locations.

Large Remote-Access VPN Solution

Table 9-9 summarizes the design decisions that the company made to meet its requirements. Figure 9-15 shows the primary components associated with the VPN solution.

Table 9-9   *Large Remote-Access VPN Solution*

Design Questions	Decision	Notes
What topology will be used for the remote-access VPN?	Hub-and-spoke topology	The corporate LAN is the hub and each individual user becomes a spoke.
What type of tunneling will be deployed?	Encrypted tunnels with IPSec	—
What type of security will be deployed?	RADIUS authentication Firewall with filters	Remote users will authenticate themselves as they connect to the corporate network. Each remote system has an installed VPN client to allow for authentication with the RADIUS server over the encrypted IPSec connection.
Is NAT required?	Yes	NAT is accomplished using the VPN concentrators.
What VPN hardware will be used?	Headquarters: Cisco 303x VPN Concentrator Remote fixed sites: Cisco 3002 VPN hardware client Remote sites: Cisco VPN client	The Cisco 3030 VPN Concentrator at headquarters supports a RADIUS server for authentication. It uses hardware encryption and is upgradeable for more functionality. The 40 fixed sites use the Cisco 3002 VPN hardware client. The 3002 VPN hardware client offers the following features: • Includes DHCP client and a DHCP Server for up to 253 stations behind the 3002 • Support for NAT for hiding stations behind 3002 • Optional 8-port 10/100 Mbps switch • Supports client mode as well as network extension mode for application flexibility

continues

Table 9-9 *Large Remote-Access VPN Solution (Continued)*

Design Questions	Decision	Notes
What VPN hardware will be used? (*Cont.*)		• Works with any operating system • Eliminates the need to add or support VPN applications on the PC or workstation • Seamless operation with existing applications The Cisco VPN client was selected for the remote devices connecting to the corporate LAN because of its ease of use and availability on a wide range of operating systems, including Windows, MAC OS, Solaris, and Linux.
What type of high availability will be deployed?	Redundant link from the corporate office to the service provider for failover	No other redundancy is planned for the network besides the redundant link. The ISP offers the VPN service and has many phone numbers available for access to their global system. If the corporate network fails, a second corporate connection comes online.

Figure 9-15 *Large Remote-Access VPN Solution*

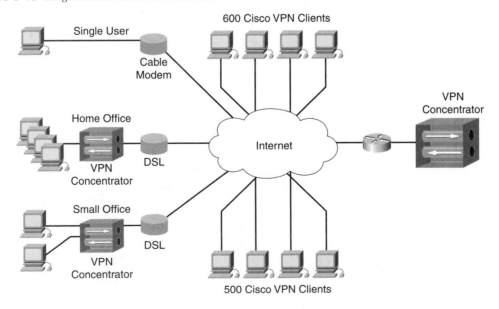

Summary

In this chapter, you learned the following key points:

- VPNs enable network connectivity for an organization, its business partners, and customers over a shared infrastructure, delivering the same policies as a private network.

- Virtual point-to-point connectivity is typically provided by a tunneling protocol.

- VPN security is provided by IPSec, user authentication, and encryption.

- For high availability and scalability, it is best to seek out a dedicated VPN concentrator platform, purpose-built to aggregate a large volume of simultaneous VPN sessions.

- Robust VPN management is a critical success factor for any large remote-access deployment. Management features are grouped into broad categories, such as configuration, monitoring, and alert functionality.

- When designing the site-to-site VPN, you need to design the topology, and incorporate resiliency and failover mechanisms.

- When remote user or branch office connectivity is critical, downtime for the VPN is not an option. Enterprises need a systemic approach to examine all the essential elements of delivering a high-availability site-to-site VPN.

- A site-to-site VPN solution will support static routing and dynamic routing protocols that are implemented elsewhere in the network.

- IPSec and GRE headers increase the size of packets being transported over a VPN.

- Site-to-site VPNs can be implemented in both small and large enterprise environments.

- Remote-access VPNs typically begin as a replacement technology for traditional remote-access servers. As high-speed Internet access and broadband connectivity emerge as cost-effective choices for consumers and businesses, the VPN becomes more strategic.

- To design a remote-access VPN, you will determine the primary applications and requirements for the system.

- You will select a VPN concentrator for a remote-access VPN based on current and future capacity projections.

- NAT along with IPScc present issues for the remote-access VPN.

- You can implement remote-access VPNs in any network from a small company to large enterprise environments.

References

Virtual Private Network Design. http://www.cisco.com/warp/public/779/largeent/design/vpn.html.

Solutions Reference Network Design (SRND) Networking Solutions Design Guides. To locate these documents, perform the following:

Step 1   Go to **http://www.cisco.com/**.

Step 2   In the Search box, enter **SRND** and click **Go**. A list of SRND Networking Solutions Design Guides appears.

Step 3   Select the Networking Solutions Design Guide that meets your needs.

A Primer for Implementing a Cisco Virtual Private Network. http://www.cisco.com/warp/public/cc/so/neso/vpn/vpne/vpn21_rg.htm.

White paper. *SAFE VPN: IPSec Virtual Private Networks in Depth.* http://www.cisco.com/warp/public/cc/so/cuso/epso/sqfr/safev_wp.htm.

Product Summary

Table 9-10 provides a brief overview of some of the products available from Cisco Systems that relate to the technologies discussed in this chapter. For a more detailed breakdown of the Cisco product line, visit http://www.cisco.com/en/US/products/index.html.

Table 9-10   *Cisco Security Products*

Cisco Security Products		
Virtual Private Networks	VPN 3080 Concentrator	10000 Simultaneous IPSec Remote-Access Users
		500 Simultaneous WebVPN (Clientless) Users (SSL VPN)
		1000 Maximum LAN-to-LAN Sessions
		100 Mbps Encryption Throughput
		HW Encryption Method
	VPN 3060 Concentrator	5000 Simultaneous IPSec Remote-Access Users
		500 Simultaneous WebVPN (Clientless) Users (SSL VPN)
		1000 Maximum LAN-to-LAN Sessions
		100 Mbps Encryption Throughput
		HW Encryption Method

Table 9-10   *Cisco Security Products (Continued)*

Cisco Security Products		
Virtual Private Networks (***Cont.***)	VPN 3030 Concentrator	1500 Simultaneous IPSec Remote-Access Users
		500 Simultaneous WebVPN (Clientless) Users (SSL VPN)
		500 Maximum LAN-to-LAN Sessions
		50 Mbps Encryption Throughput
		HW Encryption Method
	VPN 3020 Concentrator	750 Simultaneous IPSec Remote-Access Users
		200 Simultaneous WebVPN (Clientless) Users (SSL VPN)
		250 Maximum LAN-to-LAN Sessions
		50 Mbps Encryption Throughput
		HW Encryption Method
	VPN 3015 Concentrator	100 Simultaneous IPSec Remote-Access Users
		75 Simultaneous WebVPN (Clientless) Users (SSL VPN)
		100 Maximum LAN-to-LAN Sessions
		4 Mbps Encryption Throughput
		SW Encryption Method
	VPN 3005 Concentrator	100 Simultaneous IPSec Remote-Access Users
		50 Simultaneous WebVPN (Clientless) Users (SSL VPN)
		100 Maximum LAN-to-LAN Sessions
		4 Mbps Encryption Throughput
		SW Encryption Method
	VPN 3002 Client	Eliminates the need to add or support VPN applications on a PC or workstation
	IPSec VPN Service Module Cisco 7600 Series Router Catalyst 6500 Series Switch	Up to 8000 simultaneous tunnels Provides up to 1.9 Gbps 3DES IPSec throughput

continues

Table 9-10   *Cisco Security Products (Continued)*

Cisco Security Products		
Firewalls	PIX 535	Cleartext throughput: 1.7 Gbps
		Concurrent connections: 500,000
		168-bit 3DES IPSec VPN throughput: Up to 440 Mbps with VAC+ or 100 Mbps with VAC
		128-bit AES IPSec VPN throughput: Up to 535 Mbps with VAC+
		256-bit AES IPSec VPN throughput: Up to 440 Mbps with VAC+
		Simultaneous VPN tunnels: 2000
	PIX 525	Cleartext throughput: 330 Mbps
		Concurrent connections: 280,000
		168-bit 3DES IPSec VPN throughput: Up to 155 Mbps with VAC+ or 72 Mbps with VAC
		128-bit AES IPSec VPN throughput: Up to 165 Mbps with VAC+
		256-bit AES IPSec VPN throughput: Up to 170 Mbps with VAC+
		Simultaneous VPN tunnels: 2000
	PIX 515E	Cleartext throughput: 188 Mbps
		Concurrent connections: 130,000
		168-bit 3DES IPSec VPN throughput: Up to 140 Mbps with VAC+ or 63 Mbps with VAC
		128-bit AES IPSec VPN throughput: Up to 135 Mbps with VAC+
		256-bit AES IPSec VPN throughput: Up to 140 Mbps with VAC+
		Simultaneous VPN tunnels: 2000
	PIX 506E	Cleartext throughput: 100 Mbps
		Concurrent connections: 25,000
		56-bit DES IPSec VPN throughput: 20 Mbps
		168-bit 3DES IPSec VPN throughput: 17 Mbps
		128-bit AES IPSec VPN throughput: 30 Mbps
		Simultaneous VPN peers: 25

Table 9-10   *Cisco Security Products (Continued)*

Cisco Security Products		
Firewalls (*Cont.*)	PIX 501	Cleartext throughput: 60 Mbps Concurrent connections: 7500 56-bit DES IPSec VPN throughput: 6 Mbps 168-bit 3DES IPSec VPN throughput: 3 Mbps 128-bit AES IPSec VPN throughput: 4.5 Mbps Simultaneous VPN peers: 10
	Cisco SOHO 90	168-bit 3DES IPSec VPN throughput: 1 Mbps Simultaneous VPN peers: 8
	Cisco 830	168-bit 3DES IPSec VPN throughput: 7 Mbps 128-bit AES IPSec VPN throughput: 2 Mbps Simultaneous VPN peers: 10
	Cisco 1700 /w VPN Module	168-bit 3DES IPSec VPN throughput: 15 Mbps Simultaneous VPN peers: 100
	Cisco 2600XM /w AIM-VPN/BPII	168-bit 3DES IPSec VPN throughput: 22 Mbps 128-bit AES IPSec VPN throughput: 22 Mbps Simultaneous VPN peers: 800
	Cisco 2691 /w AIM-VPN/EPII	168-bit 3DES IPSec VPN throughput: 150 Mbps 128-bit AES IPSec VPN throughput: 150 Mbps Simultaneous VPN peers: 800
	Cisco 3725 /w AIM-VPN/EPII	168-bit 3DES IPSec VPN throughput: 186 Mbps 128-bit AES IPSec VPN throughput: 186 Mbps Simultaneous VPN peers: 800
	Cisco 3745 /w AIM-VPN/HPII	168-bit 3DES IPSec VPN throughput: 190 Mbps 128-bit AES IPSec VPN throughput: 190 Mbps Simultaneous VPN peers: 2000
	Cisco 7200VXR /w single SA-VAM2	168-bit 3DES IPSec VPN throughput: 260 Mbps 128-bit AES IPSec VPN throughput: 260 Mbps Simultaneous VPN peers: 5000
	Cisco 7301 with SA-VAM2	168-bit 3DES IPSec VPN throughput: 370 Mbps 128-bit AES IPSec VPN throughput: 370 Mbps Simultaneous VPN peers: 5000

NOTE   The information in Table 9-10 was derived from the Cisco website (http://www.cisco.com/go/safe/).

NOTE   Secure Socket Layer (SSL)-based VPN is an emerging technology that provides remote-access connectivity from almost any Internet-enabled location using a web browser and its native SSL encryption. SSL-based VPNs allow users to access web pages and a growing set of web-enabled services—including the ability to access files, send and receive e-mail, and run TCP-based applications—without the use of VPN client software. Although the ability to access applications does not equal that of IPSec VPNs, SSL-based VPNs are an excellent fit for user populations that require per-application/server access control or access from nonenterprise owned desktops.

SSL-based and IPSec VPNs are complementary technologies that can be deployed together to better address the unique access requirements of diverse user communities. To that extent, Cisco has enhanced its widely deployed IPSec VPN products to deliver SSL-based VPN (clientless, web browser–based) services as well, providing the benefits of both technologies on a single device. This strategy eases deployment and management by using existing installed infrastructure, while preserving customer investments in existing VPN equipment.

Standards and Specification Summary

PKCS #3: Diffie-Hellman Key Agreement Standard. http://www.rsasecurity.com/rsalabs/pkcs/pkcs-3/.

Federal Information Processing Standard (FIPS) for the Advanced Encryption Standard, FIPS-197. http://csrc.nist.gov/CryptoToolkit/aes/.

Federal Information Processing Standard (FIPS) for the Data Encryption Standard, FIPS-46-2. http://www.itl.nist.gov/fipspubs/fip46-2.htm.

Federal Information Processing Standard (FIPS) for the Data Encryption Standard, FIPS-46-3.

X9.52-1998, Triple Data Encryption Algorithm Modes of Operation.

Request For Comments (RFCs) can be downloaded from the following website: http://www.rfc-editor.org/rfc.html.

- RFC 1321, "The MD5 Message-Digest Algorithm"
- RFC 1828, "IP Authentication using Keyed MD5"
- RFC 2085, "HMAC-MD5 IP Authentication with Replay Prevention"
- RFC 1492, "An Access Control Protocol, Sometimes Called TACACS"

- RFC 1510, "The Kerberos Network Authentication Service (V5)"
- RFC 1701, "Generic Routing Encapsulation (GRE)"[*]
- RFC 2784, "Generic Routing Encapsulation (GRE)"[*]
- RFC 2890, "Key and Sequence Number Extensions to GRE"[*]

NOTE   [*] Both implementations are deployed in networks. RFC 2890 extensions are starting to be adopted.

- RFC 2866, "RADIUS Accounting"
- RFC 2865, "Remote Authentication Dial-In User Service (RADIUS)"
- RFC 2402, "IP Authentication Header"
- RFC 2406, "IP Encapsulating Security Payload (ESP)"
- RFC 2408, "Internet Security Association and Key Management Protocol (ISAKMP)"
- RFC 2409, "The Internet Key Exchange (IKE)"
- RFC 2459, "Internet X.509 Public Key Infrastructure Certificate and CRL Profile"
- RFC 2510, "Internet X.509 Public Key Infrastructure Certificate Management Protocols"
- RFC 2516, "A Method for Transmitting PPP Over Ethernet (PPPoE)"
- RFC 2637, "Point-to-Point Tunneling Protocol (PPTP)"
- RFC 2661, "Layer Two Tunneling Protocol (L2TP)"
- RFC 3193, "Securing L2TP using IPSec"
- RFC 2764, "A Framework for IP Based Virtual Private Networks"
- RFC 2631, "Diffie-Hellman Key Agreement Method"
- RFC 2246, "The TLS Protocol Version 1.0."

Review Questions

Answer the following questions to test your comprehension of the topics discussed in this chapter. Refer to Appendix A, "Answers to Review Questions," to check your answers.

1. What are the required attributes of a VPN solution?

2. What are the benefits of a site-to-site VPN?

3. Define the technique known as tunneling.

4. When is GRE tunneling used?

5. What are the key components of the IPSec framework laid out by the IETF?

6. What is the role of a certification authority (CA)?

7. Define encryption.

8. When evaluating the capabilities of the concentrator device, what questions need to be answered?

9. What are the key VPN management design considerations?

10. Define the modules associated with the CiscoWorks VPN/Security Management Solutions discussed in this chapter.

11. List the key components of site-to-site VPN design.

12. What are the four major steps to designing a site-to-site VPN solution?

13. When is it appropriate to use a hub-and-spoke design for a VPN solution?

14. When is it appropriate to use a full-mesh design for a VPN solution?

15. When is it appropriate to use a hierarchical design for a VPN solution?

16. What two steps must occur for stateless failover of a VPN connection to be successful?

17. What two steps can be taken to avoid the fragmentation of packets over a GRE/IPSec tunnel?

18. What technique should be used to add resiliency to IPSec tunnels?

19. Define a GRE tunnel.

20. List the principle advantages of a remote-access VPN solution.

21. What questions should be asked when designing a remote-access VPN?

22. What should be defined to help document the capacity planning design aspects of the remote-access VPN solution?

23. What is NAT Traversal?

24. How does split tunneling work?

25. When split tunneling is involved with a network that uses the Internet to create a VPN, it is highly recommended that a stateful inspection firewall function be configured at the spoke sites. Why?

Case Study: OCSIC Bottling Company

The purpose of this case study is to practice the key design skills discussed in this chapter. The project is to revisit the earlier design for the OCSIC Bottling Company and ensure that the VPN solution provides secure access to data and reduces the risk to network intrusions and attacks. For each identified component of the design, we are required to provide justification for our decision. The justification will provide an explanation for the options considered, and the reason behind choosing the selected option.

OCSIC international offices require an always-on connection to the headquarters to share data and e-mail. However, the cost of a dedicated connection is too high. Each international plant requires a connection to their local ISP and a VPN for secure communications over the Internet to headquarters.

Site-to-Site VPN Solution

The first task is to design a site-to-site VPN solution between the headquarters and each international plant. Table 9-11 summarizes the design decisions that the enterprise made to meet the requirements.

Table 9-11   *Design Decisions*

Design Questions	Decision	Justification
What topology will be used for the site-to-site VPN?	Hub-and-spoke topology	The corporate LAN is the hub, and each individual site becomes a spoke.
What type of tunneling will be deployed?	GRE tunnels	Each international site creates a GRE tunnel to the headquarters site and then encrypts the information through IPSec tunnel mode.
What type of security will be deployed?	IPSec tunnels Authentication with a Terminal Access Controller Access Control System Plus (TACACS+) server	The information is encrypted through the IPSec tunnel. The site-to-site tunnels are authenticated through a separate TACACS+ server.
Is NAT required?	No	All addresses are public, and the remote users are not allowed access to the Internet through the corporate network.
What VPN hardware will be used?	Central site: Cisco 3030 VPN Concentrator Remote sites: Cisco 1740 or larger	The Cisco 3030 VPN Concentrator handles both the site-to-site and remote-site VPN access. The remote-site routers support VPN tunnel end-points.
What type of high availability will be deployed?	None, except services offered by the ISP	The only resiliency incorporated into the design is that the ISP offers the VPN service and has many numbers that users can call to access their global system. If the corporate network fails, there is no corporate access.

Remote-Access VPN Solution

The next task is to design a remote access VPN solution for U.S.–based telecommuters to headquarters. Table 9-12 shows the design decisions that were made for the remote-access VPN.

Table 9-12 *Design Decision for Remote-Access VPN*

Design Questions	Decision	Justification
What topology will be used for the remote-access VPN?	Hub-and-spoke topology	The corporate LAN is the hub, and each individual user becomes a spoke.
What type of tunneling will be deployed?	L2TP tunnels	Each remote user will create an L2TP tunnel to the headquarters site and then encrypt the information through IPSec tunnel mode.
What type of security will be deployed?	IPSec tunnels Authentication with TACACS+ server	The information is encrypted through the IPSec tunnel. The site-to-site tunnels are authenticated through a separate TACACS+ server.
Is NAT required?	Provided by VPN concentrator	The VPN concentrator will perform any NAT functions needed.
What VPN hardware will be used?	Central site: Cisco 3030 VPN Concentrator Cisco VPN client for remote users	The Cisco 3030 VPN Concentrator handles both the site-to-site and remote-site VPN access.
What type of high availability will be deployed?	None, except services offered by the ISP	The only resiliency incorporated into the design is that the ISP offers the VPN service and has many numbers that users can call to access their global system. If the corporate network fails, there is no corporate access.

Revised Network Diagrams

The updated network diagrams, which reflect the site-to-site and remote-access VPN strategies presented, follow.

Figure 9-16 *Revised Network Diagram for the Site-to-Site VPN Solution*

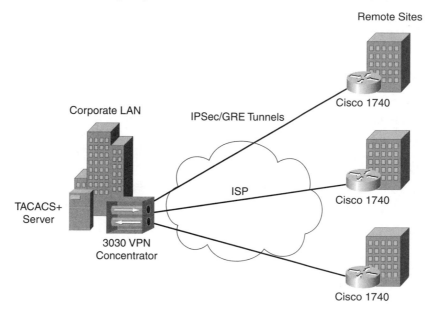

Figure 9-17 *A Network Diagram for the Remote VPN Solution*

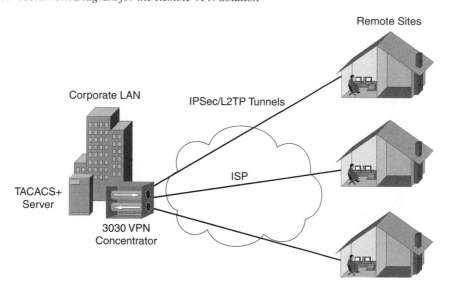

After completing this chapter, you will be able to

- Identify the wireless LAN solution
- Design wireless LANs for enhanced enterprise communications

CHAPTER 10

Designing Enterprise Wireless Networks

Simply put, a wireless local-area network (WLAN) does not require wires. It uses radio frequencies instead of a traditional media, such as copper or fiber. It provides real-time access to the network. With a WLAN, the covered area is essentially comparable to that of a wired LAN. In large applications, by deploying a series of access points throughout a building or campus, enterprises can achieve more coverage than a wired network, with the benefits of high-speed data rates and the freedom of mobility from being able to access broadband data anywhere within the WLAN.

Reviewing the Wireless LAN Solution

WLANs enable network designers to establish and maintain a wireless network connection throughout or between buildings, without the limitations of wires or cables. Cisco provides a family of WLAN products that combine the mobility and flexibility users want from a wireless system with the throughput and security they get from a wired LAN.

Mobility and ease of installation have made WLAN technology a key technology in markets such as health care, education, and retail. WLANs are also making inroads in general business environments.

This section demonstrates how to identify the necessary components of a WLAN solution, given specific mobility requirements. It describes how WLANs meet enterprise requirements, compares their architecture to a typical wired LAN configuration, and identifies the 802.11 standards and differences.

Emerging Wireless Enterprise Network Needs

A WLAN implementation adds a mobile component to the traditional office LAN and provides LAN coverage in areas where cabling is impractical or inefficient. This section describes how WLANs can meet enterprise requirements.

In a high-performance, switched environment, wireless technology can deliver Ethernet-level speeds to open areas on the campus, or high-density areas such as auditoriums and conference rooms that require network access for a large number of users. Typically, a WLAN does not replace the wired LAN. It is typically an addition or extension to the wired LAN. WLAN technology enables deployment of LANs in offices where cabling might not be cost effective or timely. The WLAN adds a nomadic or mobile dimension to the traditional office LAN. The WLAN also facilitates connectivity in meeting rooms, cafeterias, and other common areas where wired LANs are impractical.

NOTE   The IEEE 802.11 specification defines the physical and data link layer protocols associated with the transmission of data over a wireless medium.

Wireless Communication Architecture

A WLAN consists of an access point communicating over radio frequency to wireless clients, as shown in Figure 10-1. The data rate, power level, and antenna choice affect the size of the coverage area of a single wireless cell, which, in turn, affects how many access points are required in a specific implementation. This section describes the wireless communication architecture.

Figure 10-1 *Cisco Wireless Architecture*

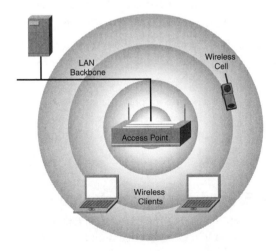

NOTE   A wireless access point is a specialized device that provides a central point of communication for all wireless stations that belong to the same Basic Service Set (BSS). Wireless stations (clients) transmit their frames to the access point (AP), which, in turn, forwards them on to the intended recipient. The AP not only moves frames between wireless stations, but also forwards them to a wired LAN.

The purpose of a BSS is to specify a group of wireless devices that is configured to communicate with one another. A BSS consists of an AP and its associated wireless clients. The wireless AP broadcasts a signal that can be received by any station within transmission range. The broadcast contains a Service Set ID (SSID), which defines the BSS that the AP belongs to. A wireless station receiving the broadcast, reads the SSID, and decides if it should join in the advertised BSS. The SSID is a name specified by the administrator (for example, "LAB" could be specified as the SSID for a WLAN). The wireless access software provides a list of SSIDs for APs that it has received and provides the user with the option of selecting the one they want to join. Acceptance of the SSID allows the station to use the AP for transmitting and receiving data.

APs can reduce unauthorized connections by specifying the MAC of stations that are allowed to connect—MAC-based authentication. Another mechanism that can help reduce unauthorized access is turning off SSID broadcasts. This way, stations that want to connect need to know the SSID (preconfigured) in advance. Other security enhancements are discussed in the section, "WLAN Security Extension—EAP."

Only one station in a wireless cell, including the access point, can send data at any one time. The bandwidth is shared among all stations. If a station wants to send data, it listens and waits for an available slot. WLANs use carrier-sense multiple access collision avoidance (CSMA/CA).

The protocols used in a wireless network cover the physical and data link layers. Therefore, a wireless LAN can transport a variety of LAN and network layer protocols, such as IP, AppleTalk, NetBIOS Extended User Interface (NetBEUI), and so on.

NOTE   CSMA/CA predates carrier sense multiple access collision detection (CSMA/CD), and is a more structured implementation of a shared medium communications algorithm. Each device must sample the physical medium to detect if the medium is in use or free before transmitting. When a station transmits a frame, the sender must indicate for how long the medium will be in use so all other members of the same shared medium know how long to wait before they can send traffic. The receiver must acknowledge each frame so that the sender knows it was received. A back-off algorithm is used to gauge how long the transmitter waits before resending a frame that was not acknowledged.

Access Point Coverage

Figure 10-2 demonstrates how different data rates affect cell size (coverage). Lower data rates allow the signal to extend further from the access point than higher data rates can. Hence, the data rate (and power level) will affect cell coverage and the number of APs required.

Figure 10-2 *Access Point Coverage*

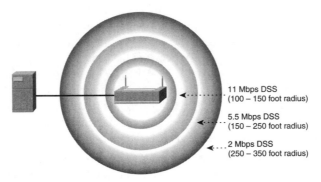

11 Mbps DSS
(100 – 150 foot radius)

5.5 Mbps DSS
(150 – 250 foot radius)

2 Mbps DSS
(250 – 350 foot radius)

The following factors affect the coverage of the AP:

- Selected data rate
  - 1 Mbps
  - 2 Mbps
  - 5.5 Mbps
  - 11 Mbps
- Power level, detailed as follows (maximum power setting varies according to individual country regulations):
  - 100 MW (20 dBm)
  - 50 MW (17 dBm)
  - 30 MW (15 dBm)
  - 20 MW (13 dBm)
  - 5 MW (7 dBm)
  - 1 MW (0 dBm)
- Antenna choice
  - Dipole
  - Omni
  - Wall mount

For a given data rate, the WLAN designer can alter the power level or choose a different antenna to change the coverage area and/or coverage shape.

NOTE   Antennas have a significant impact on the effective design of your wireless network. Proper selection requires an understanding of the various antenna types and models available for you to choose from. The following provides a brief introduction into antenna types and their usage.

An omnidirectional antenna is designed to provide a 360-degree radiation pattern. This type of antenna is used when coverage in all directions from the antenna is required. These antenna types are best used to provide coverage in large open spaces found in warehouses, retail stores, and enterprise networks. They are best placed in the center of the area serviced and in an open space. Cisco recommends where possible mounting them at 20 to 25 feet. In a small office environment, the standard dipole antenna usually provides effective coverage. The following are examples of omnidirectional antenna:

- Dipole antenna
- Yagi antenna

Directional antennas redirect the power they receive from the transmitter allowing them to provide more power in a single direction and less in all other directions. As the gain, or power of a directional antenna increases, the angle of radiation usually decreases, providing a greater coverage distance, but with a reduced coverage angle. Directional antenna provide excellent coverage in hard to reach areas or for very long distances that are 1/2 mile or greater. The following antenna types are examples of directional antenna:

- Patch antenna (wall mounted)
- Dish antenna

For more information on Cisco Aironet antennas, see http://www.cisco.com/en/US/ products/hw/wireless/ps469/products_data_sheet09186a008008883b.html.

APs have an aggregate throughput of about 6 Mbps for the 802.11b specification. With this in mind, the maximum suggested number of active clients is between 10 and 30 clients. The precise number of active clients depends on the data rates supported. That is, active clients with higher data rates necessitate fewer active clients for each AP.

Cisco wireless products support 11-Mbps communications with an indoor range (within a building) of 40 meters (130 feet) and outdoor range of 244 meters (800 feet). However, as the distance between the wireless station and the AP grows, it becomes necessary to lower transmission speed to maintain channel quality. To avoid loss of data for mobile users,

Cisco wireless products automatically switch to lower speeds, which enables users to maintain a connection in open areas of up to 610 meters (2000 feet) from the AP. These transmission distances are typical when using 100 MW transmission power with a 2.2 dBi diversity dipole antenna.

Cell Distribution

A large cell size might cause too many clients to share the available bandwidth. By reducing the AP power or antenna gain, you can reduce the cell size and share it with fewer clients. This results in more APs for a given coverage area, but provides better and more equitable performance for clients.

NOTE   A *cell* refers to the transmission range of a wireless AP.

802.11 Standards

The IEEE 802.11 standard is a group of protocol specifications for WLANs (see Table 10-1). This section describes the IEEE 802.11 standards and their differences.

Table 10-1   *IEEE 802.11 Standard*

	802.11b	802.11a	802.11g
Frequency Band	204 GHz	5 GHz	2.4 GHz
Availability	Worldwide	U.S./Asia Pacific	Worldwide
Maximum Data Rate	11 Mbps	54 Mbps	54 Mbps

The laws of radio dynamics are as follows:

- Higher data rates = Shorter transmission range
- Higher power output = Increased range, but lower battery life
- Higher frequency radios = Higher data rates, shorter ranges

The 802.11 standards define the communication protocols between wireless workstations and the network APs that bridge wireless and wired networks. The original 802.11 standard had specified support for 1- and 2-Mbps peak transfer rates. Subsequent advances in the 802.11 standard have greatly increased wireless transfer rates. The high rate amendment to the 802.11 standard, 802.11b, added 5.5- and 11-Mbps transmission speeds.

The next evolution in the standard is 802.11a, which supports transmission speeds of 36 Mbps, 48 Mbps, 54 Mbps, and ultimately 108 Mbps, using dual channels and operating on the 5-GHz Unlicensed National Information Infrastructure (U-NII) band. The 802.11a standard is not compatible with the 802.11b standard.

The 802.11g standard operates in the same unlicensed portion of the 2.4-GHz spectrum as 802.11b. Both the IEEE 802.11g and 802.11a standards provide a 54-Mbps data rate. IEEE 802.11g provides the benefit of backward compatibility with IEEE 802.11b equipment, preserving users' investment in their existing WLAN infrastructure. In addition, because it builds on 802.11b technology, 802.11g will take advantage of the years of 802.11b silicon integration and the resulting reduction in power consumption, form factor size, and cost. However, because 802.11g is limited to the same channels as 802.11b, scalability might become a factor as WLAN user density increases.

Cisco Wireless Solutions

The Cisco wireless solution includes the following components:

- APs and client adapters
- Workgroup bridges
- Wireless bridges
- Antennas

This section describes the components of a Cisco wireless solution.

Access Points and Client Adapters

An AP, as shown in Figure 10-3, is the center point in an all-wireless network, or serves as a connection point between a wired and wireless network. You can place multiple APs throughout a facility to give users with WLAN client adapters the ability to roam freely throughout an extended area while maintaining uninterrupted access to all network resources.

Figure 10-3 *Access Points and Client Adapters*

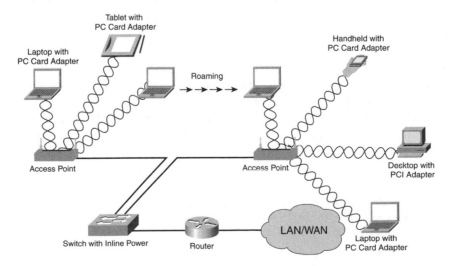

Workgroup Bridges

A workgroup bridge provides wireless connectivity to an Ethernet-enabled device. In Figure 10-4, a workgroup bridge is shown connecting Ethernet-enabled laptops and other portable computers to a WLAN, providing the link from these devices to an AP or wireless bridge.

Figure 10-4 *Workgroup Bridge*

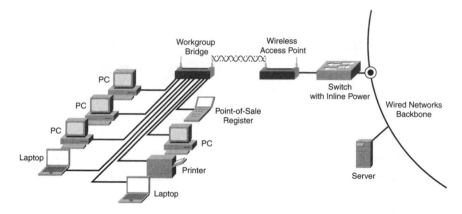

Wireless Bridges

A wireless bridge provides a means to connect two or more remote Ethernet segments over a wireless connection.

A wireless bridge is capable of communicating over greater distances than 802.11b APs and clients. Wireless bridges do this by stretching the timing constraints 802.11 puts on the return times for packet acknowledgments. This alteration of the timing values violates 802.11 specifications.

Antennas

With the appropriate antennas, a bridge in AP mode can communicate with clients in the line of sight. In contrast, APs are compliant with 802.11 and are subject to timing characteristics that impose a maximum distance limitation of 1 mile for communication with clients at any speed. AP distances vary up to 1 mile in distance depending on the antennas used.

NOTE   You should plan to work with a radio frequency (RF) designer to determine appropriate antennas for a WLAN installation.

Designing WLANs for Enhanced Enterprise Communications

WLANs are generally deployed in an enterprise campus or branch office for increased efficiency and flexibility. WLANs are emerging as an effective method to connect to an enterprise network. They are an access technology intended for LAN implementations. This section presents design recommendations for the WLAN infrastructure in enterprises.

By addressing common deployment schemes, an enterprise WLAN will provide mobility within a building or site, convenience, and flexibility.

This section describes how to design WLAN solutions for small and large enterprise networks, branch offices, and telecommuters, given specific enterprise network requirements.

Enterprise WLAN Design Considerations

When designing an enterprise wireless network solution, you must consider the RF design, the campus infrastructure, high availability, roaming, IP multicast, and quality of service (QoS). This section identifies the design considerations for an enterprise WLAN solution.

WLAN Data Rates

Data rates affect cell size. Lower data rates (such as 1 Mbps) can extend farther from the AP than can higher data rates (such as 11 Mbps). Therefore, the data rate (and power level) affects cell coverage and consequently the number of APs required.

Although six APs with a data rate of 2 Mbps might adequately service an area, it might take twice as many APs to support a data rate of 5 Mbps, and more again to support data rates of 11 Mbps.

The data rate chosen is dependent on the type of application to be supported. In a WLAN extension environment, the higher data rates of 11 Mbps and 5.5 Mbps are recommended. This gives maximum throughput and should minimize performance-related support issues. In a WLAN environment, the data rates selected are determined by the application requirements. Some clients might not support the higher data rates and might require the use of lower data rates.

It might seem logical to choose the default configuration of APs and clients, thereby allowing all data rates. However, three key reasons exist for limiting the data rate to the highest rate at which full coverage is obtained:

- Broadcast and multicast are sent at the slowest data rate (to ensure that all clients can see them), which reduces the throughput of the WLAN because traffic must wait until frames are processed at the slower rate.

- Clients that are farther away, and, therefore, accessing the network at a lower data rate, decrease the overall throughput by causing delays while the lower bit rates are being serviced.

- If an 11-Mbps service has been specified and provisioned with APs to support this level of service, allowing clients to associate at lower rates will create a coverage area greater than planned, increasing the security exposure and potentially interfering with other WLANs.

Client Density and Throughput

APs have an aggregate throughput of approximately 6 Mbps. Therefore, the maximum suggested number of active associations (active clients) is around 10 to 30 clients. You can adjust this number depending on the particular application.

A large cell size can result in an overloading of available capacity with too many clients sharing network access via the same AP. By reducing the AP power or antenna gain, you can reduce the cell size and share it among fewer clients. More APs will be required for a given coverage area, but clients receive better performance.

Client power should be adjusted to match the AP power settings. Maintaining a high setting on the client does not result in higher performance, and it can cause interference in nearby cells.

WLAN Coverage

Different enterprises have different requirements. Some need a WLAN to cover specific common areas. Others need WLANs to cover each floor of a building, the entire building including stairwells and elevators, or the entire campus including parking areas and roads.

Apart from impacting the number of APs required, the coverage requirements can introduce other issues, such as specialized antennas, outdoor enclosures, and lightning protection.

RF Environment

You can use RF design to minimize the RF radiation in coverage areas or directions not required. For example, if WLAN coverage is required only in the buildings, you can minimize the amount of RF coverage outside the building through AP placement and directional antennas.

The performance of the WLAN and its equipment depends upon its RF environment. Some examples of variables that can adversely affect RF performance are

- 2.4-GHz cordless phones
- Walls fabricated from wire mesh and stucco
- Filing cabinets and metal equipment racks
- Transformers
- Heavy-duty electric motors
- Firewalls and fire doors
- Concrete
- Refrigerators
- Sulphur plasma lighting (Fusion 2.4-GHz lighting systems)
- Air conditioning ductwork
- Other radio equipment
- Microwave ovens
- Other WLAN equipment

You should perform a site survey to ensure that the required data rates are supported in all the required areas, despite the environmental variables.

The site survey should consider the three-dimensional space occupied by the WLAN. For example, a multistory building WLAN with different subnets per floor might require a different RF configuration than the same building with a single WLAN subnet per building. In the multiple-subnet instance, a client attempting to roam to a different AP on the same floor might acquire an AP from an adjacent floor. Switching APs in a multisubnet environment would change the roaming activity from a seamless data link layer roam to a network layer roam, which would, in turn, disrupt sessions and might require user intervention.

Channel Selection

Channel selection depends on the frequencies and channels permitted for the particular region. The North American and European Telecommunication Standards Institute (ETSI) channel sets allow the allocation of three nonoverlapping channels: 1, 6, and 11.

You should allocate the channels to the cells as follows:

- Overlapping cells should use nonoverlapping channels, as shown in Figure 10-5.
- Where the same channels are required in multiple cells, make sure those cells have no overlap.

Figure 10-5 *Non-Overlapping Channels*

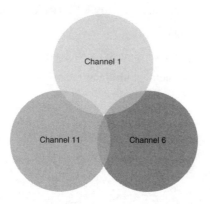

In multistory buildings, check the cell overlap between floors according to the overlap guidelines. Some resurveying and relocating of APs might be required. Retest the site using the selected channels and check for interference.

You can configure an AP to automatically search for the best channel.

IEEE 802.11a allocates 12 channels in the 5-GHz frequency range for use in North America, but does not find itself under the same design constraints as 802.11b and 802.11g. Like 802.11b, the 802.11a specification channel spacing does overlap; however, because of the signaling protocol used, Orthogonal Frequency Division Multiplexing (OFDM), it does not cause interference.

Access-Point Placement and Number

The required data rate has a direct impact on the number of APs needed in a design. For example, six APs with a data rate of 2 Mbps might adequately service an area, but it would take twice as many APs to support a data rate of 5 Mbps.

The data rate selected is dependent on the type of application to be supported. In a WLAN extension environment, higher data rates of 11 Mbps and 5.5 Mbps are recommended to provide maximum throughput and to minimize performance-related support issues.

When choosing an AP and associated client cards, consider the following:

* Processor power
* Throughput requirements
* Inline power support
* Output power support

Choose the AP that best serves the application needs and then select the appropriate client cards and accessories.

Inline Power

Inline power is particularly useful in campus and office deployments where APs are unlikely to be mounted near power outlets. Inline power eliminates the requirement for site customization to provide power outlets in ceilings or walls to support APs.

Power options include the following:

- A switch with inline power
- An inline power patch panel
- A Cisco Aironet power injector (used when inline power is not available)

NOTE   Power injectors provide inline power to APs or bridges by combining 48-VDC power with the data signal.

VLANs

Whenever possible, the WLAN should be a separate subnet from other LAN traffic, for these reasons:

- To optimize overall network performance. The WLAN media is shared and, therefore, any unnecessary broadcast or multicast traffic can impair network performance.
- To clearly identify the source of traffic for management and security issues.
- To increase the number of WLAN clients on a single VLAN and increase the possible Layer 2 roaming domain.

When a WLAN is an overlay network extension, it is not expected that WLAN VLANs mirror the wired VLANs. For example, you can implement separate VLANs per floor for the wired LAN, but only a single WLAN VLAN for the building.

Separate VLANs for WLANs are mandatory for solutions using IP Security (IPSec) Virtual Private Networks (VPNs), or static Wired Equivalent Privacy (WEP). Protocol and address filtering is applied to traffic on these VLANs. In addition, the filters are required between the wireless network and the wired network to protect the wired clients from attack from the wireless network.

Some WLAN applications, especially those using static WEP, might require one VLAN to be extended across the entire campus to support application roaming.

NOTE	The IEEE 802.11 WEP specification is a shared key encryption protocol used to secure traffic exchanged between a wireless AP and client. Shared key encryption requires that both parties be configured with identical keys. The protocol is built upon the RC4 stream cipher, and only encrypts the payload and the Integrity Check Value (ICV) of the 802.11 frame. The popularity of WEP as a security protocol initially was based on its low computational overhead and easy implementation. Since its inception in 1997, it has been demonstrated as relatively easy to break, causing other security solutions to be explored and implemented.

IP Addressing

The IP addressing of the WLAN has no direct impact on its behavior; however, address assignment can impact management. To that end, it is recommended to allocate a separate address space for WLAN clients. Separating address spaces in this way can ease security and management. Configuration of filters and Intrusion Detection Systems (IDSs) will also be simpler and WAP clients will be easier to identify. RFC 2827 filtering should be implemented to prevent the use of the enterprise network as a launching point for security breaches.

Infrastructure Availability

The WLAN can use the existing high-availability services provided by the enterprise network, such as Hot Standby Router Protocol (HSRP) and Layer 2 and Layer 3 redundancies. Therefore, it is simply an issue of providing the required availability in the WLAN.

You can address the availability of the WLAN in three ways:

- **As an overlay network**—The hard-wired LAN is the users' backup if the WLAN fails.

- **As a mobile network**—Users can move to a location where connectivity is available if the WLAN fails.

- **As a mission-critical network**—Network redundancies ensure that the failure of one component does not impact WLAN users.

Back-End System Availability

High-availability designs are required for the back-end systems to ensure that individual component failures do not have widespread impact. The back-end systems vary depending upon the WLAN security deployment options.

Access-Point Hot Standby Redundancy

The use of AP hot standby is independent of the security model chosen. In the hot standby redundancy case, two APs are configured to use the same channel in a single coverage area. Only one of the APs is active. The standby AP passively monitors the network and the primary AP. If the primary AP fails, the secondary AP seamlessly takes over to provide cell coverage. A Simple Network Management Protocol (SNMP) trap is generated to alert the administrator that the primary AP has failed.

Hot standby is not the same as HSRP. Hot standby mode designates an AP as a backup for another AP. The standby AP is placed near the AP it monitors and is configured exactly the same as the monitored AP (except for its role in the radio network and IP address). The standby AP associates with the monitored AP as a client and queries the monitored AP regularly through both the Ethernet interface and the radio interface. If the monitored AP fails to respond, the standby AP comes online, signals the primary AP radio to become quiescent, and takes the monitored AP's place in the network.

As soon as the primary AP failure is detected, user intervention is required. The user must return the backup AP (which is now in root mode) to standby mode when the primary AP comes back online. Failure to reset the standby AP results in both the primary and standby APs operating concurrently on the same channel. If two APs are online at the same time, you may end up with an IP address conflict. To avoid this, change the IP address of at least one of the APs to something other than the default IP (10.0.0.2). The addressing should reflect your IP architecture.

Roaming

The native Layer 2 mobility of the Cisco APs can support devices that stay within a single subnet. Devices that need to move from subnet to subnet must acquire a new IP address and can lose packets that might have been buffered when roaming between APs on different subnets. Seamless roaming on a WLAN requires that the AP involved be included within a single VLAN.

When a WLAN is used as an overlay network, it is possible to span the same WLAN VLAN across a building floor or multiple floors of a building. This arrangement should be sufficient to meet most user mobility requirements.

Clients that require continuous connectivity, but only within a building, should be able to be accommodated by implementing a single VLAN within all but the largest buildings.

Applications that require continuous connectivity within a campus present a challenge in providing mobility across different VLANs. Cisco routers support mobile IP, which is designed to provide this type of mobility. The issue is that almost no standard mobile IP clients are available, and those that are available do not support the operating systems of mobile clients that are likely to need mobile IP support, such as scanners and 802.11 phones.

NOTE   Mobile IP is a standards-based solution that enables Layer 3 roaming for wireless devices. Mobile IP simplifies mobility by allowing a client to move between multiple IP subnets without losing connectivity to their home network. Through the use of mobile agents and tunneling technology, connectivity is maintained as the client roams from one network to another without disrupting application-level services.

Multicast

The following considerations apply to IP multicast in WLAN environments:

- **WLAN security extensions**—The WLAN LAN extension via Extensible Authentication protocol (EAP) and WLAN static WEP solutions can support multicast traffic on the WLAN. The WLAN LAN extension via IPSec solution cannot support multicast traffic.

- **Bit rates**—The WLAN available bit rate must be shared by all clients of an AP. If the AP is configured to operate at multiple bit rates, multicasts and broadcasts are sent at the lowest rate to ensure that all clients receive them. This reduces the available throughput of the network because traffic must queue behind traffic that is being clocked out at a slower rate.

- **Snooping**—WLAN clients can roam from one AP to another seamlessly within the same subnet. If roaming multicast is to be supported, Cisco Group Management Protocol (CGMP) and/or Internet Group Management Protocol (IGMP) snooping must be turned off, because a multicast user roaming from one AP to another is roaming from one switch port to another. The new switch port might not have this stream set up, and it has no reliable way of determining the required multicast stream. Therefore, to deliver multicast reliably to roaming clients, the multicast must be flooded.

- **Application performance**—Multicast and broadcast from the AP are sent without requiring link-layer acknowledgment. Every unicast packet is acknowledged and retransmitted if unacknowledged. The purpose of the acknowledgment is to overcome the inherent unreliable nature of wireless links. Broadcasts and multicasts are unacknowledged because of the difficulty in managing and scaling the acknowledgments. This means that a network that is seen as operating well for unicast applications can experience degraded performance in multicast applications.

To ensure that multicast operates effectively and that it has minimal impact upon network performance, follow these strategies:

- Prevent superfluous multicast traffic from being sent out on the air interface. The first step is to have the WLAN on its own subnet. The second step is to determine which multicasts must be permitted by filters, and then only allow these multicasts.

- To gain the highest performance for multicast traffic and for the AP, configure the APs to run at the highest possible rate. This removes the requirement for multicast to clock out at a slower rate. This can impact the AP's range and must be taken into account in the site survey.

- If multicast reliability is a problem (indicated by dropped packets), set the AP to use a slower data rate (base rate). This will give the multicast a better signal-to-noise ratio and can reduce the number of bad packets.

- Test the multicast application for its suitability in the WLAN environment. Determine the application and user-performance effects when packet loss is higher than seen on wired networks.

QoS

QoS is quickly emerging as a requirement for wireless networks. As new technologies begin to use wireless transport services, it is necessary to be able to prioritize traffic across this low-bandwidth, high-latency medium. This section examines QoS services for wireless-enabled applications.

Voice over IP

Any application that has stringent QoS requirements must be examined carefully to determine its suitability for 802.11 unlicensed wireless networking.

Wireless QoS implementations must allow the available network resources to be prioritized. Wireless interference in the unlicensed 802.11 frequency bands can deplete these network resources, making prioritization ineffective. This might be acceptable if it only means some dropped voice or video frames, but might be unacceptable if it means dropped frames in a real-time control system.

Apart from the QoS mechanisms in 802.11, be sure to consider the throughput and forwarding rate of the systems.

Access-Point Filters

Although the AP (being a central point) is able to provide a level of queuing and prioritization for downstream traffic (AP to client), the clients must rely on mechanisms beyond the AP to prioritize their upstream traffic.

AP filters provide strict priority queuing for downstream traffic. Filters are used to assign priority on EtherType, IP port, or protocol. Therefore, protocols likely to carry latency-sensitive traffic can have a higher priority at the AP.

Proprietary QoS for 802.11 Phones

Certain client devices, such as some 802.11 phones, have an upstream proprietary QoS mechanism.

If Voice over IP (VoIP) over 802.11 is required, you should consider the use of WLAN static WEP solutions that use downstream prioritization and the proprietary upstream prioritization.

The general recommendations for 802.11 phones are as follows:

- The maximum recommended number of phones per AP is seven. This limitation is due to the number of packets that can be forwarded per second over an 802.11 link and minimizing transmission delays, rather than a bandwidth limitation of the link.

NOTE   The number of wireless phones was calculated based on the maximum number of calls that could be serviced simultaneously by an 802.11b-compliant AP with 11-Mbps bandwidth. This does not preclude you from deploying other devices with an AP, but you might wish to enable QoS for your IP phones to give them priority over other wireless devices.

- No additional control mechanisms exist, so the planned phone density (per AP) should be less than the maximum recommended to reduce the probability of over-subscription. The impact on data throughput when carrying VoIP is unknown.

- VoIP installations should follow the WLAN static WEP solution security guidelines, because 802.11 phones currently support only static WEP. Consider implementing a different call policy on the wireless network to prevent phone fraud if a WEP key is compromised.

The maximum throughput of the Cisco 802.11b AP is approximately 6 Mbps under good RF conditions and at an 11-Mbps bit rate. Under poor RF conditions or lower bit rates, the throughput will be less.

WLAN Security Design Considerations

Three different security deployment options should be considered when designing your enterprise WLAN:

- WLAN LAN extension via EAP
- WLAN LAN extension via IPSec
- WLAN static WEP

This section examines these three options in relationship to the overall design of wireless network architectures.

NOTE   The IEEE 802.1X standard was developed to provide access control services on a port-per-port basis at Layer 2 of the OSI model. The 802.1X standard relies upon the services of EAP to negotiate and implement authentication.

EAP is an open specification protocol for Point-to-Point Protocol (PPP) authentication, which supports multiple authentication mechanisms. EAP provides for negotiation of an authentication protocol between peers before allowing network layer protocols to transmit over the link. Some examples of EAP types include

- Cisco Wireless EAP (LEAP)—Developed by Cisco to provide dynamic per-user, per-session WEP encryption keys. Cisco LEAP, like other EAP authentication variants, is designed to function on top of the 802.1X authentication framework. Cisco LEAP employs its user-based nature to generate unique keying material for each client. This relieves network administrators from the burden of managing static keys and manually rekeying as needed.

- EAP-TLS is based on the Transport Layer Security (TLS) protocol (RFC 2246). TLS is a Secure Socket Layer (SSL) implementation that uses mutual authentication based on X.509 digital certificates.

- EAP-Message Digest 5 (MD5)—User name-and-password method that incorporates MD5 hashing for more secure authentication.

Both EAP and 802.1x belong to the new 802.11i specification developed to address security issues associated with WEP and the 802.11 WLAN specification.

WLAN security deployment options include the following:

- **WLAN LAN extension using EAP**—Backend systems are the Remote Authentication Dial-In User Service (RADIUS) asynchronous communications servers (ACSs) used to authenticate users.

- **WLAN LAN extension using IPSec**—Backend systems are the VPN concentrators and associated servers.

- **WLAN static WEP**—Backend systems are the application servers for the mobility application.

The security model selected for a given WLAN implementation has a substantial impact on the overall WLAN design. The three security models to consider are

- WLAN LAN extension—EAP
- WLAN LAN extension—IPSec
- WLAN static WEP

What you choose as a security model has far-reaching design implications. Whenever possible, EAP should be implemented in a WLAN. This section describes the available WLAN security extensions and their differences.

WLAN Security Extension—EAP

Cisco's implementation of EAP (also called Cisco LEAP) provides these advantages:

- Requires no user intervention
- Provides per-user authentication
- Automatically provides a dynamic WEP key, thus overcoming key management issues associated with WEP
- Supports accounting
- Does not require any additional filtering or access control
- Is multiprotocol and can carry protocols other than IP over the WLAN
- Supports the same filtering requirements at the network access layer as those for wired implementations

Although EAP is the recommended option, it might not be suitable in all cases because of these reasons:

- Requires EAP-aware APs and WLAN clients, and a client might not be available for your operating system. In this case, no EAP solution is available for your preferred authentication type. EAP-Cisco is available only from Cisco and Apple (client only). EAP-TLS protocol is supported by Microsoft on XP clients. You can use either the Microsoft client or the Cisco Aironet client utility. Cisco APs support all EAP solutions that conform to the 802.1x and EAP standard.
- You may require the security features offered by IPSec, such as Triple Data Encryption Standard (3DES) encryption, One-Time Password (OTP) support, or per-user policies.
- WLAN clients, such as scanners or 802.11 phones, might not support EAP.
- Where seamless roaming within a Layer 2 domain is required, EAP clients can take longer to roam between APs, compared to those using static WEP; this can impact some applications, such as VoIP over 802.11.

WLAN LAN Extension—IPSec

As with the WLAN EAP solution, IPSec provides a WLAN LAN extension service. However, this solution requires users to connect to the network through an IPSec-capable VPN client, even within a campus environment.

Here are some typical characteristics of a WLAN using IPSec VPNs:

- Does not require the use of EAP, and allows any client adapter to be used with a 3DES encryption.
- Allows the use of multifactor authentication systems, such as OTP systems.
- Requires the implementation of extensive filters on the network edge to limit network access to IPSec-related traffic destined to the VPN concentrator network.
- Requires user intervention. The users must launch the VPN client before they attach to the network.

NOTE   Cisco does support auto initiation of the VPN client when a defined network is detected launching the client automatically for the user.

- Does not support multicast applications.
- Requires local traffic to go through the VPN concentrator, causing traffic to cross the network multiple times, increasing traffic across the network and degrading performance.
- Clients such as scanners or 802.11 phones might not support IPSec.

WLAN Static WEP

WLAN static WEP addresses specialized clients that are application specific and support only static WEP.

Within each enterprise, small application verticals exist that can benefit from WLAN applications (specialized applications that run on specialized clients designed for mobile use). Applications requiring this type of solution might also require uninterrupted seamless coverage. Examples of potential WLAN applications that might use static WEP are as follows:

- VoIP over 802.11
- Messaging applications
- Workflow applications
- Security applications
- Package-tracking applications

NOTE   WEP currently supports only static, preshared encryption keys. Static WEP means that the administrator is responsible for distribution and placement of the encryption key on all parties that are required to exchange data with one another— no centralized key distribution and management feature exists.

Security Extension Comparison

Table 10-2 compares the three security implementation models in detail.

Table 10-2 *Security Implementation Model Comparison*

	WLAN LAN Extension via EAP	WLAN LAN Extension via IPSec	WLAN Static WEP
Protocols	Multiprotocol	Unicast only	Multiprotocol
NICs	Cisco and Apple	Any 802.11b-compliant card	Any 802.11b-compliant card
Connection to network	Integrated with Windows login. Non-Windows users enter username and password.	User must launch a VPN client and log in	Transparent to user
Clients	Laptop PCs, high-end PDAs, a wide range of operating systems supported	Laptop PCs, high-end PDAs, a wide range of operating systems supported	Any 802.11 client
Authentication	Username and password or certificates	OTP or username and password	Matching WEP key required
Privacy	Dynamic WEP with time-limited keys and TKIP[1] enhancements	3DES	Static WEP (with TKIP enhancements for Cisco clients); problematic key management
Impact on existing network architecture	Additional RADIUS server required	Additional infrastructure WLAN will be on a perimeter LAN and require VPN concentrators, authentication servers, DHCP servers	Option of additional firewall software or hardware at access layer
Filtering	None required	Extensive filtering required, limiting network access until VPN authentication has occurred	Extensive filtering required, limiting wireless access to only certain predetermined applications
Layer 2 roaming	Transparent Automatically reauthenticates without client intervention (might be slower than VPN or WEP)	Transparent May be easier to extend Layer 2 domain due to reduced broadcast and multicast traffic	Transparent

Table 10-2   *Security Implementation Model Comparison (Continued)*

	WLAN LAN Extension via EAP	**WLAN LAN Extension via IPSec**	**WLAN Static WEP**
Layer 3 roaming	Requires IP address release or renewal, or mobile IP solution	Requires IP address release or renewal, or mobile IP solution	Requires IP address release or renewal, or mobile IP solution
Management	Network is open to existing network management systems	Filtering must be adjusted to support management applications	May have application-specific management requirements; filtering must be adjusted to support the management applications
QoS	Best-effort QoS Proprietary client schemes exist but do not currently support EAP	Best-effort QoS Proprietary client schemes exist but do not currently support IPSec; IPSec tunnel prevents the use of NBAR[2] until after the VPN concentrator	Best-effort QoS unless proprietary client schemes are used, such as Symbol and Spectralink
Multicast	Supported	Not supported	Supported
Performance	WEP encryption performed in hardware on Cisco NICs for EAP-Cisco Might be performed in software for other EAP solutions	3DES performed in software, an expected throughput hit of 20–30 percent	WEP encryption performed in hardware on Cisco NICs

[1]TKIP = Temporal Key Integrity Protocol

[2]NBAR = Network-based application recognition

Cisco EAP

Cisco EAP (also known as LEAP) allows the wireless infrastructure to implement per-user authentication services at Layer 2. Building on top of the port-level security features associated with the underlying 802.1x specification, EAP provides early authentication of users during the Layer 2 connection negotiation phase. This is in contrast to other authentication schemes that are either based on the system, not user, or take place later in the connection phase at a higher layer of the OSI model. The purpose of the following section is to examine common issues related to the deployment of Cisco EAP in a wireless architecture.

In most cases, WLAN APs are connected to existing data-link layer access switches. RADIUS and Dynamic Host Configuration Protocol (DHCP) servers are located in the server module of the corporate network (see Figure 10-6). Security in the design is maintained by preventing network access in the event of a RADIUS service failure, because most of the mitigation against security risks relies on the RADIUS service. Overall, management of the security solution is hindered if DHCP services fail. The wireless clients and application processors use EAP to authenticate the WLAN client devices and end users against the RADIUS servers. Be sure to require (and check) that users choose strong passwords and set account lockouts after a small number of incorrect login attempts. This configuration can be made at the RADIUS server.

Figure 10-6 *RADIUS and DHCP Servers*

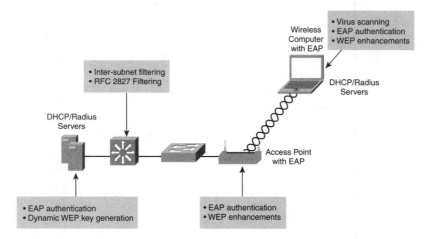

For scalability and manageability purposes, the WLAN client devices are configured to use the DHCP protocol for IP configuration. DHCP occurs after the device and end user are successfully authenticated via LEAP. After successful DHCP configuration, the wireless end user is allowed access to the corporate network. Filtering in place at the first Layer 3 switch prevents the wireless network from accessing portions of the wired network as dictated by an organization's security policy. In Cisco Security Architecture for Enterprise Networks (SAFE), for example, filtering was put in place to prevent wireless access to any department servers, voice networks, or other user networks. Network designers should give special consideration to the location of the RADIUS and DHCP servers used by EAP.

Attack Mitigation Using EAP Authentication

The use of authentication services at Layer 2 may assist in mitigating common network-based attacks. The design shown in Figure 10-6 demonstrates how the common attacks described here can be prevented through the deployment of EAP authentication:

- **Wireless packet sniffers**—Wireless packet sniffers can take advantage of any of the known WEP attacks to derive the encryption key. These threats are mitigated by WEP enhancements and key rotation using LEAP.

- **Unauthenticated access**—Only authenticated users are able to access the wireless and wired network. Optional access control on the Layer 3 switch limits wired network access.

- **Man-in-the-middle**—The mutual authentication nature of EAP combined with the Message Integrity Check (MIC) prevents a hacker from inserting itself in the path of wireless communications.

- **IP spoofing**—Hackers cannot perform IP spoofing without first authenticating to the WLAN. Authenticating optional RFC 2827 filtering on the Layer 3 switch restricts any spoofing to the local subnet range.

- **Address Resolution Protocol (ARP) spoofing**—Hackers cannot perform ARP spoofing without first authenticating to the WLAN. Authenticating ARP spoofing attacks can be launched in the same manner as in a wired environment to intercept other user's data.

- **Network topology discovery**—Hackers cannot perform network discovery if they are unable to authenticate. When authenticated via EAP, standard topology discovery can occur in the same way that is possible in the wired network.

NOTE   The initial security mechanism designed for use by the IEEE for 802.11 wireless LANs, called Wireless Equivalent Privacy (WEP), quickly proved to have some significant shortcomings. In particular, the encryption algorithm used by WEP to secure packets in transit (called RC4) is easily broken using well-known, readily available sampling techniques. This problem is compounded by the use of static keys that are typically not changed on a regular, frequent basis, making sampling that much simpler. Initially, Wireless Protected Access (WPA) emerged as an interim solution to address the security weaknesses inherent in the WEP specification. WPA, however, has been superceded by the IEEE 802.11i specification, which improves upon WEP's initial design through the implementation of the following improvements:

- **Temporal Key Integrity Protocol (TKIP)**—Provides a wrapper service to wireless packets. It extends RC4 by allowing for a larger encryption key and dynamic rekeying during data exchange. Cisco enhancements to TKIP enable per-packet keying. Rekeying, or changing of encryption keys, is also known as key rotation.

- **Message Integrity Check (MIC)**—Used to prevent packet forgery by uniquely signing every packet with a one-way forwarded, hashed signature (difficult to reverse engineer).

- **Advanced Encryption Standard**—802.11i allows for the replacement of RC4 with the more robust AES algorithm.

Attack Mitigation Using IPSec

WLAN APs connect to data-link layer switches in the Campus Backbone on a dedicated VLAN, and forward traffic from the WLAN to the wired LAN using IPSec to protect the flows until they reach the wired network.

It is important to point out that WEP is not enabled in the design shown in Figure 10-7. The wireless network itself is considered an untrusted network, suitable only as a transit network for IPSec traffic. To isolate this untrusted network, administrators should not mix the VLAN for the WLAN users with a wired network. This configuration would potentially allow hackers on the wireless network to attack users on the wired network.

Figure 10-7 *Wireless Networks Using VPNs*

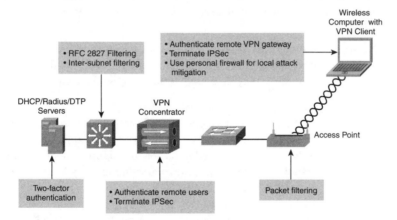

The WLAN clients associate with a wireless AP to establish connectivity to the campus network at the data-link layer. The wireless clients then use DHCP and Domain Name System (DNS) services in the Server Farm module to establish connectivity to the campus at the network layer. When the wireless client is communicating with the campus network, but before the IPSec tunnel is established, the client traffic is not considered secure. All the noted WLAN security issues are still present until the wireless client can secure communications with an IPSec VPN. Therefore, two mitigation techniques are recommended:

- Configure the AP with the ether type protocol and port filters based on a company's wireless usage policy. SAFE WLAN recommends restrictive filters that allow only the necessary protocols required for establishing a secure tunnel to a VPN gateway. These protocols include DHCP for initial client configuration, DNS for name resolution of the VPN gateways, and the VPN-specific protocols: Internet Key Exchange (IKE) on User Datagram Protocol (UDP) port 500, and Encapsulating Security Payload (ESP) (IP Protocol 50). The DNS traffic is optional, dependent on whether the VPN client needs to be configured with a DNS name for the VPN gateway or if only an IP address is suitable.

- Use personal firewall software on the wireless client to protect the client while it is connected to the untrusted WLAN network, without the protection of IPSec. In general terms, the VPN gateway delineates between the trusted wired network and the untrusted WLAN. The wireless client establishes a VPN connection to the VPN gateway to start secure communication to the corporate network. In the process of doing so, the VPN gateway provides device and user authentication via the IPSec VPN.

Even with this filtering, the DNS and DHCP servers are still open to direct attack on the application protocols themselves. Take extra care to ensure that these systems are as secure as possible at the host level. This includes keeping them up to date with the latest OS and application patches and running a Host Intrusion Detection System (HIDS).

The VPN gateway can use digital certificates or preshared keys for wireless device authentication. The VPN gateway then takes advantage of OTPs to authenticate users. Without OTP, the VPN gateways are open to brute-force login attempts by hackers who have obtained the shared IPSec key used by the VPN gateway. The VPN gateway takes advantage of RADIUS services, which, in turn, contact the OTP server for user authentication. The VPN gateway uses DHCP for IP address configuration for the WLAN client to communicate through the VPN tunnel. Security in the design is maintained by preventing network access if a VPN gateway or RADIUS service fails. Both services are required for the client to reach the wired network with production traffic.

Network designers might still consider enabling static WEP keys on all devices in an effort to add an additional deterrent against hackers. Although enhancements to WEP, such as MIC and WEP key hashing, provide effective risk mitigation to currently identified WEP vulnerabilities, the management overhead of dealing with static key changes makes this alternative less than ideal for large WLAN deployments. This management overhead could be mitigated by never changing the static WEP key, but this solution falls strongly into the "security through obscurity" category.

To further secure the DNS and DHCP services, network designers should consider using dedicated hosts for the VPN, WLAN, DHCP, and DNS deployment. This mitigates against two potential threats that could affect wired resources:

- Denial of service (DoS) attacks against the DHCP and DNS services that could affect wired users
- Network reconnaissance through the use of DNS queries or reverse-lookups

As an alternative to dedicated DNS servers, designers might consider hard coding the IP address of the VPN gateway for the VPN clients. The drawback of this solution is that if the IP address of the VPN gateway changes, every client will need to update its gateway entry.

The use of IPSec might assist in mitigating many common network-based attacks. The design shown in Figure 10-7 demonstrates how the common network attacks described here can be prevented through the deployment of VPN services:

- **Wireless packet sniffers**—Mitigated by IPSec encryption of wireless client traffic.
- **Man-in-the-middle**—Mitigated by IPSec encryption of wireless client traffic.

- **Unauthorized access**—The only known protocols for initial IP configuration, DHCP and VPN access protocols (DNS, IKE, and ESP), are allowed from the WLAN to the corporate network through filtering at the AP and Layer 3 switch. Optionally, you can enforce authorization policies on the VPN gateway for individual user groups.

- **IP spoofing**—Hackers can spoof traffic on the WLAN, but only valid, authenticated IPSec packets will ever reach the wired network.

- **ARP spoofing**—ARP spoofing attacks can be launched, but data is encrypted to the VPN gateway, so hackers will be unable to read the data.

- **Password attacks**—Mitigated through good password policies, auditing, and OTP.

- **Network topology discovery**—Only IKE, ESP, DNS, and DHCP are allowed from this segment into the corporate network.

One threat that is not mitigated is MAC/IP spoofing from unauthenticated users. ARP spoofing and IP spoofing are still effective on the WLAN subnet until the wireless client uses IPSec to secure the connection.

Small Office WLAN Design Model

In a small office, you might implement a WLAN to extend the network reach to areas where physical constraints, cost, or speed of deployment are issues. This section describes the design of Cisco WLAN solutions for small enterprise networks.

The workgroup bridge is a useful aid for network extensions, because you can extend the WLAN without having WLAN cards in the devices. The workgroup bridge can support up to eight devices. Figure 10-8 illustrates a small office WLAN design model.

Figure 10-8 *Small Office WLAN Design Model*

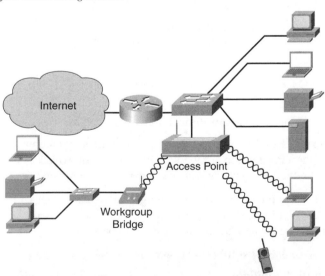

Figure 10-9 shows the WLAN on the same subnet as other users. You may want to consider filters on the APs to limit the amount of broadcast and multicast traffic sent to the WLAN. (The environment illustrated in Figure 10-9 assumes a WLAN that provides access to a server farm.)

Figure 10-9 *Example of a Small Office WLAN Design*

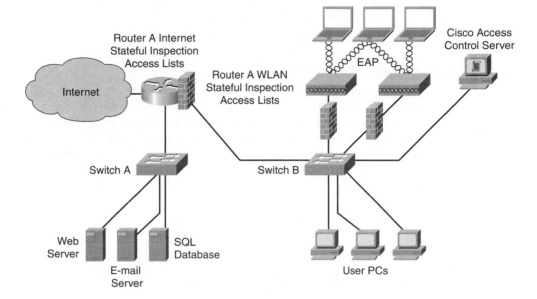

Key management via EAP systems provides the least intrusive form of security for the small office and offers the lowest cost of ownership, as it is compatible with all topologies and should require the least configuration and maintenance.

Enterprise WLAN Design Model

A WLAN is typically deployed in an enterprise network as an extension rather than a replacement. This section describes the design of WLAN solutions for large enterprise networks.

The ideal solution is to simply attach the WLAN to the existing LAN infrastructure and go from there. The caveat in this is that the WLAN is a shared media where broadcast and multicast traffic are sent at the slowest connection speed, and are buffered for equipment in power-save mode.

To create an environment where multicasts and broadcasts can be more easily controlled, it is recommended that the WLAN be a separate VLAN to the wired LAN.

You need to take into account the number of expected users on an AP and their traffic requirements in the site survey and RF design of the sites. The shared nature of a WLAN impacts the location and density of WLAN equipment, but normally does not impact the architecture.

The biggest influence on the network architecture is the mechanism to secure the WLAN. A WLAN needs a key management solution, such as network EAP, EAP-TLS, or IPSec VPNs, to make it secure enough for enterprise use.

Example: Enterprise WLAN Site Design

Acme Corporation decided to extend its network with wireless access in two conference rooms. The first decision to make is the choice of security implementation. To obtain maximum security, Acme chooses EAP. This requires the addition of Cisco ACS authentication servers to its server farm. For the wireless components themselves, two APs per conference room are installed, which provides access for up to 50 simultaneous users. Figure 10-10 shows an example site design for Acme Corporation.

Figure 10-10 *Example Site Design for Enterprise WLAN*

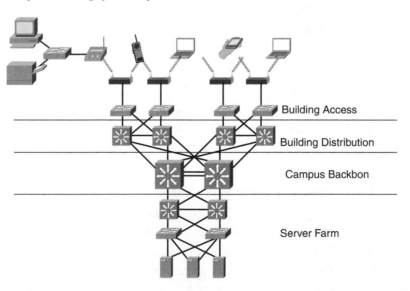

The EAP solution provides privacy over the WLAN via the dynamic WEP key, and controls access to the network by the WEP key in combination with 802.1x and the RADIUS server authentication. This creates end-to-end network security.

Example: Enterprise WLAN Remote Office Design

Corporate growth has required that a company acquire additional office space. No space is available in the company's headquarters' building, but space is available within the same complex a half-mile away. Wireless bridges are used to connect the branch office's LAN to the headquarters' LAN. The same headquarters' ACS servers provide security to the wireless components of the remote office (see Figure 10-11).

Figure 10-11 *Example Remote Office Design for Enterprise WLAN*

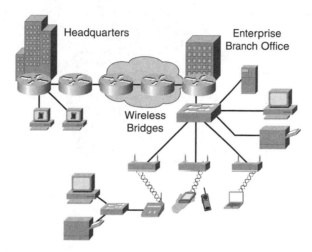

The APs are added as an overlay to the existing wired LAN, which provides some degree of mobility within the branch office. Because this is a single network using APs, clients can roam seamlessly about the office (from AP to AP) without disruption.

Remote-Access and Telecommuter WLAN Design Models

You can use a wireless base station to provide access for a location with a small number of users, such as a small remote office or a telecommuter's office. This section describes the design of Cisco WLAN solutions for remote access and telecommuters.

Strong client authentication must be required before access from the home network to the corporate network is permitted. An IPSec-based, client-initiated VPN authenticates the client and ensures that only authorized people can access the corporate network from the home network. Besides authenticating the individual access to the corporate network, VPNs also provide data privacy via strong encryption algorithms, such as 3DES.

The sample design shown in Figure 10-12 uses a broadband connection to the Internet, such as DSL or cable. The broadband router supplying this access includes an internal firewall to protect the home network from intrusion.

Figure 10-12 *Sample Telecommuter WLAN Design*

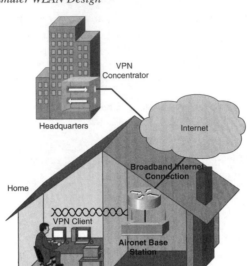

NOTE	Personal firewall software should be installed on client PCs to protect the PCs from attacks from the WLAN or the Internet. If an attacker gains access to a client PC, he can use that to launch other attacks on the corporate network later.

The Aironet base station shown in Figure 10-12 supports static 128-bit WEP to prevent unauthorized access to the home network. Data privacy is provided—independent of WEP—by the VPN for traffic traveling to and from the corporate site. General web traffic is secured by using SSL when required.

Summary

In this chapter, you learned the following key points:

- When designing an enterprise wireless network, consider the following:
    - RF design
    - Campus infrastructure
    - High availability
    - Roaming
    - IP multicast
    - QoS
- You must choose one of the following as the security model for a wireless LAN implementation:
    - EAP

— IPSec

— WEP

The choice of security model has far-reaching design implications.

- In a small office, use a WLAN to extend the network reach to areas where physical constraints, cost, or speed of deployment are issues.

- A WLAN is typically an extension to the wired LAN rather than a replacement.

- Use a Cisco wireless base station to provide access for a location with a small number of users, such as a small remote office or telecommuter.

References

Wireless Solutions. http://www.cisco.com/warp/public/44/solutions/network/wireless.shtml.

http://www.cisco.com/en/US/products/hw/wireless/index.html.

Solutions Reference Network Design (SRND) Networking Solutions Design Guides. To locate these documents, following these steps:

Step 1   Go to http://www.cisco.com/.

Step 2   In the Search box, enter **SRND** and click **Go**. A list of SRND Networking Solutions Design Guides appears.

Step 3   Select the Networking Solutions Design Guide that meets your needs.

Product Summary

Table 10-3   *Cisco Wireless Products*

Wireless Product	Transmit Power	Data Rate	Range
Cisco Aironet 350 Series Access Point	1–100 MW	IEEE 802.11b 1, 2, 5.5, and 11 Mbps	Indoors: 130–350 feet Outdoors: 800–2000 feet
Cisco Aironet 1100 Series Access Point	1–100 MW	IEEE 802.11b and g 1-54 Mbps	Indoors: 90–410 feet Outdoors: 250–2000 feet
Cisco Aironet 1200 Series Access Point	1–100 MW	IEEE 802.11a, b, and g 1-54 Mbps	Indoors: 45–410 feet Outdoors: 100–2000 feet
Cisco Aironet 350 Series Wireless Bridge	1–100 MW	IEEE 802.11b 1, 2, 5.5, and 11 Mbps	18–25 miles
Cisco Aironet 350 Series Workgroup Bridge	1–100 MW	IEEE 802.11b	Indoors: 130–350 feet Outdoors: 800–2000 feet

Standards and Specification Summary

IEEE 802.11, 1999 Edition (ISO/IEC 8802-11, 1999) IEEE Standards for Information Technology—Telecommunications and Information Exchange Between Systems—Local and Metropolitan Area Network. Specific Requirements, Part 11, Wireless LAN Medium Access Control (MAC) and Physical Layer (PHY) Specifications.

IEEE 802.11a-1999 (8802-11:1999/Amd 1:2000(E)), IEEE Standard for Information technology—Telecommunications and information exchange between systems—Local and metropolitan area networks. Specific requirements, Part 11, Wireless LAN Medium Access Control (MAC) and Physical Layer (PHY) specifications. Amendment 1, High-speed Physical Layer in the 5-GHz band.

IEEE 802.11b-1999 Supplement to 802.11, 1999, Wireless LAN MAC and PHY specifications. Higher-speed Physical Layer (PHY) extension in the 2.4-GHz band.

802.11b-1999/Cor1-2001, IEEE Standard for Information technology—Telecommunications and information exchange between systems—Local and metropolitan area networks. Specific requirements, Part 11, Wireless LAN Medium Access Control (MAC) and Physical Layer (PHY) specifications, Amendment 2, Higher-speed Physical Layer (PHY) extension in the 2.4-GHz band, Corrigendum1.

IEEE 802.11g-2003 IEEE Standard for Information technology—Telecommunications and information exchange between systems—Local and metropolitan area networks. Specific requirements, Part 11, Wireless LAN Medium Access Control (MAC) and Physical Layer (PHY) specifications, Amendment 4, Further Higher-Speed Physical Layer Extension in the 2.4-GHz Band.

IEEE 802.1X-2001 IEEE Standards for Local and Metropolitan Area Networks— Port-Based Network Access Control.

Request For Comments (RFCs) can be downloaded from the following website: http://www.rfc-editor.org/rfc.html.

- RFC 2284 PPP Extensible Authentication Protocol (EAP)
- RFC 2002 IP Mobility Support

Review Questions

Answer the following questions to test your comprehension of the topics discussed in this chapter. Refer to Appendix A, "Answers to Review Questions," to check your answers.

1 What three factors affect the size of a wireless LAN coverage area?

2 What is the role of CSMA/CA in wireless LANs?

3 How do data rates affect cell size?

4 What does the IEEE 802.11 specification define?

5 Describe the components that comprise the Cisco wireless solution.

6 Describe the role of an AP in wireless networks.

7 Describe the role of a wireless bridge in a wireless network.

8 What are some considerations when designing an enterprise WLAN solution?

9 What are three reasons for limiting the data rate to the highest rate at which full coverage is obtained?

10 What are some examples of variables that can adversely affect RF performance?

11 What are the channels used in North America for the 802.11b specification?

12 How should you allocate channels to cells?

13 What should you consider when choosing an AP and associated client cards?

14 What is an advantage of inline power?

15 Why should the WLAN be on a separate VLAN from other LAN traffic?

16 What are the three different security deployment options?

17 What are the three ways to address the availability of the WLAN?

18 What is the role of AP hot standby redundancy?

19 What are the bit rates associated with multicast and broadcast traffic on WLANs?

20 What is the recommended role of AP filters in WLANs?

21 What is the maximum number of VoIP phones per AP? Why?

22 What two mitigation techniques should be used to protect a wireless client if a VPN solution is going to be used to connect them?

23 What two ways might a wireless network be used in a small office deployment?

24 What is the typical role of a wireless LAN in an enterprise network?

Case Study: OCSIC Bottling Company

The purpose of this case study is to design a wireless network that meets the needs of the OCSIC Bottling Company.

The OCSIC Bottling Company wants to attach wireless devices to key control systems in the plants to be able to monitor and reconfigure them remotely. It also wants to implement a tracking system to track its mobile plant-material handling equipment, and provide network access for inventory accounting and control. Each component of the design will have multiple options. As each component of the design is identified, justification is given for the decision.

First, you need to design a wireless network for a North American OCSIC plant by creating a campus network diagram indicating the wireless LAN design for one of the North American plants. Each location is labeled as shown in Figure 10-13.

Figure 10-13 *Example Wireless Network Plant Layout*

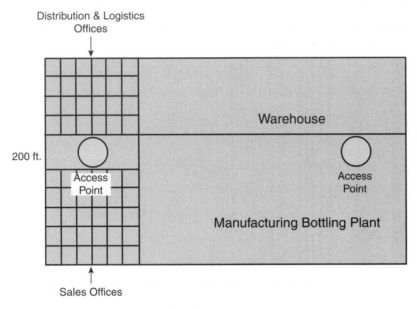

Table 10-4 shows the design decisions and the justification for those decisions.

Table 10-4 *Design Decisions for the Wireless Network*

Design Questions	Decision	Justification
How many APs are required within a typical OCSIC 60,000-square-foot district office or plant? Where should the APs be placed?	Within a typical OCSIC 60,000-square-foot district office/plant, the company will place two APs, located equidistant across the facility. APs are placed without major obstruction between the APs and the wireless devices that use the APs. The Cisco 1200 AP is selected because it can deliver 802.11b and will support 802.11a.	Coverage of the sales offices and manufacturing/bottling plant is most important.

Table 10-4   *Design Decisions for the Wireless Network (Continued)*

Design Questions	Decision	Justification
How many active devices can each AP support?	If there are 24 users, each user gets approximately 280 kbps worth of bandwidth. If there are more active users, each user gets less bandwidth.	The number of users varies depending on the amount of bandwidth each user needs.
How are channels identified for the design?	Two APs are in each building, each with its own channel.	Currently, the plans are to put two APs in each building that will have some overlap but not total overlap. The corners of the building might receive weak signals. Each AP can broadcast about 130 feet indoors.
How will you meet the inline power requirements for the design?	The Cisco 1200 AP accepts inline power or can be powered from a power brick. Preferred power will be through the inline power.	
What is the high-availability (redundancy) strategy for the design?	There will be no redundancy for the wireless design.	The wireless network is not considered to be mission-critical. If one AP fails, users can access the second one.

You have completed this exercise when you create a WLAN design that includes the following components:

- Number and placement of APs
- Number of devices each AP will support
- Channel selection
- Inline power requirements
- High availability

After completing this chapter, you will be able to

- Understand the Cisco IP Telephony solution
- Design the network for Cisco IP Telephony

CHAPTER 11

Designing IP Telephony Solutions

Built on the Cisco Architecture for Voice, Video, and Integrated Data (AVVID) network infrastructure, a Cisco IP Telephony solution delivers high-quality IP voice and fully integrated communications by allowing voice to be originated on and transmitted over a single network infrastructure along with data and video. Cisco IP Telephony solutions provide feature functionality with straightforward configuration and maintenance requirements and interoperability with a wide variety of other applications.

Reviewing the Cisco IP Telephony Solution

The flexibility and functionality of the Cisco AVVID network infrastructure provides a framework that permits rapid deployment of IP Telephony applications.

The Cisco AVVID framework, combined with multicast services and the Cisco IP Telephony solution, provides universal transport for data, voice, and video applications today.

This section describes the following:

- Cisco IP Telephony solution
- Gateways and control protocols
- Transcoders and conferencing
- Cisco IP Telephony applications

Introducing the Cisco IP Telephony Solution

The Cisco IP Telephony solution includes infrastructure components of the traditional IP network, as well as devices dedicated to voice. This section lists the components of the Cisco AVVID IP Telephony solution and explains the role of each component in the overall IP Telephony solution.

The overall goals of an IP Telephony network are to

- Provide end-to-end IP Telephony for network users
- Use the IP wide-area network (WAN) as the primary voice path with the Public Switched Telephone Network (PSTN) as the secondary voice path between sites
- Lower the total cost of ownership with greater flexibility
- Enable new applications

The Cisco IP Telephony solution makes it possible to implement a phone system that is transparent to the users. The user sees a phone that offers the same service and quality offered in a Private Branch Exchange (PBX) system, but that has unique data characteristics as well. Figure 11-1 illustrates the components of an IP Telephony solution.

Figure 11-1 *IP Telephony Components*

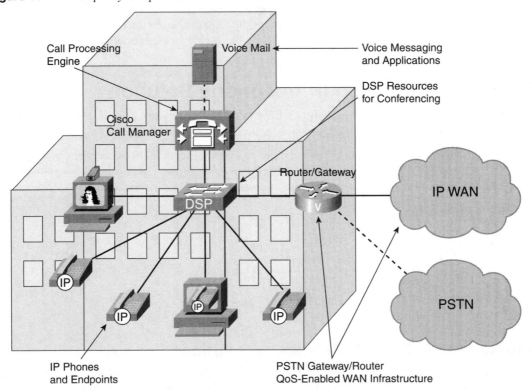

The telephony components found within the architecture, as shown in Figure 11-1, are as follows:

- **Call processing engine**—Routes calls on the network. CallManager is the primary call processing engine for Cisco IP Telephony networks. It provides call control and signaling services to client endpoints, which might include telephones or gateways.

- **IP phones**—Convert analog voice to digital IP packets so the IP network can transport them. Other endpoints require gateways.

- **Gateways**—Gateways provide access to the IP Telephony network for endpoints other than IP telephones, such as applications, WAN facilities, the PSTN, and other IP Telephony and Voice over IP (VoIP) installations:

  - **Applications**—Voice applications include voice mail, automated attendant, interactive voice response (IVR), call distribution, and others.

  - **Voice-enabled routers**—Voice-enabled routers route traffic between the campus voice network and WAN facilities.

  - **PSTN gateways**—PSTN gateways enable enterprises to send calls to other enterprises and individuals over the PSTN.

  - **VoIP gateways**—VoIP gateways, often software running within a network device, enable independent call processing agents to coordinate calls across the Internet without reliance on the PSTN.

NOTE   The role of a PSTN gateway is to provide an interface between the IP voice network and the traditional Plain Old Telephone Service (POTS) network. This feature is often enabled in a router that connects on one side to the packet voice network and on the other side to the traditional telephony network.

- **Digital signal processor (DSP) resources for transcoding and conferencing**—A DSP changes the digitization (in other words, G.711 to G.729) or provides services such as conferencing (replication of a single inbound voice stream for transport to multiple endpoints).

NOTE   Digitization of an analog voice signal is a fundamental building block of today's voice networks. The process is built on the Nyquist theorem, which defines the process for the conversion of analog signals to their digital equivalents. Nyquist's process takes the standard 4000 Hz (cycles per second) bandwidth used by an analog voice call and converts it to a digital signal using a technique called Pulse Code Modulation (PCM). PCM samples the original analog signal and converts each sample to its digital equivalent using a process known as Quantization. Quantization works by multiplying the analog bandwidth by two and then converting each sample into a digital word. The result is that the original signal is sampled 8000 times at 8 bits per sample for a total transmission rate of 64000 bits per second. The resulting signal is known as Digital Signaling level Zero (DS0), which provides a 64-kbps voice circuit.

The process of digitization takes place in a hardware component called a codec. A codec is responsible for the coding and decoding of analog voice signals.

PCM has been modified by different specifications to reduce the bandwidth required to transmit a voice signal across a digital network. The following are common audio codecs that deploy variations of PCM and the associated transmission speeds:

- **G.711**—64 kbps
- **G.723**—6.3/5.3 kbps
- **G.726**—40/32/24/16 kbps
- **G.729a**—8 kbps

In traditional corporate voice networks, the PBX was responsible for handling the following functions:

- **Call processing**—Call establishment, termination, and control functions
- **Switching**—Local path selection
- **Line termination**—Terminating voice lines from endpoints (telephones)
- **PSTN interface**—Providing connectivity to the PSTN for routing inbound and outbound calls

IP Telephony maintains these functions, but replaces them with components that enable them to be applied to an IP-based environment:

- **Call processing**—Cisco CallManager
- **Switching**—Cisco Catalyst switches
- **Line termination**—Cisco Catalyst switches/voice-enabled modules
- **PSTN interface**—Cisco routers (gateways) that are voice enabled to provide an interface to the PSTN

The next section provides a detailed overview of the various components that make up the IP Telephony solution.

Cisco CallManager

CallManager provides call processing for the Cisco AVVID IP Telephony solution. This section describes the CallManager features and introduces the deployment models.

CallManager is the software-based call-processing component of the Cisco enterprise IP Telephony solution and is a product enabled by Cisco AVVID. CallManager software extends enterprise telephony features and capabilities to packet telephony network devices, such as IP phones, media-processing devices, VoIP gateways, and multimedia applications. Additional data, voice, and video services such as unified messaging, multimedia conferencing, collaborative contact centers, and interactive multimedia response systems interact with the IP Telephony solution through the Cisco CallManager Telephony application programming interfaces (APIs).

CallManager is installed on the Cisco media convergence server and selected third-party servers. CallManager includes a suite of integrated voice applications and utilities: a software-only conferencing application; the Bulk Administration Tool (BAT); the call detail record (CDR) Analysis and Reporting (CAR) tool; and the Admin Serviceability Tool (AST).

Multiple CallManager servers are clustered and managed as a single entity. Clustering multiple call-processing servers on an IP network is a unique capability in the industry and highlights the leading architecture provided by Cisco AVVID. CallManager clustering yields scalability of up to 10,000 users per cluster. By interlinking multiple clusters, system capacity can be increased to as many as one million users in a 100-site system. Clustering aggregates the power of multiple, distributed CallManagers.

Call admission control ensures that voice quality of service (QoS) is maintained across constricted WAN links and automatically diverts calls to alternative PSTN routes when WAN bandwidth is not available.

Several basic models are available for deploying the call-processing capabilities of CallManager, depending on the size, geographical distribution, and functional requirements of your enterprise:

- Single-site call processing model
- Multisite WAN model with centralized call processing
- Multisite WAN model with distributed call processing
- Clustering over the IP WAN

NOTE   CallManager deployments are described in detail in the section, "Designing a Network for Cisco IP Telephony."

Gateways and Control Protocols

Voice, video, and data gateway protocols are required for call routing and interoperability on a network that supports IP Telephony. This section lists the various voice, video, and data gateway components of the Cisco IP Telephony solution and explains the role of each component in the overall IP Telephony solution.

Gateway selection depends on the following requirements:

- Voice, fax, and modem capabilities
- Analog or digital access
- Signaling protocol used to control gateways

Gateway selection depends on the type of platform already deployed. For example, a large campus with many Cisco Catalyst 6000 switches might opt to use the cards that fit within that chassis. A small site might use an existing Cisco IOS router with voice interface modules as an integrated solution. A non-IP voice mail system might also require gateways, which, in most cases, would be Media Gateway Control Protocol (MGCP) gateways.

Protocol selection depends on site-specific requirements and the installed base of equipment. CallManager supports the following gateway protocols:

- **Simple Gateway Control Protocol (SGCP)**—Provides control between the CallManager and digital gateways.

- **MGCP**—Provides control between the CallManager and analog gateways.

- **H.323**—Provides control between Cisco IOS integrated router gateways and CallManager.

- **Session Initiation Protocol (SIP)**—Internet Engineering Task Force (IETF) standard for multimedia conferencing over IP. SIP is an ASCII-based, application layer control protocol (defined in Request For Comments [RFC] 2543) that can be used to establish, maintain, and terminate calls between two or more endpoints.

NOTE   H.323 and SIP are two standards designed for the provisioning of VoIP services. The following section provides a brief explanation of each protocol and its function.

H.323 is the most mature solution for provisioning VoIP services. It was developed by the International Telecommunications Union Telecommunication Standardization Sector (ITU-T) and has been deployed widely in many private and public networks. The H.323 architecture consists of the following components:

- **Gateway**—Interconnects/translates between the IP network and the PSTN.

- **Gatekeeper**—Provides call routing for end terminals (VoIP terminals) to the appropriate available gateway. Gatekeeper can also distinguish between voicemail and faxes and route them to the appropriate servers.

- **Signaling protocols**—H.225, H.245, registration, admission and status (RAS), and Real-Time Transport Protocol (RTP).

- **PSTN interface**—Signaling System 7 (SS7)-capable device to allow routing of calls from the IP packet network to the PSTN. SS7 is used by the PSTN for intertoll communications and call routing.

- **VoIP application servers**—Provide authentication, billing, and network management functions.

H.323 signaling protocols perform the following functions:

- **H.225**—Creates connections between two H.323 enabled devices (VoIP phones).

- **H.245**—Provides control functions for the negotiation of features, such as codec type, fax handling, and channel selection.

- **RAS**—Controls the registration, admission, and status reporting between the gatekeeper and gateway.

  SIP is an IETF protocol specification laid out in RFC 2543 that provides an alternative method for provisioning VoIP services. SIP defines a client/server architecture that is comprised of the following components:

- **SIP**—An application layer signaling protocol that is used for the establishment and termination of voice sessions between two SIP-enabled endpoints. An endpoint is described as a user agent, of which there exists a client and server component. SIP performs similar functions to H.323's H.225 and RAS protocols.

- **Servers**—SIP servers provide call routing, device address registration, authentication and authorization, as well as call redirection services.

- **Gateways**—Performs the same function as in H.323-based networks.

NOTE   MGCP and SGCP are protocols designed to enhance the functionality and control of VoIP gateways. SGCP was developed by Cisco and Bellcore; MGCP was designed by the IETF and merged SGCP and another existing standard, known as Internet Protocol Device Control (IPDC), into one specification. Some of the services provided by MGCP are echo cancellation, attenuation, amplification, and advanced reporting.

Table 11-1 shows which protocols are supported by various Cisco IP Telephony components and services.

Table 11-1   *Gateway Protocols*

	SGCP	MGCP	H.323	SIP
Analog Gateways		√	√	
Digital Gateways	√	√		
Cisco Multiservice Access Concentrators		√	√	√
Cisco Branch Office Routers		√	√	√
Cisco Central Site Routers		√	√	√
Cisco Access Servers			√	√
Catalyst Switches	√	√	√	√

Remote branch locations might deploy Cisco 2600 or 3600 series routers that support the H.323 and MGCP protocols. For gateway configuration, an enterprise might prefer to implement MGCP rather than H.323, because MGCP offers simpler configuration and call survivability during a CallManager switchover from a primary to a secondary CallManager. Alternatively, H.323 might be preferred instead of MGCP because of the robustness of the interfaces supported.

NOTE   SGCP functionality will be included in H.323 v3.

Transcoders and Conferencing

CallManager provides access to a variety of media resources. A media resource is a software- or hardware-based entity that performs media processing functions on the voice data streams to which it is connected. Media processing functions include mixing multiple streams to create one output stream, passing the stream from one connection to another, or transcoding the data stream from one compression type to another. This section describes the types and roles of the transcoder and conferencing components of an IP Telephony solution.

Hardware Support

The DSP resources provide hardware support for the CallManager IP Telephony features. These features include hardware-enabled voice conferencing, hardware-based media termination point (MTP) support for supplementary services, and transcoding services.

Catalyst-enabled conferencing supports voice conferences in hardware. DSPs convert VoIP sessions into time-division multiplexing (TDM) streams for multiparty conference calls.

The Cisco MTP service can act either like the original software MTP resource or as a transcoding MTP resource. An MTP service can provide supplementary services such as hold, transfer, and conferencing when using gateways and clients that do not support H.323.

Transcoding compresses and decompresses voice streams to maximize use of WAN resources for VoIP traffic. A transcoder takes the output stream of one codec and converts it in real time (transcodes it) into an input stream for a different codec type. In other words, a transcoder converts a stream of one compression type into a stream of another compression type.

Transcoding (as shown in Figure 11-2) is, in effect, an IP-to-IP voice gateway service. A transcoding node can convert a G.711 voice stream into a low bit-rate compressed voice stream, such as G.729a, which is critical for enabling applications such as IVR, voice messaging, and conference calls over low-speed IP WANs. In addition, a transcoder provides the capabilities of an MTP. You can use transcoding to enable supplementary services for H.323 endpoints when required.

Figure 11-2 *Centralized MTP, Transcoding, and Conferencing Services*

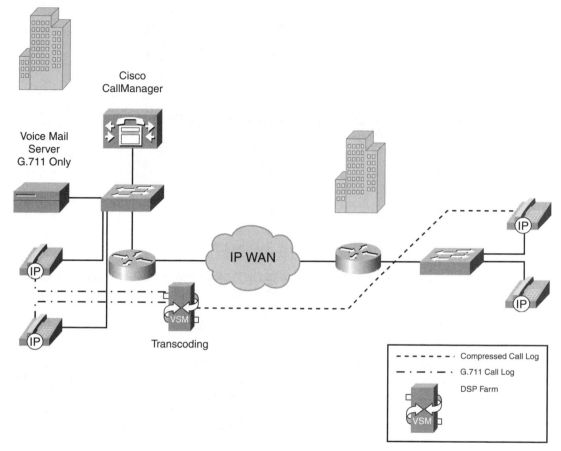

Cisco
CallManager

Voice Mail
Server
G.711 Only

IP WAN

Transcoding

- - - - - - - Compressed Call Log

- - · - · - G.711 Call Log

DSP Farm

Unicast Conference Bridge

A unicast conference bridge, as shown in Figure 11-3, is a device that accepts multiple connections for a given conference. It can accept any number of connections for a given conference, up to the maximum number of streams allowed for a single conference on that device.

There is a one-to-one correspondence between media streams connected to a conference and participants connected to the conference. The conference bridge mixes the streams and creates a unique output stream for each connected party. The output stream for a given party is usually the composite of the streams from all connected parties minus their own input stream. Some conference bridges mix only the three loudest talkers on the conference, and distribute that composite stream to each participant (minus their own input stream if they are one of the talkers).

Figure 11-3 *Unicast Conference Bridge*

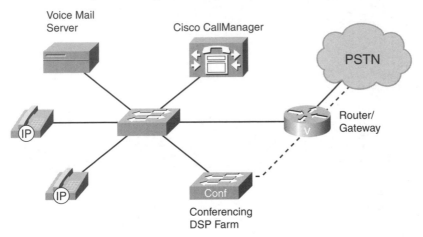

There are two types of conference bridges:

- **Software conference bridge**— A standard conference mixer that is capable of mixing G.711 audio streams. Both a-law and μ law streams might be connected to the same conference. The number of parties that can be supported on a given conference depends on the server where the conference bridge software is running and the configuration for that device.

- **Hardware conference bridge**—Has all the capabilities of a software conference bridge. In addition, some hardware conference bridges can support multiple low bit-rate stream types such as G.729, global system for mobile communication (GSM), or G.723. This allows some hardware conference bridges to handle mixed-mode conferences. In a mixed-mode conference, the hardware conference bridge transcodes G.729, GSM, and G.723 streams into G.711 streams, mixes them, and then encodes the resulting stream into the appropriate stream type for transmission back to the user. Some hardware conference bridges support only G.711 conferences.

NOTE The ITU G.711 specification for the digitization of a voice signal defines two different methods for companding: a law and μ law. *Companding* refers to the process of compressing an analog signal prior to transmission and expanding the analog signal back to its original size at the destination. This process enables bandwidth conservation and maximizes resource utilization. The two companding specifications defined by G.711 are a law and μ law. μ law is the specification used in North America, and a law is used by the rest of the world. These two methodologies are not compatible, and, therefore, conversion must take place prior to interfacing. The process of conversion is the responsibility of the μ law country.

Cisco IP Telephony Applications

The primary Cisco IP Telephony applications include the following:

- **Cisco Customer Response Solution (CRS)**— An integrated platform that simplifies business integration, eases agent administration, increases agent flexibility, and provides efficiency gains in network hosting. This single-server integrated platform includes Cisco IP IVR, Cisco IP Integrated Contact Distribution (ICD), and Cisco IP Queue Manager with automatic call distribution (ACD) features, such as skills-based routing and priority queuing.

- **Cisco Conference Connection**— A "meet-me" audio conference server that provides integrated operation with CallManager. Conferences are scheduled from an intuitive web-based conference scheduler. Conference participants call in to a central number, enter a meeting identification, and are then placed into the conference.

- **Cisco Emergency Responder**— Addresses the need to identify the location of 911 callers in an emergency, with no administration required when phones or people move from one location to another.

- **Cisco IP Contact Center (IPCC)**— Delivers intelligent call routing, network-to-desktop computer telephony integration (CTI), and multimedia contact management to contact center agents over an IP network. It combines software ACD functionality with IP Telephony in a unified solution.

- **Cisco IP Phone Productivity Services**— The Cisco IP Phone services software developer's kit (SDK) makes it easy for web developers to format and deliver content to IP phones by providing web-server components for Lightweight Directory Access Protocol (LDAP) directory access, web proxy, and graphics conversion. It also contains several sample applications.

- **Cisco Unity**— Provides convergence-based communication services, such as voice and unified messaging on a platform that offers the utmost in reliability, scalability, and performance. With Cisco Unity, users can listen to e-mail over the telephone, check voice messages from the Internet, and (when integrated with a supported third-party fax server) forward faxes to any local fax machine, increasing organizational productivity while improving customer service and responsiveness.

- **Cisco Personal Assistant**— A telephony application that operates with Cisco Unity and streamlines communications by helping users manage how and where they want to be reached.

Designing a Network for Cisco IP Telephony

You can deploy Cisco IP Telephony solutions in single-site, multisite, and clustering over IP WAN configurations. A multisite configuration deployment might support centralized or distributed call processing. Each deployment model has its own network design considerations.

Each call-processing model offers its own benefits for specific enterprise needs and situations. The challenge is to select the right model and design each component. Effective design of the underlying network infrastructure and Cisco AVVID components will provide an efficient, scalable, and available foundation for IP Telephony networks.

This section describes the following:

- Cisco CallManager cluster design considerations
- Designing single-site IP Telephony solutions
- Designing multisite with centralized call-processing IP Telephony solutions
- Designing multisite with distributed call-processing IP Telephony solutions
- Clustering over the IP WAN
- Network infrastructure design considerations
- Intelligent network services for IP Telephony and voice

Cisco CallManager Cluster Design Considerations

A Cisco CallManager cluster, as shown in Figure 11-4, might contain as many as eight servers, of which a maximum of six provide CallManager call processing to support up to 10,000 phones. This section describes how to design CallManager clusters.

Figure 11-4 *Cisco CallManager Clusters*

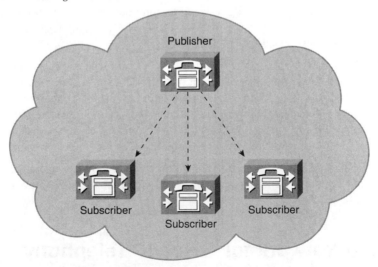

A CallManager cluster consists of two or more CallManager servers that work together. A database defines the servers in the cluster. A cluster has one publisher (main) server and up to seven additional subscriber servers. The publisher maintains one database, which it replicates to the other servers in the cluster. Logically, a CallManager cluster is a single CallManager instance.

In addition to the CallManager, you can configure other servers, including

- **Dedicated database publisher**—Synchronizes configuration changes and captures CDRs.

- **Trivial File Transfer Protocol (TFTP) server**—Stores configuration files, device loads (operating code), and ring types for downloading.

- **Music on Hold (MoH) server**—Provides the music-on-hold functionality for a CallManager cluster.

- **Computer telephony integration (CTI) manager**—Manages Telephony Application Programming Interface (TAPI), Java TAPI (JTAPI), or CTI devices.

- **Media streaming server**—A media streaming server, such as a conference bridge or MTP, is a separate server that registers with the CallManager cluster.

For large systems, Cisco recommends a dedicated database publisher and either a dedicated TFTP server or multiple load-balanced TFTP servers coresident with CallManager. For smaller systems, you can combine the functions of database publisher and TFTP server.

Cluster Deployment Guidelines

These general guidelines apply to all clusters:

- A cluster might contain a mix of server platforms, but all CallManagers within the cluster must run the same software version.

- Within a cluster, you can enable a maximum of six servers with the CallManager service, and use other servers for more specialized functions such as TFTP, database publisher, MoH, and so forth.

- All operating systems and network services that are not required on a server should be disabled to maximize the server's available resources.

There are two primary kinds of communication within a CallManager cluster (as shown in Figure 11-5):

- **Structured Query Language (SQL) database**—The SQL server database is the core element of the cluster; in fact, it defines the relationship between the publisher and subscriber. The database distributes the database that contains all the device configuration information. The configuration database is stored on a publisher server and replicated to the subscriber members of the cluster. Changes made on the publisher are communicated to the subscriber databases, ensuring that the configuration is consistent across the members of the cluster, as well as facilitating spatial redundancy of the database.

- **Intracluster runtime data**—This type of intracluster communication is the propagation and replication of runtime data, such as registration of devices, location bandwidth, and shared media resources. This information is shared across all members of a cluster running the CallManager service, and it assures optimum routing of calls between members of the cluster and associated gateways.

Figure 11-5 *Intracluster Communication*

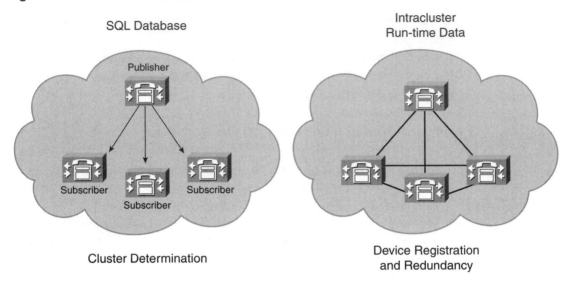

LDAP directory information is also replicated between all servers in a cluster. The publisher replicates the LDAP directory to all other servers. You can integrate CallManager information into a corporate LDAP directory, such as Microsoft's Active Directory or Netscape Directory. The replication is dependent on the integration method deployed.

Figure 11-6 shows the recommended cluster configuration for the small, medium, and large clusters.

The clustering options relate to the grouping of devices, usually phones and gateways. With the limits imposed on a single CallManager and good design practices, the minimum configuration consists of two CallManagers, which will support up to 2500 IP phones. Cisco recommends four CallManagers to support 5000 IP phones and up to six CallManagers to support up to 10,000 IP phones.

Cluster Design

In a small-scale cluster environment (up to 2500 phones) deploy both a publisher and a subscriber. The publisher stores the master copy of the database, and the subscriber is the device to which the phones register. In this scenario, the publisher is the backup server, and the subscriber is the primary server. If the subscriber fails, the publisher becomes the primary CallManager for the cluster.

In the medium-scale cluster design, there are four servers. The publisher acts as the TFTP server and is separate from the primary and backup servers. There would then be two primary systems that could register up to 5000 phones and one server as the backup server to the two primary servers.

In the large-scale cluster design, there are up to eight servers in the cluster. The same basic scenario exists as for the 5000-phone service, but, in this case, there are four primary CallManager systems and two backup systems. The publisher is separate from the primary and backup systems, and holds the master database. The TFTP server acts independently of the publisher.

Figure 11-6 *Cluster Considerations for Small, Medium, and Large Clusters*

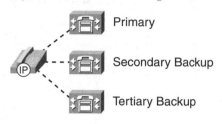

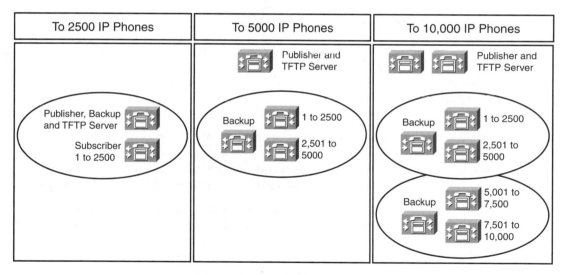

Each telephony device carries a different weight, shown in Table 11-2, based on the amount of resources it requires from the server platform with which it is registered. The required resources include memory, processor, and input/output (I/O). Each device then consumes additional server resources during transactions, which are normally in the form of calls. For example, a device that makes only six calls per hour consumes fewer resources than a device making 12 calls per hour. As a common starting point, the base weight of a device is calculated with the assumption that it makes six or fewer calls per hour during its busiest hour, or six busy hour call attempts (BHCAs).

The maximum number of IP phones that can register with a single CallManager is 2500 on the largest server platforms, even if only IP phones are registered. To calculate the number of IP phones that can register with a CallManager in a specific deployment, subtract the weighted value of non-IP phone resources from the maximum number of device units allowed for that platform. The maximum number of IP phones might be lower than this calculated number, depending on the call volume per phone. In the case of the largest servers, the maximum number of device units is 5000.

Table 11-2 *Device Weights*

	Weight BHCAs < 6	Weight BHCAs < 12	Weight BHCAs < 18	Weight BHCAs < 24
CTI Server Port	2	4	6	8
CTI Client Port	2	4	6	8
CTI Third Party	3	6	9	12
CTI Agent	6	12	18	24
CTI Route Point	2	4	6	8
Transcoder MTP	3	N/A	N/A	N/A
H.323 Gateway	3	3	3	3
H.323 Client	3	6	9	12
SCCP Client	1	2	3	4
MGCP	3	3	3	3
Conference	3	N/A	N/A	N/A

The coresident CTI manager allows a maximum of 800 CTI connections or associations per server, or a maximum of 3200 CTI connections or associations per cluster when they are equally shared between the four active CallManager servers. Associations are defined as devices that have been associated with a particular user in the CallManager user configuration.

CTI route points require some additional consideration. The base weight is two, but the multiplier is based on the number of busy hour call completions (BHCCs). To calculate the BHCC of a route point, we need to know how many calls can be expected to redirect to other ports through the route point. For example, in a typical IP IVR application, the IP IVR is expected to handle ten simultaneous calls. The configuration for this requires a CTI route point and ten CTI ports. If each IP IVR port expects six BHCC, the route point can expect to redirect six calls per hour for each port, or a total of 60 calls per hour for the route point.

The multiplier for a CTI route point is calculated by taking the sum of the BHCC for all the ports associated with the CTI route point, dividing that sum by six, and rounding up to the nearest whole number.

Designing Single-Site IP Telephony Solutions

The single-site IP Telephony model offers the ability to use the PSTN for all off-net calls. In the LAN environment, sufficient bandwidth is available for voice traffic, and the bandwidth allocations are less of a concern. In this section, you learn how to design standalone IP Telephony solutions that communicate with other IP Telephony systems over the PSTN.

The single-site model for IP Telephony, as shown in Figure 11-7, consists of a call processing agent located at a single site, with no telephony services provided over an IP WAN. An enterprise would typically deploy the single-site model over a LAN or metropolitan-area network (MAN), which carries the VoIP traffic within served buildings or geographic areas. In this model, calls beyond the LAN or MAN use the PSTN.

Figure 11-7 *Single-Site IP Telephony Model*

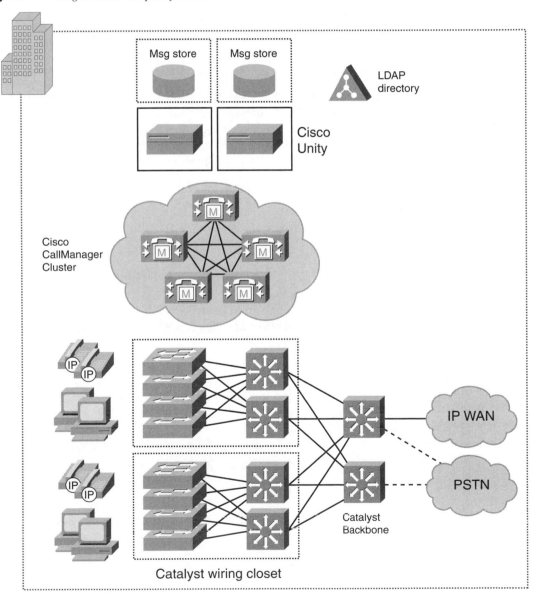

The single-site model has the following design characteristics:

- Single CallManager or CallManager cluster
- Maximum of 10,000 IP phones per cluster
- PSTN for all external calls
- DSP resources for conferencing, transcoding, and MTP
- Voice mail and unified messaging components
- G.711 codec used for all IP phone calls (80 kbps of IP bandwidth per call, uncompressed)
- Capability to integrate with legacy PBX and voice mail systems

A single infrastructure for a converged network solution provides significant cost benefits and enables IP Telephony to take advantage of the many IP-based applications in the enterprise. Single-site deployment also allows each site to be completely self-contained. There is no dependency for service in the event of an IP WAN failure or insufficient bandwidth, and there is no loss of call processing service or functionality.

In summary, the main benefits of the single-site model are

- Ease of deployment
- A common infrastructure for a converged solution
- Simplified dial plan
- No transcoding resources required, due to the use of only G.711 codecs

The dial plan for the single-site model is usually the simplest of all the deployment models because of reliance on the PSTN for all off-net calls. However, some requirements exist for the dial plan for a single site, mainly to offer various classes of service, calling restrictions, 911 and E911 services, and security.

NOTE   Enhanced 911 services (E911) refers to the Federal Communications Commission (FCC) wireless program that requires service providers to provide the telephone number of a cell phone caller that places a 911 call, and the location of the cell phone antenna that received it. The program began in 2001 and is scheduled for completion by December 2005.

For more information, visit http://www.fcc.gov/911/enhanced/.

The CallManager dial-plan architecture can handle these general types of calls:

- All internal calls within the site
- External calls through a PSTN gateway

The complexity of your dial-plan configuration depends on the number of classes of service required by your specific enterprise policy. A class of service is a set of calling restrictions applied to a certain group of devices. Some examples are

- Internal calls only
- Internal and local PSTN calls (no long-distance PSTN)
- Unrestricted calls (internal, local, and long-distance PSTN)

A single-site deployment is a subset of the distributed and centralized deployment models. The deployment should be over a stable infrastructure that allows easy migration to a voice and video network. Some guidelines specific to a single-site IP Telephony deployment include

- Know the calling patterns for the enterprise. Use the single-site model if most of the calls from the enterprise are within the same site or to PSTN users outside of the enterprise.
- Use G.711 codecs for all endpoints. This practice eliminates the consumption of DSP resources for transcoding, and those resources can be allocated to other functions, such as conferencing and MTPs.
- Use MGCP gateways for the PSTN if the enterprise does not require H.323 functionality. This practice simplifies the dial-plan configuration. H.323 might be required to support specific functionality not offered with MGCP, such as support for SS7 or Non-Facility Associated Signaling (NFAS).
- Implement the recommended network infrastructure for high-availability connectivity options for phones (inline power), QoS mechanisms, and security.

Example: Single-Site

NB is a global publishing company. The Singapore operation consists of approximately 6000 sales, printing, and writing staff members. The NB staff resides in a number of office buildings located in the vicinity of each other. In late 2000, NB added another building, the Remote building, to its campus. This additional building houses 750 employees. Rather than deploy a PBX in the new building, NB decided to deploy an IP telephony solution. The deployment includes the network component.

Single-Site Solution

The NB IP Telephony solution, shown in Figure 11-8, is a single-site design. All IP Telephony users are located in the Main building and are distributed across five floors. The CallManager, PSTN gateway, and voice mail server are also physically located in the Main building.

Figure 11-8 *Single-Site IP Telephony Solution*

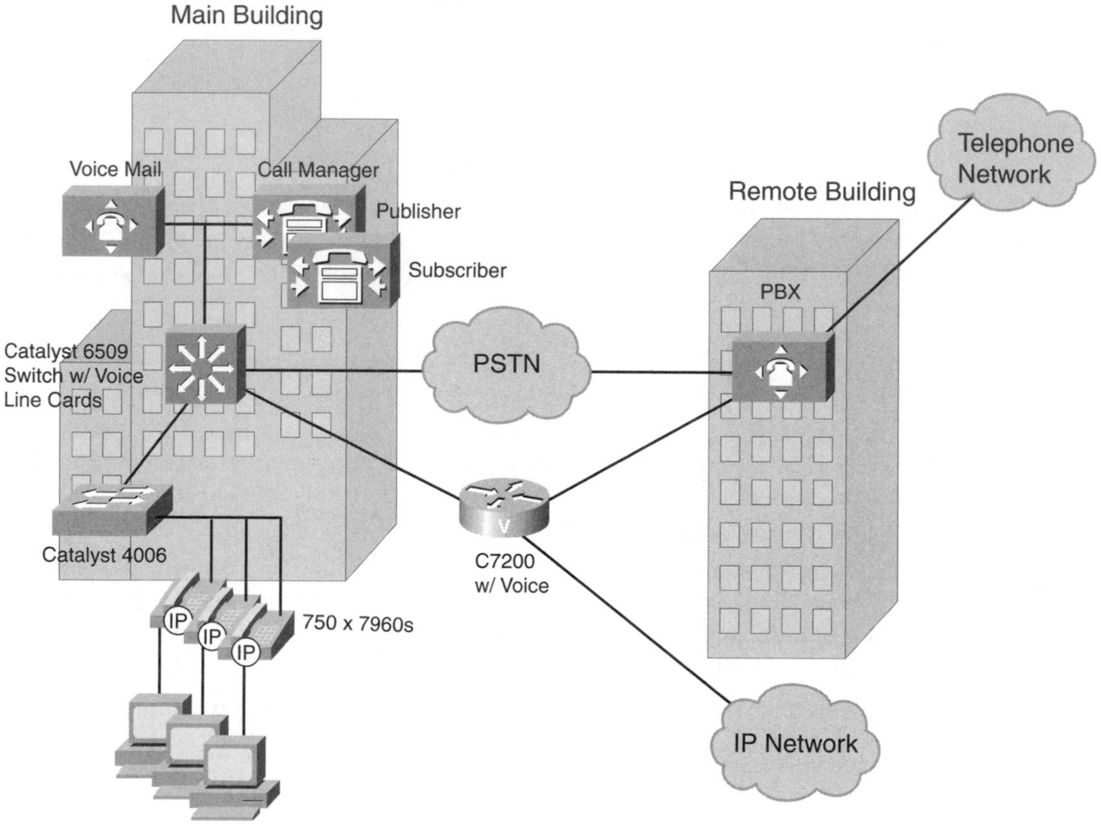

A MAN link connects the Main building to the Remote building less than 1 km away. This MAN link carries voice traffic across to the Remote building, where a gateway connects into the worldwide NB PBX network. Figure 11-8 shows the Main and Remote buildings.

The Main building has approximately 750 IP Phone 7960s. IP phones connect to 10/100 ports on the Catalyst 4006, and receive inline power from the switch. Workstations connect to switch ports in the back of the IP phone.

IP phones and workstations are on separate VLANs and IP subnets.

Cisco CallManager and Call Admission Control

The NB CallManager deployment model is single-site. No call admission control is required across the MAN. This is because the number of calls across the MAN is implicitly limited by the number of trunks connecting the gateway to the PBX.

One CallManager performs the database publishing function, and the other subscribes to the database. All IP phones register with the subscriber as the primary CallManager, and use the publisher as the secondary CallManager.

Voice Mail Integration

CallManager connects to the company's voice mail system by means of two 24-port foreign exchange station (FXS) cards in the Catalyst 6509 switch. Only 30 of the available 48 ports are used. A 9600-bps simplified message desk interface (SMDI) link connects the primary CallManager to the voice mail device.

In addition to the voice mail system, other single points of failure include

- The SMDI link is not redundant. A failure of the primary CallManager will take the voice mail system out of service. Should this situation occur, the NB strategy is to manually move the SMDI cable to the backup CallManager. Alternatively, an SMDI splitter would allow both CallManagers to be connected at the same time, and allow for automatic failover.

- Currently, both 24-port FXS cards reside in the same Catalyst 6509 chassis. A Catalyst 6509 failure will take the voice mail system out of service. As discussed earlier in this chapter, there is much to be gained in terms of resilience by adding a second Catalyst 6509.

Gateway Integration

The following three types of gateways exist:

- **H.323 gateway**—One Cisco 7200 connecting to legacy NB PBX network
- **PSTN gateway**—Three Catalyst 6509 E1 ports connecting to PSTN
- **Voice mail gateway**—Two Catalyst 6509 24-port FXS cards with 30 ports connecting to voice mail

Designing Multisite with Centralized Call Processing IP Telephony Solutions

In a centralized call processing system, as shown in Figure 11-9, CallManagers are centrally located at the hub or aggregation site, with no local call processing at the branch or remote office. This section shows you how to design a multisite IP Telephony solution with centralized call processing, given two or more locations over an IP WAN.

With centralized call processing, the CallManager cluster is located at the central site. Cisco CallManager supports a cluster of 10,000 IP phones.

A primary advantage of the centralized IP Telephony model is the capability to centralize call processing and applications. This reduces the equipment required at the remote branch, and eliminates the administration of multiple PBXs or key systems. Dedicated POTS lines or cellular phones can provide backup services. Centralized services reduce the equipment required at the remote sites and eliminate the administration and maintenance costs of multiple PBXs or key systems used in traditional telephony systems.

Figure 11-9 *Centralized Call-Processing Model*

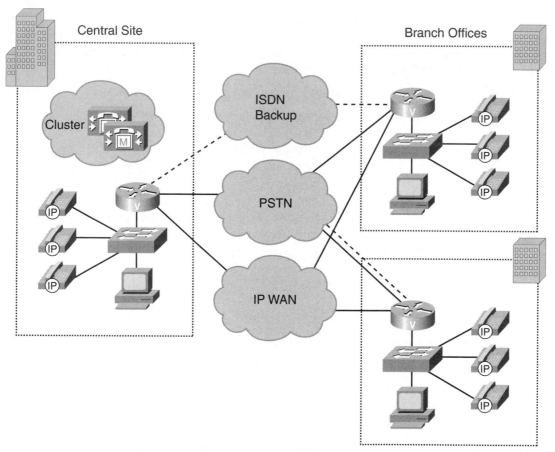

In summary, the multisite WAN model with centralized call processing provides the following benefits:

- Simplified management and administration
- No need for a specialized support staff at the remote sites
- Lower maintenance costs
- Seamless WAN connectivity of all remote sites (toll bypass savings)
- Unified dial plan
- Survivable Remote Site Telephony (SRST) that provides basic call processing at remote sites in the event of an IP WAN failure

NOTE   In deployments where IP WAN bandwidth is either scarce or expensive with respect to PSTN charges, you can configure a remote site to place all external calls through the PSTN. In this scenario, the WAN link carries only regular data and call control signaling between the centralized CallManager cluster and the remote IP phones and gateways. With the centralized call processing approach, PBX equipment is not needed at the remote sites.

Follow these guidelines and best practices when implementing the multisite WAN model with centralized call processing:

- Minimize delay between CallManager and remote locations to reduce voice cut-through delays (also known as clipping).
- Use a hub-and-spoke topology for the sites. The call admission control relies on the hub-and-spoke topology and records only the bandwidth into and out of each location.
- Limit the remote sites to the number of phones supported by the SRST feature on the branch router, or provide more branch routers.
- Configure up to four active CallManagers in the central cluster for call processing. This configuration can support a maximum of 10,000 IP phones (or 20,000 device units) when CallManager runs on the largest supported server. Devices such as gateways, conferencing resources, voice mail, and other applications consume device units according to their relative device weights.
- Each CallManager cluster can support up to 500 locations configured with call admission control. If you need more remote sites, add CallManager clusters and connect them using intercluster trunks, as in the distributed call processing model.

When using the CallManager locations mechanism for call admission control, follow these recommendations:

- You can install gateways at the central site only, at the remote sites only, or at both the central and remote sites. Use the CallManager locations mechanism to provide call admission control for the gateways at the remote sites but not at the central site. You do not need a Cisco IOS gatekeeper under these circumstances.
- Do not move devices between locations, because Cisco CallManager keeps track of the bandwidth only for the configured location of the device and not for the physical location.
- If you have more than one circuit or virtual circuit in a spoke location, set the bandwidth according to the dedicated resources allocated on the smallest link.

Designing Multisite with Distributed Call Processing IP Telephony Solutions

In the distributed call processing model, shown here in Figure 11-10, each CallManager cluster has its own set of resources and connects to the other clusters within the network via intercluster trunk links. This section helps you design a multisite IP Telephony solution with distributed call processing, given two or more locations over an IP WAN.

Figure 11-10 *Distributed Call Processing Model*

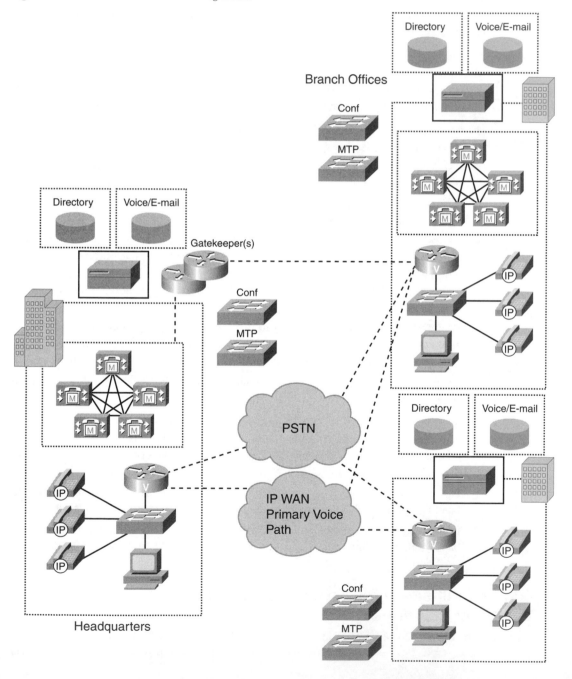

CallManager supports up to 100 sites for distributed call processing. Voice calls between sites can use the IP WAN as the primary path and the PSTN as the secondary path in the event the IP WAN is down or has insufficient resources to handle additional calls. Whether calls use the IP WAN or the PSTN can be transparent to both the calling party and the called party.

The primary advantage of the distributed call processing model is that, by using local call processing, it provides the same level of features and capabilities whether the IP WAN is available or not. Each site can have from one to eight CallManager servers in a cluster, based on the number of users. This is the predominant deployment model for sites with greater than 50 users, and each site can support up to 10,000 users. In addition, no loss of service occurs if the IP WAN is down.

The multisite WAN model with distributed call processing provides these benefits:

- Cost savings when using the IP WAN for calls between sites.
- Use of the IP WAN to bypass toll charges by routing calls through remote-site gateways, closer to the PSTN number dialed. This practice is known as tail-end-hop-off.
- Maximum utilization of available bandwidth by allowing voice to share the IP WAN with other types of traffic.
- No loss of functionality during IP WAN failure, because there is a call processing agent at each site.
- Scalability to hundreds of sites.

A multisite WAN with distributed call processing is a superset of the single-site deployment. (The best practices should include those from the single-site deployment, as well as those in the following list.) The key difference in the single-site and the multisite distributed site is how to control the voice calls over the WAN. The gatekeeper is responsible for controlling voice calls in the distributed mode. The gatekeeper performs two main functions:

- Call admission control
- E.164 dial-plan resolution

NOTE   E.164 is a ITU-T recommendation that specifies numbering plan formats used by Integrated Services Digital Network (ISDN) and Asynchronous Transfer Mode (ATM).

In the distributed model, the number of sites is limited by the hub-and-spoke environment, while the gatekeeper can scale to hundreds of sites.

A gatekeeper is one of the key elements in the multisite WAN model with distributed call processing.

A gatekeeper is an H.323 device that provides call admission control and PSTN dial-plan resolution. The following best practices apply to the use of a gatekeeper:

- Use a hub-and-spoke topology for the gatekeeper. A gatekeeper can manage the bandwidth into and out of a site, or between zones within a site, but it is not aware of the topology.

- To provide high availability of the gatekeeper, use Hot Standby Router Protocol (HSRP) gatekeeper pairs, gatekeeper clustering, and alternate gatekeeper support. In addition, use multiple gatekeepers to provide redundancy within the network.

- Use a single WAN codec, because the H.323 specification does not allow for Layer 2, IP, User Datagram Protocol (UDP), or RTP header overhead in the bandwidth request. (Header overhead is allowed only in the payload or encoded voice part of the packet.) Use one type of codec on the WAN to simplify capacity planning by eliminating the need to overprovision the IP WAN to allow for the worst-case scenario.

- Gatekeeper networks can scale to hundreds of sites, and the design is limited only by the hub-and-spoke topology.

A distributed call processing system requires call admission control, just as a centralized call processing system does. However, the mechanism for implementing call admission control differs greatly in these two types of systems.

For distributed call processing systems, you can implement call admission control with an H.323 gatekeeper as illustrated in Figure 11-11. In this design, the call processing agent registers with the IOS gatekeeper, and queries it each time the agent wants to place an IP WAN call. The IOS gatekeeper associates each call processing agent with a zone that has specific bandwidth limitations. Therefore, the IOS gatekeeper can limit the maximum amount of bandwidth consumed by IP WAN voice calls into or out of a zone.

Figure 11-11 shows call admission control with a gatekeeper. When the call processing agent wants to place an IP WAN call, it first requests permission from the gatekeeper. If the gatekeeper grants permission, the call processing agent places the call across the IP WAN. If the gatekeeper denies the request, the call processing agent can try a secondary path, such as the PSTN, or it can simply fail the call.

This design essentially consists of a call accounting method for providing admission control, in which the gatekeeper keeps track of the bandwidth consumed by the IP WAN calls. When you set the maximum bandwidth for a zone, take into account the recommendation that voice traffic should not consume more than 75% of the WAN link.

Figure 11-11 *Call Admission Control Using a Gatekeeper*

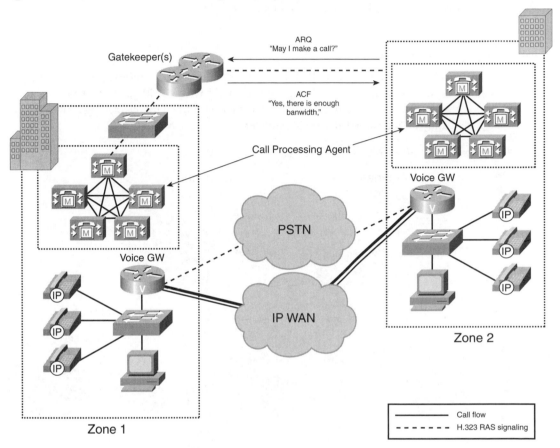

Example: Distributed Call Processing

The ACU is a public government-funded university established in 1991. The university has approximately 10,000 learners and approximately 1000 staff. Six campuses are spread across Ireland.

The current campus design does not comply with the Cisco-recommended QoS design guidelines for IP Telephony. These concerns are in regard to QoS:

- The broadcast domain is very large. IP phones might be affected by the excessive amount of broadcasts they process.

- Catalyst 1900 switches within each campus are not QoS-capable. If an IP phone and PC are connected to the same switch port, voice packets might be dropped if the PC is receiving data at a high rate.

Significant improvements can be achieved by redesigning parts of the campus infrastructure. A hardware upgrade is not necessarily required.

Distributed Call Processing Solution

The ACU recently deployed an IP Telephony solution, as shown in Figure 11-12. The solution consists of a two-CallManager cluster and a Cisco 3640 gateway at each campus, along with a number of IP phones. The six campuses are interconnected by a WAN provided by an international service provider.

Figure 11-12 *Distributed Call Processing Solution*

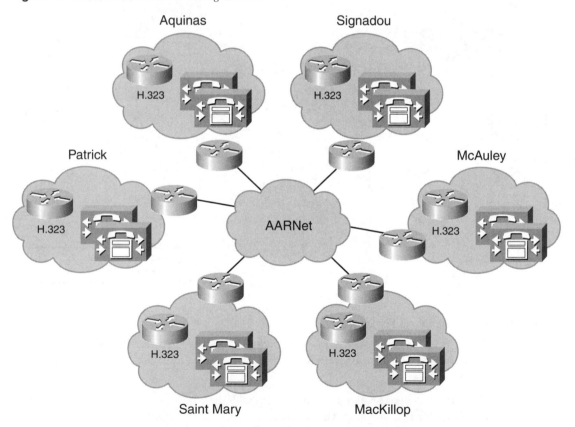

The campus, as shown in Figure 11-13, is now split into a voice VLAN and a data VLAN. Phones and PCs that connect to a Catalyst 1900 switch must now connect to different ports to achieve the VLAN separation. An additional uplink from each Catalyst 1900 switch to a Cisco 3500 Series XL switch is added. One of the two uplinks is a member of the voice VLAN; the other uplink is a member of the data VLAN. Using Interswitch Link (ISL) trunking as an alternative to having two uplinks is not recommended, as this will not provide the voice and data traffic with separate queues. The gigabit Ethernet links from the Catalyst 3500XL to the Catalyst 6000 must also be converted to 802.1Q trunks so that both voice and data VLAN can be carried across this core switch.

Figure 11-13 *MacKillop Campus Solution*

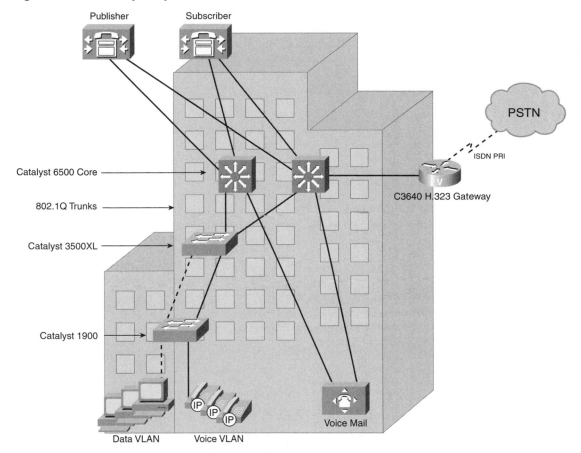

Ports on the Catalyst 3500XL that are in the data VLAN have a default class of service (CoS) of 0. Ports that are a member of the voice VLAN have a default CoS of 5. As a result, the voice traffic will be correctly prioritized after it arrives at a Catalyst 3500/Catalyst 6500 core.

In the rare case when IP phones connect directly to a Catalyst 3500XL, a PC might be connected to the rear switch port on the IP phone. In this case, the IP phones connect to the switch by means of an 802.1Q trunk. This allows voice and data packets to travel on separate VLANs, and packets can be given the correct CoS at ingress. As the network evolves over time, and the Catalyst 1900s reach end-of-life, they should be replaced with Catalyst 3500XL switches or other QoS-capable switches. This topology then becomes the standard method of connecting IP phones and PCs to the network.

Gateways

Each of the six ACU campuses has a Cisco 3640 router acting as an H.323 gateway. These gateways connect to the PSTN by means of ISDN. The number of Primary Rate Interfaces (PRIs) and bearer channels (B Channels) varies depending on the size of the campus.

For direct outward dialing (DOD), these gateways are used only as secondary gateways. The service provider's gateways are used as the primary gateways. For direct inward dialing (DID), the ACU gateways are always used.

Cisco CallManager

Each of the six campuses has a cluster consisting of two CallManager servers. One CallManager is the publisher and the other CallManager is the subscriber. The subscriber acts as the primary CallManager for all IP phones.

Each cluster is configured with two regions: one for intracampus calls (G.711) and the other for intercampus calls (G.729).

Location-based Call Admission Control (CAC) is not appropriate for ACU, as all IP phones served by each cluster are on a single campus. There are merits to a gatekeeper-based CAC for intercampus calls, but this is not currently implemented. There are, however, plans to do so in the near future.

NOTE   Location-based CAC provides call admission control using the Cisco CallManager to control all the locations, while gatekeeper-based CAC provides call admission control using gatekeeper technology.

Each CallManager is configured with 12 H.323 gateways. This is made up of intercluster trunks to the five other CallManager clusters, six service-provider PSTN gateways, and one ACU gateway at each campus.

International calls are gatekeeper routed and not sent through the local gateway. This is significant, as the service provider might deploy international gateways in the future. If a gateway was later deployed in the United States, a simple gatekeeper configuration change would allow universities to place calls to the United States at U.S. domestic rates.

Voice Mail

Prior to the migration to IP Telephony, ACU had three Active Voice Repartee OS/2-based voice mail servers with Dialogic phone boards. The plan is to reuse these servers in the IP Telephony environment. When implemented, each Repartee server will connect to a CallManager by means of SMDI and a Catalyst 6000 24-port FXS card. This provides voice mail for three of the six campuses, leaving three campuses without voice mail. It is not possible to properly share one Repartee server between users on two CallManager clusters, as there is no way of propagating the Message Waiting Indicator (MWI) across the intercluster H.323 trunk.

ACU is also considering purchasing three Cisco Unity servers for the remaining three campuses. These servers will be Skinny Station Protocol-based, so no gateways will be required.

Media Resources

Hardware DSPs are not currently deployed at ACU. Local conferencing uses the software-based conference bridge on the CallManager. Intercluster conferencing is not currently supported. Transcoding is currently not required. Only G.711 and G.729 codecs are used and supported on all deployed end devices.

Fax and Modem Support

Fax and modem traffic is not currently supported by the ACU IP Telephony network. The university is planning to use the Catalyst 6000 24-port FXS card for fax/modem relay in the future.

Clustering over the IP WAN

You might deploy a single CallManager cluster across multiple sites that are connected by an IP WAN with QoS features enabled. This section provides a brief overview of how to design a cluster over the WAN IP Telephony solution, given two or more locations.

Clustering over the WAN can support two types of deployments: local failover and remote failover. In addition, clustering over the WAN supports a single point of administration for IP phones for all sites within the cluster, feature transparency, shared line appearances, extension mobility within the cluster, and a unified dial plan. These features make this solution ideal as a disaster-recovery plan for business continuance sites or as a single solution for small or medium sites.

Local Failover

The local failover deployment model, as shown in Figure 11-14, provides the most resilience for clustering over the WAN. Each of the sites in this model contains at least one primary CallManager subscriber and one backup subscriber. This deployment model is ideal for two or three sites with CallManager servers and a maximum of 5000 and 2500 IP phones per site, respectively. This model allows for up to 10,000 IP phones in the two-site configuration and 7500 IP phones in the three-site configuration.

Figure 11-14 *Clustering over the IP WAN with Local Failover*

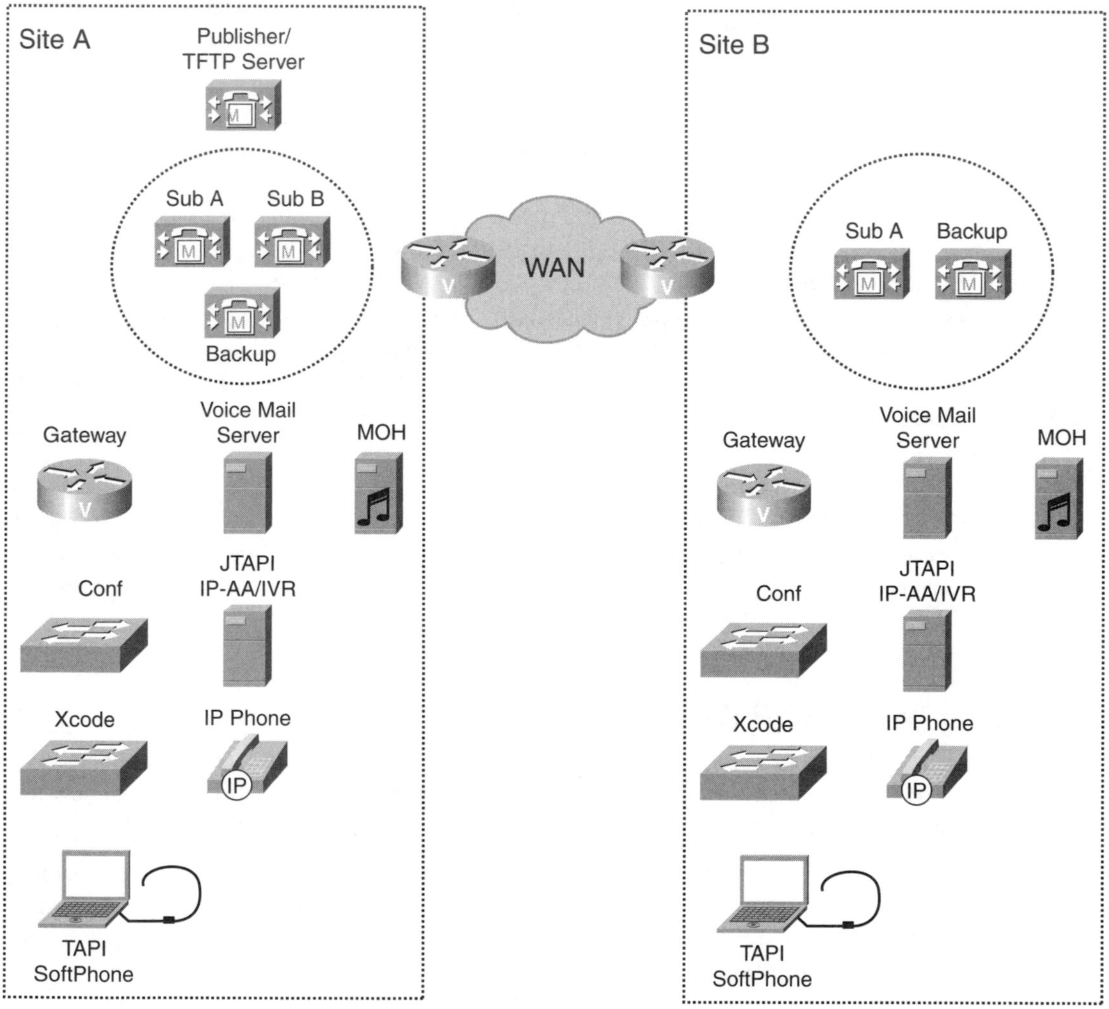

In summary, observe these guidelines when implementing the local failover model:

- Configure each site to contain at least one primary and one backup CallManager subscriber.

- Cisco highly recommends that you replicate key services (TFTP, DNS, DHCP, LDAP, and IP phone services), all media resources (conference bridges and MoH), and gateways at each site to provide the highest level of resiliency. You could also extend this practice to include a voice mail system at each site. In the event of a WAN failure, only sites without access to the publisher database might lose a small amount of functionality.

- Every 10,000 BHCAs in the cluster requires 900 kbps of bandwidth for Intracluster Communication Signaling (ICCS). This is a minimum bandwidth requirement, and bandwidth is allocated in multiples of 900 kbps.

- Allow a maximum round-trip time (RTT) of 40 ms between any two servers in the CallManager cluster. This time equates to a 20-ms maximum one-way delay or a transmission distance of approximately 1860 miles (3000 km) under ideal conditions.

Cisco CallManager Provisioning

Provisioning of the CallManager cluster for the local failover model should follow the design guidelines for device weights. If calls are allowed across the WAN between the sites, you must configure CallManager locations in addition to the default location for the other sites, to provide call admission control between the sites. If the bandwidth is over-provisioned for the number of devices, it is still best to configure call admission control based on locations. Because call admission control based on locations does not provide automatic failover to the PSTN, Cisco recommends that you over-provision the WAN for intersite calls.

As the delay increases between the CallManager servers, the bandwidth information shared between the servers for call admission control will also be delayed, possibly allowing additional calls to be set up until the ICCS bandwidth message arrives. This situation is a small risk because, even at full capacity, only a few additional calls might be set up before the bandwidth information arrives. To provide for this situation, Cisco recommends that you over-provision the priority queue for voice traffic by a few extra calls.

To improve redundancy, Cisco recommends that you enable TFTP service on at least one of the CallManager servers at each location. You can run the TFTP service on either a publisher or a subscriber server, depending on the site. The TFTP server option must be correctly set on the DHCP servers for each site. If DHCP is not in use or the TFTP server is manually configured, you should configure the correct address for the site.

Other services, which might affect normal operation of CallManager during WAN outages, should also be replicated at all sites to ensure uninterrupted service. These services include DHCP servers, DNS servers, corporate directories, and IP phone services. On each DHCP server, set the DNS server address correctly for each location.

IP phones might have shared line appearances between the sites. The ICCS bandwidth provisioned between the sites allows for the additional ICCS traffic that shared line appearances generate. During a WAN outage, call control for each line appearance is segmented, but call control returns to a single CallManager server after the WAN is restored. During the WAN restoration period, there is extra traffic between the two sites. If this situation occurs during a period of high call volume, the shared lines might not operate as expected during that period. This situation should not last more than a few minutes, but if it is a concern, you can provision an extra 2 Mbps of bandwidth to minimize the effects.

NOTE   Shared line appearances is when two or more lines on different devices share the same
directory number.

Gateways

Normally, gateways should be provided at all sites for access to the PSTN. The device pools
should be configured to register the gateways with the CallManager servers at the same site.
Partitions and calling search spaces should also be configured to select the local gateways
at the site as the first choice for PSTN access and the other site gateways as a second choice
for overflow. Take special care to ensure emergency service access at each site.

You can centralize access to the PSTN gateways if access is not required during a WAN
failure and if sufficient additional bandwidth is configured for the number of calls across
the WAN. For E911 requirements, additional gateways might be needed at each site.

Voice Mail

You can deploy Cisco Unity at all sites and integrate it into the CallManager cluster. This
configuration provides voice mail access even during a WAN failure and without using the
PSTN. Because Cisco Unity requires a unique pilot number for voice mail, you have to
configure a translation pattern at each location to translate the "virtual" messages number
at each site to the correct pilot number. You should place this translation pattern in a
partition that is in the calling search space for the devices at that location. If extension
mobility is not being used, users from one site who are visiting another site will have to dial
the voice mail pilot number directly.

Music on Hold

MoH servers should be provisioned at each site, with sufficient capacity for the expected
load. Through the use of media resource groups (MRGs) and media resource group lists
(MRGLs), MoH is provided by the on-site resource and is available during a WAN failure.

Remote Failover

The remote failover deployment model provides flexibility for the placement of backup
servers. Each site contains at least one primary CallManager subscriber and might or might
not have a backup subscriber.

Remote failover, shown in Figure 11-15, allows you to deploy the backup servers over the
WAN. Using this employment model, you might have up to six sites with CallManager
subscribers and one or two sites containing the CallManager backup server. This
deployment allows for up to 10,000 IP phones shared over the required number of sites.

Figure 11-15 *Clustering over the IP WAN with Remote Failover*

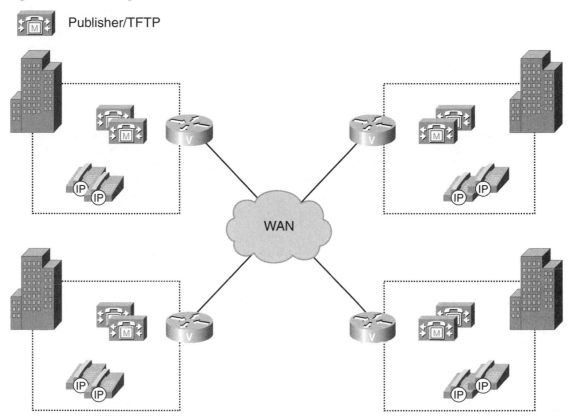

Publisher/TFTP

Remote failover allows for a deployment of three to six sites with IP phones and other devices normally registered, with a maximum of four servers. In summary, observe these guidelines when implementing the remote failover model:

- Configure each site to contain at least one primary CallManager subscriber and an optional backup subscriber if desired.

- Cisco highly recommends that you replicate key services (TFTP, DNS, DHCP, LDAP, and IP phone services), all media resources (conference bridges and MoH), and gateways at each site with IP phones to provide the highest level of resiliency. You could also extend this practice to include a voice mail system at each site. In the event of a WAN failure, only sites without access to the publisher database might lose a small amount of functionality.

- Every 10,000 BHCA in the cluster requires 900 kbps of bandwidth for ICCS. This is a minimum bandwidth requirement, and bandwidth is allocated in multiples of 900 kbps.

- Signaling or controling plane traffic requires additional bandwidth when devices are registered across the WAN with a remote CallManager server within the same cluster.

- Allow a maximum RTT of 40 ms between any two servers in the CallManager cluster. This time equates to a 20-ms maximum one-way delay or a transmission distance of approximately 1860 miles (3000 km) under ideal conditions.

Cisco CallManager Provisioning

If calls are allowed across a WAN between sites, you must configure CallManager locations in addition to the default location for the other sites to provide call admission control between the sites. If the bandwidth is overprovisioned for the number of devices, it is still best to configure call admission control based on locations. Because call admission control based on locations does not provide automatic failover to the PSTN, Cisco recommends that you overprovision the WAN for intersite calls.

As the delay increases between the CallManager servers, the bandwidth information shared between the servers for call admission control will also be delayed, possibly allowing additional calls to be set up until the ICCS bandwidth message arrives. This situation is a small risk because, even at full capacity, only a few additional calls might be set up before the bandwidth information arrives. To provide for this situation, Cisco recommends that you overprovision the priority queue for voice traffic by a few extra calls.

To improve redundancy, Cisco recommends that you enable the TFTP service on at least one of the CallManager servers at each location. You can run the TFTP service on either a publisher or a subscriber server, depending on the site. The TFTP server option must be correctly set on the DHCP servers for each site. If DHCP is not in use or the TFTP server is manually configured, you should configure the correct address for the site.

Other services, which might affect normal operation of CallManager during WAN outages, should also be replicated at all sites to ensure uninterrupted service. These services include DHCP servers, DNS servers, corporate directories, and IP phone services. On each DHCP server, set the DNS server address correctly for each location.

IP phones might have shared line appearances between the sites. The ICCS bandwidth provisioned between the sites allows for the additional ICCS traffic that shared line appearances generate. During a WAN outage, call control for each line appearance is segmented, but call control returns to a single CallManager server after the WAN is restored. During the WAN restoration period, there is extra traffic between the two sites. If this situation occurs during a period of high call volume, the shared lines might not operate as expected during that period. This situation should not last more than a few minutes, but if it is a concern, you can provision an extra 2 Mbps of bandwidth to minimize the effects.

Gateways

Normally, gateways should be provided at all user sites for access to the PSTN. The device pools might be configured to allow the gateways to register with a remote CallManager server as backup if the local CallManager server is unavailable. Partitions and calling search spaces should also be configured to select the local gateways at the site as the first choice for PSTN access and the other site gateways as a second choice for overflow. Take special care to ensure emergency service access at each site.

You can centralize access to the PSTN gateways if access is not required during a WAN failure and if sufficient additional bandwidth is configured for the number of calls across the WAN. For E911 requirements, additional gateways might be needed at each site.

Voice Mail

You can deploy Cisco Unity at all sites and integrate it into the CallManager cluster. This configuration provides voice mail access even during a WAN failure and without using the PSTN. Because Cisco Unity requires a unique pilot number, you have to configure a translation pattern at each location to translate the "virtual" messages number at each site to the correct pilot number. You should place this translation pattern in a partition that is in the calling search space for the devices at that location. If extension mobility is not being used, users from one site who are visiting another site will have to dial the voice mail pilot number directly.

Music on Hold

MoH servers should be provisioned at each site, with sufficient capacity for the expected load. Through the use of MRGs and MRGLs, MoH is provided by the on-site resource and is available during a WAN failure.

Network Infrastructure Design Considerations

IP Telephony places strict requirements on the network infrastructure. The network must provide sufficient bandwidth and quick convergence after network failures or changes. This section describes the physical network and network features required to support Cisco IP Telephony solutions.

Most IP Telephony installations are built on an existing network infrastructure, but the infrastructure might require enhancements. In the voice solution, it is critical that you prepare to allow voice traffic to have priority over all other traffic in the network. To design the infrastructure to support voice, ask the following questions:

- **What features are required for each device in the campus network?** IP phones require power. Most enterprises put IP Telephony applications on a separate VLAN with prioritization. The infrastructure must support voice to ensure success.

- **Will the physical plant in the campus support IP Telephony or is an upgrade required?** The wiring and cabling plant are critical for IP Telephony. Category 5 cabling running at least 100 Mbps throughout is generally considered critical for IP Telephony.

- **What features are required for each device at the enterprise edge?** At the edge, QoS is critical. You need to know what features are implemented in the network. Without considering the edge, users might think that the voice equipment is not performing adequately when, in fact, the network is not performing adequately.

- **Are the WAN links sufficient to support IP Telephony or is an upgrade required?** Evaluate each WAN link to determine if it will support voice.

- **Does the network provide the bandwidth required to support both voice and call control traffic?** Bandwidth must consider both voice traffic and call control traffic. Consider both in your traffic engineering efforts. In the campus network, bandwidth provisioning requires careful planning of the LAN infrastructure so that the available bandwidth is always considerably higher than the load and there is no steady-state congestion over the LAN links. This ensures that the network is responsive to the offered traffic.

NOTE   Plan to work with a voice specialist to complete a traffic engineering analysis for the network.

Layer 2 Voice Transport

As an alternative to a CallManager VoIP-based voice network, you can use the data-link layer as the transport. The most common use of a Layer 2 voice transport is to replace tie lines or create circuits or trunks from one voice-enabled network device to another voice-enabled network device, providing a point-to-point circuit.

Many enterprises have an existing Frame Relay or ATM network. Voice over Frame Relay or Voice over ATM is an option for those enterprises. For enterprises already using constant-bit-rate ATM, there is a natural match with voice capabilities. Their savings for packet voice coding is dependent on the networks support for subrate multiplexing.

For enterprises that have an existing Frame Relay network or the variable bit rate forms of ATM, transport of compressed voice can represent significant savings while providing additional flexibility of features.

VoIP over Leased Lines

VoIP over leased lines provides a method for enterprises that currently use leased lines VoIP over Serial with either Point-to-Point Protocol (PPP) or High-Level Data Link Control (HDLC) encapsulation to integrate voice into their current data leased lines.

Voice over Frame Relay

Voice-enabled routers can integrate voice, LAN, synchronous data, video, and fax traffic for transport over a public or private Frame Relay network. Cisco optimizes network bandwidth over network links by multiplexing voice and data on the same circuit or physical interface. These features are offered with Voice over Frame Relay:

- Enables real-time, delay-sensitive voice traffic to be carried over slow Frame Relay links
- Allows replacement of dedicated 64-kbps TDM telephony circuits with more economical Frame Relay PVCs or SVCs
- Uses voice compression technology that conforms to ITU-T specifications
- Allows intelligent setup of proprietary-switched Voice over Frame Relay connections between two Voice over Frame Relay endpoints
- Supports standards-based FRF.11 and FRF.12 functionality

Voice over ATM

ATM is a switching method for transmitting information in fixed-length cells, based on application (voice, video, and data) demand and priority. ATM supports a number of service classes. Each ATM service class is given a guaranteed minimum bandwidth, which ensures deterministic behavior under load, and supports complex classes of service that voice and video can take advantage of to guarantee they receive a higher priority through the network. Voice over ATM offers these features:

- Uses small, fixed-sized cells (53 bytes)
- Is a connection-oriented protocol
- Supports multiple service types
- Supports LAN and WAN traffic
- Emulates PSTN circuits using ATM virtual circuits
- Minimizes delay and delay variation

Network Bandwidth Provisioning

Properly provisioning the network bandwidth is a major component of designing a successful IP Telephony network. You can calculate the required bandwidth by adding the bandwidth requirements for each major application, including voice, video, and data. This sum then represents the minimum bandwidth requirement for any given link, and it should not exceed approximately 75% of the total available bandwidth for the link.

From a traffic standpoint, an IP Telephony call consists of two parts:

- The voice carrier stream, which consists of RTP packets that contain the actual voice samples.

- The call control signaling, which consists of packets belonging to one of several protocols, according to the endpoints involved in the call, for example, H.323 or MGCP. Call control functions are, for instance, those used to set up, maintain, tear down, or redirect a call.

Bandwidth provisioning must include not only the voice stream traffic but also the call control traffic.

Provisioning for Voice Bearer Traffic

A VoIP packet consists of the payload, IP header, UDP header, RTP header, and Layer 2 link header. At a packetization period of 20 ms, voice packets have a 160-byte payload for G.711 or a 20-byte payload for G.729. However, G.729 does not support fax or modem traffic. The IP header is 20 bytes, the UDP header is 8 bytes, and the RTP header is 12 bytes. The link header varies in size according to the Layer 2 media used.

Use the following formula to calculate the bandwidth that voice streams consume:

(Packet payload + all headers in bits) * Packet rate per second (50 packets per second when using a 20 ms packet period)

NOTE   The RTP is responsible for carrying real-time voice data in IP-enabled networks. RTP uses a timestamp in its header to tag the payload to allow proper resequencing of the data by the receiver. RTP uses the services of the UDP transport protocol to interface with IP.

Provisioning for Call Control Traffic

When provisioning bandwidth for call control traffic using centralized call control from remote sites, consider the following:

- When a remote branch phone places a call, the control traffic traverses the IP WAN (even if the call is local to the branch) to reach the CallManager at the central site.

- Signaling Connection Control Part (SCCP) and TAPI are the most common signaling protocols on the IP WAN. Other deployment patterns might use H.323, MGCP, or SIP. All the control traffic is exchanged between a CallManager and the central site, and endpoints or gateways at the remote branches.

As a consequence, the area in which to provision bandwidth for control traffic lies between the branch routers and the WAN aggregation router at the central site. The control traffic that traverses the WAN includes two categories:

- **Maintenance traffic**—Includes keepalive messages periodically exchanged between the branch IP phones and CallManager, regardless of phone activity

- **Call-related traffic**—Includes signaling messages exchanged between the branch IP phones and/or gateways and the CallManager at the central site when a call needs to be set up, torn down, forwarded, and so on

To estimate the generated call control traffic, you must determine the average number of calls per hour made by each branch IP phone.

You can determine the recommended bandwidth needed for call control traffic with these formulas:

- Bandwidth (bps) with no TAPI traffic = 150 * Number of IP phones and gateways in the branch

- Bandwidth (bps) with TAPI applications = 225 * Number of IP phones and gateways in the branch

If a TAPI application is deployed at the remote branches, the recommended bandwidth is affected, because the TAPI protocol requires more messages to be exchanged between the CallManager and the endpoints.

The following formula takes into account the impact of a TAPI application:

Bandwidth (bps) with TAPI applications = 225 * Number of IP phones and gateways in the branch

If you consider the fact that the smallest bandwidth that you can assign to a queue on an IOS router is 8 kbps, you can summarize the values of minimum and recommended bandwidth for different branch office sizes.

Traffic Engineering

Traffic engineering, as it applies to traditional voice networks, is determining the number of trunks necessary to carry a required amount of voice calls during a period of time. For designers of a voice network, the goal is to properly size the number of trunks and provision the appropriate amount of bandwidth necessary to carry the amount of traffic determined.

There are two different types of connections to consider: lines and trunks. Lines allow telephone sets to be connected to telephone switches, such as PBXs and central office (CO) switches. Trunks connect switches together. An example of a trunk is a tie line interconnecting PBXs (ignore the use of "line" in the tie line statement; it's actually a trunk).

Companies use switches to act as concentrators, because the number of telephone sets required is usually greater than the number of simultaneous calls that need to be made. For example, a company might have 600 telephone sets connected to a PBX but might only have 15 trunks connecting the PBX to the central office switch.

To perform traffic engineering on a voice network, follow the process described in Table 11-3.

Table 11-3 *Traffic Engineering*

Step	Description	Notes
1	Collect the existing voice traffic.	From the carrier, gather the following information:
		Peg counts for calls offered, calls abandoned, and all trunks busy
		Grade of service rating for trunk groups
		Total traffic carried per trunk group
		Phone bills, to see the carrier's rates
		For best results, get two weeks' worth of traffic.
		The internal telecommunications department can provide call detail records (CDRs) for PBXs. This information typically records calls that are offered, but does not provide information on calls that were blocked because all trunks were busy.
2	Categorize the traffic by groups.	In most large enterprises, it is more cost-effective to apply traffic engineering to groups of trunks serving a common purpose. For example, you might separate inbound customer service calls into a separate trunk group distinctly different from general outgoing calls.
		Start by separating the traffic into inbound and outbound directions. Group outbound traffic into distances called (for example, local, local long distance, intrastate, interstate, and so on). It is important to break the traffic by distance because most tariffs are distance sensitive.
		Determine the purpose of the calls. For example, what were the calls for? Were they used for fax, modem, call center, 800 for customer service, 800 for voice mail, telecommuters, and so on?
3	Determine the number of physical trunks required to meet the traffic needs.	If you know the amount of traffic generated and the Grade of Service required, you can calculate the number of trunks required to meet your needs. Use the following simple equation to calculate traffic flow:
		$A = C * T$
		A is the amount of traffic (in seconds), C is the number of calls originating during a period of one hour, and T is the average holding time of a call in seconds.
		It is important to note that C is the number of calls originated, not carried. Typically, the information received from the carrier or from the company's internal CDRs are in terms of carried traffic and not offered traffic, as is usually provided by PBXs.

Table 11-3 *Traffic Engineering (Continued)*

Step	Description	Notes
4	Determine the proper mix of trunks.	The proper mix of trunks is more of an economic decision than a technical decision. Cost per minute is the most commonly used measurement for determining the price breakpoint of adding trunks. Care must be taken to ensure that all cost components are considered, such as accounting for additional transmission, equipment, administration, and maintenance costs.
		There are two rules to follow when optimizing the network for cost:
		Use average usage figures instead of the busy hour, which would overstate the number of call minutes.
		Use the least costly circuit until the incremental cost becomes more expensive than the next best route.
5	Convert the number of erlangs of traffic to packets or cells per second.	The final step in traffic engineering is to equate erlangs of carried traffic to packets or cells per second. One way to do this is to convert one erlang to the appropriate data measurement, and then apply modifiers. The following equations are theoretical numbers based on PCM voice and fully loaded packets:
		One PCM voice channel requires 64 Kbps
		One erlang is 60 minutes of voice or enough traffic to keep a single port occupied for one hour.
		Therefore,
		1 erlang = 64 kbps * 3600 seconds * 1 byte/8 bits = 28.8 MB of traffic in one hour.

NOTE   Use an erlang calculator and an experienced voice network designer to perform traffic engineering for a voice network. Refer to http://www.erlang.com/calculator/ for more information and an erlang calculator.

Dial Plan Design Considerations

A well-designed dial plan is a vital component of any IP Telephony network; it applies to traditional voice networks and all the other network elements rely on it. The dial plan is essentially the endpoint selection for IP voice calls.

CallManager distinguishes between internal and external calls. The design questions to ask are

- How many calls are internal calls?
- How many calls are external calls?

CallManager provides digit transformation (translation), which is the capability to transform a called or calling number into another number. Digit translation can be used on internal as well as external calls, whether inbound or outbound.

CallManager provides the ability to restrict calls on each phone individually or on groups of phones in the same CallManager cluster. Users can be grouped into communities of interest on the same CallManager, yet share the same gateways and have overlapping dial plans. These capabilities help support multisite IP WAN deployments with centralized call processing and multitenant deployments.

Access to emergency services (911 and E911) is required by law in most areas. Because emergency services have requirements that can affect the overall design of your network, you should consider them early in the design phase. Gateways for 911 and E911 services must be highly available, and you can distribute them in many locations to meet this requirement. You can also install redundant gateways at each location to connect to the PSTN and provide routing of 911 calls.

NOTE   Creating dial plans is difficult and involved. It requires an expert in dial planning to develop an effective solution. Consult with an expert before attempting to create an enterprise dial plan.

Intelligent Network Services for IP Telephony and Voice

Intelligent network services, such as network management, high availability, security, and QoS, extend to incorporate voice-specific solutions. This section explains the role that intelligent network services play in a Cisco IP Telephony solution.

Traditional voice networks have a distinct set of voice management concepts and processes. The convergence of voice and data has brought about a similar merge of data network and voice-only management.

In fact, this merging of management tasks and processes is one of the key benefits of using a converged network as opposed to a dedicated voice-only network. However, it is still necessary to comprehend the traditional voice-only management concepts to relate the features available in that technology to the converged network management techniques.

Network management of circuit-switched data networks is often summarized by the fault, configuration, accounting, performance, security (FCAPS) model, defined in the functional model of the Open System Interconnection (OSI) management architecture and adopted by ITU-T as part of the Telecommunication Management Network (TMN) initiative. In a traditional voice environment, the approach to management is usually referred to as operations, administration, management, and provisioning (OAM&P).

IP Telephony Network Management Tools

The CiscoWorks family of tools, CallManager, and various third-party tools, as shown in Figure 11-16, provide management functions for IP Telephony networks. This section proposes network management services required to support Cisco IP Telephony solutions.

Figure 11-16 *Network Management Tools for IP Telephony*

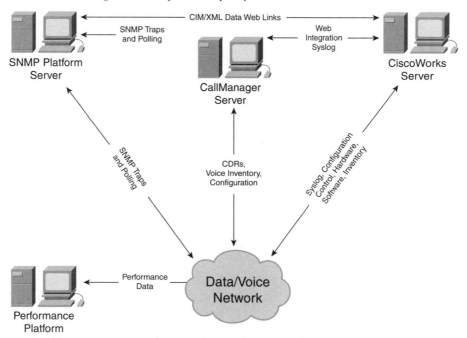

In addition to managing the routers and switches of the Cisco AVVID infrastructure, the CiscoWorks tools communicate with devices providing voice services, such as CallManager, Cisco Conference Connection, and Cisco Emergency Responder, which themselves might provide other voice management services.

CiscoWorks VoIP Health Monitor (VHM) proactively monitors Cisco voice servers and polls for reachability, interface status, environmental conditions (power supply, fan, and temperature), and application status. In addition to monitoring the voice server, VHM verifies the availability of key voice services by performing synthetic transactions, wherein the VHM server emulates the behavior of a Cisco IP Phone and performs a specific transaction. The value of synthetic transactions is that, by actually accessing these critical voice services, it is possible to verify that the services are available.

High Availability

Cisco AVVID IP Telephony is based on a distributed model, as shown in Figure 11-17, for high availability. CallManager clusters support CallManager redundancy. The gateways must support the capability to "re-home" to a secondary CallManager in the event that a primary CallManager fails, providing CallManager redundancy. This differs from call survivability in the event of a CallManager or network failure, where the call is routed to an alternate gateway, such as an MGCP gateway.

Figure 11-17 *High Availability for Voice*

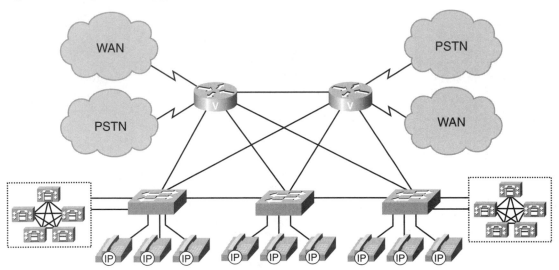

As with any capability within the network, you need to plan redundancy for critical components such as the CallManager and the associated gateway and infrastructure devices that support the voice network.

When deploying IP Telephony across a WAN with the centralized call processing model, you should take additional steps to ensure that data and voice services at the remote sites are highly available. SRST provides high availability for voice services only, by providing a subset of the call processing capabilities within the remote office router and enhancing the IP phones with the capability to "re-home" to the call processing functions in the local router if a WAN failure is detected.

If the WAN link to the branch office fails, as shown in Figure 11-18, or if some other event causes loss of connectivity to the CallManager cluster, the branch IP phones reregister with the branch router. The branch router queries the IP phones for their configuration and uses this information to build its own configuration automatically. The branch IP phones can then make and receive calls either internally or through the PSTN. The phone displays the message "CM fallback mode," and some advanced CallManager features are unavailable and are grayed out on the phone display.

When WAN connectivity to the central site is reestablished, the branch IP phones automatically reregister with the CallManager cluster and resume normal operation. The branch router deletes its information about the IP phones and reverts to its standard routing or gateway configuration.

Figure 11-18 *Remote Site Survivability*

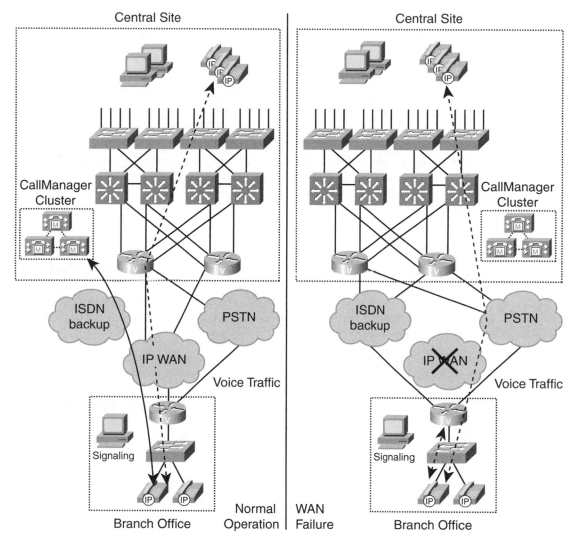

Voice Security

The subject of securing voice communications, which is always a very sensitive topic for today's communications architects, has received even more visibility recently as network convergence becomes the accepted design model. With the advent of IP Telephony, which uses IP data network devices for voice communication, the potential exists for malicious attacks on call-processing components and telephony applications.

To help safeguard against attacks, you should implement the same security precautions as in the rest of the enterprise network.

Securing the voice call processing platform and installed applications is perhaps the most vital step in securing Cisco AVVID networks.

Every enterprise should have a predefined security policy for all devices, applications, and users to follow. The strictness of the security policy depends on the level of caution required.

NOTE   For more information on securing VoIP see, "IP Communications Security Solution" at http://www.cisco.com/en/US/netsol/ns340/ns394/ns165/ns391/net_value_ proposition09186a00802327a8.html.

QoS Design Considerations

Voice, as a class of IP network traffic, has strict requirements concerning delay and delay variation (also known as jitter). Compared to most data, it is relatively tolerant of loss. To meet the requirements for voice traffic, the Cisco AVVID IP Telephony solution uses a wide range of IP QoS features, such as classification, queuing, congestion detection, traffic shaping, and compression.

The overall goal of QoS in the network is to be able to manage which applications are less likely to be affected by loss, delay, and jitter. When a network becomes congested, some traffic will be delayed or even, at times, lost. The goal is to give critical applications a higher priority for service so that they are least likely to be delayed or dropped in times of congestion. In many converged networks, voice is the most critical application. In others, voice might be used to opportunistically use bandwidth not required for data, and fall back to the PSTN in times of congestion.

When you configure campus QoS, you must consider

- **Trust boundary**—Define and enforce a trust boundary at the network edge. Classification should take place at the network edge, typically in the wiring closet or within the endpoints themselves.

- **Traffic classification**—Network design practice emphasizes that you should classify or mark traffic as close to the edge of the network as possible. Traffic class is a criterion for queue selection in the various queuing schemes used at interfaces within the campus switches and WAN devices. When you connect an IP phone using a single cable, the phone becomes the edge of the managed network. As the edge device, the IP phone can and should classify and mark traffic flows so that network QoS mechanisms can correctly handle the packets.

- **Interface queuing**—To guarantee voice quality, you must design for QoS and enable it within the campus infrastructure. By enabling QoS on campus switches, you can configure voice traffic to use separate queues, virtually eliminating the possibility of dropped voice packets as an interface buffer fills, and minimizing delay.

  Although network management tools might show that the campus network is not congested, QoS tools are still required to guarantee voice quality. Network management tools typically show only the average congestion over a relatively long sample time, minutes to tens of minutes. While useful, this average does not show the congestion peaks on a campus interface, which can occur in a period of seconds to tens of seconds.

  Transmit interface buffers within a campus tend to congest in small, finite intervals as a result of the bursty nature of network data traffic. When severe congestion occurs, any packets destined for that transmit interface are delayed or even dropped, thereby affecting voice quality. The way to prevent dropped voice traffic is to configure multiple queues on campus switches. Most Cisco Ethernet switches support the enhanced queuing services using multiple queues that can guarantee voice quality in the campus.

WAN QoS techniques depend on the speeds of the links. At speeds above 768 kbps, voice priority queuing is used to reduce jitter and possible packet loss if a burst of traffic oversubscribes a buffer. This queuing requirement is similar to the one for the LAN infrastructure.

In addition, the WAN requires traffic shaping for two reasons:

- To remain within the contracted traffic agreement with the ATM or Frame Relay network to avoid being policed and incurring dropped packets.

- To maintain comparable traffic speeds between sites linked to the Frame Relay or ATM network by different line speeds. For example, the headquarters site might use digital signature (DS)-3 and the other sites use DS-1, which can result in buffer overruns within the network and, thus, in packet loss. Traffic shaping helps prevent buffer overruns and packet loss.

In choosing from among the many available prioritization schemes, the major factors to consider include the type of traffic involved and the type of media on the WAN. For multiservice traffic over an IP WAN, Cisco recommends low-latency queuing (LLQ) for low-speed links. LLQ allows up to 64 traffic classes with the ability to specify, for example, strict priority queuing behavior for voice and interactive video, a minimum bandwidth for Systems Network Architecture (SNA) data and market data feeds, and weighted fair queuing (WFQ) for other traffic types.

Because wide-area bandwidth is often expensive, only low-speed circuits might be available or affordable when interconnecting remote sites. In these cases, it is important to achieve maximum bandwidth efficiencies by transmitting as many voice calls as possible over the low-speed link. Compression schemes, such as G.729, can compress a 64-kbps call into an 8-kbps payload. Cisco gateways and IP phones support a range of codecs that can improve bandwidth efficiency on these low-speed links in exchange for slightly increased delay.

NOTE	You should not use G.729 codecs with conferencing applications. With G.729 codecs, the quality of any conversation between multiple parties is unacceptable when more than one person talks at one time.

You can increase link efficiency further by using compressed Real-Time Transport Protocol (CRTP) on selected links. This protocol compresses a 40-byte IP, UDP, and RTP header to approximately 2 to 4 bytes across an appropriately configured link.

IP Telephony places strict requirements on IP packet loss, packet delay, and delay variation (or jitter). Therefore, you need to enable most of the QoS mechanisms available on Cisco switches and routers throughout the network.

Table 11-4 indicates the requirements for each device that forms the network infrastructure. The features are key components of the infrastructure. If the infrastructure is not planned properly, adding voice to an improperly planned network will have a disastrous effect on the voice quality. In a small- to medium-sized network, the features listed in the figure are not as critical as they are for a large enterprise. You should implement each feature to provide a reliable quality voice and integrated data network.

Table 11-4   *Recommended Device Features*

	Campus Access Switch	Campus Distribution/ Core Switch	WAN Aggregation Router	Branch Router	Branch Switch
Inline Power	√				√
Multiple Queues	√	√	√	√	√
802.1p/802.1Q	√	√	√	√	√
Traffic Classification		√	√	√	
Traffic Reclassification		√	√	√	
Traffic Shaping			√		
Link Efficiency			√	√	
Fast Link Convergence	√				

Summary

In this chapter, you learned the following key points:

- The Cisco IP Telephony solution includes infrastructure components of the traditional IP network, as well as devices dedicated to voice.
- Cisco CallManager provides call processing for the Cisco AVVID IP Telephony solution.
- Voice, video, and data gateway protocols are required for call routing and interoperability on a network that supports IP Telephony.
- Cisco CallManager provides access to a variety of media resources, software- or hardware-based entities that perform media processing functions on the voice data streams to which it is connected.
- The primary Cisco IP Telephony applications include Cisco Customer Response Solution, Cisco Conference Connection, Cisco IP Contact Center, and Cisco Unity.
- A Cisco CallManager cluster might contain up to eight servers, of which a maximum of six provide call processing to support up to 10,000 phones.
- The single-site IP Telephony model offers ability to use the PSTN for all off-net calls. In the LAN environment, sufficient bandwidth exists for voice traffic, and the bandwidth allocations are less of a concern.
- In a centralized call processing system, Cisco CallManagers are centrally located at the hub or aggregation site, with no local call processing at the branch or remote office location.
- In the distributed call processing model, each Cisco CallManager cluster has its own set of resources and connects to the other clusters within the network via intercluster trunk links.
- You might deploy a single Cisco CallManager cluster across multiple sites that are connected by an IP WAN with QoS features enabled.
- IP Telephony places strict requirements on the network infrastructure. The network must provide sufficient bandwidth and quick convergence after network failures or changes.
- The network management, high availability, security, and QoS intelligent network services extend to incorporate voice-specific attributes.

References

Voice Solutions. http://www.cisco.com/en/US/netsol/networking_solutions_index.html.

Cisco CallManager Clusters. http://www.cisco.com/univercd/cc/td/doc/product/voice/ip_tele/network/dgclustr.htm.

White paper. "Architecture for Voice, Video, and Integrated Data." http://www.cisco.com/warp/public/cc/so/neso/vvda/iptl/avvid_wp.htm.

Westbay Engineers Limited. http://www.erlang.com.

Cisco Voice Products. http://www.cisco.com/en/US/products/sw/voicesw/

Product Summary

Table 11-5 provides a brief overview of some of the products available from Cisco Systems that relate to the technologies discussed in this chapter. For a more detailed breakdown of the Cisco product line, visit http://www.cisco.com/en/US/products/index.html.

Table 11-5 *Cisco VoIP Products*

Product Class	Product	Specifications
IP Phones	Cisco IP Phone 7970G Cisco IP Phone 7960G Cisco IP Phone 7940G Cisco IP Phone 7912G Cisco IP Phone 7910G Cisco IP Phone 7905G Cisco IP Phone 7902G	Cisco IP Phones are designed to enhance productivity and address the specific needs of the variety of users in your organization. Cisco IP Phones 7970G, 7960G, 7940G, 7912G, and 7905G feature pixel-based liquid crystal display (LCD) displays, offering dynamic soft keys that guide a user through call features and functions, and can support additional information services including Extensible Markup Language (XML) capabilities. XML-based services can be customized to provide users with access to a diverse array of information such as stock quotes, employee extension numbers, or any web-based content.
Voice Gateways	7500 7400 7200 3600 2600 1700 800 AS5800 AS5400 AS5300	Cisco routers and Access servers can function as Voice Gateways when installed with the proper feature cards and IOS images.

Table 11-5   *Cisco VoIP Products (Continued)*

Product Class	Product	Specifications
Voice Servers	Cisco Media Convergence Servers	Cisco Media Convergence Servers provide highly available server platforms to host IP communications applications. These platforms address enterprise customer requirements for Cisco CallManager installations from 2 to 10,000 IP phones within a single Cisco CallManager cluster as well as providing platforms for Cisco Conference Connection, Cisco Emergency Responder, Cisco IPCC Express, IP Interactive Voice Response (IP IVR), Cisco Personal Assistant, Cisco Queue Manager, and Cisco Unity.

NOTE   For more information on Cisco Voice products, visit http://www.cisco.com/en/US/products/sw/voicesw/.

Standards and Specification Summary

Request For Comments (RFCs) can be downloaded from the following website: http://www.rfc-editor.org/rfc.html.

- RFC 3261 SIP, "Session Initiation Protocol."
- RFC 3550 RTP, "A Transport Protocol for Real-Time Applications."
- RFC 3435, "Media Gateway Control Protocol (MGCP) Version 1.0."

Review Questions

Answer the following questions to test your comprehension of the topics discussed in this chapter. Refer to Appendix A, "Answers to Review Questions," to check your answers.

1   What are the telephony components found within the Cisco IP Telephony architecture?

2   What is the role of gateways in the Cisco IP Telephony architecture?

3   What types of gateways are defined in the Cisco IP Telephony architecture?

4   What is the role of Cisco CallManager?

5 How many users can be serviced by a single CallManager cluster?

6 What is the overall goal of an IP Telephony network?

7 Gateway selection depends upon what requirements?

8 What gateway protocols does the Cisco CallManager support?

9 What is a media resource?

10 What is the definition of transcoding?

11 What is the function of a unicast conference bridge?

12 What are the two types of conference bridges?

13 What are the components of a CallManager cluster?

14 What are some general guidelines for CallManager deployment?

15 In a small-scale cluster deployment, how many servers should you deploy?

16 How many CallManagers can you deploy in a large-scale cluster design?

17 What is the maximum number of IP phones that can register with a single CallManager?

18 How does the device weighting factor affect the CallManager solution?

19 What are some possible design characteristics of a single-site model?

20 What are the three possible gateway solutions?

21 What are the primary benefits of the single-site model?

22 What is the primary advantage of a distributed call processing solution?

23 What is the role of a gatekeeper in the distributed model?

24 Describe the guidelines you should follow when implementing the local failover model for CallManager clustering across multiple sites.

25 What questions should you ask when designing an infrastructure to support voice?

26 What are two Layer 2 alternatives to a CallManager VoIP-based network?

27 What formula should you use to calculate the bandwidth that voice streams consume?

28 What are the two categories of control traffic that traverse the WAN?

29 What is traffic engineering, as it applies to traditional voice networks?

30 What should you consider when configuring campus QoS?

Case Study: OCSIC Bottling Company

The purpose of this case study is to practice the key design skills discussed in this chapter. The project is to revisit the earlier design for the OCSIC Bottling Company, and ensure that the IP Telephony solution provides the required voice services. For each identified component of the design, we are required to provide justification for our decision. The justification will provide an explanation for the options considered and the reason behind choosing the selected option.

The first task is to design an IP Telephony network for the company. Table 11-6 summarizes the design decisions that the enterprise made to meet their requirements.

Table 11-6   *Design Decisions for the IP Telephony Network*

Design Questions	Decision	Justification
Is centralized or distributed call processing most appropriate?	Distributed call processing.	Distributed call processing enables local call processing, providing the same level of features and capabilities whether the IP WAN is available or not.
How many CallManager servers will you deploy? In what locations? Which server will be the publisher? Which servers will be the subscribers? What other servers would you include in the cluster?	The company selected a multisite telephony solution for the headquarters campus location. The solution includes the following components: Distributed Cisco CallManager Eight Cisco CallManager servers including four subscribers, two backups, one publisher, and one TFTP server.	The CallManager servers can provide the call processing capability and back-up features required for a network of this size.
What gateways will you deploy? Where will the gateways be located? What function will each gateway serve?	Each district and plant has a voice-enabled router with a two-port multiflex trunk card. Headquarters uses Catalyst 6500 T1 ports for access to the PSTN.	Each voice-enabled router routes traffic between the campus voice network and WAN facilities.

continues

Table 11-6 *Design Decisions for the IP Telephony Network (Continued)*

Design Questions	Decision	Justification
What QoS strategy will you deploy to support the solution?	Implement QoS at the campus and enterprise edge. Voice will be prioritized over all other traffic priority five. Voice signaling traffic will be given a priority of four.	Classification and marking, congestion avoidance, congestion management, traffic conditioning, signaling, and link-efficiency mechanisms are all required.
What DSP resources are required for the solution?	Each voice-enabled router has the appropriate DSPs to terminate 24 voice calls. Each T1 card on the headquarters Catalyst 6500 switches has DSPs.	DSPs provide the appropriate resources to terminate 24 G.711 calls.
What transcoding resources are required for the solution?	Conferencing is done from the Catalyst 6500 located in the headquarters campus network. Transcoding resources are located in the headquarters campus network.	Transcoding supports conferencing across the headquarters campus network.
What are the network bandwidth and traffic engineering considerations?	All district sites have a T1 to the PSTN. All regional sites have a T1 to the PSTN. The corporate office has 14 T1s to the PSTN (288 trunks for 5700 people). Voice will use G.729 codecs in the WAN, and G.711 codecs for calls within each site. All devices can use either G.711 or G.729 as requested.	The traffic engineering analysis incorporates sufficient bandwidth for the anticipated call volume.

Figure 11-19 shows a CallManager design for the North American plants.

Figure 11-19 *CallManager Design*

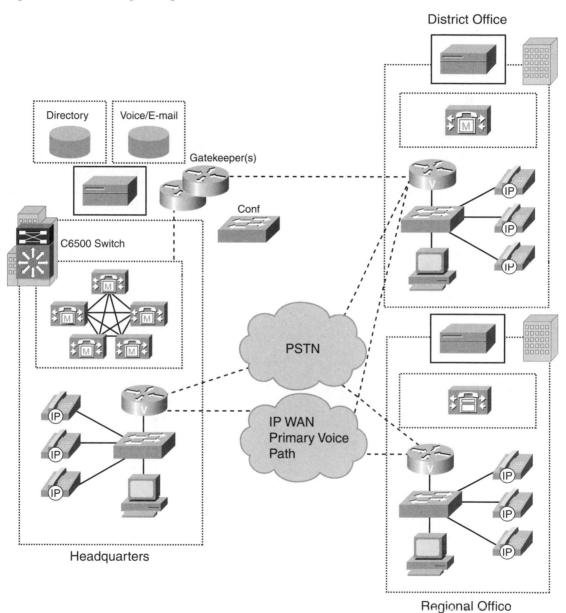

After completing this chapter, you will be able to

- Review the Cisco content networking solutions
- Design content network solutions

CHAPTER 12

Designing Content Networking Solutions

Content networking is the replication and placement of copies of content closer to the user or groups of users through caching and Content Delivery Network (CDN) technologies. Caching is the process by which content is copied and delivered to the user upon demand. CDN refers to the positioning of content closer to the user in advance of the user's request. These technologies support applications, such as corporate communication and e-learning, by providing services such as live broadcast, video and audio on demand (media on demand), and rebroadcast.

This chapter describes the components of a content networking solution, given specific content networking requirements. It also defines how to design a content networking solution to support e-commerce, web content delivery, and streaming services.

Reviewing the Content Networking Solution

More and more applications require large volumes of content to be delivered over the network. Streaming video, e-learning, and graphic-intensive websites can place a strain on an enterprise's network resources. A content networking architecture comprises several components that allow an enterprise to optimize website performance and content delivery.

Content networking extends an Internet Protocol (IP) service infrastructure to enable content services opportunities for web-driven enterprises. Content networking makes networks more efficient in delivering the content required by many applications.

This section identifies the necessary components of a content networking solution, given specific content networking requirements. This section discusses the following:

- Enterprise content networking requirements
- Content networking architecture
- Content caching
- Content switching

- Content routing
- Content distribution and management
- Intelligent networking services integration

Enterprise Content Networking Requirements

As the data (content) being accessed over the network increases in size and complexity, content networking becomes a requirement for your network. A content networking solution supports the following:

- Bandwidth optimization
- Server scalability
- Response-time reduction
- Large-scale deployment of rich content, such as video or audio

This section identifies enterprise requirements for content networking.

Users access web content more and more frequently. In addition, the content being delivered continues to increase in size and complexity. With the increase in activity and content size, enterprises can experience bandwidth bottlenecks, overloaded servers, and degraded response times. New applications, such as broadcast video and media-on-demand, can place an untenable strain on network resources.

Figure 12-1 demonstrates the difficulty of transmitting data from a corporate headquarters to a branch office. The bandwidth available at the point-of-origin inside corporate headquarters is more than sufficient to handle the data traffic requirements for any application. However, as the data moves to the destination, the available bandwidth begins to decrease to the point where network congestion can hamper application performance. However, there is sufficient bandwidth at the destination network. Content networking can address this issue in several ways:

- Moving content closer to the users reduces bandwidth requirements over the WAN or Internet and improves response time.

- Offloading server content, load balancing, and redundancy allow enterprises to scale server availability without necessarily increasing the number of servers.

- Distributing content to multiple locations in a controlled manner can enable new applications without overstressing the available network resources.

Content networking supports rich-media-intensive, distributed e-business applications for both live and on-demand streaming application support.

Figure 12-1 *Enterprise Content Networking Optimizes Bandwidth*

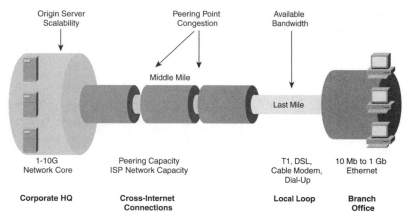

Content Networking Architecture

The Cisco content networking solutions include content edge delivery (caching), content switching, content routing, and content delivery and management. This section describes the purpose of each component of the content networking architecture.

The content networking architecture recommended by Cisco is made up of five components:

- **Content caching**—Caches select content from origin servers, and deliver specific content to a requesting user.

- **Content switching**—Provides a front end for web server farms and cache clusters, performing functions such as load balancing and availability.

- **Content routing**—Directs a user request to the optimal resource within a network based on user-defined policies, such as rules for specific content, availability of content, health or current loads for web servers or caches, and various other network conditions.

- **Content distribution and management**—Provides the mechanism for proactively distributing cacheable content from origin servers to content servers throughout the network.

- **Intelligent network services**—Enables content networking by using tightly integrated intelligent network services, such as high availability, security, quality of service (QoS), and IP multicast.

Content Caching

A content engine (CE) caches copies of data from origin servers, allowing the content to be served locally. A CE can be deployed in transparent mode, proxy mode, or reverse proxy mode. This section describes the content caching components of a Cisco content networking solution.

Caching is a demand-based replication and storage of cacheable content for the purpose of serving that same content to users making subsequent requests for it. Prime candidates for caching are typically static application data associated with a file type and file extension, such as

- **Graphics files**— .gif, .jpeg, .bmp
- **Compressed files**— .zip, .gz, .tar
- **Document files**— .txt, .pdf
- **Multimedia files**— .avi, .mov, .mpeg, .wav8

CEs store or cache copies of content from origin servers. The CE, rather than the origin server, can then process user requests reducing both network traffic and server processing. Web objects are typically cached, rather than entire web pages. Content engines can be proactively populated with specific content or simply allowed to cache requested content automatically.

Figure 12-2 shows a CE caching content in a location closer to end users than the origin server.

Figure 12-2 *Content Caching*

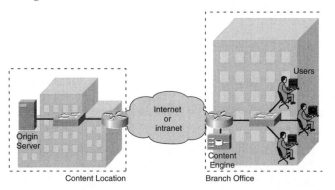

Content caching can be accomplished anywhere, either at the central site or at any remote site. At the central site, caching is deployed at the data center or within a perimeter LAN. Typically, caching takes place at the remote site, close to users.

The three deployment models for content caching include the following:

- Transparent and proxy
- Application and browser
- Reverse proxy

With each caching mechanism, you can specify how content is stored and when it is cleared from the content server.

Transparent Caching Deployment

With *transparent caching*, as shown in Figure 12-3, a user request for content (usually through a web browser) is redirected by a router or switch to a CE. (In Figure 12-3, the router is using the Web Caching Communication Protocol [WCCP] to enable content routing based on user request.) On the first request for a specific piece of content, the CE initiates a request to the origin server to retrieve the content, and then stores it locally and returns the content to the user making the request. On subsequent requests for that same piece of content, the content can be served locally, eliminating the need for a request to travel to the origin server. The CEs deployed in transparent mode are placed close to the users making the requests.

Figure 12-3 *Caching Deployment: Transparent*

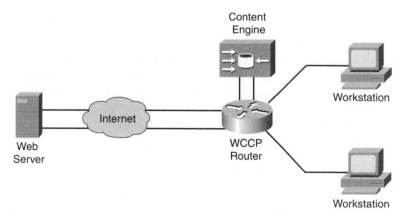

To deploy transparent caching, consider these best practices:

- Place the cache at the network edge between the user and the servers, close to the user population.

- Place the cache in the path of outbound network traffic at the network edge.
- Understand the network topology and traffic patterns.

Proxy Caching Deployment

Proxy caching, as shown in Figure 12-4, uses the CE as a proxy for all content requests. The user's browser is typically modified to send requests directly to the CE instead of the origin server. The CE then forwards the request to the origin server, if necessary, or serves the content locally. CEs in proxy mode are placed close to the users making the requests, but far enough along the servers' traffic path to intercept all such traffic. Typically, these CEs are placed in the edge, either at a WAN or Internet access point.

Figure 12-4 *Caching Deployment: Proxy*

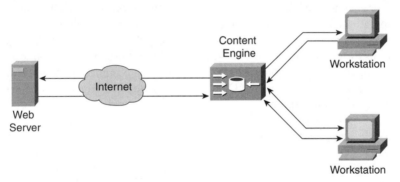

In proxy mode, end-user web browsers need to be explicitly configured to the IP address or host name of the CE, and no need exists for additional hardware, such as Layer 4 switches or WCCP-enabled routers, to intercept user requests, as in transparent caching. Enterprises are normally interested in deploying transparent network caching, but some enterprises might have a legacy requirement for a proxy (nontransparent) cache.

To deploy proxy caching, consider these best practices:

- Position the cache at the Internet edge.
- Manually configure client browsers to send all requests to the proxy. The proxy acts on behalf of the client.

Reverse Proxy Caching Deployment

With *reverse proxy caching*, as shown in Figure 12-5, static content from a server is offloaded onto a CE. Requests destined for the server are directed to the CE, which serves the content locally, freeing the server from processing multiple requests for static content. CEs in reverse proxy mode are placed close to the servers being offloaded, typically in an internal server farm or an edge server farm providing outbound web or e-commerce services.

Figure 12-5 *Caching Deployment: Reverse Proxy*

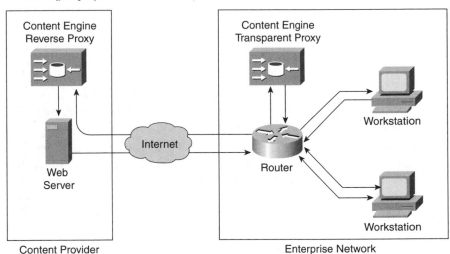

Use reverse proxy on CEs that are deployed in front of web server farms to increase the server farm capacity and improve website performance.

To deploy reverse proxy caching, consider these best practices:

- Position the reverse proxy in front of web server farms to minimize the transaction processing for the backend infrastructure.
- Deploy reverse proxies in data centers and perimeter LANs for Internet-facing web server farms.

Content Switching

Content switches provide load balancing and availability features for multiple content or application servers. This section describes the content switching components of a Cisco content networking solution.

Content switching, as shown in Figure 12-6, intelligently load balances traffic across servers or CEs based on the availability of the content and the load on the server.

Figure 12-6 *Content Switching*

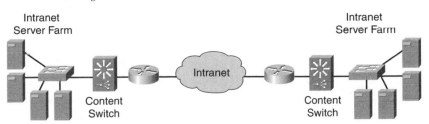

Content switches provide these services:

- Local and global load balancing of user requests across server farms or CE clusters to improve performance, scalability, and content availability
- Policy-based web traffic direction based on full visibility of uniform resource locator (URLs), host tags, and cookies.
- Enhanced denial-of-service (DoS) protection, cache and firewall load balancing, and flash-crowd management. (Flash-crowd refers to unpredictable, event-driven traffic surges that swamp servers and disrupt site services.)

With content switches, multiple web or application servers can be represented with a single IP address. The content switch load-balancing algorithms intelligently distribute content requests based on round-robin, weighted round-robin, least connections, weighted least connections, Hypertext Transfer Protocol (HTTP) header content, or URL. The content switch performs server health checks to verify content and server availability.

Content switches are "smart" devices with sophisticated load-balancing capabilities and content-acceleration intelligence. Use them to add scalability to large networks.

Content Routing

Content routing, as shown in Figure 12-7, redirects an end-user request to the best site based on a set of metrics such as delay, topology, or server load, and a set of policies such as location of content. This section describes the content routing components of a content networking solution.

Figure 12-7 *Content Routing*

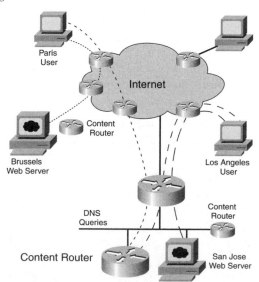

Cisco routers and switches incorporate WCCP software to enable content-routing capabilities. Additionally, Cisco offers content routers specifically designed to support large-scale mirrored websites.

Content-routing routes user requests to the replicated content site (typically a mirror site) that can serve them most quickly and efficiently. The content-routing software redirects a user request to the closest (best) replicated content site, based on network delay, using a software process called boomerang. The content-routing software load balances up to 500 sites for each domain it is configured to support.

A content router can be deployed on a network in two different ways:

- It can be set up in direct mode.
- It can be set up in WCCP mode.

Both deployments involve setting up a content routing agent at each content site within each domain you want the content router to support. Content routing agents are machines (such as CEs) that have been configured to interact with the content router.

Direct Mode Content Routing

In direct mode, the content router is configured as the authoritative Domain Name System server for the fully qualified domain name being routed. For example, to route Cisco.com, the address record in the primary DNS server for Cisco.com is changed to a name server record pointing to the content router. All requests for the IP address of Cisco.com are handled by the content router and its content routing agents. When a request arrives, a specific number of agents respond at exactly the same time. This is called a DNS race, because the agent that sent the first response received is the winner of the DNS race and is, therefore, the site to which the user will connect. Figure 12-8 provides an overview of the direct mode content-routing process.

Figure 12-8 *Overview of Direct Mode Content Routing*

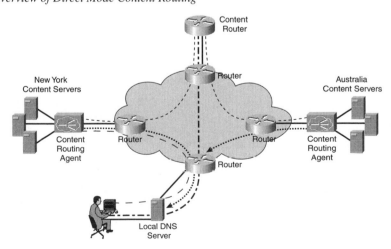

Direct mode content routing follows this process:

1 A user requests a connection from a web browser or other service.

2 A DNS request is sent to the content router.

3 The content router forwards the request to content routing agents.

4 Agents simultaneously send responses back to the local DNS server. The first response through the network contains the IP address of the best site.

5 The user connects to the best site.

WCCP Mode Content Routing

WCCP, as shown in Figure 12-9, provides the mechanism for content routers and other WCCP-enabled routers and switches to redirect user requests to the appropriate destination.

Figure 12-9 *WCCP*

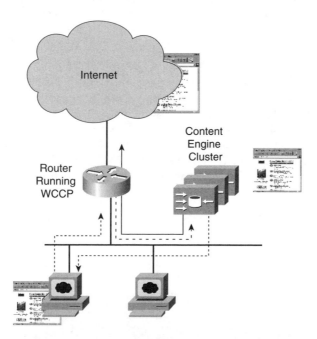

WCCP includes load balancing, scaling, fault tolerance, and service-assurance (failsafe) mechanisms; its process is described as follows:

1 A user requests a connection from a web browser or other service.

2 The WCCP-enabled router intercepts and analyzes the DNS request from the client and forwards it to the content router. Based on TCP port number, the content router determines if it should transparently redirect it to a CE. Access lists can be applied to control which requests are redirected.

3 If a CE does not have the requested content, it sets up a separate TCP connection to the end server to retrieve the content. The content returns to, and is stored on, the CE.

4 The CE sends the content to the client. Upon subsequent requests for the same content, the CE transparently fulfills the requests from its local storage.

Content Distribution and Management

Content distribution and management, as shown in Figure 12-10, provides the mechanism for importing, replicating, and managing content throughout the enterprise network. This section describes the Cisco content distribution and management components of a content networking solution.

Figure 12-10 *Distribution and Management of Content*

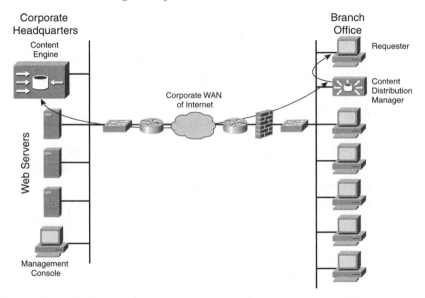

The Cisco Content Distribution Manager (CDM) is a web-browser–based tool that provides the administrative function for content networking. With the CDM, you can do the following:

- Configure and monitor CEs.
- Import and preview media.
- Generate media URLs for access from websites.
- Set maximum bandwidth usage over the WAN from the CDM to the remote CEs.
- Set maximum LAN bandwidth usage from the CEs to end-user desktops.
- Schedule content distribution by time of day and day of week, allowing content replication to occur during off-peak hours.
- Capture usage and billing data

The CDM resides at the branch office data center. Client requests for content are sent first to the CDM, which redirects the request to the most appropriate CE.

Content management is used to automatically import, maintain copies, and configure content at the edge of the network. The CDM maintains a hierarchy of CEs. This allows them to replicate content to CEs lower in the hierarchy. Replication is performed without waiting for the entire content to be received at one location before distribution to the next location begins.

The Self-Organizing Distributed Architecture (SODA) is a Cisco technology allowing content networking devices to self-organize into a single, cooperating system. The CDM defines the network policies and then automatically stores the SODA network information, building routing tables for specific content. When a device is added to the network, it automatically configures itself in the network based on the network topology and content requirements.

Intelligent Network Services Integration

Content networking requires the support of intelligent networking services. This section explains how to integrate intelligent networking services to support content networking solutions.

When implementing a content networking solution, these Cisco intelligent services should be integrated:

- **High availability**—Some of the content networking devices, like content switches and routers, are used to provide high availability for content. Redundant CEs, switches, and routers can further ensure availability for the most critical content.

- **Security**—The content being served can be highly sensitive, so in addition to the security features implemented throughout the network, you should take additional care to secure the content networking devices themselves.

- **QoS**—When content networking involves the delivery of delay-sensitive data, such as audio or video, QoS features allow such traffic to be given priority over other data traffic.

- **IP multicast**—When content networking is used to facilitate simultaneous delivery of streaming media, IP multicast must be implemented throughout the network to support the broadcast requirements.

Designing Content Networking Solutions

Cisco content networking solutions enable enterprises to build networks that can deliver e-commerce, web content delivery, and streaming media. Content networking solutions give enterprises control in allocating site resources for effective utilization.

Enterprises can deploy end-to-end content networking solutions that enable Internet data centers and branch sites to provide content and delivery services.

This section describes how to design a content networking solution to support e-commerce, web content delivery, and streaming services. This includes the following topics:

- Content networking design considerations
- Content networking solutions for web content delivery
- Content networking solutions for e-commerce
- Content networking solutions for streaming media

Content Networking Design Considerations

When planning to implement a content networking solution, consider the following:

- **Existing topology**—Before placing your content networking devices, consider the existing topology. Make sure that where your design redirects traffic for content purposes does not cause a break in the existing topology.

  For example, the existing network might have asymmetric traffic path possibilities. When you introduce a content switch or router, make sure that you do not force traffic to travel on the less favorable path. Ensure that you place redirection devices in locations that guarantee that all required traffic will reach the redirection point before traversing the WAN or Internet.

- **Compatibility with high availability**—Make sure that your content networking devices function properly with existing high-availability services.

  For example, make sure that a content switch will still be accessed when a router failover occurs, and that load-balanced devices are all configured to redirect content requests to the same locations.

- **Adequate capacity**—Make sure that your design provides sufficient capacity to avoid introducing undesirable effects.

  For example, when deciding how many CEs to install for a particular application, make sure that the processing and storage capabilities of the CEs are sufficient to handle the requests and to cache frequently requested content for a reasonable length of time (at least 24 and preferably 72 hours).

- **Caching**—Consider three important parameters when determining the sizing required for a particular cache installation:

  — Number of transactions per second required—Identifies the amount of HTTP traffic

  — Number of simultaneous connections—Defines the total number of HTTP flows that the cache will see at any single point in time

  — Size of objects—Determines the amount of disk storage required, and the object hold time

To allow a cache to function effectively and reduce the amount of network bandwidth, the minimum cache storage time should be between 24 and 72 hours. The longer objects remain on disk, the larger the hit rate, but the larger the storage requirements. Sizing the disk requirements is a function of the number of transactions per second (TPS), average object size in bytes, and the expected cache hit rate in bytes. Use this formula to determine the cache storage required for 24 hours:

Average TPS * Average object size (bytes) * Number of seconds in 24 hours * (1 − expected cache hit rate [bytes]) / 1,000,000,000

Table 12-1 describes the recommended locations for deploying caching on the network.

Table 12-1 *Content Networking Design Consideration: Caching*

Location	Environment	Transparent	Proxy (Legacy)	Reverse Proxy
Data center	Server farm			X
Campus	Server farm			X
Campus	Remote access	X		
Campus	WAN module	X		
Campus	VPN module	X		
Remote edge	Egress point	X	X	

Content Networking Solutions for Web Content Delivery

A content networking solution for web content delivery incorporates CEs to cache content closer to the users and offload internal web servers. Content switches also provide load balancing, and WCCP-enabled routers provide traffic redirection. This section describes enterprise content networking requirements for web content delivery.

A content networking implementation for web content delivery should take into account access to both internal and external web servers throughout the enterprise. The example implementation shown in Figure 12-11 includes these elements:

- **Caching**—CEs in transparent mode are placed at the edge of the remote offices to cache content originating from the headquarters' web servers or over the Internet. CEs in transparent and/or proxy mode are placed at the Internet edge in the headquarters' site, with another cluster of CEs in reverse proxy mode placed in the server farm to offload the internal web servers.

- **Content switching**—Because the caching requirements at the remote offices are minimal, no content switch is required. The clusters of CEs at the server farm and Internet edge each have an associated content switch to perform load balancing and manage redundancy.

- **Content routing**—WCCP is configured on selected Building Access or Building Distribution routers or switches at all sites to perform redirection of content requests to the appropriate CE or content switch.

Figure 12-11 *Web Content Delivery*

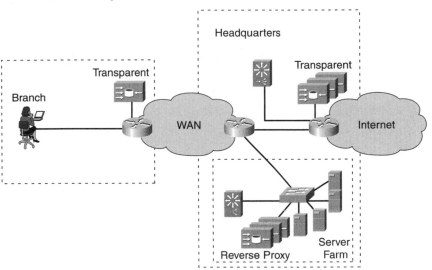

Example: Web Content Delivery

A company that is a health care provider requires the network to be available 24 hours a day, 7 days a week, with no exceptions. The company supports complex health care applications, including clinical information systems, financial information systems, and the Picture Archive and Communications System. The company is heavily regulated within the United States.

The company serves 6 of the top 10 health care systems, 22 public health institutions, and more than 300 university teaching facilities in the United States. It also operates acute care institutions, clinics, and hospitals worldwide.

The company's goal is to accelerate content delivery for customers and accelerate the delivery of Internet and intranet content for employees located at their headquarters.

Web Content Delivery Solution

The company solution, shown in Figure 12-12, deployed CEs at customer sites as part of its managed service offerings, which include a web-based order processing and registration application and a hospital scheduling application. Customers that outsource these applications deploy a CE at the customer premises. The CE supports specific Java-based health care applications. The CE at the customer site means that a customer downloads the applet once for all users to access.

Figure 12-12 *Example Web Content Delivery Network*

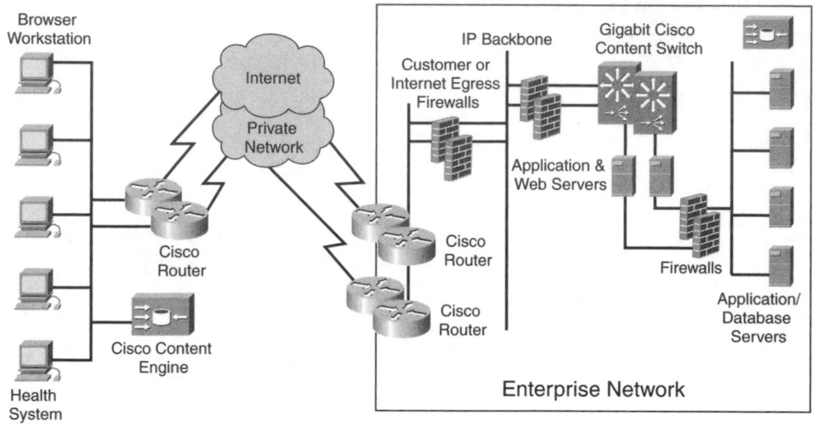

At the company's headquarters, CEs were deployed on the campus network. The content is then delivered to the LAN, which accelerates content delivery and saves WAN bandwidth.

The company network comprises redundant Cisco 3500 switches and redundant Cisco Catalyst 6500 switches. Everything within the environment is redundant, including the switch fabric back to the Cisco content switches, firewalls, and routers, across a private WAN and out to a Cisco router at the customer site.

Content Networking Solutions for E-Commerce

A content networking solution for e-commerce will typically incorporate caching and content switching. A special consideration for e-commerce is session persistence, or stickiness. This section describes enterprise content networking requirements for e-commerce.

Businesses using e-commerce need to deliver rapid transaction response time and manage peak-period volume levels, whether from seasonal increases in traffic or from unexpected surges in customer demand. Customers will return to e-commerce sites that offer consistently high levels of reliability, and they will avoid sites that deliver slow response times, difficult shopping experiences, or failed attempts to make purchases. A key component in ensuring that e-commerce sites remain open for business requires support for persistent, "sticky" network connections between customers and e-commerce servers; this prevents shopping carts from becoming lost before purchase transactions are completed.

The content networking solution for e-commerce, as shown in Figure 12-13, includes these components:

- **Caching**—A cluster of CEs is placed in the perimeter LAN containing the outbound-facing web and e-commerce servers. These CEs are deployed in reverse proxy mode to offload content from the servers.

- **Content switching**—Redundant content switches are used to load balance, and direct traffic to the appropriate CE.

Figure 12-13 *E-Commerce*

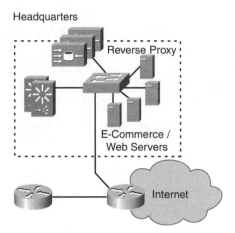

Headquarters

Reverse Proxy

E-Commerce /
Web Servers

Internet

When users are connected to a server, the content switch ensures that they stay connected to a single server for the duration of their transaction using "cookies" embedded in the user's request. The only reliable way to maintain sticky connections is to use cookies to identify individual customers. Content switches can read the entire cookie to identify the user and route the request to the correct server.

Example: E-Commerce

In the United Kingdom, a one-day event was staged to raise money for charities around the world. The goal was to end poverty and social injustice. The group sponsoring the event wanted to build a reliable e-commerce website that would enable it to effectively collect donations online during a TV broadcast. The website had to provide 100% availability, and the ability to handle extremely heavy traffic during the event. Requirements for the web were as follows:

- Provide 100% availability with a response time of less than seven seconds
- Process up to 200 credit-card transactions per second
- Handle forecasted peaks in traffic (440 hits per second, 75 kb average downloaded page size)

E-Commerce Solution

The group's solution deployed Oracle database servers and web server software, along with real-time authentication software. The group implemented Cisco content switches that could process up to 200 credit-card transactions per second, and Cisco Catalyst switches.

The Cisco content switches were used to front-end 19 web servers. The group used the intelligent keepalive capabilities of the Cisco content switches to provide 100-percent availability.

Content Networking Solutions for Streaming Media

A content networking solution for streaming media typically incorporates the entire range of content networking devices. The content distribution manager is the central management device for both media-on-demand and broadcast streaming media. This section describes the design of content networking solutions to support streaming media.

Applications, such as e-learning and corporate communications, frequently involve broadcasting media streams that are to be accessed simultaneously by multiple users throughout the network. The content networking solution for broadcasting streaming media, as shown in Figure 12-14, includes these components:

- **CDM**—The CDM enables you to configure bandwidth and distribution settings such that the streaming content will not interfere with other network traffic. It is also the central control point where the CEs that will carry the broadcast media are identified. The CDM is typically located in the server farm.

- **CE**—The CEs stream live or on-demand content to the desktop. A user logs on to a web page or application to access the high-bandwidth media over the LAN.

- **Event capture and delivery**—The Cisco IP/TV broadcast server and control server can capture and deliver live events.

- **IP multicast**—Multicast technology makes it possible for organizations to deliver live broadcasts to desktops and meeting rooms. IP multicast must be configured throughout the network to enable broadcast.

Figure 12-14 *Broadcast Streaming Media*

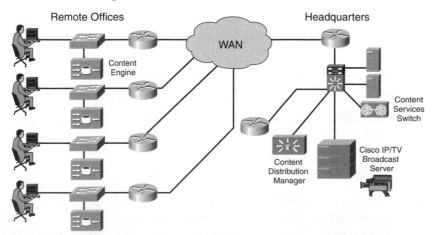

A media-on-demand solution typically involves the distribution of large video and/or audio files. The content networking solution for media on demand, as shown in Figure 12-15, includes these components:

- **CDM**—Media (content) is imported into the CDM and then replicated to the CEs according to a schedule and bandwidth constraints set by the administrator.

- **CEs**—The CEs serve the content on receiving a request from a user.

Figure 12-15 *Media on Demand*

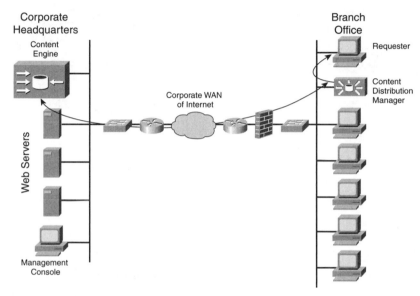

Example: Streaming Media

A major financial institution wants to deliver timely corporate information, including corporate messages and company initiatives, through a sophisticated video content delivery system. It wants a network-based system that would enable it to distribute high-quality video worldwide over IP (instead of videotape). Core requirements for a system include the ability to stage content, fully control content distribution worldwide, and limit the need for administration at remote sites.

Streaming Media Solution

As shown in Figure 12-16, the company deployed an IP-based television service for employees worldwide. Components of the content delivery network included Cisco CDM, Cisco CE, content switches, and content routers. The CEs are deployed in major offices throughout the world, although the Cisco CDM is located at the main office in Europe. The Cisco content switches provide load balancing between the CEs and the CDM. The content router is deployed for redundancy to provide redirection, speed, and performance. All video clips are stored on the company intranet and, when activated, are streamed via unicast.

Figure 12-16 *Streaming Media Network Example*

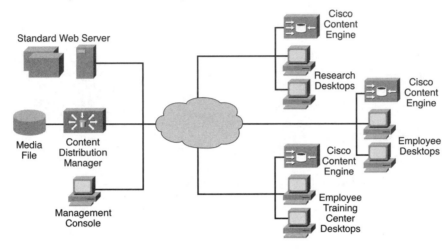

Summary

In this chapter, you learned the following key points:

- As the data (content) being accessed over the network increases in size and complexity, content networking becomes a requirement. Content networking supports

    — Bandwidth optimization

    — Server scalability

    — Response time reduction

    — Large-scale deployment of rich content, such as video or audio

- Content networking solutions include

    — Content edge delivery (caching)

    — Content switching

    — Content routing

    — Content delivery and management

- A CE caches copies of data from origin servers, allowing the content to be served locally. A CE can be deployed in transparent mode, proxy mode, or reverse proxy mode.

- Content switches provide load balancing and availability features for multiple content or application servers.

- Content routing redirects an end-user request to the best site based on a set of metrics, such as delay, topology, or server load and a set of policies, such as location of content.

- Content distribution management provides the mechanism for importing, replicating, and managing content throughout the enterprise network.

- Content networking requires the support of intelligent networking services such as high availability, security, QoS, and IP multicast.

- Make sure the content networking design does not interfere with the existing network topology or redundancy and that the solution is scaled sufficiently.

- A content networking solution for web content delivery incorporates CEs, content switches, and WCCP-enabled routers.

- A content networking solution for e-commerce typically incorporates caching and content switching. A special consideration for e-commerce is session persistence or stickiness.

- A content networking solution for streaming media typically incorporates the entire range of content networking devices. The content distribution manager is the central management device for both media-on-demand and broadcast streaming media.

References

White paper. "Accelerating Web Applications with Cisco Enterprise Content Delivery Networks." http://www.cisco.com/warp/public/cc/pd/cxsr/ces/prodlit/awace_wp.htm.

Technology Solutions—Content Networking. http://www.cisco.com/offer/tdm_home/content_network/index.shtml.

White paper. "Network Caching: Networking Challenges with Internet and Intranet Growth." http://www.cisco.com/warp/public/cc/pd/cxsr/500/tech/cds_wp.htm.

Content Networking Solutions for Large Enterprises. http://www.cisco.com/en/US/netsol/ns340/ns394/ns50/networking_solutions_packages_list.html.

Solutions Reference Network Design (SRND) Networking Solutions Design Guides. To locate these documents, perform the following:

Step 1 Go to http://www.cisco.com/.

Step 2 In the Search box, enter **SRND** and click **Go**. A list of SRND Networking Solutions Design Guides appears.

Step 3 Select the Networking Solutions Design Guide that meets your needs.

Product Summary

Table 12-2 provides a brief overview of some of the products available from Cisco Systems that relate to the technologies discussed in this chapter. For a more detailed breakdown of the Cisco product line, visit http://www.cisco.com/en/US/products/index.html.

Table 12-2 *Cisco Content Networking Products*

Product Class	Product	Specifications
Content Engines	7325 7320 565 510	Within the Cisco content networking solutions portfolio, the Cisco Application and Content Networking System (ACNS) software enables a variety of services that optimize delivery of web applications and content from the network edge to ensure enhanced speed, availability, and performance for users. ACNS software combines the technologies of transparent caching and enterprise content-delivery network (ECDN) for accelerated delivery of web objects, files, and streaming media from a single intelligent edge appliance, the Cisco CE.
Content switches	11500 Series	The Cisco CSS 11500 is available in three models—the standalone Cisco CSS 11501, the three-slot Cisco CSS 11503, and the six-slot Cisco CSS 11506. Both the CSS 11503 and CSS 11506 systems take advantage of the same high-performance, modular architecture and use the same set of I/O, Secure Sockets Layer (SSL), and session accelerator modules. Also, all three systems operate with the same WebNS software, enabling the Cisco CSS 11501, 11503, and 11506 to offer industry-leading content switching functionality within three compact, hardware platforms.
Content routers	4400 Series	The CR-4450 has three power supplies; two internal 18-gigabyte (GB) Ultra2 SCSI system drives; and one four-port 10BASE-T/100BASE-TX Ethernet/Fast Ethernet network interface.
Content Distribution Manager	4600 Series	The Cisco CDM configures network and device policy settings for edge node CE. Used to accelerate web content and save network bandwidth in a content networking architecture, the CDM can be easily integrated into existing network infrastructures. Deployed in an Enterprise or Service Provider Internet or extranet environment, the Cisco CDM and CEs provide transparent on-demand rich media streaming and static file delivery to standard PCs.
Content Switch Module	CSM 6500	The Cisco Content Switching Module (CSM) is a Catalyst 6500 line card that balances client traffic to farms of servers, firewalls, SSL devices, or Virtual Private Network (VPN) termination devices. The CSM provides a high-performance, cost-effective load-balancing solution for enterprise and Internet Service Provider (ISP) networks. The CSM meets the demands of high-speed Content Delivery Networks, tracking network sessions and server load conditions in real time and directing each session to the most appropriate server. Fault-tolerant CSM configurations maintain full state information, and provide true hitless failover required for mission-critical functions.

Standards and Specification Summary

Request For Comments (RFCs) can be downloaded from the following website: http://www.rfc-editor.org/rfc.html.

- RFC 3466, "A Model for Content Internetworking (CDI)"
- RFC 3568, "Known Content Network (CN) Request-Routing Mechanisms"
- RFC 3570, "Content Internetworking (CDI) Scenarios"

Review Questions

Answer the following questions to test your comprehension of the topics discussed in this chapter. Refer to Appendix A, "Answers to Review Questions," to check your answers.

1 What is content networking?

2 What components comprise the Cisco Content Networking solution?

3 What is the role of the Content Engine?

4 What is caching?

5 What are the three models for content caching?

6 Where does enterprise caching typically take place?

7 How does transparent caching work?

8 How does proxy caching work?

9 How does reverse proxy work?

10 Define content switching.

11 What services do content switches provide?

12 What is content routing?

13 What are the two modes a content router can be deployed in?

14 What is direct mode content routing?

15 Describe the Cisco Content Distribution and Management solution.

16 What are the Cisco intelligent solution components?

17 What are the three important parameters to consider when determining the sizing required for a particular cache installation?

18 What formula determines the cache storage required for 24 hours?

Case Study: OCSIC Bottling Company

The purpose of this case study is to practice the key design skills discussed in this chapter. The project is to revisit the earlier design for the OCSIC Bottling Company, and ensure that content networking solution provides fast access to data and reduces the load on the network between buildings at the headquarters' campus and between the headquarters office and the North American plants. For each identified component of the design, you are required to provide justification for our decision. The justification will provide an explanation for the options considered, and the reason behind choosing the selected option.

It is necessary to design a content networking solution for the company's network. Determine each location where users will need to access cached content. Figure 12-17 shows the network diagram for the headquarters and North American plants, indicating the location of each content networking device including content switches, content routers, content managers, and content distribution managers.

Figure 12-17 *Network Diagram for the Headquarters and North American Plants*

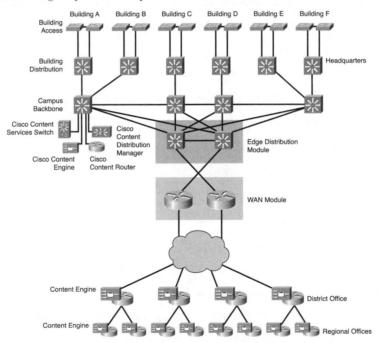

To support content networking between the headquarters and North American plant sites, the following options are included in the network:

- CEs at each plant bring content closer to the users. The CEs support specific Java-based applications. The CE at each remote site allows each plant to download the applet once for all users to access.

- CEs are deployed on the district and regional plant networks. The content is then delivered to the LAN, which accelerates content delivery and saves WAN bandwidth between headquarters and the district plants, and between the district plants and the regional plants.

- The company has an IP-based television service for employees worldwide. Components of the content delivery network included Cisco CDM, Cisco CE, Cisco content switch, and Cisco content router.

Table 12-3 summarizes the design decisions that the enterprise made to meet its requirements.

Table 12-3 *Design Decisions for the OCSIC Content Networking Solution*

Design Questions	Decision	Justification
What high-availability strategy will you deploy to support your content networking solution?	Content switches and routers provide high availability for content.	Redundant content engines, switches, and routers can further ensure availability for the most critical content, if desired.
What security strategy will you deploy to support your content networking solution?	Applications are secured with authentication and authorization based on sensitivity of the data.	The content being served can be highly sensitive so additional care is taken to secure the content networking devices themselves.
What QoS strategy will you deploy to support your content networking solution?	Audio and video data are given priority over other data types.	When content networking involves the delivery of delay-sensitive data such as audio or video, QoS features allow such traffic to be given priority over other data traffic.

After completing this chapter, you will be able to

- Review Cisco storage networking solutions

- Design a storage networking architecture with internet protocol (IP) access

CHAPTER 13

Designing Storage Networking Solutions

The Cisco storage networking solutions combine storage and networking technologies in an IP-enabled enterprise network. Storage networking allows interconnection, access, and sharing of stored data over IP, using a variety of media that includes Gigabit Ethernet, Fibre Channel, and optical networks. These technologies provide interconnection and access for network-attached storage and storage-area network (SAN) environments.

This chapter describes how the Cisco storage networking architecture meets enterprise storage networking needs. It also defines how to design a storage-networking solution with IP access, given enterprise storage networking needs.

Reviewing the Cisco Storage Networking Solution

Enterprise data storage is changing as Fibre Channel and IP networks converge toward an integrated storage-networking infrastructure. This eliminates the limitations imposed by separate SAN islands. The convergence of storage and the network enables the Cisco Architecture for Voice, Video, and Integrated Data (AVVID) storage-networking solution to integrate the technology already deployed in IP networks with new standards, protocols, and products.

The Cisco storage-networking solution fully integrates with the Cisco AVVID network infrastructure and is based on industry standards.

This section examines these individual topics:

- Enterprise requirements for storage networking
- How the Cisco storage networking architecture meets enterprise storage networking needs
- How the Cisco storage networking models use the underlying networking technology and intelligent network services
- The important standards that make storage networking possible in an enterprise network
- How to implement intelligent network services to support storage networking

Enterprise Needs for Storage Networking

With storage networking, you can distribute storage for remote access through the network's IP infrastructure. Storage consolidation and business continuance are two common applications for storage networking. This section identifies enterprise requirements for storage networking.

The rapid growth of the Internet and e-business has made data storage more important than ever. Business applications such as e-commerce, e-learning, supply-chain management, customer care, and workforce optimization add to storage requirements. IP network technology is bringing some new capabilities to the storage world.

Instead of being tied to local host computers, storage device controllers are accessed directly by distant hosts using IP technology. This lowers costs and simplifies information technology (IT) infrastructures, while allowing storage to be located remotely, subject to user and application storage access latency and data synchronization requirements.

Storage Consolidation

Enterprises that have already implemented SAN or network-attached storage architectures want to leverage the existing infrastructure to consolidate storage. With the growth of digital information, the amount of data and servers has also increased. System administrators are faced with the challenging task of managing storage and making it scalable to accommodate future needs.

When storage is directly attached to the server, scalability becomes difficult to maintain. The storage expansion capability is limited to the capacity of the server (for example, as measured by the number of input/output [I/O] controllers and devices per controller configured in the server). The nature of the small computer system interface (SCSI) bus commonly used to connect commodity disks to a commodity server makes it difficult to allocate more disk storage without interrupting and rebooting the server; thus, applications are affected.

To accommodate growth, deployment of additional storage must be accomplished quickly and have minimum or no impact on the availability of applications or data. The addition of servers with directly attached storage resources to accommodate rapid growth results in a more difficult environment to manage and poor use of resources. A pool of storage devices attached to the network creates rapid and simplified scalability. These storage devices provide server file access (network-attached storage) or block access (SAN).

A best-practice approach is to provide all servers that do not have local access to the SAN with IP access to the storage and allocate storage on demand. This storage consolidation provides centralization and simplification of storage management.

Business Continuance and Backup

Today's storage and networking architectures do not tolerate any interruption in normal operation, and enterprises are implementing stringent disaster-recovery plans to guarantee the recovery of services in a timely and cost-effective manner. Enterprise-wide information is protected and archived according to its level of criticality, the length of time allowed to recover the information, and whether the potential loss of information is acceptable.

The highest level of information protection is achieved through mirror sites: a complete replicated storage, server, network, and application infrastructure in two or more locations. The information is synchronously replicated, in real time, between the mirror sites. An enterprise must sacrifice a significant cost for this level of data protection.

A lower level of data protection includes asynchronous mirroring, which includes the information being replicated in an asynchronous manner at a selected frequency. In this asynchronous mode of replication, snapshots, or point-in-time copies of the data, are made and transferred to a remote site. The point-in-time image is used for disaster recovery and can potentially be used to perform tasks that do not require tight synchronization with the online applications (for example, data mining, reporting, and backup).

Disaster-recovery applications, such as mirroring and replication, protect against equipment or site failures to provide a highly available infrastructure. However, these applications do not protect against user errors or data corruption. Backup, with offsite storage and restore, provides protection against any kind of data loss for the retention period of the backup. Backup media are also used for long-term off-site archiving for protection of key information for future reference or audit purposes. With the growth of stored data, the backup volume required has increased, yet the timeframe allowed for backup is limited. Local backups impact the performance of the application servers, and backup management has become increasingly complex as the amount of information grows.

Backup has evolved from an architecture in which tape drives were directly attached to the servers. Network backup uses tape drives attached to a centralized backup server or to a SAN-based, networked tape library. When SANs first emerged, tape autoloader or tape libraries constituted a consolidated backup system. Snapshot technology makes it possible to back up systems online with minimum impact on the applications. Therefore, snapshot technology improves backup efficiency and reduces the impact of backup activities while increasing the restoration requirements.

Cisco Storage Networking Architecture

Storage networking is the hardware and software that enables you to consolidate, share, and access storage over a networked infrastructure. Cisco views the storage network, which is shown in Figure 13-1, as another component of the Cisco AVVID common infrastructure. This section explains how the Cisco storage networking architecture meets enterprise storage networking needs.

Figure 13-1 *Cisco Storage Networking Architecture*

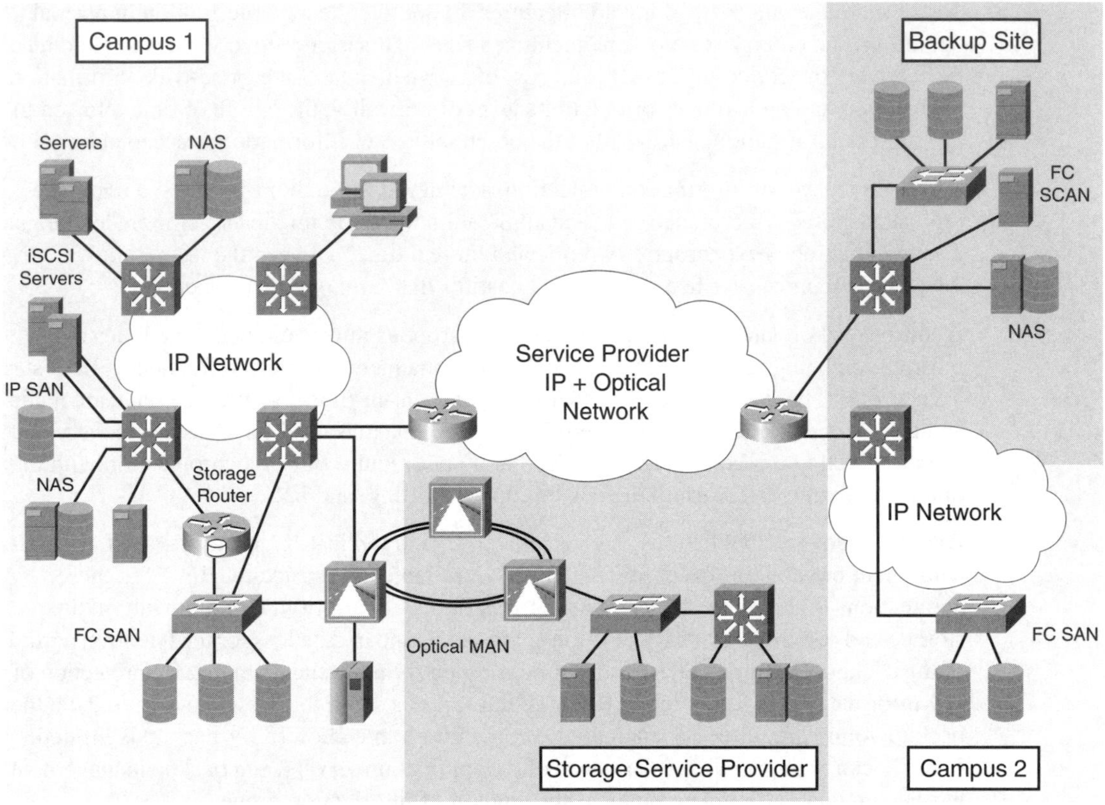

Key components of the Cisco storage networking solution are

- Network-attached storage for file-oriented access to storage

- IP access to storage for block-oriented host-to-storage communication in SANs

- Storage over the wide-area network, for the interconnection of all storage environments

- Metro optical connectivity for the efficient, high-performance transport of these storage traffic types over data-link protocols, which include 1/10 Gigabit Ethernet and other optical technologies:

    — **Fibre Channel**—Allows for high-speed information exchange, from 133 Mbps to 2 Gbps, between network devices over a fibre infrastructure. This architecture takes advantage of the physical characteristics associated with fibre data transfers to allow for quick communication between network devices such as SANs. Fibre Channel technology eliminates much of the overhead associated with regular network-based communications by using a point-to-point switched architecture. In essence, the network is used to extend the internal bus architecture of the computing device to allow data transfers to occur directly between the buffers of each interconnected SAN device.

— **Internet Small Computer System Interface (iSCSI)**—This technology is based upon the SCSI architecture, which was designed for component communications across an internal PC-based bus architecture. iSCSI, or SCSI over IP networks, takes the SCSI architecture and extends its capability to transport data over IP-based networks. This approach allows implementers of SAN solutions to not have to be reliant upon an expensive fibre-based solution. Therefore, wherever an IP-based network exists, iSCSI is capable of the transport of data between SAN devices.

— **Enterprise System Connection (ESCON)**—A proprietary interface used by IBM to interconnect switches to SAN components.

The Cisco AVVID common infrastructure supports both SAN and network-attached storage models. These complementary technologies simultaneously use the Cisco AVVID common infrastructure:

- **SAN**—Provides block-oriented access to native disk storage. It is based on a shared or switched infrastructure, often Fibre Channel. You can extend SAN to an IP infrastructure. New protocols and products are emerging that allow the integration of SANs with the IP network. Historically, SANs have been well suited to high-volume, write-intensive, transaction-driven applications.

- **Network-attached storage**—Provides file-oriented access over an IP network. Network-attached storage is implemented using customized storage appliances that run Network File System (NFS) for UNIX environments and Common Internet File System (CIFS) for Microsoft Windows NT and Microsoft Windows environments. Network-attached storage is deployed for high-performance file-sharing applications, such as engineering collaboration, NT file systems, e-mail, and web content storage.

Most enterprises deploy a combination of network-attached storage and SAN strategies to meet the wide range of application environments. Differentiation between these technologies will diminish as storage architectures converge to provide both file and block-based services.

Network Storage Models

This section describes the two network-storage models:

- SANs
- Network-attached storage

SANs

A SAN describes a dedicated, high-performance network infrastructure deployed between servers and storage resources. The storage area infrastructure is a separate, dedicated network entity optimized for the efficient movement of a large amount of raw block data to the application servers, which coordinate client access to data. In effect, SAN is an extended link between server and storage. SANs enable the extension of the storage access protocol over longer distances.

SANs are typically built using the SCSI and Fibre Channel protocols (SCSI-FCP). Fibre Channel is well suited to this application, because it can transfer large blocks of data (as is required with SCSI) while simultaneously transferring these blocks over longer distances (unlike SCSI media). Fibre Channel topologies, either loop or fabric, are built using specially designed devices that closely resemble the hubs, switches, and gateways used to build typical packet-based LANs and WANs. The SAN market has historically addressed high-end, enterprise-class storage applications where performance, redundancy, and availability are paramount in support of mission-critical, transaction-driven business systems.

NOTE   A *loop topology* is a Fibre Channel topology that allows for up to 126 devices to be connected via a shared link at any given time. Each node on the loop contends for access and once gained, creates a logical point-to-point connection with the intended end device for the purpose of the data transfer.

A *fabric topology* is a Fibre Channel topology that uses a shared switch to interconnect up to 2^{24} devices in a virtual-meshed topology.

Network-Attached Storage

LANs made it possible to connect multiple file servers with a common infrastructure for the purpose of file sharing. LANs accelerated the development of distributed multitier computing. The concept of distributed technology involves using an arrangement of inexpensive microcomputers and storage devices (disk, tape, and so forth) to reduce cost and move processing nearer the user. As computers proliferated, many incompatibilities complicated shared data access. The advent and widespread deployment of LANs encouraged workgroup clusters by offering file sharing, interoperability, and cost savings. Network-attached storage consists of a specialized file server and storage, as shown in Figure 13-2. Network-attached storage servers run optimized file systems and are installed as preconfigured storage "appliances." Because network-attached storage systems are connected to the IP network, clients are able to transfer data to and from the storage devices associated with the network-attached storage system.

Figure 13-2 *Network Storage Models*

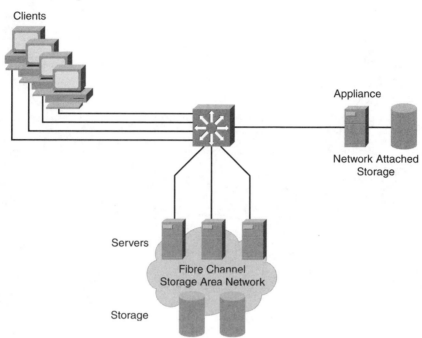

In addition, network-attached storage can directly process file-system protocols, such as NFS and CIFS. Client machines mount volumes on these disk resources, allowing virtual access to productivity applications and file data. Although these devices are capable of hosting distributed applications, these applications are typically placed on application-specific server platforms that have no responsibilities for directly attached data storage.

NOTE   SANs are typically used to access blocks of data within files for applications, such as clustered database access. Network-attached storage is typically used to access files.

Network Technology Enablers for Storage Networks

These core storage-networking technology enablers provide access and interconnection for network-attached storage and SAN environments (see Figure 13-3):

- IP
- Gigabit Ethernet (GE)
- Fibre Channel
- Optical networking

Figure 13-3 *Storage Networking Technology Enablers*

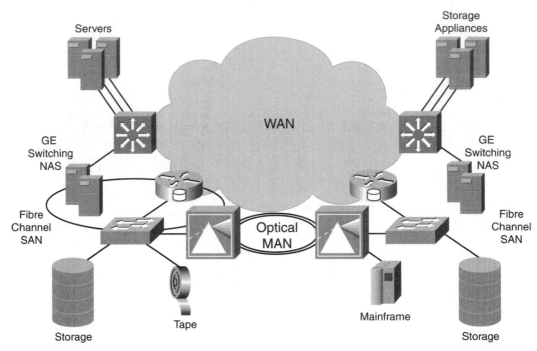

This section describes the important standards that make storage networking possible in an enterprise network.

iSCSI

The iSCSI protocol enables access to storage over TCP/IP, and Fibre Channel over IP (FCIP) links Fibre Channel SANs over IP.

The iSCSI protocol encapsulates a SCSI request in an IP packet. iSCSI is a SCSI transport protocol for mapping block-oriented storage requests over Transmission Control Protocol/ Internet Protocol (TCP/IP) networks. By making direct access to storage over IP possible, the iSCSI protocol allows IP-connected hosts to access iSCSI or Fibre Channel–connected storage.

iSCSI is fully compatible with existing IP infrastructures. With iSCSI, users can access storage across campus and WAN, allowing data center storage to scale across the enterprise.

Relying on existing IP network infrastructures, local- and wide-area routers and switches transparently extend storage access across the WAN for applications, such as remote disk copy, and tape backup and restore. In the WAN environment, TCP/IP ensures data reliability, manages network congestion, and controls WAN retransmissions.

Figure 13-4 shows how block accesses to storage are made through the interconnected IP and Fibre Channel network. The storage router acts as a bridge between Fibre Channel and the IP network. One or more TCP sessions support the communication between the SCSI initiator and SCSI targets. The key technologies that enable the transfer of blocks of data over the IP network are

- **iSCSI routers**—Enable connection of iSCSI hosts to Fibre Channel–connected storage. Along with the iSCSI router, iSCSI device drivers provide the interface between the operating system and the TCP/IP stack.

- **Optical media**—The bandwidth necessary for the timely transfer of I/O data is typically provided over optical media. Gigabit Ethernet is often used in this solution.

Figure 13-4 *iSCSI for Storage Consolidation*

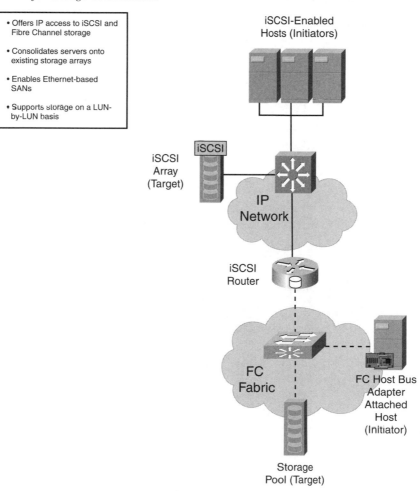

You can deploy iSCSI to provide the following:

- Remote storage over IP
- Remote backup of devices over IP to provide centralized storage management

An application must tolerate relatively high access latency to support a remote iSCSI solution over long distances. Metro Ethernet services offer a low-latency, high-volume transport alternative where available.

Figure 13-5 shows how storage devices use iSCSI to provide remote access to servers through the high-speed network. Enterprises that already have a consolidated SAN might want to preserve their investment in a centralized pool of storage and use an iSCSI router to access the SAN island. iSCSI technology with Gigabit Ethernet enables the connection of storage appliances or devices to the IP network.

Figure 13-5 *iSCSI for Remote Block Access*

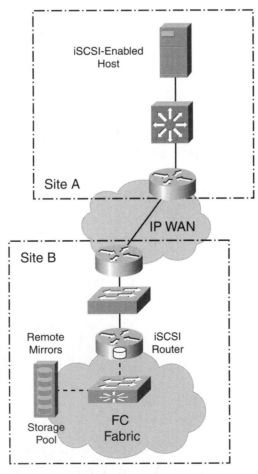

FCIP

An important technology for linking Fibre Channel SANs is FCIP. FCIP and iSCSI are complementary solutions for enabling company-wide access to storage. FCIP transparently interconnects Fibre Channel SAN islands over IP networks through FCIP tunnels, and iSCSI allows IP-connected hosts to access iSCSI or Fibre Channel–connected storage.

iSCSI and FCIP are typically used for different purposes. With iSCSI, SCSI commands and data frames are encapsulated in IP to support disk access over an IP network. With FCIP, Fibre Channel frames are encapsulated in IP so that both SCSI and non-SCSI frames can be transported over an IP network.

FCIP overcomes many shortcomings of direct-attached storage by offering these features:

- Addressing for up to 16 million nodes (24 bits)
- Loop (shared) and fabric (switched) transport
- Speeds of 1000 or 2000 Mbps (1 or 2 Gbps)
- Distance of up to 10 km with extenders
- Support for multiple protocols

The combination of FCIP and iSCSI allows enterprises to

- Interconnect SAN islands
- Provide applications including remote backup and replication, in addition to performing Fibre Channel I/O communication

Businesses expanding their storage infrastructures are faced with business continuance issues. Applications associated with disaster recovery and high availability can use FCIP as a solution for protecting their data. You can use FCIP to connect two geographically dispersed Fibre Channel storage arrays for the purpose of synchronous data storage, as shown in Figure 13-6. If the local storage array becomes unavailable, an application could use the FCIP link to access the data on the "hot backup" storage system at the remote site. It is also possible to implement remote tape backups to further protect customers' valuable information in the event of a disaster at the primary site.

FCIP differs from iSCSI as follows:

- iSCSI encapsulates SCSI commands and data in a TCP/IP packet. In this case, an IP-connected host running an iSCSI driver is accessing block-level data over an IP network.
- FCIP encapsulates Fibre Channel in IP packets. In this case, any Fibre Channel frame, SCSI/FCP or otherwise, is transported transparently in an IP packet. Fibre Channel hosts and storage communicate on both sides of an FCIP link.

Figure 13-6 *Fibre Channel over IP*

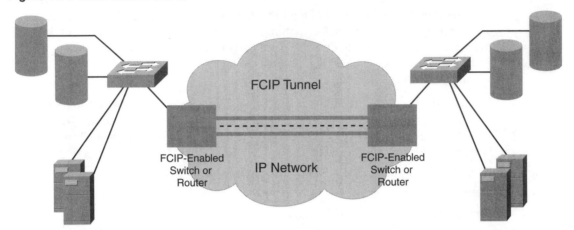

Fibre Channel
Storage Area Network   Fibre Channel
                                                                                                         Storage Area Network

FCIP extends SANs over the metropolitan-area network (MAN) and provides peer-to-peer connection between SANs. With FCIP, enterprises can use their existing MAN infrastructure. Remote data replication, or backup, is performed when use is low. Asynchronous data replication, or backup applications, require high bandwidth but are less sensitive to latency. A response time of tens of milliseconds is acceptable for backup or asynchronous replication applications, unlike interactive applications, which require the least possible storage access latency to meet overall delay bounds, including processing and multiple storage accesses.

Intelligent Network Services for Storage Networking

Standard IP services, including network management, high availability, security, and quality of service (QoS), are used to support storage networking. This section describes how to implement services to support storage networking.

Storage-area networking relies on network services to deliver performance, scalability, and availability. With IP-based storage networking, the existing IP services are used for storage networking purposes. Services that support storage networking include

- **Network management**—Apply network management principles to the network between clients and storage, any storage-specific network, and the storage servers and devices.

- **High availability**—For storage networking, availability applies not only to the network between clients and storage but also to the storage router and the storage devices themselves. Consider implementing these features:

  — **Spanning-tree enhancements**—Use 802.1w, the IEEE standard for Rapid Spanning Tree, for fast spanning-tree reconvergence in Ethernet environments. Use UplinkFast and PortFast on Catalyst switches for fast recovery from a topology change.

— **Routing protocols**—Tune Open Shortest Path First (OSPF) and Enhanced Interior Gateway Routing Protocol (EIGRP) routing protocols for very fast convergence following a network link or router failure.

— **Host multipath support**—Use multipath software above the host-based iSCSI layer to add path resiliency to an IP SAN.

— **Hot Standby Router Protocol (HSRP)**—Use HSRP to create redundancy default gateways for iSCI initiator hosts to ensure fast recovery if a gateway fails.

Two important considerations regarding storage networking are:

- **Security**—You can use IP Security (IPSec) hardware encryption to encrypt FCIP tunnels across the WAN/MAN. The iSCSI standard calls for IPSec support and requires hardware acceleration from clients. Use virtual LANs (VLANs) to isolate storage traffic within a LAN, or consider using private VLANs. You can use IP and VLAN access control lists to isolate storage within a LAN and storage-router–based access control lists to restrict access to storage. Implement Remote Access Dial-In User Service (RADIUS)/Terminal Access Controller Access Control System plus (TACACS+) to provide authentication for iSCSI initiators. You can use firewalls to prevent attacks due to static TCP ports.

- **QoS**—Use QoS to protect iSCSI traffic and prioritize it within the LAN for higher-priority queuing and switching. Use QoS to throttle non-IP storage traffic to protect FCIP traffic in a WAN/MAN.

The best QoS solution for storage networking is a separate network. Physical separation with adequate bandwidth provides an absolute QoS guarantee. A dedicated network might be expensive to provision and increase management complexity, but it is more predictable.

Many Layer 2 services exist to ensure performance in a SAN as well as to protect storage traffic from potential bottlenecks. You can implement these services to enhance performance:

- **EtherChannel**—Use EtherChannel to bundle up to 16 Gbps of bandwidth into one logical link within the LAN.

- **100-Mbps Ethernet**—Potentially use 100-Mbps built-in host network interface cards (NICs) for applications with lower performance requirements.

Designing a Storage Networking Architecture with IP Access

Block storage access has been associated with Fibre Channel SANs and file access with network-attached storage. SANs and network-attached storage are converging, as Fibre

Channel and IP networks enable an integrated storage networking architecture. Storage networks are an infrastructure that enables file access and block access over interconnected Fibre Channel and IP networks. Cisco supports the development of new protocols that allow access to Fibre Channel SANs through enterprise IP networks.

The limitations of locally connected storage solutions have led to the development of new network storage technologies, including serial SCSI and iSCSI to provide a scalable data storage infrastructure.

This section describes how to design a storage networking solution with IP access, given enterprise storage networking needs. The individual topics covered are as follows:

- Designing a storage networking architecture

- Design of an IP access storage networking solution using Cisco products and features, given enterprise storage networking needs

- Design of a storage over WAN solution using Cisco products and features, given enterprise storage network needs

- Design of a network-attached storage networking solution using Cisco components, given enterprise storage networking needs

Designing a Storage Networking Architecture

The architecture of a storage networking solution depends on the applications accessing the storage. To determine the design requirements, you must know the I/O profiles, throughput, and availability needs of the applications. This section describes a methodology that a network designer might use to design a storage networking architecture.

To plan for a storage networking implementation, you must identify the needs of the application accessing the storage by considering these factors:

- **Access pattern**—The type of access required has a major impact on the storage networking architecture. A SAN is typically used for real-time application access, but network-attached storage is typically used for individual access and backup.

- **I/O profile**—How many bytes are being read or written per second? How much bandwidth will the data transfer related to storage access use? What is the most important aspect of the data I/O for the application: throughput or latency? The transaction rate of the application can be affected by the storage networking solution. Can the application tolerate latency for transfer between storage and the server? IP access to storage might introduce a latency factor that is unacceptable for some applications. Enterprises might require a Fibre Channel SAN in such cases. For latency-sensitive applications, the geographic placement of servers relative to storage devices can be an issue, as well as the bandwidth limitations between devices.

- **Throughput**—What are the sustained throughput requirements of the application? How will the requirements scale over time? The storage networking solution will need to address the infrastructure and device needs for the expected throughput.

- **Availability**—How critical is the application data to the enterprise? What is the effect on the enterprise of the application becoming unavailable? What high-availability measures should you consider for the storage network and devices? Mirrored servers and redundant network infrastructure might be required for some applications.

Figure 13-7 lists several considerations for storage networking:

- **Performance**—Ensures that the networked channel has adequate bandwidth and flow control; the performance requirements vary depending on whether the application is for real-time or archival requirements.

- **Latency**—Ensures that the channel does not experience sufficient latency to compromise application integrity.

- **Resource management**—Ensures that network resources are monitored.

- **Fault management**—Ensures that the proper tools exist to detect, evaluate, and act on faults in the network.

- **Scalability**—Ensures that the network can be expanded without jeopardizing network stability.

Figure 13-7 *Design Considerations for Storage Networks*

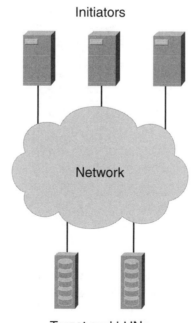

Initiators

Network

Target and LUNs

IP Access to Storage

IP access to storage provides access to block-oriented storage over IP networks. This section describes the design of an IP access storage networking solution.

Cisco extends storage consolidation beyond the data center by enabling block-oriented storage I/O over an IP network. This allows servers that might not have otherwise been eligible to connect to shared storage resources. This could include Microsoft Windows server farms, remote servers, and small server clusters in remote offices.

iSCSI encapsulates the SCSI command set and data frame into TCP/IP, and thereby allows hosts to communicate with storage over a high-speed IP infrastructure, transparently to the application.

You can implement iSCSI to access Fibre Channel–connected storage or to access storage devices that are natively connected to the IP network. Figure 13-8 shows both IP access to Fibre Channel–connected and native iSCSI-connected storage from iSCSI-enabled servers.

Figure 13-8 *IP Access to Storage Model*

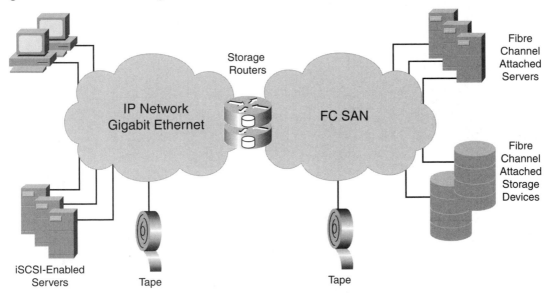

Example: IP Access to Storage

A major medical research facility's database was growing quickly, and users needed access. Hundreds of users in five separate buildings were networked into a powerful server farm made up of application servers that shared a very large, 4-terabyte Oracle database.

The organization wanted to install a storage network to support the storage access requirements at the remote locations that would support their performance and cost needs, as well as grow with them in the future.

IP Access to Storage Solution

The researchers compared a Fibre Channel–only approach with a hybrid approach that coupled an iSCSI storage network with Fibre Channel for storage access. Both configuration alternatives provided redundant Gigabit Ethernet paths from every server to the facility's 4-terabyte database.

The Fibre Channel–only alternative required a mesh of Fibre Channel switches. This approach involved stacking a large number of switches and could require multiple hops through the switches to reach the right storage array.

Although the Fibre Channel approach met the basic access requirements, that fact was overshadowed by a high probability of congestion on the interswitch links. In addition, the architecture cost exceeded the medical research facility's budget allocation.

The Cisco storage router delivers redundant iSCSI paths to a pair of Fibre Channel switches. iSCSI takes advantage of the connection-oriented TCP protocol for reliable service. Ethernet was already part of the IT network. This meant trained personnel were on board, and it simplified the storage networking installation.

Cost was an important factor in choosing iSCSI. Because the research facility already had TCP/IP and Gigabit Ethernet networks installed, the iSCSI solution fit their budget and met their storage networking needs.

The Cisco storage router met the budget constraints of the research facility and allowed the company to tune storage performance to meet the facility's requirements for volume, activity rates, and management of access conflicts. For the medical research facility, storage access was the primary need. Given that the solution would include high-performance servers, the researchers determined that it was important to directly connect those servers to the Fibre Channel switches.

The end result, shown in Figure 13-9, used the scalability and cost advantages of iSCSI via Gigabit Ethernet for storage networking and retained Fibre Channel for storage access. This hybrid approach permitted the medical research facility to reduce capital costs and meet their operational needs.

The applications were interfaced with the generic SCSI layer in the Windows hosts; this ensured that they would only see SCSI. The storage router shielded the host from any Fibre Channel considerations. This transparency gave the medical research facility complete flexibility in designing its storage network.

Figure 13-9 *IP Access to Storage Example*

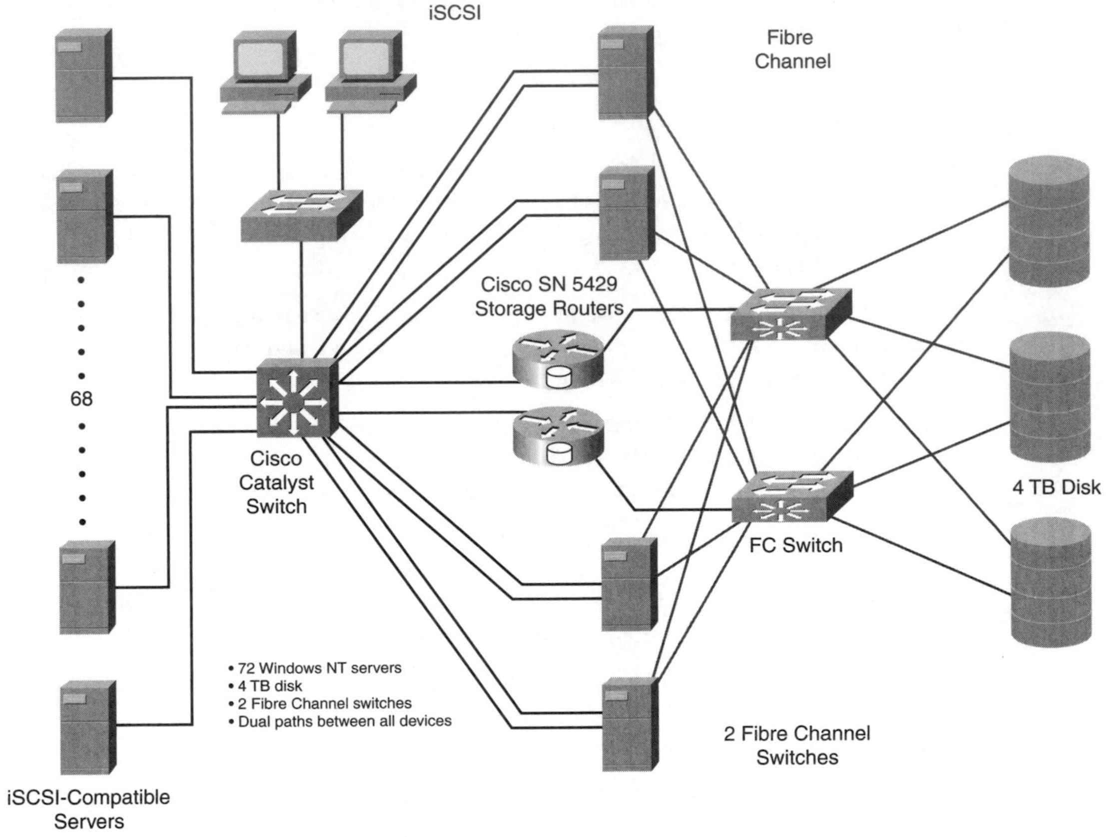

Storage over WAN

Storage over WAN, shown in Figure 13-10, enables fast, secure, and highly available storage networks interconnecting over WANs. This section describes the design of an IP access storage networking solution over a WAN.

To build a truly enterprise-wide storage resource, companies need the ability to interconnect and manage storage across WANs. The growing requirements to replicate, distribute, and manage data over relatively long distances result from several needs.

The most critical need is for backup and restore services to ensure business continuance and data protection at an offsite location. Other applications include centralized storage management, efficient data center migration, or the aggregation of multiple production databases into a single data warehouse for analysis and data mining.

Figure 13-10 *Storage over WAN Model*

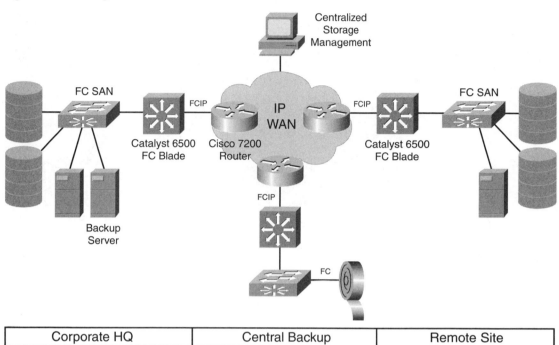

For IP-based networked storage, either network-attached storage or SAN (the traditional wide-area IP routing technologies) allow enterprises to manage storage.

For Fibre Channel– or Enterprise System Connection (ESCON)–based MAN applications up to a 10-km distance, you must bridge the storage environment to the IP network infrastructure. For Fibre Channel, the FCIP protocol provides transparent encapsulation of the complete Fibre Channel frame. This allows you to transport both host-to-storage traffic and storage-to-storage replication traffic transparently across the MAN.

Example: Storage over WAN

A large financial institution decided that its critical data needs additional protection through expanded backup procedures. The company already has multiple data centers in place, each with a Fibre Channel SAN.

Storage over WAN Solution

An FCIP solution shown in Figure 13-11 allowed the financial enterprise to add storage to each data center, and then use FCIP to perform asynchronous backup of data from one site to another. This allowed the company to take advantage of its existing IP infrastructure over the WAN and to provide additional locations for all critical data.

Figure 13-11 *Storage over WAN Model Example*

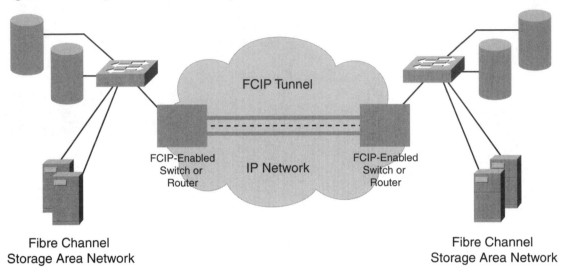

FCIP Tunnel

IP Network

FCIP-Enabled
Switch or
Router

FCIP-Enabled
Switch or
Router

Fibre Channel
Storage Area Network

Fibre Channel
Storage Area Network

Example: Storage over Optical Metro

A financial-management company is concerned about maintaining good customer relationships. It wants to adopt strategies that keep application services up and running while protecting business-critical information from corruption and loss. An outage would be devastating to the business. Brokerage firms and other financial institutions can lose millions of dollars per hour when systems are down. Even retail sales organizations can lose hundreds of thousands of dollars an hour when customers cannot place orders.

Storage over Optical Metro Solution

The company is implementing a business-continuance strategy for storage that addresses both data backup and disaster recovery. Backup and replication includes data archiving for protection against data loss and corruption, remote replication of data for distribution of content, application testing, disaster protection, and data-center migration. Real-time disaster recovery implemented with synchronous mirroring allows the company to safeguard data by guaranteeing that mission-critical data is securely and remotely mirrored to avoid any data loss in the event of a disaster, ensuring uninterrupted services to employees, customers, and partners.

The business continuance strategy and associated SAN technology, implemented with Fibre Channel and ESCON, requires a fault-tolerant, high-bandwidth, and low-latency network. For synchronous mirroring, the high-bit rate of an optical network minimizes the time necessary to complete a data transfer. This is critical to avoid negative impact on application performance.

Figure 13-12 shows a metro optical ring, implemented with the Cisco extended services platform, providing high-bandwidth transport for multiple Gigabit Ethernet LANs, Fibre Channel SANs, and mainframe environments across a single fiber pair.

Figure 13-12 *Storage over Optical Metro Example*

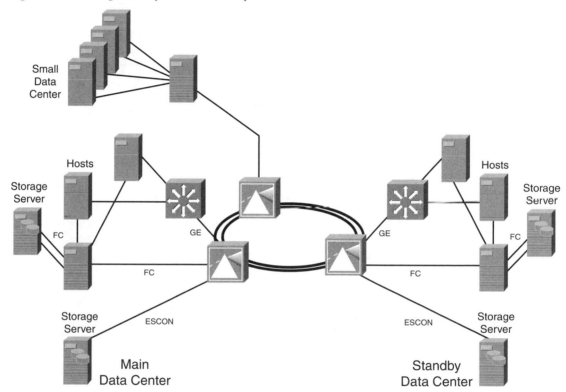

Network-Attached Storage Model

Network-attached storage provides high-performance access, data protection, and disaster recovery for file sharing over an IP network. This section describes the design of a network-attached storage networking solution.

Network-attached storage makes mainstream deployment of IP-based storage consolidation and file sharing possible. Network-attached storage is popular for many applications including collaborative development, engineering, e-mail, web serving, and general file serving. In particular, because network-attached storage abstracts storage to the file-system level, it can manage the sharing of files effectively between multiple users and applications. Figure 13-13 describes a generic network-attached storage deployment across an IP, Gigabit Ethernet network.

Figure 13-13 *Network-Attached Storage Model*

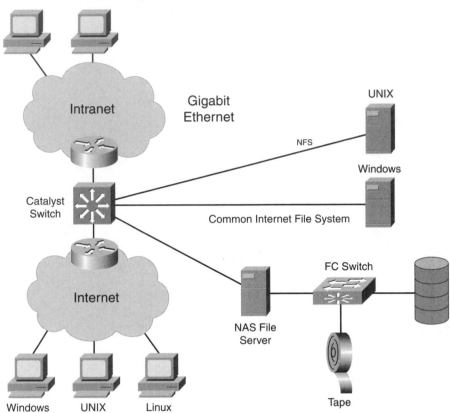

Example: Network-Attached Storage

An expanding software development company found that as it added engineering sites, its current solution for centralized code storage was becoming cumbersome and inefficient. Each site needed to maintain separate servers with dedicated storage, introducing the possibility of synchronization issues, or they had to access file servers over the WAN. Latency was not an issue, because entire files were downloaded to individual engineering workstations for modification, and then uploaded back to the servers.

Network-Attached Storage Solution

By deploying network-attached storage devices in its network, shown in Figure 13-14, the company leveraged its existing infrastructure and allowed each site to maintain its own application servers while keeping the data itself centralized, which eliminated synchronization problems. Network-attached storage requires file locking.

Figure 13-14 *Network-Attached Storage Example*

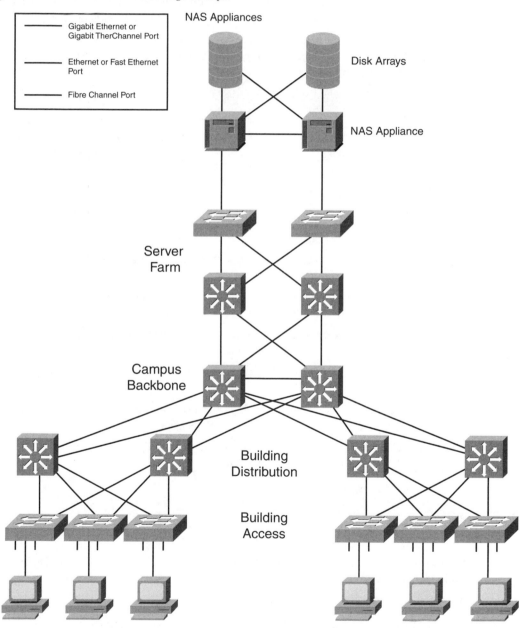

Summary

In this chapter, you learned the following key points:

- You can locate storage anywhere for access through the network's IP infrastructure. Storage consolidation and business continuance are two common applications.

- Storage networking includes the hardware and software that enables you to consolidate, share, and access storage over a networked infrastructure. The two network storage models are
  - Network-attached storage
  - SAN

- The core storage networking technology enablers that provide universal access and interconnection are
  - IP
  - Gigabit Ethernet
  - Fibre Channel
  - Optical networking

- Standard IP services, including network management, high availability, security, and QoS, are used to support storage networking.

- To determine the storage networking design requirements, you must know the application's I/O profile, throughput, and availability needs.

- IP access to storage provides universal access to block-oriented storage over IP networks.

- Storage over WAN enables fast, secure, and highly available network access storage interconnecting over WANs.

- Network-attached storage provides high-performance access, data protection, and disaster recovery for file sharing over an IP network.

- The iSCSI protocol enables access to storage over TCP/IP, while Fibre Channel over IP (FCIP) links Fibre Channel SANs over IP.

References

Storage Networking. http://www.cisco.com/go/san.

Solutions Reference Network Design (SRND) Networking Solutions Design Guides. To locate these documents, perform the following:

Step 1 Go to http://www.cisco.com/.

Step 2 In the Search box, enter **SRND** and click **Go**. A list of SRND Networking Solutions Design Guides appears.

Step 3   Select the Networking Solutions Design Guide that meets your needs.

Storage Area Networking Association. http://www.snia.org/.

Fibre Channel Industry Association. http://www.fibrechannel.org/.

SCSI Trade Association. http://www.scsita.org/.

IETF IP Storage Working Group. http://www.ietf.org/html.charters/ips-charter.html

Product Summary

Table 13-1 provides a brief overview of some of the products available from Cisco Systems that relate to the technologies discussed in this chapter. For a more detailed breakdown of the Cisco product line, visit http://www.cisco.com/en/US/products/index.html.

Table 13-1   *Cisco Storage Networking Products*

Product Class	Product	Specifications
Storage Routers	5428 5428-2	The Cisco Serial Number (SN) 5428 provides two Gigabit Ethernet ports, supporting iSCSI, for connection to standard IP networks and eight Fibre Channel fabric switch ports. RADIUS and TACACS+ authentication, logical unit number (LUN) mapping, LUN masking, and Fibre Channel zoning.
Message Delivery Service (MDS) 9000 Series Multilayer Switches	9100 Series	Up to 40 2/1-Gbps autosensing Fibre Channel ports. 20- and 40-port configurations (Cisco MDS 9120, MDS 9140), packaged in a one-rack-unit (1RU) form-factor chassis with dual-hot-swappable-power supplies and fans.
	9216	Starting with 16 2/1-Gbps auto-sensing Fibre Channel ports, the MDS 9216's expansion slot allows for the addition of any Cisco MDS 9000 Family module for up to 48 total ports. The multilayer architecture of the Cisco MDS 9216 Multilayer Fabric Switch enables a consistent feature set over a protocol agnostic switch fabric; and seamlessly integrates Fibre Channel, iSCSI, and FCIP in one system. Cisco MDS 9216 supports up to 16 2-Gbps links in a single PortChannel—links might span any port on any module within a chassis for added scalability and resilience.

continues

Table 13-1 *Cisco Storage Networking Products (Continued)*

Product Class	Product	Specifications
Message Delivery Service (MDS) 9000 Series Multilayer Switches (*Cont.*)	9506	The Cisco MDS 9506 supports up to 128 1/2-Gbps autosensing Fibre Channel ports in a single chassis and up to 768 Fibre Channel ports in a single rack—1.44 Terabits per second (Tbps) of internal system bandwidth ensures smooth integration of future 10-Gbps modules.
		Industry's highest performance Inter Switch Links (ISLs): The Cisco MDS 9506 supports up to 16 2-Gbps links in a single PortChannel—links might span any port on any module within a chassis for added scalability and resilience.
		The multilayer architecture of the Cisco MDS 9506 enables a consistent feature set over a protocol agnostic switch fabric; and seamlessly integrates Fibre Channel, iSCSI, and FCIP in one system. Flexible architecture allows integration of future storage protocols.
	9509	The Cisco MDS 9509 supports up to 224 1/2-Gbps autosensing Fibre Channel ports in a single chassis and up to 672 Fibre Channel ports in a single rack—1.44 Tbps of internal system bandwidth ensures smooth integration of future 10-Gbps modules.
		The multilayer architecture of the Cisco MDS 9509 enables a consistent feature set over a protocol agnostic switch fabric; and seamlessly integrates Fibre Channel, iSCSI, and FCIP in one system. Flexible architecture allows integration of future storage protocols.
		The Cisco MDS 9509 supports up to 16 2-Gbps links in a single PortChannel—links might span any port on any module within a chassis for added scalability and resilience.

Standards and Specification Summary

Request For Comments (RFCs) can be downloaded from the following website: http://www.rfc-editor.org/rfc.html.

- RFC 3347, "Small Computer Systems Interface protocol over the Internet (iSCSI) Requirements and Design Considerations"
- RFC 3643, "Fibre Channel Frame Encapsulation"

Review Questions

Answer the following questions to test your comprehension of the topics discussed in this chapter. Refer to Appendix A, "Answers to Review Questions," to check your answers.

1. How is the highest level of information protection achieved?

2. What is asynchronous mirroring?

3. How does snapshot technology work?

4. What are the key components of the Cisco storage networking solution?

5. What is network-attached storage?

6. What is a SAN?

7. What protocols are typically used to build a SAN solution?

8. What is the primary difference between SANs and network-attached storage?

9. Define the iSCSI protocol.

10. What are the key technologies that enable the transfer of blocks of data over the IP network?

11. What services can iSCSI provide?

12. What is Fibre Channel over IP?

13. What shortcoming(s) of direct-attached storage does FCIP overcome?

14. How does FCIP differ from iSCSI?

15. What services are supported by storage networking?

16. What are two important design considerations regarding storage networking?

17. To plan for a storage networking implementation, you must consider what factors regarding the software applications that need to access the SAN?

18. What are several considerations for designing storage networking?

Case Study: OCSIC Bottling Company

The purpose of this case study is to practice the key design skills discussed in this chapter. The project is to revisit the earlier design for the OCSIC Bottling Company, and ensure that SAN solution provides fast access to data and reduces the load on the network between buildings at the headquarters' campus and between the headquarters' office and the North American plants. For each identified component of the design, we are required to provide justification for our decision. The justification will provide an explanation for the options considered and the reason behind choosing the selected option.

Your first step is to determine the location of each storage device on the network. Create a campus network diagram for the headquarters location and the North American plants, indicating the location of each storage-networking solution.

To support IP access to storage, the company selected the following options:

- A Cisco storage router that delivers redundant iSCSI paths to a pair of Fibre Channel switches. iSCSI takes advantage of the connection-oriented TCP protocol for reliable service. Ethernet was already part of the IT network. The end result used the scalability and cost advantages of iSCSI via Gigabit Ethernet for storage networking and retained Fibre Channel for storage access.

- The applications interface with the generic SCSI layer in the Windows hosts, which see only SCSI. The storage router shielded the host from any Fibre Channel considerations.

- To support storage over the WAN, the company implemented an FCIP solution that allowed them to add storage at each plant, and then use FCIP to perform asynchronous backup of data from one site to another. This allowed them to take advantage of their existing IP infrastructure and to provide additional locations for all critical data. The company put in a T3 between the regional offices and headquarters to address the bandwidth guarantees needed.

Table 13-2 summarizes the design decisions that the enterprise made to meet the company's requirements.

Table 13-2 *Design Decisions for the OCSIC Storage Networking Solution*

Design Questions	Decision	Justification
What high-availability strategy will you deploy to support your storage networking solution?	Use 802.1w for spanning tree Use OSPF Use HSRP	802.1w provides fast spanning-tree reconvergence in Ethernet environments. OSPF provides very fast convergence following a network link or router failure. HSRP creates redundancy default gateways for iSCSI initiator hosts to ensure fast recovery if a gateway fails.

Table 13-2   *Design Decisions for the OCSIC Storage Networking Solution (Continued)*

Design Questions	Decision	Justification
What security strategy will you deploy to support your storage networking solution?	Use IP Security (IPSec) hardware encryption Use IP and VLAN access control lists	IPSec hardware encryption encrypts FCIP tunnels across the WAN. IP and VLAN access control lists isolate storage within a LAN and storage-router–based access control lists to restrict access to storage.
What QoS strategy will you deploy to support your storage networking solution?	Prioritize iSCSI traffic Use QoS to throttle non-IP storage traffic	Prioritize iSCSI traffic within the LAN for higher-priority queuing and switching. Use QoS to throttle non-IP storage traffic to protect FCIP traffic in a WAN/MAN.

Answers to Review Questions

Chapter 1

1 List the key components of the Cisco AVVID framework.

Answer: Common Network Infrastructure, Intelligent Network Services, Network Solutions

2 List the benefits that the Cisco AVVID framework offers.

Answer: Integration, intelligence, innovation, interoperability

3 What are the primary concerns of network deployment?

Answer: Performance, scalability, availability

4 What are the three metrics for gauging network performance?

Answer: Responsiveness, throughput, utilization

5 What are the major areas of concern with respect to network scalability?

Answer: Topology, addressing, routing protocols

6 What are the key availability issues that must be addressed during network deployment?

Answer: Device fault-tolerance and redundancy, link redundancy, protocol resiliency, network capacity design (planning)

7 What are the hardware components of the Cisco AVVID Common Network Infrastructure?

Answer: Clients and application servers, and network platforms

8 Name the intelligent network services you might deploy using Cisco Systems products and solutions to keep the network at peak performance.

Answer: Network management, high availability, security, quality of service, IP multicast

9 Which network solutions does Cisco provide?

Answer: VPN, wireless, IP telephony, content networking, storage networking

10 The hierarchical model that Cisco introduced nearly a decade ago divided a network into what layers?

Answer: Access layer, distribution layer, core layer

11 What are the functional areas that comprise the Enterprise Composite Network Model?

Answer: Enterprise Campus, Enterprise Edge, Service Provider Edge

12 What are the modules that the Enterprise Campus functional area is made of?

Answer: Campus Infrastructure module, Network Management module, Server Farm module, Edge Distribution module

13 What are the modules that the Enterprise Edge functional area is made of?

Answer: E-Commerce, Internet Connectivity, Remote Access and VPN, WAN

14 Name the network devices that might be deployed to build a successful E-Commerce solution.

Answer: Web servers, application servers, database servers, security devices

15 What are the major components of the Internet Connectivity module?

Answer: E-mail servers, DNS servers, public web servers, security devices, Edge routers

16 What are the major components of the Remote Access and VPN module?

Answer: Dial-in access concentrators, VPN concentrators, firewalls and intrusion detection systems, Layer 2 switches

17 What are the functions provided by the Service Provider Edge modules?

Answer: ISP, PSTN, FR/ATM/PPP

Chapter 2

1 The design of an enterprise campus network entails design of each of which modules?

Answer: Campus Infrastructure, Network Management, Server Farm, and Edge Distribution modules

2 What requirements must the design of an enterprise campus network meet?

Answer: Functionality, performance, scalability, availability, manageability, and cost effectiveness

3 List the seven steps of the campus design methodology.

Answer:

Step 1 Determine application and data requirements for each campus location.

Step 2 Design the logical network.

Step 3 Design the physical network.

Step 4 Select appropriate Cisco network devices (hardware and software).

Step 5 Select an IP addressing strategy and numbering scheme.

Step 6 Select a routing protocol.

Step 7 Design the Edge Distribution module.

4 Name at least two important factors that need to be considered when analyzing network traffic?

Answer: Traffic load measurement, traffic types, and sampling methods

5 What are the two methods used to create logical network segments?

Answer: Logical network segments may be created using VLANs, or using separate networks.

6 What are the drawbacks of campus-wide VLANs?

Answer: Large and overlapping spanning-tree domains are created, unnecessary complexities are introduced, deterministic behavior of the network is reduced, and convergence is slower.

7 List at least two methods of deploying VLANs at the access layer.

Answer: One VLAN per switch, unique VLANs per switch, and VLANs spanning multiple access switches.

8 What are the common transmission media for campus networks? Identify which one is suitable for which layer of the campus infrastructure.

Answer:

Twisted pair: Building Access

Multimode fiber: Building Distribution and Campus Backbone

Single-mode fiber: Building Distribution and Campus Backbone

9 What are the common data-link layer protocols used in campus networks? Identify the typical uses of each one.

Answer:

Ethernet: Building Access

Fast Ethernet: Building Access and Building Distribution

Gigabit Ethernet: Building Distribution and Campus Backbone

10 Specify the wiring/cable category used for Long-Range Ethernet (LRE) plus its speed range and distance limitation.

Answer: Category 1/2/3 wiring, speeds from 5 to 15 Mbps, and distances up to 5000 feet.

11 Network segmentation strategies are based on consideration of which three domain types?

Answer: Broadcast Domain, Failure Domain, and Policy Domain

12 How many spanning-tree instances exist when PVST is used? How many if CST is used? What is the modern compromise between PVST and CST called?

Answer: PVST builds and maintains one spanning tree per VLAN. CST uses one spanning tree for all VLANs. The modern compromise between PVST and CST is called Multiple (Instance) Spanning Tree or MST (802.1s).

13 Briefly compare data-link layer switching and multilayer switching.

Answer: Data-link layer switching's cost is moderate, it is simpler and less versatile, and it is typically used in Building Access and Campus Backbone. Multilayer switching is more expensive, more complex, more versatile, and it is typically used in Building Distribution and Campus Backbone.

14 What tool does Cisco offer to help in selecting a Cisco network device?

Answer: Cisco Product Advisor

15 List at least two factors that affect IP addressing strategy.

Answer: The size of the network, whether private or public addresses are needed, and whether hierarchical IP addressing is required.

16 Name at least two situations that justify use of static routing.

Answer: Static routing is primarily used for stub networks and/or small networks or to support special features such as on-demand and dial-on-demand routing.

17 List at least two considerations that influence the choice of dynamic IP routing protocol deployed.

Answer:

The enterprise policy on usage of standard as opposed to proprietary protocols, plus the knowledge and comfort of the network engineers with particular protocols

Size of the enterprise and the whether it has multiple locations (requiring hierarchical routing and summarization)

Existence of, and hence the need to support Multiaccess, Non-Broadcast-Multiaccess, Point-to-Point, and Stub networks

The need for special features such as manual/classless/per-link summarization, authentication, fast convergence, unequal metric load sharing, and so on

18 Name three of the server farm design objectives.

Answer:

The primary objectives in the design of an enterprise server farm are

- Performance
- Scalability
- Availability
- Security
- Manageability

19 Specify at lease two methods that can augment the server farm's performance and scalability.

Answer: Increase port density, add higher-speed interfaces, consider the spanning-tree implementation, and implement a modular design.

20 Name at least three server farm manageability considerations.

Answer:

- Identify critical devices and applications
- Create an operations and support plan
- Implement 24–7 monitoring of servers and network equipment
- Implement problem resolution procedures
- Create a business continuity plan in case of natural disaster

Chapter 3

1 Name the four modules that the Enterprise Edge functional area is comprised of.

Answer: E-Commerce, Internet Connectivity, Remote Acccss and VPN, WAN

2 Name at least four of the typical requirements for the Enterprise Edge functional area.

Answer: Functionality, performance, scalability, availability, manageability, cost effectiveness

3 List the eight steps of the Cisco Enterprise Edge Design methodology.

Answer:

Step 1 Characterize applications.

Step 2 Select and diagram the WAN topology.

Step 3 Select a service provider and negotiate price and features.

Step 4 Select a data-link layer WAN, remote-access, or Internet technology.

Step 5 Select a physical layer WAN, remote-access, or Internet technology.

Step 6 Select specific WAN, remote-access, and Internet features.

Step 7 Select specific Cisco network devices and hardware and software options at each location.

Step 8 Select routing protocols and IP addressing.

4 Name at least two important characteristics of network applications that need to be noted while analyzing network traffic patterns.

Answer: Minimum bandwidth needed, plus delay, jitter, and loss tolerance

5 List at least three enterprise requirements for a site-to-site WAN solution.

Answer: Bandwidth, link quality, reliability, data-link protocol characteristics, always-on or on-demand characteristics, cost

6 What are some of the valid questions for designing a branch office WAN connection? (List at least three.)

Answer:

How many users are in the branch?

What are the per-application bandwidth requirements?

What is the total bandwidth needed for applications?

What type of routing protocol is going to be used?

What are the redundancy needs of the site?

What is the effect on the business if the site is unreachable or if the site cannot reach the central servers?

Is the site supporting on-demand connectivity to other sites or users?

7 When developing the WAN module to support a regional office WAN, what questions need to be answered? (List at least three.)

Answer:

How many users are in the regional office?

What are the per-application bandwidth requirements?

What is the total bandwidth needed for applications?

What type of routing protocol is going to be used?

What are the redundancy needs of the site?

What is the effect on the business if the site is not reachable or the site cannot reach the central servers?

Is the site supporting on-demand connectivity to other sites or users?

Is the site a rally point for traffic from other sites to pass through?

Does the regional site have servers or services that are shared with other offices, either branch or core? Does this change the amount of bandwidth that the branch offices need to the core?

8 What questions/concerns need to be answered/addressed when designing the enterprise WAN backbone? (List at least three.)

Answer:

What are the per-application bandwidth requirements?

What is the total bandwidth needed for applications?

What type of routing protocol is going to be used?

What are the redundancy needs of the site?

What is the effect on the business if the site is not reachable?

Is the site supporting on-demand connectivity to other sites or users?

Is the site a rally point for traffic from other sites to pass through?

9 Name at least three criteria for selection of a service provider.

Answer: Price, speeds supported, features supported, geographies covered, service level agreements

10 What are the commonly selected data-link layer WAN technologies? (Name at least two.)

Answer: PPP, Frame Relay, ATM, X.25, and MPLS

11 What are the commonly selected physical layer WAN technologies? (Name at least two.)

Answer: Leased line, DSL, dial-up, ISDN, and Optical Carrier (SONET/SDH)

12 Explain the MP feature of PPP.

Answer: Multilink PPP (MP) allows devices to send data over multiple point-to-point data links to the same destination by implementing a virtual link. The MP connection has a maximum bandwidth equal to the sum of the bandwidths of the component links. MP can be configured for either multiplexed links, such as ISDN and Frame Relay, or for multiple asynchronous lines.

13 Name at least three service classes of ATM:

Answer: CBR, ABR, UBR, RT-VBR, NRT-VBR

14 What is the name of the online tool Cisco provides for choosing the best Cisco product for your particular needs?

Answer: Product Advisor

15 Name three routing protocols that are suitable for site-to-site WAN. Which is the most scalable and nonproprietary protocol?

Answer:

Static Routing, EIGRP, and OSPF (IS-IS is also acceptable).

OSPF (IS-IS is also a correct answer) is standards based (nonproprietary) and scalable.

16 When designing the remote-access connectivity, what important questions need to be answered?

Answer:

What type of remote-access is needed? (Site-to-site or individual user remote access)

What types of access connectivity is needed in the environment? (Dialup, broadband, or VPN)

Where is the remote-access termination point going to be? (Central site, remote site, or service provider)

Who is going to provide the actual termination endpoint of the remote access device?

17 In what situation would an on-demand remote-access solution be viable for a group of employees at a remote site?

Answer:

Sporadic need for enterprise network connectivity, not requiring an "always up" connection

Multiple users at a facility sharing the on-demand access

Prohibitive cost of installing a dedicated always-on connection

18 What are some questions to be asked about remote-access physical termination?

Answer:

What are the requirements on the termination ports? Do they have to support voice, data, and fax?

What is the cost of bringing all the users into a central site, versus the cost of maintaining modem pools in several sites? Where will the connectivity be most reliable?

How many users are going to simultaneously use the remote-access system?

Are the users mobile or fixed?

How many fixed users have access to always-on technology?

Are sites, or individual users, being terminated?

19 What are five common physical layer technologies (dialup and broadband) for enterprise remote access?

Answer: Modem dialup, ISDN, cell phone, DSL, cable modem

20 To size the central site remote-access solution, what parameters need to be determined? How would the peak bandwidth be determined?

Answer:

The total number of remote users, percentage of remote users that log in at once, and bandwidth required per user. To determine the peak bandwidth, use the following formula:

Total bandwidth required = Total number of remote users * percentage of users logged in at one time (expressed as 0.nn) * bandwidth required per user (expressed as kbps)

21 To determine Internet connectivity requirements, what are some of the basic questions that must be answered?

Answer:

Does the enterprise need a single Internet connection or multiple Internet connections? Will multiple Internet connections be furnished by a single ISP or by different ISPs?

If multiple ISPs are used, how will load balancing be done?

Which routing protocol will advertise the Internet internally, and advertise publicly available subnets externally?

Is NAT or PAT required at a router or transition device between the public and corporate network?

What security measures are required to protect the corporate network?

22 Name the major forms of NAT.

Answer: Static, dynamic, overloading, overlapping

23   What are some the common questions that must be asked when implementing a single-homed connection?

Answer:

What are the consequences if the Internet connection is lost?

Can the enterprise afford the consequences of an outage?

Will public addressing or private addressing be used in the network?

If private addressing is used inside, how many public addresses are needed to support the hosts that need static addressing? How many addresses are needed in the address pool for the users?

When selecting the ISP, what services and support does it provide?

24   What are the advantages of multihoming?

Answer: Reliability and availability (fault tolerance), load sharing, and ability to enforce policies.

25   What are the two routing options for a multihomed solution?

Answer:

Run BGP on edge routers, set them up as IBGP peers, and set up EBGP relation between these routers and their ISP counterparts.

Setup static gateways of last resort on the edge routers pointing to the ISPs, and inject gateway of last resort (default route) into the network.

Chapter 4

1   What role(s) does network modeling play in the development of a Network Management System?

Answer: Network modeling enables the development of "what if" scenarios to allow proactive determination of future network failures to assist the network staff in proactively fixing problems. It also provides the ability to do capacity planning to help determine which upgrades might be required in the future.

2   What are the five functional areas defined by the ISO for Network Management?

Answer: Fault management, configuration management, accounting management, performance management, and security management

3   Network management policies differ from network management procedures in what way?

Answer: Policies are implemented to define the plan for the network management system, and the procedures are in place to define how to respond to an event or how to interpret collected performance data.

4 What are two management styles typically found in Network Management?

Answer: Proactive and reactive

5 Define the six steps required to develop an enterprise network management strategy.

Answer:

Step 1 Plan which devices are to be managed and which are not.

Step 2 Determine what information to gather or receive from network devices.

Step 3 Set realistic, measurable goals for network management.

Step 4 Identify the tools available to collect the required data.

Step 5 Identify the monitoring goals and thresholds.

Step 6 Create plans and procedures to handle "what if" scenarios, so that when a network problem is identified, some basic procedures are in place to resolve the problem.

6 Identify the services the Network Management Module might contain.

Answer: Authentication services, access control services, network monitoring services, IDS director, Syslog, and system administration services

7 Give an example of out-of-band management.

Answer: Terminal server

8 What protocols are used by the Common Management Foundation component of CiscoWorks to discover the network?

Answer: CDP, ILMI, and SNMP

9 What are the two core components of the CiscoWorks product line used to manage LANs and WANs?

Answer: LAN Management Solution (LMS) and Routed WAN Management Solution (RWAN)

10 Define the common elements that are found in both the LMS and RWAN CiscoWorks product lines.

Answer: CD One and Resource Manager Essentials (RME)

11 In the Resource Manager Essentials application, describe the function of the Change Audit Service.

Answer: Change Audit displays changes made to managed devices.

12 What are the three modules that CiscoWorks LMS is composed of?

Answer: Campus Manager, nGenius Real-Time Monitor, and Device Fault Manager

13 Define the four RME tasks that Cisco recommends as best practices?

Answer: Maintain a configuration archive, maintain a software image archive, create a change management inventory, and run custom reports.

14 The Internetwork Performance Monitor (IPM) uses what service within IOS to generate synthetic traffic for performance measurement?

Answer: Service Assurance Agent

15 What are the RWAN modules in addition to CD One and RME?

Answer: Internetwork Performance Monitor (IPM) and Access Control List Manager (ACL Manager)

16 List three traffic types the IPM can generate a network response time baseline for.

Answer: ICMP echo, IP path echo, SNA echo, UDP, UDP jitter, Voice over IP, TCP connect, DNS, DHCP, HTTP and DLSw

17 What should you consider when sizing your network management station?

Answer:

Determine the number of managed devices.

Determine which operating systems are used in the enterprise (Windows or Solaris).

Select the appropriate CPU type, number, and speed.

Consider the amount of RAM and swap space required for polling.

Consider the amount of hard disk space required for polling data and reporting data.

18 What are some of the issues that should be considered when considering data collection strategy?

Answer: Is polling required? What data should be collected? How much bandwidth is required for polling? What are the issues regarding management protocols? What are the issues surrounding access protocols? Is out-of-band or in-band management required?

19 A single-server deployment LAN Management Solution is recommended for networks with up to how many devices or end-user stations?

Answer: 2000 network devices or 40,000 end-user stations

20 If multiple management domains are required because of sizing limitations, what are some of the logical ways to base segmentation on?

Answer: VTP domains, IP address ranges, or LAN/WAN boundaries

21 How many devices does Cisco recommend monitoring from a single RME server?

Answer: 500

22 What are some of the scaling issues associated with Cisco RME in a large site network?

Answer:

Total number of objects in inventory

Inventory updates of largest devices

Availability monitoring

Web GUI performance

Software update jobs

Configuration-change jobs

Syslog traffic level

23 What are the key questions to consider when conducting your network management design process?

Answer:

How many network management servers are needed?

What specific bundles and products will be deployed?

What components and functions of the products are most important to the network managers?

What other management tools will be present? Will any other applications be installed on a CiscoWorks network management server, for example?

How many users will the network management tools have? How many of them will use the tools simultaneously?

In the case of very large networks, what are the administrative groupings of the network devices and network management users?

Is a separate network required for network management?

Chapter 5

1 List at least three requirements for high availability.

Answer:

Ensure that mission-critical applications are available

Improve employee and customer satisfaction and loyalty

Reduce reactive information technology (IT) support costs, resulting in increased IT productivity

Reduce financial loss

Minimize lost productivity

2 List at least three requirements or techniques to achieve high network availability.

Answer:

Reliable, fault-tolerant network devices

Device and link redundancy

Load balancing

Resilient network technologies

Network design (no single point of failure)

Best practices (documented procedures)

3 Name at least one benefit of fault tolerance.

Answer:

Minimizes time periods during which the system is nonresponsive

Helps in eliminating single points of failure

Provides disaster protection

4 What is the major drawback of achieving high availability solely through device-level fault tolerance?

Answer: Higher cost

5 What is RPR?

Answer: Route Processor Redundancy (RPR) provides a high system availability feature for some Cisco switches and routers. A system can reset and use a standby Route Switch Processor (RSP) in the event of a failure of the active RSP.

6 Name at least two Layer 3 redundancy features offered by Cisco IOS Software.

Answer: HSRP or VRRP, fast routing protocol convergence, EtherChannel technology, load sharing, CEF

7 What is MST?

Answer: Multiple Spanning Tree (MST) is based on the 802.1w standard. It allows you to map several VLANs to a reduced number of spanning-tree instances.

8 Name at least one of the software features recommended by Cisco Systems to achieve high availability.

Answer:

Protect gateway routers with HSRP or VRRP

Implement resilient routing protocols such as EIGRP, OSPF, IS-IS, RIPv2, BGP

Use floating static routes and access control lists to reduce load in case of failure

9 Name at least two essential points that must be considered about the carrier network with regards to high availability.

Answer: The topology and structure of carrier network, carrier's multihoming to different vendors, carrier availability, carrier notification, and escalation procedures to reduce repair times

10 What are the five steps of the process recommended by Cisco as best practices for high availability?

Answer:

Step 1 Analyze technical goals and constraints

Step 2 Determine the availability budget for the network

Step 3 Create application profiles for business applications

Step 4 Define availability and performance standards

Step 5 Create an operations support plan

11 Name at least two problems that must be eliminated to achieve 99.99-percent availability.

Answer:

Single point of failure

Inevitable outage for hardware and software upgrades

Long recovery time for reboot or switchover

No tested hardware spares available on site

Long repair times due to a lack of troubleshooting guides and process

Inappropriate environmental conditions

12 Name at least two problems that must be eliminated to achieve 99.999-percent availability?

Answer:

High probability of failure of redundant modules

High probability of more than one failure on the network

Long convergence for rerouting traffic around a failed trunk or router in the core

Insufficient operational control

13 List at least two of the guidelines for server farm high availability.

Answer:

Use redundant components in infrastructure systems, where such a configuration is practical, cost effective, and considered optimal

Use redundant traffic paths provided by redundant links between infrastructure systems

Use optional end-system dual-homing to provide a higher degree of availability

Chapter 6

1 What are the four types of threats that networks are vulnerable to?

Answer: Loss of privacy, data theft, impersonation, and loss of integrity

2 Provide a definition of a security policy as stated in RFC 2196.

Answer: A security policy is a formal statement of the rules by which people who are given access to an organization's technology and information assets must abide.

3 Typically, which situations are defined in a network security policy?

Answer:

Acceptable use policy

Identification and authentication policy

Internet use policy

Campus-access policy

Remote-access policy

4 What are the four solutions you can implement to secure a network?

Answer:

Authentication, encryption, firewalls, and vulnerability patching

5 Define the three risk levels that can be used to categorize network resources during a risk assessment.

Answer:

Low risk—If compromised, these systems would disrupt the business or cause legal or financial ramifications.

Medium risk—If compromised, these systems would cause a moderate disruption in the business or cause minor legal or financial ramifications.

High risk—If compromised, these systems would cause an extreme disruption in the business or cause major legal or financial ramifications.

6 List the five key elements that make up the Cisco security solution.

Answer:

Secure connectivity

Perimeter security

Intrusion protection

Identity

Security management

7 List the type of network security attacks a network should attempt to defend against.

Answer:

Packet sniffers

IP spoofing

Denial of service

Password attacks

Man-in-the-middle attacks

Application-layer attacks

Network reconnaissance

Trust exploitation

Port redirection

Unauthorized access

Virus and Trojan horse

8 List three measures that can be used to mitigate the effects of denial of service.

Answer: Anti-spoof (RFC 2827 filtering), anti-DoS feature (limit TCP half-open connections), and traffic-rate limiting

9 List standard technologies that can be used to enable identification services.

Answer:

Remote Authentication Dial-In User Service (RADIUS)

Terminal Access Controller Access Control System plus (TACACS+)

Kerberos

One-time passwords (OTP)

Smart cards

Tokens

Directory services

Digital certificates

10 To mitigate the success of password attacks, what steps should be used when selecting a password?

Answer: Use OTPs to avoid plain text passwords. Ensure your passwords are a minimum of eight characters in length and are comprised of upper case letters, lower case letters, numbers, and special characters.

11 List some of the measures that you can take to reduce the risk of application-layer attacks.

Answer:

Read operating system and network log files and analyze them using log analysis applications.

Subscribe to mailing lists that publicize vulnerabilities.

Keep operating systems and applications patched.

Use IDSs to minimize application layer attacks.

12 What is port redirection?

Answer: Port redirection is a type of trust exploitation attack that uses a compromised host to pass traffic through a firewall.

13 List two of the primary vulnerabilities for end-user workstations.

Answer: Viruses and Trojan horse

14 Define a Trojan horse.

Answer: A Trojan horse is an entire application that was written to look like something else, when in fact it is an attack tool.

15 Define a perimeter LAN.

Answer: Perimeter LAN is another term for a demilitarized zone. In the context of firewalls, this refers to a part of the network that is neither part of the internal network nor directly part of the Internet.

16 List some of the security services provided by the PIX firewall.

Answer:

Network Address Translation

Port Address Translation

Content filtering

URL filtering

Authentication, authorization, and accounting (AAA) RADIUS/TACACS+ integration

Support for x.509 public key infrastructure (PKI) solutions

DHCP

PPP over Ethernet (PPPoE) support

VPN services (software and hardware)

17 What are the two complementary IDS technologies?

Answer: Host-based IDS and network-based IDS

18 Define the term attack signature.

Answer: Attack signatures are the profile for a particular attack or kind of attack. They specify conditions that must be met before traffic is deemed to be an attack.

19 What are some intrusion detection design considerations?

Answer:

Tune to make information useful and meaningful.

Reduce false positives.

Consider an event correlation engine.

Avoid sensor overruns.

Place at critical assets.

Consider issues with asymmetric routing.

20 Define the term false positives.

Answer: False positives are alarms caused by legitimate traffic or activity.

21 List at least three authentication, authorization, and accounting protocols.

Answer: RADIUS, TACACS+, Kerberos, and PKI

22 What cryptographic algorithm for encryption authentication docs Kerberos use?

Answer: Data Encryption Standard (DES)

23 Define the term certificate within the context of PKI.

Answer: A certificate is a cryptographically signed structure that guarantees the association between at least one identifier and public key. It is valid for a limited period of time, for a specific usage, and under certain conditions and limitations described in a certificate policy.

24 List the services provided by IPSec.

Answer: Data confidentiality, data integrity, data origin authentication, and anti-replay

25 List the two protocols IPSec provides for transporting user data.

Answer: Authentication Header and Encapsulating Security Payload

26 List some of the tasks that you can perform to secure a router.

Answer:

Lock down Telnet access.

Lock down SNMP access.

Control access through the use of TACACS+.

Turn off unneeded services.

Log at the appropriate levels.

Authenticate routing updates.

Deploy secure commands and control.

27   What are some common forms of DDoS?

Answer: ICMP floods, TCP SYN floods, and UDP floods

28   List the SAFE design objectives.

Answer:

Security and attack mitigation based on policy.

Security implementation through the infrastructure.

Secure management and reporting.

Authentication and authorization of users and administrators to critical network resources.

Intrusion detection for critical resources and subnets.

29   List the primary devices included in the small network Internet Connectivity module.

Answer:

SMTP server

DNS server

FTP/HTTP server

Firewall or firewall router

Layer 2 switch

Host-based IDS (HIDS)

30   Which three modules comprise the SAFE Design for Medium Networks?

Answer:

Internet Connectivity module, Campus Infrastructure module, and WAN module

Chapter 7

1   Choose three items that require QoS to manage them.

Answer: Delay, packet loss, and delay variation (b, c, e)

2   Name at least two benefits of effective QoS configurations?

Answer: Control over resources, more effective use of network resources, tailored services, and coexistence of mission-critical applications

3   Name the three types of fixed delay.

Answer: Packetization delay, serialization delay, and propagation delay

4 Explain delay variation (jitter).

Answer: Delay variation is the difference between the end-to-end trip delay of packets in the same stream. For example, if one packet in a stream takes 100 ms to go from source to the destination, and the next packet in the same stream takes 125 ms, the delay variation between the two packets is 25 ms.

5 What is a jitter buffer?

Answer: A jitter buffer is used to smooth out changes in arrival times of data packets containing voice or video. Each end station in a voice or video conversation has a jitter buffer.

6 List at least three tasks that IT managers can accomplish using QoS technologies:

Answer:

Predict response times for end-to-end services

Manage jitter-sensitive applications

Manage delay-sensitive traffic

Control loss in times of inevitable bursty congestion

Set traffic priorities across the network

Support dedicated bandwidth

Avoid and manage network congestion

7 Name the two QoS architectures (models) used in IP networks.

Answer: Integrated Services (IntServ) architecture and Differentiated Services (DiffServ) architecture

8 Within the IntServ model, which protocol is used by applications to signal their QoS requirements?

Answer: Resource Reservation Protocol (RSVP)

9 Which two of the following items are *not* in line with the IntServ model?

Answer: b and d

10 Which two of the following items are *not* in line with the DiffServ model?

Answer: a and c

11 Name the three basic levels of QoS that can be provided across a heterogeneous network.

Answer:

Best-effort service (also called lack of QoS)

Differentiated service (also called soft QoS)

Guaranteed service (also called hard QoS)

12 Classification at the trust boundary can mark packets by examining different fields. Name at least three of those fields.

Answer:

Layer 2 parameters: CoS bits, MAC address, MPLS exp

Layer 3 parameters: IP Precedence, DSCP, Source address, destination address, protocol number

Layer 4 parameters: TCP or UDP port numbers

Application-layer parameters: application signatures

13 Name and briefly explain the technique (supported by Cisco IOS) for congestion avoidance.

Answer: Weighted Random Early Detection (WRED) provides congestion avoidance by monitoring buffer depth and performing a probabilistic (random) discard, instead of waiting for buffers to fill and tail-drop all arriving packets. WRED can be configured to use either IP Precedence or to use the DSCP value when it calculated the drop probability of a packet. On VIP cards, WRED can be performed on a distributed basis (dWRED).

14 Name at least three congestion management features supported by Cisco IOS.

Answer:

First in, first out (FIFO)

Weighted fair queuing (WFQ)—Flow-based, class-based, and distributed

Low-latency queuing (LLQ)—Distributed, LLQ for Frame Relay

Priority 1 queuing (PQ)

Custom queuing (CQ)

Frame Relay PVC Interface Priority Queuing (FRPIPQ)

IP RTP Priority and Frame Relay IP RTP Priority

15 Name at least two Cisco IOS–supported traffic conditioning tools and techniques?

Answer: CAR, police, and traffic shaping

16 Name at least two QoS software traffic-shaping features within Cisco IOS?

Answer:

Generic traffic shaping (GTS)

Class-based shaping

Distributed traffic shaping

Frame Relay traffic shaping (FRTS)

17 Name the three link-efficiency mechanisms (offered by IOS QoS software) that work in conjunction with queuing and traffic shaping to improve the predictability of application services.

Answer: Link Fragmentation and Interleaving (LFI), Compressed Real-Time Protocol (cRTP), and Distributed Compressed Real-Time Protocol (dcRTP)

18 Name at least two properties or benefits of LFI?

Answer:

Reduces serialization delay

Works as a Layer 2 mechanism

Used on links of less than 768 kbps

Creates additional CPU load

19 cRTP can reduce the IP/UDP/RTP headers down to how many bytes?

Answer: It can reduce the 40-byte IP/UDP/RTP header down to 2 bytes (4 bytes with UDP CRC).

20 Based on the design guidelines for voice and video, what are the one-way requirements for these types of traffic?

Answer: Latency no more than 150–200 ms, jitter no more than 30 ms, and loss no more than 1 percent

Chapter 8

1 If an application on one host wants to send packets to three hosts on the same subnet, usage of which of the following methods will generate more traffic?

Answer: a Unicast

2 Which of the following applications is a good candidate as a multicast application?

Answer: d All of the above

3 Which of the following is not one of the characteristics of IP multicast?

Answer: c Reliable transport

4 Which of the following is not a potential disadvantage of IP multicast?

Answer: a Inefficient data delivery

5 Multicast forwarding is based on which of the following techniques?

Answer: b Reverse Path Forwarding

6 Which of the following is not a characteristic of IP multicast source-distribution trees?

Answer: **c** Require initial configuration of root (RP)

7 Which of the following is not a characteristic of IP multicast shared-distribution trees?

Answer: **d** Require easier configuration than source-based trees

8 Which of the following best describes PIM-DM?

Answer: **b** Flood and prune, source tree

9 Which of the following best describes PIM-SM?

Answer: **c** On-demand join, shared tree

10 Which of the following is not related to PIM-SM?

Answer: **a** Periodic flooding

11 Which of the following is not a characteristic of CGMP?

Answer: **b** Used by IPv4 hosts to communicate multicast group membership to the connected routers.

12 Which of the following is a characteristic of IGMP?

Answer: **d** Used by IPv4 hosts to communicate multicast group membership to the connected routers.

13 Which of the following is an IP multicast control mechanism that Cisco IOS supports?

Answer: **d** All of the above

14 Which of the following is not a major IP multicast design consideration?

Answer: **a** What is the multicast server's OS?

15 When designing IP multicast for a collapsed core (small campus) network, which device is considered the best candidate for RP?

Answer: **d** Core router

Chapter 9

1 What are the required attributes of a VPN solution?

Answer: Robust architecture, scalability, easy management, and flexibility

2 What are the benefits of a site-to-site VPN?

Answer: It extends connectivity of the network across the WAN, increases bandwidth, and offers lower cost than a leased line.

3 Define the technique known as tunneling.

Answer: Tunneling is the technique where packets of one type of protocol are encapsulated by another protocol.

4 When is GRE tunneling used?

Answer: GRE tunneling is used when multicast, broadcast, and non-IP packets need to be tunneled.

5 What are the key components of the IPSec framework laid out by the IETF?

Answer: Data integrity checks for tamper protection, source address verification, and data privacy for the packet data and packet path.

6 What is the role of a certification authority (CA)?

Answer: A certification authority digitally signs each certificate and validates the integrity of a certificate.

7 Define encryption.

Answer: Encryption is the process of converting data through an algorithm to a form that cannot be easily read.

8 When evaluating the capabilities of the concentrator device, what questions need to be answered?

Answer:

Is it a purpose-built communications platform?

Is physical redundancy designed in?

Does the product use a proven software operating system?

Can the device be proactively managed for high availability?

9 What are the key VPN management design considerations?

Answer:

Ease of configuration

Dynamic reconfiguration

Proactive monitoring and alerts

Multiple device monitoring

Robust configuration

10 Define the modules associated with the CiscoWorks VPN/Security Management Solutions discussed in this chapter.

Answer:

VPN Monitor

Cisco IDS Host Sensor

Cisco Secure Policy Manager (CSPM)

Resource Manager Essential (RME)

CiscoView (CD One)

11 List the key components of site-to-site VPN design.

Answer:

Cisco head-end VPN routers

Cisco VPN access router

IPSec and generic routing encapsulation (GRE)

Internet services from ISPs

12 What are the four major steps to designing a site-to-site VPN solution?

Answer:

Step 1 Determine the application and data needs for the VPN solution.

Step 2 Design the VPN topology between sites.

Step 3 Incorporate design resiliency and failover mechanisms.

Step 4 Choose head-end products based on predicted VPN capacity requirements.

13 When is it appropriate to use a hub-and-spoke design for a VPN solution?

Answer: When there is a single regional or headquarters location with a large number of remote offices, and the majority of all traffic is between remote sites and the regional or headquarters location.

14 When is it appropriate to use a full-mesh design for a VPN solution?

Answer: When there is a small number of total locations (regional, headquarters, or remote locations), with a large amount of traffic flowing between some (partial mesh) or all (full mesh) of the sites.

15 When is it appropriate to use a hierarchical design for a VPN solution?

Answer: With large networks that contain both a large number of remote offices, which have little traffic interaction between them, and a small number of headquarters or regional offices, which have a large number of traffic flowing between them. Hierarchical designs are the most scalable design for large networks, which require either partial or full connectivity between sites.

16 What two steps must occur for stateless failover of a VPN connection to be successful?

Answer:

One of the peers must detect the loss of connectivity.

After detected, the peer must take action to reconnect with another peer to reach the part of the private network at the same time.

17 What two steps can be taken to avoid the fragmentation of packets over a GRE/IPSec tunnel?

Answer:

Employ the MTU discovery.

Set the MTU to allow for packet expansion, such as 1400 bytes.

18 What technique should be used to add resiliency to IPSec tunnels?

Answer: Implement two IPSec tunnels in transport mode on top of GRE tunnels.

19 Define a GRE tunnel.

Answer: A GRE tunnel is a virtual interface in a router that provides many of the features associated with physical interfaces. GRE tunnels provide the ability to encapsulate multicast and broadcast packets from non-IP protocols.

20 List the principle advantages of a remote-access VPN solution.

Answer:

Reduced access charges

Reduced overhead cost

Reduced service and support costs

More successful connections

Improved scalability

Improved availability

21 What questions should be asked when designing a remote-access VPN?

Answer:

Is remote access connectivity the main focus of the solution?

What operating systems will remote users use? Determine if the VPN hardware and software client support these operating systems.

Which VPN tunneling protocol will be used on the VPN concentrator?

How will user authentication be achieved in this solution?

22 What should be defined to help document the capacity planning design aspects of the remote-access VPN solution?

Answer:

Estimate the total number of users.

Estimate the number of concurrent users.

Determine the current bandwidth of the ISP connection.

Estimate the required bandwidth for the ISP connection.

Identify the user connection method.

Forecast VPN usage growth.

23 What is NAT Traversal?

Answer: NAT Traversal (NAT-T) lets IPSec peers establish a connection through a NAT device. It does this by encapsulating IPSec traffic in UDP datagrams, using port 4500, thereby providing NAT devices with port information. NAT-T autodetects any NAT devices, and only encapsulates IPSec traffic when necessary.

24 How does split tunneling work?

Answer: When the split tunneling feature is enabled, all the traffic leaving a particular site through a router will be forwarded directly to the next hop closest to the destination of that traffic. Only traffic destined to the remote site served by the tunnel will be encapsulated.

25 When split tunneling is involved with a network that uses the Internet to create a VPN, it is highly recommended that a stateful inspection firewall function be configured at the spoke sites. Why?

Answer: Split tunneling allows an end station to directly access those hosts on the Internet. These end stations will not be protected by any firewall configured at the hub location. NAT is not a complete firewall solution.

Chapter 10

1 What three factors affect the size of a wireless LAN coverage area?

Answer: Data rate, antenna choice, power level

2 What is the role of CSMA/CA in wireless LANs?

Answer: Carrier sense multiple access collision avoidance (CSMA/CA) is used by wireless stations to determine when they can communicate. This is required because the bandwidth is shared among all stations.

3 How do data rates affect cell size?

Answer: Lower data rates allow the signal to extend further from the access point than higher data rates can. Hence, the data rate (and power level) will affect cell coverage and the number of access points required.

4 What does the IEEE 802.11 specification define?

Answer: The 802.11 standards define the communication protocols between wireless workstations and the network access points that bridge wireless and wired networks.

5 Describe the components that comprise the Cisco wireless solution.

Answer: The Cisco wireless solution includes access points, client adapters, workgroup bridges, wireless bridges, antennas, and accessories.

6 Describe the role of an access point in wireless networks.

Answer: An access point is the center point in an all-wireless network, or serves as a connection point between a wired and wireless network.

7 Describe the role of a wireless bridge in a wireless network.

Answer: A wireless bridge is capable of communicating over greater distances than 802.11b access points and clients.

8 What are some considerations when designing an enterprise WLAN solution?

Answer: When designing an enterprise wireless network solution, you must consider the radio frequency (RF) design, the campus infrastructure, high availability, roaming, IP multicast, quality of service (QoS), and security.

9 What are three reasons for limiting the data rate to the highest rate at which full coverage is obtained?

Answer: Broadcast and multicast are sent at the slowest data rate (to ensure that all clients can see them), which reduces the throughput of the WLAN because traffic must wait until frames are processed at the slower rate.

Clients that are farther away, and, therefore, accessing the network at a lower data rate, decrease the overall throughput by causing delays while the lower bit rates are being serviced.

If an 11-Mbps service has been specified and provisioned with access points to support this level of service, allowing clients to associate at lower rates will create a coverage area greater than planned, increasing the security exposure and potentially interfering with other WLANs.

10 What are some examples of variables that can adversely affect RF performance?

Answer:

2.4-GHz cordless phones

Walls fabricated from wire mesh and stucco

Filing cabinets and metal equipment racks

Transformers

Heavy-duty electric motors

Firewalls and fire doors

Concrete

Refrigerators

Sulphur plasma lighting (Fusion 2.4-GHz lighting systems)

Air conditioning ductwork

Other radio equipment

Microwave ovens

Other WLAN equipment

11   What are the channels used in North America for the 802.11b specification?

Answer: The North American and European Telecommunication Standards Institute (ETSI) channel sets allow the allocation of three nonoverlapping channels: 1, 6, and 11.

12   How should you allocate channels to cells?

Answer:

Overlapping cells should use nonoverlapping channels.

Where the same channels are required in multiple cells, make sure those cells have no overlap.

13   What should you consider when choosing an access point and associated client cards?

Answer: Processor power, throughput requirements, inline power support, and output power support.

14   What is an advantage of inline power?

Answer: Inline power eliminates the requirement for site customization to provide power outlets in ceilings or walls to support access points.

15   Why should the WLAN be on a separate VLAN from other LAN traffic?

Answer:

Optimize overall network performance. The WLAN media is shared and, therefore, any unnecessary broadcast or multicast traffic can impair network performance.

Clearly identify the source of traffic for management and security issues.

Increase the number of WLAN clients on a single VLAN and increase the possible Layer 2 roaming domain.

16 What are the three different security deployment options?

Answer:

WLAN LAN extension via EAP—Using the Extensible Authentication Protocol (EAP) to provide dynamic per-user per-session WEP to ensure privacy, in combination with 802.11x to provide access control.

WLAN LAN extension via IPSec—Using IPSec to ensure privacy and using access-point filtering, router filtering, and the VPN concentrator to provide access control.

WLAN static WEP—Using whatever privacy mechanism is available and using access-point filtering, router filtering, and the hardened application servers to provide access control. This security option is not recommended for open network access (access must be limited to specific applications).

17 What are the three ways to address the availability of the WLAN?

Answer:

As an overlay network—The hard-wired LAN is the users' backup if the WLAN fails.

As a mobile network—Users can move to a location where connectivity is available if the WLAN fails.

As a mission-critical network—Network redundancies ensure that the failure of one component does not impact WLAN users.

18 What is the role of access-point hot standby redundancy?

Answer: Access-point hot standby is not the same as HSRP. Hot standby mode designates an access point as a backup for another access point. The standby access point is placed near the access point it monitors and is configured exactly the same as the monitored access. The standby access point associates with the monitored access point as a client and queries the monitored access point regularly through both the Ethernet interface and the radio interface. If the monitored access point fails to respond, the standby access point comes online, signals the primary access-point radio to become quiescent, and takes the monitored access point's place in the network.

19 What are the bit rates associated with multicast and broadcast traffic on WLANs?

Answer: If the access point is configured to operate at multiple bit rates, multicasts and broadcasts are sent at the lowest rate to ensure that all clients receive them.

20 What is the recommended role of access-point filters in WLANs?

Answer: Access-point filters provide strict priority queuing for downstream traffic. Filters are used to assign priority on EtherType, IP port, or protocol. Therefore, protocols likely to carry latency-sensitive traffic can have a higher priority at the access point.

21 What is the maximum number of VoIP phones per access point? Why?

Answer: The maximum recommended number of phones per access point is seven. This limitation is due to the number of packets that can be forwarded per second over an 802.11 link and minimizing transmission delays, rather than a bandwidth limitation of the link.

22 What two mitigation techniques should be used to protect a wireless client if a VPN solution is going to be used to connect them?

Answer:

First, configure the access point with the ether type protocol and port filters based on a company's wireless usage policy. SAFE WLAN recommends restrictive filters that allow only the necessary protocols required for establishing a secure tunnel to a VPN gateway. These protocols include DHCP for initial client configuration, DNS for name resolution of the VPN gateways, and the VPN-specific protocols: Internet Key Exchange (IKE) on User Datagram Protocol (UDP) port 500, and Encapsulating Security Payload (ESP) (IP Protocol 50).

Secondly, use personal firewall software on the wireless client to protect the client while it is connected to the untrusted WLAN network, without the protection of IPSec.

23 What two ways might a wireless network be used in a small office deployment?

Answer: In the small office, the WLAN might be used as an overlay network, or it might be used as a replacement network.

24 What is the typical role of a wireless LAN in an enterprise network?

Answer: A WLAN is typically deployed in an enterprise network as an extension rather than a replacement. The goal is usually to obtain the benefits of WLAN with as little disruption as possible to the existing infrastructure.

Chapter 11

1 What are the telephony components found within the Cisco IP Telephony architecture?

Answer: Call processing engine, IP phones, and gateways

2 What is the role of gateways in the Cisco IP Telephony architecture?

Answer: Gateways provide access to the IP Telephony network for endpoints other than IP Phones, such as applications, WAN facilities, the Public Switched Telephone Network (PSTN), and other IP Telephony and Voice over IP (VoIP) installations.

3 What types of gateways are defined in the Cisco IP Telephony architecture?

Answer: Applications, voice-enabled routers, PSTN gateways, and VoIP gateways

4 What is the role of Cisco CallManager?

Answer: CallManager provides call processing for the Cisco AVVID IP telephony solution. CallManager is the software-based call-processing component of the Cisco enterprise IP Telephony solution and is a product enabled by Cisco AVVID. CallManager software extends enterprise telephony features and capabilities to packet telephony network devices, such as IP Phones, media processing devices, VoIP gateways, and multimedia applications.

5 How many users can be serviced by a single CallManager cluster?

Answer: CallManager clustering yields scalability of up to 10,000 users per cluster.

6 What is the overall goal of an IP Telephony network?

Answer:

Provide end-to-end IP Telephony for network users

Use the IP WAN as the primary voice path with the PSTN as the secondary voice path between sites

Lower the total cost of ownership with greater flexibility

Enable new applications

7 Gateway selection depends upon what requirements?

Answer:

Voice, fax, and modem capabilities

Analog or digital access

Signaling protocol used to control gateways

8 What gateway protocols does the Cisco CallManager support?

Answer: Simple Gateway Control Protocol (SGCP), Media Gateway Control Protocol (MGCP), H.323, Session Initiation Protocol (SIP)

9 What is a media resource?

Answer: A media resource is a software- or hardware-based entity that performs media processing functions on the voice data streams to which it is connected.

10 What is the definition of transcoding?

Answer: Transcoding compresses and decompresses voice streams to maximize use of WAN resources for VoIP traffic. A transcoder takes the output stream of one codec and converts it in real time (transcodes it) into an input stream for a different codec type.

11 What is the function of a unicast conference bridge?

Answer: A unicast conference bridge is a device that accepts multiple connections for a given conference. It can accept any number of connections for a given conference, up to the maximum number of streams allowed for a single conference on that device.

12 What are the two types of conference bridges?

Answer: Software based and hardware based

13 What are the components of a CallManager cluster?

Answer: A CallManager cluster consists of two or more CallManager servers that work together. A database defines the servers in the cluster. A cluster has one publisher (main) server and up to seven subscriber servers. The publisher maintains one database, which it replicates to the other servers in the cluster. Logically, a CallManager cluster is a single CallManager instance.

14 What are some general guidelines for CallManager deployment?

Answer:

A cluster might contain a mix of server platforms, but all CallManagers in the cluster must run the same software version.

Within a cluster, you can enable a maximum of six servers with the CallManager service, and use other servers for more specialized functions such as TFTP, database publisher, MoH, and so forth.

All operating system and network services that are not required on a server should be disabled to maximize the server's available resources.

15 In a small-scale cluster deployment, how many servers should you deploy?

Answer: In a small-scale cluster environment (up to 2500 phones), deploy both a publisher and a subscriber.

16 How many CallManagers can you deploy in a large-scale cluster design?

Answer: In the large-cluster design, there are up to eight CallManagers.

17 What is the maximum number of IP phones that can register with a single CallManager?

Answer: 2500 on the largest server platforms, even if only IP Phones are registered.

18 How does the device-weighting factor affect the CallManager solution?

Answer: Each telephony device carries a different weight based on the amount of resources it requires from the server platform with which it is registered. The required resources include memory, processor, and I/O.

19 What are some possible design characteristics of a single-site model?

Answer:

Single CallManager or CallManager cluster

Maximum of 10,000 IP Phones per cluster

PSTN for all external calls

DSP resources for conferencing, transcoding, and MTP

Voice mail and unified messaging components

G.711 codec used for all IP Phone calls (80 kbps of IP bandwidth per call, uncompressed)

Capability to integrate with legacy PBX and voice mail systems

20 What are the three possible gateway solutions?

Answer:

H.323 gateway

PSTN gateway

Voice-mail gateway

21 What are the primary benefits of the single-site model?

Answer:

Ease of deployment

A common infrastructure for a converged solution

Simplified dial plan

No transcoding resources required, due to the use of only G.711 codecs

22 What is the primary advantage of a distributed call processing solution?

Answer: The primary advantage of the distributed call processing model is that, by using local call processing, it provides the same level of features and capabilities whether the IP WAN is available or not. Each site can have from one to eight CallManager servers in a cluster, based on the number of users. This is the predominant deployment model for sites with greater than 50 users, and each site can support up to 10,000 users. In addition, no loss of service occurs if the IP WAN is down.

23 What is the role of a gatekeeper in the distributed model?

Answer: A gatekeeper is an H.323 device that provides call admission control and PSTN dial-plan resolution.

24 Describe the guidelines you should follow when implementing the local failover model for CallManager clustering across multiple sites.

Answer:

Configure each site to contain at least one primary and one backup CallManager subscriber.

Cisco highly recommends that you replicate key services (TFTP, DNS, DHCP, LDAP, and IP Phone services), all media resources (conference bridges and MoH), and gateways at each site to provide the highest level of resiliency. You could also extend this practice to include a voice-mail system at each site. In the event of a WAN failure, only sites without access to the publisher database might lose a small amount of functionality.

Every 10,000 BHCAs in the cluster require 900 kbps of bandwidth for Intra-Cluster Communication Signaling (ICCS). This is a minimum bandwidth requirement, and bandwidth is allocated in multiples of 900 kbps.

Allow a maximum round-trip time (RTT) of 40 ms between any two servers in the CallManager cluster. This time equates to a 20-ms maximum one-way delay, or a transmission distance of approximately 1860 miles (3000 km) under ideal conditions.

25 What questions should you ask when designing an infrastructure to support voice?

Answer:

What features are required for each device in the campus network?

Will the physical plant in the campus support IP Telephony or is an upgrade required?

What features are required for each device at the enterprise edge?

Does the network provide the bandwidth required to support both voice and call control traffic?

26 What are two Layer 2 alternatives to a CallManager VoIP-based network?

Answer: Voice over Frame Relay or Voice over ATM

27 What formula should you use to calculate the bandwidth that voice streams consume?

(Packet payload + all headers in bits) * packet rate per second (50 packets per second when using a 20 ms packet period)

28 What are the two categories of control traffic that traverse the WAN?

Answer: Call-related traffic and maintenance traffic

29 What is traffic engineering, as it applies to traditional voice networks?

Answer: It is determining the number of trunks necessary to carry a required amount of voice calls during a period of time.

30 What should you consider when configuring campus QoS?

Answer: Trust boundary, traffic classification, and interface queuing

Chapter 12

1 What is content networking?

Answer: Content networking is the replication and placement of copies of content closer to the user or groups of users through caching and Content Delivery Network (CDN) technologies.

2 What components comprise the Cisco Content Networking solution?

Answer:

Content caching

Content switching

Content routing

Content distribution and management

Intelligent network services

3 What is the role of the Content Engine?

Answer: A Content Engine (CE) caches copies of data from origin servers, allowing the content to be served locally.

4 What is caching?

Answer: Caching is a demand-based replication and storage of cacheable content for the purpose of serving that same content to users making subsequent requests for it.

5 What are the three models for content caching?

Answer: The three deployment models for content caching include transparent, proxy, and reverse proxy.

6 Where does enterprise caching typically take place?

Answer: Typically, caching takes place at the remote site, close to users.

7 How does transparent caching work?

Answer: With transparent caching, a user request for content (usually through a web browser) is redirected by a router or switch to a CE.

8 How does proxy caching work?

Answer: Proxy caching uses the CE as a proxy for all content requests. The user's browser is typically modified to send requests directly to the CE rather than to the origin server. The CE then forwards the request to the origin server, if necessary, or serves the content locally.

9 How does reverse proxy work?

Answer: With reverse proxy caching, static content from a server is offloaded onto a CE. Requests destined for the server are directed to the CE, which serves the content locally, freeing the server from processing multiple requests for static content.

10 Define content switching.

Answer: Content switching intelligently load balances traffic across servers or CEs based on the availability of the content and the load on the server.

11 What services do content switches provide?

Answer:

Local and global load balancing of user requests

Policy-based web traffic direction based on full visibility of URLs, host tags, and cookies

Enhanced denial-of-service protection, cache and firewall load balancing, and flash-crowd management

12 What is content routing?

Answer: Content routing redirects an end-user request to the best site based on a set of metrics such as delay, topology, or server load, and a set of policies such as location of content.

13 What are the two modes a content router can be deployed in?

Answer:

It can be set up in direct mode.

It can be set up in WCCP mode.

14 What is direct mode content routing?

Answer: In direct mode, the content router is configured as the authoritative DNS server for the fully qualified domain name being routed. All requests for the IP address of the domain name are handled by the content router and its content routing agents.

15 Describe the Cisco Content Distribution and Management solution.

Answer: The Cisco CDM is a web-browser–based tool that provides the administrative function for content networking. With the CDM, you can configure and monitor CEs, import and preview media, and generate media URLs for access from websites. You also set maximum bandwidth usage over the WAN from the CDM to the remote CEs, as well as maximum LAN bandwidth usage from the CEs to end-user desktops. You can schedule content distribution by time of day and day of week, allowing content replication to occur during off-peak hours.

16 What are the Cisco intelligent solution components?

Answer:

High availability—Some of the content networking devices, such as content switches and routers, are used to provide high availability for content. Redundant CEs, switches, and routers can further ensure availability for the most critical content.

Security—The content being served can be highly sensitive, so in addition to the security features implemented throughout the network, you should take additional care to secure the content networking devices themselves.

QoS—When content networking involves the delivery of delay-sensitive data such as audio or video, QoS features allow such traffic to be given priority over other data traffic.

IP multicast—When content networking is used to facilitate simultaneous delivery of streaming media, IP multicast must be implemented throughout the network to support the broadcast requirements.

17 What are the three important parameters to consider when determining the sizing required for a particular cache installation?

Answer:

Number of transactions per second required—Identifies the amount of HTTP traffic

Number of simultaneous connections—Defines the total number of HTTP flows that the cache will see at any single point in time

Size of objects—Determines the amount of disk storage required, and the object hold time

18 What formula determines the cache storage required for 24 hours?

Answer: Average TPS * average object size (bytes) * number of seconds in 24 hours * (1 − expected cache hit rate [bytes]) / 1,000,000,000

Chapter 13

1 How is the highest level of information protection achieved?

Answer: The highest level of information protection is achieved through mirror sites.

2 What is asynchronous mirroring?

Answer: In this asynchronous mode of replication, snapshots, or point-in-time copies of the data, are taken and transferred to a remote site. The point-in-time image is used for disaster recovery, and can potentially be used to perform tasks that do not require tight synchronization with the online applications (for example, data mining, reporting, backup).

3 How does snapshot technology work?

Answer: Snapshot technology makes it possible to back up systems online with minimum impact on the applications, by archiving only the changed data.

4 What are the key components of the Cisco storage networking solution?

Answer:

Network-attached storage for file-oriented access to storage

IP access to storage for block-oriented host-to-storage communication in storage area networks

Storage over the WAN, for the interconnection of all storage environments

Metro optical connectivity for the efficient, high-performance transport of storage traffic types, including Fibre Channel, Internet Small Computer System Interface (iSCSI), and Enterprise System Connection (ESCON), over data-link protocols, which include 1/10 Gigabit Ethernet and other optical technologies

5 What is network-attached storage?

Answer: Network-attached storage provides file-oriented access over an IP network. Network-attached storage is implemented using customized storage appliances that run Network File System (NFS) for UNIX environments and Common Internet File System (CIFS) for Microsoft Windows NT and Microsoft Windows environments. Network-attached storage is deployed for high-performance file-sharing applications, such as engineering collaboration, NT file systems, e-mail, and web-content storage.

6 What is a SAN?

Answer: SAN provides block-oriented access to native disk storage. It is based on a shared or switched infrastructure, often Fibre Channel. You can extend SAN to an IP infrastructure. New protocols and products are emerging that allow the integration of SANs with the IP network. Historically, SANs have been well suited to high-volume, write-intensive, transaction-driven applications.

7 What protocols are typically used to build a SAN solution?

Answer: SANs are typically built using the SCSI and Fibre Channel protocols (SCSI-FCP).

8 What is the primary difference between SANs and network-attached storage?

Answer: SANs are typically used to access blocks of data within files for applications such as clustered database access. Network-attached storage is typically used to access files.

9 Define the iSCSI protocol.

Answer: The iSCSI protocol encapsulates a SCSI request in an IP packet. iSCSI is a SCSI transport protocol for mapping block-oriented storage requests over TCP/IP networks. Making direct access to storage over IP possible, the iSCSI protocol allows IP-connected hosts to access iSCSI or Fibre Channel–connected storage.

iSCSI is fully compatible with existing IP infrastructures. With iSCSI, users can access storage across campus and wide-area networks, allowing data center storage to scale across the enterprise.

10 What are the key technologies that enable the transfer of blocks of data over the IP network?

Answer:

iSCSI routers—Enable connection of iSCSI hosts to Fibre Channel–connected storage. Along with the iSCSI router, iSCSI device drivers provide the interface between the operating system and the TCP/IP stack.

Optical media—The bandwidth necessary for the timely transfer of I/O data is typically provided over optical media. Gigabit Ethernet is often used in this solution.

11 What services can iSCSI provide?

Answer:

Remote storage over IP

Remote backup of devices over IP to provide centralized storage management

12 What is Fibre Channel over IP?

Answer:

FCIP transparently interconnects Fibre Channel SAN islands over IP networks through FCIP tunnels.

With FCIP, Fibre Channel frames are encapsulated in IP so that both SCSI and non-SCSI frames can be transported over an IP network.

13 What shortcoming(s) of direct-attached storage does FCIP overcome?

Answer:

Addressing for up to 16 million nodes (24 bits)

Loop (shared) and fabric (switched) transport

Speeds of 1000 or 2000 Mbps (1 or 2 Gbps)

Distance of up to 10 km with extenders

Support for multiple protocols

14 How does FCIP differ from iSCSI?

Answer:

iSCSI encapsulates SCSI commands and data in a TCP/IP packet. In this case, an IP-connected host running an iSCSI driver is accessing block-level data over an IP network.

FCIP encapsulates Fibre Channel in IP packets. In this case, any Fibre Channel frame, SCSI/FCP or otherwise, is transported transparently in an IP packet. Fibre Channel hosts and storage communicate on both sides of an FCIP link.

15 What services are supported by storage networking?

Answer:

Network management—Apply network management principles to the network between clients and storage, any storage-specific network, and the storage servers and devices.

High availability—For storage networking, availability applies not only to the network between clients and storage, but also to the storage router and the storage devices themselves.

16 What are two important design considerations regarding storage networking?

Answer: Security and QoS

17 To plan for a storage networking implementation, you must consider what factors regarding the software applications that need to access the SAN?

Answer:

Access pattern—A storage-area network is typically used for real-time application access, and network-attached storage is typically used for individual access and backup.

I/O profile—The transaction rate of the application can be affected by the storage networking solution. Can the application tolerate latency for transfer between storage and the server? IP access to storage might introduce a latency factor that is unacceptable for some applications. Enterprises may require a Fibre Channel SAN in such cases. For latency-sensitive applications, the geographic placement of servers relative to storage devices can be an issue, as well as the bandwidth limitations between devices.

Throughput—The storage networking solution will need to address the infrastructure and device needs for the expected throughput.

Availability—Mirrored servers and redundant network infrastructure might be required for some applications.

18 What are several considerations for designing storage networking?

Answer:

Performance—Ensures that the networked channel has adequate bandwidth and flow control; the performance requirements vary depending on whether the application is for real-time or archival requirements

Latency—Ensures that the channel does not experience sufficient latency to compromise application integrity

Resource management—Ensures that network resources are monitored

Fault management—Ensures that the proper tools exist to detect, evaluate, and act on faults in the network

Scalability—Ensures that the network can be expanded without jeopardizing network stability

Numerics

10BASE-T. 10-Mbps baseband Ethernet specification using two pairs of twisted-pair cabling (Categories 3, 4, or 5)—one pair for transmitting data and the other for receiving data. 10BASE-T, which is part of the IEEE 802.3 specification, has a distance limit of approximately 328 feet (100 meters) per segment.

100BASE-T. 100-Mbps baseband Fast Ethernet specification using UTP wiring. Similar to the 10BASE-T technology on which it is based, 100BASE-T sends link pulses over the network segment when no traffic is present. However, these link pulses contain more information than those used in 10BASE-T. Based on the IEEE 802.3u standard.

1000BASE-T. 1000-Mbps baseband Gigabit Ethernet specification using twisted-pair based on the IEEE 802.3ab standard.

A

AAA. authentication, authorization, and accounting (pronounced "triple a"). Network security services that provide the primary framework through which you set up access control on your router or access server. AAA protocol requirements for network access are defined in RFC 2989.

ABR. available bit rate. A service category defined by the ATM Forum for ATM networks. It relates traffic characteristics and QoS requirements to network behavior. ABR is used for connections that do not require timing relationships between source and destination. ABR provides no guarantees in terms of cell loss or delay, providing only best-effort service. Traffic sources adjust their transmission rate in response to information they receive describing the status of the network and its capability to successfully deliver data.

area border router. Router located on the border of one or more OSPF areas that connect those areas to the backbone network. ABRs are considered members of both the OSPF backbone and the attached areas. They, therefore, maintain routing tables describing both the backbone topology and the topology of thc other areas.

access server. Communications processor that connects asynchronous devices to a LAN or WAN through network and terminal emulation software. Performs both synchronous and asynchronous routing of supported protocols. Sometimes called a *network access server* or NAS.

ACD. automatic call distributor. Programmable device at a telephone call center that routes incoming telephone calls to agents (persons) within that call center. After the system determines the agent for a call, the call is sent to the ACD associated with that agent.

automatic call distribution. Device or service that automatically reroutes calls to customers in geographically distributed locations served by the same CO.

ACL. access control list. An ordered list of statements. Each statement of the ACL has a match condition and a permit or deny keyword. An object that matches the condition of a statement will, hence, be identified as permitted or denied, accordingly. If an object does not match the condition of a statement, the object is then compared to the condition of the next statement and so on, until a match is found, or all the ACL statements are exhausted. An object that does not match any of the ACL statements is treated as denied. So what happens when an object is permitted or it is denied by an ACL? The answer is that it depends on what the ACL is used for; in other words, it depends on the context or application where the ACL is applied. ACLs have several usages, among them are packet filtering on router interfaces, routing update filtering, specifying the interesting traffic for dial-on-demand routing, and so on.

ActiveX. A Microsoft Windows-specific non-Java technique for writing applets. ActiveX sometimes is said to be a superset of Java.

address. Data structure or logical convention used to identify a unique entity, such as a particular process, network interface (IP), or a network device (DECnet).

address mask. A bit combination used to describe which part of an IP network address refers to the network or the subnet and which part refers to the host. Sometimes referred to simply as mask.

administrative distance. Rating of the trustworthiness of a routing information source. Administrative distance is expressed as a numerical value between 0 and 255 in Cisco IOS Software. The higher the value, the lower the trustworthiness rating. It is configurable.

ADSL. asymmetric digital subscriber line. One of four DSL technologies. ADSL is designed to deliver more bandwidth downstream (from the central office to the customer site) than upstream. Downstream rates range from 1.5 to 9 Mbps, whereas upstream bandwidth ranges from 16 to 640 kbps. ADSL transmissions might work at distances up to 18,000 feet (5,488 meters) over a single copper twisted pair. Available data rates are affected by distance, wire gauge, and the quality of the local cable plant.

AH. Authentication Header. A security protocol that provides data authentication and optional antireplay services. The authentication header is embedded in the data to be protected (a full IP datagram).

A-law. An ITU-T companding standard used in the conversion between analog and digital signals in PCM systems. The A-law is used primarily in European telephone networks and is similar to the North American μ-law standard.

analog signal. The representation of information with a continuously variable physical quantity, such as frequency and amplitude. Because of the constant changing of the wave shape with regard to a given point in time or space, an analog signal has a virtually infinite number of states or values. This contrasts with a digital signal that is expressed as a square wave and, therefore, has a very limited number of discrete states.

anti-replay. Security service where the receiver can reject old or duplicate packets to protect itself against replay attacks. IPSec provides this optional service by use of a sequence number combined with the use of data authentication.

API. aplication programming interface. The means by which an application program talks to communications software. Standardized APIs allow application programs to be developed independently of the underlying method of communication. A set of standard software interrupts, calls, and data formats that computer application programs use to initiate contact with other devices (such as network services, mainframe communications programs, or other program-to-program communications). Typically, APIs make it easier for software developers to create the links that an application needs to communicate with the operating system or the network.

AppleTalk Remote Access. A protocol that gives Macintosh users direct access to information and resources at a remote AppleTalk site.

ARP. Address Resolution Protocol. An Internet protocol used to map an IP address to a MAC address. Defined in RFC 826.

ASBR. autonomous system border router. A router that connects multiple OSPF routing domains.

ASIC. application-specific integrated circuit. Chip that is built for a specific application.

ASN.1. Abstract Syntax Notation Number One. A formal notation used to describe data transmitted by telecommunications protocols.

ATM. Asynchronous Transfer Mode. The international standard for cell relay in which multiple service types (such as voice, video, or data) are conveyed in fixed-length (53-byte) cells. Fixed-length cells allow cell processing to occur in hardware, thereby reducing transit delays. ATM is designed to take advantage of high-speed transmission media, from T1 through OC-192c.

availability. A measurable quantity that mathematically defines a system's or service's uptime. The factors affecting availability are mean time to repair (MTTR), the time it takes to recover from a failure, and mean time between failure (MTBF), the time that passes between network outages or device failures. Decreasing MTTR and increasing MTBF increase availability. Dividing MTBF by the sum of MTBF and MTTR results in a percentage indicating availability. A common goal for availability is to achieve 99.999% ("five nines").

AVVID. Architecture for Voice, Video, and Integrated Data. Cisco AVVID is an enterprise-wide, standards-based network architecture that provides the road map for combining business and technology strategies into one cohesive model. Cisco AVVID delivers the infrastructure and intelligent network services that are essential for rapid deployment of emerging technologies and new Internet business solutions.

B

BackboneFast. A feature on the switch that reduces the Spanning Tree Protocol convergence time from 50 seconds to 20 to 30 seconds.

backplane. The physical connection between an interface processor or card and the data buses and the power distribution buses inside a chassis.

backup. A way of providing high availability by using redundant links. Backup connection can be established either via dialup or by using permanent connections.

base station controller (Wireless). A device that provides the control functions and physical links between the mobile switching center (MSC) and base transceiver station (BTS) in a global system for mobile communication (GSM) mobile wireless network. The BSC is a high-capacity telephony switch that provides handoff functions and cell configuration data and controls radio frequency power levels in BTSs. The combined functions of the BSC and BTS are called the base station subsystem (BSS).

baseband. Characteristic of a network technology where only one carrier frequency is used. Ethernet is an example of a baseband network.

Bc. committed burst. Negotiated tariff metric in Frame Relay internetworks. The maximum amount of data (in bits) that a Frame Relay internetwork is committed to accept and transmit in excess of the CIR.

Be. excess burst. Negotiated tariff metric in Frame Relay internetworks. The number of bits that a Frame Relay internetwork attempts to transmit after Bc is accommodated. Be data, in general, is delivered with a lower probability than Bc data, because Be data can be marked as DE by the network.

BECN. backward explicit congestion notification. Bit set by a Frame Relay network in frames traveling in the opposite direction of frames encountering a congested path. DTE receiving frames with the BECN bit set can request that higher-level protocols take flow control action as appropriate.

best-effort service. Also called lack of QoS, best-effort service is basic connectivity with no guarantees. This is often characterized by queues that have no differentiation between flows.

BGP. Border Gateway Protocol. Interdomain routing protocol that replaces EGP. BGP exchanges reachability information with other BGP systems. It is defined by RFC 1771.

BIND. Berkeley Internet Name Domain. An implementation of the Domain Name System (DNS) developed and distributed by the University of California at Berkeley (United States). Many Internet hosts run BIND, which is the ancestor of many commercial BIND implementations.

BISDN. Broadband Integrated Services Digital Network. (Standards and Specifications)(WAN Access) International Telecommunication Union Telecommunication Standardization Sector (ITU-T) communication standards designed to handle high-bandwidth applications, such as video. BISDN currently uses ATM technology over SONET-based transmission circuits to provide data rates from 155 to 622 Mbps and higher.

BPDU. bridge protocol data unit. Spanning Tree Protocol hello packet that is sent out at configurable intervals to exchange information among bridges in the network.

bps. bits per second.

BRI. Basic Rate Interface. ISDN interface composed of two B channels and one D channel for circuit-switched communication of voice, video, and data.

broadband. Describes media in which multiple frequencies are available to transmit information. This allows information to be multiplexed and sent on many different frequencies or channels within the band concurrently; contrast with baseband.

broadcast. Data packets that are sent to all nodes on a network.

broadcast address. A special address reserved for sending a message to all stations. Generally, a data-link broadcast address is a MAC destination address of all ones. An IPv4 broadcast address is one in which the host portion of the address is all ones. No corresponding capability exists in IPv6.

broadcast domain. Set of all devices that receive broadcast frames originating from any device within the set. Routers typically bound data-link broadcast domains, because routers do not forward data-link broadcast frames.

broadcast storm. An undesirable network event in which many broadcasts are sent across all network segments. A broadcast storm uses substantial network bandwidth and typically causes network timeouts.

BSC. binary synchronous communication (WAN Access). A character-oriented data-link layer protocol for half-duplex applications. A form of telecommunication line control that uses a standard set of transmission control characters and control character sequences for the binary synchronous transmission of binary-coded data between stations.

BSS. base station subsystem. Refers to the radio-related functions provided by the base transceiver station (BTS) and binary synchronous communication (BSC) in a global system for mobile communication (GSM) mobile wireless network.

BTS. base transceiver station (Wireless). 1. A land-based station in a global system for mobile communication (GSM) mobile wireless network that consists of transceivers and antennas that handle the radio interface to a mobile station. A base station controller (BSC) controls one or more BTSs. The combined functions of the BTS and the BSC are called the base station subsystem (BSS). 2. A transmitting/receiving station that provides service to cellular mobile units in a land mobile system. Sometimes called a land station or cell site.

Building Access submodule. A submodule within the Enterprise Composite Network Model. Contains end-user workstations, IP phones, and Layer 2 access switches for connecting devices to the Building Distribution component.

Building Distribution submodule. A submodule within the Enterprise Composite Network Model. Provides aggregation of access networks using Layer 3 switching. Performs routing, QoS, and access control.

C

CA. certification authority. In IKE, the CA is a trusted agent responsible for certificate management.

CAC. Call Admission Control. CAC mechanisms protect existing traffic from being negatively affected by new traffic requests and keeps excess traffic off the network.

connection admission control. The ATM Forum Specification defines CAC as the set of actions taken by the network during the call setup phase to determine whether a connection request can be accepted or should be rejected (or whether a request for re-allocation can be accommodated).

caching. The process by which content is copied and delivered to the user upon demand.

campus. One or more buildings with multiple virtual and physical networks, connected across a high-performance backbone.

Campus Backbone submodule. A module within the Enterprise Composite Network Model that connects distribution modules.

Campus Infrastructure module. A module within the Enterprise Composite Network Model that comprises Building Access and Building Distribution submodules.

CAR. committed access rate. In Cisco IOS, the CAR limits the input or output transmission rate on an interface or subinterface based on a flexible set of configured criteria.

Category 5. One of several grades of UTP cabling described in the EIA/TIA-568 and ISO 11801 standards. Category 5 cabling can transmit data at speeds up to 100 Mbps over limited distance.

CBR. constant bit rate. A service category defined by the ATM Forum for ATM networks. It relates traffic characteristics and QoS requirements to network behavior. CBR is used for connections that depend on precise clocking to ensure undistorted delivery.

CBWFQ. class-based weighted fair queuing. Extends WFQ functionality to provide support for user-defined traffic classes.

CDN. content delivery network. A network that provides the service of replicating and placing copies of content closer to the user or groups of users through caching and content networking technologies.

CDP. Cisco Discovery Protocol. Media and protocol independent device-discovery protocol that runs on Cisco systems, including routers, access servers, and switches. Using CDP, a device can advertise its existence to other devices and receive information about other devices on the same LAN or on the remote site of a WAN segment.

CDR. call detail record. Used in telephony networks devices, including mobile wireless network calls, the CDR contains billing information for charging purposes. In a GPRS network, the charging gateway sends the billing information within a CDR to the network service provider for that subscriber.

CEF. Cisco Express Forwarding. Scalable, distributed Layer 3 switching technology designed to enhance network performance within supported platforms.

CELP. code-excited linear prediction. A family of algorithms for compression of a digital audio stream that simulates speech using a combination of tone generators and filters. It does not allow exact reproduction of the input.

certificate. Also called a digital certificate, this is a password-protected encrypted data file that consists of user and device attributes, such as the name, serial number, company, department or IP address, and a copy of the user's public key. This method is based on the X.509 architecture. This method requires a CA to verify and sign it, thereby binding a public key to an identity for authentication. When attached to a public key, this method proves that the key has not been compromised. Usually, this method includes the owner's name and public key and the certificate's serial number and expiration date. This method allows for network scalability by attaching an identity to each device.

CGI. common gateway interface. A set of rules that describes how a web server communicates with another application running on the same computer and how the application (called a CGI program) communicates with the web server. Any application can be a CGI program if it handles input and output according to the CGI standard.

CGMP. Cisco Group Management Protocol. A Cisco-developed protocol that allows data-link layer switches to leverage IGMP (Internet Group Management Protocol) information on Cisco routers to make data-link layer forwarding decisions. CGMP provides management of group membership on switched Ethernet LANs, which allows switches to forward multicast traffic to only those ports that are interested in the traffic.

CHAP. Challenge Handshake Authentication Protocol. Security feature supported on lines using PPP encapsulation that prevents unauthorized access. CHAP does not itself prevent unauthorized access but merely identifies the remote end. The router or access server then determines whether that user is allowed access. It is defined in IETF RFC 1994.

CIDR. classless interdomain routing. A way to allocate and specify IPv4 addresses more flexibly than with the original system of address classes.

CIR. committed information rate. The rate at which a Frame Relay network agrees to transfer information under normal conditions, averaged over a minimum increment of time. CIR, measured in bits per second, is one of the negotiated tariff metrics.

Cisco CallManager. The software-based call-processing component of the Cisco enterprise IP Telephony solution. Cisco CallManager software extends enterprise telephony features and capabilities to packet telephony network devices such as IP phones, media-processing devices, VoIP gateways, and multimedia applications.

Cisco IOS. Cisco Internetwork Operating System. Cisco software that provides common functionality, scalability, and security for Cisco products. Cisco IOS allows centralized, integrated, and automated installation and management of internetworks while ensuring support for a wide variety of protocols, media, services, and platforms.

CiscoWorks. A comprehensive web-based network management solution that provides monitoring and configuration tools to simplify the administration of networks and workgroups containing Cisco internetworking products (switches, routers, hubs, and access servers).

class-based shaping. Provides the means for configuring GTS on a class, rather than on an ACL. You can enable class-based shaping on any interface that supports GTS.

classful routing protocols. Routing protocols that perform automatic summarization of network information on major IPv4 class network boundaries only (Class A, B, or C).

classless routing protocols. Routing protocols that propagate subnet mask information with each routing update to enable route summarization anywhere in the IP address, not just on major class network boundaries (Class A, B, or C).

CLI. command-line interface. A syntactic user interface that allows interaction with the application or operating system though commands and optional arguments entered from a keyboard. Cisco IOS, UNIX operating systems, and DOS provide CLIs. Contrast with GUI.

CM. cable modem. Device used to connect a PC to a local cable TV line and receive data at much higher rates than ordinary telephone modems or ISDN. A cable modem can be added to or integrated with a set-top box, thereby enabling Internet access via a television set. In most cases, cable modems are furnished as part of the cable access service and are not purchased directly or installed by the subscriber.

CMF. Common Management Foundation. A set of shared application services for the CiscoWorks network management solution.

CO. central office. The local telephone company office in which all local loops in a given area terminate and where circuit switching of subscriber lines occurs.

codec. COder-DECoder. Integrated circuit device that transforms analog acoustic signals into a digital bit stream (coder) and digital signals back into analog signals (decoder).

Software that uses a DSP software algorithm to compress/decompress digital speech or audio signals.

collision domain. A single CSMA/CD network in which a collision will occur if two devices attached to the system transmit at the same time. Ethernet uses CSMA/CD. Repeaters and hubs extend the collision domain; LAN switches, bridges, and routers do not.

connectionless. Term used to describe data transfer without the existence of a physical or virtual circuit.

connection-oriented. Term used to describe data transfer that requires the establishment of a physical or virtual circuit connecting the end points of the transfer.

content cache. A device that accelerates content delivery for end users by transparently caching frequently accessed content and then locally fulfilling content requests rather than traversing the Internet/intranet to a distant server.

Content Distribution Manager. A device that performs all the management functions needed to control content distribution accessible through a browser interface.

content networking. A technology for optimization of web content delivery that proactively distributes cacheable content from origin servers to content servers at the edges of the network, and keeps content fresh.

controlled load service. Allows applications to have low delay and high throughput even during times of congestion. For example, adaptive real-time applications, such as playback of a recorded conference, can use this kind of service. IOS QoS uses RSVP with (WRED) to provide this kind of service. Controlled load service is a queue-entry discipline that accelerates packet discard as congestion increases.

convergence. The agreement of a group of interconnected internetworking devices running a specific routing protocol on the network topology of an internetwork after a change in that topology.

Speed and capability of a group of interconnected switches to rebuild a spanning tree following a topology change.

COPS. Common Open Policy Service. To achieve centralized monitoring and control of RSVP signaling, IOS Software offers COPS with RSVP.

CoS. class of service. An indication of how an upper-layer protocol requires a lower-layer protocol to treat its messages.

In Ethernet networks, CoS is signaled using three bits in the 802.1Q/P header. Closely related to type of service in networks implemented using Cisco routers and switches.

In SNA subarea routing, CoS definitions are used by subarea nodes to determine the optimal route to establish a given session. A CoS definition comprises a virtual route number and a transmission priority field.

CPE. customer premises equipment. Terminating equipment, such as terminals, telephones, and modems installed at customer sites, and connected to the telephone company network. Can also refer to any telephone equipment supplied by the telephone company residing on the customer site.

CPU. central processing unit. Computing part of a computer or networking device.

CQ. custom queuing. Reserves a percentage of the available bandwidth of an interface for each selected traffic type. If a particular type of traffic is not using the bandwidth reserved for it, other traffic types might use the remaining reserved bandwidth.

crossbar. A type of high-performance switching fabric found in high-end Cisco switches.

cRTP. Compressed Real-Time Transfer Protocol. A method to conserve bandwidth, which compresses IP headers from 40 bytes to 2 or 4 bytes, offering significant bandwidth savings. cRTP is sometimes referred to as RTP header compression. Configured on each link individually, it is often used within networks transporting delay-sensitive traffic over narrow links.

cryptography. The principles, means, and methods for making plain information unintelligible, and for restoring the processed information to intelligible form.

CSMA/CD. carrier sense multiple access collision detect. A media-access mechanism in which devices that are ready to transmit data first check the channel for a carrier. If no carrier is sensed for a specific period of time, a device can transmit. If two devices transmit at once, a collision occurs and is detected by all colliding devices. This collision subsequently delays retransmissions from those devices for a random length of time. Ethernet and IEEE 802.3 use CSMA/CD access.

CST. Common Spanning Tree. Using the same spanning tree for multiple VLANs. CST has been the model endorsed by the 802.1Q committee (as opposed to per-VLAN spanning tree, endorsed by Cisco Systems).

CSU. channel service unit. Digital interface device that connects end-user equipment to the local digital telephone loop. It terminates the service provider circuit. Often referred to together with DSU, as CSU/DSU.

CTI . computer telephony integration. The name given to the merger of traditional telecommunications (PBX) equipment with computers and computer applications. The use of caller ID to retrieve customer information automatically from a database is an example of a CTI application.

D

daemon. A program that is not invoked explicitly but that lies dormant, waiting for a condition or conditions to occur.

dark fiber. An installed optical fiber infrastructure through which no light is being transmitted or installed fiber optic cable not carrying a signal.

data-link layer. Layer 2 of the OSI reference model. This layer responds to service requests from the network layer and issues service requests to the physical layer. It provides reliable transit of data across a physical link. The data-link layer is concerned with physical addressing, network topology, line discipline, error notification, ordered delivery of frames, and flow control. The IEEE divided this layer into two sublayers: the MAC sublayer and the LLC sublayer. Sometimes simply called link layer.

DCE. data circuit-terminating equipment. The equipment that (a) performs functions, such as signal conversion and coding, at the network end of the line between the DTE and the line, and (b) might be a separate or an integral part of the DTE or of intermediate equipment.

The interfacing equipment that might be required to couple the DTE into a transmission circuit or channel and from a transmission circuit or channel into the DTE.

DDR. dial-on-demand routing. Technique whereby a router can automatically initiate and close a circuit-switched session as transmitting stations demand. The router spoofs keepalives so that end stations treat the session as active. DDR permits routing over ISDN or telephone lines using an external ISDN terminal adaptor or modem.

DE. discard eligible. Frame Relay header bit, that when set, allows traffic to be dropped preferentially. It is used when the network is congested to ensure the delivery of unmarked traffic. The Frame Relay network sets it when a traffic stream violates its traffic contract. It might also be set by Frame Relay clients to identify less critical traffic.

delay. The amount of time it takes a packet to reach the receiving end-point after being transmitted from the sending point. Three types of delay are packetization delay, serialization delay, and propagation delay. Packetization delay is the amount of time it takes to make the data ready as packet payload (packetize); with voice and video, this includes the time to sample and encode the analog signals. Serialization delay is the amount of time it takes to place the bits of the data packets onto the physical media. Propagation delay is the amount of time it takes to transmit the bits of a packet across the physical media links.

designated bridge. Bridge that incurs the lowest path cost when forwarding a frame from a segment to the root bridge.

designated router. OSPF router that generates LSAs for a multiaccess network and has other special responsibilities in running OSPF. Each multiaccess OSPF network has a designated router that is elected by the OSPF hello protocol. The designated router enables a reduction in the number of adjacencies required on a multiaccess network, which in turn reduces the amount of routing protocol traffic and the size of the topological database.

DHCP. Dynamic Host Configuration Protocol. Provides a mechanism for allocating IP addresses dynamically so that addresses can be reused when hosts no longer need them. DHCP is defined in RFC 2131.

dial backup. Feature that provides protection against WAN downtime by allowing the network administrator to configure a backup serial line through a circuit-switched connection.

dial peer. Used in packet voice networks to identify call source and destination endpoints and to define the characteristics applied to each call leg in the call connection. Attributes that are defined in a dial peer and applied to the call leg include codec, QoS, VAD, and fax rate. In Cisco devices, plain old telephone service and voice-network dial peers can be defined.

dialup. Communications circuit that is established by a switched-circuit connection using the dial telephony circuits, usually over the PSTN.

DID. direct inward dial. Allows a user outside a company to dial an internal extension without needing to pass through an operator or attendant. The dialed digits are passed to the PBX, which then completes the call.

DiffServ. Differentiated service (DiffServ) is a multiple service model that can satisfy differing QoS requirements. However, unlike the IntServ model, an application using differentiated service does not explicitly signal (to router) before sending data. For differentiated service, the network tries to deliver a particular kind of service based on the QoS per-hop behavior (PHB) associated with the differential services code point (DSCP) within each packet.

digital signature. Value computed with a cryptographic algorithm and appended to a data object in such a way that any recipient of the data can use the signature to verify the data's origin and integrity.

distance vector routing protocols. Class of routing algorithms that use a relatively simple measure, such as the number of hops in a route, to define the best path toward a destination network. Distance vector routing algorithms call for each router to send its entire routing table in each update, but only to its neighbors. Distance vector routing algorithms can be prone to routing loops, but are computationally simpler than link-state routing algorithms. A common algorithm used to build the routing table is the Bellman-Ford algorithm.

DLCI. data-link connection identifier. Value that identifies a virtual circuit (VC) in the physical link connecting client equipment and a Frame Relay network edge device. In the basic Frame Relay specification, DLCIs are locally significant. Connected devices might use different values to specify the same destination device, and the same DLCI also might be used on different physical links. The optional global addressing extension to the Frame Relay Forum (FRF) Local Management Interface (LMI) specification makes DLCIs globally significant.

DNS. Domain Name System. DNS is used on the Internet for translating names of network nodes into addresses. DNS is Internet Standard 13. The protocol definitions are spread over several RFCs.

DOCSIS. Data-over-Cable Service Interface Specifications. Technical specifications for equipment at both subscriber locations and the headends of cable operators. Adoption of DOCSIS will ensure interoperability of equipment throughout the infrastructures of system operators.

DoS. denial of service. An incident in which a user or organization is deprived of the services of a resource it would normally expect to have. Typically, the loss of service is the inability of a particular network service, such as e-mail, to be available or the temporary loss of all network connectivity and services.

DSCP. differential services code point. A 6-bit bit-pattern in the IPv4 ToS octet.

DSL. digital subscriber line. Public network technology that delivers high bandwidth over conventional copper wiring at limited distances. The types of DSL include ADSL, RADSL, HDSL, SDSL, and VDSL. All are provisioned via modem pairs, with one modem located at a central office and the other at the customer site. Because most DSL technologies do not use the whole bandwidth of the twisted pair, there might be capacity remaining for a voice channel.

DSLAM. digital subscriber line access multiplexer. A device that connects many digital subscriber lines to a network by multiplexing the DSL traffic onto one or more network trunk lines.

DSP. digital signal processor. A software-configurable CPU that processes analog to digital (and vice versa) data streams. Performs audio/video coding and transcoding, including compression.

DTMF. dual-tone multifrequency. Tones generated when a button is pressed on a telephone.

DWDM. dense wavelength division multiplexing. Optical transmission of multiple signals in a single optical fiber over closely spaced wavelengths in the

1550 nm region. (Frequency spacings are usually 100 GHz or 200 GHz, which corresponds to 0.8 nm or 1.6 nm.)

dynamic address resolution. Use of an address resolution protocol to determine and store address information on demand.

dynamic routing. Routing that adjusts automatically to network topology or traffic changes. Also called adaptive routing.

E

E&M. earth and magnet (more commonly "ear and mouth") signaling arrangement generally used for switch-to-switch or switch-to-network trunks. E&M is available on analog and digital interfaces. The term originally comes from the term earth and magnet; earth represents the electrical ground and magnet represents the electromagnet used to generate tone.

E.164. 1. An ITU-T recommendation for international telecommunication numbering, especially in ISDN, BISDN, and SMDS. An evolution of standard telephone numbers. 2. The name of the field in an ATM address that contains numbers in E.164 format.

E1. Channelized digital transmission scheme used internationally that carries data in up to 32 64-kbps channels at an aggregate rate of 2.048 Mbps. Available data rates are 1.920 Mbps when the line carries voice signaling, 1.984 Mbps when just framed and, rarely, 2.048 Mbps over an unframed line. E1 lines can be leased for private use from common carriers.

EAP. Extensible Authentication Protocol. Framework that supports multiple, optional authentication mechanisms for PPP, including clear text passwords, challenge-response, and arbitrary dialog sequences. EAP is defined in RFC 2284.

echo. Audible and unwanted leak-through of one's own voice into one's own receive (return) path. A signal from the transmission path is returning to one's ear through the receive path.

echo cancellation. Method for removing unwanted signals from the main received voice telephony signal.

E-commerce module. A module within the Enterprise Composite Network Model. The E-commerce module enables enterprises to successfully deploy e-commerce applications.

Edge Distribution module. A module within the Enterprise Composite Network Model that aggregates the connectivity from the various elements at the Enterprise Edge module and routes the traffic into the Campus Backbone submodule.

EDI. electronic data interchange. Electronic communication of operational data, such as orders and invoices, between organizations.

EGP. exterior gateway protocol. Internet protocol for exchanging routing information between autonomous systems. Documented in RFC 904. Not to be confused with the general term exterior gateway protocol. EGP is an obsolete protocol that was replaced by BGP.

EIGRP. Enhanced Interior Gateway Routing Protocol. Advanced version of IGRP developed by Cisco. Provides superior convergence properties and operating efficiency. A hybrid, it combines the advantages of link-state protocols with those of distance vector protocols.

e-mail. Widely used application in which text messages are transmitted electronically between end users over various types of networks using various network protocols. Underlying network application protocols include SMTP and POP.

encryption. Application of a specific algorithm to data so as to alter the representation of the data making it incomprehensible to those who do not have access to the algorithm and key required to reverse the process.

Enterprise Campus. A functional area within the Enterprise Composite Network Model. Comprises the modules required to build a highly robust campus network in terms of performance, scalability, and availability. This area contains all the network elements for independent operation within one geographic location.

Enterprise Composite Network Model. A model of enterprise campus networks that logically and physically segregates the campus along functional boundaries.

Enterprise Edge. A functional area within the Enterprise Composite Network Model. Aggregates the connectivity from the various elements at the edge of each enterprise campus network.

enterprise network. The comprehensive network that connects an organization. It includes all LAN, campus, metropolitan, and WAN links, and equipment.

ESCON. Enterprise System Connection. An IBM channel architecture that specifies a pair of fiber-optic cables, with either LEDs or lasers as transmitters and a signaling rate of 200 Mbps.

ESP. Encapsulating Security Payload. A security protocol that provides data privacy services, optional data authentication, and antireplay services. ESP encapsulates the data to be protected.

EtherChannel. Combines multiple Fast Ethernet links up to 800 Mbps or Gigabit Ethernet links up to 8 Gbps. EtherChannel provides fault-tolerant, high-speed links between switches, routers, and servers. Without EtherChannel, connectivity options are limited to the specific line rates of the interface.

Ethernet. Baseband LAN specification invented by Xerox Corporation and developed jointly by Xerox, Intel, and Digital Equipment Corporation. Ethernet networks use CSMA/CD or switches, and run over a variety of cable types at 10 Mbps. Current Ethernet implementations are defined in the IEEE 802.3 series of standards.

ETSI. European Telecommunications Standards Institute. A nonprofit organization that produces voluntary telecommunications standards used throughout Europe.

F

failover. A backup operational mode in which the functions of a system component (for example, a processor, server, network, or database) are assumed by secondary system components when the primary component becomes unavailable through either failure or scheduled downtime.

failure domain. A group of Layer 2 switches connected together is called a Layer 2-switched domain. The Layer 2-switched domain can be considered as a failure domain, because a misconfigured or malfunctioning workstation can introduce errors that will impact or disable the entire domain.

Fast EtherChannel. Bundled Fast Ethernet links that appear as one logical interface.

Fast Ethernet. Any of a number of 100-Mbps Ethernet specifications. Fast Ethernet offers a speed increase ten times that of the 10BASE-T Ethernet specifications while preserving such qualities as frame format, MAC mechanisms, and MTU. These similarities allow the use of existing Ethernet applications and network management tools on Fast Ethernet networks. Based on an extension to the IEEE 802.3 specification.

FCAPS. fault, configuration, accounting, performance, and security. A model of network management that divides the required activities into fault management, configuration management, accounting management, performance management, and security management.

FECN. forward explicit congestion notification. Bit set by a Frame Relay network to inform the DTE receiving the frame that congestion was experienced in the path from source to destination. The DTE receiving frames with the FECN bit set can request that higher-level protocols take flow-control action as appropriate.

Fibre Channel. A technology for transmitting data between computer devices at data rates from 100 to 400 Mbps over optical fiber or copper. Fibre Channel is optimized for connecting servers to shared storage devices and for interconnecting storage controllers and drives.

fiber optics. A medium used for the transmission of information (audio, video, or data). Light is modulated and transmitted over high-purity, hair-thin fibers of glass or plastic. The bandwidth capacity of fiber-optic cable is much greater than that of conventional coaxial cable or copper wire.

FIFO. first in, first out. The default queuing algorithm on high-speed interfaces, requiring no configuration. FIFO is a queuing algorithm in which packets arriving at the queue are serviced based upon arrival times. It is the default for Cisco devices on high-speed interfaces (greater than 768 Kbps).

firewall. A network appliance, or software running in a router or access server, which provides isolation between any connected public networks and a private network. A firewall router uses access lists and other methods to ensure the security of the protected network.

flat addressing. Scheme of network addressing that does not use a logical hierarchy to determine association. For example, MAC addresses are flat. Bridging protocols must flood packets throughout a flat network to deliver the packet to the appropriate location.

fragmentation. Process of breaking a packet into smaller units when transmitting over a network medium that cannot support the original size of the packet.

frame. Logical grouping of information sent as a data-link layer unit over a transmission medium. Often refers to the header and the trailer used for synchronization and error control that surround the user data contained in the unit. The terms cell, datagram, message, packet, and segment also are used to describe logical information groupings at various layers of the OSI reference model and in various technology circles.

Transmission unit within time division multiplexed media. For example, a T1 frame is 193 bits, and an E1 frame is 256 bits.

Frame Relay. Industry-standard, switched data-link layer protocol that handles multiple virtual circuits using HDLC-derived encapsulation between connected devices. Frame Relay is more bit efficient and less robust than X.25, the protocol for which it generally is considered a replacement.

FR PIPQ. Frame Relay PVC Interface Priority Queuing. Provides an interface-level PQ scheme in which prioritization is based on destination PVC rather than packet contents.

FRTS. Frame Relay traffic shaping. Applies only to Frame Relay PVCs and SVCs. FRTS provides parameters that are useful for managing network traffic congestion.

FTP. File Transfer Protocol. Application protocol, which is part of the TCP/IP protocol family, used for transferring files between network nodes. FTP is an Internet Standard defined in RFC 959.

full mesh. Term describing a network topology in which devices are directly connected to every other device with either a physical circuit or a virtual circuit. A full mesh provides a great deal of redundancy. It usually is reserved for network backbones, because it can be very expensive to implement.

FXO. Foreign Exchange Office. An FXO interface is intended to connect to the PSTN central office. It is the interface offered on a standard telephone. Cisco's FXO interface allows an analog connection to the PSTN central office or to a station interface on a PBX.

FXS. Foreign Exchange Station. An FXS interface connects directly to a standard telephone and supplies ring, voltage, and dial tone. Cisco's FXS interface allows connections to basic telephone service equipment, key sets, and PBXs.

G

G.711. Defines the 64-Kbps PCM voice coding technique. One of the ITU-T G-series recommendations, G.711 encoded voice is the expected format for digital voice delivery in the PSTN or through PBXs. This coding technique allows reproduction of the input stream.

G.723. Defines a compression technique that can be used for compressing speech or audio signal components at a low bit rate as part of the H.324 family of standards. This codec has two bit rates associated with it: 5.3 and 6.3 Kbps. The higher bit rate is based on MP-MLQ technology and provides a somewhat higher quality of sound. The lower bit rate is based on CELP and provides system designers with additional flexibility. It is one of the ITU-T G-series recommendations.

G.729. Describes a CELP compression in which voice is coded into 8-kbps streams. There are several variations of this standard (G.729, G.729 Annex A, and

G.729 Annex B) that differ mainly in computational complexity; all provide speech quality similar to 32-kbps ADPCM. It is an ITU-T G-series recommendation.

gatekeeper. The component of an H.323 conferencing system that performs address resolution and call admission control (bandwidth management).

Telecommunications: H.323 entity that provides address translation and control access to the LAN for H.323 terminals and gateways. The gatekeeper can provide other services to the H.323 terminals and gateways, such as bandwidth management and locating gateways. A gatekeeper maintains a registry of devices in the multimedia network. The devices register with the gatekeeper at startup and request admission to a call from the gatekeeper.

gateway. A device that performs application layer conversion of information from one protocol stack to another. In the IP community, it originally referred to a routing device. Today, the term router is used to describe nodes that perform this function.

GBIC. Cisco Gigabit Interface Converter. The industry-standard GBIC is a hot-swappable input/output device that plugs into a Gigabit Ethernet port or slot, linking the port with the network. Cisco GBICs can be interchanged on a wide variety of Cisco products and can be intermixed in combinations of 1000BASE-T, 1000BASE-SX, 1000BASE-LX/LH, 1000BASE-ZX, or 1000BASE-CWDM interfaces on a port-by-port basis. As additional capabilities are developed, these modules make it easy to upgrade to the latest interface technology, maximizing investment protection. Cisco GBICs are supported across a variety of Cisco switches, routers, and optical transport devices.

Gb. gigabit. Approximately 1,000,000,000 bits.

Gbps. gigabits per second.

GBps. gigabytes per second.

GFR. Guaranteed Frame Rate. A service category defined by the ATM Forum for ATM networks. It relates traffic characteristics and QoS requirements to network behavior. GFR is a frame-aware service that only applies to virtual channel connections (VCCs), because frame delineation is not usually visible at the virtual path level.

Gigabit EtherChannel. Bundled multiple Gigabit Ethernet links, which appear as one logical interface.

Gigabit Ethernet. Standard for a high-speed Ethernet at 1 Gbps, approved by the IEEE 802.3z standards committee in 1996.

GPRS. general packet radio service. A service defined and standardized by the ETSI. GPRS is an IP packet-based data service for GSM networks.

GRE. generic routing encapsulation. Tunneling protocol developed by Cisco that can encapsulate a wide variety of protocol packet types inside IP tunnels, creating a virtual point-to-point link to routers at remote points over an IP internetwork. By connecting multiprotocol subnetworks in a single-protocol backbone environment, IP tunneling using GRE allows network expansion across a single-protocol backbone environment. GRE is defined in RFC 2784.

GSM. global system for mobile communication. A second-generation (2G) mobile wireless networking standard defined by ETSI that is deployed widely throughout the world. GSM uses TDMA technology and operates in the 900-MHz radio band.

GTS. generic traffic shaping. Provides a mechanism to control the flow of outbound traffic on a particular interface. It reduces outbound traffic flow to avoid congestion by constraining specified traffic to a particular bit rate. Traffic adhering to a particular profile can be shaped to meet downstream requirements, eliminating bottlenecks in topologies with data-rate mismatches.

Guaranteed Rate Service. Also called hard QoS, this is an absolute reservation of network resources for specific traffic. Guaranteed services use QoS tools including RSVP and CBWFQ.

GUI. graphical user interface. A navigational user interface that allows interaction with the application or operating system through selection of menu items or icons using a pointing device, such as a mouse. Apple MacOS and Microsoft Windows provide GUIs. Contrast with CLI.

H

H.225.0. An ITU recommendation that governs session establishment and packetization. H.225.0 actually describes several different protocols: RAS, use of Q.931, and use of RTP. It is specified for use by H.323.

H.245. An ITU recommendation that governs endpoint control. It is specified for use by H.323.

H.323. An ITU-T recommendation that allows dissimilar packet communication devices to communicate with each other by using a standardized communication protocol. H.323 defines a common set of codecs, call setup and negotiating procedures, and basic data transport methods.

headend. End point of a broadband cable network. All stations transmit toward the headend; the headend transmits toward the destination stations.

header. Control information placed before data when encapsulating that data for network transmission.

HIDS. host intrusion detection system. Host-based security service that monitors and analyzes system events for the purpose of finding (and providing real-time or near real-time warning of) attempts to access system resources in an unauthorized manner.

hierarchical addressing. Scheme of addressing that uses a logical hierarchy to determine location. For example, IP addresses consist of network numbers, subnet numbers, and host numbers, which IP routing algorithms use to route the packet to the appropriate location.

hierarchical routing. The complex problem of routing on large networks can be simplified by reducing the size of the networks. This is accomplished by breaking a network into a hierarchy of networks, where each level is responsible for its own routing.

high availability. An intelligent network service that, when carefully implemented, ensures adequate connectivity for mission-critical applications through fault tolerance, device redundancy, redundant physical connections, and route redundancy.

HMAC. Hash-based Message Authentication Code. A mechanism for message authentication using cryptographic hash functions. HMAC can be used with any iterative cryptographic hash function, for example, Message Digest 5 (MD5) or Secure Hash Algorithm 1 (SHA-1), in combination with a secret shared key. The cryptographic strength of HMAC depends on the properties of the underlying hash function.

HSRP. Hot Standby Router Protocol. Provides high-network availability and transparent network topology changes. HSRP creates a Hot Standby router group with a lead router that services all packets sent to the Hot Standby address. Other routers in the group monitor the lead router, and if it fails, one of the standby routers inherits the lead position and the Hot Standby group address. HSRP is documented in RFC 2281.

HTML. Hypertext Markup Language. Simple hypertext document formatting language that uses tags to indicate how a given part of a document should be interpreted by a viewing application, such as a web browser. The World Wide Web Consortium (W3C) maintains the HTML standard.

HTTP. Hypertext Transfer Protocol. The protocol used by web browsers and web servers to transfer files, such as text and graphic files. HTTP is defined in RFC 2616.

I

IBGP. Internal Border Gateway Protocol. IBGP is a variant of the BGP protocol used within an autonomous system.

ICMP. Internet Control Message Protocol. Network layer Internet protocol that reports errors and provides other information relevant to IP packet processing. Documented in RFC 792.

ICMP flood. Denial-of-service attack that sends a host more ICMP echo request (ping) packets than the protocol implementation can handle.

ICND. Interconnecting Cisco Network Devices. Cisco training course.

IDS. intrusion detection system. Security service that monitors and analyzes system events for the purpose of finding (and providing real-time or near real-time warning of) attempts to access system resources in an unauthorized manner.

IEEE. Institute of Electrical and Electronics Engineers. Professional organization whose activities include the development of communications and network standards. IEEE LAN standards are the predominant LAN standards today.

IEEE 802.1. IEEE specification that describes an algorithm that prevents bridging loops by creating a spanning tree. Digital Equipment Corporation invented the original algorithm. The Digital algorithm and the IEEE 802.1 algorithm are not exactly the same, nor are they compatible.

IETF. Internet Engineering Task Force. Task force consisting of more than 80 working groups responsible for developing Internet standards. The IETF operates under the auspices of ISOC.

IGMP. Internet Group Management Protocol. Used by IP hosts to report their multicast group membership requests to an adjacent multicast router. IGMP is defined in RFC 3376.

IGMP snooping. An IP Multicast constraining mechanism that runs on a Layer 2 LAN switch. IGMP snooping requires the LAN switch to examine (snoop) some Layer 3 information (IGMP join/leave messages) in the IGMP packets sent between the hosts and a router or Layer 3 switch.

IGP. Interior Gateway Protocol. Internet protocol used to exchange routing information within an autonomous system. Examples of common Internet IGPs include EIGRP, OSPF, IS-IS, and RIP.

IGRP. Interior Gateway Routing Protocol. IGP developed by Cisco to address issues associated with routing in large, heterogeneous networks.

IKE. Internet Key Exchange. IKE establishes a shared security policy and authenticates keys for services (such as IPSec) that require keys. Before any IPSec traffic can be passed, each router/firewall/host must verify the identity of its peer. This can be done by manually entering preshared keys into both hosts or by a CA service. IKE is defined in RFC 2409.

ILMI. Integrated Local Management Interface. Specification developed by the ATM Forum for incorporating interface management capabilities into the ATM UNI.

in-band signaling. Transmission of control information within a content stream also used for information transmission.

Integrated IS-IS. Routing protocol based on the OSI routing protocol IS-IS but with support for IP and other protocols. Integrated IS-IS implementations send only one set of routing updates, making it more efficient than two separate implementations. Formerly called Dual IS-IS. Use of Integrated IS-IS for routing in a TCP/IP network is defined in RFC 1195.

intelligent network services. These services essentially add intelligence, extra qualities, and features to the network infrastructure above and beyond merely moving datagrams. Intelligent network services include network management, high availability, security, QoS, and IP multicast.

interarea routing. Term used to describe routing between two or more logical areas.

Internet. The largest global internetwork, connecting tens of thousands of networks worldwide and having a "culture" that focuses on research and standardization based on real-life use. Many leading-edge network technologies come from the Internet community. The Internet evolved in part from Advanced Research Projects Agency Network (ARPANET), at one time, called the Defense Advanced Research Projects Agency (DARPA) Internet. Not to be confused with the general term internet.

Internet Connectivity module. A module within the Enterprise Edge functional area of the Enterprise Composite Network Model. This module provides internal enterprise users with connectivity to Internet services.

internetwork. Collection of networks interconnected by routers and other devices that functions (generally) as a single network. Sometimes called an internet, which is not to be confused with the Internet.

InterNIC. An organization that serves the Internet community by supplying user assistance, documentation, training, a registration service for Internet domain names, and other services. Formerly called NIC.

intra-area routing. Term used to describe routing within a logical area.

Intranet. A closed, organization-wide network that includes LANs and WANs. It frequently uses open standards, such as TCP/IP, instead of proprietary protocols traditionally used for LANs and WANs.

Intrusion Detection. Security service that monitors and analyzes system events for the purpose of finding (and providing real-time or near real-time warning of) attempts to access system resources in an unauthorized manner.

IntServ. A multiple service model, in other words, it can accommodate multiple QoS requirements. Each application is expected to request a specific kind of service from the network before it sends data. The request is made using explicit signaling.

IP. Internet Protocol. Network layer protocol in the TCP/IP stack offering a connectionless internetwork service. IP provides features for addressing, type of service specification, fragmentation and reassembly, and security. Defined in RFC 791.

IP address. An address assigned to hosts using TCP/IP. An IPv4 network address belongs to one of five classes (A, B, C, D, or E) and is written as four octets separated by periods (dotted decimal format), or eight hexadecimal digits. Each address consists of a network portion, which includes the network number and an optional subnetwork number and a host number. A subnet mask, or CIDR prefix, is used to extract the network portion from the IP address. The network number, extended using a single subnet mask for that network, can be used for routing in all routing protocols. More modern routing protocols can route on the network portion constructed using variable length subnet masks. The host number is used to address an individual host within the network or subnetwork. Also called an Internet address. In IPv6, the address is 128 bits that are displayed using eight 16-bit groups. Each group is presented using up to four hexadecimal digits and separated by colons.

IP datagram. Fundamental unit of information passed across the Internet. Contains source and destination addresses along with data and a number of fields that define such things as the length of the datagram and the header checksum. The IPv6 header is similar in purpose, though very different in structure.

IPM. Internetwork Performance Monitor. CiscoWorks tool used to isolate performance problems, locate bottlenecks, diagnose latency and jitter, and perform trend analysis of network response time.

IP multicast. A packet routing technique that allows IP traffic to be propagated efficiently from one source to a number of destinations or from many sources to many destinations. Rather than sending duplicate packets, one to each destination, only one packet is sent out each interface on which a multicast group identified by a single IP destination group address is registered. This can greatly reduce the required bandwidth.

IPng. IP next generation. The first name for the IPv6.

IP Phone. Device that enables termination of voice communications within the IP network. Cisco IP telephones are centrally managed by the Cisco CallManager. They might be powered inline through Ethernet connections, reducing the need to protect wall power outlets to maintain voice power.

IP precedence. Use of three bits from the term-of-service octet in the IP header to provide limited prioritization for IP packets in a routed network.

IPSec. Internet Protocol Security. A framework of standards that provides data confidentiality, data integrity, and data authentication between participating peers. IPSec provides these security services at the IP layer. IPSec uses IKE to handle the negotiation of protocols and algorithms based on local policy and to generate the encryption and authentication keys to be used by IPSec. IPSec can protect data flows between a pair of hosts, between a pair of security gateways, or between a security gateway and a host.

IP spoofing. A network attack that occurs when an attacker outside your network pretends to be a trusted user by using an IP address that is within the range of IP addresses for your network or by using an authorized external IP address that you trust and to which you want to provide access to specified resources on your network. Should an attacker get access to your IPSec security parameters, that attacker can masquerade as the remote user authorized to connect to the corporate network.

IP Telephony. The transmission of voice calls over data networks that use the IP. IP Telephony is the result of the transformation of the circuit-switched telephone network to a packet-based network that deploys voice-compression algorithms and flexible and sophisticated transmission techniques to deliver services using only a fraction of the aggregate bandwidth required by traditional digital telephony.

IPv4. Internet Protocol version 4.

IPv6. Internet Protocol version 6. Replacement for the current version of IP (version 4). IPv6 includes support for flow ID in the packet header, which can be used to identify flows. Formerly called IPng (IP next generation).

ISAKMP. Internet Security Association and Key Management Protocol. An Internet IPSec protocol (documented in RFC 2408) that negotiates, establishes, modifies, and deletes security associations. It also exchanges key-generation and authentication data (independent of the details of any specific key-generation technique), key establishment protocols, encryption algorithms, or authentication mechanisms.

ISDN. Integrated Services Digital Network. Communication protocol offered by telephone companies that extended the digital network to the customer premises to carry data, digital voice, and other source traffic integrated as a single service.

IS-IS. Intermediate System-to-Intermediate System. OSI link-state hierarchical routing protocol whereby intermediate systems (routers) exchange routing information based on a single configurable metric to determine network topology.

ISL. Inter-Switch Link. Cisco-proprietary protocol that maintains VLAN information as traffic from multiple VLANs flows between switches and routers on a single physical link.

ISO. International Organization for Standardization. International organization that is responsible for a wide range of standards, including those relevant to networking. ISO developed the OSI reference model, a popular networking reference model.

ISOC. Internet Society.

ISP. Internet service provider. Company that provides Internet access to other companies and individuals.

ITU-T. International Telecommunication Union Telecommunication Standardization Sector. International body that develops worldwide standards for telecommunications technologies. A United Nations agency, the ITU-T carries out the functions of the former Consultative Committee for International Telegraph and Telephone (CCITT).

IVR. interactive voice response. Term used to describe systems that provide information in the form of recorded messages over telephone lines in response to user input in the form of spoken words or DTMF signaling. Examples include banks that allow you to check your balance from any telephone and automated stock quote systems.

J–K

Java. An object-oriented programming language developed at Sun Microsystems to solve a number of problems in modern programming practice. The Java language is used extensively on the World Wide Web, particularly for applets.

jitter. The interpacket delay variance; that is, the difference between interpacket arrival and departure. Jitter is an important QoS metric for voice and video applications.

Analog communication line distortion caused by the variation of a signal from its reference timing positions. Jitter can cause data loss, particularly at high speeds.

jitter buffer. Dejitter buffers are used at the receiving end to smooth delay variability and allow time for decoding and decompression. They help on the first talk spurt to provide smooth playback of voice traffic.

JTAPI. Java Telephony application programming interface. A call control model developed by Sun Microsystems.

Kbps. kilobits per second.

Kerberos. Standard for authenticating network users. Kerberos offers two key benefits: It functions in a multivendor network, and it does not transmit passwords over the network. Kerberos is described in RFC 1510.

L

L2 switching (L2-switched). Switching based on Layer 2 (data-link layer) information. The current generation of Layer 2 switches are functionally equivalent to bridges. The exposures in a large bridged network include broadcast storms, spanning-tree loops, and address limitations.

L2TP. Layer 2 Tunneling Protocol. An IETF-standards track protocol defined in RFC 2661 that provides tunneling of PPP. Based upon the best features of L2F and PPTP, L2TP provides an industry-wide interoperable method of implementing Virtual Private Dialup Networking (VPDNs). Communications transactions between the LAC and the LNS support tunneling of a single PPP connection. A one-to-one relationship among the PPP connection, L2TP session, and L2TP call.

L3 switching. Integrates routing with switching to yield very high routing throughput rates typical of L2 switches and offering Network layer (L3) routing services and data-link layer (L2) termination.

LAN. High-speed, low-error rate data network covering a relatively small geographic area (up to a few thousand meters). LANs connect workstations, peripherals, terminals, and other devices in a single building or other geographically limited area. LAN standards specify cabling and signaling at the physical and data-link layers of the OSI model. Ethernet at various rates is the most widely used LAN implementation technology.

latency. Delay between the time a device transmits a packet and when that packet is received at the destination.

Delay between the time a device requests access to a network and the time that it is granted permission to transmit.

Delay between the time a device receives a frame and the time the frame is forwarded out the destination port.

LDAP. Lightweight Directory Access Protocol. A protocol that provides access for management and browser applications, which enables read/write interactive access to the X.500 Directory.

leased line. Transmission line reserved by a communications carrier for the private use of a customer. The enterprise perceives a leased line as a type of dedicated line.

LEC. local exchange carrier. A telephone company that provides customer access to the public switched telephone network through one of its central offices.

LFI. link fragmentation and interleaving. A solution for queuing delay situations. With LFI, large packets are fragmented into smaller frames and interleaved with small voice packets. It is similar in effect to FRF.12, Frame Relay Fragmentation, available with Frame Relay.

link-state routing protocols. Routing algorithm in which each router floods information regarding the cost of reaching each of its neighbors (link-state) to all nodes in the internetwork. Link-state algorithms create a consistent view of the network and, therefore, are not prone to routing loops. They achieve this at the cost of relatively greater computational complexity and more widespread traffic (compared with distance vector routing algorithms).

LLC. Logical Link Control. The higher of the two data-link layer sublayers defined by the IEEE. The LLC sublayer handles error control, flow control, framing, and MAC-sublayer addressing. The most prevalent LLC protocol is IEEE 802.2, which includes both connectionless and connection-oriented variants.

LLC2. Logical Link Control, Type 2 (TCP/IP). A connection-oriented OSI LLC-sublayer protocol. LLC2 specifies one of three types of service. Type 1 provides unacknowledged connectionless service, Type 2 provides connection-oriented service, and Type 3 provides acknowledged connectionless service. Class I devices support only Type 1 service. Class II devices support Type 1 and Type 2 services. Class III devices support Type 1 and Type 3 services. Class IV devices support all three types of services.

LLQ. low-latency queuing. Feature that brings strict priority queuing to CBWFQ. Strict priority queuing allows delay-sensitive data, such as voice, to be dequeued and sent first (before packets in other queues are dequeued), giving delay-sensitive data preferential treatment over other traffic.

load balancing, load sharing. In routing, the capability of a router to distribute traffic over all its network ports that are the same distance from the destination address. Good load-balancing algorithms use both line speed and reliability information. Load balancing increases the use of network segments, thus increasing effective network bandwidth.

local loop. Line from the premises of a telephone subscriber to the telephone company CO.

loop-start signaling. A method of signaling where a DC closure is applied to a phone line (loop), and the start of DC current flow indicates a change from on-hook to off-hook.

loss. Loss (or packet loss) is a comparative measure of packets faithfully transmitted and received to the total number that were transmitted. Loss is expressed as the percentage of packets that were dropped.

LRE. Long Range Ethernet. For buildings with existing Category 1/2/3 wiring, the LRE technology provides connectivity at speeds from 5 to 15 Mbps (full duplex) and distances up to 5000 feet. LRE technology delivers broadband service on the same lines as plain old telephone service (POTS), digital telephone, and ISDN traffic.

LSA. link-state advertisement. Routing information advertised (multicast) by OSPF that contains information about neighbors and path costs. The receiving routers use LSAs to maintain their routing tables. The equivalent in IS-IS is called an LSP.

M

MAC. Media Access Control. Lower of the two sublayers of the data-link layer defined by the IEEE. The MAC sublayer handles access to shared media, such as whether token passing or contention will be used.

MAC address. Standardized data-link layer address that is required for every port or device that connects to an Ethernet-based LAN. Other devices in the network use these addresses to locate specific ports in the network and to create and update routing tables and data structures. MAC addresses are 6 bytes long and are controlled by the IEEE. Also known as a hardware address, MAC layer address, and physical address.

MAN. metropolitan-area network. Network that spans a metropolitan area. Generally, a MAN spans a larger geographic area than a LAN but a smaller geographic area than a WAN.

Mb. megabit. Approximately 1,000,000 bits.

MB. megabyte. Depending on the context, it can mean either 1,000,000 or 1,048,576 (2^{20}) bytes.

Mbps. megabits per second. A bit rate expressed in millions of binary bits per second.

MCU. multipoint control unit. An H.323 endpoint that provides the capability for three or more terminals and gateways to participate in multipoint conferences.

MD5. Message Digest Algorithm 5. A one-way hashing algorithm that produces a 128-bit hash. Both MD5 and Secure Hash Algorithm (SHA) are variations on MD4 and are designed to strengthen the security of the MD4 hashing algorithm. Cisco uses hashes for authentication within the IPSec framework. Also used for message authentication in Simple Network Management Protocol (SNMP) version 3. MD5 verifies a communication's integrity, authenticates the origin, and checks for timeliness.

MGCP. Media Gateway Control Protocol. A merging of the Internet Protocol Device Control (IPDC) Protocol and the Simple Gateway Control Protocol (SGCP). MGCP is defined in RFC 2705.

MIB. Management Information Base. Database of network management information that is used and maintained by a network management protocol, such as Simple Network Management Protocol (SNMP) or Common Management Information Protocol (CMIP). The value of a MIB object can be changed or retrieved using SNMP or CMIP commands, usually through a GUI network management system. MIB objects are organized in a tree structure that includes public (standard) and private (proprietary) branches defined in ASN.1.

MIC. media interface connector. The Fiber Distributed Data Interface (FDDI) de facto standard connector.

MM fiber. multimode fiber. Uses a light emitting diode (LED) as the light source. The low power output and modal dispersion limits the distance at which the signal can be distinguished reliably.

MPEG. *Motion Picture Experts Group.* Standards for compressing video. MPEG1 is a bit-stream standard for compressed video and audio optimized to fit into a bandwidth of 1.5 Mbps. MPEG2 is intended for higher quality video-on-demand applications and runs at data rates between 4 and 9 Mbps. MPEG4 is a low-bit-rate compression algorithm intended to provide acceptable quality over dedicated connections as narrow as 64 Kbps. MPEG-7 is a standard for description and search of audio and visual content. Work started on MPEG-21 "Multimedia Framework" in mid-2000.

MPLS. Multiprotocol Label Switching. Switching method that forwards network layer traffic using a label. This label instructs the routers and the switches in a network where to forward the packets based on preestablished routing information determined as the packet entered the network. MPLS is defined in RFC 3031.

MST. Multiple Spanning Tree. This standards-based model (802.1s) allows building a spanning tree for multiple VLANs that have similar topologies. MST is the new alternative over CST and Cisco PVST+.

MTBF. mean time between failure. The average number of hours between failures for a particular device.

MTU. maximum transmission unit. Maximum packet size, in bytes, that a particular interface can transmit without fragmentation.

μ-law. A North American companding standard used in conversion between analog and digital signals in pulse code modulation (PCM) systems. Similar to the European a-law.

multicast. The transmission of packets from a single source to multiple destinations in a way which conserves network bandwidth by reducing the duplication of packets sent.

multilayer switching. Filtering and forwarding protocol data units (PDUs) on the basis of MAC addresses, network addresses, or other upper layer PDU headers.

N

NANP. North American Numbering Plan. A specification for assigning telephone numbers in North America. It implements the E.164 international standard in this region.

NAS. network access server. Cisco platform (or collection of platforms) that interfaces between the packet world (for example, the Internet) and the circuit world (for example, the PSTN).

NAT. Network Address Translation. Mechanism for reducing the need for globally unique IP addresses. NAT allows an organization with addresses that are not globally unique to connect to the Internet by translating those addresses into globally routable address space. Also known as Network Address Translator.

NBAR. network-based application recognition. Cisco IOS Software feature used for real-time network traffic analysis to support QoS requirements.

NBMA. nonbroadcast multiaccess. Term describing a multiaccess network that either does not support broadcasting (such as Frame Relay) or in which broadcasting is not feasible (for example, an SMDS broadcast group or an extended Ethernet that is too large).

NetBEUI. NetBIOS Extended User Interface. An enhanced version of the NetBIOS protocol used by network operating systems, such as LAN Manager, LAN Server, Windows for Workgroups, and Windows NT. NetBEUI formalizes the transport frame and adds other functions. NetBEUI implements the OSI LLC2 protocol.

NetBIOS. Network Basic Input/Output System. An application programming interface (API) used by applications on an IBM LAN to request services from lower-level network processes. These services might include establishing and terminating sessions and transferring information.

Network Management module. A module within the Enterprise Composite Network Model. This module performs intrusion detection logging, system logging, and Terminal Access Controller Access Control System Plus (TACACS+)/RADIUS and one-time password (OTP) authentication, as well as network monitoring and general configuration management functions.

NFS. Network File System. As commonly used, a distributed file system protocol suite developed by Sun Microsystems that allows remote file access across a network. In actuality, NFS is simply one protocol in the suite. NFS protocols include NFS, remote-procedure call (RPC), eXternal Data Representation (XDR), and others. These protocols are part of a larger architecture that Sun refers to as open network computing (ONC).

NIC. network interface card. Board that provides network communication capabilities to and from a computer system. Also called an adapter.

NIDS. Network Intrusion Detection System. Security service that monitors and analyzes system events for the purpose of finding (and providing real-time or near real-time warning of) attempts to access system resources in an unauthorized manner.

NMS. network management system. System responsible for managing at least part of a network. An NMS is generally a reasonably powerful and well-equipped computer, such as an engineering workstation. NMSs communicate with agents to help keep track of network statistics and resources.

nonrepudiation service. Security service that provides protection against false denial of involvement in a communication.

nonstub area. OSPF area that carries a default route, static routes, intraarea routes, interarea routes, and external routes. Nonstub areas are the only OSPF areas that can have virtual links configured across them and are the only areas that can contain an ASBR.

NTP. Network Time Protocol. Protocol built on top of TCP that ensures accurate local time keeping with reference to radio and atomic clocks located on the Internet. This protocol is capable of synchronizing distributed clocks within milliseconds over long time periods. The current version of NTP is defined in RFC 1305.

O

OAKLEY. A key establishment protocol (proposed for IPSec but superseded by IKE) based on the Diffie-Hellman algorithm, and designed to be a compatible component of ISAKMP.

ODR. on-demand routing. A routing mechanism that uses Cisco Discovery Protocol (CDP) to propagate the IP prefix. ODR is appropriate for hub-and-spoke topologies.

OPNET. The vendor of the simulation tool used in the ARCH course.

OSI. Open System Interconnection. International standardization program created by ISO and ITU-T to develop standards for data networking that facilitate multivendor equipment interoperability.

OSI protocol stack. Set of related communications protocols that operate together and, as a group, address communication at some or all of the seven layers of the OSI reference model. Not every protocol stack covers each layer of the model, and often a single protocol in the stack addresses a number of layers at once. TCP/IP is a typical protocol stack.

OSI reference model. Open System Interconnection reference model. Network architectural model developed by ISO and ITU-T. The model consists of seven layers, each of which specifies particular network functions, such as addressing, flow control, error control, encapsulation, and reliable message transfer. The lowest layer (the physical layer) is closest to the media technology. The lower two layers are implemented in hardware and firmware, whereas the upper five layers are implemented only in software. The highest layer (the application layer) is closest to the user application. The OSI reference model is used universally as a method for teaching and understanding network functionality.

OSPF. Open Shortest Path First. Link-state, hierarchical IGP routing algorithm proposed as a successor to RIP in the Internet community. OSPF features include least-cost routing, multipath routing, and load balancing. OSPF was derived from an early version of the IS-IS protocol. The current version of OSPF is defined in RFC 2328.

OTP. one-time password. Type of authentication that permits a user to enter a password one time for all applications and systems.

out-of-band signaling. Transmission of control traffic using frequencies or channels other than the frequencies or channels normally used for information transfer. Out-of-band signaling often is used for error reporting in situations in which in-band signaling can be affected by whatever problems the network might be experiencing. The SS7 signaling system of the PSTN is an example of out-of-band signaling.

P

p2mp. point-to-multipoint. Wireless communication between a series of receivers and transmitters to a central location. Cisco p2mp typically is set up in three segments to enable frequency reuse.

p2p. point-to-point. Wireless communication between one receiver and one location. p2p has a higher bandwidth than p2mp because, among other reasons, it has less overhead to manage the data paths only one receiver exists per transmitter.

packet sniffer. Device that monitors traffic on a network and reports on problems on the network.

PAP. Password Authentication Protocol. An authentication protocol that allows Point-to-Point Protocol (PPP) peers to authenticate one another. The remote router attempting to connect to the local router is required to send an authentication request. Unlike Challenge Handshake Authentication Protocol (CHAP), PAP passes the password and the host name or username in the clear (unencrypted). PAP does not itself prevent unauthorized access; it merely identifies the remote end. The router or access server then determines whether that user is allowed access. PAP is supported only on PPP lines.

partial mesh. Network topology in which devices are only directly connected to some other nodes in the network. A network topology in which every node is connected to at least two of the nodes is described as well connected. A partial mesh does not provide the level of link redundancy of a full-mesh topology but is far less expensive to implement. Partial-mesh topologies generally are used to connect peripheral networks that distribute traffic to a fully meshed backbone.

password sniffing. Passive traffic interception, usually on a local-area network, to gain knowledge of passwords.

PAT. port address translation. IP address translation method that allows a router to forward packets from several sessions or flows between a private internetwork and the Internet. PAT allows the router to forward packets between a private IP network and the Internet using a single public IP address to support multiple actual users.

PBX. private branch exchange. Digital or analog telephone switch located on the subscriber premises and used to connect private and public telephone networks.

PCM. pulse code modulation. A technique of encoding analog voice into a 64-kbps data stream by sampling with 8-bit resolution at a rate of 8000 times per second.

PDN. public data network. Network operated either by a government (as in Europe) or by a private concern to provide computer communications to the public, usually for a fee. PDNs enable small organizations to create a WAN without the equipment costs of long-distance circuits.

pilot network. A part of an existing live network used to test designs, hardware compatibility, and new software.

PIM. Protocol Independent Multicast. Multicast routing protocol that allows the addition of IP multicast routing on existing IP networks. PIM is unicast routing protocol independent and can be operated in two modes: dense and sparse.

PIM-DM. PIM dense mode. Actively attempts to send multicast data to all potential receivers (flooding) and relies upon their self-pruning (removal from group) to achieve desired distribution.

PIM-SM. PIM sparse mode. Relies upon an explicit joining method before attempting to send data to receivers of a multicast group.

ping. Packet Internet groper. An Internet Control Message Protocol (ICMP) echo message and its reply. Ping is often used in IP networks to test a network device's reachability.

PKI. public key infrastructure. A system of certification authorities (CAs) (and, optionally, registration authorities [RAs] and other supporting servers and agents) that perform some set of certificate management, archive management, key management, and token management functions for a community of users in an application of asymmetric cryptography.

policy domain. A collection of networks under single management.

POP. point of presence. A physical location within a service provider network where users dial-in.

Post Office Protocol. Internet application protocol providing e-mail services. An Internet Standard, POP is defined by RFC 1939.

PortFast. Feature used on switched ports where only end-user stations are directly connected. There is no delay in passing traffic, because the switch immediately puts the port to the forward state. It reduces the number and duration of SPT convergence events.

POS. packet-over-SONET/SDH. Technology that enables core routers to send native IP packets directly over SONET/SDH frames. Essentially, an IP packet is placed into PPP (RFC 1661), encapsulated in HDLC-like framing (RFC 1662), and finally placed into a SONET/SDH payload (RFC 2615).

POTS. plain old telephone service. Basic service supplying standard single-line telephones, telephone lines, and access to the public switched network.

PPP. Point-to-Point Protocol. Successor to Serial Line Internet Protocol (SLIP) that provides router-to-router and host-to-network connections over synchronous and asynchronous circuits. Whereas SLIP was designed to work with IP, PPP was designed to work with several network layer protocols, such as IP, IPX, and AppleTalk Remote Access (ARA). PPP also has built-in security mechanisms, such as CHAP, PAP, and EAP. PPP relies on two protocols: Link Control Protocol (LCP) and Network Control Protocol (NCP). PPP is defined in IETF RFC 1661.

PPPoE. PPP over Ethernet. Allows a PPP session to be initiated on a simple Ethernet-connected client. PPPoE can be used on existing customer premise equipment. PPPoE preserves the point-to-point session used by ISPs in the current dialup model. It is the only protocol capable of running point-to-point over Ethernet without requiring an intermediate IP stack. PPPoE is most often used to connect a host to a cable modem.

PPPoA. PPP over ATM adaptation Layer 5 (AAL5) (specified in RFC 2364) uses AAL5 as the framed protocol, which supports both PVCs and SVCs. PPPoA is primarily implemented as part of an ADSL. PPPoA relies on RFC 1483/2684, operating in either logical link control-Subnetwork Access Protocol (LLC-SNAP) or virtual circuit multiplexer mode. A customer premises equipment (CPE) device encapsulates the PPP session for transport across the ADSL loop and the DSLAM.

pps. packets per second.

PPTP. Point-to-Point Tunneling Protocol. A protocol that allows the Point-to-Point Protocol (PPP) to be tunneled through an IP network. RFC 2637 describes the PPTP protocol.

PQ. priority queuing. Queue management and service discipline that prioritizes traffic at a network interface. Four traffic priorities can be configured. A series of filters based on packet characteristics (source IP address and port) is defined to cause the router to place critical traffic in the highest queue and other traffic in the lower three queues. The queue with the highest priority is serviced first until empty; the lower queues are then serviced in sequence. It is possible for higher-priority traffic to starve lower-priority traffic by consuming all the bandwidth.

PQ-CBWFQ. priority queuing-class-based weighted fair queuing. Feature that joins strict priority queuing and CBWFQ. Strict priority queuing allows delay-sensitive data, such as voice, to be dequeued from a single priority queue and sent first (before packets in other queues are dequeued), giving delay-sensitive data preferential treatment over other traffic. It is also called low-latency queuing (LLQ).

PQ-WFQ. priority queuing-weighted fair queuing. Also called IP RTP Priority. Queuing mechanism that provides a strict priority queuing scheme for delay-sensitive data, such as voice.

PRI. Primary Rate Interface. ISDN interface to primary rate access. Primary rate access consists of a single 64-Kbps D channel plus 23 (T1) or 30 (E1) B channels for voice or data.

prototype network. A separate (non-live) network used to test designs, new hardware, and software versions before deployment.

proxy. 1. An entity that, in the interest of efficiency, essentially stands in for another entity. 2. A special gateway that relays one H.323 session to another.

PSTN. public switched telephone network. General term referring to the variety of telephone networks and services in place worldwide. The PSTN includes POTS and ISDN services.

PVC. permanent virtual circuit. Virtual circuit that is permanently established. PVCs save bandwidth, and operations and processing costs associated with circuit provisioning, and tear down in situations where certain virtual circuits must exist all the time. In ATM terminology, called a permanent virtual connection.

PVST. per-VLAN spanning tree. Support for IEEE 802.1q trunks to map multiple spanning trees to a single spanning tree. PVST+ can coexist with CST.

Q

QoS. quality of service. Measure of performance for a transmission system that reflects its transmission quality and service availability.

queue. Generally, a list of elements waiting to be processed.

queuing delay. Amount of time that a data packet must wait in a queue before it can be transmitted onto a statistically multiplexed physical circuit.

R

RA. registration authority (security). An optional public key infrastructure (PKI) entity (separate from certification authorities [CAs]). It does not sign either digital certificates or certificate revocation lists (CRLs) but is responsible for recording or verifying some or all of the information needed by a CA (particularly the identities of subjects) to issue certificates and CRLs and to perform other certificate-management functions.

RADIUS. Remote Authentication Dial-In User Service. Responsible for receiving user connection requests, authenticating the user, and then returning all configuration information necessary for the client to deliver service to the user. It includes a database for authenticating connections and for tracking connection time. RADIUS is defined in RFC 2865.

RAS. registration, admission, and status protocol. Protocol that is used between endpoints and the gatekeeper to perform management functions. RAS signaling function performs registration, admissions, bandwidth changes, status, and disengage procedures between the VoIP gateway and the gatekeeper.

Remote Access Server. One of a family of devices that provide remote-access services to clients.

RED. random early detection. Congestion avoidance algorithm in which some percentage of packets are dropped when congestion is detected and before the queue in question overflows completely.

Remote Access and VPN module. A module within the Enterprise Edge functional area of the Enterprise Composite Network Model. This module terminates VPN traffic, forwarded by the Internet Connectivity module, from remote users and remote sites.

RFC. Request for Comments. Document series used as the primary means for communicating information about Internet protocols and related technical details. Some RFCs are designated by the Internet Architecture Board (IAB) as Internet standards. Most RFCs document protocol specifications, such as Telnet and FTP, but some are humorous or historical. RFCs are available online from numerous sources.

RIP. Routing Information Protocol. IGP supplied with UNIX BSD systems. The most common IGP in the Internet. RIP uses hop count as a routing metric. Version 2 of RIP, RIPv2 is defined in RFC 2453. RIP Next Generation (RIPng) is defined for use with IPv6.

RMON. remote monitoring. Remote Network Monitoring MIB specification described in RFC 2819 that defines objects for managing remote network monitoring devices. The RMON specification provides numerous monitoring, problem detection, and reporting capabilities.

root bridge. The root, or start, of the spanning tree in a switched network. It exchanges topology information with designated bridges in a spanning-tree instance and notifies all other bridges in the network when topology changes are required. This exchange prevents loops and provides a measure of defense against link failure.

routing protocols. Protocols that accomplish routing through the implementation of a specific routing algorithm. Examples of routing protocols include EIGRP, OSPF, and RIP.

RP. rendezvous point. PIM-SM distributes information about active sources by forwarding data packets on the shared tree. Shared tree requires a rendezvous point to be administratively assigned. Source routers send multicast data up the shared tree to RP, and RP, in turn, sends the multicast data down the shared tree to the interested recipient.

RPF. reverse path forwarding. A multicasting technique in which a multicast datagram is forwarded out all but the receiving interface if the receiving interface is the one used to forward unicast datagrams to the source of the multicast datagram.

RPR. Route Processor Redundancy. Provides a high system availability feature for some Cisco switches and routers. A system can reset and use a standby Route Switch Processor (RSP) in the event of a failure of the active RSP. RPR reduces unplanned downtime and enables a quicker switchover between an active and standby RSP in the event of a fatal error on the active RSP. When you configure RPR, the standby RSP loads a Cisco IOS image upon boot up and initializes itself in standby mode (but Multilayer Switch Feature Card (MSFC) and Policy Feature Card [PFC] are not operational). In the event of a fatal error on the active RSP, the system switches to the standby RSP, which reinitializes itself as the active RSP, reloads all the line cards, and restarts the system; switchover takes 2 to 4 minutes.

RPR+ allows a failover to occur without reloading the line cards. The standby route processor takes over the router without affecting any other processes and subsystems. The switchover takes 30 to 60 seconds (core dump upon failure is disabled).

RSA algorithm. The Rivest, Shamir, and Adelman algorithm. Named after the inventors of the technique, RSA is a public key cryptographic system that can be used for encryption and authentication.

RSP. Route Switch Processor. Processor module in the Cisco 7500 series routers that integrates the functions of the Route Processor (RP) and the Switch Processor (SP).

RSTP. Rapid Spanning Tree Protocol. The 802.1w standard defines Rapid Spanning Tree Protocol. This protocol incorporates many of the Cisco proprietary enhancements to the 802.1D classic STP, and it also introduces new enhancements to it.

RSVP. Resource Reservation Protocol. Protocol that supports the reservation of resources across an IP network. Applications running on IP end systems can use RSVP to indicate to other nodes the nature (bandwidth, jitter, maximum burst, and so on) of the packet streams they want to receive. Also known as Resource Reservation Setup Protocol.

RTCP. RTP Control Protocol. Protocol that monitors the QoS of an IPv6 RTP connection and conveys information about the ongoing session.

RTP. Real-Time Transport Protocol. Protocol designed to provide end-to-end network transport functions for applications transmitting real-time data, such as audio, video, or simulation data, over multicast or unicast network services. RTP provides such services as payload type identification, sequence numbering, time stamping, and delivery monitoring to real-time applications.

RWAN. Routed WAN Management Solution. CiscoWorks solution used to configure, administer, and maintain a Cisco routed wide-area network (WAN).

S

SA. security association. An instance of security policy and keying material applied to a data flow. Both IKE and IPSec use security associations, although security associations are independent of one another. IPSec security associations are unidirectional and are unique in each security protocol. An IKE SA is used by IKE only, and, unlike the IPSec security association, it is bidirectional.

SAA. Service Assurance Agent. Network performance measurement agent in Cisco IOS Software that provides a scalable, cost-effective solution for service level monitoring.

SAFE. Security Architecture for Enterprise Blueprint. Flexible, dynamic blueprints for security and VPN networks, built on the Cisco Architecture for Voice, Video, and Integrated Data (AVVID), that enable businesses to securely take advantage of e-business economies and compete in the Internet economy.

SAN. storage area network. An emerging data communications platform that interconnects servers and storage at Gigabit Ethernet speeds. By combining LAN networking models with the core building blocks of server performance and mass storage capacity, SAN eliminates the bandwidth bottlenecks and scalability limitations imposed by previous SCSI bus-based architectures.

SBM. subnetwork bandwidth manager. To enable admission control over IEEE 802-styled networks, IOS QoS software offers SBM.

scheduling. Assigning packets to one of multiple queues (based on classification) for expedited treatment throughout the network.

SDH. Synchronous Digital Hierarchy. A standard technology for synchronous data transmission on optical media. It is the international equivalent of SONET.

SDSL. single-line digital subscriber line. One of four DSL technologies. SDSL delivers 1544 Mbps both downstream and upstream over a single copper twisted pair. The use of a single twisted pair limits the operating range of SDSL to 10,000 feet (3048.8 meters).

sender registration. In PIM-SM, as soon as an active source for group G sends a packet to the router that is attached to this source, the router is responsible for registering the multicast address and its source with the RP. The source router encapsulates the multicast data from the source in a special PIM-SM message, called the Register message, and unicasts that data to the RP.

Server Farm module. A module within the Enterprise Composite Network Model. It contains servers providing application, file, print, e-mail, and Domain Name System (DNS) services to internal users.

service level. Various levels and quality of services defined for each service type. For example, the service type called quality of sound might have service levels defined for telephone, broadcast, and digital CD.

Service Provider Edge. A functional area described within the Enterprise Composite Network Model. The modules in this area are not implemented by the enterprise itself, but are necessary to enable communication with other networks. It most often uses different WAN technologies provided by SPs.

SGCP. Simple Gateway Control Protocol. A protocol that controls voice over IP gateways by an external call control element (called a call agent). This has been adapted to allow SGCP to control switch ATM Circuit Emulation Service circuits (called endpoints in SGCP). The resulting system (call agents and gateways) allows the call agent to engage in Common Channel Signaling (CCS) over a

64-kbps circuit emulation service (CES) circuit, governing the interconnection of bearer channels on the CES interface.

SHA-1. Secure Hash Algorithm 1. An algorithm that takes a message of less than 264 bits in length and produces a 160-bit message digest. The large message digest provides security against brute-force collision and inversion attacks. SHA-1 [NIS94c] is a revision to SHA, which was published in 1994.

shared tree. Shared (multicast distribution) trees use a single common root (per one or more or all multicast groups) placed at some administratively chosen point in the network. This shared root is called a rendezvous point (RP). Source traffic is sent toward the RP on a source tree; the traffic is then forwarded down the shared tree from the RP to reach all the receivers, unless the receiver is located between the source and the RP, in which case it will be serviced directly.

single-mode fiber. Uses lasers as the light source and is designed for the transmission of a single wave or mode of light as a carrier. The single ray of light can be distinguished more reliably at longer distances compared to multimode fiber.

SIP. session initiation protocol. Protocol developed by the IETF as an alternative to H.323. SIP features are compliant with IETF RFC 2543, published in March 1999. SIP equips platforms to signal the setup of voice and multimedia calls over IP networks.

SLA. *See* SLC.

SLC. service level agreement (SLA). A key component of a service level contract (SLC). The SLC specifies connectivity and performance agreements for an end-user service from a provider of service. A service provider might provide wide-area or hosted application services. Bandwidth, round-trip response, loss characteristics, and network services are part of the SLA specifications.

SLIP. Serial Line Internet Protocol. The standard protocol for point-to-point serial connections using a variation of TCP/IP. A predecessor of Point-to-Point Protocol (PPP).

SMDS. Switched Multimegabit Data Service. (WAN Access) A high-speed, packet-switched, datagram-based WAN networking technology offered by telephone companies.

SMI. Structure of Management Information. RFC 1155 specifying rules used to define managed objects in the MIB.

SMTP. Simple Mail Transfer Protocol. Internet application protocol providing e-mail services. SMTP is defined in RFC 2821.

SN. storage networking. SN provides customers with universal access to storage solutions and products for an open standards-based architecture. SN combines intelligent Fibre Channel, Ethernet, and optical networking offerings to build scalable data center storage networks and extend storage networks through IP and optical technologies. Major technology areas include NAS and SAN.

SNA. Systems Network Architecture. A large, complex, feature-rich network architecture developed in the 1970s by IBM. Similar in some respects to the Open System Interconnection (OSI) reference model but with a number of differences, SNA essentially is composed of seven layers.

SNMP. Simple Network Management Protocol. Network management protocol used almost exclusively in TCP/IP networks. SNMP provides a means to monitor and control network devices, and to manage configurations, statistics collection, performance, and security.

SONET. Synchronous Optical Network. A standard framing for transporting a wide range of digital telecommunications services over optical fiber. SONET is characterized by standard line rates, optical interfaces, and signal formats.

source tree. The simplest form of a multicast distribution tree with its root at the router closest to the multicast source and branches forming a spanning tree through the network to the receivers or to the ultimate routers connected to the multicast group members. Because this tree uses the shortest path through the network, it is also referred to as a shortest path tree (SPT).

SPAN. Switched Port Analyzer. A feature of the Cisco Catalyst series switches that extends the monitoring capabilities of existing network analyzers into a switched Ethernet environment. SPAN mirrors the traffic at one switched segment onto a predefined SPAN port. A network analyzer attached to the SPAN port can monitor traffic from any of the other Catalyst switch ports.

SPI. security parameter index. A number that, together with a destination IP address and security protocol, uniquely identifies a particular security association. When IKE is used to establish the security associations, the SPI for each security association is a pseudo-randomly derived number. Without IKE, the SPI is manually specified for each security association.

SPF. shortest path first algorithm or Dijkstra's algorithm. Routing algorithm that iterates on length of path to determine a shortest path spanning tree. Commonly used in link-state routing algorithms, it runs on every routing device in the network.

spoofing. The act of constructing a packet stream claiming to be from an address other than the actual source. Spoofing is designed to foil network security mechanisms, such as filters and access lists.

SPT switchover. PIM-SM includes the capability for last-hop routers (that is, routers with directly connected members/recipients) to switch to the shortest path tree and bypass the RP if the traffic rate is above a set threshold (called the SPT-threshold). This behavior is called SPT switchover.

static route. Route that is explicitly configured and entered into the routing table. Static routes take precedence over routes chosen by dynamic routing protocols.

storage networking. Provides customers with universal access to storage solutions and products in an open standards-based architecture. Storage networking combines intelligent Fibre Channel, Ethernet, and optical networking offerings to build scalable data center storage networks, and extend storage networks through IP and optical technologies. Major technology areas include NAS and SAN.

STP. Spanning Tree Protocol. Bridge protocol that uses the spanning-tree algorithm, enabling a learning bridge to dynamically work around loops in a network topology by creating a spanning tree. Bridges exchange BPDU messages with other bridges to detect loops, and then remove the loops by shutting down selected bridge interfaces. Refers to both the IEEE 802.1 Spanning Tree Protocol standard and the earlier Digital Equipment Corporation Spanning Tree Protocol upon which it is based. The IEEE version supports bridge domains and allows the bridge to construct a loop-free topology across an extended LAN. The IEEE version generally is preferred over the Digital Equipment version. Sometimes abbreviated as STP.

stub area. OSPF area that carries a default route, intraarea routes, and interarea routes but does not carry external routes. Virtual links cannot be configured across a stub area, and they cannot contain an ASBR.

subnet. In IP networks, a network sharing a particular subnet address. Subnetworks are networks arbitrarily segmented by a network administrator to provide a multilevel, hierarchical routing structure while shielding the subnetwork from the addressing complexity of attached networks.

SVC. switched virtual circuit. Virtual circuit that is dynamically established on demand and is torn down when transmission is complete. SVCs are used in situations where data transmission is sporadic.

switch. Network device that filters, forwards, and floods frames based on the destination address of each frame. The switch operates at the data-link layer of the OSI model.

General term applied to an electronic or mechanical device that allows a connection to be established as necessary and terminated when there is no longer a session to support.

In telephony, a general term for any device, such as a PBX, that connects individual phones to phone lines. *See also* PBX and PSTN.

switched LAN. LAN implemented with LAN switches.

switching. Process of taking an incoming frame from one interface and delivering to another interface for transmission. Routers use Layer 3 switching to route a packet, and traditional LAN switches use Layer 2 switching to forward frames. *See also* Layer 2 switching and Layer 3 switching.

syslog. Dedicated server that logs system messages.

T

T1. Digital WAN carrier facility. T1 transmits DS-1–formatted data at 1.544 Mbps through a TDM network, using AMI or B8ZS coding.

TACACS+. Terminal Access Controller Access Control System plus. Authentication protocol extended by Cisco that provides remote-access authentication and related services, such as event logging. User passwords are administered in a central database rather than in individual routers, providing a scalable network security solution.

TAPI. Telephony Application Programming Interface. A call control model developed by Microsoft and Intel.

Tbps. terabits per second. 1,000,000,000,000 bits per second.

TCP. Transmission Control Protocol. Connection-oriented transport layer protocol that provides reliable full-duplex data transmission. TCP is part of the TCP/IP protocol stack.

TDM. time-division multiplexing. Technique in which information from multiple channels can be allocated bandwidth on a single wire based on preassigned time slots.

Telnet. Standard terminal emulation protocol in the TCP/IP protocol stack. Telnet is used for remote terminal connection, enabling users to log in to remote systems and use resources as if they were connected to a local system. Telnet is defined in RFC 854.

TFTP. Trivial File Transfer Protocol. Simplified version of FTP that allows files to be transferred from one computer to another over a network, usually without the use of client authentication (for example, username and password). TFTP is defined in RFC 1350.

throughput. Specifies the rate of information arriving at, and possibly passing through, a particular point in a network system.

tie-line. A dedicated circuit that connects enterprise PBXs together.

ToS. type of service. An indication of how an upper-layer protocol requires a lower-layer protocol to treat its messages. In many IP networks, this is signaled using the three precedence bits in the type-of-service octet of the IP header. More recent implementations use DSCP in the DS field of the IP header.

touch-tone. Use as an adjective, not a noun; for example, touch-tone telephone, touch-tone telephone buttons, and so forth.

traffic policing. Process used to measure the actual traffic flow across a given connection, and compare it to the total admissible traffic flow for that connection. Traffic outside of the agreed upon flow can be discarded immediately or tagged (where some field is changed) and discarded en route if congestion develops. Traffic policing is used in ATM, Frame Relay, and other types of networks. Also known as admission control, permit processing, and rate enforcement. Most often implemented on ingress ports to protect a transport network from greedy traffic flows, it is frequently implemented using a leaky bucket algorithm.

traffic shaping. Use of queues to smooth surges that can congest a network. Data is buffered and then sent into the network in regulated amounts to ensure that the traffic fits within the promised traffic envelope for the particular connection. Traffic shaping is used in ATM, Frame Relay, and other types of networks. Also known as metering, shaping, and smoothing. Most often configured on egress ports to ensure compliance with agreed connection traffic rates to avoid traffic policing, it is frequently implemented using a token bucket algorithm.

Trojan horse. Computer program that appears to have a useful function but also has a hidden and potentially malicious function that evades security mechanisms, sometimes by exploiting legitimate authorizations of a system entity that invokes the program.

trunk. Physical and logical connection between two switches across which network traffic travels. A backbone is composed of a number of trunks.

In telephony, a phone line between two COs, between a CO and a PBX, or between two PBXs.

trust boundary. The network edge where QoS markings are accepted (or rejected) is referred to as the trust boundary.

TTL. Time to Live. A field within the IP header; its value is decremented every time the packet enters a router. When the value of TTL drops to zero, the packet is dropped and a TTL expired message is sent to the sender of the packet. The purpose of the TTL field in the IP packet is that during periods when there are routing loops, the packet's TTL eventually drops to zero and the packet is dropped.

tunneling. A dual encapsulation mechanism by which a protocol at some layer in the protocol stack is transported by another protocol operating at the same layer.

twisted pair. Describes copper media in which the wires are twisted around each other in a spiral to reduce crosstalk or electromagnetic induction between the pairs of wires. The ordinary copper wire that connects homes and many business computers to the PSTN uses a single pair for each analog telephone line.

U

UBR. unspecified bit rate. A service category defined by the ATM Forum for ATM networks. It relates traffic characteristics and QoS requirements to network behavior. UBR allows any amount of data up to a specified maximum to be sent across the network, but there are no guarantees in terms of cell loss rate and delay.

UDP. User Datagram Protocol. Connectionless transport layer protocol in the TCP/IP protocol stack. UDP is a simple protocol that exchanges datagrams without acknowledgments or guaranteed delivery, requiring that error processing and retransmission be handled by other protocols. UDP is defined in RFC 768.

unicast. Traffic from a single source sent to a single network destination.

UNIX. Operating system developed in 1969 at Bell Laboratories. UNIX has gone through several iterations since its inception. These include UNIX 4.3 BSD (Berkeley Standard Distribution), developed at the University of California at Berkeley, and UNIX System V, Release 4.0, developed by AT&T.

UplinkFast. A spanning-tree maintenance mechanism that enables the switch to put a redundant path (port) into active state within a second.

UPS. uninterruptible power supply.

utilization. Measures the use of a particular resource over time, usually expressed as a percentage, where the usage of the resource is compared with its maximum operational capacity.

UTP. unshielded twisted-pair. Four-pair wire medium used in a variety of networks. UTP does not require the fixed spacing between connections that is necessary with coaxial-type connections. Six types of UTP cabling are commonly used.

V

VACL. VLAN access control list. A VACL contains an ordered list of access control entries (ACEs).

VAD. voice activity detection. When enabled on a voice port or a dial peer, silence is not transmitted over the network, only audible speech. When VAD is enabled, the sound quality is slightly degraded, but the connection uses much less bandwidth.

VBR. variable bit rate. A service category defined by the ATM Forum for ATM networks. It relates traffic characteristics and QoS requirements to network behavior. VBR is subdivided into a real-time (RT) class and nonreal-time (NRT) class. VBR (RT) is used for connections in which a fixed timing relationship exists between samples. VBR (NRT) is used for connections in which no fixed timing relationship exists between samples but that still need a guaranteed QoS.

VLAN. virtual LAN. Group of devices on one or more LANs that are configured (using management software) so that they can communicate as if they were attached to the same wire, when in fact they are located on a number of different LAN segments. Because VLANs are based on logical instead of physical connections, they are extremely flexible.

VLSM. variable-length subnet masking. Capability to specify a different subnet mask for the same network number on different subnets. VLSM can help optimize available address space.

voice mail. Voice messaging is a service expected by most users of a telephone system. It provides the facility to divert their incoming calls to a voice mailbox when they are unable to answer their telephones.

VoIP. Voice over IP. The capability to carry voice over an IP-based Internet with POTS-like functionality, reliability, and voice quality. VoIP enables a router to carry voice traffic (for example, telephone calls) over an IP network. In VoIP, the DSP output is collected over 20 or 30 milliseconds and placed in UDP datagrams. These datagrams are transported using IP packets with RTP. Skinny Client Control Protocol (SCCP), H.323, and SIP provide session (call) control.

VPN. Virtual Private Network. Uses tunneling and encryption at the network layer to enable IP traffic to travel securely over a public TCP/IP network.

VRRP. Virtual Router Redundancy Protocol. VRRP is similar to HSRP, but it is standards based and it has some advantages over HSRP.

VTP. VLAN Trunking Protocol. VTP reduces administration in a switched network by distributing VLAN information through all switches in the VTP domain. VTP is a Cisco-proprietary protocol that is available on most of the Cisco Catalyst Family products.

vty. virtual type terminal. Commonly used as virtual terminal lines.

W

WAN. wide-area network. Data communications network that serves users across a broad geographic area and often uses transmission devices provided by common carriers. ATM, Frame Relay, PPP, SMDS, and X.25 are examples of common data-link layer protocols found in WANs.

WAN module. A module within the Enterprise Edge functional area of the Enterprise Composite Network Model. The WAN module includes all WAN technologies that provide circuits between geographically separated locations. FR, ATM, and PPP are frequently encountered data-link technologies.

WCCP. Web Cache Communication Protocol. A protocol for communication between routers and web caches. Two versions exist: WCCP version 1 (WCCPv1) and WCCP version 2 (WCCPv2). The two versions are incompatible. Cisco IOS Software images can support either of the two versions or both.

web. World Wide Web (also called WWW). A client/server system based on HTML and HTTP.

WFQ. weighted fair queuing. Queuing algorithm that identifies conversations (in the form of traffic streams), separates packets that belong to each conversation, and ensures that capacity is shared fairly between these individual conversations. WFQ is an automatic way of stabilizing network behavior during congestion and results in increased performance and reduced retransmission. It is the default on interfaces at and below 2.048 Mbps.

wildcard mask. A 32-bit quantity used in conjunction with an IP address to determine which bits in an IP address should be ignored when comparing that address with another IP address. A wildcard mask is specified when configuring access lists.

wiring closet. Specially designed room used for wiring a data or voice network. Wiring closets serve as a central junction point for the wiring and the wiring equipment that is used for interconnecting devices. They are sometimes called distribution facilities.

workgroup. Collection of workstations and servers on a LAN that are designed to communicate and exchange data with one another.

WRED. weighted random early detection. Queuing method that ensures that high-precedence traffic has lower loss rates than other traffic during times of congestion by dropping some percentage of packets when congestion is detected and before the queue in question overflows. The drop probability can be configured differently for each of multiple traffic classes.

X–Z

X.25. ITU-T standard for defining how connections between DTE and DCE are maintained for remote terminal access and computer communications in PDNs.

xDSL. Group term used to refer to ADSL, HDSL, SDSL, and VDSL. All are emerging digital technologies using the existing copper infrastructure provided by the telephone companies. xDSL is a high-speed alternative to ISDN.

XML. extensible markup language. A standard maintained by the World Wide Web Consortium (W3C). It defines a syntax that lets you create markup languages to specify information structures. Information structures define the type of information, for example, subscriber name or address, not how the information looks (bold, italic, and so on). External processes can manipulate these information structures and publish them in a variety of formats. Text markup language designed to enable the use of SGML on the World Wide Web. XML allows you to define your own customized markup language.

zone. In H.323, the collection of all terminals, gateways, and MCUs managed by a single gatekeeper. A zone includes at least one terminal and can include gateways or MCUs. A zone has only one gatekeeper. A zone can be independent of LAN topology and can be comprised of multiple LAN segments connected using routers or other devices.

INDEX

Numerics

10-Mbps Ethernet, 37
100-Mbps Ethernet, 37
1000-Mbps Ethernet, 37
3DES (Triple DES), 208

A

AAA (authentication, authorization,
  and accounting), 231
    Kerberos, 233–234
    PKI, 234–235
    RADIUS, 231
    TACACS+, 232–233
ABR (Available Bit Rate), 96
Access Control List Manager (ACLM), 149
access control lists (ACLs), 39
access layer, 12
access patterns, 534
access points, 401
    cell coverage, 402–403
    cell distribution, 404
    Cisco wireless solutions, 405
    hot standby redundancy, 413
    placement and numbers, 410
ACLM (Access Control List Manager), 149
ACLs (access control lists), 39
active monitoring, 150
addressing, 6
AES (Advanced Encryption
  Standard), 208
AH (Authentication Header), 238
analyzing network traffic patterns, 31
antennas, 403
application layer attacks, 220
applications
    Cisco IP Telephony solution, 447
    IP multicast, 317
    security, 243
architectures
    Cisco content networking solutions, 497
    Cisco storage-networking solution, 523

communication (WLANs), 401
    access point coverage, 402–403
    cell distribution, 404
network management, 151
QoS
    DiffServ, 283
    IntServ, 282
SAFE, 244–245
ARP spoofing, 426
ATM, 93–96
attack signatures, 228
attacks
    application layer attacks, 220
    DDoS, 242
    DoS attacks, 217
    IP spoofing, 216
    man-in-the-middle attacks, 219
    mitigation
        EAP authentication, 422–423
        IPSec, 424–426
    network reconnaissance, 220–221
    packet sniffers, 214–215
    password attacks, 218
    port redirection attacks, 222
    trust exploitation, 221
    unauthorized access attacks, 222
    viruses and Trojan horses, 222–223
authentication (VPNs), 353
Authentication Header (AH), 238
autonomous solutions, 113
availability, 6, 132
    campus networks, 29
    Campus Network, 16
    Enterprise Edge, 19, 85
    parallel, 185
    server farms, 58
    storage networks, 535
    WLANs, 412
Availability Manager, 145, 159
AVVID (Cisco Architecture for Voice, Video, and
  Integrated Data) framework, 3, 141
    benefits, 9
    Common Network Infrastructure, 8–9
    components, 8
    Intelligent Network Services, 8-10
    network solutions, 8, 11
    overview, 7

J–L

T

W

X–Z

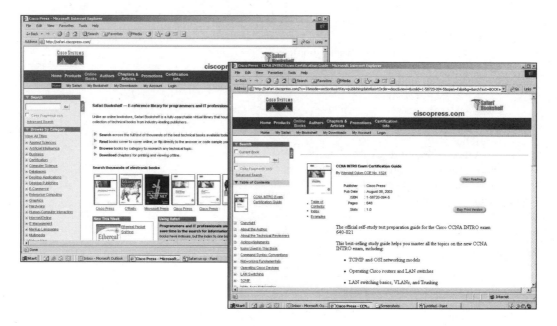